THE ROUGH GUIDE TO

CRETE

This thirteenth edition updated by
Marc Dubin

Contents

WILDFLOWER MEADOW NEAR AYÍA GALÍNI

Introduction to **Crete**

With its fabulous beaches and crystalline seas, Crete has everything you could want of a Greek island. But it also has a great deal more: as the birthplace of Zeus and cradle of Europe's earliest civilization, Crete can boast a history longer even than classical Greece, and reminders of its extraordinary past are scattered all over the island. It's also a substantial and multifarious land in its own right, with cosmopolitan cities as well as unspoilt, hidden villages, dramatic gorges and mountains high enough to be snow-capped through spring into summer.

Because the island is so big, it is far from dominated by visitors. Indeed, thanks to a flourishing agricultural economy – including some surprisingly good vineyards – Crete is one of the few Greek islands that could probably support itself without holiday-makers. So although tourism is an important part of the economy, traditional life also survives, along with the **hospitality** that forms part of that tradition. There are plenty of visitors, of course, and the populous **north coast** can be as sophisticated as you want it; here you'll find every facility imaginable and, in places, crowds of package tourists determined to exploit them to the full. But in the less-known coastal reaches of the **south** it's still possible to escape the development, while the high mountains and agricultural plains of the interior are barely touched. One of the most rewarding things to do on Crete is to rent a car and head for more remote villages, often just a few kilometres off some heavily beaten track. Here the island's customs, its everyday life, dialects, song, traditional dress and festivals, and above all its welcome to strangers, survive to an extent that's exceptional in modern Europe.

The **mountains**, which dominate the view as you approach Crete by air or sea, run from one end of the island to the other, and make all but the shortest journey inland an expedition. They are perhaps the island's greatest surprise and biggest reward, providing welcome relief in the heat of summer, giving Crete much of its character, and making the place feel much larger than it really is. Cut through by gorges and studded by caves, they offer fabulous **walking** too, from easy strolls to strenuous climbs,

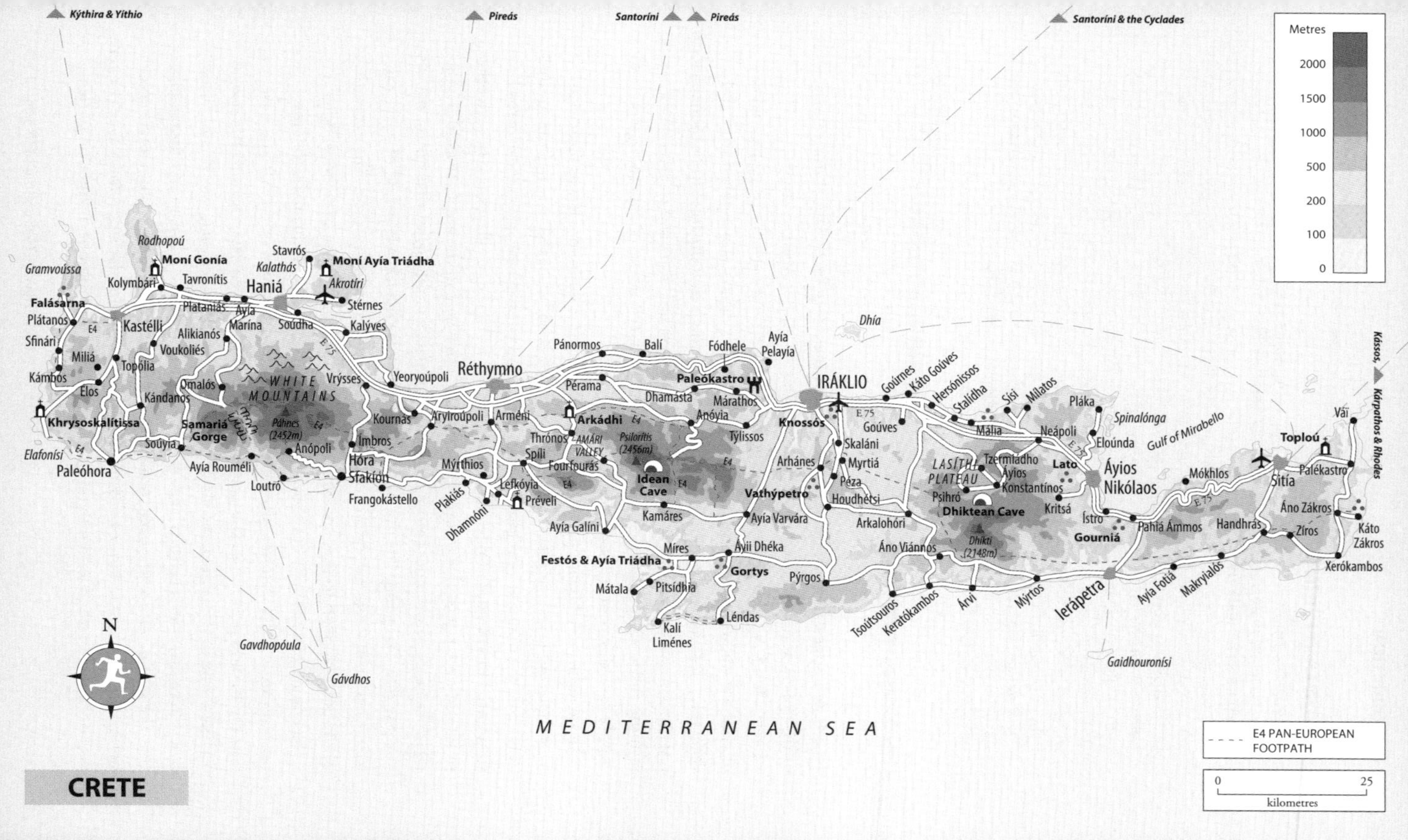
CRETE
MEDITERRANEAN SEA
Metres
2000
1500
1000
500
200
100
0
E4 PAN-EUROPEAN FOOTPATH
0
25
kilometres
N
Kýthira & Ýthio
Pireás
Santoríni
Pireás
Santoríni & the Cyclades
Kássos, Kárpathos & Rhodes
Gramvoússa
Falásarna
Plátanos
Sfinári
Kámbos
Miliá
Elos
Khrysoskalítissa
Elafonísi
Paleóhora
Kastélli
Topólia
Kolymbári
Rodhopoú
Moní Gonía
Tavronítis
Plataniás
Voukoliés
Alikianós
Kándanos
Soúyia
Omalós
Samariá Gorge
Ayía Rouméli
Ayía Marína
Haniá
Kalathás
Stavrós
Moní Ayía Triádha
Akrotíri
Stérnes
Soúdha
Kalýves
WHITE MOUNTAINS
Páhnes (2452m)
Anópoli
Loutró
Vrýsses
Ímbros
Hóra Sfakíon
Frangokástello
Kournás
Yeoryoúpoli
Réthymno
Aryiroúpoli
Arméni
Mýrthios
Plakiás
Dhamnóni
Lefkóyia
Préveli
Spíli
Thrónos
AMÁRI VALLEY
Fourfourás
Ayía Galíni
Pánormos
Pérama
Arkádhi
Psiloritis (2456m)
Idean Cave
Kamáres
Balí
Dhamasta
Anóyia
Fódhele
Paleókastro
Márathos
Týlissos
Ayía Pelayía
Dhía
IRÁKLIO
Knossós
Arhánes
Vathýpetro
Ayía Varvára
Míres
Festós & Ayía Triádha
Áyii Dhéka
Gortys
Mátala
Pitsídhia
Kalí Liménes
Léndas
Pýrgos
Skaláni
Myrtiá
Péza
Houdhétsi
Arkalohóri
Goúrnes
Káto Goúves
Goúves
Hersónissos
Stalídha
Mália
Sísi
Mílatos
Neápoli
LASÍTHI PLATEAU
Tzermiádho
Áyios Konstantínos
Psihró
Dhiktean Cave
Dhíkti (2148m)
Áno Viánnos
Tsoútsouros
Kerátokambos
Árvi
Mýrtos
Pláka
Spinalónga
Eloúnda
Lato
Áyios Nikólaos
Kritsá
Ístro
Gourniá
Pahiá Ámmos
Gulf of Mirabello
Mókhlos
Ierápetra
Ayía Fotiá
Makryialós
Gaidhouronísi
Handhrás
Sitía
Toploú
Vái
Palékastro
Áno Zákros
Zíros
Káto Zákros
Xerókambos
Gavdhopóula
Gávdhos
E4
E75

MOUNTAIN HIKING

There are few places in the world where high **mountains** so close to the sea combine with an often perfect climate. This is a paradise for climbers, birdwatchers, botanists and nature lovers, but above all for **walkers** – whether on a brief stroll or a week-long hike. A network of ancient footpaths and shepherds' trails allows you to walk all day and barely see a soul. Yet, should you want to, you can always find a village, and Cretan hospitality ensures that almost wherever you end up you will eat well and spend the night in comfort. The grand-daddy of Crete's treks is the **E4**, the long-distance European footpath that traverses the island, taking in many of the highest peaks en route. To walk the entire length takes weeks, but there are plenty of sections that are easily accessible and where you can hike for a few hours. Some of the best of these are in the southwest, where the path splits: one branch following the coast and another winding through the heights of the Lefká Óri; the magnificent Samariá Gorge links the two.

One striking feature of Crete's topography is the sheer number of spectacular **gorges** that slash their way through the mountains. In addition to Samariá, there are at least fifty more gorges in the Lefká Óri alone, many hardly visited at all. On a hot summer's day, heading down a gorge is the ideal hike: you're usually shaded from the sun's ferocity, with an empty beach and a welcome swim to reward you at the end. Arrange for someone to collect you so you don't have to toil back up, and you have the makings of a perfect day.

as well as a huge variety of habitats for **wildlife**, including many large birds of prey. For birdwatchers and wildflower spotters, Crete has no end of treats in store.

Cretan **food** can also prove an unexpected bonus. There's an increasing awareness of culinary traditions based on magnificent, locally sourced, sun-ripened fruit and vegetables, foraged herbs and home-reared meat, much of it organic. In fashionable city restaurants, grandma's recipes are being rediscovered and reworked to great effect, while in more rustic village or beachside tavernas, the age-old magic of superb ingredients, simply served, has never been forgotten.

An extraordinary **history** plays a large part in Crete's appeal, too. It was more than four thousand years ago that the island's story began to be shaped, when, from around 2000 BC, the **Minoans** developed an advanced and cultured society at the centre of a substantial maritime trading empire: the first real European civilization. The artworks produced on Crete at this time are unsurpassed anywhere in the ancient world, and it seems clear, as you wander through the Minoan palaces and towns, that life on the island in those days was good. For five hundred years, by far the longest period of peace the island has seen, Crete was home to a civilization well ahead of its time. The excavations of the great Minoan palaces are among the island's prime tourist attractions today.

Recent genetic research has shown that the Minoans were indigenous to Crete, pushing aside older theories stipulating origins from Anatolia or the Middle East, and the island's position as strategic **meeting point** between east and west has played a crucial role in its subsequent history and culture. The Greek flag was finally raised over Crete just over a century ago, in 1913. For two thousand years and more before that the island was fought over by others – subject to Rome, Byzantium and Venice before being subsumed into the Turkish Ottoman empire. During World War II Crete was occupied by the Germans and Italians, gaining the dubious distinction of being

THE OLD HARBOUR AND LIGHTHOUSE OF HANIÁ AT SUNSET

A RURAL ISLAND

Despite the rapid growth in the last fifty years of towns like Haniá, Réthymno and particularly Iráklio, Crete remains a land rooted in the **countryside**. Almost everyone seems to have some connection to the land – a smallholding where they grow fresh produce or a village where parents or grandparents still live. The villages, each with its own character and traditions, are the island's pulse, where the pace of the year is determined by the agricultural calendar. Here you can still find everyday life lived as it has been for centuries, where potters craft clay into ewers and jars, weavers make rugs in traditional patterns and growers cart their olives to the local press.

the first place to be successfully invaded by parachute. Each one of these diverse rulers has left some mark, and more importantly they have imprinted on the islanders a personality toughened by constant struggles for independence.

Where to go

Every part of Crete has its loyal devotees who will argue fervently in defence of their favourite spot. On the whole, though, if you want to get away from it all you should head for the ends of the island – west, towards Haniá and the smaller, less well-connected places along the south and west coasts, or east to Sitía and beyond. Wherever you're staying, you won't have to go far inland to escape the crowds.

At the centre of the northern coast the sprawling capital, **Iráklio** (Heraklion), is home to a magnificent **archeological museum** and lies just a few kilometres from **Knossós**, the greatest of the **Minoan palaces**. You'll find other reminders of history all over Crete, but the best known are mostly here, near the heart of the island; above all **Festós** and **Ayía Triádha** in the south (with Roman **Górtys** to provide contrast) and the palace of **Mália** on the north coast.

As for **beaches**, you'll find great ones almost anywhere on the north coast. From Iráklio to Áyios Nikólaos there's very heavy development, and most package tourists are aiming for the resort hotels in this region. These places can be fun if nightlife and crowds are what you're after – particularly the biggest of them, like **Mália**, **Hersónisos** and **Áyios Nikólaos**. The majority of the island's most luxurious **hotels** and **inclusive resorts** are near Áyios Nikólaos, overlooking the Gulf of Mirabello especially around **Eloúnda**.. Further east things get quieter: **Sitía** is a place of real character, and beyond it on the east coast are a number of laidback resorts as well as the beautiful palm beach at **Vái**, a favourite with day-trippers from across the island, and the relatively little-visited Minoan palace near modern **Zákros**. To the west there's more development around both **Réthymno** and **Haniá**, the most attractive of the island's big towns. Other places at this end of the island tend to be on a smaller scale.Along the **south coast**, where the mountains frequently drop straight down to the sea, resorts are more scattered. Only a handful of places are really developed – **Ierápetra**, **Ayía Galíni**, **Mátala**, **Paleóhora** – with a few more, like **Plakiás** and **Makriyialós**, on their way.

AYÍA TRIÁDHA

AVERAGE MONTHLY TEMPERATURES AND RAINFALL (IRÁKLIO)

	Jan	Feb	Mar	Apr	May	Jun	Jul	Aug	Sep	Oct	Nov	Dec
Max/min (°C)	14/7	14/8	15/9	20/12	23/15	27/19	29/22	29/22	27/19	24/17	20/13	17/11
Max/min (°F)	60/48	60/48	63/48	68/54	73/60	81/66	84/72	84/72	81/66	75/63	68/55	63/52
Rainfall (mm)	153	118	90	38	20	8	3	123	95	83	122	89

For many people, unexpected highlights also turn out to be the island's **Venetian forts** and defensive walls and bastions – dominant at Réthymno, Iráklio and Haniá, magnificently isolated at **Frangokástello**, and found in various sizes and stages of ruin all over Crete. The **Byzantine churches** and remote **monasteries** dotted across the island, many containing stunning medieval **wall paintings**, are also unexpected treasures. Smaller Cretan **towns**, supply centres for the island's farmers, are always worth visiting for their vibrant markets, shops and tavernas, while Réthymno and Haniá boast atmospheric, cluttered old centres, whose narrow alleys are crammed with reminders of the Venetian and Ottoman eras.

The mountains and valleys of the interior deserve far more attention than they get, too. Only the **Lasíthi** plateau in the east and the **Samariá Gorge** in the west see really large numbers of visitors, but turn off the main roads almost anywhere and you'll find villages going about their daily agricultural routine, often in the midst of astonishingly beautiful scenery. This is especially true in the west, where the Lefká Óri – the **White Mountains** – dramatically dominate every view; but the **Psiloritis** range in the centre of the island also offers magnificent scenery and mountain villages, along with some of the island's finest walking, while the easterly **mountains** of Sitia are far less explored.

When to go

The combination of high **mountains** and warm seas, together with a position as far south as any in Europe, makes for an exceptionally long season: you can get a decent tan in Crete right into October and swim at least from April until early November. **Spring** is the prime time to come: in April and May the island is relatively empty of visitors (except over Easter), the weather clear and not overpoweringly hot, and every scene is brightened by a profusion of wildflowers.

By mid-June the rush is beginning. **July** and **August** are not only the hottest, the most crowded and most expensive months, they are also intermittently blighted by fierce winds and accompanying high seas; the north coast is particularly prone to these. In September the crowds gradually begin to thin out, and **autumn** can again be a great time to visit – but now the landscape looks parched and tired, and there's a feeling of things gradually winding down.

Winters are mild, but also vaguely depressing: except around Christmas/New Year's, many places are shut, it can rain sporadically, sometimes for days, and there's far less life in the streets. In the mountains it snows, even to the extent where villages can be cut off; on the south coast it's generally warmer, soothed by a breeze from Africa.

Author picks

Our authors have explored every corner of Crete in order to uncover the very best it has to offer. Here are some of their favourite things to see and do.

Unspoilt villages You can escape the coastal crowds and heat by heading inland almost anywhere. Try these for starters: Aryiroúpoli (see page 229), Áyios Konstandínos (see page 144), Kefáli (see page 299) and Zarós (see page 101).

Amazing adventures Bungee jump into a 140m gorge at Arádhena (see page 282), windsurf at Koureménos (see page 167), or trek down the sensational Samariá Gorge, Europe's longest (see page 273).

Fresh from the sea Feasting on fish and crustaceans in sight of the sea is a tip-top Cretan treat. Four of the best places to do it are *Akrogiali* (see page 247), *Caravella* (see page 307), *Hióna* (see page 167) and *Kalliotzina* (see page 180).

Brilliant beaches Among hundreds of superb beaches standouts include tropical-fantasy Elafonísi (see page 300), the idyllic white-sand Bálos Bay (see page 290) and the Caribbean-style palm beach at Vái (see page 164).

Cretan castles If castles are your thing Réthymno's Fortezza (see page 195), Frangokástello (see page 288), and the stirring island forts of Spinalónga (see page 138) and Gramvoúsa (see page 295) won't disappoint.

Caves and caverns Crete has thousands of caves, many of which can be explored. The Sfendóni (see page 211), Melidhóni (see page 207) and Dhiktean (see page 145) caverns are all well worth a trip.

Intriguing islands The seas surrounding Crete are dotted with dozens of offshore islands and islets. Spinalónga (see page 138), Gramvoúsa (see page 295), Gaidhouronísi (see page 183) and Gávdhos (see page 314) each have a distinct character.

Magnificent museums Iráklio's magnificent Archeological Museum is unique and world-class (see page 57) but the museums at Haniá (see page 240) and Sitía (see page 159) are also well worth a visit.

Our author recommendations don't end here. We've flagged up our favourite places – a perfectly sited hotel, an atmospheric café, a special restaurant – throughout the Guide, highlighted with the ★ symbol.

BUNGEE JUMPING, ARÁDHENA GORGE

FRESH SEAFOOD – A TAVERNA STAPLE

20

things not to miss

It's not possible to see everything Crete has to offer in one trip – and we don't suggest you try. What follows, in no particular order, is a subjective selection of the island's highlights, including world-famous archeological sites, stunning mountain ranges, lively resorts and great beaches. All highlights are colour-coded by chapter and have a page reference to take you straight into the Guide, where you can find out more.

1

2 3

4

5

1 LOUTRÓ

See page 277

Accessible only by boat or on foot, this idyllic retreat on the edge of its own bay is the perfect place to get away from it all.

2 TRADITIONAL MUSIC AND DANCE

See page 209

Crete's musical traditions are thriving, and traditional music and dance is widely performed at tavernas, weddings, baptisms and saint's day celebrations across the island – often featuring the *lýra* and *laúto*.

3 KNOSSÓS

See page 72

Crete's biggest attraction, this 3500-year-old Minoan palace is a sprawling maze of royal chambers, grand staircases, storerooms and workshops.

4 ARCHEOLOGICAL MUSEUM, IRÁKLIO

See page 57

The finest collection of Minoan artefacts in the world, with a refurbished-since- 2010 setting to do them justice.

5 LASÍTHI PLATEAU

See page 142

Traditional village life continues on this fertile mountain plateau, famed for its windmills, where you'll also see a riot of springtime wildflowers.

6 ELAFONÍSI

See page 300

Turquoise waters, rose-tinted sands and a shallow, warm lagoon make this subtropical-island beach one of Crete's most exotic locations.

7 WINDSURFING

See page 167

Koureménos Beach is Crete's top windsurfing spot, with constant winds almost year-round.

8 WILDLIFE

See page 344

Crete's spectacular flora and fauna ranges from ubiquitous vultures to rarities like the *kri-kri* wild ibex and delicate mountain orchids. Several beaches are nesting sites for the endangered loggerhead turtle.

9 HIKING

See pages 6, 31 and 41

Crete's countless walking opportunities include spectacular gorge hikes that take you from the mountains to the sea.

10 HANIÁ

See page 237

Wander the streets of Haniá's old town to discover its beautiful harbour and haunting vestiges of a Minoan, Venetian and Ottoman past.

9

11 ÁYIOS NIKÓLAOS

See page 128

With plenty of restaurants, bars and clubs, this is one of the island's most vibrant and picturesque towns, arrayed around a supposedly bottomless lake.

12 LEFKÁ ÓRI

See page 270

The Lefká Óri, or White Mountains, often snow-capped until late May or early June, dominate the western end of the island, offering some unbeatable walking and hiking adventures.

13 BEACHES

See page 296

From great swathes of sand at the north-coast resorts to tiny pebble coves overshadowed by stunning mountains in the south, Crete has beaches to suit any taste.

14 CAVES

See page 207

The awesome Melidhóni Cave is just one of hundreds dotted around the island, many of which can be visited.

15 MONÍ ARKÁDHI

See page 203

The most celebrated of Crete's numerous monasteries has a fine Venetian church and is an emblem of the island's struggle for independence.

11

13

14

15

16 RÉTHYMNO

See page 190

Lose yourself in the old quarter of Réthymno, an elegant town dominated by its Venetian fortress and fine nearby beach.

17 BYZANTINE FRESCOES

See page 84

Some of the finest Byzantine frescoes in Greece are to be found in Crete's country churches.

18 THE KAFENÍO

See page 36

Focal point of traditional Cretan life, the kafenío is a great place for lively discussions or games of *távli* (backgammon) while downing a coffee, an ouzo or a fiery *rakí*.

19 THE AMÁRI VALLEY

See page 211

A beautiful valley, with old churches and spectacular mountain views, which epitomises Cretan rural life.

20 WINE

See page 37

Wine has been made in Crete for around 4000 years, but in recent years the island has seen a boom in boutique wineries and high quality wines.

18
19
20

Itineraries

There are as many potential itineraries as there are visitors to Crete, and you'll no doubt want to create your own to reflect personal interests, whether those be mountain climbing, bird-watching or lying on the beach. The itineraries below should begin to give a flavour of what the island has to offer.

THE GREAT ISLAND

The Grand Tour, taking in the best-known destinations. Allow at least two weeks, taking time off for the beaches and hikes along the way.

❶ **Iráklio** The inevitable starting point, Crete's capital boasts a world-class archeological museum, and is the easiest base from which to visit the ruins at Knossós. See page 52

❷ **Áyios Nikólaos** Home to the finest of Crete's luxury resort hotels, this is a charming if mostly modern town with good restaurants and nightlife. See page 128

❸ **Sitía** Laidback capital of the far east, offering excellent food, subtle charms and an escape from mass tourism. See page 156

❹ **Zákros** A tiny, isolated seaside hamlet with a lovely pebble beach and one of the four great Minoan palaces. See page 168

❺ **Mátala** From hippy hideout in the 1960s to crowded resort today, Mátala and its beachside caves have managed to retain a unique charm. See page 113

❻ **Réthymno** A university city with an enchanting old town, a big sandy beach and beautiful countryside within easy reach. See page 190

❼ **Haniá** The island's second city is for many its most attractive; gateway to the mountains of the west and with plenty of sophisticated charm. See page 237

THE EAST: MINOANS, MOUNTAINS AND BEACHES

This itinerary presents a little of everything the east of the island has to offer, with ample opportunities for getting to the beach or hiking into the hills. You could easily do it in four days, or break the journey into day-trips from a base almost anywhere in the east.

❶ **Knossós** The greatest of the Minoan palaces, Knossós lies in the countryside just behind Iráklio. Partly reconstructed and with many of the original frescoes copied, it's an extraordinary sight. See page 72

❷ **Mália** Both the island's most notorious resort and an important Minoan palace, in a glorious seaside setting. Some of Crete's sandiest beaches lie between here and Knossós. See page 94

❸ Karfí An ancient Minoan site on a limestone pinnacle, with spectacular views over the coast and the Lasíthi plateau. Little survives of the site itself, but the journey, the taxing hike up and the chance to visit the plateau afterwards are irresistible. See page 145

❹ Spinalónga This island and one-time leper colony can be reached only by boat, with swimming opportunities nearby. See page 138

❺ Gourniá A unique Minoan town set on the isthmus at Crete's narrowest point, Gourniá allows a glimpse of the lives of ordinary Cretans four thousand years ago. See page 150

❻ Mýrtos A tranquil, laidback spot on the sunny south coast where there's little to do but lie on the beach, swim, eat and drink. See page 184

❼ Ayía Triádha Tiny and enigmatic, Minoan Ayía Triádha has glorious views of both mountains and sea, with easy access to both. It's also very near the major palace at Festós, and the Roman ruins of Górtys. See page 109

❽ Zarós A wholly traditional village in the shadow of the Psilorítis mountains, Zarós offers some great places to stay and to eat, as well as lovely walks. See page 101

WALKING IN THE WEST: CASTLES AND CHURCHES

The castles, monasteries and painted Byzantine churches that litter the west are set among some of Crete's finest hiking territory and most spectacular mountain scenery. This itinerary takes you to a selection; all of them also offer tremendous opportunities for short walks.

❶ Moní Arkádhi The island's most important monastery – with a fine Venetian-era church – is a shrine to the nineteenth-century independence struggle. A branch of the E4 path passes the monastery, which is also close to superb walking in the Amári valley. See page 203

❷ Moní Préveli Another of Crete's great monastic settlements, Préveli played a heroic role in World War II. Walk down to Palm Beach directly below, or longer hikes head up the river behind the beach. See page 226

❸ Frangokástello An imposing fourteenth-century Venetian fort between the beach and forbidding mountains. Two little-known gorges are nearby. See page 288

❹ Church of Panayía and Sotíra, Roústika Some of Crete's most spectacular mountain roads lie between Frangokástello and Roústika, a drive through great walking country. The Byzantine church has some of the finest medieval frescoes in Crete. See page 228

❺ Chapel of Metamórphosis Sotírou, Mesklá Hidden away in a mountain village close to Haniá, this chapel celebrating Christ's transfiguration has superb frescoes dating from the fourteenth century. There are some great rural tavernas nearby, too. See page 268

❻ Moní Goniá, Kolymbári On the coast at the base of the Rodhopoú peninsula, where few roads penetrate, this seventeenth-century monastery played a stirring role in Crete's wars against the Ottomans – and has cannonballs lodged in its walls to prove it. See page 264

❼ Topólia Fascinating village with a frescoed Byzantine church at the head of a lovely inland ravine. See page 301

❽ Moní Khrysoskalítissa This much-venerated monastery, close to fine beaches, is reached through verdant countryside studded with ancient churches. See page 299

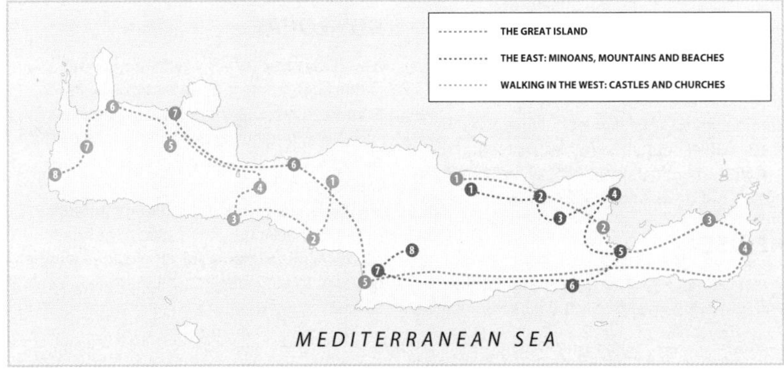

Sustainable travel

More and more people are becoming aware of the importance of travelling responsibly and minimising the impact on the environment during their adventures. What follows is a list of suggestions to make your trip to Crete as sustainable as possible.

CHOOSE LOW-IMPACT STAYS

One of the main concerns in Crete is overbuilding. You can help by spending your tourist cash on stays at restored older buildings where possible since all-new construction relies excessively on Portland concrete, whose manufacture and deployment are intensely polluting and energy intensive. Lime-based mortar is superior from every viewpoint and preferred in quality, sensitive restoration projects. One worthwhile project in this vein is based at Vámos in the Haniá district (www.vamosvillage.gr), which has been carefully restored in line with the local environment, employing people from the village and supporting nearby producers. Whilst deep in Haniá province, Milia village (https://milia.gr) has been reimagined as one huge eco-lodge without sacrificing such amenities as wi-fi. The lodge features solar panels and on-site organic food production on the farms of the property. In the far east of Crete, White River Cottages (www.whiterivercottages.com/traditional-houses-crete) is based in an abandoned pastoral hamlet just inland from mass-market coastal resort Makriyialós and offers a more authentic stay but with all the amenities just a short drive (or long walk) away.

RE-USE

Arrive with a rugged, reusable water bottle, and your hosts will be only too happy to point you towards a potable water source. Many hill villages have unrestricted-access public fountains, which were often the only local water source before indoor plumbing became routine. Many tourist shops also sell sturdy reusable tote bags made of sustainable fibres like raffia palm, or better yet, bring one from home.

VOLUNTEER

Amazingly, considering the level of development just inland, loggerhead sea turtles (Caretta caretta) still nest every summer on the Réthymno town beach. Volunteering with their ongoing conservation project (https://archelon.gr/en/volunteer/project-areas/crete-rethymno) is a great way to help preserve this incredible species and their habitat.

BUY LOCAL

If available, buy locally wherever you can. Fantastic produce is abundant on the island, from fresh fish caught just a few miles from your hotel to olive oil produced in the olive groves inland. There are also local brands created and distributed on the island that are worth trying. Instead of buying the big international labels you're used to at home, products like Temenia soft drinks, for example, based in a Haniá district village, make a great alternative.

WHITE RIVER COTTAGES

7

ELOUNDA

Basics

Getting there

By far the easiest way to get to Crete is to fly. The vast majority of visitors are Northern Europeans on package tours that include a direct charter flight. Many of these charter companies sell flight-only tickets on their planes, and there's an increasing number of direct scheduled flights too. Overland routes are long, tortuous and expensive, so we've included only the briefest details here. If your starting point is outside Europe the most cost-effective way to reach Crete may well be to get to London – or Amsterdam, Frankfurt or another Northern European hub – and pick up an onward flight from there.

The chief disadvantage of direct flights to Crete is a lack of flexibility; for greater choice, you may have to fly to Athens and take a domestic flight or ferry from there (see page 27).

There are two main **airports on the island**: at **Iráklio** (Heraklion) for the centre and east, and at **Haniá** (Chania) for the west; both have scheduled international services with budget airlines, regular charters from across Europe and numerous daily flights from Athens. **Sitía** in the far east is now an international airport, but flights from Britain and Eire are limited.

When **buying flights** it always pays to shop around, and bear in mind that many websites don't include charter or budget airlines in their results. Be aware too that a **package deal**, with accommodation included, can sometimes be as cheap as, or even cheaper than, a flight alone: there's no rule that says you have to use your accommodation every night, or even at all.

Flights from the UK and Ireland

There are **direct flights** from the UK to Crete on British Airways (http://ba.com), with budget airlines easyJet (http://easyjet.com), Ryanair (http://ryanair.com), and Jet2 (http://jet2.com), or with charter airlines. Don't expect them to be cheap though: unless you book far in advance, there are few bargains to be had. **Fares** depend on the season, with the highest in July, August and during Easter week. But May, June and September are also popular, and since no direct flights operate through the winter (most run from April to mid-October), bargains are rare at any time. In theory, you can fly from Gatwick to Iráklio for as little as £100 return with carry-ons only, but you'll have to move very fast to find fares this low. Realistically you can expect to pay £200–400 return at most times of the year; much more if you leave your booking for too late.

British Airways operates almost daily flights from Gatwick to Iráklio as well as several weekly from Heathrow, and two to three a week from Heathrow to Haniá. EasyJet flies to Iráklio from Gatwick (twice daily) and from Manchester, Edinburgh, Luton and Bristol; and to Haniá daily from Gatwick. Jet2 has flights to Iráklio from Leeds-Bradford, Glasgow, Manchester, Edinburgh, East Midlands and Newcastle. Ryanair flies to Haniá from Stansted up to 4 weekly), and from Leeds, Manchester (up to 3 weekly), Bristol, East Midlands and Newcastle (2 weekly).

Most **charter operators** offer very similar flight-only deals, either through their own websites or through package and specialist operators; prices from airports outside London are generally somewhat higher. In summer there are direct charters to Iráklio from numerous regional airports in the UK; the biggest operator is Tui (www.tui.co.uk) and they also go to Haniá.

If you can't find a direct flight, want more flexibility or are travelling out of season, consider travelling **via Athens** (some flights are also routed via Thessaloníki), with a domestic flight or ferry from there to Crete. Scheduled flights include Aegean (http://aegeanair.com) from Heathrow, Manchester and Edinburgh to Athens; British Airways from Heathrow to Athens and Gatwick to Thessaloníki; easyJet from Gatwick, Manchester, Bristol or Edinburgh to Athens and Gatwick, Luton or Manchester to Thessaloníki; Ryanair from Stansted to Athens and Thessaloníki; and Jet2 from several regional airports to Thessaloníki. From

A BETTER KIND OF TRAVEL

At Rough Guides we are passionately committed to travel. We believe it helps us understand the world we live in and the people we share it with – and of course tourism is vital to many developing economies. But the scale of modern tourism has also damaged some places irreparably, and climate change is accelerated by most forms of transport, especially flying. We encourage all our authors to consider the carbon footprint of the journeys they make in the course of researching our guides.

Athens or Thessaloníki you will then have to arrange onward transport to Crete (see page 27).

From Dublin there are direct charters to Crete (rarely less than €400 return), while Ryanair, Aegean and Aer Lingus (http://aerlingus.com) all fly direct to Athens on an overnight schedule with fares starting at around €100 each way, though more commonly three times that amount. These all operate in summer only – at other times of year you'll have to make at least one stop en route to Greece, in London or elsewhere.

Flights from the USA and Canada

Delta (http://delta.com), United (http://united.com) and Emirates (http://emirates.com) operate **direct nonstop flights** from New York JFK to Athens, daily for most of the year, while American (http://aa.com) flies five times a week from Chicago via Newark, as well as to Athens between May and October. Code-sharing airlines can quote through fares with one of the above, or a European partner, from **virtually every major US city**, connecting either at New York or a European hub such as London or Frankfurt. From Athens there are reasonably priced add-on flights to Crete (see page 27).

Fares vary greatly, so it's worth putting in a little time on the internet, or using a good travel agent; book as far ahead as possible to get the best price. Round-trip prices range from US$800 out of season to $1800 in high summer; from the west coast, expect to pay ten to twenty percent more. Remember too that you may be better off getting a domestic flight to New York or Philadelphia and heading directly to Athens from there, or flying to London (beware of changing airport changes there) or another European city and travelling on from there.

As with the US, airfares **from Canada** vary depending on where you start your journey, and whether you take a direct service. Air Canada Rouge (http://aircanada.com) flies to Athens out of Toronto three to five times weekly, and from Montreal two to four times weekly, between May and October. Air Transat (http://airtransat.com) also has summer-only flights from Toronto (weekly) and Montreal (twice a week) to Athens. Otherwise, you'll have to choose among one- or two-stop itineraries on a variety of European carriers, or perhaps Delta via New York; costs run from Can$800 round trip in low season from Toronto to well over double that from Vancouver in high season.

For all of the above optons, a **connecting flight to Crete** will add €100–150 roundtrip, depending on season and airline.

Flights from Australia and New Zealand

There are **no direct flights** from Australia or New Zealand to Greece; you'll have to change planes in Southeast Asia, the Gulf or Europe. Tickets bought direct from the airlines tend to be expensive; travel agents or Australia-based websites generally offer much better deals on fares and have the latest information on limited specials and included stopovers.

Return fares **from Australia** start from around Aus$1000, rising to around Aus$2600 depending on season, routing, validity, number of stopovers, etc. The shortest flights and best fares are generally with airlines like Emirates (http://emirates.com), in partnership with Qantas (http://qantas.com), and Etihad (http://etihadairways.com), who fly you direct to Athens from their Gulf hubs, though you'll also find offers on Swiss (http://swiss.com), KLM (http://klm.com) and other European carriers. **From New Zealand**, prices are slightly higher: from around NZ$1300, rising to over NZ$3500 in high season.

If Greece is only one stop on a longer journey, you might consider buying a **Round-the-World** (RTW) fare, although Greece never seems to be included in any of the cheaper deals, which means you might have to stump up over Aus$3000/NZ$3500 for one of the fully flexible multi-stop fares from One World or the Star Alliance. At that price, you may be better off with a cheaper deal and a separate ticket to Greece once you get to Europe.

Flights from South Africa

There are currently **no direct flights** from South Africa to Greece. Indirect routes include Emirates (http://emirates.com) or Etihad (www.etihad.com) via the Gulf, or just about any of the major European airlines through their domestic hub. Prices start at around R14,000 for a good low-season deal, to double that in high season or if the cheaper seats have gone.

Overland from the UK, Ireland and the rest of Europe

As a result of the horrific track wreck at Témbi in early 2024, **Greek rail routes** have been greatly reduced, and once you reach Crete there are no trains at all. However, that doesn't necessarily mean that you can't travel most of the way to Crete by **train**, provided you have three or four days to spare and accept that it will almost always work out more expensive than flying. Travelling by train offers the chance to stop over on the way; with an InterRail (for European residents only) or Eurail (for all others) pass you could take in Greece as part of a wider rail trip around Europe. The most practical route from Britain crosses France and Italy before embarking on the ferry from Bari or Brindisi to Pátra. If you're determined to go all the way by train, there are a number of alternative routes across Europe to either Belgrade or Sofia, each of which has connections to Thessaloníki, from where you can get an onward train to Athens. Booking well in advance (essential in summer) and going for the cheapest seats on each leg, you can theoretically buy individual tickets to Iráklio for around £225/€250/$290 each way. Using rail passes will cost you more, but give far more flexibility. For full details, check out The Man in Seat 61 website (http://seat61.com).

Driving to Crete can also be worth considering if you want to explore en route or are going to stay for an extended period. The most popular **route** is again down through France and Italy to catch one of the Adriatic ferries. The much longer alternative through Eastern Europe only makes sense if you want to explore the Greek mainland on the way.

Once in **Italy**, regular car and passenger ferries link Venice, Ancona, Bari and Brindisi with Pátra (Patras, at the northwest tip of the Peloponnese). From here you can cut across country to Pireás for daily ferries to Crete, or head down through the Peloponnese to Yíthio, from where there are a couple of weekly sailings to Kastélli Kissámou in western Crete.

Internal flights to Crete

Flying to Crete **via Greece** doesn't necessarily mean going through Athens, although the vast majority of people do so. **From Athens** Olympic (www.olympicair.com) offer at least seven flights a day to Iráklio in peak season, and there are also as-frequent services with Sky Express (www.skyexpress.gr). Olympic also fly several times daily to Haniá, and at least daily in season to Sitía. Journey time is less than an hour, and flying is good value when weighed against a ferry trip: one-way **prices** for civilised departure times start from around €70, though expect to routinely pay in excess of €100 each way. There are also daily direct flights **from Thessaloníki** to Iráklio on Olympic and (expensively) to Haniá, daily with Ryanair,

Ferries to Crete

There are overnight services every day throughout the year from **Pireás** (the port of Athens) to Iráklio and Haniá, plus daytime services in summer and at other peak periods. There are also much slower ferries, once or twice a week, to Sitía and Kastélli Kissámou. The latter goes via Yíthio in the Peloponnese, and the island of Kýthira. Ferries are operated by ANEK (www.anek.gr; Haniá and Sitía), Minoan Lines (http://minoan.gr; Iráklio and Haniá) and Avlemon (210 808 1967; Kastélli and the Peloponnese route); information on all the routes can also be found at www.openseas.gr and www.ferries.gr.

Pireás is about an hour from Athens airport by bus (#X96; at least 2 an hour, day and night; €5.50), or easily reached on the Metro from central Athens; from the airport metro also serves Pireás' 'Dimotiko Theatro' station, a short walk inland from the quays for Aro-Saronic island services, but a long way from the quay and gates used by Crete bound-ferries. A taxi from the airport will cost around €50. You can buy **tickets** online, or from dozens of agencies in Pireás or in central Athens, as well as from booths on the docks near the boats. If you're taking a car or want a cabin it's worth booking ahead, but deck-class tickets are always available on the spot except at major holiday dates when boat capacity is controlled for safety reasons.

These cheapest tickets give you the run of almost the entire boat, excluding the cabins, some reserved seating and the upper-class restaurant and bar. Most of the ferries serving Crete are modern and reasonably luxurious, with plenty of café and "pullman seating" areas inside, though often without a huge amount of deck space. If you are travelling deck class, it's worth getting on board reasonably early to claim a good space. Cabins are also available, ranging from four-berth, shared inside cabins (all en suite and perfectly adequate) up to deluxe suites with huge picture windows.

Prices are similar on all the routes: minimum €42 deck class, €70 for a berth in a basic cabin, and €100–130 per person in a luxurious double, with cars going for €80 and motorbikes for €30.

Agents and operators

Just about every mainstream **tour operator** includes Crete in its portfolio. You'll find far more interesting alternatives, however, through small **specialist agencies**. As well as traditional village-based accommodation, many of these offer **walking** or **nature holidays** and cater for other special interests such as **yogakayaking** or **cycling**.

PACKAGE OPERATORS

Grecian Tours Australia, 085 2796 8599, http://greciantours.com.au. A variety of accommodation and sightseeing tours, plus flights.

Hidden Greece UK, 020 8004 9095, www.hidden-greece.co.uk. Specialist agent putting together tailor-made packages to smaller destinations at reasonable prices.

Homeric Tours US, 800 223 5570, http://homerictours.com. Hotel packages, individual tours, escorted group tours (though none exclusively to Crete), and fly/drive deals. Good source of inexpensive flights.
Olympic Holidays UK, 020 8492 6868, www.olympicholidays.com. Huge package holiday company specializing in Greece; all standards from cheap-and-cheerful to five-star, and often a good source of last-minute bargains and cheap flights.
Sunvil Holidays UK, 020 8568 4499, www.sunvil.co.uk. High-quality outfit offering a wide range of small hotels, apartments and villas in western Crete (including remote Paleóhora and Loutró), plus fly-drives
True Greece USA, 1 800 817 7098, http://truegreece.com. Upmarket escorted travel and custom-made trips catering for special interests such as cooking, golf and wedding packages, but no specifically Cretan off-the-shelf offerings.

VILLA AND APARTMENT HOLIDAYS

Cachet Travel UK, 020 8847 8700, http://cachet-travel.co.uk. Attractive range of villas, boutique hotels and apartments right across the island, plus walking tours and fly-drives.
Pure Crete UK, 01444 880 404, http://purecrete.com. Village villas and characterful converted cottages and farmhouses in western Crete, plus walking, wildlife and other special-interest trips.
Simpson Travel UK, 020 8392 5858 or 020 8392 5747, www.simpsontravel.com. Classy villas (including family-size), upmarket hotels and village hideaways across the island, but mostly in Réthymno and Haniá districts.

WALKING AND WILDLIFE TOURS

Inntravel UK, 01653 617001, www.inntravel.co.uk. Hotel-to-hotel and single-centre self-guided walking holidays, mostly in western Crete.
Jonathan's Tours 6971 974559 , www.guidedwalks.com.net or htttps://greekwalking.com. Family-run walking holidays with a highly experienced guide – English, but based in France and Crete.
Naturetrek UK, 01962 733051, www.naturetrek.co.uk. Spring and autumn botanical and bird-watching tours.
Ramble worldwide UK, 01707 817260, www.rambleworldwide.co.uk/europe/greece. Big, specialist walking-holiday company with several annual options on Crete.
The Travelling Naturalist UK, 01305 267994, http://naturalist.co.uk. Wildlife holiday company that runs excellent birding and wild-flower-spotting trips to Crete.

SPECIALIST AND ACTIVITY TOURS

Big Blue Swim UK, 01905/978028, https://thebigblueswim.com. Week-long, open-water swimming tours based in south-westerly Hóra Sfakíon, with optional day trip – weather permitting – by small boat to Gávdhos islet.
Classic Adventures USA, 1 800 777 8090, http://classicadventures.com. Two twelve-day biking tours, either the less demanding Land of Zorba, or the self-explanatory more 'extreme' one.
Sportif UK, 01273 844919, http://sportif.travel. Windsurfing packages and kitesurfing packages.
Yoga Escapes UK, 020 7584 9432, www.yoga-escapes.com. Autumn yoga retreats with 5-star accommodation near Haniá.
Yoga Rocks UK, 020 3286 2586, http://yogaholidaysgreece.com. Yoga courses near sandy Áyios Pávlos bay, an isolated south coast location near the Triópetra rock formation.

Getting around

Crete is, on the whole, pretty easy to get around. The main towns and resorts along the north coast are linked by an excellent road and a fast and frequent (almost hourly in summer) bus service. Elsewhere the road network has been extensively upgraded, and most villages see at least one daily bus. However, if you're keen to escape the crowds and experience some of Crete's more remote beaches and spectacular mountain scenery, you'll need to get off the main roads; for at least some of your time it's worth considering renting some transport or setting out on foot – or better still, a combination of the two.

By bus

The only form of public transport on Crete, **buses** cover the island remarkably comprehensively. Modern, fast and efficient services run along the main north-coast road every hour or more, though off the major routes standards vary. The ones used primarily by tourists (to Omalós and Hóra Sfakíon for the Samariá Gorge, for example, or to Festós and Mátala) tend also to be modern and convenient. Those that cater mainly for locals are often older vehicles that run once daily as transport to market or school – into the provincial capital very early in the morning and back out to the village just after 2pm, which means they're of little use for day-trips. There are few places not accessible by bus, though, and if you combine buses with some walking you'll get about extremely cheaply, if not always especially quickly.

Buses on Crete are run by a consortium of companies jointly known as the **KTEL**. That this is not one single company is most obvious in Iráklio where there are two separate bus terminals, serving different directions. On the whole, buses to a given village run from the provincial capital – Iráklio, Réthymno and Haniá, or in Lasíthi province from Áyios Nikólaos and Sitía. There are also a number of small-scale services that cross inter-provincial borders. Timetables, fares and online booking for western Crete (Réthymno and Haniá) can be found at www.e-ktel.com and for the east (Iráklio and Lasíthi) at www.ktelherlas.gr; printed timetables are generally available from bus stations and tourist offices.

Prices remain reasonable: each hop between the major north-coast towns – Iráklio to Réthymno or Áyios Nikólaos, for example, or Réthymno to Haniá – costs €7–8 one way.

By taxi or tour bus

Local **taxis** are exceptionally good value, at least as long as the meter is running or you've fixed a price in advance; from Iráklio airport to Hersónisos, for example, would be about €35, or the 90km from Haniá airport to Paleóhora around €100. Much of their business is long-distance, taking people to and from the villages around the main towns (at some city taxi ranks and all major airports, there's a printed list of prices to the most common destinations). If you want to visit somewhere where there's only one bus, or spend some time hiking and get a ride back, it's well worth arranging for a taxi to pick you up: four people together in a taxi will pay little more per person than on the bus.

It's also quite easy to negotiate a day or half-day **sightseeing** by taxi, although this may require some Greek, and over long distances can become expensive. A simpler alternative for a one-off visit is to take a **bus tour**. Travel agents everywhere offer the obvious ones – the Samariá Gorge or Vái beach – and a few offer more adventurous alternatives: some of the best of these are detailed in the Guide.

By car or motorbike

Renting a **car** or **bike** (or bringing your own), will give you a huge amount of extra freedom to explore and to check out mountain villages and isolated beaches. Most people seem to do this for at least part of their stay, and there are numerous operators in every resort, the vast majority of them offering modern, reliable vehicles and competitive rates.

Do take the time, however, to check out any vehicle carefully before driving off. You and the agent should inventory existing scratches and dents together. More importantly, take care while driving, as Greece has a very high **accident rate** compared with Northern Europe or North America. This is in part due to the state of the roads and the nature of the countryside: although many minor roads have been upgraded in recent years, they are still mountainous and winding, and you'll frequently pass without warning from a smooth, modern surface to a stretch of potholed track. Signage is also poor in many places, or hidden behind vegetation, and road traffic rules often ignored. On the narrower parts of the main north-coast highway – an excellent road for the most part, being improved gradually between Hersónissos and Sitía – to near-motorway standard – you're expected to drive with at least two wheels on the hard shoulder to allow faster vehicles to overtake. This is also due to Cretan driving habits – the north-coast highway is not for the faint-hearted, and vehicles barging in from minor side roads without care are the norm everywhere.

Fuel costs are relatively high, with regular, 95-octane unleaded (*amólyvdhi*) currently around €1.9080 per litre on the north coast, but often over €2 in more remote areas; diesel is a little cheaper. It's easy to run out after dark or at weekends, especially in the extreme east and west of the island; most rural stations close at 7 or 8pm and some shut at weekends, particularly Sunday When touring in these areas it's wise to maintain a full tank, especially when a weekend or national holiday is approaching.

Rules of the road

EU and UK **driving licences** are valid in Crete, and in practice you can rent a vehicle with almost any valid national licence: however, non-EU drivers are legally required to have an International Driving Permit (acquired before leaving home through organizations such as the AAA; https://mwgaaa.com), and the lack of one could cause problems should you have a run-in with the police. It is compulsory to wear **seat belts** and for motorcyclists to wear **helmets** – fines for violations are draconian – and children under the age of 10 are not allowed to sit in the front seats of cars. There has also been a major crackdown on **drink-driving** in recent years, with random checks and roadblocks especially on weekend nights designed to catch clubbers heading home in the early hours of the morning around major towns and resorts, or even those exiting a taverna at 11pm. **Parking** can also be a headache, especially in the big towns, where it's rarely obvious where you are and are not allowed to park, or how to pay when you do so. When in doubt, park a bit out of the centre in obviously unregulated spaces and walk into town; parking tickets start at €80 for basic violations.

If you are involved in any kind of **accident** with another driver or property damage it's illegal to drive away; wait for the traffic police to appear, breatha-lyse all drivers and take statements from all drivers involved before compiling a report, which you should be given a copy of and you can theoretically be held

SIX SCENIC DRIVES

The Far West A circuit from Kastélli Kissámou, down the west coast and back on the inland roads via Élos offers a bit of everything: stunning coastal vistas, traditional villages, mountains and gorges. See page 295

North to South West of Réthymno, a choice of roads crosses the island towards Frangokástello and Plakiás, each more spectacular than the next. See page 228

Amári Valley and Psiloritis Heading southeast from Réthymno, the Arkádhi monastery marks the entry to the Amári valley, whose east side, especially, offers glorious mountain scenery. See page 211

Iráklio to Réthymno Take the old road via Anóyia for a complete contrast to the coastal highway, or combine with the Amári route for a total circumnavigation of Crete's highest mountain. See page 85

Lasíthi plateau Beautiful, however you approach it: try a complete circuit, climbing up from the north coast and back through Neápolis. See page 142

The Far East Barren and lonely: from Sitía, head east to Vái beach, south through Zákros and Xerókambos, then back on the inland road via upland Zíros. See page 162

at a police station for up to 24 hours. If this happens, ring your consulate (though calls will be forwarded to the pertinent embassy in Athens) immediately to get a lawyer, and don't make a statement to anyone who doesn't speak, and write, very good English. **On-the-spot fines** can be issued for minor traffic infringements such as speeding or crossing a central double white line; from around €80 to €300 depending on the gravity of the offence. The address on the ticket will detail the office in the nearest town to which you should go to pay the fine.

Car rental

Car rental starts at around €35 a day or €200 a week in high season for the smallest model, including unlimited mileage, tax and insurance; outside peak season, prices drop by about 25 percent. An open-top jeep or a van will cost up to three times as much; jeeps can be fun, but there's little point going for a fancy vehicle – you'll rarely get a chance to drive at great speed, and small cars are an advantage when parking or negotiating narrow village streets.

Many package holidays will include a car, and if not there's a great deal to be said for organizing your rental in advance, when you may well get a much better deal. If you go for a Cretan company, pick one that is local to where you intend to head or, if you're touring around, one that has offices around the island to ensure that there's help available should you need it.

Almost all agencies require a **credit card** to swipe as a deposit against any damage caused; minimum **age requirements** vary from 21 to 25. Be sure to check that full insurance and a **collision damage waiver** is included (or take out a separate car hire excess insurance in advance, generally far cheaper) and note that damage to tyres and the underside of the vehicle is usually excluded from the insurance, so take care on bumpy dirt roads. Likewise, damage to the interior – handle read/side-view mirrors in a gingerly manner.

Motorbikes and mopeds

Motorbikes, **mopeds**, **scooters** and **quad bikes** are also widely available to rent in Crete, at prices starting at around €20 a day (€120/week) for a 50cc scooter, and €30 a day (€190/week) for a 200cc trail bike. Reputable establishments demand a full motorcycle driving licence for any engine over 100cc, and you will usually have to leave your passport (sometimes a valid credit card is acceptable) as security. For smaller models up to about 100cc displacement any driving licence with an AM class entitlement will do.

The smaller bikes and scooters are ideal for pottering around for a day or two, but don't regard them as serious transport: Crete is very mountainous and small scooters simply won't go up some of the steeper hills, even carrying only one person. Be sure not to run beyond the range of your petrol tank either, as they're not designed for long-distance travel and there are few filling stations outside the towns. For serious exploration, or to venture into the mountains, you really need a motorbike or a more powerful scooter. Folk without the necessary license will be steered towards quad bikes – which ironically are unstable and dangerous, and not recommended.

Although motorbikes are enormous fun to ride around, you need to take more than usual care: there's an alarming number of **accidents** each year among visitors and locals because basic safety procedures are not followed. It's only too easy to come to grief on a potholed road or steep dirt track, especially at night. You should never rent a bike that you feel you can't handle, or is too underpowered to support two riders, and always use a **helmet** (a legal requirement), despite the fact that many locals don't – fines levied at checkpoints are draconian Quite apart from any injuries, you're likely to be charged a criminally high price for any repairs needed for the bike, so make sure that you are adequately **insured**. Note that some travel insurance policies specifically exclude injuries sustained while riding/driving a rented vehicle. Local hospital casualty wards and clinics are wearily familiar with road-rash injuries sustained on two-wheelers.

CAR RENTAL AGENCIES IN CRETE

Alianthos 28320 32033, http://alianthos-group.com. Cars and bikes, with offices at the airports and across western Crete.
Blue Sea 2810 221 215, www.bluesearentals.com. Cars and bikes in Iráklio and elsewhere.
Clubcars 28410 25868, http://clubcars.net. Áyios Nikólaos, Iráklio airport and other locations in the east.
Kosmos Athens HQ 210 92 34 696, 28210 63035, http://kosmos-carrental.com. Iráklio, Réthymno, Haniá,Sitía.
Motor Club 2810 222 408, www.motorclub.gr. Cars and bikes in Iráklio and many resort locations.

Walking, cycling and local boats

There are plenty of **walking** opportunities for visitors. Choices range from local strolls inland from almost any resort to organized tours through the Samariá Gorge and the challenging E4 trans-European footpath, which crosses the island from west to east. If you have the time and stamina, walking is probably the single best way to see the island. There are suggestions for hikes, from easy strolls to serious climbing, throughout the Guide: check out, too, our list of specialist walking-tour operators (see page 28).

Cycling

The popularity of **cycling** has been growing in Crete – **mountain bikes** can be rented in most resorts of any size, and many of the rental places offer organized local excursions. Any significant distance, however, generally involves steeply mountainous terrain and, in summer, fierce heat. Even so, provided you're reasonably fit, riding a bike offers an incomparable view of the island and guarantees contact with locals whom the average visitor could never meet. A number of companies offer tours involving group exploration of the island by bike (see page 28). If you're really keen you can bring your own bike by plane (it's normally free within your ordinary baggage allowance) or by sea if you're coming from Italy or Athens (in which case it should go free on the ferry).

Boats and local ferries

Around the island numerous **local ferry services** run to offshore islets and isolated beaches, plus all long the southwest coast; these are detailed throughout the Guide. Some adventure travel operators (see page 28) offer tours around the coast by **sea kayak**.

Accommodation

There are vast numbers of beds available for tourists in Crete, and most of the year you can rely on turning up pretty much anywhere and finding something. At Easter and in July and August, however, you can run into problems unless you've booked in advance, especially in the more popular resorts and cities.

The big **hotels** and self-catering complexes in the larger resorts are often pre-booked by package-holiday companies for the whole season. Although they may have vacancies if you just turn up, non-package visitors are far more likely to find themselves staying in smaller, simpler places which usually describe themselves simply as "**rooms**", or as apartments or studios. Standards here can vary from spartan (though invariably clean) to luxurious, but the vast majority are purpose-built blocks where every room is en suite, and where the minimal furnishings are well adapted to the local climate – at least in summer.

Single rooms are rare, and generally poor value – you'll often have to pay the full double-room price or haggle for around a third off; on the other hand, larger groups and **families** can almost always find triple and quadruple rooms or two-bedroom apartments, and fancier hotels may have family **suites** (two rooms sharing one bathroom), all of which can be very good value.

Hotels

The tourist police set official **star categories** for hotels, from five-star down to no-star; all except the top category have to keep within set price limits. You may occasionally still see the old letter system (L, luxury, is five-star, then A to E). Ratings correspond to the common facilities available (lifts, conference rooms, spa, gym, dining room, pool etc), a box-ticking exercise which doesn't always reflect the actual quality of the rooms; there are plenty of 3-star hotels which are in practice smarter and more comfortable

ACCOMMODATION PRICES

There are typically three **seasons** that affect accommodation prices in Crete: October to April (low), May, June and September (mid) and July and August (high) – though Easter and the first two weeks of August may fall into a higher category still.

Each accommodation reviewed in this Guide is accompanied by a price category, based on the cost of a standard double room in high season. Price ranges don't include breakfast, unless stated otherwise. For camping, price categories are given per pitch, while for hostels, dormitory bed price categories are indicated as well as private rooms.

€ = under €80
€€ = €80–150
€€€ = €151–300
€€€€ = over €300

than nearby 4-star outfits. A "boutique" category allows some hotels to escape the ratings straitjacket on the grounds of location or historical significance.

2-star hotels and below have only to provide the most rudimentary of continental **breakfasts** – sometimes optional for an extra charge – while 3-star and above will usually offer a buffet breakfast including fruit salad, cheeses, cold meats, eggs and cereals plus poor coffee.

Rooms and apartments

Many places categorized as apartments or rooms are every bit as comfortable as hotels, and in the lower price ranges are usually more congenial and better value. Traditionally **rooms** (*dhomátia* – but usually spotted by a "Rooms for Rent" or *Zimmer Frei* sign) were literally a room in someone's house, a bare space with a bed and a hook on the back of the door, where the sparse facilities were offset by the disarming hospitality you'd be offered as part of the family. Such places are now rare, however, and these days almost all are purpose-built (though many still family-run), with comfortable en suites, air-conditioning and balconies – at the fancier end of the scale you'll find studio and apartment complexes with marble floors, pools, bars and children's playgrounds. Many have a variety of rooms at different prices, so if possible always ask to see the room first. Places described as **studios** usually have a small **kitchenette** – a fridge, sink and a couple of hotplates in the room itself – while **apartments** generally have at least one bedroom and separate kitchen/living room. The popularity of sites like Airbnb, combined with the economic crisis, has also led to something of a flood of individuals renting largely unregulated rooms or apartments. Many are wonderful, but make sure you know exactly what you're getting, and its location.

AIR CONDITIONING AND WI-FI

Almost all modern rooms and apartments have **air conditioning**, but it's sometimes an optional extra and you'll be charged an additional €5 or so a night for the remote so you can use it. If there's no a/c, we'll mention it in the listings. **Wi-fi** is ubiquitous, and even the most basic places tend to have it; there's very rarely a charge (you're more likely to be charged extra, ironically, in more expensive hotels), but the signal may not extend to the rooms (or if it does, not to every room), and it's often pretty slow.

Rooms proprietors sometimes ask to keep your **passport**: ostensibly "for the tourist police", but in reality to prevent you leaving with an unpaid bill. Some may be satisfied with just taking down the details, and they'll almost always return the documents once you get to know them. In the larger resorts, though, the only way to keep hold of your passport may be to pay in advance.

Villas and longer-term stays

Although one of the great dreams of Greek travel is finding an idyllic coastal **villa** and renting it for virtually nothing for a whole month, there's no chance at all of your dream coming true in modern Crete. All the best villas are contracted out to agents and let through foreign operators. Even if you do find one empty for a week or two, renting it in Crete usually costs far more than it would have done to arrange from home. Specialist operators (see page 28) represent some superb places, from simple to luxurious, and costs can be very reasonable, especially if shared between a few people.

Having said that, if you do arrive and decide you want to drop roots for a while, you can still strike lucky if you don't mind avoiding the coast, and are happy with relatively modest accommodation. Pick an untouristed inland village, get yourself known and ask around; you might still pick up a wonderful deal. And there are also plenty of apartments on Airbnb,

SEVEN GREAT ESCAPES

Looking to get away from it all and escape the crowds? Look no further:

Akrogiali, Kissamos Rooms on the beach, accessed by boat. See page 247

Miliá Eco Village Abandoned mountain hamlet restored as lovely, candle-lit accommodation. See page 303

Moní Koudhoumá This remote seaside monastery welcomes pilgrims and gives them a bed. See page 121

Thalori, Káto Kapetanianá. Not far from Koudhoumá but a complete contrast; luxury restored houses in an isolated, largely abandoned mountain village. See page 121

Vailakakis, Sarakiníko, Gávdhos The island of Gávdhos is about as far off the grid as you can hope to get in Europe. See page 318

Vilaeti Traditional Guesthouses, Áyios Konstantínos Night-time on the Lasíthi plateau is magical: a taste of timeless mountain Crete. See page 147

Zakros Palace Apartments, Zákros High above the beach, gorge and palace of Zákros in the isolated far east. See page 173

booking.com and the like, rarely super-luxurious but often good value at short notice. Out of season your chances are much better – even in touristy areas, between October and March (sometimes as late as April and May) you can bargain for a very good rate, especially for stays of a month or more. Travel agents are another good source of information on what's available locally, and many rooms places keep an apartment on the side or know someone with one to rent.

Youth hostels

Two excellent, long-established, traditional-style hostels survive on Crete – in Réthymno and Plakiás – along with two new backpacker-style places each in Iráklio and Haniá (Iráklio also has an old official youth hostel, not recommended). Facilities are basic – you pay €12–15 a night for a dormitory bed (€20 in Haniá) on which to spread your sleeping bag – but they offer cheap meals, kitchen facilities, a good social life and an excellent grapevine for finding work or travelling companions.

Camping

There are about a dozen official **campsites** in Crete see https://www.camping.info/en/country/greece/crete for a list of them and on the whole they're not very comfortable, tending to be dominated by camper vans and with very hard earth. Several do have spectacular seafront locations, though. Prices start at around €5/night per person, but they mount up once you've added a charge for a tent (generally about €3.50 for a two-person model or €5 for something larger), and the same again for a vehicle and for everyone in your group – you're looking at €18–30 a night for two people, tent and vehicle in high season.

Camping outside an official campsite (with or without a tent) is against the law – enforced in most tourist areas and on beaches. Nevertheless, with discretion and sensitivity it can still be done: the police crack down on people camping rough on (and littering) popular mainstream tourist beaches, but there are still places on the south and west coasts where the practice is fairly common.

From May until early September, it's warm enough to **sleep out** in just a lightweight sleeping bag (though the nights can be too chilly in mountainous zones). A waterproof bag or groundsheet is useful to keep out spring or autumn damp, and a foam pad lets you sleep in relative comfort almost anywhere.

Food and drink

Cretans spend a lot of time socializing outside their homes, and sharing a meal is one of the chief ways of doing it. The atmosphere is invariably relaxed and informal, with pretensions and expense-account prices rare outside the fancier hotels. Greeks are not prodigious drinkers – tippling is traditionally meant to accompany food – though there are plenty of bars in the tourist resorts and you can always get a beer, a glass of wine or an ouzo at a café.

The **food** in Crete may be simple, but at its best it is magnificent –piquantly flavoured with the herbs that scent the countryside. Organic production, local

EATING OUT PRICES

Each restaurant and café reviewed in this Guide is accompanied by a price category, based on the cost of a two-course meal (or similar) for one, including a non-alcoholic drink.

€ = under €20
€€ = €20–30
€€€ = €31–45
€€€€ = over €45

sourcing and foraging for ingredients are not fads or recent developments here, but central to the way people have always eaten; most Cretans have access to a smallholding of some kind, or if not to local street markets where the island's superb agricultural produce is sold. In the better tavernas, the bulk of the produce used will be fresh, local and naturally organic. There's a **food and drink glossary** in Contexts (see page 357).

Breakfast, fast food and snacks

Greeks generally don't eat much in the way of **breakfast**, more often opting for a mid-morning snack from the bakery. Some of the best rooms places and fancier hotels will serve up fresh fruit and yoghurt, eggs straight from the hen and home-made breads and pastries; more often, though, "continental" breakfast consists of cardboard-flavoured orange squash, stewed coffee of tea, processed cheese and meats, plus pre-packaged butter, honey and jam (confusingly called *marmeládha*). In the resorts, there are plenty of places offering bacon and eggs too.

Picnics and snacks

Picnic ingredients are easily available at supermarkets, bakeries and greengrocers, most of which open early. Yoghurt, bread, eggs, fruit, cheese, salami, olives and tomatoes are always easy to buy. Note that Greek **cheese** isn't all feta (salty white sheep's cheese); tasty local varieties include creamy *myzíthra*, *káskavali*, and *graviéra*; the last – a peppery, mature, full-fat sheep's cheese – is particularly good.

At **bakeries**, you'll find oven-warm flaky pies filled with cheese (*tyrópita*), spinach (*spanakópita*), wild greens or sausage or, better still, stuffed with creamy cheese and sprinkled with icing sugar and cinnamon (*bougátsa*). In the tourist areas many bakeries also cater for northern European palates by turning out croissants, doughnuts and even wholemeal, multi-grain and rye breads.

Ubiquitous **fast-food** snacks include **souvláki** – small kebabs on wooden sticks, which as *píta-souvláki* are served stuffed into a doughy bread (more like Indian naan than pitta bread) along with salad and yoghurt – and, even better, doner-kebab-like **yíros píta**. You'll also find places serving **pizza** (usually excellent at specialist places and awful in tavernas) and **tost** (bland ham-and-cheese toasties).

Seasonal **fruits** are exceptionally inexpensive. Look out for what's on offer in the markets or by the roadside: cherries in spring; melons, watermelons, plums and apricots in summer; pears and apples in autumn; kiwi between October and May, oranges and grapes most of the time. They even grow small bananas in the area around Árvi– an endeavour heavily subsidized by the EU.

Tavernas and restaurants

Most Cretan restaurants describe themselves as **tavernas**, though you can also get a meal at an *estiatório* or a *psistariá* as well as in ouzerís and many others. **Estiatória** are very similar to tavernas but specialize in the baked dishes known as *mayireftá* (see page 36), and tend to be simpler, less expensive, and perhaps more traditionally Greek. **Psistariés** are restaurants that offer grilled or spit-roasted meat, usually over charcoal. A **psarótaverna** is a taverna that specializes in fish or other seafood. **Ouzerís**, superficially resembling bars, specialize in ouzo and mezédhes; a *rakádhiko*, very fashionable these days, is the equivalent, but serving *rakí* as tipple. They are well

OLIVE OIL AND THE CRETAN DIET

Great claims are made for the **Cretan diet** – comparative studies have shown that the island has (or had) one of the longest-lived and least diseased populations in the world – and any local will be happy to lecture you on the life-enhancing properties of good **olive oil** (plus a little wine or *rakí* in moderation). As increasing amounts of meat and dairy produce are added to the everyday diet, the health benefits are falling away, but with plentiful locally produced olive oil, cereals, and sun-ripened vegetables and fruit, this still feels like a very healthy place to eat.

worth trying for the marvellous variety of **mezédhes** (small plates of food) they serve, although the most authentic are to be found in the larger towns where there's a local customer base to keep them on their toes. At the better places several plates of mezédhes will effectively substitute for a meal (though it may not work out any cheaper if you have a healthy appetite, and mezédhes are also served at many tavernas). Wherever you eat, chic appearance is not a good guide to quality; often the most basic place will turn out to be the best, and in swankier restaurants you may well be paying for the linen and stemmed wineglasses.

Sometimes at traditional tavernas and *estiatória* there's no visible menu (by law there must be one to consult somewhere, however) and you're taken into the **kitchen** to inspect what's on offer: uncooked cuts of meat and fish, simmering pots of stews or vegetables, trays of baked foods. Even where there is a **menu** (usually in English as well as Greek) it's often a standard printed form that bears little relation to what is actually on offer: again, check the kitchen or display case.

A basic taverna meal with house wine or Greek beer will **cost** around €18–25 per person. Add a better bottle of wine, seafood or more careful cooking, and it could be €25–40 a head; you'll rarely pay more than that. If you're unsure about the **price** of something, ask before ordering since it always seems to turn out more expensive if you wait until after you've eaten. Fish is almost always priced by weight, uncleaned (see page 36). There's always a small **cover charge** (€0.50–1.50 per person), which includes the bread you'll inevitably be given, though you have the right to refuse – and not pay – for this.

TAVERNA ADVICE AND HOURS

Cretans generally eat late: **lunch** is served 2–4pm, **dinner** at 8.45–11pm. You can eat earlier than this, but you're likely to get indifferent service at a tourist establishment or find yourself eating alone everywhere else. If you can't wait that long, do what the locals do: take an aperitif along with a few mezédhes.

The **opening hours** we quote in our reviews throughout the Guide should be taken as indicative rather than set in stone; if you want to sit talking and drinking till the early hours (as many locals do), you'll rarely be thrown out. And if the proprietor has been up till 3am, it's no surprise if he should choose to open a little later than usual the next day.

Prices are supposedly inclusive of all taxes and service, but an extra **tip** of around five percent or simple rounding up of the bill is always welcome.

Greek dishes and Cretan specialities

As Cretan restaurants increasingly adapt themselves to tourists, you'll find that some of the advice below no longer applies in the resorts, where you're more likely to get western European-style service (places much patronized by the French, for example, offer fixed-price set menus). On the other hand, the better tavernas have started to recognize the value of their culture and serve more consciously **traditional foods** cooked in more traditional ways.

A typical Greek meal consists of various shared salads and appetizers (often in the form of **mezédhes**) and a main meat or fish dish. They may be brought to the table at much the same time as there's no strict concept of courses – if you really want the main course later, stagger your ordering throughout your evening..

VEGETARIANS AND VEGANS

Although there are scarcely any **vegetarian** or **vegan** restaurants as such, you will find that you can eat extremely well in Crete. Quite apart from the fact that meals based on eggs, pizza or pasta are available in all the towns and resorts, as are traditional snacks like *tyrópita*, the increased interest in local cuisine, as well as pressure from tourists, has seen far more vegetable dishes appear on local menus. Many mezédhes like tzatziki, *dolmádhes* (stuffed vine leaves) and *yígandes* (large haricot beans in tomato sauce) are naturally meat-free and dairy-free; you'll find excellent salads everywhere; *yemistá* (stuffed vegetables) are usually meat-free but might be made with broth; and there are frequently vegetable-baked dishes including ratatouille-like *briám*, *imám bayaldí* (stuffed aubergine/eggplant) and *bouréki* (potato, courgette/zucchini and cheese bake) on the menu. Vegans will be in for a harder time, given the Cretan love of cheese and yogurt.

FABULOUS RURAL TAVERNAS

The best food is often found off the beaten track.

Kafenío Sto Skholio Anídhri. See page 311

Piperia Pefkí. See page 180

Taverna Plateia M ýrthios. See page 225

Taverna Tzitzifia Tzitzifés. See page 258

Taverna Vilaeti Áyios Konstantínos. See page 146

Vegera Zarós. See page 103

Salads and vegetables are traditionally served as the first course and usually shared. If you ask for 'salad' you'll invariably be brought *horiátiki saláta* – the so-called **Greek salad**, including feta cheese: wonderful as it is there are plenty of cheaper alternatives without cheese. Vegetable dishes are often very good in themselves and, if you order a few between several people, can make a satisfying meal. The **main dish** of meat or fish generally comes on its own except for maybe a piece of lemon or half a dozen chips (fries); lamb (or better still goat if it's available) is usually the best meat, local and excellent, if a little pricier than alternatives. Check out the kitchen for **oven-baked dishes** (*mayireftá*, such as *moussakás, pastítsio* (macaroni pie), meat or game stews, *yemistá* (stuffed tomatoes or peppers), the oily vegetable casseroles called *ladherá*, and oven-baked meat and fish), which are generally delicious and less expensive than straight meat or fish dishes.

Traditionally, restaurants didn't serve much in the way of **dessert** – the Greek practice is to visit a *zaharoplastío* or patisserie for pastries, coffee and liqueurs once the main meal is over – but these days more often than not you'll be offered something on the house, the kérasma: fresh fruit, halva or báklavas, often accompanied by a glass of ubiquitous *rakí*.

In season, **fish** is varied and delicious, but in summer visitors get a restricted choice as industrial-scale trawling is prohibited locally from June to September. It is also relatively expensive: if the prices on the menu seem phenomenally high, that's generally because they are **per kilo**; €55 a kilo will work out at €19 or so a head/portion. Most tavernas will encourage you to go into the kitchen to see what's available and when you've selected your fish they'll weigh it (uncleaned) to determine the actual price (a larger fish, shared between two or more, is generally tastier and better value; don't leave it to the waiter to choose, or you may well get the biggest). Cheaper, tasty alternatives include small **sardine** or picarel-style fish, eaten whole flash fried, fish soups and stews, and (more expensively) **squid**, octopus and shellfish.

Traditional **Cretan specialities** increasingly find their way onto menus too: some of the more common among dozens of typical dishes are snails and rabbit, both often served stewed with onions or, in the case of snails, ***bourbouristí*** (sauteed with garlic and rosemary but no red sauce). Look out too for savoury stuffed pastries. Another speciality you shouldn't miss if you get a chance is *hórta* – the wild greens that grow in abundance on the Cretan hills from autumn through springtime. These are gathered and boiled to be served up lukewarm (or sometimes cold), dressed with olive oil and vinegar or lemon juice, and can be delicious – or at the very least good for you. Although you can eat them all year round, spring and autumn are the best times, when they grow vigorously in cooler and damper conditions. Best, and most local are the misnamed ***stamnagáthi*** (spiny chicory) whose season starts in February.

Cafés and bars

The traditional Cretan coffee shop – the **kafenío** – filled with old men arguing and playing *távli*

RAKÍ – A SHOT OF HOSPITALITY

Rakí, known more often in western Crete as *tsikoudhiá*, holds a special place in the Cretan heart, and is central to traditional Cretan hospitality. No matter the time of day, if you're invited into a Cretan home you'll be presented with a glass of water, a morsel of cheese or a home-made sweet, and a shot of *rakí*, the local firewater. Many tavernas will offer you a shot after your meal, too, though this may be a more commercial (and hangover-inducing) product. Distilled from grape pomace – the leftovers from winemaking – the real stuff is home-made in hundreds of tiny stills (and a few bigger, communal ones) in villages the length of the island. Each is unique – Cretans pride themselves on being able to detect the most subtle distinctions in taste and quality – all are fiercely potent, and the best have a wonderfully clean yet fiery effect. Accept it if you can; quite apart from the danger of causing offence if you refuse, you'll rarely regret saying yes – and this is a gesture of welcome that still marks Crete out as a uniquely hospitable place.

(backgammon, a national obsession; most places will lend you a set) is still found in every village, though increasingly beleaguered under the onslaught of global mass culture. In the towns and resorts its place has largely been taken over by modern **cafés** and elegant **patisseries** (*zaharoplastía*).

Actual **bars** are rare except in the bigger resorts, but you can get a beer or glass of wine at almost any time in any café or taverna, and the modern cafés that proliferate in the major towns and cities generally become bars by night.

Coffee and kafenía

Traditional Greek **coffee** is what most Westerners would call "Turkish", tiny cups filled with a thick, black, heady concoction. It makes a great start to the day or a pick-me-up later – once you've acquired the taste and learned to leave the grounds behind in the cup. Most Cretans drink it medium-sweet or *métrio*; if you want no sugar at all, ask for *skéto*, while *varýglykó* is very sweet indeed. If you want Greek coffee, ask for a *kafé ellinikó* – many Cretan *kafenío* proprietors assume foreigners will want ordinary coffee (usually instant), so by choosing it you'll rise greatly in their estimation. *Kafenía* also serve ouzo, brandy, beer, various teas (*tsái*), soft drinks and juices. Some close at siesta time, but many remain open from early in the morning until late at night.

Cappuccino and other stylish coffees, including iced *freddoccino*, are rarely available at *kafenía*, but are of course the staple of more modern cafés. The universal drink of young Greece, however, is **frappé**. This is simply instant coffee powder, ice and water, whizzed to a froth and served with a glass of cold water: but it is infinitely better than that makes it sound, and the quintessential taste of a Greek summer. Again, you can have it *skéto*, *métrio* or *glykó* and with milk (*me gála*) or without.

Ouzo and rakí

In a *kafenío* or ouzerí, the prime time for an **ouzo** is 6–8pm, before dinner and after the afternoon nap. Ouzo, an aniseed-flavoured spirit, is served by the glass or *karafáki* (a 200ml vial or miniature bottle); add water or ice to taste, and watch the clear liquid turn cloudy white from the interaction of anethole with water or ice. Traditionally every ouzo was automatically accompanied by a small plate of mezédhes on the house – cheese, cucumber, tomato, a few olives, sometimes octopus or a couple of small fish – and this is a tradition that has made a welcome comeback; if you want something more substantial, you can always order more. **Rakí** is a burningly strong, unflavoured spirit, usually consumed as a digestif.

Wine

Wine is the usual accompaniment to a meal in a restaurant or taverna. If you don't specify what you want, you'll be served the **house wine**, traditionally poured cold from the barrel into tin jugs (*kantária*) or glass carafes in either kilo (litre), half- or quarter-kilo measures. Often the wine is home-made and a source of great pride: this can be excellent, it's invariably interesting and it's always relatively inexpensive. In more touristy places it may be from a wine box or barrel produced by one of the big co-ops, but again is

CRETAN WINE

With the increase in tourism and a new breed of fancier restaurants has come a demand for a more polished product, and Cretan viniculture is developing rapidly; increasing numbers of vineyards offer tours and tastings (see page 79 and http://winesofcrete.gr). **Cretan wines** come in many varieties; the hot, dry summers are more suited to producing dry red wines – dark and powerful – than whites. Six traditional grape varieties thrive on the island – *kotsifáli, thrapsathíri, liátiko, mandilariá, roméïko* and *vilána* – and there are four appellation wine-growing areas: Pezá, Dafnés, Sitía and Arhánes, the last still using some vineyards cultivated by the Minoans almost four thousand years ago.

Pezá brands like Minos red and white, which you can get everywhere, are generally palatable if rather boring. The **Arhánes** wine region also produces some pretty good red and white vintages, most notably by a co-operative that sells its wines under the Arhánes brand name. The **Sitian** wines Topiko (medium-dry with a hint of sherry) and Myrtos are both good everyday whites to drink with seafood. In the west, Kissamos red is another good bet. But the really interesting wines come from a proliferation of **smaller, boutique producers**: look out for names including Lyrarakis and Michalakis from the Pezá region; Dafnés producers Douloufakis and Idaia; Economou from Zíros in the far east; or in the west, Manousakis, near Vrýsses, and Karavtakis, from the Kolymbári region.

always local and very drinkable – which is more than can be said for the few bottles of overpriced wine stored on a hot, dusty shelf in the average taverna. If you want to taste the house wine before committing yourself to a *kanáta*, this should never be a problem.

Retsína is also produced locally, and always available. This pine-resinated wine, which usually comes in half-litre bottles, is an acquired taste, but some varieties are extremely good (particularly those produced by the Central Union of Haniá Wine Producers). It's also exceptionally cheap: a half-litre generally costs less than €1 in the supermarket, much the same as a half-litre of beer.

The media

Greeks are great devourers of newsprint – although few would propose the Greek mass media as a paradigm of objective journalism. Papers are almost uniformly sensational, while state-run TV and radio are often biased in favour of whichever party happens to be in government. Foreign news is easily available in the form of foreign publications flown in, often on the day of printing and cable TV news channels.

Newspapers

British newspapers are widely available in resorts and the larger towns at a cost of €2–4 for dailies, or €4–6 for Sunday editions. Many, including the *Guardian*, *Times*, *Mail* and *Mirror*, have slimmed-down editions printed in Greece which are available the same day; others are likely to be a day old. At bigger newsagents you'll also be able to find *USA Today* and *Time*.

MOVIES

Cretan **cinemas** show the regular major release movies, which in the case of English-language titles will almost always be in English with Greek subtitles (only children's films are dubbed). In summer, **open-air screens** operate in all the major towns and some of the resorts, and these are absolutely wonderful. You may not hear much, thanks to crackly speakers and locals chatting away throughout, but watching a movie under the stars on a warm night is simply a great experience.

Radio

Crete's airwaves are cluttered with **local stations**, many of which have plenty of music, often traditional. In resort areas some have news bulletins and tourist information in English. The mountainous nature of much of the island, though, means that any sort of radio reception is tricky and rather spotty: if you're driving around you'll find that you constantly have to retune. The two state-run networks are ER1 (a mix of news, talk and pop music) and ER2 (traditional and pop music).

Virtually any radio station from around the world is of course available over the internet, though, and quite a few on satellite TV channels.

Television

Even if your hotel advertises **satellite TV**, the only English-language channels usually included are CNN and BBC World. However, most evenings you'll find English-language films and mini-series, with subtitles, on at least a couple of the main Greek channels.

Festivals and cultural events

Most of the big Greek popular festivals have a religious origin, so they're observed in accordance with the Greek Orthodox calendar. This means that Easter, for example, can fall as much as three weeks to either side of the Western festival.

On top of the main religious festivals, there are scores of local fiestas, or **paniyíria**, celebrating the patron saint of the village church. Some of the more important are listed below; the *paramoní*, or **eve of the festival**, is often as significant as the day itself, and many of the events are actually celebrated on the night before. If you show up on the morning of the date given you may find that you have missed most of the music, dancing and drinking. With some 330-odd possible saints' days you're unlikely to travel for long without stumbling on something. Local tourist offices should be able to fill you in on events in their area. Twelve **public holidays** are dotted through the year (see page 47), during which banks and many shops and businesses close.

EASTER'S HOLY FLAME – A PAGAN RITE?

The flame from which all the Easter candles are lit has its source at Christ's Tomb in the Church of the Holy Sepulchre in Jerusalem; here the Patriarch of the Greek Orthodox Church celebrates the ceremony of the Holy Fire each Holy Saturday. From Jerusalem the flame is transported on a special flight to Athens, and within hours distributed by land, sea and air to churches throughout mainland Greece and the islands.

These ceremonies around the rebirth of light closely mirror the ancient Greek worship of Persephone, daughter of Demeter, goddess of the earth. In legend, Persephone was banished to the darkness of Hades for the winter, returning joyously to the light of day every spring.

Easter

Easter is by far the most important festival of the Greek year. It is an excellent time to be in Crete, both for the beautiful and moving religious ceremonies and for the days of feasting and celebration that follow. If you make for a smallish village, you may well find yourself an honorary member for the period of the festival. This is a busy time for Greek tourists as well as international ones, though, so book ahead.

The first great ceremony takes place on Holy Thursday evening, with Crucifixion hymns chanted in major churches. On **Good Friday** evening the Descent from the Cross is lamented in church. At dusk, the *Epitáfios*, Christ's funeral bier, lavishly decorated by the women of the parish, leaves the sanctuary and is paraded solemnly through the streets. **Late Saturday** evening sees the climax in a majestic mass to celebrate Christ's triumphant return. At the stroke of midnight all the lights in each crowded church are extinguished and the congregation plunged into darkness until the priest appears, holding aloft a taper to light the candles of the nearest worshippers. The flame is passed from person to person until the entire church – and the outer courtyard, standing room only for latecomers – is ablaze with burning candles. These are carried home through the streets, inside wind shields, and are said to bring good fortune to the house if they arrive still alight.

The lighting of the flames is the signal for celebrations to start, the Lent fast to be broken and, in many Cretan villages, for effigies of Judas to be burned. The traditional greeting, as fireworks and dynamite explode all around you in the street, is *Khristós Anésti* ("Christ is risen"), to which the response is *Alithós Anésti* ("Truly He is risen"). On **Easter Sunday** there's feasting on roast lamb.

The Greek equivalent of **Easter eggs** are hard-boiled eggs (painted red on Holy Thursday), which are baked into twisted, sweet bread-loaves (*tsourékia*) or distributed on Easter Sunday. People rap their eggs against their friends' eggs, and the owner of the last uncracked egg is considered lucky.

JANUARY

Jan 1: New Year's Day Also celebrated as the Feast of St Basil (Áyios Vasílios).

NAME DAYS

In Crete, everyone gets to celebrate their birthday twice. More important, in fact, than your actual birthday, is the "**Name Day**" of the saint whose name you bear. Greek ingenuity has stretched the saints' names (or invented new saints) to cover almost everyone, so even pagan Aris or Socrates get to celebrate. Altough in truth everyone named for a pagan personality also has an Orthodox baptismal name – e.g. Pandora Anna. If your name isn't covered, no problem – your party is on All Saints' Day, eight weeks after Easter.

The big name-day celebrations (Ioannis/Ioanna on January 7th or Yeoryios on April 23rd for example) can involve thousands of people, and traditional naming conventions guarantee that families get to celebrate together. In most families the eldest boy is still named after his paternal grandfather, and the eldest girl after her grandmother, so all the eldest cousins will share the same name, and the same name day. Any church or chapel bearing the saint's name will mark the event – some smaller chapels will open just for this one day of the year – while if an entire village is named after the saint, you can almost guarantee a festival. To check when your name day falls, see www.namedays.gr.

Jan 6: Epiphany Marks the baptism of Jesus and the end of the twelve days of Christmas. Baptismal fonts, lakes, rivers and seas are blessed, especially harbours, where the priest or bishop traditionally casts a crucifix into the water, with local youths competing to recover it.

FEBRUARY & MARCH

Carnival (Apókries) Festivities span three weeks, climaxing during the seventh weekend before Easter; big in Kalýves, Haniá and Réthymno.

Clean Monday (Kathará Dheftéra) The beginning of Lent, 7 weeks before Easter, is a traditional time to fly kites and to feast on all the things that will be forbidden over the coming weeks.

Meat Scent Thursday (Tsikhnopémpti) The last day before Lent when meat may be consumed. All *psistaiés* (grillhouses) are booked solid that evening.

March 25: Independence Day and the Feast of the Annunciation Both a religious and a national holiday, with military parades in many towns and dancing to celebrate the beginning of the revolt against Ottoman rule in 1821, and church services to honour the news given to Mary that she was to become the Mother of God. There are special celebrations in Paleóhora.

APRIL

Easter (Páskha);20 April, 2025; 12 April 2026; 2 May, 2027. Widespread celebration for the most important festival of the year; Good Friday and Easter Monday are public holidays. Shops open on Saturday.

April 23: Áyios Yeóryios St George, the patron saint of shepherds and their flocks, is commemorated with big rural celebrations throughout Crete, with much feasting and dancing. There's a major celebration in Así Goniá.

MAY

May 1: May Day The great urban holiday – most people make for the countryside to picnic. In the towns, demonstrations by the Left claim the day as Labour Day. If 1 May falls on a weekend, the official holiday will take place on a week-dayjust after.

May 20–27: Anniversary of the Battle of Crete Celebrated in Haniá and a different local village each year, with veterans' ceremonies, sporting events and folk dancing.

May 21: Áyios Konstandínos The feast of St Constantine who, as emperor, championed Christianity in the Byzantine Empire, and his mother, Ayía Eléni (St Helena) who recovered the True Cross from the Holy Land, with services and celebrations at churches and monasteries named after these saints, especially Arkádhi monastery; also a very popular name day.

JUNE

Whit Monday (Áyion) Pnévma fifty days after Easter, this is both a religious holiday and a secular one marking the start of the summer season.

June 24: Summer Solstice/John the Baptist Bonfires the night before, and widespread celebrations.

Late June: Naval Week Naval celebrations culminating in fireworks – especially big at Soúdha, and Haniá's old port fortress.

JULY & AUGUST

Early July: Réthymno Cretan Diet Festival A week of celebration of Cretan food and wine, along with traditional music and dancing (https://cretandietfestival.gr/en/home).

July to mid-Sept: Iráklio Festival A wide variety of cultural events from drama and film to traditional dance and jazz, at scattered sites (especially in the dry moat of the medieval walls) through most of the summer.

July to mid-Aug: Sitía Kornaría Festival Concerts, dance, theatre and food.

July & Aug: Áyios Nikólaos Lato Festival Cultural and sporting events throughout the summer.

Aug 6: Metamórfosi/Transfiguration Another important feast day. Especially celebrated in Voukoliés (Haniá), Máles (Ierápetra) and Zákros.

Aug 12: Áyios Mathéos The feast of St Matthew sees celebrations in Kastélli Kissámou.

Aug 15: Dormition of the Virgin (Kímisis tís Panayías) A huge holiday throughout Greece, the great feast of the Assumption (the Dormition in Greek) is a day when people traditionally return to their home village, often creating problems for unsuspecting visitors who find there's no accommodation left. Services in churches begin at dawn, but latecomers usually arrive for the bread, lamb and wine served in the churchyard at the end of the service around lunchtime. The neighbourhood of Neápoli is a main centre for this feast.

Aug 24: Áyios Eftýhios Celebrated especially in the southwest corner of the island, where many infants are given this name; there are festivities at Kándhanos near Soúyia (Haniá).

Aug 24: Áyios Títos The patron saint of Crete is celebrated all across the island, and with a big procession in Iráklio.

Aug 29: Áyios Ioánnis A massive name-day pilgrimage to the church of Áyios Ioánnis Gonión on the Rodhopoú peninsula in Haniá.

Late Aug: Kritsá Cretan Wedding A "traditional" wedding laid on for the tourists – quite a spectacle, nonetheless.

SEPTEMBER & OCTOBER

Sept 14: Áyios Stavrós/Holy Cross Celebrated with festivities at Tzermiádho and Kalamáfka.

Oct 11: Mihaíl Arhángelos The feast of the archangel is especially popular at Potamiés (Lasíthi).

Mid-Oct: Chestnut Festival Celebrated in Élos and other villages of the southwest where chestnuts are grown.

Oct 28: Óhi Day A national holiday with parades, folk dancing and speeches to commemorate prime minister Metaxas' one-word reply to Mussolini's 1940 ultimatum: Óhi! ("No!").

NOVEMBER & DECEMBER

Nov 7–9: Anniversary of the explosion at the monastery of Arkádhi One of Crete's biggest gatherings.

Dec 6: Áyios Nikólaos The patron saint of seafarers. Many chapels are dedicated to him around the island's coastline, including the one at the resort named after him, where processions and festivities mark the day.

Dec 25 & 26: Christmas It's less all-encompassing than Easter, but Christmas is still an important religious feast, and one that increasingly comes with all the usual commercial trappings: decorations, gifts and alarming outbreaks of plastic Santas on rooftops an balconies. Both Christmas Day and 26 December are public holidays.

31 Dec Paramoní of Aï Vassili Adults play cards for money, and divide a *vasillópita* cake, inside of which is baked a coin. The person whose slice contains the coin has good luck for the coming year.

Sports and outdoor activities

Although, not surprisingly, watersports are tremendously popular in Crete, there are perhaps fewer opportunities to take part than you might expect. Away from the coast, it's the mountains that are the great lure, with plenty of hiking options, from gentle strolls to long-distance mountain paths, and above all the great gorge walks, above the south coast. The mountains also offer the opportunity for more strenuous adventure activities.

Watersports

In all the resorts you'll find **waterski** boats that spend most of their time hauling people around on bananas or other inflatables, or towing parachutes for **parascending**. Sometimes there are jet skis too, but it's rare to find boats or windsurfers to rent. **Windsurfing** is particularly good in the far east, however, with a major centre at Kouréménos Beach (see page 166). **Scuba-diving** is also growing in popularity, largely due to the relaxation of government controls. There are centres where you can learn to dive in all the major north-coast resorts, but the best diving is probably off the south coast – especially around Plakiás – and in the far east, where there are fewer facilities. There isn't much life left in the Mediterranean, but these waters have more than most, and they're also exceptionally clear, while the rocky coast offers plenty of caves and hidden nooks to explore. **Kayaking** is growing in popularity, too, especially around the southwest coast, where some tour operators offer organised excursions (see page 28).

Hiking, cycling and climbing

There are great **walks** everywhere inland, and many of the best are pointed out throughout the Guide. If you're planning any serious hiking – including any of the various gorges – stout shoes or trainers are essential and **walking boots** with firm ankle support recommended, along with protection against the sun and adequate water supplies. Walking is much better in the spring and autumn than in the fierce heat of midsummer, especially as there will be far more animal and plant life then. Be aware that paths are none too well marked, and even those that start out clear may peter out as you climb into the mountains – always try to get local advice before setting out on anything at all challenging, and never hike alone.

In most of the resorts you can rent **mountain bikes**, and many of the rental places lead organized rides, which vary from easy explorations of the countryside to serious rides up proper mountains.

Crete also offers some exciting possibilities for **climbers**: contacts for the local mountaineering clubs (EOS) in Iráklio, Réthymno and Haniá are given in their respective listings, or see https://climbincrete.com.

Horseriding and adrenaline sports

A handful of adventure operators offer **adrenaline sports** including climbing, canyoning, abseiling and bungee – the Arádhena Gorge (see page 283) offers Europe's second-highest **bungee jump**. There are also opportunities for **horseriding** and, believe it or not, it is even possible to **ski** in Crete in winter: there's a tiny ski lift on the Nídha plain above Anóyia, while the *Kallergí Refuge* in the White Mountains (see page 273) may also open for ski parties. Don't come specially, however.

FIVE GREAT GORGE HIKES

Arádhena A challenging and spectacular trek. See page 283

Áyio An easy path through a lonely gorge to a great beach. See page 118

Roúvas An inland gorge, climbing high into the mountains. See page 101

Samariá Always crowded, always extraordinary. See page 273

Zákros, Gorge of the Dead A straightforward walk downhill from the eponymous village, rewarded with a Minoan palace and a welcome swim at a good beach. See page 169

ADVENTURE SPORTS OPERATORS

Crete is a great place for adventure holidays, and there are numerous companies across the island offering everything from mountain biking and canyoning to trekking and horseriding. Watersports and diving operators are also listed throughout the Guide.

CLIMBING/ADRENALINE SPORTS

Cretan Outdoor Adventures https://www.cretanadventures.gr/en.Guided and self-guiding hikes in western Crete also river trekking in Réthymno's Kourtaliótiko canyon. and a Via Ferrata in the little visited Ateroúsia Mountiains above the central south coast.

Liquid Bungy 6937 615 191, www.bungy.gr. White-knuckle bungee jumping at the Arádhena Gorge, Haniá.

Trekking Plan (aka Mounain Services) www.cycling.gr. Rock climbing, mountaineering, via Ferrata. ski touring on Psiloritís and the `Lefká Ori, plus canyoning, abseiling, kayaking and mountain biking in Haniá province.

HORSERIDING

Plakias Horse Riding Center 28320 31196 or 6942011620, www.cretehorseriding.com. Horse and donkey rides and instruction outside Plakiás; you can also enquire at Alianhos Car Rental in Plakiás.

Zoraïda's Horseriding 28250 61745, https://www.zoraidas-horseriding.com. Daily morning and evenin ridesfrom their stables at Kavrós beach, in Haniá district.

WALKING AND CYCLING

Cretan Adventures Evans 10, Iráklio, 28103 32772, www.cretanadventures.gr. Hiking, cycling, via ferrata and a huge variety of other adventure and family activities, especially in western Crete.

Cycling Creta 6947 308 452, https://cyclingcreta.gr. Cycle tours and training at all levels, including e-bike tours, from a base near Hersónisos, also straight rentals of various kinds of bike.

Olympic Bike 6944 220513, https://olympicbike.com. Gentle bike tours and serious mountain biking, mostly in central Crete, from a base in Réthymno.

Strata Walking Tours Platía Tzanakaki, Kastélli Kisámou, 28220 24249, http://stratatours.com. Guided treks and day-walks in Crete's the far west.

Travel essentials

Accessible travel

It is all too easy to wax lyrical over the attractions of Crete – the stepped, narrow alleys, the ease of travel by bus and ferry, the thrill of clambering around the great archeological sites. Travellers who use a wheelchair or have limited mobility or vision may not be so impressed. Uneven pavements, steep streets, and lack of facilities in ancient towns will always be an issue. Few of the major archeological sites or museums are at all wheelchair-friendly and nor, on the whole, are the towns and resorts.

Having said that, new hotels and apartments, along with modern museums, are subject to **EU legislation**; new hotels must have at least one room with disabled access and increasingly take people with disabilities into account in their design. With a little forward planning, it's possible to enjoy an inexpensive and trauma-free holiday in Crete. A quick web search will find a number of organizations that can help, including numerous small specialist agencies. One resort hotel, the *Eria* (+30 28210 62790, https://eria-resort.gr), in Maleme near Haniá, has been **designed specifically** for visitors with disabilities and their carers, with facilities including rental of most equipment you might need (from oxygen to hoists), physiotherapy, accessible airport transfers and so on. Inevitably, it's not cheap.

Many other hotels and apartments are accessible, and even mainstream operators and the large package companies now provide information on access, although such advice rarely extends to what happens when you venture beyond the front door.

A **medical certificate** of your fitness to travel, provided by your doctor, is extremely useful; some airlines or insurance companies may insist on it. You should also carry extra supplies of any required **medicines** and a prescription including the generic name in case of emergency. It's probably best to assume that any special equipment, drugs or clothing you may require is unavailable in Crete and will need to be brought with you.

Costs

The **cost** of travelling in Greece has dropped only slightly since the economic crisis, with inflation currently running at just over two percent; nonetheless it remains an EU country and member of the euro, and prices in shops and cafés are broadly comparable to other EU countries. In general, though, your needs are simple here and public transport, accommodation and taverna meals are among the less inflated items.

Average costs depend very much on where and when you go. The cities and major resorts are unsurprisingly more expensive, and costs increase substantially in July, August and at Easter. A per person **budget** of €60/£55/$70 a day will get you a share of a plain double room with bath or shower, breakfast, a picnic or simple taverna lunch, bus rides, museum tickets, a couple of beers and a decent evening meal. You could save a bit on this by camping or staying at hostels and catering for yourself, while for €80–100/£70–90/$90–115 you could upgrade your room, squeeze in a few extra drinks, and share the rental of a motorbike or small car.

Entry charges for archeological sites and museums vary from €2 to around €10 for an important site such as Knossós; entrance to state-run sites and museums is **free** on Sundays and public holidays between November and March.

Most shops have fixed prices, so **bargaining** isn't a regular feature of tourist life. It is worth negotiating over rooms, though, especially off-season, or for vehicle rental, especially for longer periods.

Tipping is not essential anywhere, though taxi drivers generally expect it from tourists and most service staff are very poorly paid. Restaurant bills incorporate a service charge; if you want to tip, rounding up the bill is usually sufficient. If you are offered hospitality by a local they are likely to insist on paying – and offering cash can be seen as offensive. The best solution is to offer to reciprocate, making clear that it's on you next time.

Crime and personal safety

Crete, along with Greece as a whole, remains one of Europe's safest regions, with a low **crime** rate and a deserved reputation for honesty. If you leave a bag or wallet at a café, you'll most likely find it scrupulously looked after, pending your return. Nonetheless theft and muggings do happen. With this in mind, it's best to lock rooms and cars securely (don't leave valuables even in locked cars), and to keep your valuables hidden, especially in cities. Civil unrest, in the form of strikes and demonstrations, is also on the increase but while this might inconvenience you, as a visitor you'd be very unlucky to get caught up in any trouble.

In more remote localities **women** may feel slightly uncomfortable travelling alone. The traditional villagers may not understand why you are unaccompanied and might not welcome your presence in their exclusively male *kafenía* – often the only place where you can get a drink. Travelling with a companion, you're more likely to be treated as a *xéni*, a word meaning both (female) stranger and guest.

Police and potential offences

Though the chances are you'll never meet a member of the national **police force**, the *Ellinikí Astynomía*, Greek cops expect respect: in Crete, on the whole, they're pretty laidback, but they can be harsh if you cross them, and police practice often falls short of northern European norms. If you need to go to the police, always try to do so through the Tourist Police (171), who should speak English and are used to dealing with visitors. You are required to **carry suitable ID** on you at all times – either a passport or a driving licence. A certified photocopy of your passport front page will do for the beach.

The most common causes of a brush with the law are beach **nudity**, **camping** outside authorized sites, **public inebriation** or lewd behaviour. In 2009 a large British stag group dressed as nuns was arrested in Mália and held for several days, having managed to combine extreme drunkenness with a lack of respect to the church and in 2020 a group of foreigners was arrested for causing a brawl in one of the tourist resorts. Also avoid taking **photos in forbidden areas** such as airports. Such areas are usually marked with a sign featuring an old-style bellows camera with a red 'X' through it.

Drug offences are treated as major crimes, particularly since there's a mushrooming local addiction problem. The maximum penalty for "causing the use

DISCOUNTS AND STUDENT CARDS

State-run museums and archeological sites offer free entry to under-18s, senior citizens, students, teachers and journalists from the EU with proper identification, and substantial reductions for other nationalities; private attractions may also offer reduced prices, especially for children.

Full-time students are eligible for the **International Student ID Card or app** (ISIC; www.isic.org), which entitles the bearer to special air and ferry fares and discounts at numerous shops and attractions. For Americans there's also a health benefit. You only have to be 26 or younger to qualify for the **International Youth Travel Card**, which costs the same and carries the same benefits – it's not strictly a student ID, but will probably work. Teachers qualify for the **International Teacher Identity Card (ITIC)**, offering insurance benefits but limited travel discounts.

As well as the benefits listed above, **senior citizens** are entitled to cut-price fares on some buses, ferries and domestic flights. You'll need to have proof of age to hand.

of drugs by someone under 18", for example, is life imprisonment and an astronomical fine. Foreigners caught in possession of even small amounts of marijuana get long jail sentences if there's evidence that they've been supplying the drug to others. Things are changing slowly CBD or HHC edibles or smokables are increasingly available through the Hemp Oil chain of shops, with outlets on Crete in Haniá and Hersónisos.

Electricity

The **electricity** supply is 220 volt AC. Plugs are the standard European variety of two round pins and you should pick up an adapter before you leave home, as they can be difficult to find locally (only at electrical merchants). North American appliances (unless they're dual voltage) will also require a transformer.

Entry requirements

EU nationals need only a valid **passport** for entry to Greece, and are not stamped in on arrival or out upon departure (in other words, you can stay as long as you like). UK, US, Australian, New Zealand, Canadian and most non-EU Europeans can stay as tourists for ninety days (cumulative) in any six-month period; make sure your passport is stamped to avoid problems on exit. Your passport must be valid for three months after your arrival date.

Visitors from non-EU countries, unless of Greek descent, are very rarely granted **extensions** to tourist visas. If you overstay you're liable to be deported (at vast expense) or will be hit with a large fine upon departure when you attempt to leave. Visa requirements by country and a full list of Greek embassies and consulates overseas can be found at www.mfa.gr.

Health

Covid19 has ceased to be an urgent concern to visitors to Greece, but if you have had a course of inoculations since 2020 it's not a bad idea to bring an official certificate detailing when you had them, should there be another panic while you are in Crete. There are no other required **vaccinations** for Greece, though it's wise to ensure that you are up to date on tetanus and polio. The main **health risks** faced by visitors involve overexposure to the sun, over-indulgence in food and drink, or bites and stings from insects and sea creatures. **Drinking water** is safe pretty much everywhere, though it doesn't always taste great; in the mountains, it often comes straight from the same spring used by the bottling factories. Despite this, almost everyone drinks the bottled stuff instead.

EU nationals are entitled to free medical care upon presentation of a **European Health Insurance Card** (EHIC). The UK, US, Canada, Australia and New Zealand have no formal healthcare agreements with Greece (other than allowing for free emergency trauma treatment), so insurance is highly recommended. Brits can obtain a global health insurance card for free treatment in public hospitals and clinics on Crete at https://overseas-healthcare.nhsbsa.nhs.uk/get-healthcare-cover-travelling-abroad/start

For serious medical attention you'll find English-speaking **doctors** (mainly private) in all the bigger towns and resorts. There are also hospitals in all the big cities. For an **ambulance**, phone 166.

Pharmacies, drugs and contraception

For minor complaints, head for the local pharmacy (**farmakío**). Greek pharmacists are highly trained and dispense a number of medicines which elsewhere could only be prescribed by a doctor. In the larger towns and resorts there'll usually be one who speaks good English. Pharmacies are usually closed evenings and Saturday mornings, but all should have a schedule on their door showing the night and weekend duty pharmacists in town.

If you regularly use any form of **prescription drug**, you should bring along a copy of the prescription, together with the generic name of the drug; this will help you replace it, and avoids problems with customs officials. In this regard, you should be aware that **codeine is banned** in Greece, and if you import any you might find yourself in trouble, so check labels carefully; it's a major ingredient of Panadeine, Veganin, Solpadeine, Codis and Nurofen Plus, to name just a few. If you have a prescription, you should be OK.

Contraceptive pills are sold over-the-counter at larger pharmacies, though not necessarily the brands you may be used to; a good pharmacist should come up with a close match. **Condoms** are inexpensive and ubiquitous – just ask for *profylaktiká* (less formally, *plastiká* or *kapótes*) at any pharmacy, sundries store or corner *períptero* (kiosk). Sanitary towels and **tampons** are widely sold in supermarkets.

Insurance

Even though EU health care privileges apply in Greece (see page 44), you'd do well to take out **insurance** before travelling to cover against theft, loss, illness or injury. Before paying for a whole new policy it's worth checking whether you are already covered: some all-risks home insurance policies may

ROUGH GUIDES TRAVEL INSURANCE

Looking for travel insurance? Rough Guides partners with top providers worldwide to offer you the best coverage. Policies are available to residents of anywhere in the world, with a range of options whether you are looking for single-trip, multi-country or long-stay insurance. There's coverage for a wide range of adventure sports, 24-hour emergency assistance, high levels of medical and evacuation cover and a stream of travel safety information. Even better, roughguides.com users can take advantage of these policies online 24/7, from anywhere in the world – even if you're already travelling. To make the most of your travels and ensure a smoother experience, it's always good to be prepared for when things don't go according to plan. For more information go to www.roughguides.com/bookings/insurance.

cover your possessions when overseas, and many private medical schemes offer coverage extensions for abroad. Some form of insurance may be included if you paid for your holiday with a **credit card**, too.

Rough Guides strongly recommends taking out private **travel insurance**; there are plenty of deals online (it's rarely good value when bought from a travel agent). Most policies exclude so-called **dangerous sports** unless an extra premium is paid: in Crete this could include horseriding, windsurfing, jet skiing, mountaineering and motorbiking.

If you need to make a **medical claim**, you should keep receipts for medicines and treatment, and in the event you have anything stolen or lost, you must obtain an **official statement** from the police or the airline that lost your bags. With a rise in the numbers of fraudulent claims, most insurers won't even consider one unless you have a police report.

Internet

In the resorts and bigger towns there's **free wi-fi** in the majority of hotels and rooms places, as well as in most cafés and tavernas. **Internet cafés** are dying out as a result, though you can usually find something (often packed with local kids, gaming online): rates are around €2–4/hr.

LGBTQI+ travellers

"Out" gay Greeks are rare, and "out" local lesbians rarer still. Foreign same-sex couples will be regarded, away from the big resorts, with some bemusement but accorded the same standard courtesy as straight foreigners. There are no specifically **LGBTQI+ resorts** on Crete like other Greek islands, but there are plenty of gay-friendly bars and clubs in towns like Haniá and Iráklio, as well as beaches with a LGBTQI+ scene. Gay Pride is usually held in Iráklio and takes place across two days at the end of June.

Living in Crete

Many habitual visitors fall in love with Crete and end up as part- or full-time residents, more likely buying property than renting it, and most probably retired or self-employed rather than working at relatively low Greek wages. EU citizens are entitled to stay indefinitely and to work in Crete; though even then this is a highly bureaucratic society were getting a job (at least legally) is fraught with paperwork, as are the everyday needs of getting a phone, power and the like. It's beyond the scope of this book to go into detail, but there's plenty of assistance available locally, above all from the existing expat community who've done it all before. The website http://livingincrete.net is also an excellent resource. It is worth noting that since Brexit, UK citizens are no longer able to live, work or retire in Greece without the proper papers.

Work

Work opportunities in Crete are severely limited and, EU membership notwithstanding, **short-term unskilled work** is often badly paid and undocumented. The old standby of work on the harvests is now dominated by immigrants from Albania, South Asia and Eastern Europe, and appallingly paid even if you can find it.

There's a far better chance of employment in **tourism**, or teaching English. Many bars, tavernas and hotels have seasonal jobs, for which you should turn up early in the season and ask around. Your chances will be better if you can speak more than one language (ideally including Greek!), and if you are female. Men, unless they are trained chefs, find it harder to find any work, even washing up.

On a similar, unofficial level you might be able to work in a **tourist shop**, or (if you've the expertise) helping out at a watersports centre. Perhaps the best type of tourism-related work, however, is that of courier/greeter/group coordinator for a **package holiday company**. Most of these jobs are filled well in advance, but people may leave or fall ill – get yourself known to the reps, locally or on their airport runs, and you may get lucky.

Teaching English is largely a winter job, in the big towns where the language schools are. It's relatively well paid, but almost impossible to get into without a bona fide TEFL certificate.

Mail

Post offices are open Monday to Friday from 7.30am to 2pm. **Airmail letters** take 3–7 days to reach the rest of Europe, 5–12 days to North America, a little longer for Australia and New Zealand. As anywhere, post offices tend to have long queues, so if all you want is a stamp (*grammatósimo*) you're better off buying it when you buy your postcards, or from almost any *períptero* (kiosk) and most minimarkets. Postage for postcards and letters up to 20g is the same for all international destinations, currently €0.85. For about €3 extra you can use the express service (*katepígonda*), which cuts delivery time by a couple of days.

Ordinary **postboxes** are bright yellow, express boxes dark red, but it's best to use those by the door of a post office if possible, since days may pass between collections at others.

Maps

Maps of Crete are easily available all over the island, but you'll almost certainly find a better one at home. Having said that, even the best maps seem to have a number of significant errors. For drivers this is rarely more than a minor irritation, but hikers should take care not to rely solely on a single map and to confirm directions locally wherever possible.

The best maps for **driving and general use** is the Terrain 1:200,000 product; some of the better free car-rental maps are also surprisingly useful – they may be small-scale and covered in adverts, but they tend to be updated regularly, which means that they often show the main roads more accurately than many more professional-looking rivals. The Greek tourist authorities also provide a downloadable map at http://visitgreece.gr.

If you want more detail, for **hiking** for example, the best maps are from Greek cartographer Anavasi (http://anavasi.gr), who cover the island in three GPS-compatible regional 1:100,000 maps and also produce seven excellent 1:25,000 or 1:30,000 hiking maps covering the most popular areas, including the White Mountains, Mount Psiloritis and the far east.

SHHHH! SIESTA TIME

The hours **between 3 and 5.30pm**, the midday *mikró ýpno* (**siesta**), are sacrosanct and indeed protected by law – it's not acceptable to visit people, make phone calls to strangers or cause any sort of loud noise (especially with motorcycles) at this time. Quiet is also legally mandated **between 11pm and 8am** in residential areas.

Money

Currency in Crete is the euro (€). Euro coins are issued in denominations of 1, 2, 5, 10, 20 and 50 cents and 1 and 2 euros; euro notes come in denominations of 5, 10, 20, 50, 100, and 200 euros. Up-to-date exchange rates can be found on www.xe.com.

Banks and exchange

The airports at Haniá and Iráklio should always have an **exchange desk** operating for passengers on incoming international flights, as well as ATMs – but at peak periods there's often a queue and it's well worth taking some euros to tide you over the first few hours. You'll generally get a better rate if you buy euros in advance, provided you shop around and pre-order, rather than waiting until you get to the airport.

Banks are normally open Mon–Thurs 8.30am–2.30pm, Fri 8.30am–2pm, while outside these hours larger hotels can often change paper money, albeit with hefty commissions. When using a bank, always take your passport with you and be prepared for at least one long queue – often you have to line up once to have the transaction approved and again to pick up the cash. Rates and commissions vary considerably, even between branches of the same bank, so ask first.

ATMs and credit cards

ATMs are plentiful, and can be found in all the resorts and towns of any size, though you shouldn't expect to find them in rural areas or the smaller resorts (especially on the south coast). They're easy to use, with your normal PIN, though you won't know exactly what exchange rate you're getting or how much you're being charged. In most cases rates and commission are no worse than the alternatives, however, and you can avoid some of the charges and uncertainty by using a prepaid holiday money card in euros, or a specialist travel card such as Revolut (http://revolut.com).

PUBLIC HOLIDAYS

Jan 1 New Year's Day/tou Aï Vassili
Jan 6 Epiphany/Ta Ayia Theofánia
Feb/March Clean Monday, 7 weeks before Easter
March 25 Independence/Annunciation Day
April/May Good Friday and Easter Monday (see page 39 for dates)
May 1 May Day
May/June Whit Monday, 7 weeks plus on day after Easter
Aug 15 Dormition of the Panagía (Moher of God); commemorates the defiance of the Italian ultimatum in 1941
Dec 25/26 Christmas Day. In Greece gifts are exchanged on 1 January.

Major **credit cards** are widely accepted, but only by the more expensive stores, hotels and restaurants: they're useful for renting cars, for example, but not widely accepted by the cheaper tavernas or rooms places. Using a credit card in an ATM (as opposed to a debit card) means you'll be charged interest from the moment you do so.

Opening hours and public holidays

It's difficult to generalize about Cretan **opening hours**, which are notoriously erratic. Nonetheless the general pattern is that on Monday, Wednesday and Saturday shops are open 8.30am–2.30pm, and on Tuesday, Thursday and Friday 8.30am–2pm and 5.30–9pm; offices will generally follow similar hours. In tourist areas, though, stores and offices may stay open right through the day – certainly the most important, state-run **archeological sites and museums** do so. As far as possible, opening hours for these are quoted in the Guide, but they change with exasperating frequency, depending on staff availability. If you're planning a special journey try to confirm in advance, or time your visit for the core hours of 9am–2pm; many close on Tuesdays. **Churches and monasteries** are generally open through the day, though they, too, may well close for an afternoon siesta.

Phones

There's excellent **mobile phone** coverage throughout Crete, and you should be able to pick up a signal just about anywhere. To use your own phone you may u need to call your provider to ensure that you have international roaming switched on: there are no roaming charges within the EU, so EU nationals pay the same price for calls, texts and data to numbers in their home country as they would at home. Post-Brexit, UK users should check costs with their provider; US users should also check that their phone will work in Europe – it must be triband. If you do have to pay, most networks offer good-value European add-ons, essential if you plan to use data (otherwise, make sure data roaming is switched off). Remember that you'll be charged for incoming as well as outgoing calls. If you plan to use a phone extensively for local calls you might well be better off buying a Greek **pay-as-you-go** SIM card (from around €15); you may have to have your phone unlocked to use this, but most Greek mobile shops can do this for a small fee. You also must have the phone registered as an anti-terrorism precaution.

Calling on regular phones is pretty straightforward, and all the resorts and towns of any size will have **call boxes**, invariably sited at the noisiest street corner. These work only with **phonecards** (*tilekártes*), widely available from kiosks and newsagents in various denominations starting at €4. They offer fairly good value even for international calls, especially within Europe. A **calling card** may make international calls cheaper; either one provided by your own operator at home, accessed by a freephone number and charged directly to your domestic account (these are convenient, but rates vary), or a prepaid card which you can buy from many local kiosks and newsagents (compare rates, as different cards offer better value for different countries).

Avoid making calls from your **hotel** room, as a huge surcharge will be slapped on, though you shouldn't be charged to access a free calling card number.

Smoking

Despite governmental campaigns against the practice, Greeks remain among the heaviest **smokers** in Europe, and although legally you're not allowed to smoke indoors in restaurants, bars or public offices, in practice the law is widely disregarded. No-smoking areas are increasingly enforced these days, an even in winter outdoor seating is accordingly popular.

PHONE CODES AND NUMBERS

The international dialling code for Greece is +30. To make an international call, dial the international access code (in Greece it's 00), then the destination's country code, before the rest of the number. Note that the initial zero is omitted from the area code when dialling the UK, Ireland, Australia and New Zealand from abroad.

Australia international access code + 61
New Zealand international access code + 64
UK international access code + 44
US and Canada international access code + 1
Ireland international access code + 353
South Africa international access code + 27

USEFUL PHONE NUMBERS

Ambulance 166
Fire service 199
Forest fire reporting 191
Operator (domestic) 132
Operator (international) 139
Police/emergency 100
Tourist police 171

Time

Greek **summertime** begins at 2am on the last Sunday in March, when the clocks go forward one hour, and ends at 2am on the last Sunday in October when they go back. This change is not well publicized locally, and visitors miss planes and ferries every year. Greek time is always 2hr ahead of Britain. For North America, the difference is usually 7hr for Eastern Standard Time and 10hr for Pacific Standard Time – but bear in mind that daylight saving starts 2–3 weeks earlier and ends a week later than in Europe.

Toilets

In **toilets** throughout Crete you're expected to toss paper in a wastebasket, not in the bowl: learn this habit, or you'll block the pipes. There's almost always a sign to remind you, but even if not you should do so, except in the most modern and upmarket hotels. Public toilets are rare except in the towns, usually in parks or squares, often subterranean. Otherwise try a bus station or pay for a coffee somewhere. It's worth carrying toilet paper with you – though it's provided by any attendants at public facilities, there may be none in tavernas and cafés.

Tourist information

The **National Tourist Organization of Greece** (*Ellinikós Organismós Tourismoú*, or EOT; http://visitgreece.gr) maintains offices in major European capitals, and in New York. On the island, **local tourist offices** in the major towns and many smaller resorts provide an array of maps, timetables and leaflets as well as details of local accommodation, sometimes offering a booking service as well. The economic crisis is taking a heavy toll, though, and most have drastically shortened their hours and reduced staffing; some have closed altogether. In their stead, local **travel agencies** are always helpful and many voluntarily act as improvised tourist offices; many of these are listed in the Guide. The **tourist police** may also be helpful: a branch (or often just a single delegate) of the local police, they should have some knowledge of English and deal with complaints about restaurants, taxis, hotels and all things tourist-related; call 171 for information and help, and see individual town accounts for local addresses.

Travelling with children

Children are worshipped and indulged in Crete, arguably to excess – wherever you go on the island, your kids will be very welcome. Greek children sleep in the afternoon and stay up late. You'll see plenty of kids at tavernas, joining in with the adult food and conversation.

While there's not much in the way of specifically child-oriented holidays to Crete, many hotels and newer apartment complexes have children's pools and small playgrounds, and most tour operators will be able to book you something suitable. Some of the fancier resort hotels have kids' clubs and activities, while almost all hotels and rooms places have three- and four-bed rooms (or can add a cot to a regular room, at minimal or no extra cost); many have small apartments with fridges and simple cooking facilities, too. There are several water parks along the north coast (see page 245), and activities like gorge-hiking or boat trips can become real adventures (though don't be overambitious – they can also be really gruelling in the heat). Younger kids may also enjoy the "tourist train" rides that operate in and around many of the major towns and resorts. Under-18s get **free entry** to state-run museums and archeological sites, and reduced prices at most attractions.

Baby food and **nappies** (diapers) are readily available and reasonably priced.

Iráklio

RUINS OF THE MINOAN PALACE, MALIÁ

Iráklio

The province of Iráklio sees more tourists than any other in Crete. They come for two simple reasons: the string of big resorts that lies to the east of the city, just an hour or so from the existing airport, and the great Minoan sites, almost all of which are concentrated in the centre of the island. Knossós, Mália and Festós are in easy reach of almost anywhere in the province, and there are excellent beaches all along the north coast.

Iráklio itself is a big, boisterous city – the fifth largest in Greece. Strident and modern, it's a maelstrom of crowded thoroughfares, building work and dust, and, in high summer, its great sites are packed. Penetrate this facade, however, and you can discover a vibrant working city with a myriad of attractive features that do much to temper initial impressions. **East of the city**, the startling pace of **tourist development** is all too plain to see. In peak season, it can be hard to find a room in this monument to the package tour, and expensive if you do, though some of the resorts, most notably **Mália** and **Hersónisos**, do at least have good beaches and lively nightlife. As a general rule, the further east you go, the better things get: head inland even briefly and a more appealing Crete – of olive groves, tidy villages and picturesque mountain vistas – reveals itself.

West and south of Iráklio, the beaches are smaller and the coastline is less amenable to hotel builders. To the west, there's just one small, classy resort – in the bay at **Ayía Pelayía** – a few isolated hotels and, in the hills behind, a number of interesting old villages. **Mátala** is the only resort of any size in the south, and a day-trip route takes in the major archeological sites of **Górtys**, **Festós** and **Ayía Triádha**. The rest is traditional farming country; the **Messará plain**, in particular, has been a vital resource since Minoan times, and its importance is reflected in the number of large and wealthy villages here.

Iráklio city

The best way to arrive in **IRÁKLIO** (**Ηράκλειο**) is from the sea: the traditional approach and still the one that shows the city in its best light, with Mount Yioúhtas rising behind, the heights of the Psilorítis range to the southwest and, as you get closer, the great fortress guarding the old harbour entrance and the city walls encircling and dominating the oldest part of town.

The reality when you arrive is less romantic: modern ferries are far too large for the old harbour and dock at giant concrete wharves alongside, while on closer inspection what little remains of the **old city** has been heavily restored, often from the bottom up. The slick renovations often look unnaturally pristine and polished alongside the grime that coats even the most recent buildings – a juxtaposition that seems neatly to sum up much about modern Iráklio. While the city will never be one of the jewels of the Mediterranean, the ebullient friendliness of its people and an infectious cosmopolitan atmosphere may well tempt you into giving it more than the customary one-night transit.

Brief history

A Roman port, Heraclium, stood hereabouts and the city readopted its name only at the beginning of the twentieth century. Founded by the **Saracens**, who held Crete from 827 to 961, it was originally known as **El Khandak**, after the great ditch that surrounded it, later corrupted by the Venetians to **Candia** – or Candy, as Shakespeare titled it in *Twelfth Night* – a name also applied to the island as a whole. This Venetian

MÁTALA BEACH

Highlights

1 Iráklio Crete's bustling capital boasts great restaurants and cafés, a vibrant market and an impressive harbour fortress, as well as an outstanding archeological museum with the world's finest collection of Minoan artefacts. See page 52

2 Knossós Crete's major tourist attraction, the world-famous palace of Knossós remains the most impressive of the Minoan sites. See page 72

3 Górtys Capital of Crete in Roman times, this site has plenty of ruins to explore, including the imposing remains of Áyios Títos, the island's first Christian church. See page 104

4 Festós and Mália palaces These two outstanding ancient sites in picturesque locations are superb examples of Minoan architecture. See pages 107 and 95

5 Museum of Cretan Ethnology, Vóri An outstanding folk museum in a mountainous, rural area of great beauty. See page 112

6 Mátala In striking contrast to the brash north-coast resorts, Mátala is on a thoroughly human scale, though still with lots going on late into the night. Nearby are plenty of quieter escapes, and it's within easy reach of many of the major sights. See page 113

HIGHLIGHTS ARE MARKED ON THE MAP ON PAGE 54

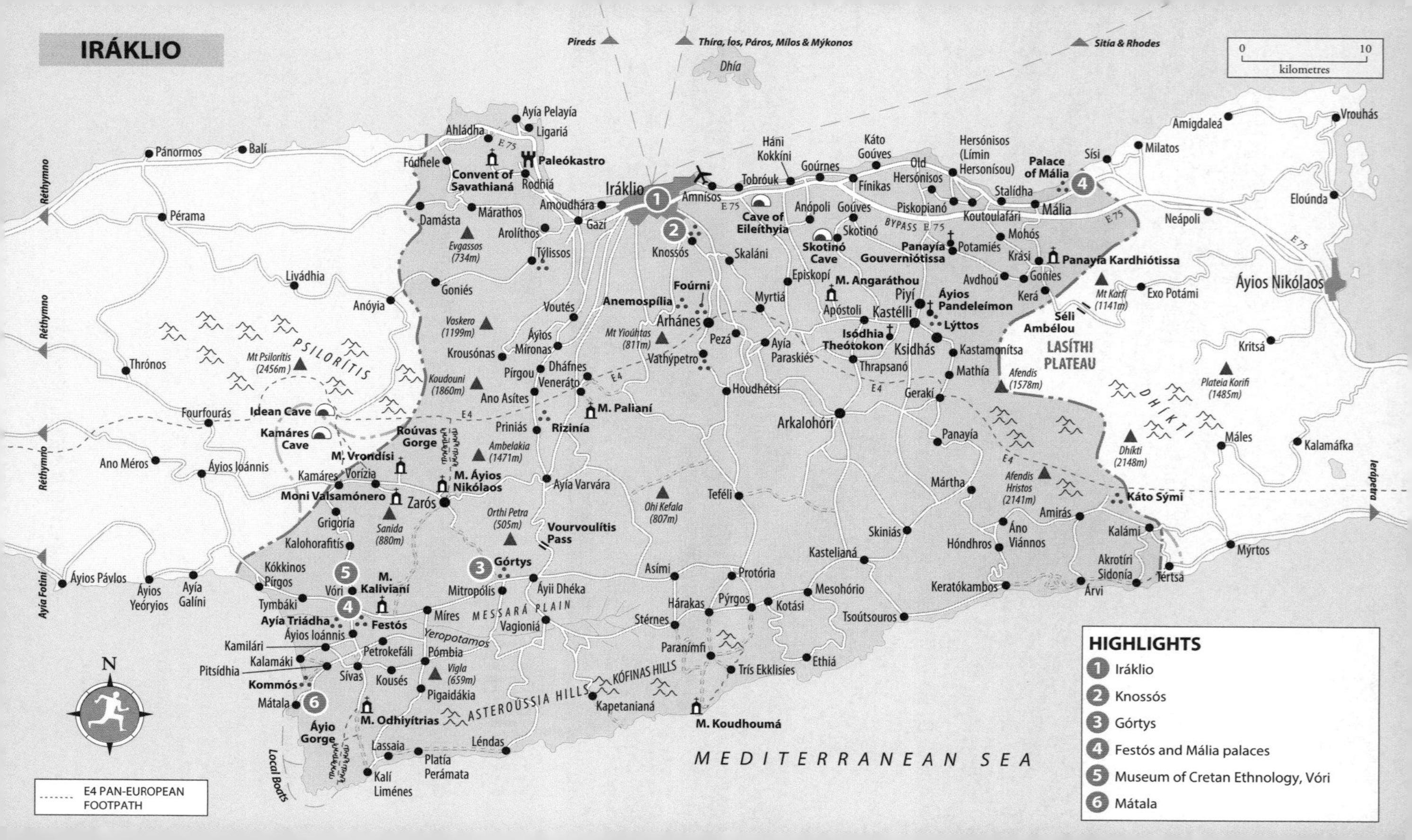

IRÁKLIO

HIGHLIGHTS

1. Iráklio
2. Knossós
3. Górtys
4. Festós and Mália palaces
5. Museum of Cretan Ethnology, Vóri
6. Mátala

E4 PAN-EUROPEAN FOOTPATH

0 10 kilometres

N

Pireás
Thíra, Íos, Páros, Mílos & Mýkonos
Sitía & Rhodes
Dhía
Réthymno
Ayía Fotiní
Ierápetra
Local Boats
MEDITERRANEAN SEA

Ayía Pelayía
Ahládha
Ligariá
Pánormos
Balí
Fódhele
Convent of Savathianá
Paleókastro
Rodhiá
Iráklio
Amnísos
Tobróuk
Háni Kokkíni
Goúrnes
Káto Goúves
Fínikas
Old Hersónisos
Hersónisos (Límin Hersonísou)
Palace of Mália
Sísi
Milatos
Amígdaleá
Vrouhás
Eloúnda
Neápoli
Mália
Stalídha
Koutoulafári
Piskopianó
Pérama
Damásta
Márathos
Amoudhára
Gazi
Arolíthos
Evgassos (734m)
Týlissos
Knossós
Cave of Eileíthyia
Anópoli
Goúves
Skotinó
Skotinó Cave
Panayía Gouverniótissa
Potamiés
Mohós
Krási
Panayía Kardhiótissa
Goníes
Avdhoú
Kerá
Mt Karfí (1141m)
Exo Potámi
Áyios Nikólaos
Livádhia
Anóyia
Goniés
Skaláni
Episkopí
M. Angaráthou
Piyí
Áyios Pandeleímon
Séli Ambélou
Kritsá
Fourni
Anemospília
Myrtiá
Apóstoli
Kastélli
Lýttos
LASÍTHI PLATEAU
Voutés
Voskero (1199m)
Áyios Míronas
Krousónas
Arhánes
Mt Yioúhtas (811m)
Pezá
Ayía Paraskiés
Isódhia Theótokon
Ksidhás
Kastamonítsa
Thrónos
PSILORÍTIS
Mt Psiloritis (2456m)
Koudouni (1860m)
Pírgou
Dháfnes
Veneráto
Vathýpetro
Thrapsanó
Mathía
Afendis (1578m)
Plateia Korifi (1485m)
DHÍKTI
Ano Asítes
Houdhétsi
Geraki
Fourfourás
Idean Cave
M. Paliani
Arkalohóri
Kamáres Cave
Roúvas Gorge
Priniás
Rizinía
Panayía
Dhíkti (2148m)
Máles
Kalamáfka
Ano Méros
Áyios Ioánnis
M. Vrondísi
Ambelakia (1471m)
M. Áyios Nikólaos
Kamáres
Vorízia
Ayía Varvára
Ohi Kefala (807m)
Tefeli
Mártha
Afendis Hristos (2141m)
Káto Sými
Moni Valsamónero
Zarós
Orthi Petra (505m)
Vourvoulítis Pass
Grigoría
Sanida (880m)
Skiniás
Amirás
Ano Viánnos
Hóndhros
Kalámi
Kalohorafitís
Górtys
Asími
Kasteliana
Mýrtos
Kókkinos Pírgos
Áyios Pávlos
Áyios Yeóryios
Ayía Galíni
Vóri
M. Kaliviani
Mitropólis
Áyii Dhéka
Protória
Mesohório
Keratókambos
Akrotíri Sidonía
Tértsa
Árvi
Tymbáki
Míres
MESSARÁ PLAIN
Hárakas
Pýrgos
Kotási
Tsoútsouros
Ayía Triádha
Festós
Áyios Ioánnis
Yeropotamos
Vagioniá
Stérnes
Kamilári
Petrokefáli
Pómbia
Paranímfi
Ethiá
Kalamáki
Pitsídhia
Sívas
Kousés
Vigla (659m)
Trís Ekklisíes
KÓFINAS HILLS
Kommós
Pigaidákia
ASTEROÚSSIA HILLS
Kapetanianá
Mátala
M. Odhiyítrias
M. Koudhoumá
Áyio Gorge
Lassaia
Léndas
Platía Perámata
Kalí Liménes
E75
E4
BYPASS E75

capital was, in its day, one of the strongest and most spectacular cities in Europe; a trading centre, a staging-point for the Crusades and, as time wore on, the front line of Christendom. The **Turk Ottomans** finally conquered the city after 21 years of war, which culminated in a bitter siege from May 1667 to September 1669. Under its new Ottoman rulers, the city's importance declined in relation to Haniá's, but it remained a major port and the second city in Crete. It was here, too, that the incident occurred which eventually put an end to Ottoman occupation of the island (see page 63). Finally united with **Greece**, Iráklio's future prosperity was assured by its central position.

Almost all that you see today dates only from the last sixty years or so, partly because of the heavy bombing the city suffered during World War II, but above all thanks to Crete's (until recently) booming agriculture, industry and tourism. In 1971, Iráklio regained the official title of island **capital**, and the city is now the wealthiest per head in the whole of Greece. During the boom years the authorities undertook ambitious projects to spruce up and refurbish the city centre, and some of the results are truly impressive.

The harbour

The obvious starting point is the **harbour**, now home to fishing boats and a pleasure marina but still guarded over by an impressive sixteenth-century **Venetian fortress**, generally known by its Turkish name of **Koúles** (charge), emblazoned with the Lion of St Mark. The causeway leading to the fort is a favourite place for a stroll and for locals to fish: at night, when the fortress is floodlit, it's a fine place to watch the ferries coming and going. Inside, the sturdy walls protect a series of chambers in which the defenders must have enjoyed an overwhelming sense of security. There are tremendous views from the roof, and recent restoration has been minimal – information boards and mulitmedia presentations dot the otherwise barren spaces.

The Arsenali

On the landward side of the harbour, the vaulted **Arsenali** are marooned in a sea of traffic scooting along Koundouriótou, the harbour road. A typically ambitious Venetian military project, they were completed in four stages between the fifteenth and seventeenth

IRÁKLIO ORIENTATION

Virtually everything of interest in Iráklio lies within the old walled city, with the majority of the sights clustered in the northeastern corner. Despite the city's rather cheerless reputation, parts of the old town can be genuinely picturesque, not least the weighty **Venetian defences**: the harbour fortress and the massive walls framing the old quarters. Focal to this area are **Venizélou** and **Eleftherías** squares, and most of the churches and museums – including the **Archeological Museum**, with the world's foremost collection of Minoan antiquities – are just a few minutes' walk from either.

The most vital thoroughfare, pedestrianized **Odhós 25-Avgoústou** (see page 63), lined with souvenir shops, banks and travel or shipping agencies, links the harbour with the commercial city centre. West of here, behind Platía Venizélou, is the grandly named **El Greco Park**, which is in reality more of a garden. On the opposite side of 25-Avgoústou are some of the more interesting of Iráklio's older buildings, including the church of **Áyios Títos** and the Venetian Loggia. At its southern end, 25-Avgoústou opens into Platía Venizélou, which forms a junction for central Iráklio's other main arteries: **Kalokerinoú** heads westwards down to the Pórta Haníon and out of the city; straight ahead, Odhós 1821 – a fashionable shopping street – heads southwest; and the adjacent Odhós 1866 is given over to the animated **market** (see pages 64 and 71).

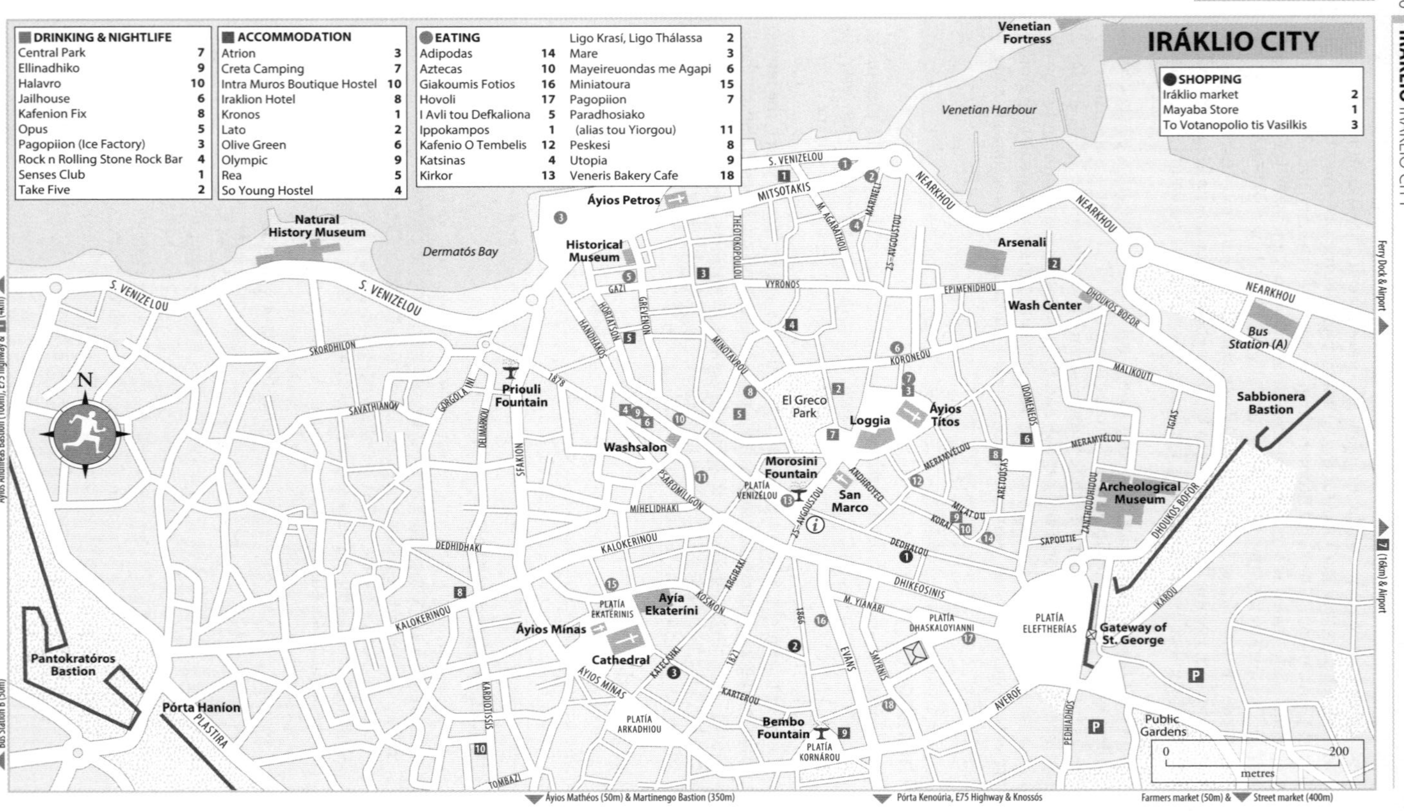
IRÁKLIO CITY
DRINKING & NIGHTLIFE
Central Park 7
Ellinadhiko 9
Halavro 10
Jailhouse 6
Kafenion Fix 8
Opus 5
Pagopiion (Ice Factory) 3
Rock n Rolling Stone Rock Bar 4
Senses Club 1
Take Five 2
ACCOMMODATION
Atrion 3
Creta Camping 7
Intra Muros Boutique Hostel 10
Iraklion Hotel 8
Kronos 1
Lato 2
Olive Green 6
Olympic 9
Rea 5
So Young Hostel 4
EATING
Adipodas 14
Aztecas 10
Giakoumis Fotios 16
Hovoli 17
I Avli tou Defkaliona 5
Ippokampos 1
Kafenio O Tembelis 12
Katsinas 4
Kirkor 13
Ligo Krasí, Ligo Thálassa 2
Mare 3
Mayeireuondas me Agapi 6
Miniatoura 15
Pagopiion 7
Paradhosiako (alias tou Yiorgou) 11
Peskesi 8
Utopia 9
Veneris Bakery Cafe 18
SHOPPING
Iráklio market 2
Mayaba Store 1
To Votanopolio tis Vasilkis 3
Venetian Fortress
Venetian Harbour
Natural History Museum
Dermatós Bay
Áyios Petros
Historical Museum
Arsenali
Wash Center
Bus Station (A)
Sabbionera Bastion
Priouli Fountain
Washsalon
El Greco Park
Loggia
Áyios Títos
Morosini Fountain
San Marco
Archeological Museum
Ayía Ekateríni
Áyios Mínas
Cathedral
Bembo Fountain
Gateway of St. George
Public Gardens
Pantokratóros Bastion
Pórta Haníon
PLATÍA VENIZÉLOU
PLATÍA EKATERINIS
PLATÍA DHASKALOYIANNI
PLATÍA ELEFTHERÍAS
PLATÍA ARKADHIOU
PLATÍA KORNÁROU
0 200 metres
N
Ferry Dock & Airport
7 (16km) & Airport
Áyios Andhréas Bastion (100m), E75 highway & 1 (4km)
Bus Station B (50m)
Áyios Mathéos (50m) & Martinengo Bastion (350m)
Pórta Kenoúria, E75 Highway & Knossós
Farmers market (50m) & Street market (400m)

centuries as this became the most important dockyard of the Venetian fleet in the eastern Mediterranean. The elongated ship sheds originally stretched to the water's edge – they were substantially shortened in order to build the road. In their heyday as many as fifty galleys at a time could be built here, or dragged ashore to be overhauled and repaired. They fell into disuse following the Ottoman conquest.

IRÁKLIO SUMMER FESTIVAL

The **Iráklio Summer Festival** runs from July to mid-September. Exhibitions, concerts and plays, mostly open-air, are put on by groups from around the world – some of which are top-notch – at venues across the city. Details are available online at http://nowheraklion.com/festival.html and from the tourist office (see page 68).

The city walls

Iráklio's **city walls** were originally thrown up in the fifteenth century, the strongest bastion in the Mediterranean, in places up to 15m thick. They were constantly improved as Crete became increasingly isolated in the path of westward Ottoman expansion; their final shape owes much to the architect Michele Sanmicheli, who arrived here in 1538 having previously designed the fortifications of Padua and Verona.

The fabric of the walls is incredibly well preserved, and many new sections are being excavated and restored along the seafront. The easiest place to get a close-up view is at the **Gateway of St George**, one of the old city's main gateways, whose restored subterranean vaults now house temporary exhibitions – it's approached down steps from the middle of Platía Eleftherías. Only the external side of the gate (on Ikárou) survives, the inner gateway having been levelled in the nineteenth century to build the Dhimokratías thoroughfare. Nearby, if you follow Odhós Pedhiádhos south from Platía Eleftherías you can climb to the dusty track that runs around the top of the ramparts all the way to the **Áyios Andhréas Bastion**, overlooking the sea in the west. You can't actually see much of the walls from up here, but there are fascinating views of town and at the major gates you pass there are stairs down to the road. To follow the walls in the other direction, simply head west along the coast for a little over 1km from the harbour until you reach this mighty bastion.

Nikos Kazantzákis' tomb

On the **Martinengo Bastion**, facing south, is the **tomb of Nikos Kazantzákis**, Crete's greatest writer (see page 58). Despite his works being banned for their unorthodox views, Kazantzákis' burial rites were performed at Áyios Mínos Cathedral, although he was not permitted burial in a cemetery – hence the interment on the bastion – and no priests officially escorted his body up here. His simple grave is adorned only with an inscription from his own writings: "I hope for nothing, I fear nothing, I am free". When she died, on Kazantzákis' birthday in 2004, aged 101, the author's wife Eleni Samiou Kazantzákis was buried in a grave alongside his. At the weekend, Iraklians gather here to pay their respects – and to enjoy a free, grandstand view of the matches played by the city's football team Ergotelis (see page 71) in the stadium below.

City gates

For the most impressive views of the city's defences, stroll out through one of the elaborate gates, the **Pórta Haníon** at the bottom of Kalokerinoú or the **Pórta Kenoúria** at the top of Odhós Evans, and admire them from the outside. Both of these portals date from the second half of the sixteenth century, when the majority of the surviving defences were completed. At the Pórta Kenoúria, the walls are over 40m thick.

The Archeological Museum

Xanthoudhídhou 2 • Charge • www.heraklionmuseum.gr

NIKOS KAZANTZÁKIS

Crete's best-known writer, **Nikos Kazantzákis**, was born in Iráklio in 1883 in the street now named after him. His early life was shadowed by the struggle against the Ottomans and for union with Greece. Educated in Athens and Paris, Kazantzákis travelled widely throughout his life, working for the Greek government on more than one occasion (serving briefly as Minister for Education in 1945) and for UNESCO, but above all writing. He produced a vast range of works, including philosophical essays, epic poetry, travel books, translations of classics such as Dante's *Divine Comedy* into Greek and, of course, the novels on which his fame in the West mostly rests. **Zorba the Greek** (1946) was his first and most celebrated novel, but his output remained prolific to the end of his life. Particularly relevant to Cretan travels are *Freedom or Death* (1950), set amidst the liberation struggle, and the autobiographical *Report to Greco*, published posthumously in 1961 (Kazantzákis died in Freiburg, West Germany, in 1957 after contracting hepatitis from an unsterilized vaccination needle during a visit to China).

Kazantzákis is widely accepted as the leading Greek writer of the twentieth century, and Cretans are extremely proud of him, despite the fact that most of his later life was spent abroad, that he was banned from entering Greece for long periods, and that he was excommunicated by the Orthodox Church for his vigorously expressed doubts about Christianity. This last detail gained him more notoriety when his *The Last Temptation of Christ* was filmed by Martin Scorsese, amid much controversy, in 1988. The Church was also instrumental in working behind the scenes to deny him the Nobel Prize, which he lost by one vote to Albert Camus in 1957. Many critics now regard much of his writing as overblown and pretentious, but even they admit that the best parts are where the Cretan in Kazantzákis shows through, in the tremendous gusto and vitality of books like *Zorba* and *Freedom or Death*. Kazantzákis himself was always conscious, and proud, of his Cretan heritage.

Iráklio's **Archeological Museum** is one of the major reasons to visit the city. It houses far and away the most important collection of **Minoan art and artefacts** anywhere in the world, and a visit to Knossós or the other sites will be greatly enhanced if you've been here first. The museum is almost always crowded (at least in summer) and often becomes overwhelmed by coach parties, with an endless procession of guided tours in all languages monopolizing the major exhibits. Given this, it's advisable to visit early, late or around lunchtime.

Rooms 1–3: Prehistory and the early Minoans

The museum begins on the ground floor with the earliest signs of human settlement in Crete, around 7000 BC. Highlights in Room 1, which covers the earliest years, are the gold and rock-crystal **jewellery** in Case 12, and the **fertility figurines** in cases 4 and 10. Rooms 2 and 3 cover the middle Bronze Age or late prepalatial period (2200–1700 BC). A tomb discovered at Malía unearthed the stunningly intricate **pendant of two bees around a golden disc** (Case 19); the disc is supposedly a drop of honey that they are storing in a comb. Among the miniature sculpture, don't miss the **clay bull** (Case 22) with tiny acrobats clinging to its horns, an early sign of the popularity of bull sports, or the clay statuettes (Case 21) of sanctuary worshippers – their arms crossed or placed on the chest in reverent attitudes – as well as the *taxímata* (ex votos) representing parts of the human body the deity was requested to heal, a custom still followed in churches all over Greece today. In Case 11 there is a display of intricately engraved seal stones, including one from ancient Mesopotamia, suggesting early contact between the island and its near eastern neighbours; case 23 shows the later development of seals and of writing.

Room 3 covers the first palaces at Knossós, Festós and Malía, with displays on daily life, economy and administration. There is a stunning collection of Kamáres ware from the Festós palace (Cases 27–34) – regarded as the peak of this artistic development

– exemplified by the so-called "**royal dinner service**" (Case 35) which includes a magnificent vase with white flowers sculpted in high relief.

Rooms 4–5: the New Palace period

The **New Palace period** (Neopalatial, 1700–1450 BC) represented the high point of Minoan civilization, exemplified by the huge wooden model of Knossós displayed here. The **Jug of Reeds** (Case 41) is a superb and typical example of the new styles tthat replaced Kámares pottery. Technological advances in material, higher temperature firing and faster pottery wheels also enabled an evolution in form and design. Vases became more slender and there was a move away from spiral designs as floral and marine decoration took centre stage. Other highlights include the fascinating "**Town Mosaic**" from Knossós (Case 37), consisting of a series of glazed plaques depicting multistorey Minoan houses, beautiful pieces that probably fitted together to form a decorative scene; and the celebrated **Festós Disc** (Case 51), a circular slab of clay upon which hieroglyphic characters have been inscribed in a spiral pattern. The disc is frequently described as the earliest-known example of printing, since the impressions of hieroglyphs were made with stamps before it was fired. The various signs are divided into groups, believed to be words; some are repeated, leading scholars to suggest that what is represented on the disc may be some form of prayer or hymn. Various claims of decipherment have been made over the years, and some scholars argue that the disc is a nineteenth-century hoax; none of these theories have gained much scientific credibility, however.

A beautiful **gaming board** (Case 39) from the Corridor of the Draughtsboard at Knossós, made of ivory, blue paste, crystal, and gold and silver leaf, with ivory pieces, is a reminder of the luxurious life which at least some Minoans could enjoy. A fascinating example of domestic architecture comes at the end of the Neopalatial period in the form of a model of a modest **Minoan dwelling** (Case 36) from Arhánes; features include a light well, small rooms and tiny windows to keep out the bright Cretan sun and fierce winds, while the roof terrace above is similar to those seen on village houses throughout Crete today. Also worth a look here is the unique ceramic portrayal of lively dolphins plunging among cockles and seaweed (Case 41), perhaps originally the stand for a large vase. Finally, two small **clay cups** (Case 53) may hold important clues to the history of Minoan writing, of which little survives. These vessels bear inscriptions written in Linear A script – developed from cumbersome hieroglyphics – using cuttlefish ink. This use of ink suggests the existence of other suitable writing materials (possibly imported papyrus or even domestically produced palm-leaf paper) that have since perished in the Cretan climate.

Room 6: daily life

Room 6 displays objects used in daily life – giant *píthoi* (storage jars), bronze vessels, saws and weights – as well as artefacts attesting to the Minoan love of sports and spectacles. The famous "**Bull Leaping**" fresco from Knossós (Case 60) depicts acrobats performing somersaults over the back of a charging bull, while a carved ivory **figurine of a bull-leaper** (Case 63) was part of an unusual, sculpted composition with other figures. The **Boxers' Rhyton** (Case 62) is a black steatite vase from Ayía Triádha depicting gloved boxers (who appear to be wearing tassled helmets) and wrestlers in combat. A wonderfully vibrant set of ceramic **figurines of dancers** circling a *lyra* player (Case 59) from Palékastro is typical of the later Minoan period, influenced by Mycenean styles – with less naturalism and more stereotyped designs. Also here are a number of great bronze **double axes** erected on wooden poles. The double axe was an important cult symbol for the Minoans, and huge axes like these were placed in shrines and palaces.

Rooms 7–8: Minoan Religion

The star exhibit in Room 7 is the famous **Harvesters Vase** (Case 75), the finest of a pair of (steatite, or soapstone) vases from Ayía Triádha. It depicts with vivid realism a procession returning home from the fields; the harvesters are led by a strangely dressed character with long hair and a big stick, possibly a priest, and accompanied by musicians, one of whom is waving a sistrum (a percussion instrument that sounds rather like a maraca). The other vase (Case 71) shows what appears to be a chieftain receiving a report from an official. Some **bronze figurines** (Case 74) depict worshippers making the ritual "salute" gesture to the deity while leaning backwards. Also of note here is the renowned **Bull's Head Rhyton** (Case 79), a sacred vessel used in religious ceremonies and found in the Little Palace at Knossós. Carved from black steatite with inlaid eyes and nostrils (the wooden horns are new), the bull is magnificently naturalistic. Another imposing alabaster rhyton, or libation vessel, is carved in the form of a lioness's head (Case 87).

Also here are two representations of the **snake goddess** (Case 83), both wearing tight-waisted, breast-baring dresses and decorated aprons, and each with snakes coiling around their hands; they may equally be priestesses engaged in sacred rituals. The so-called **"Ring of Minos"** (Case 78) was found seventy years ago close to the Knossós palace. After disappearing while in the possession of a local priest, the solid gold ring emerged again when one of the priest's descendants sold it to the museum. Highly important for its depiction of Minoan religion, the ring is engraved with a scene showing a goddess with worshippers as well as a sailing boat. The magnificent **rock crystal rhyton** (Case 89), from the palace at Zákros, has a handle of beads and a collar that hides a join between two pieces encased in gold: beauty aside, this exhibit is always singled out by the guides as an example of the painstaking reconstruction undertaken by the museum – when discovered, it was broken into over three hundred fragments. Almost as striking is the **Peak Sanctuary Rhyton** (Case 90), a green stone vessel on which a low relief scene depicts a mountain shrine, with horns of consecration decorated with birds and wild goats. Originally covered in gold leaf, this discovery provided valuable information on Minoan religion.

Rooms 9–10: the Late Palace Period

Rooms 9–10 are devoted to the final period of the palace culture (1450–1300 BC), mainly at Knossós, and the objects are considerably less exciting. In pottery, similar decorative themes continued to be used, but with a new formalism and on new types of vessel, which has been taken as a sign that Mycenaean influences were beginning to take hold. Items of note here include a small **group of clay figures** (Case 98) – from a tomb at Kamilári (see page 116) near Festós – taking part in what seems to be a ritual dance inside a circle decorated with the horns of consecration. It's a very crude work but wonderfully effective and reminiscent of the *pentozalis* danced by Cretan men today. The martial arts are represented by some fine gold sword hilts and a fabulous reconstructed **boar's tusk helmet** (Case 105) which also makes an appearance on an amphora from Arhánes (Case 108). Taken with the other weapons and military equipment displayed here, these items can be seen as further proof of the subordination of Minoan culture to the more warlike Mycenaean in this period.

Also from Arhánes comes a curious **horse burial** (between cases 107 and 108) found in a fourteenth-century BC tholos tomb. The corpse of the horse is believed to have been a sacrifice in honour of the possibly royal personage buried in the same tomb. After slaughter the beast had been systematically dismembered, and its parts carefully placed in the position in which they are now displayed.

Rooms 11–12: late settlements, sanctuaries and tombs

The final rooms in the ground floor's Minoan section deal with the artefacts from the palaces and tombs of the late and post-palatial periods. The outstanding exhibit here is the magnificent **Ayía Triádha sarcophagus** (Case 127), which, with its unique and elaborate painted-plaster ornamentation, is one of the masterpieces of Minoan art. Dating from the fourteenth century BC, it is the only stone sarcophagus yet to have been found in Crete and was discovered in a tomb beside the palace at Ayía Triádha; it had probably been used for a royal burial. On one side is a depiction of an animal sacrifice, with a bull already dead on the altar and two goats tied up awaiting their fate. On the other are two scenes, perhaps of relatives making offerings for the safe passage of the deceased. The ends feature an image of goddesses riding in a chariot drawn by griffins, and of two women in a chariot pulled by goats above a procession of men. Unlike the palace frescoes, nothing has been restored or reconstructed, making this in many ways even more striking.

Towards the end of the Bronze Age (c.1100–1000 BC) the Minoans were fleeing from the coasts before successive waves of Dorian invaders, and attempted to maintain their culture in inaccessible parts of the island such as the settlement high above the Lasíthi Plateau at Karfí (see page 145). From this remote settlement came terracotta figurines, utensils and vessels as well as large figures of the "**goddess with raised hands**" (Case 117), their anguished features seeming to foreshadow the end. New types of ritual vessel are typified by the rhyton in the shape of a **chariot drawn by bodyless oxen** (Case 117), giving the work a somewhat abstract quality.

Much of the rest of these rooms is taken up with a collection of **lárnakes** (clay coffins) from various periods, their painted decoration reflecting the prevailing pottery style. The Minoan burial position of the knees drawn up to the chest explains the small size of the coffins – and also suggests that the bodies would have been placed in them soon after death, before the onset of rigor mortis. They come in two basic shapes: chests with lids and "bathtubs" (which may well have been used as such during their owners' lifetimes, as many have plugholes). From Room 12 stairs lead to the rooms on the second floor.

Room 13: Minoan palace frescoes

Room 13, the **Hall of the Frescoes**, is perhaps the most interesting in the museum. Frescoes are among the greatest achievements of Minoan art: they were originally painted directly onto wet plaster, using mostly plant dyes but also colours from mineral sources and even shellfish – a technique which has ensured their relatively unfaded survival. Only tiny fragments of original fresco survived, but they have been painstakingly reconstituted and mounted on matching backgrounds, giving as true an impression of the entire fresco as possible. The job of the restorers was helped to an extent by knowledge of the various conventions, which matched Egyptian practice: men's skin, for example, was red, women's white; gold is shown as yellow, silver as blue and bronze, red.

Most of the frescoes displayed come originally from **Knossós**, and date from the Neopalatial period (1700–1450 BC). Along the left hand wall as you enter (Cases 129–131) are four large panels from the enormous fresco which led all the way along the **Corridor of the Procession** at Knossós; an artist's impression shows how the whole might originally have looked. Two groups of youths are shown processing towards a female figure, presumably a priestess or a goddess. The **fresco of griffins** (Case 138) came from the throne room at the palace, while the elegant **Priest-King** (Case 137) – or Prince of the Lilies as Sir Arthur Evans (see page 323) described him – once decorated a corridor near the palace's west entrance. A great painted relief of a **bull's head** (Case 139), transmitting agony and power, contrasts with a beautifully simple fresco of **swimming dolphins** (Case 142) from the queen's apartment, while nearby a heavily restored fresco depicts the elegantly attired **ladies of the court** (Case 140). Among other fresco fragments displayed, one of the most interesting is the **"Saffron Gatherer"** (Case 144). Originally reconstructed by Evans and his team as a boy, it has since been decided that this in fact represented a blue monkey; the two versions are shown side by side. Finally, one of the most celebrated fresco fragments is **"La Parisienne"** (Case 141), so dubbed for her bright red lips, huge eyes, long hair and fancy dress, but in reality almost certainly a priestess or a goddess.

Rooms 14–17: Early Iron Age

After the dazzling magnificence of the Minoan frescoes the post-Minoan period can seem like something of an anticlimax, but some of the exhibits are definitely worth a look. Highlights include, in Room 15, three large **bronze hammered figurines** of Apollo and Artemis with their mother, Leto, from the eighth-century BC sanctuary of Apollo Delphinius at Dríros (Case 159); Room 17 has a display of figurines and artefacts found at the remote mountain shrine of **Káto Sými** (Case 165) near Áno Viánnos in the southeast of Iráklio province (see page 124). As the objects on view from Minoan, Greek and Roman periods demonstrate, this is one of the few shrines in Crete where worship continued without interruption from prehistorical times to the end of antiquity. Notable pieces include bronze figurines of worshippers and ivory-handled swords from the Minoan age, and a figurine from the Hellenistic period of a lyre-playing Hermes (to whom the Greeks dedicated Káto Sými).

Rooms 18–19: Late period cemeteries

Rooms 18–19 display finds from cemeteries in the period following the Dorian invasions to the fourth century BC. Finds include a fine collection of **jewellery and gold leaf** from Knossós (Case 187), as well as some wonderful animal votive vases depicting a rooster, a hare and an owl (Case 196).

Rooms 20–25: Classical and Roman periods

Displays of finds from Cretan city states, sanctuaries and cemeteries take up most of the rest of the collection. Highlights here include two Roman mosaics from a villa at Hersónisos, one depicting a cock fight. Room 23 displays the accumulations of an Iráklio doctor and antiquities collector, the **Yiamalakis Collection**, which covers pieces from every ancient Cretan period, from Neolithic to Roman. Among interesting items displayed are a collection of Roman oil lamps, on which are featured some fairly saucy erotic images as well as some stunning gold jewellery. From here, you can take the stairs to the ground floor.

Rooms 26–27: Archaic and Classical Sculpture

The collection concludes on the ground floor with a display of sculpture from the Archaic (Room 26) and Classical (Room 27) periods. The post-Minoan era in Crete tends to be overlooked due to the overwhelming interest in Minoan civilization, but there are some very fine pieces here including, from the Archaic period, a fine limestone lintel from a seventh-century temple at **Prinías** (Rizinía), with worshippers wearing sacred headdresses, and panthers parading beneath their feet. The Classical collection has a wonderfully executed **group of statues** from Górtys depicting Pluto, Persephone (holding a sistrum) and Kerberos (Cerberus), the triple-headed "hellhound" guardian of the underworld. A marble statue of **Aphrodite** holding a bowl, a Roman copy of a fifth-century BC work by Alkamenes, comes also from Górtys. There's also a superbly carved second-century AD **Roman sarchophagus** found at Mália, as well as a number of other outstanding examples of the sculptor's craft including an imposing image of a **bearded philosopher**, also from Górtys. Along the walls are a series of **portrait busts** of members of Rome's imperial families, including images of the emperors Augustus, Trajan and Marcus Aurelius.

The exit from here brings you to the **shop** and **café**, the latter with a pleasant shaded terrace. From here you can look down into the ruins of the seventeenth-century **Venetian monastery of St Francis**, the discovery of which delayed the progress of the museum's 2006–2013 renovation.

Platía Eleftherías

The south facade of the Archeological Museum faces **Platía Eleftherías (Liberty Square)**, the city's biggest square. On its southern and western flanks, a line of pavement cafés

STREET OF THE AUGUST MARTYRS

The name of the city's major thoroughfare, in full **Odhós Martýron 25-Avgoústou 1898** (the 25th of August Martyrs), commemorates a bloody incident at the very end of Ottoman rule in Crete. In 1898 under the aegis of the great powers of post-Napoleonic Europe (France, Italy, Russia and Britain), an autonomous Cretan state with an Executive Council was formed under Ottoman sovereignty, regarded by most Cretans as a prelude to union with Greece. On August 25 a detachment of British soldiers was escorting Council officials along this street from the harbour when they were attacked by a violent mob of Muslim Cretans, smarting at what they saw as the betrayal of their birthright. In the bloody riot that ensued, hundreds of Christian Cretans lost their lives as well as seventeen British soldiers and the British Honorary Consul. This stirred the British to take reprisals and, on the principle of an eye for an eye, they rounded up and hanged seventeen of the Muslim Cretan ringleaders and put many more in prison. Shortly after this, the British navy sailed into the harbour and the city was cleared of Ottoman troops. The following November the last Turkish military forces left the island they had controlled for 230 years.

face a rather uninspiring central concourse dotted with gum trees and benches, and skirted by busy roads. Mainly due to its size the square is one of the city's most popular venues for political demonstrations, but most of the time is used by locals for strolling, chatting and sitting out. There's a small bust of Nikos Kazantzákis (see page 58) and a larger-than-life statue of Eleftherios Venizelos (the leading figure in the struggle for union with Greece), on the ramparts, looking remarkably like Lenin. Beyond the statue, you reach the entrance to the **public gardens**, as often as not half taken over by a funfair, but otherwise relatively peaceful. In the square's southeast corner, a flight of steps descends to a vaulted passage leading to the sixteenth-century St George Gate (see page 57). On its western side the square is linked to Platía Venizélou by the pedestrianized street **Dedhálou**, lined with many of Iráklio's top designer clothing stores.

Odhós 25-Avgoústou

Pedestrianized **Odhós 25th (Ikostipémptis)-Avgoústou**, which heads up from the harbour past or towards many of the city's major attractions, takes its name from one of the final acts in the ending of Ottoman domination of the island at the end of the nineteenth century.

Áyios Títos

Platía Áyios Títou • Free

On the left of Odhós 25-Avgoústou as you climb, the church of **Áyios Títos** commands a lovely little square. Originally Byzantine, but wholly rebuilt by the Venetians in the sixteenth century, it was adapted by the Turks as a mosque and rebuilt by them after a major earthquake in 1856. The Orthodox Church renovated the building after the Muslim population left Iráklio, and it was reconsecrated in 1925. A bejewelled reliquary inside contains the skull of St Titus (see page 357), originally brought here from his tomb in Górtys; his body was never found. In the Middle Ages, the skull was regularly and ceremonially exhibited to the people of Iráklio, but was later taken to Venice, where it stayed from the time of the Turkish Ottoman conquest until 1966, when it was returned. On August 25 each year, a major procession from the church marks St Titus' Day.

San Marco and around

Beyond Platía Ayíou Títou, at the northern end of 25-Avgoústou, stands the Venetian City Hall with its famous **loggia**, reconstructed after earthquake damage

1

was compounded by the rigours of World War II. Just beyond here, at the entrance to Platía Venizélou, is the church of **San Marco**, its steps usually crowded with sightseers spilling over from the square. It was the city's cathedral in the Venetian era (two interesting carved gravestones survive in what was the altar area), and was later converted to a mosque. Neither building has found a permanent role in its refurbished state, but both are generally open to house some kind of exhibition or craft show.

Platía Venizélou

Platía Venizélou (also known as Fountain Square or Platía Leondarión, Lion Square), formerly the Venetian Piazza San Marco, opens off 25-Avgoústou opposite San Marco church. Ringed by busy cafés, its focal point is the magnificent **Morosini fountain**, which dates from the final years of Venetian rule and upon its inauguration in 1628 became the city's main source of fresh water. Inspired by the city's governor, Francesco Morosini, the work took fourteen months to complete. The fountain was supplied with water from Mount Yioúhtas near Arhánes and reached the city along a 15km-long aqueduct. The fountain's basin is mounted on a circular base and is composed of eight lobes, thus enabling many people to fill their water-jars at the same time. The lobes are decorated with scenes from Greek mythology in carved relief, mainly Tritons, dolphins and nymphs as well as the arms of the Doge, the city councillors and Morosini himself. Originally the whole thing was topped by a giant statue of Poseidon, but even without him it's impressive: the lions on guard are two to three hundred years older than the rest of the structure.

Odhós 1866: the market

Daily 8am–8pm (though individual stalls vary; some close on Sun, while many take a siesta from around 2–5pm)

South of Platía Venizélou, across busy Odhós Dhikeosínis, **Odhós 1866** is packed throughout the day with the stalls and customers of Iráklio's main **market**. This is one of the few living reminders of an older city, with an atmosphere reminiscent of an oriental bazaar. There are stalls piled high with luscious fruit and vegetables, as well as butchers' and fishmongers' stalls and others selling a bewildering variety of herbs and spices, cheese and yoghurt, leather and plastic goods, CDs, tacky souvenirs, an amazing array of cheap kitchen utensils, pocket knives and just about anything else you might conceivably need.

Platía Kornárou

At the top of the Odhós 1866 market, **Platía Kornárou** makes a pleasantly tranquil contrast. The focal point of the square is a beautiful hexagonal Ottoman-era **pumphouse**, heavily restored, which now houses a café run by the municipality, a meeting place for elderly locals, who converse at the tables under the trees. The small sixteenth-century Venetian drinking fountain beside the café – the **Bembo fountain** (named after its designer Zuanne Bembo) – was the first to supply the city with running water. It incorporates a headless Roman torso imported from Ierápetra.

Platía Ayías Ekaterínis

Three churches ring the **Platía Ayías Ekaterínis**, a quiet escape from the busy shopping streets close by. The **cathedral of Áyios Minas**, a rather undistinguished nineteenth-century building, is notable mainly for its size and the gaudiness of its decoration. Just in front stands its tiny forerunner, the medieval **church of Áyios Minás**, whose gilded and elaborately decorated altarpiece contains some interesting icons.

Museum of Christian Art

Platía Ayías Ekaterínis • Charge • http://iakm.gr

The most interesting church on Platía Ayías Ekaterínis, **Ayía Ekateríni**, is now a wonderful **museum** dedicated to the Cretan School of **icon painting**. Originally a dependency, founded in the tenth century, of the Mt Sinai monastery of St Catherine, , this building – dating from the sixteenth century – was its main church. The monastery also incorporated a **monastic school** which, up to the end of Venetian rule, was one of the centres of the Cretan Renaissance, a last flourish of Eastern Christian art following the fall of Byzantium. Among the school's students were Vitzentzos Kornaros, author of the Cretan classic long poem*Erotókritos*, and many leading Orthodox theologians; most importantly, however, it served as an **art school** where Byzantine tradition came face to face with the influences of the Venetian Renaissance.

Among the greatest of the school's pupils was the late sixteenth-century painter **Mihailis Dhamaskinos**, and six of his works – including the *Adoration of the Magi*, the *Last Supper* and *Christ Appearing to the Holy Women* – form the nucleus of the collection. It was the much-imitated Dhamaskinos who introduced perspective and depth to Byzantine art, while never straying far from the strict traditions of icon painting. The most famous Cretan painter of them all, Domenicos Theotokopolous, known today as **El Greco**, took the opposite course, wholeheartedly embracing Italian styles, to which he brought the influence of his Byzantine training. Although there is little evidence, it's generally accepted that these two – Dhamaskinos and El Greco – were near contemporaries at the school, though the only El Greco works now on the island are in Iráklio's Historical Museum.

Other exhibits include examples of **Venetian arts and crafts**, especially stone carving and wood sculpture, both of which display strong Byzantine overtones, as well as sections devoted to church vestments and plate.

The Priouli fountain

Northwest of Platía Ayías Ekaterínis close to Dermatás Bay lies the impressive **Prioúli fountain**, built in 1666 at the very end of the Venetian period at the behest of city governor Antonio Priouli, during the long siege of the city by Turkish forces. Sited in what was then the old Jewish quarter, the fountain is based on the form of a Greek temple with Corinthian capitals and crowned with a triangular pediment. It used an underground source to supply the city with water after the Ottomans had destroyed the aqueducts. Following the Ottoman conquest the fountain was restored, as a plaque bearing a calligraphic Turkish inscription informs.

The Historical Museum

Sofoklí Venizélou 27 • Charge • www.historical-museum.gr

The **Historical Museum** is one of the most dynamic in Iráklio, with frequent events and interesting temporary exhibitions. The fascinating permanent collection – with many interactive displays – helps fill the gap which, for most people, yawns between Knossós and the present day, and since it's always essentially deserted, wandering around is a pleasure.

The ground and first floors

The **ground floor**, if you're working through the galleries chronologically, is the place to start; it contains sculptures and architectural fragments from the Byzantine, Venetian and Turkish periods. There are some beautiful pieces, especially a fifteenth- or sixteenth-century tiered fountain from a Venetian palace. The **first floor** has religious art, wall paintings and documents from the same periods, plus a reconstruction of a typically domed Cretan church. Here also are two works by **El Greco** – the small *View* *of Mount Sinai and the Monastery of St Catherine* (painted around 1570) and the even smaller *Baptism of Christ* (1567). Sadly – considering the hundreds of canvases by El Greco displayed in the museums of Spain and elsewhere – these are the only works by Crete's greatest painter to be seen on the island of his birth.

The upper floors

The museum's **upper floors** bring things up to date with reconstructions of the studies of the writer Nikos Kazantzákis (see page 58) and of the Cretan statesman (and briefly Greek prime minister) Emanuel Tsouderos; photos and documents relating to the occupation of Crete by the Germans, plus the odd helmet and parachute harness; and a substantial selection of folk art – particularly textiles. There's also the reconstructed interior of a Cretan farmhouse, and a small **café** with sea-view terrace.

The fountain of Idomeneas

Constructed in the late seventeenth century following the fall of the city to the Turks, the small but elegant Ottoman **fountain of Idomeneas** is set into a wall to the rear of the Historical Museum, partly obscured in the evening by diners on the terrace of a nearby, reccomendable taverna. It was a favourite location of Kazantzákis (who was born nearby); the author mentions it in his novel *Kapetan Mihalis*. It's worth a look and consists of two columns with floral capitals flanking an arched niche. In the niche, a marble slab bears a calligraphic Turkish inscription; the water fell into a marble basin below.

The Natural History Museum

Sofoklí Venizélou • Charge • www.nhmc.uo.gr

Spectacularly housed in a converted power plant overlooking the Bay of Dermatás, the **Natural History Museum** examines the ecosystems of the eastern Mediterranean along with Crete's geological evolution, the arrival of man, and the environment as it would have appeared to the Minoans. Exhibits over four floors display fossils, rocks, minerals and caves, and the flora and fauna of modern Crete. For kids there's the **Discovery Centre** in the basement, a wonderful hands-on interactive natural playground with microscopes and a mock-up marine exploration boat. There's plenty on dinosaurs and extinct species too, including a huge 4.5m-high prehistoric Cretan mammoth, reconstructed from fossil remains; and there's an **earthquake simulator** and a planetarium. The **"Living Museum"** on Level 1 has live specimens of frogs, reptiles and mice found in Crete. An emphasis on respect and care for the environment, and on species endangered by tourism and development, is a welcome reflection of the growing awareness of these issues on the island.

City beaches

It's easy to escape the city for a few hours to lie on the **beach**. The simplest course is to head east, beyond the airport, to the municipal beach at **Amnísos** or to the marginally quieter **Tobróuk** beach. Beaches to the west are less prone to aircraft noise but are also more commercialized. Buses for the beaches leave from Platía Eleftherías (see page 68).

Eastern beaches

To the east of the city, past the airport, the old road along the coast runs past a series of sandy strands. A few areas are fenced off as pay beaches with showers, changing rooms and other facilities, but between them are plenty of free spots. **Amnísos** is perhaps the pick here, with tavernas and food stalls immediately behind the beach, and showers and loungers for rent; there's good sand and clean water, too, although the stream of

THE NEW AIRPORT

As of 2027, Iráklio will get a new airport well inland past the village of Arkalohóri, supposedly 25 minutes' drive from the city centre. It will be established around the huge existing runway of a disused air-force base. Track progress of his project at www.heraklion-airport.gr/en/the-new-airport/

planes coming in directly overhead to land can be wearing. Amnísos itself is a famous name in Minoan archeology, and through a fence you can glimpse the remains of the small settlement here. This was apparently a port for Knossós, from which the Cretan forces engaged in the Trojan War are said to have set sail, and it was in a villa here that the unusual **Fresco of the Lilies** was found – now on display in the Archeological Museum.

Just beyond Amnísos, the beach at **Tobroúk** is arguably even better, with more tavernas and drinks stalls, slightly fewer people, and relative peace to be found if you walk a little way along the sand.

Western beaches

The beaches to the **west** of the city are less atmospheric and more exposed to the wind and waves than the eastern ones – which makes them popular with local surfers and kitesurfers. Cutting through Iráklio's prosperous western suburbs, you end up on a road which runs through the strip-development of **Amoudhára**, finally ending up at the luxury *Creta Beach* hotel complex, unappealingly sited immediately before the power station and a cement works. **Amoudhára beach** lies on the other side of the many hotels along this road, and getting to it is not always easy; although the beach is open to the public, there are very few access roads. One is located just west of the *Creta Beach* hotel.

ARRIVAL AND DEPARTURE — IRÁKLIO CITY

BY PLANE

Iráklio airport The existing airport (Heraklion; 2810 397 800, http://heraklionairport.net) is right on the coast, 4km east of the city. Bus #1 leaves for Platía Eleftherías (every 20min until 11pm; €2, cash only) from the car park in front of the terminal; buy your ticket at the booth before boarding. There are also plenty of taxis outside, with prices to major destinations posted – it's €15–20 to the centre of town depending on traffic; agree on the fare first.

Airlines Olympic (http://olympicair.com) and Sky Express (www.skyexpress.gr) are the main domestic operators, with a few daily flights to Athens; Sky sometimes serves several smaller islands in between, as well as Rhodes. Ryanair (http://ryanair.com) flies domestically only to Thessaloníki (http://www.skyexpress.gr). British Airways, EasyJet, Jet2 links to various UK aiports from April to November and charter airlines have direct flights from the UK in summer.

Destinations Athens (12 daily; 50min); Kássos (1 daily; 1hr); Kós (1–2 daily; 1hr); Rhodes (1–daily; 1hr); Sitía (1 daily; 30min); Thessaloníki (at least 1 daily; 1hr 15min).

BY FERRY

Ferry dock From the wharves where the ferries dock, the city rises directly ahead in steep tiers. If you're heading for the centre on foot, for the Archeological Museum or the tourist office, cut straight up the stepped alleys behind the bus station (from where there are buses to the centre) onto Doúkos Bófor and to Platía Eleftherías (about a 15min walk). For accommodation, though, and to get a better idea of the layout of Iráklio's main attractions, it's simpler to follow the main roads: head west along the coast, past Bus Station A and on by the Venetian harbour before cutting left towards the centre on Odhós 25-Avgoústou.

Operators and destinations Minoan Lines, 25-Avgoústou 17 (2810 399 800, http://minoan.gr) and ANEK/Superfast, Dhimokratías 11 (2810 308 000, http://www.anek.gr) have nightly ferries to Athens (9pm/9.30pm; 8hr 30min), with extra services in summer and at peak times; ANEK also operate the *Prevelis*, departingoncd weeekly to to Sitía (3hr), Kássos (6hr), Kárpathos (8hr), Hálki (11hr) and Rhodes (13hr). Seajets (https://www.seajets.com) (and Minoan runs daily each morning in summer to Thíra (Santoríni; 1hr 50min–2hr 20min) for the day trip market – returns in the late afternoon, some continuing to Páros ((5hr 30min).

Tickets and timetables A primary local agent is Paleologos Travel, 25-Avgoústou 5 (Mon–Fri 9am–8pm,

1

Sat 9am–3pm; 2810 346 185, www.ferries.gr), who have current timetables and can sell tickets for all ferries. You can also check timetables at www.openseas.gr.

BY CAR

Arriving in town by car, the best bet is to head for one of the signposted city-centre car parks (€3–10/day depending on location). One of the best is the large museum car park on Ikárou, 70m downhill from the Archaeological Museum, which uses space below the city walls and has plenty of shade.

BY BUS

Make sure you check the current timetables and ticket prices online before you travel; you can check bus timetables and buy tickets at http://ktelherlas.gr.

Bus Station A On the main road between the ferry dock and the Venetian harbour, Bus Station A serves all the main north-coast routes; west to Réthymno and Haniá and east along the coastal highway to Hersónisos, Mália, Áyios Nikólaos and Sitía, as well as southeast to Ierápetra and points en route. There's a left luggage office here (daily 6am–9pm; €3/bag/day).

Destinations Arhánes (14 daily, fewer at weekends; 30min); Ay. Nikólaos (20 daily; 1hr 30min); Ay. Pelayía (6 daily; 30min); Haniá (16 daily; 3hr); Hersónisos (every 30min; 45min); Ierápetra (7 daily; 2hr 30min); Kastélli (6 daily, fewer at weekends; 1hr); Lasíthi plateau (Mon & Fri 12.45pm; 1hr 30min); Mália (every 30min; 1hr); Pezá (13 daily, fewer at weekends; 40min); Réthymno (16 daily; 1hr 30min); Sísi (daily 3pm; 1hr 30min); Sitía (5 daily; 3hr 15min).

Bus Station B Buses for the southwest (Festós, Mátala and Ayía Galíni) and along the inland roads west (Týlissos, Anóyia and Fódhele) operate out of Bus Station B just outside Pórta Haníon, a 15min walk from the centre down Kalokerinoú (or jump on any city bus heading along this street).

Destinations Anóyia (3 daily; 1hr); Ay. Galíni (6 daily; 2hr 15min); Festós (4 daily; 1hr 30min); Mátala (4 daily; 2hr); Míres (10 daily; 1hr 30min).

GETTING AROUND

By bus Only the further-flung sites and beaches really justify taking a bus. For the beaches, head for Platía Eleftherías; westbound bus #6 stops outside the *Capsis Hotel* and heads out through the Pórta Haníon (past Bus Station B); eastbound #7 departs every 15min or so from the tree-shaded stop opposite. Knossós buses start from the city bus stands alongside Bus Station A and pass through Platía Eleftherías; airport buses also pass through the square. It's easier and cheaper to buy tickets (€1.20 for city and airport, €1.70 to the beach or Knossós; day pass €5) before you board, from machines in Platía Eleftherías and elsewhere, or from the many kiosks.

Bike and car rental 25-Avgoústou is lined with rental companies, but you'll often find better deals on the backstreets nearby; it's always worth asking for discounts. Try the reliable Blue Sea, Kosmá Zótou 7, just off the bottom of 25-Avgoústou (2810 241 097, www.bluesearentals.com); Kosmos, 25-Avgoústou 15 (2810 34 6173, www.kosmos-carrental.com); Caravel, ferry-port 3 and at the airport (2810 300 150, https://caravel.gr, http://caravel.gr); Heraklion, in the *Hotel Rea*, Kalimeráki 1 (2810 223 638); or Alianthos at the airport (28320 332033, http://alianthos-group.com). All offer free delivery to hotels and the airport.

Taxis Taxi stands can be found in Platía Eleftherías, Platía Kornárou, Odhós Dhikeosínis by the market, at the bottom of 25-Avgoústou and at the bus stations; alternatively call 2810 210 102 or 2814 003 084. Prices should be displayed on boards at the taxi stands.

INFORMATION AND TOURS

Tourist office The Info Point, Platía Nikifórou Foká (inside the government offices just above Platía Venizélou, the Lion-Fountain Square), is open Mon–Fri 8.30am–2.30pm (2813 409 777; www.heraklion.gr).

Travel agencies 25-Avgoústou is crammed with shipping and general travel agents; Paleologos Travel, 25-Avgoústou 5 (Mon–Fri 9am–8pm, Sat 9am–3pm; 2810 346 185, www.ferries.gr) sells tickets for all ferries.

Tours Excellent small-group food and drink tours of the city as well as wine-tasting in the nearby countryside are led by Yioryios at Vintage Routes Crete (28103 33 583); a good free walking tour (tips expected!) operates every Tuesday (6944 500 072, www.facebook.com/Heraklionfreetour/about/). Two rival companies operate hop-on, hop-off bus tours, offering a good overview of the city with stops at all the major sights and museums. The route stays almost entirely outside the walls, so doesn't include the city centre, but they do go out as far as Knossós; a 48hr ticket notionally costs around €16, though if you hesitate their ubiquitous touts may offer you a better deal.

ACCOMMODATION

SEE MAP PAGE 56

Finding a room can be difficult in high season. **Inexpensive places** are mainly concentrated in the streets above the Venetian harbour to the west of Odhós 25-Avgoústou. More **luxurious hotels** mostly lie closer to Platía Eleftherías and near Bus Station A. Noise can be a problem wherever you stay.

Atrion Hronáki 9, http://atrion.gr. This attractive, modern, business-style hotel, with all the comforts that implies – marble-clad bathrooms, minibar, silent a/c – combines luxury with a personal touch and a friendly welcome. Top-floor suites have stunning views. Breakfast included. €€

Intra Muros Boutique Hostel Monís Kardhiotíssis 30, www.intramuroshostel.com. One of two excellent backpacker-style hostels in Iráklio, offering mixed four-, six- and 12-bunk rooms, a female-only six-bed dorm and a tiny, shared-bathroom double. The bunks are curtained off for privacy, there are lockers (bring your own padlock), and well kitted-out kitchen and shower facilities, plus a communal roof terrace with views and a great traveller atmosphere. Slightly out of the way, but in a quiet neighbourhood within easy walking distance of the centre. €

Iraklion Hotel Kalokerinoú 128, https://iraklionhotel.gr. Not in the most attractive part of town, but this comfortable, good-value well-run place is close to Platía Ekaterínis (Cathedral Square) and handy for Bus Station B. Rooms come equipped with fridge and satellite TV, and many of those on the third and fourth floors have fine views out to sea. Cheap parking on site. €€

Kronos Agárthou 2, www.kronoshotel.gr. This two-star hotel has a fabulous location by the central seafront, though the busy surrounding streets can mean some traffic noise. The en-suite rooms have a/c, TV, fridge and balcony, some with wonderful sea views (slight extra cost). €

★ **Lato** Epimenídhou 15, http://lato.gr. Stylish boutique hotel in a great central location opposite the Venetian harbour, with luxurious a/c rooms sporting (in many cases) fine balcony views over the port. Excellent rooftop bar and restaurant in summer. Breakfast included. €€

★ **Olive Green** Idhomonéos 22, corner Meramvellou, http://olivegreenhotel.com. Classy and very comfortable modern hotel that claims to be both eco-friendly and high-tech (every room has a tablet to control lighting, a/c, etc). The beautifully designed rooms, in several categories including triples and quads, have powerful showers separate from the sink and loo. Impressive buffet breakfast included. €€€

Olympic Platía Kornárou 43, Modern, business-style hotel in a great location. The a/c rooms, with laminate flooring and blonde-wood furnishings, are quiet and well equipped, if a little small. Breakfast included. €€

★ **Rea** Kalimeráki 1, 2810 223 638, www.hotelrea.gr. A great budget option, this friendly, comfortable and clean *pension* enjoys a quiet but central position. Some of the nicer rooms are en suite, others share a bathroom. €

So Young Hostel Almyroú 22, corner Erotokrítou, www.hostelworld.com/st/hostels/p/286668/so-young-hostel/. The other backpacker place in town, *So Young* has curtained bunks in six- and eight-bed mixed or female-only dorms in a very central location. Modern design and equipment, including individual reading lights and electric sockets for each bed, and a well-equipped kitchen. €

CAMPING

Creta Camping Káto Goúves, 16km east of Iráklio, http://cretacamping.com. The surroundings are bleak, but this is a big, well-organized site right on the seafront and close to Cretaquarium, with facilities including restaurant, minimarket, wi-fi, beach bar and beach loungers, as well as car rental and organized tours. Decent shady pitches and also tents to rent. €

EATING

SEE MAP PAGE 56

There's no shortage of excellent places to eat in Iráklio, though **prices** are generally slightly higher than anywhere else on the island. For good quality and reasonably priced food, you need to get away from the more obvious tourist haunts, above all the main squares of Venizélou and Eleftherías (though the former is a great coffee stop). For snacks and picnics the **market** has plenty of fresh produce, there are minimarkets everywhere, open long hours daily, plus a couple of bigger central supermarkets.

CAFÉS

Kirkor Platía Venizélou 29, 2810 242 705. The cafés fronting the Morosini fountain on Platía Venizélou specialize in luscious pastries to accompany a strong mid-morning coffee. *Kirkor* is one of *the* place to sample authentic *bougátsa* (a deliciously creamy cheese pie, sweet or savoury, served warm and sprinkled with sugar and cinnamon); also excellent *loukoumádhes* (dough fritters in honey) and *tyrópita*. If you can't get a table, *Fyllo...Sofíes*, next door, is an excellent alternative; both claim to have been founded in 1922. €

Mare S Sofoklí Venizélou, corner Platía Xenía, 2810 241 946. Stylish café-bar with a wonderful setting and spectacular glass seaview terrace. Serves a range of snacks and light lunches (burgers, sandwiches, pasta and risotto), and good cocktails at night. €€

Miniatoura Monís Odhiyitrías 11, Platía Ayías Ekaterínis, 2810 334 019. Café and wine bar with tables out on the quiet cathedral square. Join the locals for a coffee or snack by day, or come later for the excellent wine list and regular Greek music or jazz evenings. €€

Utopia Hándhakos 51, 2810 341 321. Locals flock here for the cakes and biscuits, served on fancy stands, and above all for the chocolate fondue and chocolate fountains – not cheap, but irresistibly indulgent. At night they also serve more than sixty different beers from all over the world, along with "beer meze" (sausages, mainly), but even then, most people are here for the chocolate and cake. €€

Veneris Bakery Cafe Yiannitsón 12 at Smyrnis, 2810 313 666. Simple, self-service place with tables in a courtyard alongside an excellent bakery, serving inexpensive coffee, bread and cakes hot from the oven, fresh juices and tasty sandwiches. €

1

RESTAURANTS

Adipodas Koraí 13, 2810 343 236. Modern ouzerí-style restaurant popular among young locals, with tables outside on a street that's lively late at night. Plenty of mezédhes choices, or larger dishes like bifteki, shrimp risotto or a huge mixed grill for sharing. €€

Aztecas Hándhakos 22, 2810 220 334. Popular Mexican restaurant with warm pink decor, serving inexpensive Mexican tacos, fajitas, beers, tequila and jugs of sangria. €€

Giakoumis Fotios Theodhosáki 5, 2810 284 039. The little alley connecting the market with Odhós Evans boasts several tavernas catering for market traders and their customers as well as tourists. Established in 1935, *Giakoumis* claims to be the city's oldest taverna: although it's very touristy, locals reckon it still serves up some of the best *païdhákia* (lamb chops) on the island – some tribute, given the competition – as well as traditional *mayiréfta*. You can wash it all down with house wine produced by Lyrarakis, a noted Pezá winery. €€

Hovoli Platía Dhaskaloyiánni 3, 2810 220 320. If all you want is a *yíros* and a beer, or some plain grilled meat, this is the pick of several simple, inexpensive places on this leafy square just off Platía Eleftherías. €

★ **I Avli tou Defkaliona** Lysimáhou Kalokerinoú 8, 2810 244 215. An Iráklio classic, and thus always busy. The *avlí* (courtyard) in question, where the outdoor seating is, has as a focus the ornate Venetian-era Idomenéa fountain (sadly no longer flowing). The winter interior seating is as pleasant. You can easily fill up just on *mezedhákia* (small starter plates); order by number off the Greek-only menu, friendly wait staff tell you if it's off or sold out that night. The pepper salad has some quite tangy ones hidden in sauce, the *keftedákia* (meatballs) are fluffy and almost a mains portion, *volví* (wild hyacinth bulbs) are a rakí classic never found in tourist tavernas, and the houserakí itself will leave a clear head the next day. €

★ **Ippokampos** Sofoklí Venizélou 3, 2810 280 240. The first of a row of places with glassed-in, sea-view terraces (there's also a pleasant dining room for cooler days) immediately west of the harbour, *Ippokampos* serves excellent fish and seafood at competitive prices (sardines €6.50, red mullet €12). Highly popular with locals, it's often crowded late into the evening, and you may have to queue or turn up earlier than the Greeks eat. €€

★ **Kafenio O Tempelis** Milátou 7, corner Meramvélou, 6977 744 660. Hugely popular, this place has tables spilling out onto the pedestrianised streets surrounding it. There's a great variety of well-priced mezédhes and mains plus a short selection of excellent daily specials which might include the likes of chickpeas with spinach and tahin, stuffed courgette flowers or goat in red sauce. €

Katsinas Lohagoú Marinéli 14, Platía Pireós, 2810 221 027. A simple, economical and friendly ouzerí/grill serving tasty mezédhes and traditional dishes at outdoor tables. Authentic homemade food, with hand-cut chips, good seafood and meat dishes. €

Ligo Krasí, Ligo Thálassa Lohagoú Marinélli Ioánni Mitsotáki 18 Anglon Square, 2810 300 501. This mezedhopolío, very popular with locals, serves up a good selection of seafood mezédhes, as well as simple grilled meat, on a small terrace on a busy corner facing the harbour from the northwest. At the end of the meal there's often a dessert and *rakí* on the house. €€

Mayeirevondas me Agapi Koronéou 21, 2810 335 119. Wonderful spick and span little spot with just half a dozen indoor tables; look for the large English sign, "Cooking with Love". Inside the ebullient Sofía prepares a range of superb home-style *mayireftá* (oven-cooked dishes) every day; the *yemistá* (stuffed tomatoes) and beef stew are particularly recommended. Best at lunchtime, as some dishes may run out by evening. €

Pagopiion Papayiamalí 1, Platía Áyiou Títou, www.pagopoieion.gr. The pricier restaurant of one of Iráklio's most stylish bars (see page 71), with stripped stone walls, wooden tables and retro chairs. The menu offers international dishes and modern versions of traditional Greek food, with pasta, risotto and pizzas; an expansive wine list has bottles from little-known but excellent small vineyards. €€€

Paradhosiako (alias Tou Giorgou) Vourvahon 9, 28103 42927. Secluded, no-nonsense old-town taverna with courtyard seating and intriguing *objet trouvé* interior, reached through a pedestrian passage. Grills, mezédhes and a few dishes of the day are the stock in trade. Their tyrokafterí is some of the best in Greece, with plenty else like yaprákia (stuffed vine leaves) beets, and hórta for vegetarians. Their country sausage (chewy and stringy) are avoidable. Inexpensive beer, rakí or bulk wine to wash it down. Despite those sausages, among the best budget meals in town. €

★ **Peskesi** Kapetán Haralambí 6–8, 2810 288 887. Traditional Cretan dishes concocted with a creative twist are served inside a lovingly restored mansion (mentioned in Kazantzákis's *Freedom and Death*) with hidden nooks and secluded patios. Everything is locally sourced, including veg from the restaurant's own farm and an exclusively Cretan wine list. €€

DRINKING AND NIGHTLIFE

SEE MAP PAGE 56

As a university town, Iráklio has plenty of places to let your hair down. Young Cretans tend to be more into sitting and chatting over background music than dancing; long extents of Koraí and the surrounding pedestrianized streets are packed with alfresco cafés that become **bars** as the lights dim and the volume ramps up. The bigger **clubs** are generally away from the central zone; they tend to play Western music (and lots of techno) interspersed with Greek pop. Most don't open their doors before 11pm, with the crowds drifting in after 1am and dancing until dawn. For livelier, and earlier, partying head to one of the nearby resorts or look out for posters advertising beach parties in summer.

BARS

Central Park Arkoléondos 19, El Greco Park, http://central-park.gr. Big, busy cocktail bar and café with one of the city's most popular terraces for those who want to see and be seen. There's a substantial menu (until almost midnight) that goes beyond the usual snacks; big screens; and an almost permanent crowd.

Halavro Milátou 10, 6945 699 292. Beautiful, busy bar/café in a mostly derelict building with entrances on both Koraí and Milátou. The main area is in a roofless courtyard lit with fairy lights where they serve cocktails (and good food, though few order it) and DJs set up as the evening wears on.

Jailhouse Ayiostefanitón 19, 6973 334 093. Friendly rock bar in what turns out inside to be an ancient stone building on two levels; a gathering place for Iráklio's alternative crowd who hang out here until the live music starts next door at *Rolling Stone*.

Kafenion Fix Aretoúsas 2 at Meramvélou, 2810 289 023. Traditional café and bar, busiest in the evenings, with tables set out under the trees of an attractive platía. There's no music, so this is a popular place for a quiet, early drink and great if you want to make yourself heard.

Opus Kapetán Haralábi 3, 2810 225 151. In a superbly restored Venetian-Ottoman structure, part of which was once a prison – hence the sturdy walls – this atmospheric wine bar offers dozens of Greek wines. They also serve cocktails and some interesting food.

Pagopiion (Ice Factory) Platía Áyios Títos, 2810 346 028. Stunning bar with arty decor inside Iráklio's former ice factory. Much of the old building has been preserved, including a lift for hauling the ice from the basement freezer and a fascistic call to duty in German Gothic script on one wall – a remnant of Nazi occupation of the factory in World War II. Be sure to visit the toilets, which are in an artistic league of their own. An outdoor terrace faces the church of Áyios Títos and an attractive square.

Take Five Arkoléondos 7, El Greco Park, 28150 05650. One of the oldest bars in Iráklio, *Take Five* began as a rock bar in the 1980s and is now a slick pavement café with an indoor bar, playing jazzy music; it's a favourite late-night hangout for a slightly older crowd.

CLUBS AND LIVE MUSIC VENUES

Ellinadhiko Milátou 14, 6975 820 408. Relatively small downtown club with a fun atmosphere and predominantly local crowd, who've moved on from the surrounding bars. Greek and international tunes along with themed party nights.

Rock n Rolling Stone Rock Bar Ayiostefanitón 19, 6987 400 593. Attached to the *Jailhouse* bar, this is a rock club with a great atmosphere, sweaty, late-night live rock and punk bands, and rock DJs – Wednesday is Greek rock night.

Senses Club Papandréou 277, Amoudhára, 6944 269 733. A lively, summer-only club with a party atmosphere, 5km west of the city by Amoudhára beach, playing various genres of international music including dance and r'n'b. Good theme nights and special events.

SHOPPING

SEE MAP PAGE 56

In addition to Iráklio's **central market** (see page 64) there's a **farmers' market** selling wonderful produce every Mon, Wed & Fri (10am–2pm) in Yeoryiádhi park, which is adjacent to the Public Gardens, southeast of Platía Eleftherías, and a huge **street market** every Sat morning in an open area off Leonídhou, a little further out in the same direction. **Upmarket shops**, especially those selling jewellery, clothes and fabrics, cluster around Dedhálou, Odhós 1821 and Odhós Evans (east and west of the market respectively) and along Kalokerinoú heading west from here.

Iráklio market Odhós 1866. One of the best markets on the island, good for food and herbs – bargain-priced saffron and unique Cretan dried thyme – as well as cheap practical goods, leatherware, hats and tourist items like beach towels and T-shirts. Daily 8am–8pm (though individual stalls vary; some close on Sun, while many take a siesta 2–5pm).

Mayaba Store Dedalou 20, 2810 287 241. Gift store that sells a whole range of items, from handcrafted trinkets to furniture pieces. It almost looks like the home of a bohemian collector.

To Votanopolio tis Vasilkis Karteroú 35, 2810 244 452. *Vassiliki's Herbalists* sells Cretan herbs, seeds, essential oils, soaps and herbal tonics, but above all their own teas, made from local ingredients, one of which is guaranteed to cure you of pretty much whatever ails you. A lovely shop, with staff only too eager to help.

DIRECTORY

Banks and money The main branches face 25-Avgoústou, many of them with ATMs; there are more machines at banks along Dhikeosínis.

Football Two of Iráklio's football clubs, OFI and Ergotelis, featured in the Greek Superleague (the top division) early this century, until financial problems brought both to their knees. OFI clawed their way back to the top division in 2018, but Ergotelis remain near the bottom of the professional leagues. The former play at the Dhimótikou stadium, Platía Ayía Varvára in the Kaminia district on the west side of town, Ergotelis at the stadium below the Martinengo Bastion (see page 57).

1

Hospitals The city's main general hospital is the Venizelio, on the Knossós road south out of town (2810 368 000); there are slightly better facilities at the University Hospital (2813 402 111), 6km southwest of the city.
Laundry Washsalon, Evgenikoú and Ayiostefanitón (Mon & Wed 9am–5pm, Tues, Thurs & Fri 9am–8pm, Sat 9am–3pm) and Wash Center, Leoforos 62 Martýron 118 (2810 372 373, daily 9am–9pm), both do good service washes.
Left luggage In addition to the left luggage in Bus Station A (see page 68), most hotels will look after your bags free for a few days if you've stayed, as will bike rental companies.
Mountaineering and hiking The local EOS is at Dhikeosínis 53 (2810 227 609, http://eos-her.gr); they organise regular walks and climbs in the local mountins.
Pharmacies Plentiful on the main shopping streets. At least one will be open 18hr a day on a rota basis; check the list on the door of any pharmacy. There are also traditional herbalists in the market.
Post office Main office in Platía Dhaskaloyiánnis, off Eleftherías (Mon–Fri 7.30am– 5pm).
Public toilets In El Greco Park, the public gardens, Platía Kornárou, Platía Ayías Ekaterínis, at the bus stations and at the Archeological Museum (no need to pay entrance charge).

Knossós

...a dancing place
All full of turnings, that was like the admirable maze
For fair hair'd Ariadne made, by cunning Daedalos

Homer, *The Odyssey*

KNOSSÓS (**Κνωσός**), 5km south of Iráklio on a low, largely artificial hill, was by far the largest of the **Minoan palaces**, thriving more than three and a half thousand years ago at the heart of a highly sophisticated island-wide civilization. Long after Minoan culture had collapsed, a town on this site remained powerful, rivalling Górtys well into the Roman era. Today it is the most famous – and most visited – of all Crete's tourist attractions. No matter when you come, you won't get the place to yourself, but with luck you will have the opportunity to appreciate individual parts of the palace during the brief lulls between groups. In summer the best time of day to avoid the crowds is in the last couple of hours before closing time, which also has the advantage of being cooler. If you get the opportunity to come back a second time, it will all begin to make a great deal more sense.

Brief history

The discovery and excavation of the palace is among the most amazing tales of modern archeology. Until the start of the twentieth century, Knossós was a place thought to have existed only in mythology. **Heinrich Schliemann**, the German excavator of Troy, suspected that a major Minoan palace lay under the various tumuli here, but was denied the permission to dig by the local Ottoman authorities. Today's Knossós, whose fame rivals any such site in the world, is primarily associated with **Sir Arthur Evans**, who bought the site, and excavated and liberally "restored" the palace at the start of the twentieth century. His bust is one of the first things to greet you at the site. The autocratic control he exerted, his working standards and procedures, and, above all, the restorations he claimed were necessary to preserve the building have been a source of furious controversy among archeologists ever since (see page 323). It has become clear that much of Evans's upper level, the *Piano Nobile*, is pure conjecture. Even so, his guess as to what the palace might have looked like is certainly as good as anyone else's, and it makes the other sites infinitely more meaningful if you have seen Knossós first. Without the restorations, it would be hard to visualize the ceremonial stairways, strange top-heavy pillars and brightly frescoed walls that distinguish Knossós – and almost impossible to imagine the grandeur of the multistorey palace. To get an idea of the size and complexity of the palace in its original state, take a look at the cutaway drawings on sale outside; they may seem somewhat fantastic, but are probably not too far from reality.

The Palace of Knossós

Charge • 2810 231 940, buy advance tickets online at https://knossos-palace.gr

As soon as you enter the **Palace of Knossós** through its West Court, it is clear how the legends of the labyrinth grew up around it. Even with a map and description, it can be very hard to work out where you are.

The remains you see are mostly those of the **second palace**, rebuilt after the destruction of around 1700 BC (see page 325) and occupied – with increasing Mycenaean influence – through to about 1450 BC. At the time, it was surrounded by a town of considerable size. The palace itself, though, must have looked almost as much of a mess then as it does now – a vast bulk, with more than a thousand rooms on five floors, which had spread across the hill more as an organic growth than a planned building, incorporating or burying earlier structures as it went. In this, Knossós simply followed the pattern of Minoan architecture generally, with extra rooms being added as the need arose. It is a style of building still common on Crete, where finished buildings seem to be outnumbered by those waiting to have an extra floor or room added when need and finance dictate.

The difficulty in understanding the site is not helped by the fact that you are no longer allowed to wander freely through the complex: instead, a series of **timber walkways** channels visitors around. This is particularly true of the Royal Apartments, where access to many rooms is denied or reduced to partial views from behind glass screens. The walkways also make it almost impossible to avoid the guided tours that congregate at every point of significance en route. The upside of this is that if you wait

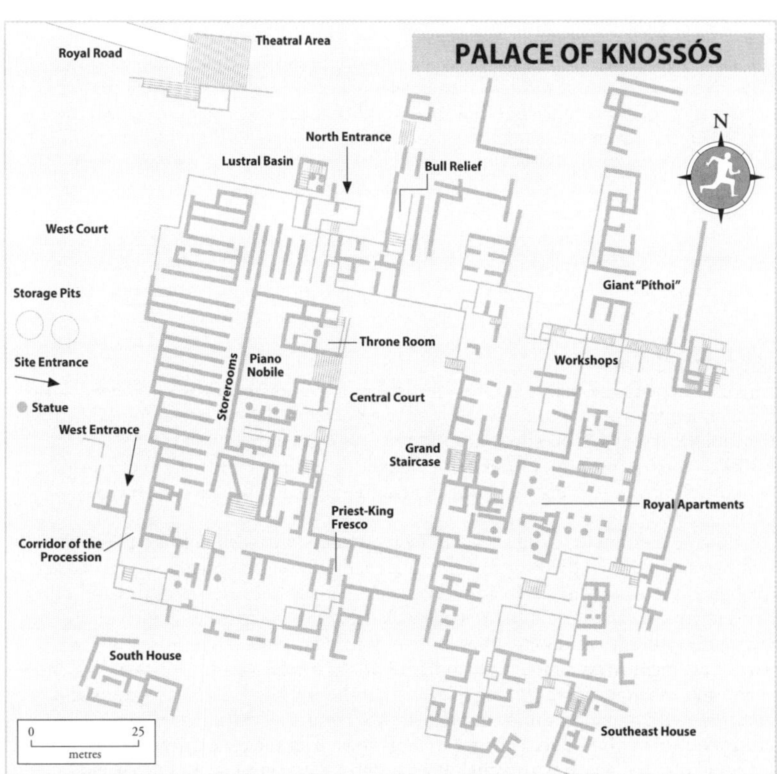

THE LEGEND OF THE MINOTAUR

Knossós was the court of the legendary **King Minos**, whose wife Pasiphae, cursed by Poseidon, bore the **Minotaur**, a creature half-bull, half-man (see page 342). The **labyrinth** was constructed by Daedalos to contain the monster, and every nine years (some say every year) seven youths and seven maidens were brought from Athens as human sacrifice, until finally **Theseus** arrived to slay the beast and, with Ariadne's help, escape its lair. Imprisoned in his own maze as punishment for the escape, Daedalos later constructed the wings that bore him away to safety – and his son **Ikaros (Icarus)** to his untimely death. The legend has inspired writers from Homer to Dante, who famously depicts the beast in his vision of Hell:

Into the chasm was that descent: and there
At point of the disparted ridge lay stretch'd
The infamy of Crete, detested brood
Of the feign'd heifer: and at sight of us
It gnaw'd itself, as one with rage distract.

Dante, *Inferno*, Canto XII

anywhere long enough a tour will come along and give you a free explanation of what you're looking at, which you can inspect in detail when the crowd has moved on.

The West Court

The **West Court**, across which you approach the palace, was perhaps a marketplace or, at any rate, the scene of public meetings. Across it run slightly raised walkways leading from the palace's West Entrance to the Theatral Area and once presumably on to the Royal Road. There are also three large **circular pits**, originally grain silos or perhaps depositories for sacred offerings, but used as rubbish tips by the end of the Minoan era. When these were excavated, remains of early dwellings – visible in the central pit, dating from around 2000 BC and thus preceding the first palace – were revealed. The walls and floor surfaces were found to have been coated with red plaster, and these are among the earliest known remains on the site.

Following the walkway towards the **West Entrance** nowadays, you arrive at stones marking the original wall of an earlier incarnation of the palace, then the facade of the palace proper, and beyond that a series of small rooms of which only the foundations survive.

The first frescoes

Anyone entering the palace by the West Entrance in its heyday would have passed through a guardroom and then followed the **Corridor of the Procession**, flanked by frescoes depicting a procession, around towards the south side of the palace; the walkway runs alongside. A brief detour down the stairway near the West Entrance would enable you to view the **South House** (see page 77) before entering the palace proper.

Following the walkway, you come to the reproduction of the **Priest-King Fresco** (which Evans dubbed the Prince of the Lilies, although some scholars are convinced the figure is female or not even a royal personage at all); the original of this and other Knossós frescoes are in Iráklio's Archeological Museum (see page 57). A revealing glimpse into Evans's mindset comes from an article he wrote in the London *Times* when this fragmentary figure came to light: "…the head is wearing a crown, which terminates in a row of five sloping lilies… That the *fleur-de-lis* of our Edwards and Henrys should find a prototype in prehistoric Greece is a startling revelation". The nearby viewing point offers a chance to look down over the palace. Apparently, a whole series of large and airy frescoed chambers, perhaps reception rooms, once stood here.

The Central Court

The **Central Court**, the heart of the palace, is aligned almost exactly north–south. The courtyard paving covers the oldest remains found on the site, dating back to Neolithic times. In Minoan times high walls would have hemmed the courtyard in on every side, and the atmosphere would have been very different from the open, shadeless space that survives. Some say this was the scene of the famous bull-leaping, but that seems unlikely: although the court measures almost 50m by 25m, it would hardly be spacious enough to accommodate the sort of intricate acrobatics shown in surviving pictures, let alone an audience to watch.

The Throne Room

The entrance to one of Knossós's most atmospheric survivals, the **Throne Room**, is in the northwestern corner of the central courtyard; you'll spot the room by the queues of people waiting to press their faces against the glass to view it. In the room, a worn stone throne sits against the wall of a surprisingly small chamber; along the walls around it are ranged stone benches and, behind, there's a copy of a fresco depicting two griffins. In all probability, this was the seat of a priestess rather than a ruler – there's nothing like it in any other Minoan palace – but it may have been an innovation wrought by the Mycenaeans, since it appears that this room dates only from the final period of the palace's occupation. Opposite the throne, steps lead down to a lustral basin – a sunken "bath", probably for ritual purification rather than actual bathing, with no drain.

The Piano Nobile

Alongside the Throne Room, a stairway climbs to the first floor and Evans's reconstructed **Piano Nobile**. One of the most interesting features of this part of the palace is the view it offers of the palace storerooms with their rows of *píthoi* (storage jars). There's an amazing amount of storage space here, in the jars – which would mostly have held oil or wine – and in sections sunk into the ground for other goods. The rooms of the *Piano Nobile* itself are again rather confusing, though you should be able to pick out the Sanctuary Hall from stumps that remain of its six large columns. Opposite this is a small concrete room (complete with roof), which Evans "reconstructed" directly above the Throne Room. It feels entirely out of place; inside, there's a small display on the restoration of the frescoes, and through the other side you get another good view over the Central Court. Returning through this room, you could climb down the very narrow staircase on your right to arrive at the entrance to the corridor of storerooms (fenced off) or head back to the left towards the area where you entered the palace.

The Royal Apartments

On the east side of the central courtyard, the **Grand Staircase** leads into the **Royal Apartments**, clearly the finest of the rooms at Knossós, though sadly you can't enter any of them. The **staircase** itself is an architectural masterpiece, not only a fitting approach to these sumptuously appointed chambers, but also an integral part of the whole design, its large well allowing light into the lower storeys. Light wells such as these, usually with a courtyard at the bottom, are a common feature of Knossós and a reminder of just how important creature comforts were to the Minoans, and how skilled they were at providing them.

For more evidence of this luxurious lifestyle, look no further than the **Queen's Suite**, off the grand **Hall of the Colonnades** at the bottom of the staircase. The main living room is decorated with the celebrated dolphin fresco and with running friezes of flowers and (earlier) spirals. On two sides it opens to courtyards that let in light and air; the smaller one would probably have been planted with flowers. It is easy to imagine the room in use, scattered with cushions and hung with rich drapes, curtains placed between the pillars providing privacy and cool shade in the heat of the day. Guides will describe all this but it is of course almost entirely speculation – and some of it pure con. The dolphin fresco, for example, was found in the courtyard, not the room itself, and would have been viewed from inside or above as a sort of *trompe l'oeil*, like looking out of a glass-bottomed boat. There are many who argue, convincingly, that grand as these rooms are, they are not really large or fine enough to have been royal quarters. Those would more likely have been in the lighter and airier rooms that must have existed in the upper reaches of the palace, while these lower apartments were inhabited by resident nobles or priests.

Whether or not you accept Evans's names and attributions, the rooms remain an impressive example of the sophistication of Minoan architecture. The **Queen's Bathroom**, its clay tub protected behind a low wall (and probably screened by curtains when in use), is another fine example, as is the famous "flushing" lavatory (a hole in the ground with drains to take the waste away – it was flushed by a bucket of water).

On the floor above the queen's domain, the Grand Staircase passes through a set of rooms that are generally described as the **King's Quarters**. These are chambers in a considerably sterner vein. The staircase opens into a grandiose reception area known as the **Hall of the Royal Guard**, its walls decorated in repeated shield motifs. Opening off it is the ruler's personal chamber, the **Hall of the Double Axes** – a room that could be divided to allow for privacy while audiences were held in the more public section, or the whole opened out for larger functions. Its name comes from the double-axe symbol, so common throughout Knossós, which here is carved into every block of masonry.

The drainage system

From the back of the queen's chambers, you can emerge into the fringes of the palace where it spreads down the lower slopes of the hill. This is a good point at which to consider the famous **drainage system** at Knossós, some of the most complete sections of which are visible under grilles. The snugly interconnecting terracotta pipes ran underneath most of the palace (here, they have come more or less direct from the Queen's Bathroom), and site guides never fail to point them out as evidence of the advanced state of Minoan civilization. Down by the external walls you get a clear view of the system of baffles and overflows designed to slow down the runoff and avoid flooding.

The Palace Workshops

From the bottom of the slope, you get a fine impression of the scale of the whole palace complex and can circle around towards the north, climbing back inside the palace limits to see the area known as the **Palace Workshops**. Here, potters, lapidaries and smiths appear to have plied their trades, and this area is also home to the spectacular **giant píthoi**; people queue to have their photograph taken with the jars towering over them. From here there's also a good view of the Bull Relief fresco in the restored north entrance.

Around the North Entrance

Circling around the palace, you can re-enter by the **North Entrance**. Beside the gateway is a well-preserved **lustral basin**, and beyond that, a guardroom. As you head up towards the central courtyard, a flight of stairs doubles back to allow you to examine the copy of the **Bull Relief** close up.

Just outside the North Entrance, the **Theatral Area** is one of the more important enigmas of this and other Minoan palaces. An open space resembling a stepped amphitheatre, it may have been used for ritual performances or dances, but there's no real evidence of this, and again there would have been very little room for an audience if that was its function.

Beyond it, the **Royal Road** sets out: originally this ran to the Little Palace, perhaps with branches heading north to the palace's harbour at Amnísos and west across the island; nowadays, however, it ends after about 100m at a brick wall beneath the modern road. Alongside are assorted structures variously interpreted as stores, workshops or grandstands for viewing parades.

The south side

Of the lesser structures that crowd around the palace, a number of houses on the south side are particularly worth noting. The one known simply as the **South House**, reconstructed to its original three floors, seems amazingly modern, but actually dates from the late Minoan period (c.1550 BC). The dwelling is believed to have belonged to an important official or noble, since it encroaches on the palace domain. In the **Southeast House** of the same period, a cult room with a sacred pillar was discovered, as well as stands for double axes and a libation table.

Outlying remains

Numerous small sites dot the fields surrounding the palace, most of them barely visited, perhaps because unless you get lucky all you can do is stare in through their fences.

Caravanserai

Across a little valley from the south side of the palace, accessed from about 250m down the road south

The **Caravanserai** was where travellers visiting Knossós would rest and water their animals. The restored building contains two elegant rooms, as well as a large stone footbath still with running water from an ancient spring. There's a good view of the palace from the surrounding fields.

Little Palace and Royal Villa

Off the road to Iráklio, about 200m northwest of the palace • Both occasionally open for special visits; details from ticket office

Among the most important of Knossós' outlying buildings are the **Little Palace**, on a site which also contains a mansion and many Roman remains, and the **Royal Villa**, facing the palace from the slope to the northeast.

Villa Dionysos

300m up the road to Iráklio from the site entrance

The first-century CE **Villa Dionysos** lay near the centre of the Roman city of Cnossus. The villa has extremely fine polychrome mosaics, and once restoration work is complete it is planned to open it up to the public. For details on the progress of the restoration, contact the Knossós ticket office.

Villa Ariadne

About 100m along the road to Iráklio from the site entrance • Not open to the public

The **Villa Ariadne** was built by Arthur Evans as his home-from-home during excavations. Later, the house served as a military hospital during the German siege of Iráklio and, following the city's fall, as the residence of the German commander of Crete. It was where General Kreipe was based when he was kidnapped (see page 334), and the villa's dining room was also where the German army signed the treaty of surrender on May 9, 1945. Although not open to the public, nobody seems to mind if you walk up the drive past the gatehouse to have a look at the house's exterior and lush gardens.

ARRIVAL AND DEPARTURE **KNOSSÓS**

By bus Local bus #2 (every 15min; €1.70 each way) starts from the city bus stands alongside Bus Station A,

1

passes through Platía Eleftherías and leaves town along Odhós-1821 and Evans.

By taxi A taxi from the centre of Iráklio will cost around €12.

By car From the centre of Iráklio head out through the Pórta Kenoúria; from anywhere else on the island turn directly off the bypass onto the badly signed Knossós road. There's a free car park immediately before the site entrance; avoid paying exorbitant rates for the private car parks, whose touts will attempt to wave you in.

TOURS

Tours Official guides, who are self-employed, can be hired at the site entrance; the tour lasts 1hr 30min and the guide expects to receive a minimum of €100 per tour. This fee will be divided between the number making the tour (thus four people will pay €25 each). To get the lowest rate (€10 per person) you will need to wait until the guide has gathered ten customers. The maximum number of people allowed per tour is 14. There are also audio guided tours, which you can enjoy using your smartphone (average €20 per person).

South of Iráklio: wine country

The countryside south of Knossós is dominated by the bulk of **Mount Yioúhtas** (811m), which rises alone from a landscape otherwise characterized by gently undulating agricultural country. Seen from the northwest, the mountain has an unmistakably human profile, and was traditionally identified with Zeus. The ancient Cretans claimed that Zeus lay buried underneath the mountain; given that the god is immortal, this furnished proof for other Greeks of the assertion that "All Cretans are liars" – it may even have been the original basis of this reputation.

As you leave Knossós behind, the nature of the journey south is transformed almost immediately: the road empties and the country becomes greener. Almost any road in this area makes for a beautiful drive, past vineyards draped across low hills and through flourishing farming communities. Just a couple of kilometres from the archeological site, at the head of the valley, an extraordinary **aqueduct** arches beside the road. This looks medieval and was built on the line of an earlier Roman aqueduct, but is in fact less than two hundred years old, having been constructed during the brief period of Egyptian rule (1832–40) to provide Iráklio with water. A little further on, the junction where you turn right towards Arhánes seems a singularly unthreatening spot today, yet it was here, on April 26, 1944, that General Kreipe was kidnapped (see page 334). The site is now marked by a lofty modern monument.

Much of the interest in this region centres around **Arhánes**, where there's an **Archeological Museum** and easy access to three fascinating **Minoan sites** at Foúrni, Anemospília and on the summit of Mount Yioúhtas itself. Nearby at **Vathýpetro** the remarkable remains of a Minoan vineyard can be seen, at the heart of what remains one of the island's chief **wine-growing areas**: many winemakers open their doors to the public, especially at **Pezá**.

Northeast of Pezá, the village of **Myrtiá** boasts a museum devoted to Crete's most famous literary name, Nikos Kazantzákis, and just south of here a road meanders through hilly farm country well inland from the big resorts, into a region known as the **Pedhiádha. Thrapsanó** constitutes an important pottery centre, and other diversions include the ancient site of **Lýttos** and some notable **frescoed churches** around **Kastélli**.

Arhánes

ARHÁNES (**Αρχάνες**) is a large and prosperous agricultural centre, substantial enough to have a one-way traffic system and be served by hourly buses from Iráklio. The streets in the central area are narrow and confusing, and the best advice for drivers is to park up near the square and explore on foot. There are tavernas and cafés around the main square, as well as numerous flashy modern bars, reflecting the region's agricultural prosperity. From mid-July to mid-August a colourful daily **street market**, selling local crafts and delicacies, takes place in the old quarter.

The richness of the land around Arhánes is nothing new: this area was a major centre of **Minoan civilization**, and there are a number of important sites in and around town, including a hypothesized fifth palace to rival those at Festós and Mália. Most are relatively recent discoveries, having been excavated over the last few decades, and not all of the excavations have been fully published. Consequently, these sites are neither particularly famous nor especially welcoming to visitors, but many of the finds are nonetheless important; indeed, some of the greatest treasures of the Iráklio archeological museum come from this region. A site right in the heart of modern Arhánes is described as the **Summer Palace**, and may have functioned as such for Knossós in the way that Áyia Triádha apparently did for the Festós palace, but this is largely speculation. Still, what remains is impressive and through the chain-link fence you can see evidence of a substantial walled mansion, representing only a small part of what once stood here. Piecemeal excavation is still going on at other sites in the centre too, but much is hidden beneath more modern buildings. If you make the Archeological Museum your first stop, you can find out more about the status of these sites and pick up a leaflet (with town map) on things to do in the area.

Arhánes Archeological Museum

Miháli Kalohristianáki, an alley just off the upper, north-bound, one-way street, about 80m north of the main square • Charge • 2810 752 712

Imaginatively laid out in a single room, the **Arhánes Archeological Museum** displays some exceptional finds from the town and surrounding sites. Near the entrance are

WINE TASTING AROUND PEZÁ

Locals claim, with some justification, that **wine** has been made in the area around Pezá for four thousand years, probably using grape varieties not far removed from the Kotsifáli and Mandilariá (for red), Plytó and Vilána (white) that are extensively cultivated today. Cretan wines, traditionally very much *vin ordinaire*, are becoming increasingly sophisticated, and a number of wineries open their doors to visitors. Most require appointments, but all of the following allow unplanned visits – though even here it's safest to call in advance. For more information there is a useful wines of Crete **map** available from vineyards and tourist offices, as well as a website: www.winesofcrete.gr.

Boutari Skaláni, on the Myrtiá road, www.boutari.gr/vineyard/scalarea-estate. Not far south of Knossós lies the spectacular modern Fantaxometocho estate, owned by one of Greece's biggest winemakers (https://winesofgreece.org/wineries/boutari-crete-domaine-fantaxometocho/). Specializing in organic production methods, they make excellent wines. Charge.

Douloufakis Dháfnes, https://douloufakis.wine. Little over 10km from Pezá as the crow flies, this award-winning family winery is more easily reached direct from Iráklio, on the road heading southwest towards Festós and Mátala. Worth visiting for a particularly good tour of the whole process, from vine to bottle. Charge.

Lyrarakis About 5km southeast of Pezá on the road to Arkalohóri,Long-established family vineyards and winery making a selection of excellent single-variety and single-region wines – the white 100% Vilána and Melissáki are particularly good. Charge.

Mesarmi Houdhétsi, on the left as you enter the village from Áyios Vasílios, 6972 665 599. A wine shop which offers tastings of Pezá and Cretan wines as well as olive oil and cheese. The proprietor, Stella Vassilaki, is a Master of Wine. Best to call ahead as there may be events on. Charge.

Peza Union Pezá, on the Kastélli road at the eastern edge of town, https://pezaunion.gr. The union of agricultural cooperatives of Pezá produces olive oil as well as wine, from the vines and trees of many small producers. Free tours of their exhibition centre are followed by wine tasting session and a small meze. Charge.

Stylianoú Winery Kounavi, 3km north of Pezá and signed once you reach the village, http://stilianouwines.gr. A pleasant drive through the vines takes you to the welcoming Stylianoú family vineyard, where they have been producing wine for four generations. Following a tour you can taste their four wines (three reds and a white), as well as the family-produced olive oil, a wonderfully peppery number. Free.

some well-preserved Minoan **lárnakes** (clay coffins, complete with the bones found in them) from **Foúrni** (see page 80) dating from around 1800 BC. Displayed nearby is a replica of a **sistrum** (a simple, tambourine-like musical instrument); the original, also from the cemetery at Foúrni, is in the Iráklio Archeological Museum and dates from around 2000 BC; it may well be the oldest surviving musical instrument in Europe. A photo shows a detail of the famous Harvesters Vase from the Iráklio museum, depicting a sistrum in use.

There are fascinating finds, too, from **Anemospília** (see page 80), where human sacrifices appear to have taken place in the temple. A copy of the **dagger** found lying on the sacrificial victim is displayed here, with a curious motif of a hybrid animal – resembling a deformed boar – carved on the blade. There's also a copy of the seal stone that the priest was wearing on his left wrist, and of the terracotta feet of a wooden statue that was destroyed in the fire that followed the destruction of the temple; again, the originals are in the Iráklio museum.

Other items to look out for include small terracotta cups that contained the ochres used to paint frescoes on the walls in the palaces and villas, and an imaginative display of **pottery shards** that evidences five thousand years of human occupation in this town: crude works of the third millennium BC are succeeded by the various Minoan periods, then Greek, Roman, Byzantine, Venetian and Turkish pieces, down to broken pots of the present day. There are also fragments of Minoan wall painting and many everyday domestic objects, ranging from a wine-press and giant *píthoi* to jewellery and jugs.

Arhánes churches

Numerous ancient churches are scattered through the town, though there's no guarantee that you'll find any open. Right on the main square an incongruous whitewashed clock tower marks out one, with a fine collection of icons; elsewhere, there are Byzantine frescoes in the church of **Ayía Triádha** on the fringes of town and at the church of **Asómatos** to the east, where the superb fourteenth-century works include a horrific *Crucifixion* and a depiction of the fall of Jericho, with Joshua in full medieval armour.

Foúrni

Immediately west of Arhánes • Free • Cross the bypass west of Arhánes and then walk for about 10min up a steep, very rocky trail

The size of the **burial ground at FOÚRNI** (**Φούρνι**) is evidence of the scale of the Minoan community that once thrived around Arhánes; the site was used throughout the Minoan period, with its earliest tombs dating from around 2500 BC (before the construction of the great palaces), and the latest from the very end of the Minoan era. The structures include a number of early tholos tombs – round, stone buildings reminiscent of beehives – each of which contained multiple burials in sarcophagi and *píthoi*. Many simpler graves and a circle of seven Mycenaean-style shaft graves were also revealed at Foúrni, making it by far the most extensive Minoan cemetery known. In "Tholos A", a side-chamber was found that revealed the undisturbed tomb of a woman who, judging by the jewellery and other goods buried with her, was of royal descent and perhaps a priestess. Her jewellery is now on display at the Iráklio Archeological Museum, as is the skeleton of a horse apparently sacrificed in her honour.

Anemospília

2km northwest of Arhánes

ANEMOSPÍLIA (**Ανεμοσπήλια**) is enlivened by a spectacular setting and a controversial story, though the site itself can only be viewed through a fence. The approach road heads north from Arhánes: coming from Iráklio, you enter the one-way street and almost immediately turn sharp right, back on yourself, just past a small chapel. Following the road leading northwest out of the town, you begin to climb across the

HUMAN SACRIFICE IN ANCIENT CRETE?

The temple at Anemospília appears to have been destroyed in the midst of a ceremony involving **human sacrifice** – the only evidence of such a ritual found in Minoan Crete. This came as a severe shock to those who liked to portray the Minoans as the perfect peaceable society, but the evidence is hard to refute. Three skeletons were found in the western room: one had rich jewellery, indicative of a priest; another was a woman, presumably a priestess or assistant; the third was curled up on an altar-like structure, and, according to scientists, was already dead when the building collapsed and killed the others. A large bronze knife lay on top of this third skeleton. Outside the western room, another man was crushed in the corridor, apparently carrying some kind of ritual vase. These events have been dated to roughly the time of the earthquakes that destroyed the first palaces and, in the circumstances, it seems easy to believe that the priests might have resorted to desperate measures in a final attempt to appease the gods who were laying waste to their civilization.

northern face of Mount Yioúhtas, winding around craggy rocks weirdly carved by the wind (Anemospília means "Caves of the Wind") until you reach the fenced site held in a steep curve of the road.

What stood here was a **temple**, and its interpretation has been the source of outraged controversy among Minoan scholars since its excavation at the beginning of the 1980s. The building, apparently destroyed by an earthquake around 1700 BC, is a simple one, consisting of three rooms connected by a north-facing portico, but its contents are not so easily described.

Mount Yioúhtas

A couple of kilometres south of Arhánes, a track leads towards the summit of **MOUNT YIOÚHTAS (Γιούχτας)**, a relatively easy drive. You can also climb the mountain in little over an hour from Arhánes, but it seems rather unsatisfying to do this only to discover other people rolling up on their motorbikes or in taxis (the summit is an optional diversion on the E4 European path as it crosses Crete: coming from the east it follows the track mentioned above, then winds steeply down to Arhánes, to rejoin the main route, via the footpath). At the summit, the **panoramic views** are the main lure, back across Iráklio especially, but also west to Psiloritis and east to Dhíkti. Up here, too, is a small chapel, and the trappings of the annual *paniyíri* (festival), which is celebrated on August 15 and attracts villagers from all around. The impressive remains of a **Minoan Peak sanctuary** dating from the early second millennium BC occupy the north side of the hill, partly built over by a telecommunications station. It very likely served as a cult centre, attracting pilgrims from Arhánes and Knossós, both of which can be seen from the summit. An enormous number of votive offerings, including jewellery, figurines and libation vessels, were unearthed in the excavations and are now on display in the museum at Iráklio. On the shoulders of the mountain, not easily accessible, are caves associated with the local Zeus cult.

Vathýpetro

4km south of Arhánes • Free

The site of **VATHÝPETRO (Βαθύπετρο)** feels somewhat neglected, and is poorly signposted off the road south of Arhánes, beneath Mount Yioúhtas. Nonetheless, the remains of this large **Minoan villa**, which once controlled the rich farmland south of Arhánes, are well worth visiting. It was found when excavated to contain a remarkable collection of everyday items – equipment for making wine and oil, and other tools and simple requisites of rural life. Still surrounded by vineyards with a valid claim to be the oldest in the world (wine has been produced here since the second millennium BC), the house was originally a substantial building of several storeys, with a courtyard enclosing a shrine, and fine large rooms – especially on the east side. The basement workrooms, however, were the scene of the most interesting discoveries, comprising agricultural equipment and a remarkably well-preserved **winepress**, which can still be seen in situ.

Houdhétsi

HOUDHÉTSI (**Χουδέτσι**) lies on a side road that links two major north–south thoroughfares, from Arhánes towards Pýrgos and from Pezá to Arkalohóri and Áno Viánnos. The village is distinguished from its agricultural neighbours by the presence of the music workshop, **Labyrinth** (https://labyrinthmusic.gr), the home base of *lyra* player Ross Daly of Irish descent but resident for decades in Greece and Crete. Although the centre is only open to people attending their seminars it has led to the creation here of some excellent places to eat and to stay; there are summer outdoor Friday-night concerts in Labyrinth's gardens.

Myrtiá

The main reason to visit **MYRTIÁ** (**Μυρτιά**) is for the **Kazantzákis Museum**, dedicated to the writer and philosopher Nikos Kazantzákis (see page 58). Only the seriously committed will spend long here, but it's a lovely drive to the village on almost deserted roads. Myrtiá itself is larger than you'd expect – as are so many of these villages – and bright with flowers planted in old olive-oil cans.

Kazantzákis Museum

In the village square • Charge • www.kazantzaki.gr

The **Kazantzákis Museum** occupies a cluster of buildings in the village square, where Nikos Kazantzákis's parents once lived. Its collection includes a vast quantity of ephemera relating to the great author and philosopher: diaries, photos, manuscripts, first editions, translations into every conceivable language, playbills, stills from films of his works, costumes and more. There's also a video documentary in Greek.

Thrapsanó

The large village of **THRAPSANÓ** (**Θραψανό**), 4km south of the Pezá–Kastélli road, has for centuries been an important **pottery-making** centre. Workshops still thrive

THE IRISH LYRA PLAYER

One of the more remarkable stories of Cretan music is that an Irishman, **Ross Daly**, has become one of its most famous names. Born in England of Irish parents, he grew up in Asia and North America, the family settling wherever the work of his physicist father happened to take them. Daly first visited Crete in 1971 and was strongly attracted to its traditional music, studying in that same decade under master *lyra* player Kostas Mountakis, in Haniá. Part of his early career was spent in Anóyia teaching *lyra* to local children, but once he had become a *lyra* virtuoso he was not content to stay within the confines of Cretan music and began to synthesize what he had learned in Crete and Greece with music from other cultures such as Turkey, the Balkans, India and Afghanistan.

Daly now performs worldwide with his ensemble, Labyrinth, a unit comprising Russian, Greek and Cretan musicians, but always returns to his home in Crete. In addition to the *lyra*, he now plays a variety of instruments, including the *laoúto* (lute), *oud*, *rabab* (Afghan lute), *sarangi* (South Asian*bouzoúki*) and a special *lyra* with twenty-one strings instead of the usual three.

in the village and along the roads out towards Vóni and Evangelismós, and many of them welcome visitors to admire the potters' skills, although there's not a great deal on offer to buy. There is, though, a good range of earthenware: *píthoi* are evident throughout Thrapsanó, not only in workshops but upturned in the main square and on the backs of parked pick-up trucks. These giant *píthoi*, little changed from Minoan times, nowadays have a new export market in northern Europe, where they are popular decorative features for urban gardens.

Kastélli and around

The chief village of the Pedhiádha, **KASTÉLLI** (**Καστέλλι**), or Kastélli Pedhiádhos, is a pleasant place to pause for a while. Chiefly an agricultural centre whose prosperity derives from the olive groves and vineyards spread across the surrounding hills, the town goes its own way, largely unaffected by the tourist zone on the coast below. There's a good taverna and peaceful accommodation, far from the madding crowd; otherwise the main attraction is the surrounding countryside, where winding lanes are traced by elderly oak and plane trees.

Áyios Pandeleímon

Less than 3km north of Kastélli, off the Hersónisos road, signposted to "Paradise Tavern" • Free

Should you decide to see only one of the many churches in this area, make it **Áyios Pandeleímon** (**Άγιος Παντελεύμον**), a large building set in a grove of oaks and planes around a spring which was very likely a sanctuary in ancient times. Inside the church are imposing though weathered frescoes of the soldier saints (on the north wall) and an unusual scene of Ayía Ánna nursing the infant Mary. The structure of the church, probably dating from the early thirteenth century, is interesting for the way it incorporates parts of the original tenth-century basilica and uses as columns some much older fragments, probably taken from Lýttos. The **aqueduct** that once transported water to the ancient city passes close by, and you may spot parts of it as you drive around. This idyllic spot also shelters the small *Paradise Taverna*, run by the eccentric Nikolaides family.

Ancient Lýttos

2km north of Ksidhás, east of Kastélli, between two small chapels that serve as useful landmarks as you approach

Ancient **LÝTTOS** (**Λύττος**), occupying a magnificent position in the foothills of the Dhíkti range, was a prominent city of Dorian Crete, mentioned by Homer as leading the Cretan contingent in the Trojan War. Later it was one of the most powerful city-states of Classical Greece during the centuries prior to the Roman conquest, and was the bitter enemy of Górtys, Ierápytna (modern Ierápetra) and especially Knossós. When Lýttos engaged these three in a **war** for control of the island (221–219 BC), it overreached itself; while its army was launching an attack on Ierápetra, Knossós seized the opportunity to destroy the unguarded city, leaving it in ruins and taking its women and children into captivity. Hellenistic historian Polybios vividly describes how, on their return to Lýttos, the troops broke down in tears at the sight, refused to enter their devastated homes and went for succour to Lappa (see page 230) near Réthymno, one of its few allies. The city was eventually rebuilt, however, and enjoyed a small-scale renaissance under the Romans through to Byzantine times.

The site

Sadly, what is visible above ground today in no way reflects Lýttos's ancient status, as no systematic archeological exploration has yet taken place. Nevertheless, what you can see underlines the fact that when the riches of Lýttos are finally excavated – including what is said to be the island's largest theatre, now lost – it will be an important site. Below the church of Tímios Stavrós, built over a large fifth-century basilica with

1

FRESCOED CHURCHES AROUND KASTÉLLI

Many of the villages around Kastélli have frescoed medieval **churches**. Look out for signs as you drive around; they're usually worth seeking out simply for the journey off the main routes, even if you can't get in. In addition to the splendid **Áyios Pandeleímon**, one of the more famous is the fifteenth-century **Isódhia Theotókou** , with fine Byzantine frescoes, near the village of **Sklaverohóri** just a couple of kilometres west of Kastélli. The key is available from the house with a vine trellis about 50m before the church, on the right. Some 6km further west, down a side road beyond Apostolí, **Moní Angaráthou** is in another pretty location. Although the monastery's church dates from the last century, the surrounding buildings date mainly from the sixteenth century and include a picturesque white-walled courtyard with palms, orange trees and cypresses. Another church is **Áyios Yeóryios** at **Ksidhás** (officially renamed in 1980 as Lýttos), about 3km east of Kastélli, which has frescoes dated by an inscription to 1321.

stones from the ancient city, are the bastions and curtain of an enormous **city wall**. The church is believed to mark the centre, or agora, of Lýttos. The church of **Áyios Yeóryios** (which has fragmentary frescoes) is also constructed from stones scavenged from Lýttos: incorporated into the outer wall is a fine fragment of carved acanthus foliage. Nearby, the ancient city's **bouleterion** or council chamber has been excavated, with visible platforms and benches. Spend half an hour roaming through the vines and olive groves on the surrounding slopes and you'll come across partially excavated dwellings, delicately carved tombstones, half-buried pillars and the enormous foundation stones of buildings waiting to be unearthed.

ARRIVAL AND DEPARTURE — SOUTH OF IRÁKLIO: WINE COUNTRY

By car The old road out via Knossós is much the most pleasant route, but directions can be confused by the presence of the new road, which cuts across the island via Pezá and Houdhétsi, often extremely close to the older road. The loop via Kastélli and the coast makes for a satisfying circuit.

By bus Buses from Iráklio (Bus Station A) can take you into wine country.

Destinations Arhánes (Mon–Fri 14 daily, Sat 9, Sun 4; 30min); Kastélli (Mon–Fri 6 daily, Sat 4, Sun 2pm; 1hr); Pezá (Mon–Sat 13 daily, Sun 2; 40min); Houdhétsi (Mon–Sat 2 daily, Sun 7.30am; 1hr).

ACCOMMODATION AND EATING

This is not remotely a touristy area, but you'll find somewhere to eat in most villages; if you stay you become very much part of the life of these thriving rural centres.

ARHÁNES

Arhontiko Villa On the edge of the village, http://arhontikoarhanes.gr. This mansion has been converted to provide four beautiful apartments for up to four guests each. Furnished with antiques and with dark wood floors and ceilings and exposed brickwork, they also come with kitchenette, wi-fi and TV. €€

Kalimera Archanes Just north of the main square, www.archanes-village.com. Lovingly restored old house that offers four villas and studios for two to five people around a tranquil, leafy courtyard. All have well-equipped kitchens; delicious breakfast included. €€€

Likastos Southwest corner of the main square, 2810 752 433. Excellent and friendly taverna, with good prices – *païdhákia* (lamb chops), *horta* (wild greens). The wholemeal bread is outstanding, and you'll get at least one tasty dessert on the house. With very good, well-priced house wine and an attractive terrace for people-watching, you couldn't really ask for more. €

HOUDHÉTSI

Petronikolis Traditional House In the centre of the village, https://petronikolis.gr. Traditional building in the heart of the village, whose bare stone walls have been scrubbed to within an inch of their lives. Comfy studios and apartments are very well kitted out, with cooking facilities, TV, wi-fi, CD players and more, and there's an on-site café-restaurant and good-sized pool. Studio €, apartments €€

KASTÉLLI

Hotel Kalliopi Off the main road, near the central crossroads, https://kalliopi-hotel.gr. If you want to stay entirely away from tourist centres and get a taste of modern agricultural Crete, you'd be hard-pressed to do better than this. Despite initial appearances the rooms, and a couple of apartments, are as rural as they get, especially if you are in the annexe at the back, amid kitchen gardens and olive groves behind the small pool. The tile-floored rooms are simple but comfortable, and the proprietors are very friendly. €

Taverna Iridha Just off the west side of the square where you arrive coming from Iráklio, 28910 32023. Authentic country taverna that serves up traditional dishes such as goat in tomato sauce, or mezédhes, along with plenty of seafood and salads. You can also just stop in for coffee or a juice. €

MYRTIÁ

Kambaeti Kazantzákis 48, 200m uphill from the Kazantzákis museum, 28130 14051. Very welcoming and attractive taverna with a tree-shaded terrace, offering carefully prepared Cretan cuisine at bargain prices. A variety of *orektiká* (try the avocado vinaigrette) and main dishes are on offer. €

West of Iráklio

Heading west from Iráklio, the modern **E75 highway**, cut into the cliffs, is – in daytime at any rate – as fast a road as you could hope to find. In simple scenic terms it's a spectacular drive, but with very little in the way of habitation; there are only a couple of developed beach resorts and the "birthplace of El Greco" at **Fódhele** until the final, flat stretch before Réthymno. Once beyond the western city beaches, the highway starts to climb into the foothills of the Psiloritis range as they plunge straight to the sea. As you ascend, keep an eye out for the immaculately crafted medieval fortress of **Paleókastro**, built into the cliff right beside the road; it's easy to miss, so completely do the crumbling fortifications blend in against the rocks.

If you're in no hurry, try the **older roads west**, curling up amid stunning mountain scenery and archetypal rural Crete, with tracks tramped by herds of sheep and goats, isolated chapels or farmsteads beside the road, and occasionally a village. There's a choice of routes at Arólithos (see page 88); the road that goes further inland, through the village of Týlissos and on via Anóyia (see page 208), has more to see and passes through the **Malevísi**, a district of fertile valleys filled with olive groves and vineyards renowned in Venetian times for the strong, sweet Malmsey wine much favoured in western Europe. England became a major market for the wine, and the growth of the shipping trade between Candia (Iráklio) and English ports caused Henry VIII to appoint the first-ever British consul to the island in 1522.

Ayía Pelayía

AYÍA PELAYÍA (**Αγία Πελαγία**), some 15km from Iráklio, appears irresistibly inviting from the highway far above, a sprinkling of white cubes set around a deep blue bay. Closer up, the attraction is slightly diminished: development is rapidly outpacing the

THE E75 HIGHWAY

The **E75 highway**, which crosses the north of the island, linking Haniá in the west to Sitía in the east, is one of the most **dangerous** in Greece. The fact that in many places it is a two-lane road with a hard shoulder has not prevented local drivers from turning it into an unofficial four-lane highway: slow-movers are expected to straddle the line demarcating the hard shoulder, thus allowing faster cars to overtake at will. A reluctance by some tourists to follow this unwritten rule often leads to dangerous tailgating until the way is cleared for the driver in a hurry. Other hazards on this road are posed by small or badly positioned **signs**, frequently posted far too late. Missing your exit can mean travelling a considerable distance to the next one, as they are not as frequent as you might expect. Further dangers can include unexpected traffic lights where the highway passes close to a town, and **left turns**, which can be particularly scary at night when you must deal with the dual hazards of crossing opposing traffic and the possibility of someone ploughing into your rear while you're waiting to do so.

1

capacity of the narrow, taverna-lined beach, and is beginning to take its toll on the village. However, the water is clear and calm, the **swimming** excellent and there's a superb view, too, of all the ships that pass the end of the bay as they steam into Iráklio – spectacular at night, when brightly lit ferries go by. Despite the development, and although the beach can get very crowded with day-trippers from Iráklio at weekends, Ayía Pelayía retains a slightly **exclusive** feel, partly thanks to a couple of upmarket hotels on the promontory immediately beyond the village.

Waterskiing, parasailing and motorboats are all available on the town beach; if you feel in need of a little more space, you can head to one of several other small beaches nearby, though none could be described as empty or unspoilt. As you continue out of the far end of Ayía Pelayía it is possible to walk to three small coves on the coast as it curls around to the north and west: **Kladhisós**, **Psaromoúra**, with just a summertime bar, and finally **Mononáftis**. In the other direction, **Ligariá**, to the east, has a little harbour and a number of tavernas – most of the time it's very quiet, but summer weekends can get busy. There's a turning off the E75 signposted directly to Ligariá, or you can get there off the road down into Ayía Pelayía.

ARRIVAL AND DEPARTURE — AYÍA PELAYÍA

By car As it descends towards Ayía Pelayía, the side road splits. The right-hand fork leads to a car park at the southern end of the beach; the other winds round to enter the town from the back, where there's an even larger car park (€2/day).

By bus There are six direct buses a day from Iráklio (30min; Bus Station A); if you take a long-distance bus bound for Réthymno or Haniá, you face a steep 3km walk down from the drop-off point on the highway.

INFORMATION AND ACTIVITIES

Travel agencies There's no tourist office here, but plenty of travel agencies who can help with rooms and general information as well as tours and car rental; JK Tours on Neofýtou Pedhióti (the street between the northern corner of the car park and the beach; 2810 811 400, https://www.jk-tours.gr; April–Oct) is particularly helpful.

Scuba-diving There are two good diving centres: Divers Club Crete (2810 811 755, www.diversclub-crete.gr), in the middle of Ayía Pelayía's main beach, and the European Diving Institute (6936 922801, https://eurodiving.ne) at Ligariá.

ACCOMMODATION

Almost every building in the centre of Ayía Pelayía seems to offer rooms, studios or apartments, but even so in peak season it can be hard to find a vacancy. The greatest concentration of places is immediately **behind the beach**, especially on the road down from the car park by Vassilis supermarket ("Beach Road"). Prices for all of this increase dramatically in August.

Creta Sun Hotel On the road behind the village, 2810 811 626. Flower-decked complex with exceptionally helpful proprietors, offering well-kept studios around a pool, all with kitchenette and many with terrace or balcony (sea view extra); four-night minimum stay required at peak times. €

Irini Beach Road, 2810 811 455. Cheery if rather basic two-room apartments above *The Home*, a lurid pink ice-cream parlour/café, just a few metres from the beach. Apartments sleep 2–6, with balcony, TV and kitchen. €

Out of the Blue East of the centre, www.outoftheblueresort.com. This five-star luxury resort complex, part of the Greek Capsis chain sits on a private peninsula, comprising five hotels, seven pools, luxury villas with private pools and three private beaches. It even has its own Minoan Amusement club. €€€

Renia Beach Road, http://renia.gr. Modern block comprising one- and two-bedroom apartments overlooking a decent-sized pool. The decor is a little spartan, but there's a tiny gym (and fish spa), and breakfast is included. €

Zorba's Beach Road, 2810 811 074, http://zorbas.gr. Pleasant apartments and studios with cooking facilities and balcony – many of which offer a sea view – above a shop just seconds from the beach. €

EATING AND DRINKING

For food, it's hard to look past the obvious attractions of Ayía Pelayía's seafront **tavernas**, which stretch in a solid row behind the beach, interrupted only by the odd bar. There are plenty of cheaper options in the village, including a number of takeaway outfits and small supermarkets for the makings of a picnic on the beach. Nightlife is mostly based at the numerous waterfront **bars**.

Mouragio Towards the southern end of the beach, 2810 811 070. Also known as *Stella's* after its ebullient owner, this is among the better-value beachfront restaurants. It serves much the same Greek menu as all the others, with an emphasis on seafood, but is distinguished by the warmth of the welcome. €€

Taverna Lygaria (Sirocco) Lygaría beach, http://lygaria.gr. A good choice for plain, if rather touristy, food, in a great location right above the beach. They have loungers for customers' use and also some excellent studio rooms. €€

Fódhele

FÓDHELE (**Φόδελε**) is firmly established on the tourist circuit as the birthplace of the painter **El Greco** (1541–1614), although there's virtually no hard evidence to substantiate the claim, and most experts now believe that he was born in Iráklio. Nonetheless, it's an enjoyable place to visit: a lovely village in a richly fertile, peaceful valley, surrounded by orange and lime groves. On the far side of the river as you drive up are a couple of small Byzantine chapels, and there's an ancient church in the village, a number of craft shops and some tavernas with riverside terraces. While you're here, take a few minutes to study the plaque in the main square, made of stone from Toledo (where Domenico Theotokopoulos settled, produced the bulk of his most famous works and earned the name El Greco). The plaque was presented to Fódhele in 1934 by the University of Valladolid as an authentication of the locale's claim to fame, which must be responsible in some measure for its current prosperity, whatever scholars may say now.

Museum of El Greco

Overlooking the valley, about 1km from Fódhele up a signed track • Charge • https://psfodele.gr

They used to claim that the ancient building housing the **Museum of El Greco** was the artist's birthplace; without that excuse the museum is, frankly, a waste of time. Given his status in the history of art, there is a niche in the museum market for a venue dedicated to the life and history of this Cretan genius; unfortunately this is an opportunity missed. What you get are a few very poor reproductions and a tedious amount of "evidence" attempting to fix the artist's birthplace as Fódhele. That said, it is a pleasant spot, and directly opposite is the impressive church of the Panayía.

Church of the Panayía

Opposite the Museum of El Greco • Free • 2810 288 484

The mainly fourteenth-century **Church of the Panayía** is charming. This exquisite, drum-domed church was built over an eighth-century basilica, and the baptismal font in the floor beside the church (deep enough for total immersion) dates from the earlier building. There are also a number of fine thirteenth- and fourteenth-century frescoes. Beneath the orange groves surrounding the church are the remains of the medieval village it once served.

Rodhiá and around

RODHIÁ (**Ροδιά**) is a sizeable inland village looking back down over Iráklio; looking up from the city at night, you can see its twinkling lights on the hillside. Travelling on the old road west from Iráklio, you pass under the new highway, and immediately start to climb south into the hills. Almost straight away, there's a right turn signposted to Rodhiá, where a couple of *kafenía* allow you to rest up and enjoy the views.

Convent of Savathianá

5km northwest of Rodhiá • Free

The isolated **Convent of Savathianá** (**Σαββαθιανά**) is set amid barren mountaintops, reached only by narrow tracks. It's an extraordinary place, a lush oasis filled with flowers and birdsong, redolent of a more tranquil age. Founded during the Venetian period, the settlement is beautifully kept by its diligent nuns, who cultivate fruit trees and sell home-made jam to visitors. There are three small chapels within the complex, which gained further celebrity in 1991 when an eighteenth-century icon entitled *Lord Thou Art Great*, identical to the one at Tóplou (see page 163), was discovered; both were painted by Ioannis Kornaros.

Márathos and around

Just beyond Arólithos (**Αρολήθος**) – a tacky and artificial "traditional village" aimed squarely at tourists – the road forks; the route to the right seems far less used, though it used to be the main route from Iráklio to Réthymno. Some 9km northwest of Arolíthos this road passes through **MÁRATHOS** (**Μάραθος**), famous for the honey that seems to be on sale at every house. Márathos is an attractive place with a couple of *kafenía* where you can break the journey (this road runs through very few other villages of any size); not far beyond the village, it's possible to cut down by an unpaved but reasonable track to Fódhele (see page 87).

Týlissos

15km southwest of Iráklio; the archeological site is signposted to the left as you approach the village from the east and is fronted by a car park • Charge • There are three daily buses to Týlissos village (a few minutes' walk from the site) from Iráklio's Pórta Haníon (Bus Station B); buses continue towards Anóyia

TÝLISSOS (**Τύλισος**) is a name famous in the annals of Minoan archeology as one of the first sites to be excavated, and the thriving modern village has a fair claim to four thousand years of continuous human occupation. Local archeologist Joseph Hatzidhakis, working at the beginning of the twentieth century, revealed evidence of structures from the early Prepalatial period (c.2000 BC), but interest focuses primarily on three large **villas** (known as Houses A, B and C) from the **Neopalatial** era. They were probably not as isolated in the country-house sense as they seem today, but may well have been part of a thriving community, or even a staging post on the route west. The existence of a rather simpler villa at Sklavókambos, on the road halfway from here to Anóyia, may lend weight to this latter theory. Týlissos shared in the destruction of the palaces in about 1450 BC, but new buildings then arose, among which was the cistern in the northeast corner of the site. Following the arrival of the Dorians, Týlissos developed into a Greek city of the Classical period, issuing its own coinage. This later construction tends to make it a bit harder to get a clear picture of the form of the Minoan structures.

The site

While it's not always the easiest of sites to interpret, Týlissos is a lovely place to wander round, with few visitors, pine trees for shade, and some evocative remains, including staircases and walls still standing almost 2m tall. Immediately beyond the fence, vineyards and rich agricultural land suggest a seductive, but probably illusory, continuity of rural life. **Houses A and C** are of extremely fine construction and design (C is the more impressive), while little remains of **House B** apart from its ground plan, although it does contain some of the oldest relics.

House A

A building of finely dressed ashlar stone, **House A** has a **colonnaded court** at its heart with a window lighting the staircase to the west side of this. In storerooms on the north side, some large reconstructed *píthoi* can be seen with holes near their bases for tapping the contents (probably oil). A number of Linear A tablets also came to light in this area. In the south wing, the main rooms open onto a light well, with the central room having a **lustral basin** – in this case more like a sunken bath – just off it. A stand for a double axe, similar to finds from Knossós, was found in the **pillar crypt**, along with

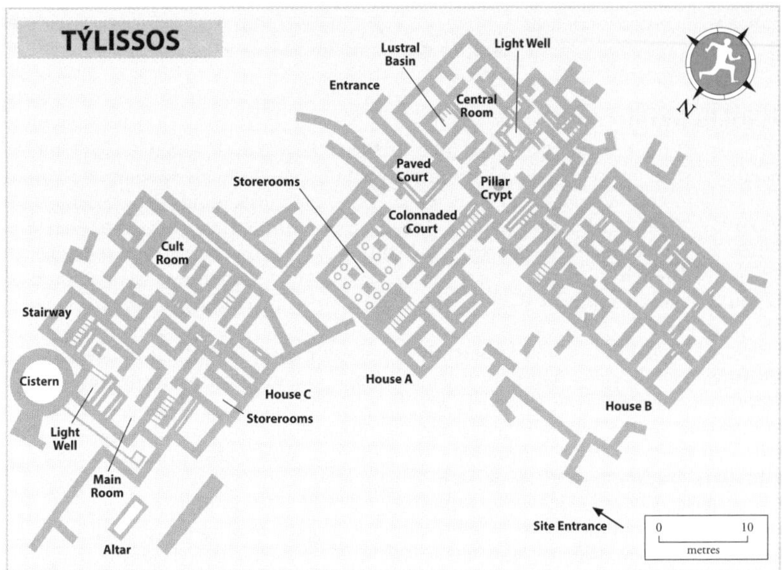

three enormous bronze cauldrons (now in the Iráklio Archeological Museum) that originally prompted the site's excavation. Throughout the house, fragments of painted stucco were found, leading archeologists to postulate the existence of a luxurious second storey to this dwelling, which had fallen in over time.

House C

House C, with a fair amount of concrete reconstruction, contains a **cult room** with a central pillar, storerooms and, at its northern end, the living area, where a paved main room would have been illuminated by a light well on its eastern side. At the end of one of many corridors (a Minoan speciality), a staircase would once have led to an upper floor. There is also evidence of a drainage system, while outside the house, beside the cistern, lies a **stone altar** from the Classical period.

East of Iráklio

East of today's airport and the city beach at Amnísos there's almost continuous development all the way to Mália, as what little remains of the coastal landscape is torn apart to build yet more hotels, apartments and beach complexes. You're in package-tour country here and the resorts of **Hersónisos** and **Mália**, above all, are big, brash and packed with visitors all summer long. There are one or two highlights and escapes along the way, though: the isolated **Skotinó Cave** near Goúves, the impressive **Cretaquarium** at Goúrnes, the **old villages** in the hills behind Hersónissos, and, just beyond the clubs and beach of Mália, a fine **Minoan palace** that will transport you back three and a half millennia. From Hersónisos or Mália, you can also head inland to climb towards the **Lasíthi plateau**.

GETTING AROUND — EAST OF IRÁKLIO

By bus Buses from Iráklio (Bus Station A) serve the coastal resorts, running at least every 30min through Háni Kokkíni and Káto Goúves to Hersónissos and Mália, with stops near all the major hotels. All the resorts also put on tours to big

1

attractions like Cretaquarium and Water City.

By car The E75 Highway runs a short way inland, bypassing all the major attractions and resorts; you'll need to turn off onto the old road to access any of them.

Háni Kokkíni

The first distinct centre east of Iráklio is **HÁNI KOKKÍNI** (**Χάνι Κοκκίνι**), a grubbily nondescript resort with a long but rather pebbly beach. There's a **Minoan villa** at the western end of town (free) – known as Nírou Háni or simply Niros. Dating from the Neopalatial period, it must have been beautifully sited above the water when it stood alone. With the road now cutting it off from the beach, it is harder to appreciate; what you see is a site the size of a large modern house (stairs on the south side led to an upper storey), with remaining walls standing to around waist height.

In the hills behind – a few kilometres to the southwest – is the locked **Cave of Eileíthyia**, which gets a mention in the *Odyssey* as one of Odysseus's stopovers on his way home from Troy. Eileithyia was the Minoan goddess of childbirth and this cave was used as a place of worship and pilgrimage from tate Neolithic times to the fifth century AD. Many figurines and votive objects were found in the cave, and its central stalagmite, a metre and a half high, is thought to have played some role in ceremonies here, perhaps as an altar. The Minoan villa and the cave share the same guardian and if free, he may be willing to accompany those with their own transport to open the cave. Information on both sites is available from the friendly *Taverna To Kyma*, almost opposite the villa, which also has the guardian's phone number.

Goúrnes and around

At **GOÚRNES** (**Γούρνες**), 15km from Iráklio, there's a break in the overdeveloped coastal strip where, just west of the village, a mammoth former US air force base awaits redevelopment. One thing that has been built here, and currently stands surrounded by broken fences and crumbling buildings, is the **Cretaquarium**, a spectacular marine aquarium rpeatedly signposted from the highway.

Cretaquarium

Goúrnes • Charge • https://cretaquarium.gr

The excellent **Cretaquarium**, boasting thirty tanks (some huge) housing everything from menacing sharks to dazzling jellyfish, is a great experience, especially for kids who are well catered for. Part of the Hellenic Centre for Marine Research, the venture is genuinely educational, scientific and non-profit-making, as well as great fun – especially the virtual reality section. Most of the island's fish and crustaceans are included among the 250 species and more than 2500 specimens on display, and unless you're a marine biologist the audio-guide (€3) is well worth it, giving loads of fascinating background information on the creatures you're looking at.

Water City water park

Anópoli, 4km inland from Goúrnes and Háni Kokkíni, 15km from Iráklio • Charge • https://watercity.gr

The giant **Water City** rivals nearby Acqua Plus for the title of most impressive water park on the island, with many of the rides taking advantage of the natural hillside over which the place is built. There's the usual array of slides, pools, snack bars and fast-food outlets, though they can struggle to cope with the crowds in high season.

The Skotinó Cave

About 6km inland from Káto Goúves, 3km by road from the village of Skotinó • Open daylight hours • Free

The **Skotinó Cave** is one of the largest and most spectacular on the island. It's an uphill hike from the coast (get detailed directions before you set out), or an easy drive, passing through **Goúves** village, which makes an encouraging contrast to the coastal strip and is a good spot to pick up refreshments – there are a couple of decent tavernas. The cave itself is well signed from the village of **Skotinó** (**Σκοτεινό**), which means "dark", the last part on a rough track where the cave entrance is marked by a pair of chapels.

Some 160m deep, the cave is divided into four levels, with an awesomely huge main chamber; it's unattended and you can scramble down as far as you dare, with plenty of natural light at first, though you'd be brave to explore the further recesses alone. It was first investigated by Arthur Evans and more scientifically explored during the 1960s by French and Greek archeologists. A considerable number of bronze and ceramic **votive offerings** were found (the earliest dating back to early Minoan times), suggesting that this was an important shrine. The cave remained in use well into the Greek and Roman eras, when the goddess Artemis was worshipped in what is thought to have been a substitution for an earlier Minoan female fertility deity, possibly Brytomartis. In the chapel of Ayía Paraskeví above, *tamata* (ex votos) left by pilgrims continue a tradition of supplication to the (now Christian) deity that has persisted on this same spot for well over four thousand years.

Hersónisos and around

HERSÓNISOS (**Χερσόνησος**) – more correctly **Límin Hersonísou**, the Port of Hersónisos; Hersónisos is one of the villages in the hills just behind – is the first of the big resorts east of Iráklio, a boisterous, sprawling and rather seedy place catering to mainly Dutch, Irish and Italian package tourists, replete with all the trappings of mass tourism. If you're looking for tranquillity and Cretan tradition, forget it; this is the world of concrete high-rise hotels, video bars, fast-food shops and eurodiscos. The town's main artery is a 2km-long street (Odhós Venizélou) parallel to the sea, a seemingly endless ribbon of bars, travel agents, amusement arcades, tacky shops, car and bike rental dealers and traffic jams. That said, the resort has plenty of life, lots of competition to keep food and drink prices down, and some really attractive rooms and restaurants in the hill villages behind; there are also decent sandy **beaches** both to the west and to the east. The one thing you may struggle to find in July or August is a room.

The esplanade

Along the modern seafront, a solid line of restaurants, bars, bars and more bars is broken only by the occasional souvenir shop or fish spa. In their midst you'll find a small **pyramidal fountain** with broken mosaics of fishing scenes. This dates from the Roman era and is the only real relic of the ancient town of **Chersonesos**, a thriving port from Classical Greek through to Byzantine times, handling trade from inland Lýttos (see page 83). The busy pleasure **harbour** to the west of the fountain is built over the ancient Roman one, and in odd places along the seafront you can see remains of Roman harbour installations, mostly submerged. The headland above the harbour is a popular spot to watch the sun set; you can explore the excavated remains of an impressively large, early Christian basilica there, complete with mosaic floors, while on the far side the remains of ancient Roman fish tanks can be seen cut into the rock. Other than these, most daytime interest is on the fringes of Hersónisos.

Star Beach Water Park

On the beach immediately east of Hersónisos • Charge Free entry, but charges for most activities • www.starbeach.gr

Star Beach Water Park hugs the coast immediately east of town, with some fine beach areas as well as pools, slides, bars and restaurants, and a wide range of watersports from banana boats to kitesurfing. Activities for young children are generally free, as are the pools and wi-fi, but everything else has to be paid for, from loungers to bungee jumping. At night they host club nights and foam parties.

Lychnostatis Open-Air Museum

On the eastern edge of Hersónisos, beyond Star Beach • Charge • www.lychnostatis.gr

The entertaining **Lychnostatis Open-Air Museum** of folk culture is worth a visit, particularly if you haven't had a chance to see the "real thing" inland. Set in a reasonably authentic-looking recreation of a traditional Cretan village in a pleasant location next to the sea, the various exhibits relate to a way of life rapidly disappearing from the island. There are orchards and herb gardens, and live displays of local crafts, such as ceramics and weaving, as well as collections of lace, embroidery and traditional costumes within the main house. Concerts of traditional music and dance are frequent, and they occasionally stage more elaborate "dance spectaculars" in the evening, as well as seasonal special events like grape-treading in the autumn.

Aqua World

Just off Venizélou in Hersónisos, at the bottom of the road to Piskopianó • Charge • https://aquaworld-crete.com

A small aquarium displaying many of the fish and sea creatures found off the island's coast, **Aqua World** also has a selection of snakes, lizards and tortoises outside in the reptile garden. Scots-run, Aqua World has an environmental ethos, and many of the creatures it houses have been rescued or were unwanted pets.

Acqua Plus

4km inland from Hersónisos on the route to the Lasíthi plateau, by the golf club • Charge • http://acquaplus.gr

Acqua Plus is a big water park that competes with Water City to offer the greatest variety of slides and other activities for all ages. It's a good day out, with an attractive setting in a natural bowl of hills and a fair amount of shade.

Labyrinth Park

4km inland from Hersónisos on the route to the Lasíthi plateau, not far from Acqua Plus • Charge • http://labyrinthpark.gr

Labyrinth Park is a fun theme park with a Minoan theme, and makes a good day out for younger kids. The centrepiece is a maze (or Labyrinth) that will keep you going for an hour or so, and there's also mini-golf, quad bikes, archery and more (for each of which there's a small charge), plus a lazer maze inside a Trojan Horse, and an escape room.

Piskopianó and around

In the hills immediately behind Hersónisos, the three pretty **hill villages** of **Piskopianó** (**Πισκοπιανό**), **Koutoulafári** and **"old" Hersónisos** present a glimpse of a more traditional Crete. They're far from unspoilt – Piskopianó is directly above the harbour and an easy walk away, with Koutoulafári a little further, so plenty of people come up here in the evenings to the busy tavernas and to nights of Cretan dancing – but they're certainly more peaceful than the coast.

Museum of Rural Life

Piskopianó • Charge • 28970 23303

The one real sight in the villages around Hersónisos, the impressive **Museum of Rural Life**, is one of the best of its kind, though closed at the moment. It's housed in a nineteenth-century village mansion with attached olive mill, modernized to form the bulk of the museum, and a more traditional workshop/barn; displays cover all aspects of rural life from carpentry to olive-oil and *rakí* production, and above all there are some very fine examples of traditional weaving.

ARRIVAL AND DEPARTURE

HERSÓNISOS AND AROUND

By bus Buses run between Hersónisos and Iráklio (Bus Station A) effectivelyv every 30min (45min), and to Áyios Nikoláos only marginally less frequently. Buses make stops along the main street (Odhós Venizélou).

By taxi For short hops around town, or up to the hill villages, there's a taxi stand at the western end of Venizélou. You can also call for one on 28970 22098.

INFORMATION AND ACTIVITIES

Travel agencies In the absence of a tourist office, travel agencies are the best source of information; they're everywhere, offering a huge variety of local tours as well as horseriding, scuba, boat trips and car rental.

Boat trips A wide variety of boat trips to local beaches and islands are on offer from the harbour; it's around €25 for the popular day-trip to Sísi (see page 141). Fishing trips are also on offer (tackle provided) for around €30 (3hr).

Horseriding Finikia (6945 924 112, https://hersonissos-horseriding.com) offer riding tours into the hills and on the beach (from €50), as well as lessons, from their base close to Star Beach.

ACCOMMODATION

Although you should have little problem finding somewhere to stay outside the peak season of July and August, much accommodation is allocated to package-tour operators and what remains is not cheap. Hotels in the centre are subject to a fair amount of **noise** both from traffic and – after dark – the pulsating nightlife. If you have a car or don't mind a short taxi ride or 20min walk, it's best to head inland to the hill villages for better quality and more peaceful surroundings.

Caravan Camping On the beach at the eastern end of Hersónisos, by Lychnostatis, 28970 22025. Small campsite in a brilliant location right on the water. Not much room, so pitches for tents can be tight-packed; they also have hexagonal concrete "bungalows", with just enough space for a double bed, sink and fridge. €

Creta Maris On the coast northwest of the centre, www.cretamaris.gr. The ritziest place in town, hogging the best part of the beach, with every facility you'd expect from a vast, luxury, all-inclusive resort, including bungalows designed to mimic a traditional village, seven pools, gym, spa and a wedding chapel. €€€

Elgoni Apartments Piskopianó, right at the top of the hill above the museum, 28970 21237. Welcoming, good-value, family-run place offering well-equipped studios, apartments and maisonettes in a lovely setting with pool and bar, and great views. The decor is looking a bit tired but it's still a good deal. €

Galaxy Villas Koutouloufári, towards the eastern end of the village near the Sports Café, www.galaxy-villas.com. Comfortable, well-equipped modern villa/apartments, sleeping up to four, in a complex with pool and bar, and views down over the coast. €

EATING AND DRINKING

There's no shortage of places to eat and drink in the resort, although quality is not always a priority, especially among the **water-front** places, whose location is so irresistible that they don't need to try too hard. Better food and a more relaxed atmosphere are to be found out of town in the **hill villages**, where many tavernas have roof terraces with views towards the coast.

Argo Navárhou Neárhou 26, round the corner from the harbour, 28970 22134. Much quieter and with a more personal welcome and traditional Greek feel than elsewhere on the main seafront. They offer home-style Greek classics plus an international menu, and there's also a tranquil bar, popular with an older crowd. €

★ **Elliniko Estiatorio John** Kaniadáki 4, off the south side of Venizélou slightly east of the church, 28970 24138. The name means simply 'Greek Restaurant', and that's exactly what it is – a place where locals come (many have takeaways) for a daily selection of freshly made *mayireftá*. There is a menu but no one uses it; simply look at the day's dishes displayed behind glass and tell owner/chef Yiannis what you want; very little English is spoken. Come at lunchtime, because many dishes run out early. €

La Scala Ayía Paraskeví 83, at the heart of the waterfront, 28970 24777. The most glamorous of the central seafront restaurants, with candlelit tables right down on the sand as well as on a terrace above it, serving a huge menu of fresh fish, pizza, pasta and Greek standards at much the same prices as its neighbours. €

Niki's 25 Mártiou 12, at the eastern end of the seafront, 2897 029372. The international menu is not significantly better (or cheaper) than elsewhere, but it's a little further from the centre so less manic than other places, with great views and a totally irresistible line in chat to draw in potential diners. €

Oniro Koutouloufári, on the lower street through the eponymous village, 28970 23840. The terrace here has some of the best coastal views of all, which is reflected in the prices. Specials such as pork or lamb shanks are slow-cooked in a wood oven; try also the aubergine stuffed with veal and cheese or *exohikó* (lamb in filo pastry). €€

★ **Pithari** Koutouloufári, at the crossroads on the upper street through the village, 28970 21449. Touristy, like

1

everywhere up here, but with well-prepared authentic Cretan dishes and a large roof terrace. Try the likes of rabbit *stifádho* or lamb Pithari (baked in filo with potato and spinach). €€

NIGHTLIFE

Hersónisos is renowned for its **nightlife** and there's certainly no shortage of it. A night's partying kicks off around the many **bars** ringing the harbour; this is dancing on tables territory, so if you fancy a quiet drink, head for the fringes of town or to the hill villages. Later on, the larger **disco-pubs** and **clubs** in the streets leading up to and along Eleftheríou Venizélou are the places to be seen.

El Paradiso Ayía Paraskeví 83. This late-night club right at the heart of the waterfront sees occasional appearances by visiting DJs, playing predominantly house and club tunes.

New York Ayía Paraskeví 30, right on the water, http://new-york.gr. Glitzy club that's also a café and beach club, with sunbeds, by day, and a flashy cocktail bar. DJ Yiannis plays funk, Greek pop and techno.

Star Beach Water Park On the beach immediately east of the resort, http://starbeach.gr. The water park (see page 91) houses a megaclub, with wild foam parties on Sunday nights (free) and frequent appearances by international DJs.

Mália

MÁLIA (**Μάλια**) is, perhaps, the most notorious resort in Crete: brash, commercial, with a reputation for wild nightlife. The **beach**, long and sandy as it is, becomes grotesquely crowded at times. Having said that, it can be a great place to stay if you're prepared to enter into the spirit of things – party all night and sleep all day – with the bonus of a genuine town that existed before the tourists came, and a fabulous **Minoan palace** just down the road. Locals are also working hard to crack down on the more extreme behaviour, partly because the place's reputation was starting to keep people away – these days it's a lot less extreme than it once was.

The beaches

Beaches stretch either side of Mália. If you're prepared to walk a bit you'll be rewarded with better sands and fewer people, though solitude is a distant dream. The **central beach** stretches east from the bottom of Beach Road; in summer, you'll need to walk through the mass of bodies for about another fifteen minutes before you find somewhere to spread out. At this eastern end of the beach is a small **church** backed by dunes and patches of marshy ground alive with frogs. You can also swim out to a tiny **offshore islet**: the rocks here are sharp for barefoot exploring, but your efforts will be rewarded by a (perpetually locked) white chapel and rock pools alive with crabs, shellfish and sea urchins on the islet's seaward side.

There are beaches west of the resort centre, but the most tempting lie to the east: **Sun Beach**, about 2.5 km from the centre, where there are free trampolines and pools, plus plenty of loungers, drinks, amusements and watersports; **Tropical Beach**, with more

MÁLIA ORIENTATION

Mália consists of two distinct parts, lying on opposite sides of the old highway (Venizélou). The heart of tourist life lies to the north towards the **beach**, where two main streets snake for a good kilometre towards the sea: one, **Zahariádhi**, from the major junction near the western end of town; the other, **Dhimokratías**, a little further east. The streets merge into one after about 300m, and along them you'll find supermarkets, souvenir shops, travel agents, cafés, restaurants, video bars and nightclubs. To walk the length of this will take you about fifteen minutes – longer if you allow yourself to be enticed by the sales patter along the way, or after midnight, when it's at its busiest. At the end there's a car park, a small harbour and access to the beach.

South of the main road is the **old town**, with its narrow, twisting alleyways and whitewashed walls. Here you can still find traces of traditional life, as Mália determinedly clings to what remains of its self-respect.

loungers but fewer buzzing banana boats and parascenders; and finally **Potamos**, at the mouth of a small river very close to the palace, with loungers and a café.

The Palace of Malia

3km east of Mália, just off the old highway • Charge • 28970 31957 • Any bus passing along the main highway should stop at the turn-off for the site

Though much less imposing than either Knossós or Festós, the **Palace of Mália** in some ways surpasses both. For a start, it's a great deal emptier, and you can wander among the remains in relative peace. And while no reconstruction has been attempted, the palace was never reoccupied after its second destruction, so the ground plan is essentially intact. The excavations are by no means complete; inside and beyond the fenced site to the north and west, digs are still going on, as an apparently sizeable town comes slowly to light.

Of the **ruins** you see today, virtually nothing stands much more than 1m above ground level apart from the giant *píthoi* that have been pieced together and left about the place like sentinels: the palace itself is worn and brown, blending almost

1

imperceptibly into the landscape. With the mountains behind, it's a thoroughly atmospheric setting. It's also easier to comprehend than Knossós, and if you've already seen the reconstructions there, it's easy to envisage this seaside palace in its days of glory. Basking on the rich agricultural plain between the Lasíthi mountains and the sea, it retains a real flavour of an ancient civilization with a taste for the good life.

Though the palace is accessible by bus, it's also easily reached on foot – a 40min **walk** from Mália – or you could rent a **bike** for the easy, flat ride out to the site, and stop for a swim on the way back.

Brief history

First discovered by Joseph Hatzidhakis early in the twentieth century, the site's excavation was handed over to the French School at Athens in 1922. As at Knossós and Festós, there was an earlier palace dating from around 1900 BC, which was devastated by the earthquake of about 1700 BC. The remains you see today are those of the palace built to replace this, which functioned until about 1450 BC, when it was destroyed for the last time. From this site came the famous **gold pendant** of two bees that can be seen in the Iráklio Archeological Museum and on any local postcard stand. It was allegedly part of a hoard that was plundered; the rest of the collection now resides (as the "Aegina Treasure") in London's British Museum. The beautiful **leopard's-head axe**, also in the museum at Iráklio, was another of the treasures found at Minoan Malia.

The West Court

The main palace is to the right of the site entrance, approached through the **West Court**. As at the other palaces, there are raised pathways leading across this, with the main one heading south towards the area of the eight circular **storage pits**. These probably held grain; the pillars in the middle of some would once have supported a protective roof. In the other direction, the raised walkway takes you to the building's north side, where you can pick up the more substantial paved road that apparently led to the sea.

The North Court

Entering the palace itself through a "door" between two rocks and jinking right then left, you arrive in the **North Court**, by the storerooms and their elaborately decorated, much-photographed giant *píthoi*. Off to the right are the so-called Royal Apartments, on the far side of which is a well-preserved lustral basin or bath. Nearby lies the **Archive Room**, where a number of Linear A tablets were unearthed. Straight ahead is the **Pillared Hall**, which the excavators, encouraged by the discovery of some cooking pots, think may have been a kitchen (the relative location is almost exactly the same as that of the palace kitchen at Zákros). Above the hall, a grand dining room would have looked out over the courtyard.

The Central Court

Mália's **Central Court**, a long, narrow area, about 48m in length by 22m wide, is only slightly smaller than the main courtyards at Knossós and Festós. Look out for the remains of the columns that once supported a portico at the northern end, and for traces of a similar portico down the eastern side. Still-visible post-holes were discovered between these columns by the excavators, suggesting that the court could be fenced in – possibly to protect the spectators during the bull-jumping games that may have been held here. Behind the eastern portico are more storerooms, now under a canopy. In the centre of the court is a shallow pit that may have been used for sacrifices; if this was indeed its purpose then, along with Anemospília (see page 80), these are the only such Minoan sacrificial areas to have been discovered.

On the west side of the courtyard are the remains of two important stairways. The first led to the upper floor beside what is termed the **Royal Lodge** or Throne Room, which overlooks the courtyard. The second, in the southwest corner, comprises the bottom four steps of what was the main ceremonial staircase to the first floor, still impressive in its scale. Beside this is the curious *kernos*, or **altar**. The purpose of this heavy limestone disc, with 34 hollows around its rim and a single bigger one in the centre, is disputed: one theory suggests an altar where, at harvest time, samples of the first fruits of the Cretan crops would be placed in the hollows as offerings to a fertility goddess, while other theories have it as a point for tax collecting or even an ancient gaming board.

The rooms along the west side of the court also merit exploration. Between the two staircases ran a long room that may have gone straight through to the upper floor, like a medieval banqueting hall. Behind this is the **Pillar Crypt**, where the double-axe symbol was found engraved on the two main pillars. Behind the Pillar Crypt runs yet another corridor of storerooms; only accessible through areas which had some royal or religious significance, these would doubtless have been depositories for things of value – the most secure storage at the palace.

Agora and Crypt

Beneath a canopy to the west of the northern end of the palace lies the **Agora** (or Hypostyle Hall). This building consists of a number of rooms – apparently shops or market stalls – and two interconnected halls of uncertain function, described as the **Crypt**. Benches run round three sides of the Crypt, leading some to speculate that this was some form of council chamber.

Area "M"

A gate from the Crypt leads to **area "M"** (or Mu – the site is divided up by archeologists using the letters of the Greek alphabet), in a second fenced area almost as large as the palace itself. Here a large section of the town dependent on the palace is protected by a spectacular canopy. You can walk above and around it on a suspended walkway, looking down on workshops, dwellings, some preserved up to roof level, and streets that give a clear idea of the considerable scale of the complex community that surrounded the palace. In one small area a section of wood-beamed roof has been reconstructed, and there's a series of what are believed to have been ritual or **cult rooms**. Several of the other cult rooms yielded statuary, libation vessels and other artefacts connected with religious ceremonies.

Archeologists are still trying to piece together exactly what connection this complex had with the palace. Was it possibly the "monastery" of a priesthood serving the palace but living separately from it, or could it have served as a temporary home for the whole palace elite while some restoration or repair was carried out to the palace proper? Many of the most interesting finds from this area are in the museum at Áyios Nikólaos (currently closed), but at the site entrance there's a small **exhibition** on the excavations (especially the more recent ones) which is well worth a look, and includes a model of area "M" as it might have looked.

The Golden Pit

Turn right (west) on leaving the palace site, and then right again along a dirt track that heads northeast towards the sea; the fenced pit lies some 300m down the track, just before the islet of Ayía Varvára, visible offshore

Some 500m north of the palace, close to the sea and outside the main fenced area, is the *Chrysolakkos* or **Golden Pit**, apparently a large, multi-chambered mausoleum dating from the Protopalatial period. Its elaborate construction suggests a royal burial-place, as does the wealth of grave goods discovered here, among them the gold honeybee pendant now at the Iráklio Archeological Museum.

Area "E"

Along the entry road leading back to the main road, on the east side there are **more excavations** (fenced off) in a zone designated **area "E"**, which further underline the scale of the urban area surrounding the palace. There are many substantial buildings

1

here, including a large mansion where fragments of painted plaster were discovered, suggesting a sumptuously decorated interior.

ARRIVAL AND INFORMATION — MÁLIA

By bus Arriving by bus you'll be dropped at the central junction on the main road (Venizélou) heading through the town. There are services to and from Iráklio (Bus Station A) virtually every 30min (1hr), and to Áyios Nikoláos at least hourly (40min).

Travel agencies There are travel agents everywhere: Sunny Holidays, 25 Martíou 9 in the old town (28970 32120), are particularly helpful and can advise on rooms, rent you a car or book you on a tour.

ACCOMMODATION

Many **rooms** are taken up by the package industry, and in peak season finding somewhere to stay may not be easy. Your best bet if you want any sleep is to avoid the Beach Road area: try one of the numerous rooms signed in the old town or on the fringes of the new. You'll save a lot of schlepping around by booking though a travel agent.

Bella Elena Omiroú 5, old town, inland from Kalesma restaurant, 28970 21204. Very good value studios and apartments, all with kitchen, many with good-sized balconies, in a small complex around a pool. Breakfast available. Works mostly via third-party websites. €

Kristalli Hotel Apartments Pávlou Melá 700, on the Lasíthi road in the old town, https://kristalli-hotel.com. Well looked-after modern standard double rooms, studios and apartments, the latter two types having kitchens, around a bar and pool, with a friendly welcome. In a quiet part of town, though your fellow guests may be partying late. €

EATING AND DRINKING

Mália's **restaurant** owners jostle for your custom at every step, especially along Beach Road; none is particularly good, but they know their clientele – *moussaká*, pie and chips and all-you-can-eat Mexican, Indian or Chinese places abound. You're far better off in the **old town** where, around the Platía Ayíos Dhimítrios, you can choose from a variety of more elegant bars, tavernas and restaurants, most open only in the evening. If you're shopping for picnic food, look out for the tasty bananas sold at stalls throughout the centre: chances are they'll have been grown in the fields around the town.

Elizabeth and Stablos Platía Áyios Dhimítrios, old town, 28970 31320. Elegant decor, decent mezédhes, fresh fish and good barrel wine, plus an attractive upstairs terrace opposite the little church, make this a popular and appealing spot. €€

Kalesma Omírou 8, off the top of 25 Martíou, old town, 28970 33125. Located in a quiet backstreet with a classy terrace and blown-glass light fittings, this is Mália's most stylish restaurant. Famous for its meze platters, it also offers well-prepared traditional dishes and a good selection of Cretan wines. €€

Zorbas 25 Martíou 17, 28970 32433. Attractive, economical old-town pizzeria with a roof terrace and a wood-fired oven in which they roast their speciality meats and produce excellent pizzas – also available to take away. €€

NIGHTLIFE

Beach Road is transformed during the hours either side of midnight, when the profusion of **bars**, **discos** and **clubs** erupt into a pulsating cacophony. Most of them have touts outside trying to lure you in, and in most you can see through glass doors what you'll be letting yourself in for. The bigger, better clubs cluster around the point where the two beach roads meet. There are plenty of "English pubs", too. Vast crowds of 18–30s – many in organized groups – stagger between the bars and clubs, and while the worst excesses of past years have been left behind, you do still get the odd confrontation.

Candy Club Dhimokratías 112, junction of Beach Road, https://candymalia.eu. With a dress code above the door stating "less is more" this place lies at the throbbing heart of the Beach Road madness. A huge venue with three bars, two dance stages, VIP area and more, playing house and electro, plus big-name performaners and DJs; they also organise paint parties and cruises.

ZigZag Club Dhimokratías 101, https://zigzagclubmalia.com. Manic bar and club where one of the party tricks is to set the bar on fire; not for the faint-hearted, though they also have big name house DJs, including the likes of Judge Jules, every Friday and Saturday.

Towards the Lasíthi plateau

The one inland route that visitors follow in any numbers is the drive up to the **Lasíthi plateau** (see page 142). The main route heads inland from Hersónisos, initially towards Kastélli (see page 83), and then east through the Aposelémis valley to Potamiés and Goníes. The attractions are charmingly simple: scenery that becomes increasingly mountainous as you climb towards the plateau; old trees spreading beside the road, and still older churches in the villages. Alternative routes – each dramatically wild and lonely, with spectacular views – wind up from Stalídha and Mália.

Panayía Gouverniótissa

On the road up from Hersónisos, about 8km from the highway • Free

The monastery of **Panayía Gouverniótissa** (**Παναγία Γκουβερνιώτισσα**); Dormition of the All-Holy Mother of God (Assumption of the Virgin) is one of the oldest in Crete. Restoration work on the buildings, mostly complete, has been undertaken largely by local people, and the place is now run as a museum rather than a working religious building. At the heart of the complex, a tiny **chapel** stands in a peaceful garden with a lemon tree; inside are restored **frescoes** dating from the fourteenth century, with a fine *Pandokrátor* adorning the dome. There are also small museums of folklore and icons, and a welcoming café.

Avdhoú

In the village of **AVDHOÚ** (**Αβδού**) there are fine, very faded frescoes from the fourteenth and fifteenth centuries in three **churches**: Áyios Andónios, Áyios Konstantínos and Áyios Yeóryios. The churches should be open; if not, enquiries in the village cafés should produce the necessary keys.

Krási

The village of **KRÁSI** (**Κράσι**), just off the main road on the route to Mália, is curiously named – curious because Krási. with a differeent accent, translates as "wine", but the village's fame is in fact based on water, in the form of a curative spring that is reputed to be especially good for stomach complaints. This is situated under stone arcading in the shade of an enormous **plane tree**, which is claimed to be two thousand years old and the largest in Europe, with a girth that cannot be encircled by twelve people. Flanking the tree are a couple of **tavernas**.

Panayía Kardhiótissa

3km south of Krási • Charge

The convent of **Panayía Kardhiótissa** (**Παναγία Καρδιώτισσα**) – Our Lady of the Heart – is one of the most important places of worship on Crete, with an annual celebration on September 8. The buildings date from the twelfth century, and though the heavily refurbished exterior of the monastery looks like whitewashed concrete, the interior is undeniably spectacular, with restored **frescoes** throughout. These came to light only in the 1960s, when they were discovered beneath accumulated layers of paint. There is also a copy of a famous twelfth-century icon of the Panayía, the original of which was taken to Rome in 1498. According to legend, successive attempts by the Turks to steal this copy were thwarted when it found its way back to adjacent Kerá village, despite being chained to a marble pillar; the pillar is now in the monastery yard, while the chain (kept inside the church) is believed to alleviate pain when wrapped around the bodies of the afflicted. There's an attractive little museum too.

The ascent to Séli Ambélou

Beyond the village of Kerá, the road winds on into the Dhiktean mountains, and the views become progressively more magnificent. To the left, **Mount Karfí** looms ominously, its summit more than 1100m above sea level. This spire-like peak (*karfí* means "nail" in Greek) was one of the sites where the Minoan civilization made its last stand, following the collapse of the great centres after the twelfth century BC. There's a scary-looking track to the site of **ancient Karfí** (see page 145), some 5km away, from the car park at the ludicrously named **Homo Sapiens Village**.

The road continues to climb to the dramatic pass of **SÉLI AMBÉLOU** (**Σέλι Αμπέλου**), flanked by ruined stone windmills. Beyond, the Lasíthi plateau suddenly unfolds before you. Almost straight ahead, on the far side of the plateau, the highest peaks of the nearby mountain range dominate the landscape, with **Mount Dhíkti** – all 2148m of it – at their heart.

Southwest from Iráklio

Crossing the island on the southwest route is not, on the whole, the most exciting of drives: on the western outskirts of Iráklio you turn south, under the highway, following the signs to Festós and Míres. From the beginning, the road climbs, heading up to the island's spine through agricultural country renowned for its vineyards. In the Middle Ages this was traditionally the **Malevísi**, or Malmsey, wine-producing region (see page 85) and the area is very much part of the revival of Cretan viniculture, especially around **Dháfnes** (see page 118). Wine tours aside, highlights along this route include an ancient site at **Rizinía** and picturesque medieval **monasteries** at Veneráto and **Zarós**, the latter a particularly pleasant village with great accommodation choices, surrounded by fine **walking country** and with a small lake nearby.

GETTING AROUND **SOUTHWEST FROM IRÁKLIO**

By car The main road is the fast route via Veneráto and Ayía Varvára, but you can also follow a scenic detour via Voutés, Áyios Mýronas and Pýrgou, a wonderful undulating ride through some lovely out-of-the-way villages.

By bus Buses from Iráklio's Bus Station B (Mon–Sat 10 daily; fewer on Sun) follow the main road across the island, heading for Festós and Mátala or Ayía Galíni via Tymbáki. Míres, in the heart of the Messará plain, is the southern junction for switching between these various routes. Áno Asítes (5km north of Priniás) also has a bus service from the same station (Mon–Fri 7 daily; Sat 2; 50min); 2 of these a day continue to Priniás.

Ancient Rizinía

Just beyond a hairpin bend 3km south of Áno Asítes a sign (to "Prinías archeological site") directs you up a short, just about driveable track, with the acropolis and chapel of Áyios Pandeleímon visible above • Free

2km north of Priniás, a pair of remarkable **rock-cut tombs** can be seen, part of the cemetery of **Ancient Rizinía** (**Ριζινία**), which occupied the flat-topped hill to the east. Founded at the end of the Bronze Age, possibly by Minoans fleeing the Dorian invasion of the north coast, Riziniá later flourished as a Greek city and the remains of two temples have been discovered on the acropolis. Although not a lot remains of the ancient town, the sheer quantity of broken shards littering the ground is evidence that this was once a substantial conurbation. Nosing around, you'll come across the footings of ancient dwellings, with steps and porches clearly identifiable. When you eventually reach the landmark whitewashed **chapel of Áyios Pandeleímon**, at the northern tip of the peak, you're greeted with astonishing **views** in all directions, especially north towards Iráklio, with the island of Dhía beyond.

Moní Palianí

A well-signed 2km detour from the village of Veneráto • Free

MONÍ PALIANÍ (**Παλιανή**) is an ancient monastic foundation (dating perhaps from as early as the seventh century) and now a thriving convent. At its heart grows a sacred ancient **myrtle tree** (said to be as much as a thousand years old), its every twig hung with *tamata* (ex votos) and credited with healing powers. There's a powerful feeling that the rituals centred on the tree predate the monastery, and even Christianity itself, by some centuries. Around the tree is a tranquil, plant-filled courtyard with a thirteenth-century chapel to one side. In a small shop you can also buy lace, embroidery and other items hand-crafted by the nuns.

Ayía Varvára

AYÍA VARVÁRA (**Αγία Βαρβάρα**) is the chief village of this region, a place known as the **omphalós** (navel) **of Crete**. The great chapel-topped rock that you see as you arrive is held to be the very point around which the island balances, its centre of being – not that this makes for any great tourist attraction. There are plenty of cafés and shops along the main street, but they cater mostly for local farmers in search of a bag of fertilizer or a tractor part.

Zarós and around

As a village, **ZARÓS** (**Ζαρός**), 14km west of Ayía Varvára, is attractive enough, but at first sight little different from many others nearby. A number of things distinguish it, however. For locals, it is known above all for its **spring waters**, which are bottled and sold all over Crete (the bottling plant is at the far edge of the village); the waters also feed a small artificial lake. It's an excellent **walking** centre too, within easy reach of a couple of interesting **monasteries**, and has some excellent accommodation and food. To the west, a beautiful drive on relatively good, empty roads follows the flank of the Psiloritis range towards Kamáres (see page 210) and eventually on to Réthymno or down to Ayía Galíni.

Folklore and Geological Museum

Just off Zarós' main street near the church of Áyios Yeóryios • Charge

Zarós' **Folklore and Geological Museum**, housed inside a restored mansion, is a labour of love realized by the village's Folklore Association. In addition to the usual collection of furnishings, tapestries and antique household implements the upper floor has a huge geological collection, assembled by a local geologist, displaying stones and fossils as well as a few Minoan and Roman artefacts.

Lake Vótomos

Just 1km or so out of Zarós, well signed for both walkers and drivers, deep-green **Lake Vótomos** (**Βότομος**) is overlooked by rocky heights. Tiny as it is, it's a lovely setting, and the lake, full of trout, is the starting point for numerous hikes. The lakeside bar and taverna *Limni* is run by the same family as the *Eleonas Traditional Resort* (see page 102), and they are also responsible for much of the excellent local waymarking that helps walkers find their way around.

Moní Áyios Nikólaos

The pick of the well-marked paths that start at Lake Vótomos is the climb past **MONÍ ÁYIOS NIKÓLAOS** (**Άγιος Νικόλαος**; 1km) and through the Roúvas Gorge (2.5km) to the chapel of Áyios Ioánnis (5.2km). You can also drive to the monastery by heading west on the main road out of Zarós, and then 2km up a signed road. The monastery itself is now dwarfed by a vast blue-domed concrete church, which seems totally out of place here. Nevertheless, the older institution behind remains very welcoming, and the elderly monks will usually offer some refreshment to passers-by as well as opening the chapel so you can view the fourteenth-century paintings within.

Roúvas Gorge

Above Moní Áyios Nikólaos, the track snakes back and forth across an increasingly steep mountainside before reaching the entrance to the **ROÚVAS GORGE** (**Ρούβας**). The

1

gorge provides a spectacular walk on a good path, tough going at times despite the wooden walkways that help in the steeper sections. At the top lies the chapel of **Áyios Ioánnis**, on the main E4 trans-island walking route (the gorge walk itself is signed as the E4, but it's certainly not part of the main path). Here the easy option is to turn around and head down the way you came for a well-earned drink by the lake, a couple of hours away. With an early start and plenty of provisions you could take a more ambitious course and head east on the E4 to Áno Asítes, picking up a taxi back from there; but be warned that this is a good 20km of high-altitude mountain walking on rough paths – the rewards are spectacular views and plenty of bird and plant life.

Moní Vrondísi

3km west of Zarós; some signs read "Áyios Antónios" • Free

Fourteenth- to seventeenth-century **MONÍ VRONDÍSI** (**Βροντίσι**) is a gloriously peaceful foundation overlooking the Koutsoulídhi valley with views towards Festós and the Gulf of Messará. Beyond the entrance, guarded by a pair of prodigious plane trees, a tranquil courtyard surrounded by monks' cells (mostly empty) fronts the monastery's simple limestone **church**. Inside are some fine fourteenth-century **frescoes**, including a moving depiction of the Last Supper, and a collection of icons taken from the nearby church of Áyios Fanoúrios. Vrondísi itself has given up the finest of its artworks, including six great panels by Dhamaskinos, to the Museum of Christian Art in Iráklio (see page 65). For most locals, however, the attraction of Vrondísi is not art, but the cool water gushing from a fifteenth-century Venetian fountain, with figures of Adam and Eve, near the entrance. Here you can fill up your empty bottles with fine mountain spring water (the same stuff that's bottled down the road) for free.

Moní Valsamónero

Signposted from the village of Vorízia • Free

All that survives of **MONÍ VALSAMÓNERO** (**Βαλσαμόνερο**) is its church, Áyios Fanoúrios. It's some survival though; it houses some of the best **frescoes** in Crete, painted in the fifteenth century by Konstantinos Rikos and depicting scenes from the life of the *Panayía* (All Holy Mother of God)), images of various saints and a fine *Pandokrátor*.

ARRIVAL AND ACTIVITIES — ZARÓS AND AROUND

By bus One bus daily from Iráklio's Bus Station B (Mon–Sat 1.30pm, Sun 7am; 50min).

Cookery lessons The *Vegera* restaurant in Zarós offers cookery lessons for groups of at least 4), during which you prepare a five-course classic Cretan meal, then sit down and eat it (4–5hr; €30 including food and drink); they also organise farm activity days and afternoons eating with locals. 6970 579 395, www.vegerazaros.gr.

ACCOMMODATION

★ **Eleonas Traditional Resort** In the hills behind Zarós – follow signs from the bottling plant or from the lake, http://eleonas.gr. The traditionally built villas here are set in gardens, where native plants are labelled, at the base of the mountains; facilities include kitchen, TV, DVD and CD player and a fireplace; the more attractive (and more expensive) original villas are slightly larger, with galleried bedrooms. There's also an excellent taverna using local produce (breakfast is included) plus a pool (heated in spring and autumn), five-a-side football pitch. They also organise activities such as wine-tasting, produce their own hiking map and rent mountain bikes. They have a 3-night minimum stay for most rooms. €€

Idi Hotel On the road to Lake Vótomos, www.idi-hotel.gr. A comfortable place to get away from it all with a big garden pool (and indoor pool for winter) and tennis court, though the pine-panelled rooms are a little old-fashioned. There's a roaring spring directly outside the hotel, and an abandoned watermill, while the hotel's taverna specializes in the trout that splash around in the trout farm behind. Breakfast included. €€

★ **Rooms Keramos** Zarós village, signed off the main street, https://www.studiokeramos-zaros.gr/index.php/en. A bourgeois house in the village has been converted into a warren of individually decorated rooms with fridge, a/c and heating. Most have balconies with village and mountain views, and some have fine brass bedsteads. It's the exceptional warmth of the old-fashioned welcome that makes this place really special, though; that, and the amazing breakfasts with home-made pies and pastries. €€

EATING AND DRINKING

Limni Lake Vótomos, 28940 31211. The only restaurant actually on the lakeside, *Limni* serves excellent food, beautifully presented; earthy bread comes with sage-flavoured olive oil, tzatziki, olives and tomato salsa. The lake trout is the inevitable special, and tasty it is too, for it could hardly be fresher. *Orektiká* include trout carpaccio. Evenings here can be magical (providing you remember to bring mosquito repellent) and it's perhaps the only place in Crete where you'll have turtles and geese begging for food alongside the usual cats. €€

Vegera Main street, Zarós village, www.vegerazaros.gr. From the same hospitable family running *Keramos*, and with an all-female kitchen, *Vegera* offers traditional, local food. There's a superb buffet, based on whatever is fresh and in season; it's usually excellent and there are plenty of interesting veggie dishes too, although despite the name which in Greek means an early evening drinks gathering, this is not a vegetarian restaurant. €

The Messará plain

South of Ayía Varvára the road becomes genuinely mountainous until, at the Vourvoulítis Pass (650m), you enter the watershed of the Messará. The **MESSARÁ PLAIN** (**Μεσσαρά**), a long strip running east from the Gulf of Messará, is the largest and most important of Crete's fertile flatlands. Bounded to the north by the Psiloritis range and the lower hills that run right across the centre of the island, to the east by the Dhiktean mountains, and to the south by the narrow strip of the Asteroússia and Kófinas hills, it is watered, somewhat erratically, by the Yeropótamos. Heavy with olives, and increasingly with the fruit and vegetable cash crops that dominate the modern agricultural economy, the plain has always been a major centre of population and a mainstay of the island's economy. There is much evidence of this, not only at the ancient sites of **Górtys**, **Festós** and **Ayía Triádha**, but at a wealth of lesser, barely explored sites; today's villages exude prosperity, too, surrounded by neat and intensive cultivation.

GETTING AROUND — **THE MESSARÁ PLAIN**

By car As you descend to the plain by a series of long, looping curves, the main road heads west through Áyii Dhéka towards Míres, Festós and Mátala. A left turn eastwards takes you across far less travelled country (see page 121) and all the way to Ierápetra.

By bus Buses from Iráklio's Bus Station B (Mon–Sat 10 daily; fewer on Sun; 1hr 30min) head for Míres, the transport hub of the Messará plain. From here they continue variously to Mátala or Ayía Galíni via Tymbáki; the majority of these buses call at Áyii Dhéka and Górtys before Míres, and many continue via Festós.

Áyii Dhéka

ÁYII DHÉKA (**Άγιοι Δέκα**) is the first village you reach on the Messará and the most interesting. The place takes its name from ten early Christians who were martyred here around 250 AD, at the behest of Emperor Decius. The **Holy Ten** are still among the most revered of Cretan saints: regarded as martyrs for Crete as much as Christianity, they were the first in a heroic line of Cretans who laid down their lives to oppose tyrannical occupation.

On the west side of the village are two churches associated with the holy ten: the older, originally Byzantine **church** is signed to the south of the main road. Inside, there's an icon portraying the martyrdom of the saints and the marble block on which they are supposed to have been decapitated, complete with the imprints of their knees. Signed from here is a relatively modern **chapel** on the edge of the village beneath which, visible from the exterior, is a crypt where you can see six of their tombs. Both churches are generally open in daylight hours; it's well worth taking the short walk between them to get a sense of how close to the busy main road rural Crete remains. You'll see reminders of the village's ancient past everywhere: Roman statues, pillars and odd blocks of masonry are reused in modern houses, propping up walls or simply lying about in yards.

Górtys

2km west of Áyii Dhéka • Charge • 28920 31144

The remnants of the ancient city of **GÓRTYS** (**Γόρτυς**), known traditionally as Gortyn or Gortyna, are scattered across a large, fragmented area, covering a great deal more than the fenced site beside the road that most people see. One of the mightiest states of classical Crete, it reached the peak of its power in Roman times when it grew to become the island's largest city, as well as a provincial capital. The best way to get some idea of the ancient city's scale is to follow the path through the fields from the village. This heads out more or less parallel to the road, opposite the chapel of Áyii Dhéka, and is an easy walk of little over 1km to the main site; along the way you'll skirt most of the major remains.

Brief history

Settled from at least Minoan times, when it was a minor subject of Festós, Górtys began its rise to prominence under the **Dorians**. By the eighth century BC it had become a significant commercial power and in the third century BC it finally conquered its former rulers at Festós. The society was strictly regulated, with a citizen class (presumably Dorian) ruling over a population of serfs (presumably "Minoan" Cretans) and slaves. Even for the citizens, life was as hard and ordered as it was in Classical Sparta.

Evidence of early Górtys has survived thanks largely to the remarkable **law code** found here, and to a lesser extent through treaties known to have existed between the Górtys of this era and its rivals, notably Knossós. **Hannibal** fled to Górtys, where he stayed briefly after his defeat by Rome, and later the city helped the **Romans** to conquer Crete. This enabled it to avoid the fate of many other cities (such as Knossós) that opposed the invaders and were destroyed. It was during the Roman era, from 67 BC onwards, that the city reached its apogee,. As the seat of a Roman praetor, with a population estimated at 300,000, it was made the capital of the province of Crete and Cyrenaica, ruling not only the rest of the island but also much of Egypt and North Africa. It was here that **Christianity** first reached Crete, when St Titus was despatched by St Paul to convert the islanders, but after the **Saracen** invasion in the ninth century, when much of the city was razed, Górtys was abruptly abandoned.

South of the road: the Roman city

In the fields en route to the site, it is the **Roman city** that dominates; this once stretched from the edges of Áyii Dhéka to the far banks of the Mitropolitanos river (then known as the Lethe) and from the hills in the north as far south as the modern hamlet of Mitrópolis, where a Roman basilica with good mosaics (now covered) has been excavated. For most people, though, the ruins along the main path, with others seen standing in the distance, and the tantalizing prospect of what lies unexcavated beneath hummocks along the way, are quite enough. Individually, or in another setting, these might seem unimpressive, but with so many of them, abandoned as they are and all but ignored, they are amazing – you almost feel as if you've discovered them for yourself. The sites that have been excavated here are mostly seen only through locked fences, but the ground everywhere is littered with pillars and broken masonry.

The **Praetorium** (the Roman governor's palace) has the most extensive remains, a vast pile built originally in the second century, rebuilt in the fourth, and occupied as a monastery right up to the time of the Venetian conquest. Excavations in this area have revealed impressive foundations, flights of steps, walls and marble columns once belonging to imposing buildings, all indicating how much more still lies beneath the olive groves waiting to be discovered. Within the same fenced area is a courtyard containing fountains and the **Nymphaeum**. Somewhere near here, too, was the terminus of the main aqueduct that brought water from the region of modern Zarós. About 100m to the west of the Praetorium area is the **Temple of Pythian Apollo**, the most important of the Roman city's temples, later converted to a church, while the nearby **theatre**, though small, is very well preserved. Some 50m north of here are the substantial remains of the **Temple of Isis and Serapis**.

The main site

Directly opposite the entrance to the main, fenced site, be sure not to miss the 1600-year-old **olive tree** that has grown around pillars from the ruins of the ancient site – a surreal attraction in its own right. Plenty of other trees that seem almost as venerable surround it; the bus stop sign is nailed to one. As you enter the site, there's an impressive collection of **statuary** in a small pavilion backing onto the **café**, demonstrating the high standard of work achieved here during the city's halcyon days.

Áyios Títos

The apse of the church of **Áyios Títos** is much the most famous image of Górtys, and the thing that immediately grabs the eye. This is the only part of the church that has survived intact, but the shape of the whole structure is easy enough to discern. When it was built (around the end of the sixth century), it would have been the island's chief church, and it is the best remaining example of an early Christian church in the

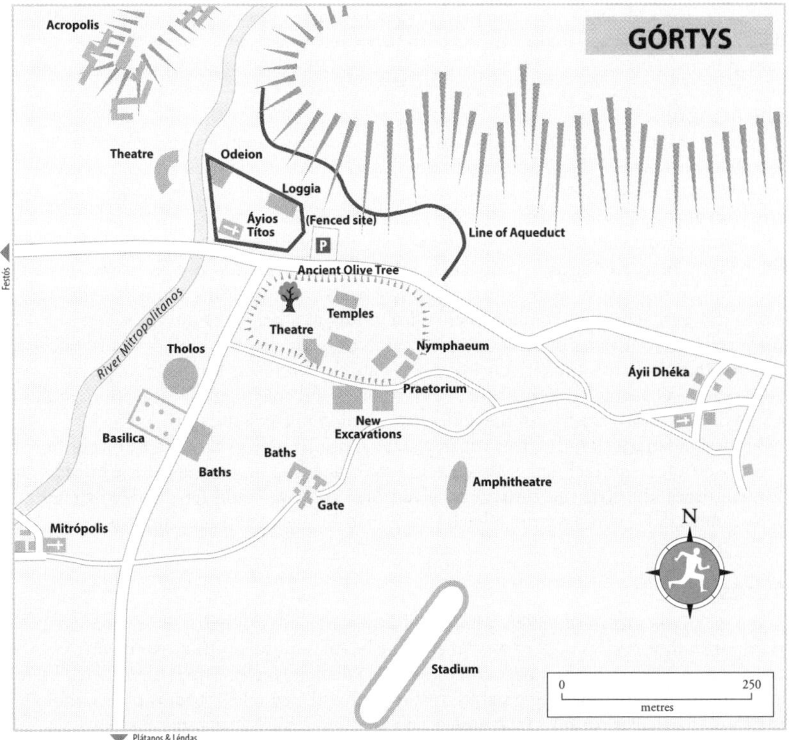

Aegean: you can see the extent to which it is still revered from the little shrine at the end of one of the aisles. The church's column capitals bear the monogram of the sixth-century Byzantine emperor Justinian.

The Odeion

Beyond the church lies an area that was probably the ancient forum, and beyond this the most important relic of ancient Górtys, the **Odeion** (or covered theatre) and its **law code**. The law code – a series of engraved stones some 9m long and 3m high – dates from around 500 BC, but it presumably codified laws that were long established by custom and practice. It provides a fascinating insight into a period of which relatively little is otherwise known; the laws are written in a very rough Doric Cretan dialect and inscribed alternately left to right and right to left, so that the eyes can follow the writing continuously (a style known as boustrophedon, after the furrows of an ox plough). The code is not a complete system of law but rather a series of rulings on special cases, and reflects a strictly hierarchical society in which there were at least three distinct classes – citizens, serfs and slaves – each with quite separate rights and obligations. Five witnesses were needed to convict a free man of a crime, while one could convict a slave; the rape of a free man or woman carried a fine of a hundred *staters*, while the same offence committed against a serf was punishable by a mere five-*stater* fine. The laws also cover subjects such as property and inheritance rights, the status of children of mixed marriages (that is, between free people and serfs) and the control of trade.

The panels on which the law is inscribed are now incorporated into the round Odeion, which was erected under Trajan in around 100 AD and rebuilt in the third or fourth century (the brick terrace which protects the inscriptions from the elements is modern). The Odeion is just the latest incarnation of a series of buildings on this site in which the code has apparently always been preserved – obviously, this was a city which valued its own history.

The Acropolis

With your own transport, you can reach the acropolis by following the road across the river towards Míres and Festós and taking a fork on the right signed "to the Acropolis of Górtys"; this road goes through the village of Ambeloúzos, where you should turn right immediately after the village sign; the route then climbs and you shortly need to turn right along a road signed to Apomarmá and Gérgeri; soon, a sign on the right will alert you to the acropolis, visible off to the right, a 5min walk away uphill

The **Acropolis of Górtys** occupies a hilltop above the river. Hardly anyone makes the hike up here, shying away from such a stiff climb in the heat, but the ruins are surprisingly impressive, with Roman defensive **walls** and a building known as the *kástro* (though apparently not a castle) still standing to a height of 6m in places. The surrounding lesser remains are among the earliest on the site and include scant relics of a Greek **temple** that was later converted to a church. From this hilltop vantage point, you also get a fine overview of the layout of Górtys and the ongoing excavations, and it's possible to trace the line of the aqueducts coming in from the north.

Beside the fenced site, the **river** runs by an abandoned medieval mill and on the far bank you can see a much larger **theatre**, in rather poor repair, set against the hillside. In Roman times, the river ran through a culvert here and you could have walked straight across; nowadays, you have to go back to the road-bridge to explore this area.

Míres

The large market town of **MÍRES** (**Μοίρες**), 10km west of Áyii Dhéka, serves as a transport hub for buses further west and to the beaches of the south coast; if you're travelling to Mátala, or west beyond Festós then you'll normally switch buses here. There are plentiful facilities including **banks**, **restaurants** and a couple of **rooms** places, though there's no particular reason to stay unless you are stranded while waiting for a bus.

ARRIVAL AND DEPARTURE — MÍRES

By bus You may need to change buses at Míres to get to Mátala or Tymbáki and Ayía Galíni; or to continue by taxi If you've missed the last bus or are heading to somewhere like Léndas or Kamilári.

Destinations Ayía Galíni (6 daily; 45min); Festós (6 daily; 20min); Iráklio (10 daily; 1hr 30min); Mátala (5 daily; 30min).

By taxi There are usually taxis waiting by the bus station, otherwise try 28920 25055 or 6948 084 598.

Festós

10km west of Míres • Charge • 28920 42315

In a wonderfully scenic location on a ridge at the eastern end of the Messará plain, the **palace of FESTÓS** (**Φαιστός**) enjoys a stunning setting, overlooked by the snowcapped peaks of Psiloritis and with magnificent views east across the plain. While no traces of frescoes were found here, and few other artworks, this doesn't mean that the palace wasn't luxurious: the materials (marble, alabaster, gypsum) were of the highest quality, there were sophisticated drainage and bathing facilities, and remains suggest a large and airy dining hall on the upper floors overlooking the court. Bear in mind, as you explore, that part of the palace is missing: there must have been more outbuildings on the south side of the site, where erosion has worn away the edge of the ridge, and a corner of the Central Court itself has collapsed.

The West Court

You enter the palace from above, approaching the northwest corner of the complex through the Upper Court, then into the **West Court** and integral **Theatral Area**. There

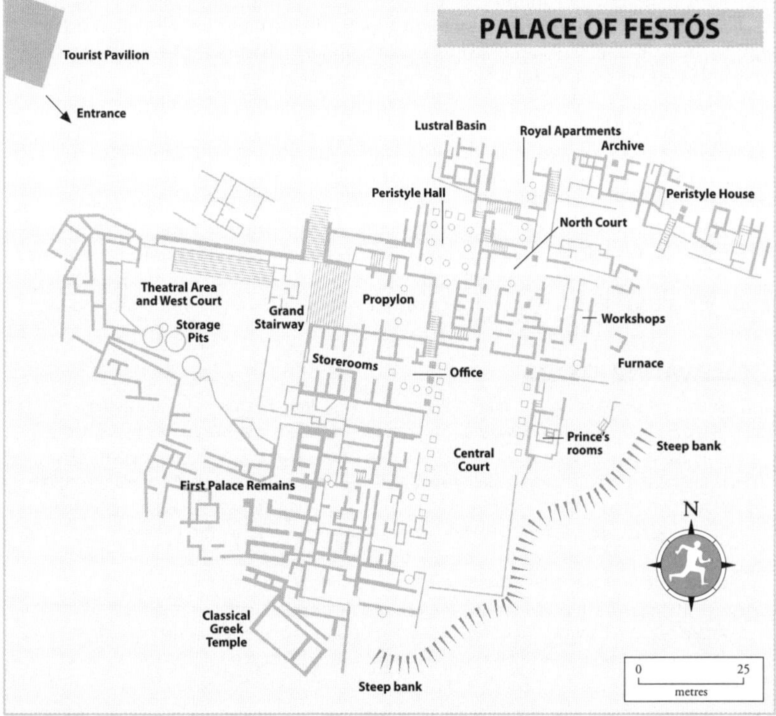

are raised walkways leading across the courtyard, and one of them runs right up the steps that form the seats of the Theatral Area (accorded this title by archeologists who supposed it was used for viewing some kind of performance or spectacle). On the west side of the court are circular walled pits, probably for storing grain. The West Court itself is a rare survival from the original palace; the main walkway leads not up the stairs into the new palace but past them and into the entrance to the old palace. From there, much of the facade of the old palace can be seen as a low wall in front of the Grand Stairway which leads into the newer building. When the palace stood, of course, this would not have been apparent; then, the court was levelled at the height of the bottom step of the stairway.

The Grand Stairway and storerooms

The **Grand Stairway** was a fitting approach to Festós, a superbly engineered flight of twelve shallow stone steps, 14m wide. Some of the steps are actually carved from the solid rock of the hill, and each is slightly convex in order to improve the visual impact. This remarkable architectural innovation anticipated similar subtleties of the Parthenon at Athens by twelve centuries. The entrance facade was no doubt equally impressive – you can still see the base of the pillar which supported the centre of the doorway – but it's hard to imagine from what survives. Once inside, the first few rooms seem somewhat cramped: this may have been deliberate, either for security purposes or as a ploy to enhance the larger, lighter spaces beyond. At the end would have been a blank wall, open to the sky, and a small door to the right that led onto stairs down towards the grand Central Court. Standing in the entrance area now, you can look down over the **storerooms**, and going down the stairs, you can get closer to them through a larger room that once served as an office. Exposed here is a storeroom from the old palace, with a giant jar still in place and another barred cellar to the right lined with more amphorae. At the far end, more *píthoi* stand in a room apparently used to store olive oil or other liquids; there's a stool to stand on while reaching in and a basin to catch spillage, while the whole floor slopes towards a hole in which slops would have collected.

The Central Court

From the stores "office", quite an elaborate room, you pass into the **Central Court**, which is by far the most atmospheric area of the palace. In this great paved court, with its scintillating **views**, there is a rare sense of Festós as it must have once been. Look north from here in the direction of the Psiloritís range and you can make out a black smudge to the right of a saddle between the two peaks. This marks the entrance to the Kamáres Cave (see page 210), a shrine sacred to the Minoans and the source of the famous hoard of elaborate Kamáres ware pottery. Even without the views – which would have

EXCAVATING FESTÓS

In legend the home of Rhadamanthys, brother of King Minos, **Festós** was excavated by Federico Halbherr (also responsible for the early work on Górtys) at almost exactly the same time as Evans was working at Knossós. The style of the excavations, however, could hardly have been more different. Here, reconstruction has been kept to an absolute minimum, to the approval of most traditional archeologists: with the exception of the Royal Apartments in the site's northeast corner, it's mostly foundations that scarcely rise above ground level.

As at Knossós (see page 72), most of what survives is what the excavators termed the **Second Palace**, rebuilt after its destruction around 1700 BC and occupied until c.1450 BC. But at Festós, the first palace was used as a foundation for the second, and much of its well-preserved floor plan has been uncovered by the excavations. Fascinating as these superimposed buildings are for the experts, they can make Festós confusing for casual visitors to interpret.

been blocked by the two storeys to either side when the palace was standing – the courtyard remains impressive. Its north end, in particular, is positively and unusually grand: the doorway, flanked by half-columns and niches (possibly for sentries) covered in painted plaster, can be plainly made out. To the left as you face this are a couple of *píthoi* (left there by the excavators) and a stepped stone that some claim was an altar, or perhaps a block from which athletes would jump onto bulls, or maybe just a base for a flowerpot.

Along each of the lengthy sides of the courtyard ran a covered **portico** or veranda, the bases of whose supports are still visible. In the southwest corner are various rooms that probably had religious functions; beyond these are parts of the old palace that are mostly fenced off. Also here, right at the edge of the site, are the remains of a **Greek temple** of the Classical era, evidence that the site was occupied long after the Minoans and the destruction of the palace.

The Royal Apartments

Heading up through the grand north door – notice the holes for door pivots and the guardroom just inside – a corridor leads through the **North Court** towards the **Royal Apartments**. These have been covered and shut off to prevent damage from people walking through, and it's hard to see a great deal of the queen's rooms, or the king's rooms behind them. Above the king's quarters is a large **Peristyle Hall**, a colonnaded courtyard much like a cloister, open in the centre. On the north side, this courtyard was open to take in the view of Psiloritis: it must have been a beautiful place, and perhaps also one of some religious significance. Staircases linked the hall directly with the Royal Apartments (and the **lustral basin** on the north edge of the king's rooms); nowadays it's easier to approach from the palace entrance, turning left up the stairs from the Propylon.

Palace dependencies

Continuing past the royal quarters on the other side, you come to a series of buildings that almost certainly predate much of the palace. Among the first of these is the so-called **Archive**, where the famous **Festós Disc** (see page 59) was discovered in one of a row of mud-brick boxes. A little further on is the **Peristyle House**, probably a private home, with an enclosed yard similar in design to the Peristyle Hall. From here, stairs lead back down to the level of the Central Court, into the area of the palace **workshops**. In the centre of another large courtyard are the remains of a furnace, probably used for metalworking or as a kiln. The small rooms roundabout were the workshops, perhaps even the homes, of the craftsmen. As you walk back to the Central Court, another suite of rooms – usually described as the **Prince's Rooms** – lies on your left, boasting its own small peristyle hall.

ARRIVAL AND INFORMATION — FESTÓS

By bus Bus services to Festós are frequent, with 6 a day from Iráklio; there are also less frquent direct buses to and from Mátala and Ayía Galíni.

ACCOMMODATION AND EATING

As you enter the site there's a **tourist pavilion** that serves drinks and food. **Rooms** can be found in villages such as Vóri (see page 111) and Kamilári (see page 116), as well as in Míres or Tymbáki. A major bonus of staying in the area is that if you get to the site early you may have a couple of hours of relative peace before the coaches start rolling in, some time after 10am. Áyios Ioánnis (see page 112), not far away on the Mátala road, makes a good **lunch stop** after or between sites. Alekos in Vóri makes a good stop after visiting Phaistos and Ayía Triáda (see below).

Ayía Triádha

44km west of Festós, on the far side of the hill • Charge • 27230 22448

In sharp contrast with unadorned Festós, **AYÍA TRIÁDHA** (**Αγία Τριάδα**) has provided some of the finest known Minoan **artworks**. These include frescoes, three famous vases of carved black steatite – the "Harvesters Vase", the "Boxers' Rhyton" and the "Chieftain Cup" – and a unique painted sarcophagus, all of which are on display in the Iráklio Archeological Museum. Yet the site – discovered and excavated at the beginning of the twentieth century by the Italian School under Federico Halbherr – remains something of an enigma. Nothing exists to compare it with in what is known of Minoan Crete, nor does it appear in any records; even the name has had to be borrowed from a nearby modern chapel.

As ever, the ruins enjoy a magnificent **location**, looking out over the Gulf of Messará. The modern view takes in the coastal plain, with Tymbáki military airstrip in the foreground, but in Minoan times the sea would have come right up to the base of the hill, very close by. Despite this beauty and wealth, Ayía Triádha is clearly not a construction on the same scale as the great palaces: the most commonly accepted explanation is that it was some kind of royal villa, but it may equally have been the home of an important prince or a wealthy ship-owing merchant, a building of special ceremonial significance, or even (as more recent theories have it, based on the quantity of records and storage found here) simply an administrative centre.

The remains, in which buildings of several eras are jumbled, are confused and confusing. This matters little, however, for it is the **atmosphere** of Ayía Triádha that really makes the place – the absence of crowds, the beauty of the surroundings and the human scale of the villa.

The site

To your left as you climb down to the site are the bare ruins of a **Minoan house** older than most of the other remains (the villa was broadly contemporary with the

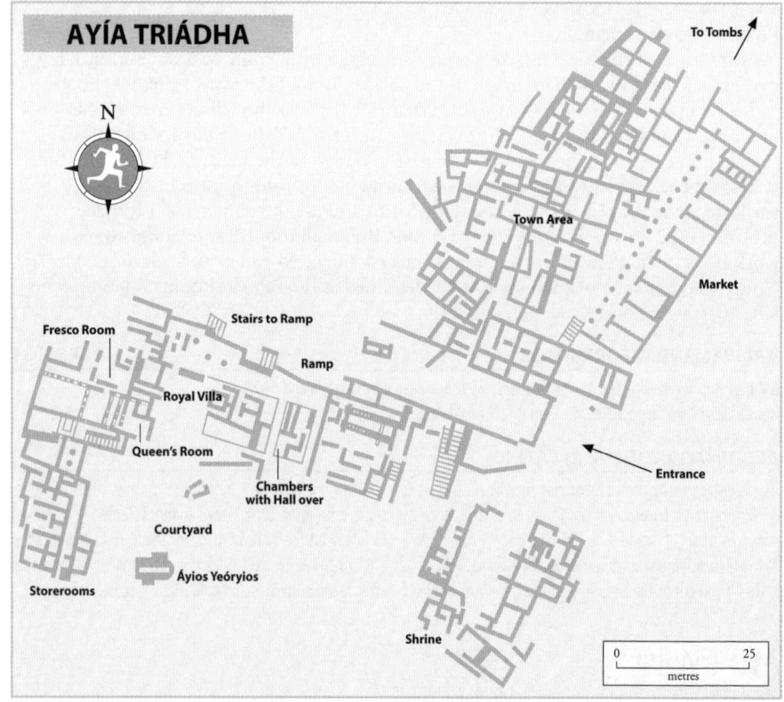

new palace at Festós), and beyond them a **shrine** that contained a frescoed floor and walls now on show in the Iráklio Archeological Museum. If you keep to the higher ground here, you come into the courtyard of the villa, perhaps the best place to get an impression of its overall layout. The L-shaped building enclosed the courtyard only on its north and west sides, and the north side is further muddled by a much later hall – apparently a Mycenaean *megaron* – built over it. To the south of the courtyard is the early fourteenth-century chapel of **Áyios Yeóryios**, in which there are fragments of some fine frescoes.

The Royal Villa

The **Royal Villa** now lies under covers below the level of the courtyard, but in Minoan times it would not have appeared this way: the builders made use of the natural slope to create a split-level construction, and entrances from the courtyard would have led directly into upper levels above those you see today. The finest of the rooms were those in the corner of the "L", looking out over the sea; here, the best of the frescoes were found, including the famous "Stalking Cat". The quality of workmanship can still be appreciated in these chambers, with their alabaster-lined walls and gypsum floors and benches. Beside them to the south is a small group of storerooms with a number of *píthoi* still in place; some bear scorch marks from the great fire that destroyed the palace about 1450 BC. From the hall and terrace out front, you can walk around the **ramp** that runs beneath the north side of the villa. The Italian excavators named this the *Rampa al Mare*, and it seems that it would have once run down to the sea.

The town area

By far the most striking aspect of the **town area**, which occupies the slope below the villa, is the **market**, a row of stores that are once again unique in Minoan architecture. The stores, identically sized and fronted by a covered portico, run in a line down the hill; in front of them is an open space and, across that, the houses of the town. There's only one problem with the easily conjured image of the Minoan populace milling around the market while their rulers looked benignly on from above: this area dates from the declining years of the Minoan culture and is contemporary not with the villa, but with the Mycenaean *megaron* erected over it. Beyond the stores (and outside the fence) lies the **Cemetery**, where remains of two tholos tombs and many other graves were found, including the one containing the Ayía Triádha sarcophagus.

Tymbáki

West of Festós the final stretch of the Messará plain, with its acres of polythene greenhouses and burgeoning concrete sprawl, must be among the ugliest places in Crete. **TYMBÁKI (Τυμβάκι)** may also be the island's drabbest town. It's a sizeable place, which means there are cafés and restaurants along the main street, stores and banks, and even a couple of hotels, but there's no reason to stay longer than you have to. Just beyond, a turning leads to **Kókkinos Pýrgos** on the coast. Here, too, plastic and concrete are the overwhelming images, and more inviting **beaches** in this area are to the south around Kalamáki (see page 117), Kommós (see page 116) and the developed resort of Mátala (see page 113).

Vóri

The road **north from Festós** confirms the rule that on Crete all you have to do is turn off the main road to escape into almost another world. **VÓRI (Βόροι)** is a sizeable place, very close to Festós and barely 1km off the main highway, yet it's almost entirely off the beaten track, a pleasant working village going about its daily routine. That some tourists do come here is largely due to its outstanding ethnology **museum**. If you're

1

heading for the Amári Valley and Réthymno from Vóri, you can spurn the main road and take a lovely, climbing drive via Kalohorafitís and Grigoría to **Kamáres** (see page 210); this also offers an alternative route back to Iráklio via Zarós (see page 101).

Museum of Cretan Ethnology

Hidden away in a pedestrian backstreet behind the church • Charge • http://bit.ly/2Pl3w5L

Though much copied, Vóri's **Museum of Cretan Ethnology** is still probably the best example of its type on the island, worth seeking out for a comprehensive survey of traditional country life in Crete. In 1992 it won the European Museum of the Year award and in 2011 made *The Daily Telegraph*'s list of Europe's Top 50 small museums, though stripped of support by the austerity-hit Greek government, it now struggles for funds.

The museum's collection is a fascinating miscellany of agricultural implements, building tools and materials, domestic utensils, furniture, pottery, musical instruments, weaving and embroidery, all well labelled. There are sections on the production of olive oil, winemaking and the distillation of *rakí*, as well as a display of the myriad herbs and medicinal plants used by Cretans since ancient times. A collection of baskets is especially interesting, the various designs including beehives, eel traps, cheese-drainers, animal muzzles and snail containers. The section on social organization has a case dedicated to the islanders' valiant struggle against Nazi occupation during World War II.

ACCOMMODATION AND EATING — VÓRI

★ **Taverna Alekos** Well signed close to the centre of the village, 28920 91094. Great little taverna with an enchanting courtyard planted with pomegranate and olive trees, serving straightforward Cretan village food, including snails, as well as pizzas for the tourists. There's a variety of salads on offer, and house specials include tasty *païdhákia* (lamb chops) and succulent oven-baked chicken. You can also stop in just for a drink, as an alternative to the *kafenía* in the village square. €

Vrondos Apartments Signed towards Faneromi, past St. Anthony Church, http://vrondos-apartments.com. Slightly outside the Vóri, these are four simple apartments very much away from it all. In a modern house on a quiet street, each apartment can accommodate up to four people; some have their own veranda. There is a shared outdoor space with a BBQ area and there are some shared bicycles you can make use of. €

Áyios Ioánnis

The road **south from Festós** passes the Ayía Triádha turn-off and soon approaches the village of **ÁYIOS IOÁNNIS** (**Άγιος Ιωάννις**) at the bottom of the hill. It's a handy stop for food or drinks, and it's worth taking the time to look at the venerable church of **Áyios Pávlos**. Right opposite the chapel a minor road heads west towards Kamilári and Kalamáki (see page 116), while the main route continues south towards Mátala.

Áyios Pávlos

500m beyond the Taverna Ayios Ioannis in a walled cemetery on the left side of the road • Normally open

Encircled by cypresses, the tiny, drum-domed church of **Áyios Pávlos** is one of the oldest on the island. Parts of it, in fact, date back to pre-Christian times, perhaps part of a Roman shrine to a water deity focused on the **well** at the back of the graveyard. The area to the rear of the church is the most ancient, with the dome probably added in the fourteenth century and the narthex, or porch – with its Venetian pointed arches – in the sixteenth. Inside, some interesting **frescoes** are dated by a frieze to 1303 and have images of the Evangelists Matthew and Luke, as well as a lurid representation of the punishments of Hell with souls being molested by serpents. This is one of the very few churches on Crete dedicated to St Paul, who was none too taken with the islanders, describing them in one of his epistles as "liars, evil beasts and lazy gluttons". To the side of the church, a charnel house contains the (visible) bones of corpses removed from the nearby tombs after a period of time to "free up" space.

EATING **ÁYIOS IOÁNNIS**

Taverna Ayios Ioannis On the main road, 28920 42006. Picturesque roadside taverna serving excellent food at tables in a garden under a shady vine trellis; the house speciality of charcoal-grilled rabbit is recommended, and the lamb is tasty, too. Service tends to be slow at busy times. €

The southwest coast

The best known of the beach resorts in the south of Iráklio province is **Mátala**, but this is far from the end of the story for this part of the coastline. There are much less crowded sands at nearby **Kommós** with its fine Minoan site, and at **Kalamáki**, and alternative bases just a short way inland at **Pitsídhia**, a well-established overflow for Mátala, and **Kamilári**, a charming hill village. Throughout this corner of Crete many properties have been bought by foreigners (Germans especially in this area), and many of the small villages have incongruously fancy villas in their midst. Nonetheless, head inland and you'll find lovely, quiet countryside, the villages surrounded by their crops of oranges, pomegranates or olives. One excursion well worth making is to the **Moní Odhiyítrias** and **Áyio Gorge**, where you can follow a verdant ravine down to the sea.

South of the Messará, two more beaches beckon – **Léndas** and **Kalí Liménes**. In an undeveloped way, Léndas is quite a busy place. Kalí Liménes, 20km south of Míres, is hardly visited at all, perhaps due to its role as a bunkering station for off-loading oil tankers. The roads around here are all passable but mostly very slow: the Asteroússia Hills, which divide the plain from the coast, are surprisingly precipitous. The only completely paved **routes** to this part of the coast are from Áyii Dhéka or Górtys to Léndas, and from Míres to Kalí Liménes via Pómbia. Both itineraries offer great views back over the Messará plain before toiling on through a quintessentially Cretan mountain landscape, where clumps of violet-flowering wild thyme cling to the verges in early summer, and shepherds slow your progress as they herd their flocks of goats along the road at dusk.

Mátala

You may still meet people who will assure you that **MÁTALA** (**Μάταλα**), with its cave-dwelling hippy community, is *the* travellers' beach on Crete. But that history bears about as much relation to modern reality as Mátala's role in legend as the place where Zeus swam ashore in the guise of a bull with Europa on his back, or its former glory as one of the chief ports of ancient Górtys. The entry to the village should prepare you for what to expect: a new road littered with very un-Cretan roundabouts, followed by a couple of kilometres of new hotels, "Welcome to Mátala" signs and extensive car and coach parking areas. In fairness it's far quieter at night, once the tour buses have paraded home, but the town never feels anything other than touristy. On the plus side, there's a spectacular **beach**, the atmosphere is boisterous, and you'll never be short of somewhere to enjoy a cocktail at sunset; with the caves lit up at night, the beach is an impossibly romantic setting.

MÁTALA ORIENTATION

For all its fame, Mátala is a very small place – you can walk through town and see all it has to offer in ten minutes. It consists basically of a single pedestrian street, running behind the **beach**: the **market** (where tourist tat has almost squeezed out the fruit and veg stalls) and many of the places to eat lie to the right, while the "**old town**", such as it is, is crammed against the rocks to the left. Car and bike rental, ATM and currency exchange can all be found on the first part of the street as you enter town. A widening of the main road close to the entrance to town we call the "first square"; the town's **main square** is immediately behind this.

THE MÁTALA CAVES

Nobody knows quite who originally built the **Mátala caves**, which are entirely artificial, but it seems likely that they were first hollowed out as Roman or early Christian **tombs**: they have since been so often reused and added to that it is virtually impossible to tell. The cliff in which they are carved is soft enough to allow surprisingly elaborate decor: some caves have windows and doorways as well as built-in benches or beds (which may originally have been grave slabs), while others are mere scooped-out hollows. Local people inhabited the caves, on and off, for centuries, and during World War II they made a handy munitions dump, but it was in the 1960s that they really became famous, attracting a large and semi-permanent foreign community. Name a famous hippy, and there'll be someone who'll claim that they lived here – the most frequently mentioned are Cat Stevens, Bob Dylan and Joni Mitchell ("they're playin' that scratchy rock and roll beneath the Matala moon" crooned the latter on *Carey*, from her 1971 album, *Blue;* and the wind that wrecked sleep and scattered dust is still often in from Africa).

It has, however, been a very long time since the caves were cleared, and nowadays they're a fenced-off **archeological site** (charge), open by day to visitors but patrolled by the police – and floodlit – every night.

Red Beach

When the crowds on the town beach get too much, you can scramble over the hill for twenty or thirty minutes to **Red Beach**, which, with its reddish-gold sand, nudists and scruffy, seasonal *kantína*, does its best to uphold Mátala's traditions. To get there, simply follow "Hotel Street" away from town, where a track becomes obvious; it can be quite hard going in parts. There's a slightly longer, easier route from town – look for the white-painted arrows pointing up from the main street.

ARRIVAL AND DEPARTURE — MÁTALA

By car Coming in by car you'll need to use the car park by the beach (€2), signed on the right as you enter the resort; if this is full (as it often is in high season) there's limited paid parking in Hotel Street (€3), or you can retrace your route and seek a place on the entry road.

By bus Arriving by bus you'll be dropped right at the entrance to town.

Destinations Iráklio (5 daily; 2hr); Míres (5 daily; 30min).

INFORMATION AND ACTIVITIES

Travel agencies Cretan Travellers (28920 45732, http://cretantravellers.gr) offers car and bike rental, ATM, currency exchange and information on rooms and excursions.

Horseriding Melanouri Stables (28920 45040, http://melanouri.com), on the western edge of Pitsídhia (see page 115), offers a variety of rides, from a 1hr trip to the beach (€25) to a ride by the olive groves (€50).

ACCOMMODATION

Finding a room should be no problem and, out of season, you may well be in a position to bargain. Most of the options below are on **"Hotel Street"**, left off the main road as you enter town, which is almost entirely lined with purpose-built places, all of them with parking.

★ **Fantastic** Hotel St, www.fantastic-matala.com. There may be a touch of hyperbole in the name, but these studios, standards double rooms and larger apartments are among the best in the street. On the town side of the street, with a private entrance at the back directly onto the town square. €

Matala Bay Hotel On the entry road, www.matalabay.gr. One of many bigger hotels that have sprung up along the road into town, this is within easy walking distance of the beach, with a good-sized pool restaurant and pool bar. Regular rooms in the main block, plus studios and apartments nearby, sharing the facilities. €€

Matala Camping Above the car park, close to the beach, 28920 45720. This campsite with shady tamarisk trees is fine if you don't mind camping on sand; there's a busy bar, and August can bring a rowdy party atmosphere. €

Matala View Hotel St, 28920 45114. Simple rooms, mostly with small balconies, as well as some larger studios and apartments, on the quiet side of Hotel St. Breakfast available at extra cost. €

Nikos Hotel St, The fanciest of the places on Hotel St, with very well-kept rooms and studios around a charming plant-filled courtyard, plus one "penthouse" with a sea view. Direct access to town from the back. Now managed by Nikos' two children. €€

★ **Sunshine Matala** Hotel St, www.sunshinematala.com. Friendly, comfortable *pension* with classily renovated rooms and suites for up to 3, andwith a/c, fridge and TV, plus larger apartments and villas on the quieter side of the street. Doubles €, apartments/villas €€

Zafiria On the main street as you enter Mátala, www.zafiria-matala.com. The longest-established hotel in town, with a prime position. Most of the balcony rooms have been done up, but even so can be a little dark, but they're comfortable and there's a good pool. Breakfast included. €€

EATING AND DRINKING

La Scala Far end of the beach above the harbour, 6981 388 135. Big Greek/Italian place with a wonderful terrace overlooking the bay; more elegant than most and only marginally more expensive. €€

Petra and Votsalo Seafront beyond the market, 28920 45361. Attractive taverna above the beach with a good reputation for fresh fish and a loyal clientele. Slightly pricier than nearby places, but worth the extra and has a nice line in creative salads with pasta and seafood. €€

Skourvoulianos Just off the main street towards the square, 6985 739 869. One of the newer places in town, with a simple but authentic menu, and the day's specials listed on a blackboard. Go for the likes of *yemistá* (stuffed veg), *soutzoukákia* (meat balls baked in sauce) or sea bream. €€

Zouridhakis Alley leading up to the main square, 28920 45352. There appear to be two bakeries here but in fact it's just one big place, with bread, ice cream, cakes and fresh rice pudding. Good for a breakfast of pastries, juice and coffee – they also serve eggs. €

NIGHTLIFE

The chief entertainment in the early evening is watching the invariably spectacular crimson **sunset** from the beach or one of the beachfront cafés. Later on the main square is ringed with quiet bars, while livelier places are crammed together at the far end of town, where on busy nights they merge into one big party.

Hakuna Matata Main street at far end of town, 6947 343 688. A bar/café/taverna that's open all day, distinguished by the pirate ship's prow hanging out over the water, and the fact that you have to walk through the premises to reach the far end of town. There's plenty of choice of food, but that's not really the point; the place really comes alive at night, serving cocktails and with dancing and frequent live bands.

Marinero Main street Red Beach, a bit out of town of town, 6986 750 860. Next door to *Hakuna Matata*, and also open all day, though with less emphasis on food; the music here tends to be more rock-oriented, and they also have DJs, theme nights and live music, often in competition.

Port Side Main street, 6945 983 886. A bistro bar with an enviable location, its candlelit tables on a terrace hanging over the beach just at the start of the nightlife zone.

Pitsídhia

An alternative base to Mátala, marginally cheaper and certainly more peaceful, **PITSÍDHIA** (**Πιτσίδια**) sprawls around the main road about 5km inland. This is already a well-used option, and far from unspoilt, but it's a congenial Greek village with plenty of rooms, decent places to eat and an affable young international crowd. Head up the hill away from the main road for more peace and atmosphere – there are numerous rooms places and tavernas up here.

ARRIVAL AND DEPARTURE — PITSÍDHIA

By bus All Mátala-bound buses pass through Pitsídhia, and on the return journey to Míres and Iráklio.

MÁTALA FESTIVAL

Honouring its hippy past, on the first weekend in July the town launches into the three-day **Mátala Festival** (http://www.matalabeachfestival.org), when thousands of local and foreign hippies descend on the town to paint it all the colours of the rainbow (mainly road surfaces and street furniture, plus any convenient bits of naked flesh). The rest of the weekend is spent gyrating to "days of yore" tribute bands on the beach stage – don't forget your bell-bottoms and kaftan.

1

ACCOMMODATION

Pension Nikos Inland from the town square, http://pitsidia-nikos.gr. It's less fancy than it looks from the outside, but this is a tranquil spot offering comfy rooms and two-room apartments with balcony and fridge. There's a communal kitchen supplied with coffee and the basics, and a roof terrace with fabulous views. The same owners have a couple of villas in the countryside nearby. €

Vrisi Studios and villas Just off the main road, near the bakery, www.pitsidia-vacation.com. Modern studios and larger bedroom apartments accommodating up to five people, around a small pool; they also rent some nearby villas for up to 6 people. Studios/apartments €, villas €€

Kommós

The archeological site of **KOMMÓS** (**Κομός**), a Minoan harbour town that was probably the main port for Festós and Ayía Triádha, lies on the coast west of Pitsídhia, at the southern end of a sandy shore that extends all the way to Kalamáki (see page 117). The northwesterly winds that often lash the beach and fill the sea with whitecaps would suggest that this was not the best place for a harbour, but the sea level would have been a couple of metres lower in Minoan times, when a reef, still just about visible offshore, provided shelter. On calm days, the **beach** here is lovely, with great views, a taverna at one end, a few loungers, and plenty of room to escape the crowds.

Ancient Kommós

Though it's clear that this is a major site, and visitor facilities have been built, the excavations remain closed – though you can get a pretty good view through the fence. There are three main **excavation areas**, none of them more than a stone's throw behind the beach. The **northern area**, on a low hill close to the sea, contains domestic dwellings, among which is a large house with a paved court and a limestone winepress. The **central group** – behind a retaining wall to prevent subsidence – has houses from the Neopalatial era, with well-preserved walls and evidence, in the fallen limestone slabs, of the earthquake of around 1700 BC. A rich haul of intact pottery was found in this area, much of it in the brightly painted Kamáres style.

The most remarkable finds, however, came in the **southern sector**. Minoan remains here include a fine stretch of **limestone roadway**, 3m wide and more than 60m long, rutted from the passage of ox-drawn carts, heading away inland, no doubt towards Ayía Triádha and Festós. To the south of the road, one building contains the longest stretch of **Minoan wall** on the island: over 50m of dressed stone. The function of this enormous structure isn't known but it could conceivably have been a palace, or it may have had a storage purpose connected with the port. Some of the nearby dwellings to the north of the roadway were also of elaborate construction, and a substantial number of fresco fragments unearthed by the excavators hint at sumptuous interior decorations. Just south of here another large building was a ship shed or **dry dock**, 30m long and 35m wide, with its seaward end open to the sea; it's now partly overlaid by a later Greek structure – probably a warehouse.

Kamilári

The attractive hill village of **KAMILÁRI** (**Καμιλάρι**) has numerous attractive **accommodation** options, plus plenty of **bars, cafés and tavernas**, some of which, thanks no doubt to the expat community, are surprisingly sophisticated. As you approach the village on the Festós road, you'll see signs (hard to follow; the final stretch is on foot, and the tomb is at the top of a hill) to an early **Minoan tomb**, one of the oldest and best preserved in Crete. Dating from about 1900 BC, the tomb was a circular structure with a large dome, inside which communal burials took place, while cult rituals were carried out in adjoining rooms. The stone walls still stand 2m high in parts; important clay models depicting worship at a shrine and a circular group of dancers unearthed here are now in the Iráklio Archeological Museum.

ACCOMMODATION AND EATING — KAMILÁRI

Acropolis Main Street, in the centre of the village, 28920 42582. One of a number of tavernas in and around the main street, this is not that far above the rest in terms of its cooking, but does have the most attractive terrace. House specials include lamb in the oven and there's decent barrelled house wine. €

★ **Apartments Ambeliotissa** On the hill as you climb towards the village from the Festós road, http://ambeliotissa.com. A very welcoming, child-friendly place with excellent a/c studios and apartments, some with mezzanine sleeping areas, in and around a house in its own grounds, with excellent pool and playground, café, communal barbecue and TV room. €

Kafeneio Kentriko Main Street, in the centre of the village, 28920 42191. This *kafenío* opened its doors almost a century ago and is now run by an ebullient female proprietor. It serves mezédhes, and there's a little terrace almost opposite. €

Sifogiannis In the heart of the village, 28920 42410. This flower-bedecked building has simple rooms that come with a/c, coffee-making facilities and fridge. There's also a roof terrace and communal kitchen. €

Xenonas Apartments In the village, www.xenonas.com. Four apartments sleeping two to four people, classily decorated in a traditional, blue-and-white Greek style. Potted plants and flowers abound in the outdoor areas. €

Kalamáki

Some 3km from Kamilári, **KALAMÁKI** (**Καλαμάκι**) is a small beach resort, popular with locals, with a rather unfinished look. Though not particularly attractive, Kalamáki does have a large, uncrowded, windswept beach that stretches right down to Kommós, plenty of good-value seafront **accommodation**, almost all of it in four- or five-storey blocks, and a pleasantly backwater atmosphere.

ACCOMMODATION AND EATING — KALAMÁKI

For food, it's hard to look beyond the **seafront tavernas**, especially as eating there will allow you to use their loungers and parasols. All have standard Greek menus with an emphasis on fish.

Alexander Beach At the southern end of the seafront, http://alexandros-kalamaki.com. In a quiet spot on the edge of town, this beachfront hotel has a/c rooms with fridge and balcony, plus its own restaurant. There's also a stone-built villa complex on the hill behind with fully equipped apartments (sleeping up to 5) and great views. Free beach loungers and breakfast included at hotel. €

★ **Kiknos Studios** Beachfront in the centre of town, http://kiknos.com. Exceptionally well-run place with classy touches that you'd expect in a far pricier establishment. Studios have kitchenette, fridge and big balconies, most with sea view (the few that don't cost less); there's also a great rooftop room, with the entire roof and its fabulous views to yourself. Free loungers on the beach. €

Rooms Psiloritis Set back a little from the northern end of the main beach, http://psiloritis-hotel.com. Great value – a rambling, slightly ramshackle hotel with numerous sea-view terraces and plain en-suite rooms with fridge. €

Taverna Avra Northern end of the beach, 2721 027709. A good choice if you want to use the sun-loungers, as it's in a quieter part of the beach away from the centre. Fresh fish and good Cretan standards are served on tree-shaded waterfront and roadside terraces. €

Taverna Delfinia Central beachfront, 28920 45697. Small, popular fish taverna with a bright, modern look – stripped pine tables, white chairs – serving excellent fresh fish, plus locally sourced meat and veg. €€

Inland from Mátala

Though there's not a great deal to seek out, it's enjoyable simply to drive around the villages of the southern Messará. Just north of Pitsídhia you can turn off the main road towards **SÍVAS** (**Σίβας**), a lovely village, but one of the most obviously affected by visitors, largely thanks to the rather bizarrely located *Shivas Village Resort*, a luxury resort on the edge of the village. Beyond Sívas you can continue to wander the back roads through villages like **Kousés**, where there are more rooms and places to eat, and on to the large agricultural centre of **Pómbia**, from where you can head south to the coast at Kalí Liménes (see page 118).

Moní Odhiyítrias

7km south of Sivas • Daily during daylight hours • Free, though you're encouraged to buy their excellent oil, honey or *rakí* • Just beyond Sívas, a paved road is signed south to Moní Odhiyítrias and Kalí Liménes – while the first half of this road, as far as the monastery, is excellent, the second half is a rough, mountainous dirt track

Even with excellent road access, **MONÍ ODHIYÍTRIAS** (**Οδηγύτριας**), founded in the fourteenth century, exudes a powerful sense of isolation, and except on summer weekends it sees few visitors. They make those visitors welcome, though, and there's usually someone to show you round this little walled oasis in the midst of the bare mountains: there's a flower-filled courtyard, fifteenth-century icons and frescoes in the church and a horse-powered olive-press, as well as a small collection of ancient agricultural implements and a crumbling tower to climb.

The Áyio Gorge

Opposite the Moní Odhiyítrias entrance you'll see signs for a track leading south to the Áyio Gorge • It's 1hr of relatively easy walking from Moní Odhiyítrias to the gorge entrance; you can also reach the gorge from a spot further down the (now unpaved) Kalí Liménes road, about 25min from the gorge entrance

ÁYIO GORGE (**Άγιο**) offers a lovely and relatively easy hike of about an hour (once you're in the gorge) down to a welcoming beach. The name ("Holy Gorge") refers to the fact that many of the caves that pockmark its sides are said to have been occupied by Christian hermits, especially during the period of the Ottoman occupation. One of them, just 250m from the sea, was a site of early Christian worship, later enclosed as the fourteenth- to fifteenth-century church of Áyios Andónios. This is a beautiful building, with an ancient well outside (whose water, sadly, is not drinkable); the cave itself is not visible, locked within the inner sanctum of the church. Finally, the **beach** is ample reward for the walk, an expansive semi-deserted pebble cove with beautifully clear, calm water.

ACCOMMODATION AND EATING — INLAND FROM ÁTALA

You'll find places to eat and tastefully restored houses, some of them for rent, in many of the villages you pass through. **Sívas** in particular has a couple of excellent tavernas on the main square, and some good accommodation options.

Horiatiko Spiti (Village House) 150m west of the main square in Sívas, http://horiatiko-spiti.de. A converted old house with beautiful, fully equipped studios and a duplex apartment sleeping up to five, all with full kitchen and wi-fi. In high season (July–Aug) there may be a minimum stay required. Studios €, apartments €€

Kalí Liménes and around

KALÍ LIMÉNES (**Καλοί Λιμένες**) was an important port in Roman times, the main harbour of Górtys (see page 104) and the place where St Paul put in as a prisoner aboard a ship bound for Rome, an incident described in the Bible in Acts 27. Paul wanted to stay the winter here but was overruled by the captain of the ship and the centurion acting as his guard; on setting sail, they were promptly overtaken by a storm, which drove them past Clauda (the island of Gávdhos) and on, eventually, to shipwreck on Malta. Today, Kalí Liménes is once again a port, for oil tankers this time, which – despite a sweeping beach to the east – has rather spoilt its chances of becoming a full-blown resort. It also has a real end-of-the-road feel, especially out of season, though summer weekends can see crowds of Irakliots descend.

A village of less than fifty souls, it must be said the isolation and loneliness does have a certain appeal, and the procession of tankers gives you something to look at as they discharge their loads into bunker tanks on an islet (named Áyios Pávlos after St Paul) just offshore. There's a solitary **taverna** on the harbour, but the nearest accommodation is at Khrysóstomos, 4km east. Some small cove beaches are accessible beneath the cliffs to the west – on foot only – while to the east is the kilometre-long, pebbly Makriá Ámmos beach where people camp out around the *Taverna Gorgona*. Beyond here, the eastern end of the beach is nudist. With a full day you could also hike up to Moní

Odhiyítrias and down through the gorge to Áyio beach (see page 118), having made arrangements at the harbour for a boat to pick you up at the end; you can also get a taxi-boat from Léndas.

East of Kalí Liménes

Leaving Kalí Liménes to the east, a road follows the coast for 18km all the way to Léndas. Smooth and tempting at first, it later it becomes an extremely rough dirt track and although passable with a standard car, you'll need to take it very slowly. In the first few kilometres, still on asphalt, you'll pass a few small tavernas, a couple of which have rooms, around the village of **Lassaia**, tumbling down a hill to a bay with a good sandy beach, and **Khrysóstomos**, the next bay. Beyond there are plenty more scruffy beaches, but the coast is blighted by plastic greenhouses and there's only one place with any sort of permanent habitation: **Platía Perámata**, a sandy little village with a couple of stores, a few basic rooms and usually the odd camper.

ACCOMMODATION AND EATING — AROUND KALÍ LIMÉNES

Palio Limani Harbourside, Kalí Liménes, 2892 097009. The "Old Port" has a pleasant raised terrace with harbour view, serves economical Cretan standards and fresh fish and has wi-fi. €

Villa Koutsakis Khrysóstomos, 4km east of Kalí Limenes, 28920 97468. A selection of rooms plus a couple of apartments in a modern building. In a very isolated spot, with a good restaurant, immediately above the beach. A couple of the rooms are very basic indeed, but most have big balconies overlooking the sea and many have cooking facilities. €

Léndas

The reputation of **LÉNDAS** (**Λέντας**) as a hippy resort, a fishing village where you can hang out by the beach and camp for free, is somewhat outdated: these days it's a tidy whitewashed seaside village with an easygoing air. For a quiet break, you could hardly choose better: it's still small, low-key and a little alternative, but it's no longer especially cheap, nor the sort of place where campers are welcomed on the beach. Having said that, scores of people *do* camp on the sand at **Dytikós**, just over the headland to the west, a predominantly nudist beach where the old ethos is still very much alive and where there are some good taverna/bars with rooms. Most of the facilities you'll need, including a couple of supermarkets and internet cafés, are located on the main square. There are few other facilities: no fuel or ATM, for instance.

Léndas beaches

The **beach** in Léndas itself is narrow and grey: for better alternatives you can take the obvious path over the headland from the western end of the town beach to the 1km-long stretch of sand at **Dytikós** or head east, where a rough path or a dirt track (signed from the bend on the road) will take you towards **Petrákis Beach**, with rooms and taverna, and **Loutrá**, a bay 5km to the east with a decent beach, small fishing boat harbour and more places to stay and eat. From Loutrá you could take a more ambitious hike, 6km inland up the scenic **Trakhoúla gorge** to Krótos. From here you may find a bus (check times before leaving), or you can take a taxi the 10km back to Léndas.

Ancient Levín

Just above the village, right on the main road • Free

Ancient Levín (or Leben) was an important centre of healing, with an *asklepion* sited by a spring of therapeutic waters. At its height, from the third century BC onward, the sanctuary maintained an enormous temple and was a major centre of pilgrimage. The ruins spread over an extensive area (not confined to the fenced site – you'll see remains throughout the village) and include a temple and a bath complex with tunnels and arches through which the water once flowed. Above all, there's a lovely third-century

BC Hellenistic black, red and white pebble mosaic (beneath a canopy) depicting a mythical creature: half horse, half sea-monster. Adjacent to the site are the more substantial remains of an early Christian basilica, with a much smaller eleventh-century chapel still standing in their midst.

ARRIVAL AND DEPARTURE — LÉNDAS

By bus The only bus to Léndas is an early afternoon service from Míres. This caters mainly for local schoolchildren (it heads from Léndas to Míres early in the morning) so doesn't run every day, or in mid-summer. In its absence, take the bus to Míres and a taxi from there.

By taxi A taxi to or from Míres will cost around €30; all the way to Iráklio around €90. Local taxis include http://taxilentas.com (6971 929 250) and http://lentas-taxi.com (6944 274 827).

ACTIVITIES

Boat trips Visits to local beaches and day-trips to places like the isolated seaside Koudhoumá monastery (see page 121) can be arranged through the *Petrakis Beach* hotel (see page 120; 28920 95345, http://petrakisbeach.com; around €30 including lunch and drinks).

Cretan Outdoor Adventures Based at Dytikós, in the laid-back *Café Relax*, they organize adventure activities including trekking, canyoning, climbing and abseiling, from around €50 (2892 095240, http://cretan-outdoor-adventures.com).

ACCOMMODATION

There's plenty of accommodation – most of it in good, modern studio-style **rooms** – though in peak season space can be at a premium.

Casa Doria Loutrá beach at the end of a rough, unpaved road, http://casadoriacrete.com. Italian-run "slow life" hotel and restaurant right above the beach, with simple, brightly decorated rooms, a laidback atmosphere and Italian-influenced food. A fabulous place, but very isolated and relatively pricey for what you get (rooms have neither fridge nor TV). Breakfast included. €€

Levin Apartments Immediately to the east of the main part of the village, http://levin.gr. Lovely modern studios and apartments, some with two bedrooms and big balconies overlooking the sea; the original apartments (Levin) are cheaper but not as nice. €

Niki's Rooms Centre of Léndas, behind Zorbas and El Greco, http://nikisrooms-lentas.gr. Super-friendly place with inexpensive rooms equipped with kettle and fridge, around a lovely flower-filled courtyard; a couple of upper-floor rooms have views (at extra cost), but there's a shared roof terrace for those who don't. Niki's daughters run several other rooms places around town. €

Petrakis Beach Petrákis Beach, 2km east of the village, http://petrakisbeach.com. Welcoming taverna-rooms place with excellent-value rooms all of which have sea view, terrace and fridge; there are also two rooms in the round tower alongside the main building. Free beach loungers, and Aris, the proprietor, also organizes boat trips, parties and other activities. €

Studios Gaitani Western end of the beach, http://studios-gaitani.gr. Studios and apartments with kitchenette and satellite TV immediately above the beach, with huge, rickety-looking balconies hanging over it. Loungers for guests' use on the beach. The same owners have a more modern apartment complex (*Gaitani Village*, with pool) in the hills immediately above town. €

Villa Tsapakis Dhytikós Beach, http://villa-tsapakis.gr. These bougainvillea-fronted rooms come with fridge and TV, and and some with sea view. They also have studios (with kitchenette) and apartments, and their taverna, *Odysseas*, is the meeting point for everyone staying or camping at Dhytikós. €

Zorbas Towards the eastern end of the beach, http://zorbas-lentas.gr. Balcony rooms and studios directly above the beach, most with sea views, above a decent taverna, in conjunction with which they offer very good-value half-board deals. They also have a stone-built apartment complex overlooking the village with a pool and great views. €

EATING AND DRINKING

Tavernas in Léndas are generally very good, serving above-average Greek food with great **sea views**. Léndas' **nightlife** is confined to a handful of bars, although in summer there are frequent beach events at Dhytikós or Petrákis Beach (the latter often lays on minibus transfers from town) – look out for the posters.

Blue Café On the rocks past the western end of the beach, 6972 822 152. A romantic spot to lounge over evening drinks while watching the moon rise over the bay, as people have been doing here since the resort's earliest days.

Lions On the square, 28920 95208. By day a quiet café with a pleasant garden terrace; at night it revs up (a little) with louder music and dancing (from 9pm), plus cocktails. There's even the occasional live band. This is about as wild as Léndas gets.

Panther Bar On the square, 28920 95389. A long-time

Léndas favourite, *Panther* has a sea-view roof terrace for coffee by day or breezy cocktails later, and cranks up the music (rock, reggae, jazz and Latin) inside as the evening wears on.

Porto Lentas Down by the water at the western end of the beach, 6982 379 199. Good and friendly taverna in a great location on the beach; check out the day's dishes in the kitchen, and the not-too-pricey fresh fish. €€

★**Taverna El Greco** www.lentas-elgreco.com. A particularly good restaurant with a large leafy terrace above the beach. The food is mostly traditional Greek – the day's baked dishes are on display in the kitchen – but cooked with exceptional care using the best local ingredients. There's an unusually good wine list, too, and they also have rooms. €€

The southeast coast

East of Léndas there's barely any access to the coast before the far east of the province, where there are low-key beach resorts at **Tsoútsouros** and **Keratókambos**, though for hardy walkers the secluded monastic community at **Moní Koudhoumá** is an escapist's dream. The road that gives access to these places, east across the Messará from Áyii Dhéka through Asími to Áno Viánnos, is an enjoyably solitary drive through fertile farming country in the shadow of the **Dhiktean mountains**. There's not a great deal to stop for along the way, but there are plenty of solid traditional villages with *kafenía* and places to eat. The more substantial village of **Áno Viánnos** has plenty of spots for a lunch break, as well as some ancient churches.

GETTING AROUND — THE SOUTHEAST COAST

By car The direct route from Iráklio to Áno Viánnos is via the farming town of Arkalohóri, joining the west–east route at Mártha. Alternatively, you can head south from Houdhétsi (see page 82), joining the west–east road near Pýrgos.

By bus Buses run from Iráklio via Arkalohóri to Áno Viánnos (Bus Station A; Mon–Fri 9.30am, 1.15pm & 3pm, Sat 9.30am & 3pm, Sun 7.30am), but none follow the route across the Messará.

Kapetanianá

The village of **KAPETANIANÁ** (**Καπετανιανά**), overshadowed by Mt Kofínas at the edge of the Asteroússia range, is most directly approached by heading south across the plain from Áyii Dhéka to Loúkia, from where it is a spectacular and lonely mountain drive. Natural beauty aside, the reason to come here is *Thalori*, an extraordinary getaway created from the largely abandoned hamlet of Káto Kapetanianá, many of whose houses have been carefully restored as guesthouses.

ACCOMMODATION — KAPETANIANÁ

Thalori Káto Kapetanianá, http://thalori.com. Twenty or so classily restored houses, sleeping 2 to 6 people, scattered through the village. Each is unique, but they share bare stone walls, handmade wooden furniture, traditional carpets, fireplaces or wood-burners, some type of cooking facility, quality sound systems and bathrooms, and a wonderful sense of isolation. There's communal life in the restaurant – the only place to eat for miles around so fortunately it's good and serves local produce – and at the mountain-edge pool. They also organise a wide range of activities, from hiking and moutain biking (free bikes available) to climbing and canyoning. There's real peace here, fabulous views over the south coast and plentiful opportunities to explore wild Crete; the downside is that you're a long way from anywhere – even the nearest beach is a scary 5km drive away. €€

Moní Koudhoumá

The remote **MONÍ KOUDHOUMÁ** (**Κουδουμά**), on the coast almost due south of Iráklio, nestles in a seaside cove with an inviting pebble beach at the foot of a cliff, surrounded by pinewoods. Arriving here is a distinctly end-of-the world experience, and the handful of remaining monks spend most of the year alone. Donations by pilgrims and benefactors have financed a considerable rebuilding programme since the year 2000 and facilities for both monks and pilgrims have vastly improved. The monks see few

1

visitors outside of the feast of the Panayía Koudhoumá in August (when up to fifteen thousand pilgrims descend on the monastery), but are extremely welcoming to those that do turn up, and will offer you food and a mattress in one of the dormitories set aside for "pilgrims". While the monks will not accept payment for their hospitality, a donation to monastery funds is unlikely to be refused. If you think the magic of the place may persuade you to prolong your stay, you should bring supplies with you. The nights here are exquisitely serene, broken only by the sound of the sea splashing against the rocks. While you're visiting the monastery, be sure to make the fifteen-minute walk west along the coast to the spectacular **cave** ("Avakospilios") where the founder monks lived during the building of the first monastery in the eighteenth century.

ARRIVAL AND DEPARTURE — MONÍ KOUDHOUMÁ

By car You can drive the 24km to the monastery on a reasonable unpaved road south from Stérnes, but the final switchback cliff face section is scary, with no barriers – allow at least 1hr 30min for the journey each way.

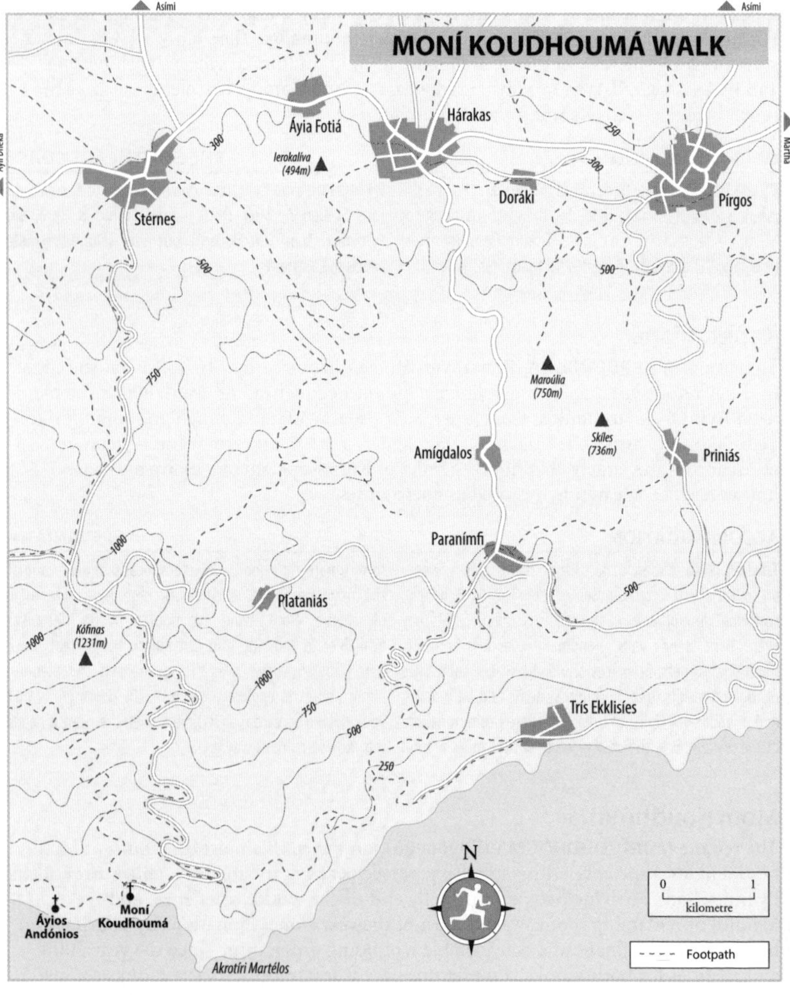

On foot It's possible to reach the monastery on foot, most easily by heading south from Hárakas on a paved road to the hamlet of Paranímfi, where you can get local directions onto the path that leads directly to the monastery, or continue on a reasonable dirt track to Trís Ekklisíes (with tavernas and rooms), from where it's 7km or so along a coastal path. Alternatively, you can hike all the way from Pýrgos via Priniás (20km; 4–5hr).

Pýrgos

PÝRGOS (**Πύργος**) is the biggest village in these parts, with plenty of facilities. Along the main street – which sees a lively **market** take place every Tuesday morning (all over by noon) – you'll find a couple of decent **tavernas** and, at the eastern end of the thoroughfare, the fourteenth-century **church** of Áyios Yióryios and Áyios Konstantínos, with some superb fresco fragments. The key is available from the house (no. 137) to the right of the church gate.

ACCOMMODATION — PÝRGOS

Hotel Arhontiko On the main road into town, 28930 23118. Comfortable, modern hotel mostly used by local business travellers, hence plenty of parking and extras including a/c, TV and kitchenette. €

Tsoútsouros

Some 11km of asphalt road winds alarmingly down from Káto Kastelianá, on the highway, to **TSOÚTSOUROS** (**Τσούτσουρος**). Despite the drama of the approach, Tsoútsouros itself is not immediately attractive; the central beach is narrow, rocky and grey, while the village straggles in an untidy line behind it, with an ugly concrete harbour/marina as a focus. Nonetheless the place is growing into a small resort, and the little bay does have its attractions – it's peaceful, with good stretches of beach backed by shady tamarisks in both directions. On summer weekends, and in the first two weeks of August, it can be very busy with local tourists; out of season, from October to April, most places close.

ACCOMMODATION AND EATING — TSOÚTSOUROS

For **accommodation**, the best places are at the eastern end of the village, where there's a better beach and it's generally more attractive despite the newer development; prices tend to be dramatically lower out of season.

Faidra Apartments Far eastern end of seafront, beyond Zorba's, https://faidrasapartments.com. Simple two-room balcony apartments with kitchenette, some with sea view. If there's no one around, ask at *Zorba's*. €

Mouratis Eastern end of seafront, 28910 92244. A large, modern place above a taverna comprising good value studios and apartments with cooking facilities for up to six people, many with big seafront balconies. €

Petra & Fos Western end of the seafront near the harbour, 28910 92345. Good pizzas from a wood-fired oven, plenty of well-prepared Greek dishes, plus fresh fish and good barrelled wine. There's also a comfortable café which is lively throughout the day, with breakfast until noon and cocktails after sundown. €

San Georgio Central seafront, by the harbour, www.sangeorgio.gr. Sizeable hotel (by Tsoútsouros standards) offering simple, smallish rooms with fridge; some have a balcony and sea view. There's a pleasant garden at the back and a café where you can get breakfast (extra). €

★ **Zorba's** Eastern end of seafront, http://zorbas-taverna.com. The pick of the resort's tavernas, with an attractive terrace and food and wine that's home-produced or locally sourced. Main dishes include daily specials such as pork with tomato and feta. Its two excellent-value rooms – only available outside July and August (when they're needed for staff) – are generously proportioned, with fridge, kettle and sea-view balconies. €

Keratókambos

KERATÓKAMBOS (**Κερατόκαμπος**), 10km east of Tsoútsouros, is accessed by a spectacularly winding mountain road from Hóndhros, near Áno Viánnos, or on a good paved road along the coast from Tsoútsouros. Though you would not at first sight describe Keratókambos as a pretty place – a single street of mismatched houses interspersed with cafés and tavernas facing a narrow, grey, shingly beach – it grows on you if you stay long enough to get over first impressions; it's peaceful and friendly, with good food and rooms. The beach, too, is better than it appears, with sandy, shallow water for a long way offshore.

In theory Keratókambos is three separate villages, though in practice they run into one another. Keratókambos itself, with the best of the beach, is immediately east of the junction where the Hóndhros road meets the coast; **Kastrí**, immediately west of the junction, has most of the facilities; while **Pórto Kastrí**, where an ugly modern concrete harbour has been built, lies a couple of hundred metres west of here.

ACCOMMODATION AND EATING — KERATÓKAMBOS

Filoxenia Kastrí, http://philoxeniaapartmentscrete.gr. Clean, modern en-suite rooms for two to eight people, right on the Kastrí seafront behind a lovingly tended, flower-filled garden. Studio-style rooms come with TV and kitchenette. €

Komis Studios In Keratókambos proper, 28950 51390. These lovingly designed, multi-level studio apartments in a garden setting come equipped with antique furnishings, minibar and TV. There's also a larger suite sleeping up to five. Breakfast included. €

Pan Apartments Above the village on the road down from Hóndhros, https://pan-appartments.de. There are numerous rooms places attractively sited above the village, with fine views out to the Libyan Sea. *Pan* is a good choice: modern studios and larger apartments come with kitchenette, spectacular sea view and a pretty garden. Minimum three-night stay. €

Taverna Kriti Kastrí, 28950 51231. One of the best local tavernas, serving good, earthy, traditional Cretan food; try the "special omelette", for example, with tomato, onion, potato and pepper. They also serve meat dishes and fresh fish at good prices, and have simple rooms. €

Áno Viánnos

ÁNO VIÁNNOS (**Άνο Βιάννος**), clinging to the southern slopes of the Dhíkti range, is a large village where almost everyone passing seems to pull over to break their journey. Given the narrow streets and lack of parking this can be unfortunate, but the air of busy chaos – with farmers' pick-ups the vehicle of choice – seems appropriate, somehow, in what was traditionally the administrative and market centre of this part of southeastern Iráklio province. Its importance has waned as the coastal settlements have grown but it's still a busy place, and there are some interesting churches to see as well as plenty of places to eat and drink. The sharper, cooler air up here is refreshing too.

The **churches** are signposted from the main street, up the narrow alleys in the upper part of the town. The most interesting is fourteenth-century Ayía Pelayía, with a magnificent, if damaged, fresco of the Crucifixion on the back wall.

EATING — ÁNO VIÁNNOS

Kafenion O Platanos On the main road at the east end of the village. The most atmospheric of the local places to eat, serving mezédhes at tables under an ancient and gigantic plátanos (plane tree). €

Káto Sými

East of Áno Viánnos the road to Árvi turns off at **Amirás**, alongside a giant memorial to Cretans killed in World War II. A few kilometres further, 1km beyond Péfkos, you can turn left for a scenic detour to the village of **KÁTO SÝMI** (**Κάτο Σύμη**) and its atmospheric **ancient sanctuary of Hermes and Aphrodite**. The trip is worth it for the adventure as much as anything – an intimidating drive up into the mountains round first-gear hairpins, all on asphalt, with a rocky scramble around the site, surrounded by pine forest, to reward you at the end.

Káto Sými itself has another **war memorial**, commemorating five hundred people put to death in 1943 when it and six other settlements were destroyed in retaliation for an attack on a German patrol.

EATING — KÁTO SÝMI

Taverna Afrodite Main street in Káto Sými, www.aphrodite-tavern.gr. A good taverna for a meal before or after you visit the site; waters from the ancient spring splash in troughs at the entrance. It has a fine terrace looking out over stands of plane trees, and serves a variety of tasty salads as well as the usual Cretan standards. They also sell home-made mountain honey. €€

The Sanctuary of Hermes and Aphrodite

Known locally as **Kryá Vrísi** (cold spring), the **Sanctuary of Hermes and Aphrodite** is laid out across a series of broad ledges on a mountainside where a prodigious spring gushes clear, ice-cold water all year round. There is evidence of a **shrine** here dating back to prehistoric times; adopted by the **Minoans**, it became a holy place of overwhelming importance, as evidenced by the thousands of votive clay and bronze figurines and vases brought here by pilgrims, many of which are now on display in the Iráklio Archeological Museum. In Greek and Roman times the shrine continued to be an important centre of pilgrimage, now to Hermes Dendrites and Aphrodite.

The spring still flows high up on the eastern side of the site, just outside the fence. Here too is an enormous hollow plane tree, which seems old enough to have witnessed many of the sacrifices and ceremonies that took place here in ancient times. The most obvious remains are in this corner of the site, including vestiges of temples, altars and cult rooms dating from all periods. Today most of the spring water disperses down the mountainside via plastic pipes to irrigate the olive groves below, but enough escapes to create several small waterfalls that you'll have passed on the way up.

ARRIVAL AND DEPARTURE — THE SANCTUARY OF HERMES AND APHRODITE

By car Start the ascent to the ancient site near the *Taverna Afrodite* in the village's main street. Uphill beyond the taverna follow wooden signs to Omalos Kristos, a chapel much higher in the mountains. You may be confused by turnings and junctions as you climb higher, but always stay on the asphalt. Eventually, some 3km above the village, a sign in Greek announces the site; the sturdy fence should be visible just above you, and although the site is almost always locked, the remains can easily be viewed by making a circuit of the perimetric fence.

Lasíthi

PALM TREES ON THE BEACH AT VAÍ

Lasíthi

Eastern Crete is dominated by the elegant resort of Áyios Nikólaos and the exclusive tourism it attracts, but get beyond "Ag Nik" (as it's known to the majority of English-speaking visitors) and its environs and you can experience some of the most striking highlands and wilderness coastlines on the island. Áyios Nikólaos itself, along with the pretty neighbouring resort of Eloúnda, is lively and cosmopolitan and has some of the most luxurious hotels on the island, although budget travellers are also catered for with a range of economical rooms and apartments. It's easy to escape into the surrounding hills and mountains, too. To the north, beyond Eloúnda and its beaches, you come to the brooding islet of Spinalónga, once a redoubtable Venetian and Ottoman fortress, later a leper colony. The town of Kritsá, with its famous frescoed church and textile sellers, and the imposing ruins of ancient Lató, also make for an enjoyable short excursion, while slightly further afield the Lasíthi plateau – a high mountain plain with picturesque villages and abundant greenery – makes a great day-trip from the coast, even better if you stay overnight.

The **far east** of Crete marks a dramatic change in scenery and tempo. Although much of it is rocky, barren and desolate, it is an area of great natural beauty, and on the whole the towns and villages are slower and quieter, with life conducted at an easier pace than in the rest of the province. The main town in the area, **Sitía**, is an attractive, traditional place where tourism has had little visible effect. The Minoan workers' village at **Gournía** is definitely worth a stop en route while, at the island's eastern tip, the famed palm-studded beach at **Vái** and the Minoan palace at **Káto Zákros** are the major tourist attractions. **Palékastro**, between the two, has plenty of accommodation within easy reach of isolated beaches while the island's southeast corner is about as escapist as you could wish.

Along the south coast, there is generally far less development. **Ierápetra** is the major town in these parts, with a scenic harbour from where boats sail to the offshore desert island of **Gaidhouronísi**. In each direction from here, towards **Mýrtos** and **Makríyialos**, lies a string of low-key resorts.

Áyios Nikólaos

The capital of the province of Lasíthi, the coastal town of **ÁYIOS NIKÓLAOS** (**Άγιος Νικόλαος**) has obvious attractions. Set on a hilly peninsula around a supposedly bottomless **lake**, in a lovely setting overlooking the **Gulf of Mirabéllo** ("Beautiful View"), it is wonderfully picturesque, with dozens of excellent cafés, restaurants and bars around the lake, the harbour and the nearby coast. Curiously, what the town doesn't have is an outstanding beach, so the five-star hotels are all some way out – mostly to the north, around Eloúnda – where they have private access to the coast.

By day, things to do in town are pretty limited – most people simply spend the day recovering from the night before. For the majority of visitors the days are taken up strolling the area around **Lake Voulisméni**, nosing around in the shops, or heading to one of the local **beaches**, all of which have Blue Flag status. There's also a wide choice of **boat trips** around the bay (see page 133).

SHEEP IN THE SNOWY MOUNTAINS OF LASÍTHI

Highlights

❶ **Áyios Nikólaos** A centre of upmarket tourism with good restaurants and buzzing nightlife. See page 128

❷ **Spinalónga** Fortified island whose impregnable isolation later made it an ideal location for a leper colony. See page 138

❸ **Lasíthi plateau** This highland plateau is a farming area where cloth-sailed windmills, multicoloured wildflowers and soaring eagles compete for your attention. See page 142

❹ **Kritsá** Home to one of Crete's most famous frescoed Byzantine churches, this traditional village is also a centre of weaving and lacemaking. See page 147

❺ **Sitía** Set around a beautiful bay is this attractive and easy-going resort with a couple of interesting museums and plenty of after-dark diversions. See page 156

❻ **Koureménos Beach** Not far from the exotic palms and crowds of tourists at Vái, the island's best windsurfing spot offers simpler beach pleasures, with plenty of more sheltered sands nearby. See page 166

❼ **Káto Zákros** With a romantically sited Minoan palace flanked by a cluster of fish tavernas and simple places to stay, Káto Zákros is a delightful seaside hamlet in which to relax. See page 169

HIGHLIGHTS ARE MARKED ON THE MAP ON PAGE 130

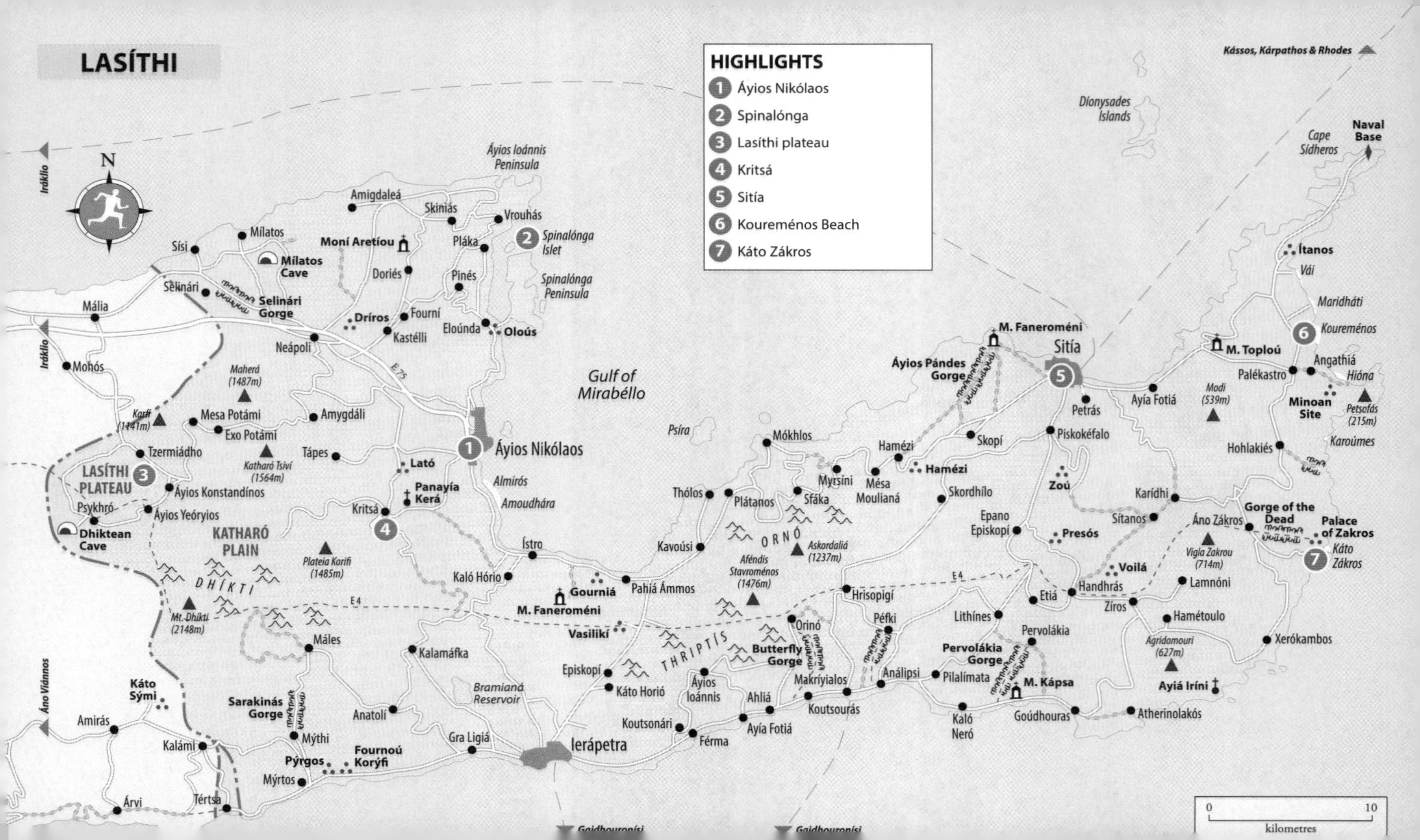

LASÍTHI
HIGHLIGHTS
1 Áyios Nikólaos
2 Spinalónga
3 Lasíthi plateau
4 Kritsá
5 Sitía
6 Koureménos Beach
7 Káto Zákros
Kássos, Kárpathos & Rhodes
Dionysades Islands
Naval Base
Cape Sídheros
Íraklio
Íraklio
Áno Viánnos
Gaidhouronísi
Gaidhouronísi
N
Áyios Ioánnis Peninsula
Spinalónga Islet
Spinalónga Peninsula
Gulf of Mirabéllo
Amigdaleá
Skiniás
Vrouhás
Mílatos
Sísi
Moní Aretíou
Pláka
Mílatos Cave
Doriés
Pinés
Selinári
Selinári Gorge
Mália
Dríros
Fourní
Eloúnda
Oloús
Kastélli
Neápoli
E75
Mohós
Maherá (1487m)
Karfí (1141m)
Mesa Potámi
Exo Potámi
Amygdáli
Tzermiádho
Katharó Tsiví (1564m)
Tápes
Lató
Áyios Nikólaos
LASÍTHI PLATEAU
Áyios Konstandínos
Panayía Kerá
Almirós
Amoudhára
Psykhró
Áyios Yeóryios
Kritsá
Dhiktean Cave
KATHARÓ PLAIN
Plateia Korifi (1485m)
DHÍKTI
Ístro
Kaló Hório
Mt. Dhíkti (2148m)
E4
Gourniá
M. Faneroméni
Pahiá Ámmos
Vasilikí
Máles
Kalamáfka
Bramiana Reservoir
Káto Sými
Sarakinás Gorge
Anatolí
Amirás
Mýthi
Gra Ligiá
Ierápetra
Kalámi
Pýrgos
Fournoú Korýfi
Mýrtos
Árvi
Tértsa
Psíra
Mókhlos
Thólos
Plátanos
Myrsíni
Sfáka
Hamézi
Hamézi
Mésa Moulianá
Kavoúsi
ORNÓ
Askordaliá (1237m)
Aféndis Stavroménos (1476m)
THRIPTÍS
Hrisopigí
Orinó
Butterfly Gorge
Péfki
Episkopí
Káto Horió
Áyios Ioánnis
Ahliá
Makríyialos
Análipsi
Koutsonári
Koutsourás
Férma
Ayía Fotiá
M. Faneroméni
Áyios Pándes Gorge
Sitía
Skopí
Skordhílo
Piskokéfalo
Petrás
Zoú
Epano Episkopí
Presós
Lithínes
Pervolákia
Pervolákia Gorge
Pilalímata
M. Kápsa
Kaló Neró
Goúdhouras
Atherinolakós
Ayía Fotiá
Modi (539m)
M. Toplóu
Palékastro
Angathiá
Hióna
Minoan Site
Petsofás (215m)
Karoúmes
Hohlakiés
Ítanos
Vái
Maridháti
Koureménos
Karídhi
Sítanos
Voilá
Handhrás
Etiá
Ziros
Áno Zákros
Vigla Zakrou (714m)
Gorge of the Dead
Palace of Zakros
Káto Zákros
Lamnóni
Hamétoulo
Agridomouri (627m)
Xerókambos
Ayiá Iríni
0
10
kilometres

Brief history

In antiquity, Áyios Nikólaos was the port for the city of **Lató** (see page 148), though this settlement faded in the Roman period and seems to have been abandoned in Byzantine times. The Venetians built a fortress – of which nothing remains – and gave the surrounding gulf its name, Mirabéllo. In succeeding years the town came slowly back to life, and by the nineteenth century the port was again busy; following union with Greece in 1913, Áyios Nikólaos was confirmed as the **capital** of Lasíthi province. A quiet harbour town for most of the last century, Áyios Nikólaos was discovered in the 1960s by international tourism and has barely looked back since.

2

Áyios Nikólaos beaches

The beach closest to the heart of things is the shingly little cove of **Kitroplatía**, surprisingly pleasant despite being right in the heart of town, though invariably crowded. The main **municipal beach** (with entry fee), beyond the marina on the southwest side of town, is no less busy. Beyond here there's a constant stream of people walking to the patch of sand at Vótsalo, or beyond it to the excellent sandy beach at **Almyrós,** 2km from the centre, or using bus or bike to reach the good beaches at Kaló Hório and beyond (see page 150). In the other direction, heading north, many locals simply dive off the rocks along Aktí Koundoúrou, though the first real sand in this direction is at tree-shaded **Ammoúdi**, another municipally run beach about 1km out of town – again, usually packed. Beyond are more little beaches en route to Eloúnda.

Folk Museum

Paleológou 1, near the bridge • Free

The **Folk Museum** has a small, slightly chaotic but interesting display of handicrafts (especially embroidery), costumes, pottery, cooking utensils and old Cretan goat-leather bagpipes. The displays include a recreation of a traditional Cretan bedroom, and a collection of weaponry with numerous revolution-era firearms.

The Archeological Museum

Paleológou 74, at the top of the hill north of the lake • 28410 24943

The town's **Archeological Museum** holds a great deal of interest. Highlights include the extraordinary **Goddess of Mýrtos**, the museum's star exhibit, a goose-necked early Minoan clay jug (c.2500 BC). There's also gold jewellery from early Minoan tombs at Mohlós (2300–2000 BC) and some fine examples of Vasilikí ware, named after the early Bronze Age site on the isthmus of Ierápetra where it was first discovered. Recent finds from the palaces at Maia and Zakros are also displayed, including a curious **model house** from Mália with a pitched roof and chimneys – both foreign concepts in Minoan architecture – and a beautiful **gold pin** (of unknown provenance) bearing an intricately crafted bramble motif and a tantalizingly long inscription in the undeciphered Linear A script on the reverse. There are fine late Minoan **clay sarcophagi**, or *lárnakes*, too, decorated with birds, fish and the long-tentacled octopuses that seems to have so delighted Minoan artists. There's also a rare Minoan **infant burial** displayed exactly as found at its site at Kryá, near Sitía.

Áyios Nikólaos church

1km north of town in the grounds of the *Minos Palace Hotel* • Free • Ask for the key at the hotel's reception desk, leaving passport or driving licence as deposit

The Byzantine church of **Áyios Nikólaos**, from which the modern resort takes its name, is, perhaps appropriately, stranded in the grounds of a five-star hotel. It's worth the effort to get there, though, to see some of the earliest **fresco** fragments found in Greece, dating back to the eighth or ninth century. The geometric patterns and motifs that survive are the legacy of the Iconoclastic movement, which banned the figural representation of divine images in religious art.

ARRIVAL AND DEPARTURE — ÁYIOS NIKÓLAOS

By bus The bus station is northest of the centre in the new town. There are local buses to the centre (July & Aug only) roughly every 30min (7.15am–10pm), or it's a short taxi ride. On foot, it's a steep up-and-down walk; head uphill and turn right along Knossoú and its continuation Kornárou, which will bring you out high above the lake; taking a left

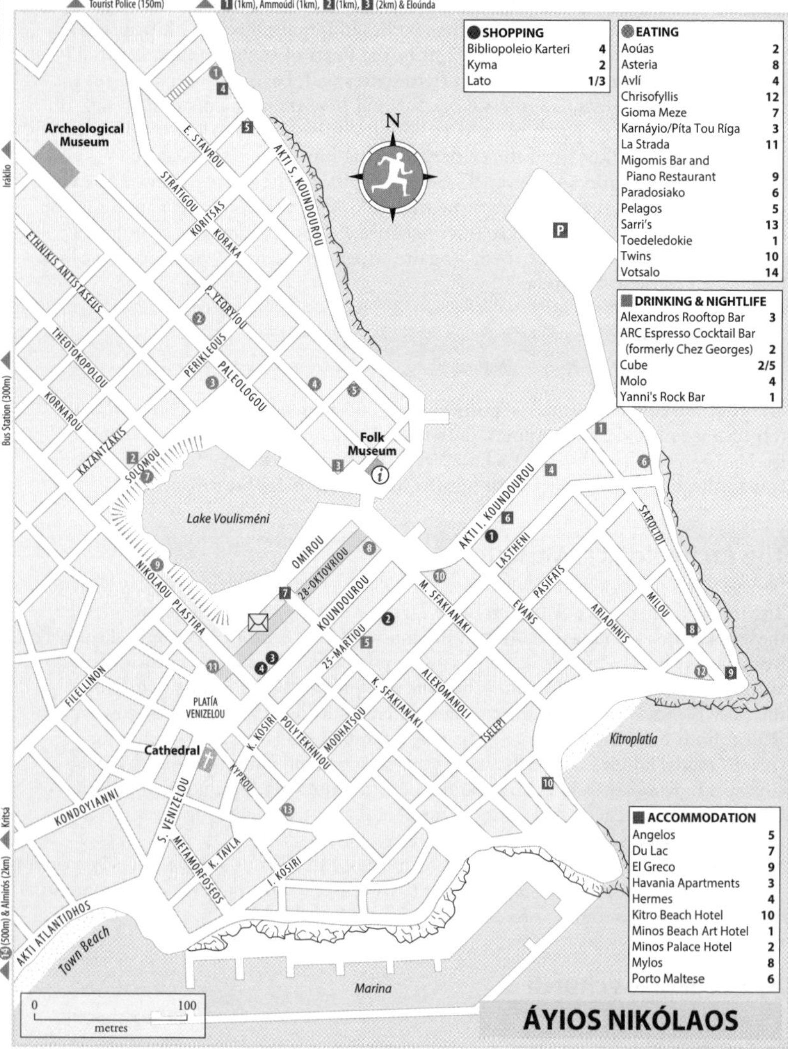

here to join Paleológou will lead you back down to the harbour area. Check timetables and book tickets at http://ktelherlas.gr; on Sundays most services are restricted to the point of vanishing.

Destinations Eloúnda (hourly 7am–9pm; 20min); Ierápetra (9 daily; 1hr); Iráklio (20 daily; 1hr 30min); Ístro (12 daily; 30min); Kritsá (Mon–Fri 8 daily, Sat & Sun 4 daily; 15min); Pláka (6 daily; 30min); Sitía (6 daily; 1hr 45min).

By car If you're driving in, follow the one-way system up the hill to Platía Venizélou, and then down into the picturesque areas past the souvenir stores that line Koundoúrou and parallel 25 Oktovríou. Parking in the central areas is a nightmare, so you're better off leaving your vehicle in the car parks at the harbour or near the marina.

GETTING AROUND AND INFORMATION

Bike rental There are dozens of outlets, mainly in the harbour area. For scooters, small motorbikes and high-quality mountain bikes, try the friendly and reliable Manolis, Aktí S. Koundoúrou 11, facing the waterfront (28410 24940, https://manolisbikes.com; April–Nov daily 8am–10pm).

Car rental Clubcars, 28-Oktovríou 24 (daily 8am–9pm; 28410 25868, http://clubcars.net).

By taxi There are ranks in Platía Venizélou and outside the Folk Museum; or call 28410 24000 or 28410 24100.

Tourist information The tourist office (April, May, Oct & Nov daily 10am–6pm; June–Sept daily 8am–10pm; closed Dec–Feb; 28410 22357, www.agiosnikolaoscrete.com), by the bridge over the lake oulet, is particularly helpful, stocking lots of maps and brochures.

Tourist police The tourist police are at Erythrou Stavroú 47 (28410 91409).

TOURS AND ACTIVITIES

Boat trips Daily trips to Spinalónga, plus various fishing, barbecue, beach and sunset tours, often with meals included, leave from around the harbour. Longer trips to Mókhlos (see page 153) and the island of Psíra (see page 153) are also sometimes available. Pelagos Dive Centre (28410 24376, http://diverete.com) offers small-group trips to Spinalónga and Mókhlos as well as private charter of a small yacht.

Cycling and adventure Martinbike at the *Sunlight Hotel* (6930 554 664, www.martinbike.com), on the coast road towards Eloúnda, organize cycle tours, some seriously challenging, and rent quality mountain and road bikes. Explore Agios Nikolaos (6970 193 573, www.exploreagn.com) offer excellent hiking, climbing, cycling and sea-kayaking experiences.

Horseriding and flower finding Fourni Horses (6940 846 019) organise lovely rural trail rides from their base in the hills behind Eloúnda. In spring and late autumn, rambles to discover the flora of Crete are run by Julia Jones (28410 42177, https://www.intocrete.net/features/wildflowers.asp).

Scuba and watersports Pelagos Dive Centre, based at the *Minos Beach Hotel* (28410 24376, http://divecrete.com), is a quality operation that also has a waterski boat, rents out kayaks, motorboats and sailing dinghies by the hour, and can arrange private sailing excursions. Happy Divers (28410 82546, http://happydivers.gr), based on the beach in front of the *Hermes* hotel with branches in Eloúnda and at a couple of big hotels, and Underwater Crete, based in the *Hotel Mirabello* on the Eloúnda road (28410 22406, http://creteunderwatercenter.com), are also reliable.

ACCOMMODATION

SEE MAP PAGE 132

Except in peak season, you're unlikely to have a problem finding a **room** in Áyios Nikólaos; however, with accommodation scattered on hilly streets all over town you may get footsore. If you haven't booked, start at the tourist office, which has information on current availability.

★ **Angelos** Aktí S. Koundoúrou 16, 28410 23501. Welcoming small hotel on the seafront, offering excellent a/c balconied rooms with TV and fridge plus fine views over the Gulf. No breakfast, but there's a supermarket, owned by the same people, directly beneath; ask here for information if there's no one around. €

★ **Du Lac** 28 Oktovríou 17, https://dulachotel.gr. Perhaps the most unexpected bargain in Áyios Nikólaos. The generous-sized rooms and studios are classily in designer style, exceptionally well-equipped, and in a prime location overlooking the lake. Not all rooms have lake views, however, and night-time noise can be a problem, as you're right in the heart of things. €

El Greco Aktí Themistokleous 1, https://hotelelgreco.eu. Fabulously located seafront hotel that's not as fancy as it first appears. Rooms at the front come with fantastic sea views from their balconies (well worth paying the slight bit extra) and all are equipped with fridge, minibar and tea-making facilities. €

Havania Apartments Havania Beach, about 2.5km north of the centre, www.havania.com. Slightly old-fashioned but clean and well-equipped apartments with a family atmosphere (some units sleep 5) and great location and facilities. There's a seafront pool and pool bar (with home-made food), a private pontoon from which you can get straight in the sea, and a good beach just 100m away. €

Hermes Aktí S. Koundoúrou 21, 28410 28253. Luxurious four-star seafront hotel with a large rooftop saltwater pool and every facility, from minibar to satellite TV. Frequent online discounts. Breakfast included. €€

Kitro Beach Hotel Nikoláou Pangálou 3, 28410 28931.

2

Standard-looking but somewhat modern hotel in a great location overlooking Kitroplatía beach, offering balconied rooms (sea view extra) with fridge and TV, and plenty of tavernas nearby. €€

★ **Minos Beach Art Hotel** Aktí Ilía Sotírhou On the promontory 1km north of town, http://minosbeach.com. One of the first of the luxury hotels to be built – during the 1960s – which means its rooms and bungalows enjoy a setting and spaciousness that younger rivals can only dream of, with almost 1km of private coastline just outside town. Original artworks sprinkle the grounds, and there's every facility you could hope for, including private pools at the fancier villas. €€€

Minos Palace Hotel On the pensinsula opposite the Minos Beach, www.minospalace.com. The most appealing of a clutch of big 5-star hotels just outside town, this is a veritable village in its own right, with views out across the Gulf as well as back towards town – the pricier suites have a private pool. Lovely rooms and every facility including private beach with watersports. Breakfast included. €€€€

★ **Mylos** Sarolídi 24, https://pensionmylos.com. Exceptionally welcoming pension where guests are often plied with homemade cakes and sweets. The rooms, including some singles and triples, are spotless, and most have balconies and spectacular views over the Gulf; all have TV and fridge. €

Porto Maltese Aktí I Koundoúrou, http://porto-maltese.com. Small boutique hotel created from an old mansion set back above the quayside. Each room is different, though all have been beautifully decorated; some are cozily small, others have balconies and wonderful harbour views (plus some inevitable noise from late-night revellers). Breakfast available. €€

EATING

SEE MAP PAGE 132

There are tourist-oriented **tavernas** (invariably employing zealous greeters) all round the lake, with little to choose between them apart from the different perspectives you get on the passing fashion show. Have a drink here, perhaps, or a mid-morning coffee – but choose somewhere else to eat. The places around Kitroplatía are generally fairer value, but again you pay for the location – the more authentic and better-value establishments tend to be less obvious, tucked away in the backstreets behind the tourist office or close to Platía Venizélou.

CAFÉS

Asteria Aktí I. Koundoúrou, 28410 22452, https://asteriacafe.eu Nicely old-fashioned café with a waterfront terrace fronting the harbour, and another on the second-floor balcony. One of the oldest in town and great for people-watching. €

Migomis Bar and Piano Restaurant Nikoláou Plastíra 22, 28410 23904. High above the bottomless lake, *Migomis* has a matchless view, arguably the best in town, and prices not significantly higher than any other fancy café; a great place for afternoon or evening drinks. Their elegant piano restaurant next door is a little over-the-top in terms of both price and decor, but perhaps worth it if you've booked a terrace-edge table to feast on that view. €

★ **Toedeledokie** Aktí S. Koundoúrou 19, 28410 25537. Café "toodle-oo" is a friendly, low-key café- run by Lucia, a Dutch artist whose works decorate the interior. There's a great parasol-shaded terrace above the sea opposite, international papers to read, yummy toasties, sandwiches and milkshakes; at night, it morphs into a chilled, candle-lit bar. €

★ **Votsalo** Vótsalo beach, south of the marina, 28410 28048. *Votsalo* continues to get the sun long after the beach it overlooks is in shade, so it's a lovely late-afternoon spot, but also busy during the day as it's directly over the water, with steps down into the sea and, behind, a little pebble beach that is effectively private. A good selection of salads, sandwiches, coffees and drinks. €

RESTAURANTS AND TAVERNAS

Aoúas Paleológou 44, 28410 23231. Very good, inexpensive traditional Cretan food, served in a plant-covered, trellissed courtyard. A bit out of the way, so can often be half-empty and lifeless. €

★ **Avlí** Pringipou Yeoryíou 12, 6980 555 887. Delightful garden ouzerí offering a wide mezédhes selection (with plenty of vegetarian options), as well as more elaborate dishes such as pork in wine, or lamb with artichokes slow-cooked in a traditional oven. Booking advisable. €€

Chrisofyllis Aktí Pangálou, 28410 22705. Attractive, stylish and creative *mezedhopolío* with reasonably priced mezédhes and creative Greek food (grilled octopus with broad beans and fava, or local pasta with saffron, shrimp and feta) served on a sea-facing terrace close to Kitroplatía beach. Some interesting wines too. €€

Gioma Meze Dhyonisíou Solomoú 10, above the lake, 28411 02056. Very popular place with some of the finest lake views. There's an excellent wine list and knowledgeable waiters, but it's best to avoid some of the fancier innovations (smoked chicken spring rolls, mussels in ouzo) and stick to plainer fare like grilled sardines or prawns. Booking essential if you want the best view. €€€

★ **Karnáyio/Píta Tou Ríga** Paleológou 24, 28410 25968. What appear to be two separate establishments in fact share a colourful terrace above the lake, where you can order from either menu. *Karnáyio* is a modern incarnation of a traditional ouzerí serving tasty mezédhes while *Píta tou Ríga* is an upmarket kebab joint – their speciality *píta tou ríga* comes with added bacon and cheese. The place attracts a young, local crowd and there's *lyra* and *laoúto* (lute) music most Fri & Sat evenings. €€

La Strada N. Plastíra 5, 28410 25841. There's decent

risotto, pizza and pasta plus reasonably priced fish dishes at this popular, Greek-Italian restaurant; get a table on their spectacular terrace above the lake for some of the best views in town. €€

Paradhosiako Akti Themistokléous 9, on the seafront near the harbour, 28410 21666 or 6977266744. Excellent ouzerí/*rakádhiko*, very popular with locals, serving a range of straightforward but excellent meze. €€

★ **Pelagos** Stratígou Kóraka and Kateháki 10, 28410 82019. Housed in an elegant mansion, this stylish (mainly) fish taverna has an attractive leafy garden terrace that complements the excellent food: fresh fish by the kilo is pricier than usual, but there are more modest options like grilled octopus, rice with seafood or pasta dishes. Booking advisable. €€€

★ **Sarri's** Kýprou 15, 28410 28059. Great little budget neighbourhood taverna in a quiet corner above the yacht marina, with outdoor tables in a platía overlooking an ancient church. The meze with wine is exceptional value and they also have daily specials like lamb in lemon sauce or chicken in the oven: breakfast is served, too. €

Twins Aktí Iosif Koundoúrou, 28410 22611. Large and always-buzzing pizzeria with tables right on the harbour and a busy takeaway business. The pizzas are good, and they also have sandwiches, salads, burgers and the like. €€

THE MIRABELLO FESTIVAL

Each year, Áyios Nikólaos mounts a summer-long cultural festival, **"The Mirabello"**, which includes music, dance and theatre from Crete, Greece and other parts of Europe. Keep an eye out for posters advertising the various events or ask at the tourist office.

2

DRINKING AND NIGHTLIFE

SEE MAP PAGE 132

One thing that Áyios Nikólaos undeniably does well is **nightlife**. A string of bars along the pedestrianized Aktí I Koundoúrou on the east side of the harbour play cool sounds to customers chatting on their waterside terraces, many with dancefloors inside that fill as the night wears on. There are bars on the opposite side of the harbour too, though fewer of them. More raucous music venues and clubs crowd the bottom of 25-Martíou (known as "Soho Street") as it heads up the hill – though few seem to survive in the same incarnation for long.

Alexandros Rooftop Bar Kondhyláki 1, 28410 24309. The name says it all; a great eyrie for a relaxed drink overlooking the lake, becoming increasingly rowdy as the cocktails take effect. The music playlist dates from the 60s to the present day but is mostly oldies, and gets louder later, encouraging punters to take to the small dancefloor. Happy hour till 10.30pm.

ARC Espresso Cocktail Bar (formerly Chez Georges) V. Kornaroú 2, 28410 26130. Chilled café/ bar with possibly the best views in town, from high above the east side of the lake. Coffee and snacks by day, cocktails and drinks at night.

Cube 25-Martíou 9. One of the longest-established of the clubs on 25-Martíou, *Cube* boasts theme nights, local DJs and a broad sweep of music.

Molo Aktí Iosif Koundoúrou 6, 28410 26250. One of a string of harbourside cafés with waterside terraces, *Molo* rarely closes; it's a café and local hangout by day and a cocktail bar in the evening; later on the action moves inside for dancing, club nights and occasional live music. Daily 8am–early hours.

Yanni's Rock Bar Aktí Iosíf Koundhoúrou 3, 28410 23581. Long-running classic rock music bar, with a party atmosphere and a soundtrack of 70s and 80s music, blues, hard rock and heavy metal.

SHOPPING

SEE MAP PAGE 132

The prime shopping street in town is Koundoúrou as it heads uphill from the harbour: head up to Platía Venizélou and then back down on 28-Oktovríou and you'll have seen most of what's on offer – from jewellery and fashion to souvenirs and sponges, photography to pharmacies and dive gear to delis.

Bibliopoleio Karteri Koundoúrou Roússou 5 and 28-Oktovríou 4, 28410 22272. Near Platía Venizélou, with entrances on both streets, *Karteri* has a good selection of books in English, plus maps and guides.

Kyma Koundoúrou 22. A huge variety of women's clothing, bags, jewellery, shoes and accessories from a range of local designers. On the whole it's not cheap, though.

Lato 28-Oktovríou 6 and Aktí I Koundoúrou 11, 28410 27478. Two separate shops, one next to *Karteri* and one on the harbourfront, each with a huge selection of quality Cretan and Greek oils, honey, wine, soap, olives, cosmetics and all sorts of natural products.

DIRECTORY

Banks and money Banks and exchange places are mostly found along Iosíf Koundoúrou and 28-Oktovríou, where there are several ATMs. The tourist office also changes money at reasonable rates.

Hospital The hospital is at the northwestern end of Paleológou, one block beyond the Archeological Museum (28413 43000).

Post office 28-Oktovríou, above the lake m–2.30pm).

The Gulf of Mirabéllo

North of Áyios Nikólaos, the swankier hotels are strung out along the **Gulf of Mirabéllo** coast road, especially as you approach the busy little resort of **Eloúnda**. The gulf's best-known attraction is the islet and former leper colony of **Spinalónga**, easily accessed from either Eloúnda or the hamlet of **Pláka**. Leaving Áyios Nikólaos, the road soon begins to climb; looking across the bay, you can make out the islands of Psíra and Mókhlos against the stark wall of the Sitía mountains, while nearer at hand mothballed supertankers are moored among the small islands sheltering in the lee of the peninsula.

Eloúnda

ELOÚNDA (**Ελούντα**) is a town with a split personality: surrounded by the most expensive hotels in Crete, and by fancy apartment and villa developments, it has plenty of jewellery and fashion stores and some pricey seafront restaurants; on the other hand, on the fringes there's a much more earthy resort, with plenty of inexpensive rooms and cafés that compete to provide the biggest, cheapest English breakfast. At the heart of town is an enormous seafront square ringed by cafés and restaurants, banks and post office, stores and hotels; virtually everything is here, or within a short walk. There are small beaches all around, though many of the best are monopolized by the big hotels; a good, sandy **municipal beach** stretches out north from the centre, and there are numerous popular swimming spots further out in this direction, along the road to Pláka.

ARRIVAL AND INFORMATION — ELOÚNDA

By bus Buses stop on the main square, where tickets can be bought from the kiosk.

Destinations Áyios Nikólaos (hourly 7.30am–9.20pm; 20min); Pláka (6 daily; 10min).

By car You have to pay to park in the seafront square (tickets from the booth); there's free parking behind the beach.

Travel agents Elounda Happy Travel (6972 600 567, https://eloundahappytravel.gr) is located along the main road in town. They can provide general information and assist with finding accommodation, as well as changing money and arranging tours and car rental.

ACTIVITIES AND TOURS

Most of the activity operators listed in Áyios Nikólaos (see page 133) will also pick up in Eloúnda, or have bases here.

Boat trips Boats leave the harbour every 30min from 9.30am to 5pm for the trip to Spinalónga (€15 return; 6974 385 854, https://eloundaboat.gr); longer day-trips taking in local beaches (around €30, kids half price), and fishing trips, are also available from them or from others around the harbour such as Elounda Boat Cruises (6970 802 409).

Fake Train trips Two rival tourist trains offer local trips, some of which venture way up into the hills (from €10), starting from the harbour square.

Watersports Petros is a large watersports centre at Ayía Paraskeví beach, about halfway between Eloúnda and Pláka (6944 932 760, https://spinalonga-windsurf.com). They have self-drive boats to hire (from €80 per hour, as well as paddleboards, waterskiing and wakeboarding. April–Oct daily 10am–7.30pm.

ACCOMMODATION

Many of the most **exclusive hotels** in Crete are sited around Eloúnda, offering **spectacular villas** with private pools costing thousands of euros a night; these are almost always far less expensive booked as part of a package. As for more ordinary accommodation, if you're having problems finding somewhere, try Olous Travel or one of the other agencies in the centre of town.

Akti Olous On the road to the causeway, Four-star seafront hotel where comfortable balcony rooms come with a/c, TV and fridge; many have a sea view. There's a bar and pool on the roof, with great views, and a seafront café flanked by a small beach. Breakfast included. **€€€€**

Corali Studios Behind the far end of the town beach, https://coralistudios.com. A sizeable complex, *Corali* (together with neighbouring *Portobello Apartments*, with slightly simpler apartments, under the same management) has good, modern a/c studios and apartments with cooking facilities, many with a sea view, and a pool and bar in the garden area behind. €

Delfinia Rooms On the waterfront just south of the centre, www.pediaditis.com.gr. *Dolphins* offers simple apartments in a great position right at the heart of things and directly above the sea (most have balconies with views). Decor and facilities are basic, but they're good value for what you get. Information from the family's bookshop on the main square. Four-night minimum stay in summer. €

Elounda Peninsula 2km south of Elounda, http://eloundapeninsula.com. Spectacular gated hotel draped across its own private peninsula. Accommodation is in duplex suites or larger villas, all with private pools, and there's virtually every facility you could wish for, including spa, tennis courts, 9-hole golf course, sandy beach and kids' clubs. Part of a complex with the *Elounda Mare* and *Porto Elounda* hotels, which share the same beaches and facilities, but offer some more standard hotel rooms. €€€€

Marin Studios Behind the town beach, close to town, 6972 314 067. Bigger and better than they appear from the front, these quiet apartments and studios, set well back from the road, are well equipped – with kitchens and balconies or terraces – and run by a helpful family. €

Milos Rooms In the upper part of town south of the centre, 28410 41641, http://pediaditis.com.gr. Under the same management as *Delfinia*, this is a more modern complex with rooms, studios and apartments surrounding a pool and bar. There's also a kids' play area, and prettily planted gardens. Information from the family's bookshop on the main square. €

Olive Grove Just off the square, on the road heading inland, https://olivegrove.com.gr. Big, modern two-bedroom apartments with full kitchen in a complex with pool and pool bar. The latter is open to non-residents and hosts occasional music nights. €

Paradisos Taverna Just outside town, signed down a track off the Áyios Nikólaos road, 28410 41631. Offering rural simplicity, this is an exceptionally quiet spot with an idyllic setting on the landward side of the Oloús lagoon. Simple rooms come with fridge and a very warm welcome. It also has an excellent garden taverna (see page 137). €

Traditional Homes of Crete http://traditional-homes.gr. Excellent restored stone-built houses (many ancient with original features), sleeping up to four, on the heights in and around the village. All come with parking, wi-fi, a/c, kitchen, terraces, views and private or shared pool. Also large two-room apartments, close to the town beach. €

EATING AND DRINKING

Eloúnda has a good choice of **tavernas** and restaurants in all price categories, and just off the square you'll also find a couple of excellent bakeries. **Nightlife** is quiet, centring on the cafés and bars around the main square; for anything wilder, head to Áyios Nikólaos (see page 135).

Babel West side of the main square, 28410 42336. A large and busy bar/café/pub with decent breakfasts and burger and pizza style eats. It's one of the liveliest spots in town, with big-screen sports, and music and dancing as the night wears on. €€

Dimitris On the square facing the church, 28410 41822. It has all the atmosphere of a transport café, but *Dimitris'* kitchen serves up good grilled meat dishes, as well as Greek standards, at economical prices. €€

★ **Ergospasio** Waterfront at the start of the causeway to Oloús, 28410 42082. Elegant ouzeri-taverna inside an old stone-built carob processing plant. The interior is bright and stylish and there's a seafront terrace plus another on the first floor. The menu is short, and decently priced for the location, but the speciality is meat spit-roasted in a glass-fronted wood-burning oven. €€

★ **Ferryman** Waterfront, south of the harbour, 28410 41230. Glitzy place named for the 1970s BBC TV series *Who Pays the Ferryman?* in which it featured. Expensive, but justly popular for the candlelit tables right above the water and short menu of interesting variations on traditional Greek recipes, many cooked in the hi-tech wood oven or giant barbecue – pork belly *yíros*-style, fish of the day. Booking advised. €€

★ **Kanali** Across the bridge at the far end of the Oloús causeway, 28410 42075. Excellent modern *psarótaverna* (fish restaurant) with a lovely setting on the edge of the lagoon, where tables sit on covered terraces. The fish (priced by kilo) is not cheap, but some of the best you'll find. Reservations recommended. €€€

Megaro Waterfront, south of the harbour, 28410 42220. Friendly place with a pontoon terrace on the water and some of the best prices on the waterfront. They serve fresh, well-prepared fish, seafood and steaks, as well as good salads and veggie dishes like stuffed red peppers.

★ **Paradisos Taverna** Just outside town, signed down a track off the Áyios Nikólaos road, www.elounda-paradisos.gr. An idyllic taverna with rooms (see page 137) on the landward side of the Oloús lagoon. Prices for fish and meat are very reasonable, with farmed *tsipoúra* (bream), and dishes like *kontosoúvli* (spit-roast pork). The day's specials are chalked up on the blackboard.

SHOPPING

Eklektos A. Papandréou 40, http://bookshopincrete.com. A great little English bookshop on the main road 100m uphill from the square in the direction of Áyios Nikólaos; they have an excellent selection of new and secondhand books and stock guides, maps and gifts. Also, helpful local advice.

The Spinalónga Peninsula

The barren **SPINALÓNGA PENINSULA** (**Σπιναλόγκα**) – often known as "big Spinalónga" to distinguish it from the more famous island of the same name – lies directly offshore from Eloúnda, forming a huge sheltered bay in front of the resort. It is linked to the mainland only by a narrow causeway, all that remains of a once-substantial now-sunken isthmus less than 2km from the centre of Eloúnda; it's an easy walk along the coast or short drive (though the sharp turning off the main road can be hard to spot). Protected by the causeway are the remains of Venetian salt pans, now fallen into disrepair, which are worth checking for migrating birds in the spring. Also here are the remains of stone windmills and the "French" canal, while all around on both sides you'll find people swimming from small patches of **beach** or basking on flat rocks. On the far side of the peninsula there are more tiny patches of sand – you can walk across to the nearest in a further thirty minutes or so. These are lovely spots, and apparently isolated, but become horrendously overcrowded in the middle of the day when boat tours make their lunch stops here.

Oloús

The ancient "sunken city" of **OLOÚS** (**Ολούς**) lay around the far end of the causeway to Spinalónga, mainly to the south and east, where a number of structures can be made out beneath the waves. Though it is known chiefly for having been the port of Dríros (see page 140), what little remains is **Roman**: there's a fenced enclosure behind the *Kanali* restaurant in which you can see the floor of a fourth-century Roman **basilica** with an odd, almost patchwork-style black-and-white mosaic, and among the rocks a little further round (watch out for sea urchins) are traces of harbour installations, now submerged as a result of the rise in sea level over the past couple of millennia. The site has never been excavated, and this is about the extent of what is visible, but it's a worthwhile trip for the setting, especially if you combine it with a swim and a drink at the *Kanali*.

Spinalónga

Charge • Boats run here every 30min in season (April–Oct) from both Eloúnda and Pláka; most give you 1hr on the island, though you can take a later boat back if there's room; it's also on many day-trips from Áyios Nikólaos; or many hotels will arrange a private transfer – often good value for a group of five or more

The imposing fortress rock of **SPINALÓNGA** (**Σπιναλόγκα**), at the northern end of the bay protected by "big Spinalónga", is a prime target for boat trips from Áyios Nikólaos, Pláka and, above all, Eloúnda. The **fortress**, which entirely covers the island, was founded by the **Venetians** in 1579 to defend the approach to the gulf and the sheltered anchorages in the bay. With its battlements, guard towers and seemingly impregnable walls, it bears all the hallmarks of the Italian republic's brilliant military architecture. Like their other island fortresses, it proved impregnable and was only handed over to the Turks by treaty in 1715, some fifty years after the rest of Crete had surrendered.

The infamous part of the island's history is much more recent, however. For the first fifty years of the twentieth century, Spinalónga was a **leper colony**, the last in Europe. Lepers were sent as outcasts – long after drugs to control their condition had rendered such measures entirely unnecessary – to a colony that was primitive in the extreme and administered almost as if it were a detention camp. Its jail was frequently used for lepers who dared complain about their living conditions.

Even today, if you can escape the visitors, there's an unnerving sense of isolation when the boat leaves you here, at a jetty from which a long tunnel leads up into the fortified centre. There are still just two easily sealed entrances: this tunnel, and a jetty on the seaward side (which you see if you approach from Áyios Nikólaos) leading up to the old **castle gate** with its lion of St Mark. Inside the castle a real town grew up – Ottoman Turkish buildings mostly, adapted by the lepers using whatever materials they could find. Although everything is in decay, you can still pick out a row of stores and some houses that must once have been quite grand. A couple have been restored to make a small **museum**, with photos and artefacts outlining the island's history.

Pláka

PLÁKA (**Πλάκα**), about 5km north of Eloúnda, lies directly opposite Spinalónga and was once the mainland supply centre for the leper colony. Boats still make the short trip across, nowadays carrying tourists, and the formerly decaying hamlet has become quite chichi, overlooked by a vast luxury hotel and with many of its houses done up by foreign owners or villa companies. It's still an attractive, tranquil place, though, with a couple of excellent tavernas and crystal-clear water – though the beach is made up of large, uncomfortable pebbles.

2

ARRIVAL AND DEPARTURE PLÁKA

By bus There are six daily buses to and from Eloúnda (10min) and Áyios Nikólaos (30min).

Boat trips Boats cross to Spinalónga from quaysides at the southern end of the village by the big car park and at the far end by the *Spinalonga* taverna, where there's more parking (April–Oct every 30min 9am–6pm; €8 return; https://plakaboat.gr); the *Spinalonga*'s boat also does a complete circuit of the island – allowing a fuller appreciation of the impregnable bastion – and offers fishing trips (€80/hr for up to four people) with the catch cooked up at the taverna on your return.

ACCOMMODATION AND EATING

Athina Villas In the heart of the village, http://spinalonga.eu. A modern complex of comfortable studios and apartments with kitchens and balconies, wi-fi and TV, many with sea views. Contact the owner for winter stays. €

Domes of Elounda 500m south of the village, http://domesofelounda.com. An expansive collection of suites and luxury villas, all with either outdoor hot tub or private pool and with magnificent views over the bay towards Spinalónga. The villas, especially, offer sybaritic luxury; there's also a private sandy beach with watersports, 5 pools, 4 restaurants, a spa, kids' club and magnificent service. €€€

Taverna Giorgos Southern end of village, 28410 41353. The best setting in town, with a large terrace facing out to sea opposite Spinalónga island. The fish is caught with their own boat but is pricey, although kalamari and octopus are more reasonable. €€

★ **Taverna Spinalonga** At the far end of the village, 28410 41804. With a lovely seafront terrace looking across to Spinalónga, this big, welcoming taverna at the far end of the village has some of the lowest prices locally (*moussakás* or grilled octopus), especially for fish (priced per kilo), fresh from the day's catch. €€

The Áyios Ioánnis peninsula

The triangular **Áyios Ioánnis peninsula**, north of Áyios Nikólaos, and northeast from Neápoli,is surprisingly wild and little travelled, with narrow roads running through remote farming hamlets with few facilities; the only sight of any significance is the remains of the ancient city of **Dríros**. The E75 north-coast highway delineates the northern edge of the peninsula; coming from the west it leaves Mália behind and embarks almost immediately on a long climb inland – rising at first through the **Selinári Gorge**, where travellers would traditionally stop at the chapel and pray to St George for safe passage. It's a tremendously engineered road, but bypasses the major town of **Néapoli** and anywhere else of note, and there's little to see until you emerge high above Áyios Nikólaos to spectacular views of the Gulf of Mirabéllo.

If you've time to dawdle, consider the minor roads across the peninsula: they make a great alternative route from Eloúnda to the west or to the Lasíthi Plateau. There's little specific to see, but there are wonderful views of the Gulf of Mirabéllo, while the larger villages offer plenty of places to eat and drink. A steep, narrow lane winds up from Eloúnda through **Páno Eloúnda** (location for most of the filming of the Greek TV series of *Island*) and **Pinés** towards **Fourní** and **Kastélli**, meeting up with the E75 highway outside Neápoli.

GETTING AROUND

THE ÁYIOS IOÁNNIS PENINSULA

By bus There's a steady stream of buses heading to and from Áyios Nikólaos along the E75 highway, most of which call at Neápoli (around 20 daily in each direction), but otherwise virtually no public transport on the peninsula.

By car Road maps of Crete, unreliable at the best of times, seem particularly hopeless on the peninsula; the Anavasi 1:100,000 Lasíthi map (see page 46) is the most trustworthy. Most significantly, there is no direct route around the coast, even on dirt roads, though some maps mark one. Follow the signposts and the asphalt, however, and you should eventually reach your destination.

2

Vrouhás and around

Beyond Pláka, the road leaves the coast and starts to climb towards **VROUHÁS** (**Βρουχάς**). Here, and in the surrounding country, you'll see many traditional stone windmills, mostly ruined: the winds that drove them are now being harnessed by a substantial **wind farm** on the ridges above. From Vrouhás and nearby **Skiniás**, rough tracks are signed to local **beaches**, plunging steeply down to isolated but unattractive pebble coves in a jagged, rocky coastline; there are small, seasonal tavernas at both hamlets.

Inland just beyond Skiniás, a signed, paved road climbs towards the lonely, fortress-like, sixteenth-century **Moní Aretíou**, surrounded by cypresses and cedars. Recently restored, it often appears deserted, though a couple of monks do remain and the gate and church of Ayía Tríadha are usually open. Beyond, you can continue, on a paved road that initially winds through utterly barren mountain tops, to **Doriés**, where the church of Áyios Konstantínos holds an icon of the *Panayía* (All-Holy Mother of God), the oldest known on the island, dating from the fourteenth century. The church is sited near the heart of the village and lies down a little path off the main road (marked by a small monument in the form of a church). The cream-and-brown-painted house next to it is that of the *papás*, who may be available to open the church for you.

Dríros

3km east of Neápoli • Open daylight hours • Free • On the northeastern edge of Neápoli, on the old road as it goes under the E75, is a road signed to Kouroúnes, Nofaliás and Skiniás; after 2km, a signed turn-off on the right leads a further 1km to a dead end beneath a rocky hillside – the stepped path up to the site can clearly be seen from the parking area inside the fence

The earliest remains found at ancient **DRÍROS** (**Δρήρος**) date back to the eighth century BC, and the city flourished for the next seven hundred years as an important ally of Knossós, but a deadly enemy of Lýttos (see page 83). Dríros declined in importance prior to the end of the second century BC, when many of its citizens emigrated to Miletus in Asia Minor (see page 142).

The site

Scrambling over piles of collapsed stones – ruins of the ancient city – you come eventually to a stone building under a corrugated canopy: the eighth-century BC **Temple of Apollo Delphinios**, one of the earliest known temples in all of Greece, in the centre of which can be seen the remains of a sunken hearth. Among the discoveries here were three hammered bronze statuettes (some of the earliest known, now in the Iráklio Archeological Museum) and two Eteocretan inscriptions – Greek letters used to write a Cretan, possibly Minoan, tongue. The temple was dedicated to a cult that celebrated Apollo transformed into a dolphin, a guise the god used when guiding Greek sailors; that the chief sanctuary of Miletus in Asia Minor was devoted to the same cult is further evidence of a link between this area and the founding of the colony there (see page 142). As you look around today, it's hard to believe that this temple once lay on the edge of the bustling **agora**, or market square. This was approached by a flight of steps – visible on the west side of the canopy, to the left of the doorway. Another flight of steps joined the temple on the east side, and to the south is a huge **cistern** constructed in the third century BC, now crammed with wild fig trees.

Neápoli

Despite its size, strategic location and history – it was the birthplace of Pope Alexander V – **NEÁPOLI** (**Νεάπολη**) sees virtually no tourists other than those who stop for a coffee in the square between buses or as they drive through. A charming provincial town, it was formerly the capital of Lasíthi (a role now assumed by Áyios Nikólaos) and remains the seat of the local government and of the provincial courts; it's a peaceful place for a stopover, and it is from here that one of the roads up to the Lasíthi plateau sets out. Around the expansive, sleepy main square, where the buses stop, are a post office, banks, tavernas and *kafenía*. You'll also see signs to an archeological museum, which has been closed for years and shows no signs of reopening, and an enjoyable folklore museum (July & Aug daily 10am–3pm & 6–9pm; free), housed in the old High School close to the square.

Sísi

SÍSI (**Σίσι**), a fair-sized resort on the western edge of the Áyios Ioánnis peninsula, in many ways has more in common with the nearby holiday centres of Iráklio province than with the rest of Lasíthi. Certainly during the day it can be crowded with day-trippers from Hersónissos and Mália, whose tour boats moor up in the harbour. That gloriously picturesque **harbour**, overlooked by a string of cafés, bars and tavernas, is the chief attraction here, though there are also some attractive cove **beaches** to the east. The best of these has been taken over by the *Kalimera Kriti* resort, but you can still get there by going to Avláki beach (itself very pleasant), and following the path around the rocks from there.

ARRIVAL AND INFORMATION — SÍSI

By bus A couple of buses a day heading between Áyios Nikólaos and Iráklio call at Sísi, the timetable dependent on the time of year. If you walk or get a taxi the 2.5km to the highway junction, you can also pick up buses there (at least 20 daily in each direction).

Travel agents AIS Travel (28410 71712), 50m up the main street from the seafront, is a helpful travel agency that can provide a village map, bus timetables and assistance with everything from accommodation to tours.

ACCOMMODATION

Many of Sísi's visitors stay in modern **apartment complexes** scattered about the surrounding countryside. Because these are so widespread – and mostly pre-booked in high season – the best tactic is to ask around at the tavernas near the harbour or at AIS Travel. There are also plenty of "Rooms for Rent" signs along the roads as you approach the village.

Bella Vista Overlooking the sea from the hills just over 1km west of town, http://bellavistasissi.com. Large, modern complex of studios and apartments with balconies (many with sea view), fully equipped kitchens and wi-fi in communal areas. In the gardens there's a big pool and pool-bar. €

Camping Sisi On the rocky shore just over 1km west of town, http://sisicamping.gr. Campsite with a fabulous seafront location (though you can't actually swim from the shore here), shady pitches, and excellent facilities including swimming pool, restaurant, kitchen, laundry and wi-fi. €

Porto Sisi Hotel On the seafront, east of the harbour, http://portosisi.com. Luxurious hotel/apartment complex with the best location in town, right on the seafront. Comfortable, well-equipped apartments come with kitchen and pool, though you pay for the privilege, especially if you want a sea view. €

EATING AND DRINKING

Angistri Facing out to sea, round the corner from the main harbour, 28410 71794. With the inevitable international menu featuring pizza and pictures of food to point at, *Angistri* also attracts locals for its competitively priced home-style food and fresh fish. €

Mike's Place Tucked down a side street behind the AIS travel agency, 2841 089883. Despite the anglicized name this is a thoroughly Greek taverna, serving home-style fish and meat dishes on a pleasant terrace shaded by a rubber tree. Mains are affordable, and the dish of the day is always excellent. Good local barrelled wine and free ouzo and *rakí*. €€

Skipper Café Above the harbour, 28410 71068. With an immaculate setting above the harbour, *Skipper* is a great place to admire the sunset over a beer or cocktail from an extensive list. Also open throughout the day for coffee, snack food and more beer. Occasional live Greek music.

Mílatos

An unpretentious settlement with a line of tavernas fronting the sea, **MÍLATOS** (**Μίλατος**) is very little developed, possibly because of its uncomfortable pebble beach and its relative isolation – a good twenty-minute drive from the E75 highway. Although you'd never guess it from what remains today, the place has a distinguished past; **ancient Miletus** even earns a mention in Homer's *Iliad* as one of the seven Cretan cities that sent forces to fight at Troy. In mythology – backed up by recent archeological finds – it was from Mílatos that Sarpedon (King Minos's brother, whom the king had defeated to take the throne) sailed to found Miletus, which was destined to become one of the greatest of all cities in Asia Minor. The site of the ancient city lies to the east of the beach, but there's little to see there: the place faded into obscurity in antiquity and by Roman times no longer existed.

Mílatos Cave

3km east of Mílatos village • Open daylight hours • Free

More a series of caverns than a single cave, the **Mílatos Cave** is something of a place of pilgrimage for Cretans. It appears to go back indefinitely, and with adequate lighting (bring a torch) you might be able to discover just how far. Less adventurously, there's a small chapel to explore right at the entrance, a memorial to the events that earned the cave its notoriety. In 1823, during one of the early rebellions against the Ottomans, some 2700 Cretans (that, at least, is the number claimed) took refuge in the cave, were discovered and besieged. Eventually, having failed to break their way out, they were offered safe conduct by the Muslim commander – only to be killed or taken away into slavery as soon as they surrendered.

ARRIVAL AND DEPARTURE — MÍLATOS

By car Mílatos is pretty much a dead end. Beyond the cave there are dirt roads that continue east, but there's no through route to the eastern half of the Áyios Ioánnis peninsula. What you can do, though, is zigzag up towards Neápoli, a beautiful drive on mostly well-paved roads.

ACCOMMODATION AND EATING

Much of the accommodation is in **apartments** in the surrounding countryside, but there are also some excellent beachfront rooms. Almost everything clusters near the small church at the junction where the main road hits the waterfront: shops and car and bike rental places as well as tavernas, cafés and rooms.

Akrogiali Seafront, right by the junction, 28410 81343. The tavernas lined along the seafront are almost all excellent; they're popular weekend outings for locals. *Akrogiali* is a particularly good spot, specializing in fish (priced per kilo) but with a broad, home-style menu for all tastes. €€

Porto Bello Villas At the western end of the seafront, http://portobello-villas.gr. Simple apartments (for up to 5) and studios in a lovely seaside setting close to the harbour with saltwater pool and satellite TV; there's an exceptionally friendly welcome from Ioanna and Paris. Excellent breakfast included. €

★ **Taverna-Apartments Sokrates** East along the waterfront, https://socrates-rooms.gr. This excellent seafront taverna serves a range of mezédhes and Cretan dishes on a spacious terrace. There's good charcoal-grilled meat (try the *païdhákia*) or oven-baked lamb (€9.50), as well as fish landed by the village boats. Accommodation consists of bright and airy modern apartments or studios with kitchen, balcony and sea view. €

The Lasíthi plateau

Every day, scores of bus tours toil up to the **LASÍTHI PLATEAU** (**Οροπέδιο Λασιθίου**) to view what is promoted as a sea of white-cloth-sailed windmills. In reality there are very few working mills left, and those that continue to operate do so only for limited periods; others are marketing features next to tavernas. The drive alone is worthwhile, however, even if you don't see a single unfurled sail, and the plain is a fine example of rural Crete at work.

If you **stay overnight** you'll see far more than on a day-trip, as the tour parties leave and a great peace settles over the plateau. The excesses of Mália or Hersónissos seem a world away as you climb into your bed to the sound of braying donkeys and a tolling church bell, and wake to the cock's crow the next morning. Early in the day you'll often see a diaphanous white mist floating over the plain and its windmills sparkling in the sun. The winters are severe here – up to 50cm of snow is not unusual – so the **best time to visit** is at either end of the summer season. In late spring, the pastures and orchards are almost alpine in their covering of wildflowers, an impression reinforced by the snow lingering on the higher peaks of the Dhíkti massif, while in autumn, the fruit trees can barely support the weight of their crop. Whatever time of year you come, though, bring some warm clothing, as the nights can get extremely cold.

Tzermiádho

TZERMIÁDHO (**Τζερμιάδο**), on the plateau's northern edge, is the largest village and one of the least touristy; in the village centre old shops that seem virtually unchanged in fifty years include sellers of hand-loom weaving and embroidery. There's also a post office and bank (with ATM) as well as an excellent old-fashioned bakery, several *kafenía* and good tavernas. In addition, Tzermiádho offers access to the Minoan site of Karfí and the Kronos Cave.

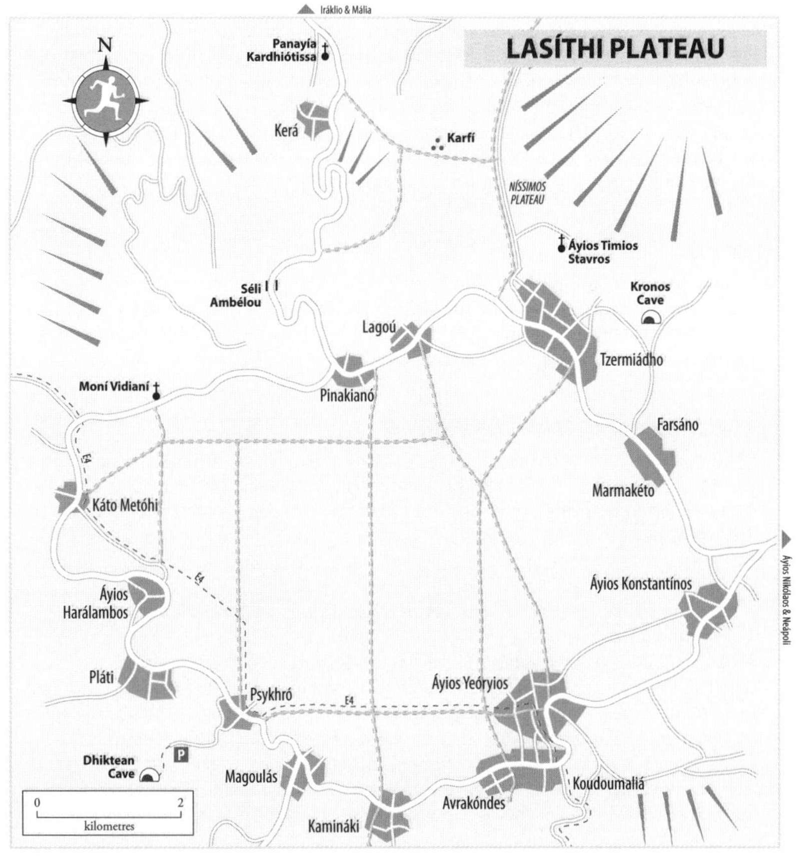

Kronos Cave

Follow signs from the centre of Tzermiádho or from the edge of Marmakéto, on the main road southeast of Tzermiádho; a path and stone steps take you the final 500m to the narrow cave entrance • Open daylight hours • Free, though there's often a guide to show you around and lend out torches, who will expect a small payment

In the **Kronos Cave**, known to archeologists as Trápeza, Evans and Pendlebury discovered remains and tombs dating back to Neolithic times. Though the cave is small, footing is slippery and treacherous, so a guide (and torch) comes in handy. In any event it helps to have someone point out the ancient tombs: in Minoan times, communal burials took place here, and many funerary offerings were discovered.

Áyios a Konstandínos

ÁYIOS KONSTANTÍNOS (**Άγιος Κονσταντίνος**) lies close to the point where the Neápoli road emerges onto the plain. As a result, it is the first (and last) village many people visit when doing a plateau circuit, and is therefore packed with souvenir stores. Some of the embroidery and weaving is very fine; in the best, natural dyes from onions, walnuts and other sources are still used. There's also an excellent taverna.

Áyios Yeóryios

ÁYIOS YEÓRYIOS (**Άγιος Γεόργιος**) is one of the largest and least touristy of the plateau villages, with a lovely, little-visited **Folk Museum** (April–Oct Mon–Sat 10am–5pm; €1.50). Housed in a low-ceilinged, windowless farmhouse preserved much as it would have been in the early twentieth century, it's full of rural tools and artefacts including a great wine-press, which doubled as the family bed. Below is a bourgeois house of the same period with displays of old pictures, including many photos of Cretan author Nikos Kazantzákis (see page 58), and between the two a section on shops and trade, including old barbers' and blacksmiths' equipment.

Psykhró

PSYKHRÓ (**Ψυχρό**), a simple community strung out along a tree-lined street, is the plateau's chief destination: the base for visiting the **Dhiktean Cave**, legendary birthplace of Zeus. There are tavernas along the main street, but in practice hardly anyone stops, preferring to continue straight to the cave itself.

THE LASÍTHI PLATEAU WINDMILLS

When you finally come upon the Lasíthi plateau laid out below you, it seems almost too perfect – a patchwork circle of tiny fields enclosed by the bare flanks of the mountains. Closer up, almost every centimetre is given over to the cultivation of potatoes, apples, pears, cereals and just about anything else that could conceivably be grown in the cooler climate up here. The area has always been fertile, its rich alluvial soil washed down from the mountains and watered by the rains that collect in this natural bowl. In spring, there can be floods, which is why the villages all cluster on the higher ground around the edge of the plain, but in summer, the **windmills** traditionally come into use, pumping the water back up to the drying surface. Although the plateau was irrigated in Roman times – and inhabited long before that – this system was designed by the Venetians in the fifteenth century, bringing the plain back into use after nearly a century of enforced neglect (during which time cultivation and pasture had been banned after a local rebellion). Where they survive, the windmills have barely changed, and although many have been replaced by more dependable petrol-driven pumps, they have been making a comeback in recent years, thanks to EU funding and tourism. The 26 stone windmills standing guard on the ridges above the plain, also mostly ruined, were traditional grain mills.

The Dhiktean Cave

1km southwest of Psykhró • Charge • From Psykhró a signed side road takes you up to a car park (the €2 parking charges are strictly enforced) from where the cave is a 10min climb on a steep, rocky path, or a longer but easier walk up a paved track; you can also go up by mule (€10 one way, €15 return)

According to legend, it was in the **Dhiktean Cave** that Zeus was born to Rhea. Zeus's father, Kronos, had been warned that he would be overthrown by a son, and accordingly ate all his offspring. On this occasion, however, Rhea gave Kronos a stone to eat instead and left the baby Zeus concealed within the cave, protected by the Kouretes (see page 341), who beat their shields outside to disguise his cries. From here, Zeus moved to the Idean Cave, on Psilorítis (see page 209), where he spent his youth. This, at least, is the version generally told here, and though there are scores of variations on the myth, it is undeniable that the cave was a cult centre from the Minoan period onwards, and that explorations around the start of the twentieth century retrieved offerings to the Mother Goddess and to Zeus dating through to Classical Greek times.

2

THE ASCENT TO KARFÍ

From Tzermiádho, there's an ascent to the ancient Minoan site of **Karfí** (**Καρφί**) one of the most dramatic places in Crete, perched on the southeast slope of Mount Karfí with an opportunity to see some of the area's spectacular birds of prey. The climb, some 6km, takes around 2hr on foot from Tzermiádho, less than half that if you drive as far as you can; you'll need sturdy footwear and, in summer, plenty of water. There are a number of shady places for a picnic on the way up, or even at the site itself.

The start of the route up is located on Tzermiádho's western edge at the side of the district health centre, opposite a blue sign marked, in English, "To the Timios Stavros church". Follow the road as it winds gently for the first couple of kilometres up to the Níssimos plateau. On this miniature plateau, turn left onto a dirt track and keep left, aiming for a small, whitewashed chapel. Leave any transport near the chapel, from just to the right of which the ascent begins, a final 30min through a rocky landscape patrolled by agile goats; there are no signs at the bottom, but the way is obvious and once climbing you'll come across numerous battered waymarks.

THE SITE

At the end of the climb the **archeological site**, with magnificent views over the coast, spreads across the saddle between the summit of Mount Karfí (the location of an ancient peak sanctuary), to the west, and the pinnacle of Mikrí Kopràna (topped by a trig point), to the east. In this cluster of crude, stone-built, single-storey dwellings, founded in the twelfth century BC, Minoan refugees fleeing from the Dorian advance attempted to preserve vestiges of their ancestral culture. For the three thousand or so inhabitants who lived here prior to the site's peaceful evacuation around 1000 BC, life must have been a grim struggle, lashed by the winds and prey to the vicious winter elements. But this very inaccessibility was of great defensive value and preserved the settlement from attack, while the cultivation of the Níssimos plateau below provided food and pasture for livestock.

Among the ruins, excavated in the 1930s by John Pendlebury, it's hard to make out anything other than a mass of fallen stones intersected by paved alleyways. The most substantial structure is what the archeologist described as the **Great House**, an important building still retaining its walls and where a number of bronze artefacts were discovered. Behind this, just to the north, a **shrine** was located, containing remarkable, metre-high terracotta goddesses with arms raised in blessing (now in the Iráklio Archeological Museum).

While you're up here there's a good chance you'll see the odd griffon vulture gliding majestically overhead, or maybe even the much rarer lammergeier, or bearded vulture, now down to a handful of isolated pairs in Crete.

Concrete steps and electric lighting have made the cave an easy place to visit, although some of the magic and mystery has inevitably been lost. The steps lead you on a circular tour, passing the bottom of the cave where you are confronted with an artificial lake. The one experience that has survived the alterations is the view back from the depths of the cave towards the peephole of light at the entrance, framed in a blue haze caused by the damp atmosphere. It's not hard to believe the tales that this was the infant Zeus's first sight of the world destined to become his kingdom.

2

To avoid the crowds and fully savour the cave's mystical qualities, try to arrive early (coaches start to arrive around 11.30am).

Moní Vidianí

Beyond Psykhró, you can complete a circuit of the plateau on a far less travelled road via the villages of Pláti, with its many tapestry sellers, Áyios Harálambos and Káto Metóhi, to meet with the direct route back to the coast at Pinakianó. Between Káto Metóhi and Pinakianó is the **Moní Vidianí**, one of whose restored buildings houses the tiny **Natural History Museum of Dhíkti** (aka Bearded Vulture Information Centre; charge). Though not wildly inspiring, the informative display, well labelled in English, covers local fauna, concentrating especially on the lammergeier or bearded vulture, with many stuffed specimens. There's also a peaceful café and shop selling local olive oil as well as icons painted at Vidhianí monastery.

ARRIVAL AND GETTING AROUND — THE LASÍTHI PLATEAU

By car The quickest and easiest routes up to the plateau are from the north and northwest, from Mália and Hersónissos (see page 98). The approach from Neápoli is far slower – a tortuous 30km climb, first south and then west into the mountains that ring the sunken plateau. Once you do finally make it, you'll find a circular road linking the villages on the plateau's edge.

By bus There are no public buses to the plateau, though tours run from all parts of the island.

On foot Once on the plateau, you can easily walk through the fields from one village to another – the paths between Áyios Yeóryios and Káto Metóhi via Psykhró even form part of the E4 Pan-European walking route. Whichever route you choose the path is rarely direct, but it's easy enough to pick your way by the trails: crossing the whole plain, from Psykhró to Tzermiádho, takes 1hr 30min or less. More ambitiously, you can also hike up to the plateau, most directly from Kritsá in the east, or on the E4 path from Kastélli to the north. A good time to take a walk here is the early evening, when you'll encounter the villagers on their carts, donkeys and pick-ups making their way back home.

ACCOMMODATION AND EATING

TZERMIÁDHO

★ **Kronio** Village centre, http://kronio.eu. Traditional Cretan dishes come with a French twist here, thanks to the proprietor's Gallic wife. It's very good value – if you're hungry and in no hurry, try the meze menu, with eighteen meze dishes, main course, wine and dessert for two. They also rent classy modern rooms and apartments with pool in Marmakéto, very nearby. €

ÁYIOS KONSTANDÍNOS

★ **Taverna Vilaeti** On the main street, www.vilaeti.gr. A beautifully restored old stone building, much more elegant

CLIMBING MOUNT DHÍKTI

A former guardian of the Dhiktean Cave, the genial Petros Zervakis leads regular ascents (May–Sept) of **Mount Dhíkti** (**Δίκτι**), which include an overnight stay at a refuge, supper under the stars and a 5am start for the summit. It's not a terribly difficult climb, but you'll need stout walking boots or shoes and a sleeping bag. The cost (around €50 per person) depends on the number of people in the group; Petros also organizes hikes to spot wildflowers (mid-April to mid-June) and birds (April–Sept). For details, ring or call in at his family's taverna *Petros*, facing the cave car park (6972 442 293 or 28440 31316).

MINOANS ALIVE AND WELL ON THE LASÍTHI PLATEAU

A genetic study carried out in 2013 into the **origins of the Minoan civilization** has gone a long way to undermining Sir Arthur Evans' belief that the Minoans had a north African or Nile delta origin. The study – by a team from Greek and US universities – compared the **DNA** of four-thousand-year-old ancient Minoan skeletons buried in a cave ossuary near to the village of Áyios Harálambos with those of the modern inhabitants of the Lasíthi plateau and Crete, as well as north Africa and other parts of Europe. The results of the genetic analysis showed little connection with African populations and a remarkably strong affinity with **modern Cretans**, particularly those living on the Lasíthi plateau. This may in part be due to the plateau's isolation (the first road did not arrive here until the 1970s), and the use of the heights above the plateau as a refuge by late Minoan groups fleeing the Dorian invasions (see page 357). Researchers also found that the skeletons were similar to those of modern-day Cretans, suggesting that the Minoans would have been similar in build and body size to today's islanders.

Evans believed the civilization had been introduced by a group that had migrated from a superior culture elsewhere, most likely Egypt; the new research, however, seems to suggest that the Minoans were descended from Neolithic populations that migrated to Europe from the Middle East and Anatolia, and created what we now call Minoan civilization once established on the island.

than you'd expect in this setting, serving exceptionally good traditional food (most of it local and organic) at standard prices. €€

Vilaeti Traditional Guesthouses Information at Taverna Vilaeti on the main street, www.vilaeti.gr. Lovely, fully equipped restored village apartments and stone-built cottages, all with fireplaces for winter and full kitchens with the basics supplied. Larger cottages sleep up to seven. Two-night minimum; superb breakfast included. €

ÁYIOS YEÓRYIOS

Hotel Maria Hidden away in the backstreets; information at Hotel Rea on the main street, run by the same family, 28440 31774. A sweet, old-fashioned place with framed embroidery on the walls and tiny bathrooms. Some of the double beds are on the Lilliputian side too – they also have three- and four-bed rooms. €

PSYKHRÓ

Stavros Taverna centre of the village, 28440 31497. Friendly and economical taverna serving traditional Cretan staples and grills with produce from the family farm. Also open for breakfast. €

Taverna Dionysos Magoulás, around 1km east of Psykhró, 28440 31672. Roadside taverna offering quiet rooms with balconies (a couple at the back have a great view over the plain) and good traditional food using local produce. €

Taverna Halavro Above the Dhiktean Cave car park, 28440 31402. Better than you'd expect, considering the captive audience, providing fresh juices and snacks for cave visitors, as well as meze, and lamb or pork roasted in a wood oven. €

Kritsá and around

The "traditional" village of **Kritsá**, 9km inland of Áyios Nikólaos, is a popular destination for tour buses and day-trippers. Despite some commercialization this is a trip well worth making, offering as it does a break from the frenetic pace of the coast; buses run frequently from the main station in Áyios Nikólaos. Easily included in a trip up here are the remarkable church of **Panayía Kerá** and the ancient site of **Lató**, both of which are worthwhile sights in their own right.

Panayía Kerá

About 1km before Kritsá on the Áyios Nikólaos road • Charge

Inside the lovely Byzantine church of **PANAYÍA KERÁ** (**Παναγία Κερά**) is preserved perhaps the most complete and certainly the most famous set of **Byzantine frescoes** in Crete.

The frescoes were applied in stages between the mid-13th and early 14th centuries. They are distinguished by their vivid facial expressions, rich colours and garments, plus the presence of many rarely depicted scenes from the Apocryphal Gospels. More canonical scenes in and above the central aisle include the Nativity, Herod's Massacre of the Innocents, the Presentation of Christ to Simeon, the Baptism complete with water creatures in the Jordan River, the Last Supper with Judas reaching for the fish of the believers, the Ascension and Paradise including the Good Thief. They're originally from the fourteenth and early fifteenth centuries, though all have been retouched and restored to such an extent that they're impossible to date accurately. Those in the **south aisle**, through which you enter, depict the life of Anne, mother of Mary – her marriage to Joachim and the birth of Mary – and the early life of Mary herself up to the journey to Bethlehem. In the **centre** of the church, the oldest part, dating originally from the twelfth century, Mary's story is continued and there are scenes from the life of Christ, including the Nativity, Herod's banquet and a superb Last Supper. And in the **north aisle** there are vivid depictions of the Second Coming and Judgement, along with the delights of Paradise and assorted interludes from the lives of the saints (especially St Anthony). Throughout, the major scenes are interspersed with small portraits of saints and apostles. After years of prohibition, photography without flash is now allowed inside the church.

Lató

4km north of Kritsá • Charge • 28410 22462

On the outskirts of Kritsá a lovely rural drive takes you to the archeological site of **LATÓ** (**Λατώ**). The city, originally Doric, flourished through to Classical times but its ruins are little visited, presumably because visitors and archeologists on Crete are more concerned with the Minoan era. That it was an important place is clear from the sheer extent of the ruins, which spread in every direction. It is also a magnificent setting, sprawled across the saddle between the twin peaks of a dauntingly craggy hill. Standing on the southernmost peak you get magnificent views down onto the white cluster of **Áyios Nikólaos** (Lató's ancient port), with the gulf and Oloús (a major rival of Lató in its heyday) beyond, as well as inland to the valleys and peaks of the Dhiktean mountains.

The site

You enter the site 200m or so below the ruins, following a rough path up to a rectangular area with a **gateway**, which would have been the city's original entrance. Continuing to climb up the street from here, you can see stores and workshops abutting the city wall on the right, with defensive towers and gateways into residential areas on the left. Higher up still, the pentagonal space of the **agora** was a meeting place

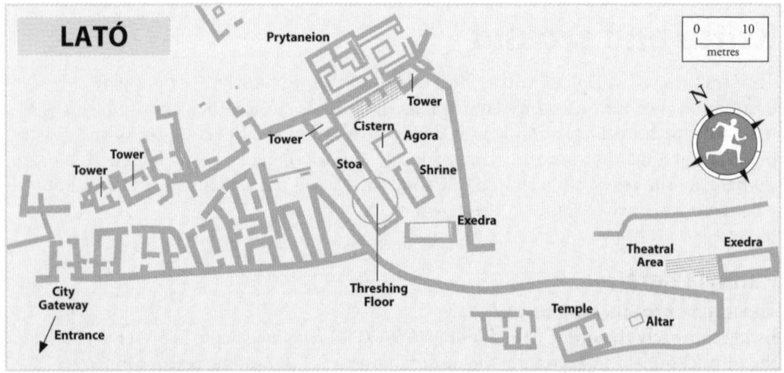

THE KATHARÓ PLAIN

If you have a couple of hours to spare, take the magnificent drive up to the **Katharó plain** (**Καθαρό**), 16km above Kritsá. From the top of the village, a winding asphalt road ascends steeply through woods of holm oaks where the air soon becomes crisper, even in summer. There are plenty of potential picnic spots, and roadside boards display maps of the various areas, some marking the routes of amazingly well-preserved Minoan trading paths, no doubt used to access the plateau in ancient times. When you finally reach the plain – a fertile upland similar to Lasíthi (see page 142), though far smaller, less intensely cultivated or visited and, at 1150m, some 300m higher – you will find a few scattered dwellings occupied in summer by farmers and shepherds.

INFORMATION AND TOURS

On the Katharó plain itself, the unexpected and welcome **Kafeníon Zervas** (open all year except when snowed in, daily 9am–8pm, 28410 22478) run by the amiable Yiannis Siganos, an expert on all aspects of the plateau, displays photographs of the plateau's flora and fauna, as well as information about the fossils of large mammals found here: 500,000 years ago this was apparently the preserve of hippos and elephants.

The plateau's **flowers**, including spectacular orchids, are exceptional; local expert Steve Lenton conducts **guided walks** to look at them, also taking in local wildlife, history, geology and paleontology (March–Nov pre-booked only; https://exploring-katharo.com).

2

for citizens that incorporates a tier of steps on its northern side, reminiscent of the theatral areas at Minoan sites such as Knossós and Festós. The steps ascend between the remains of two towers to the **prytaneion**, or council hall, with small rooms at the rear that held the city's archives. In the centre of the agora are a deep square cistern and a shrine, flanked on the western side by a colonnaded **stoa**, a shady place to shelter from the elements. The southern end of this has been cut through by a relatively modern circular threshing floor. The **exedra** nearby was a sort of public seating area, and in the southeast corner of the site is another exedra and a further broad flight of steps in the Minoan style, here officially dubbed the "Theatral Area". This leads to a raised terrace containing a well-preserved fourth-century BC temple.

Kritsá

KRITSÁ (**Κριτσά**), known as "the largest village in Crete", actually feels more like a small town, its main street lined with tourist stores selling local weaving, ceramics, carved olive wood, leather goods and embroidery. It enjoys a splendid **setting**, with views back over the green valley up which you arrived and the mountains rising steeply behind. You get little impression of this at street level, other than an awareness that you are climbing quite steeply, so try to get out onto one of the balconies or roof terraces of the *kafenía* and tavernas along the main street, from where you can look back over the town and towards Áyios Nikólaos. The more attractive part of the village is the upper half, beyond the square; this is also where you'll find the bulk of the better shops.

ARRIVAL AND DEPARTURE — KRITSÁ AND AROUND

By bus Buses from Áyios Nikólaos to Kritsá (8 daily Mon–Fri, 4 daily Sat & Sun; 15min) terminate in the village square (they also drop off and pick up outside Panayía Kerá) and immediately turn round for the return journey.

By car If you arrive by car, use the signposted car park on the way into the village, as there's no chance of finding a parking place in the narrow streets.

ACCOMMODATION

Argyro Main road as you enter Kritsá, www.argyrorooms.com. Clean, pleasant and economical rooms with balconies, many with views across the olive-tree-lined valley. The small courtyard café serves an excellent breakfast (extra). €

East of Áyios Nikólaos: the isthmus

The main road south and then east from Áyios Nikólaos is not wildly exciting – a drive through barren hills dotted with new developments and villas above the occasional sandy cove – though in places the engineering of the new road is breathtaking. Beyond the reed-fringed beaches at Almyrós and Amoudhára (with watersports and giant inflatables) there's little temptation to stop until you reach the cluster of increasing development around **Ístro**, 10km south of Áyios Nikólaos, which has tavernas and minimarkets, and paths winding steeply down to a couple of excellent small **beaches**. Inland from here lies the pretty village of **Kaló Hório**, from where scenic mountain roads head south, while just beyond lies the turn-off to the isolated hilltop **Moní Faneroméni**. Continuing east along the coast, you pass the remarkable Minoan site at **Gourniá**. Just beyond, the main road south across the isthmus towards Ierápetra turns off, allowing detours to another important early Minoan site at **Vasilikí** and to the ancient village of **Episkopí**, with its splendid Byzantine church.

2

Ístro and around

ÍSTRO (**Ίστρο**), a strip of development along the road, offers scattered accommodation and superb **beaches**: follow the signs from town to Voúlisma – sandy, beautiful, but very crowded in summer – or Áyios Pandelímon, down a variety of dusty tracks, which is slightly less spectacular, but bigger and much less crowded. Both have beach bar/cafés.

Moní Faneroméni

5km east of Ístro, take the signed exit on the left; the route, asphalted in its early stages, later a track, climbs dizzily inland for 6km

It's a bit of an effort to get to **MONÍ FANEROMÉNI** (**Μονή Φανερωμένη**), but the **view** when you finally arrive must be among the finest on Crete. To get into the rather bleak-looking monastery buildings (free), knock loudly. When you gain entry you will be shown (by one of the monks currently in residence) up to the **chapel**, built into a cave sanctuary where a sacred icon of the Panayía n was miraculously discovered – the reason for the foundation of the monastery in the fifteenth century. The **frescoes**, although seventeenth-century and thus quite late, are impressive – especially that of the *Panayía Theotókou*, the Mother of God.

Gourniá

20km east of Áyios Nikólaos; a hazardous turning off the E75 onto a dirt track • Charge • 28420 93028

VIEWS FROM THE MOUNTAIN ROUTE SOUTH

An alternative route to the south coast, or simply a wonderfully scenic drive from the coast, leads inland from Ístro, via **Kaló Hório**. From Kaló Hório the road starts to climb seriously, and at **Prína** there are a couple of fine old **churches**: Metamorfósi on the main square is nineteenth-century, but incorporates much older features, including a fine fresco, while Áyios Yeóryios dates from the fourteenth century, with frescoes almost as old inside. From Prína you can head straight for Ierapétra, but a far more spectacular route leads southwest towards **Kalamáfka**, a wealthy and historic village, full of running water, and with plenty of tavernas frequented by visiting locals. They visit for two reasons: the cave-**chapel of Tímios Stavrós**, 224 steep steps above the village, which houses a miraculous icon, and the **views**, which if you find the right spot are said to take in both coasts simultaneously. From here you can simply turn round and head back, or a rather easier road continues to the south coast, past a scenic reservoir (great for birdwatching) at **Bramianá**.

GOURNIÁ (Γουρνιά), slumped in the saddle between two low peaks on a dusty track by the highway, is the most completely preserved **Minoan town** in Crete, and in its small scale contains important clues about the lives of ordinary people and the nature of the communities from which the Minoan palaces evolved. A look at the map tells you much about ancient Gourniá's strategic importance, controlling the narrow isthmus and the relatively easy communication this gave with the southern seaboard at modern Ierápetra. The overland route avoided a hazardous sea voyage around the eastern cape – a crucial factor in ancient times, especially in winter when sailing usually stopped because of rough seas.

As you leave Gourniá, it's tempting to cross the highway and take one of the paths north through the wild thyme to the sea for a swim. Don't bother – this seemingly innocent little bay acts as a magnet for every piece of floating detritus dumped off Crete's north coast. Do be sure to look back at the site, though; as the E75 climbs the hill opposite, its street plan is laid out like a map.

Brief history

There is evidence of occupation at Gourniá as early as the third millennium BC, but the remains you see today are those of a town of the **Neopalatial** period (c.1500 BC). Around 1450 BC, as happened elsewhere, the town was destroyed by fire. Limited rebuilding occurred during the era of **Mycenaean** rule at Knossós – and the shrine may date from this late period – but the site was soon abandoned again and disappeared beneath the soil where it lay unsuspected until the awakening of archeological interest in the nineteenth century. Arthur Evans, as usual, was the first to scent Minoan occupation of this area, and then a young American, Harriet Boyd-Hawes, started digging in 1901. The site, a budding archeologist's dream, made her reputation.

The site

Gourniá's narrow, cobbled alleys and stairways – built for pack animals rather than carts – intersect a throng of one-roomed houses centred on a main square and the house of a local ruler or, more likely, governor. The settlement is not a large place, nor impressive by comparison with the palaces at Knossós and elsewhere, but it must have been at least as luxurious as the average Cretan mountain village of as little as fifty years ago. Its desolation today only serves to heighten the contrast with what must have been a cramped and raucous community 3500 years ago; bear in mind that the fenced site occupies only part of the original town, which would have stretched all the way to the sea and a small harbour.

Among the dwellings to the north and east of the site are some that have been clearly identified, by tools or materials discovered, as the homes of **craftspeople**: a carpenter, a smith and a potter. It's easy to imagine a cramped and raucous community here three and a half thousand years ago, though worth remembering that the rooms may not have been as small as they appear – many of them are in fact basements or semi-basements reached by stairs from the main rooms above, and the floor plans of those did not necessarily correspond with what you see today. The houses themselves were mainly built of stone on the lower courses and mud-brick above, with plaster-daubed reeds for roofing, the latter a building technique still used in modern Greek island construction.

The Palace and shrine

The **palace** (or governor's quarters) occupied the highest ground, to the north of a courtyard containing a familiar L-shaped stairway. With a smaller court at its heart, the whole is a copy in miniature of the palaces at Knossós and Festós. About 20m to the north of the palace, a **shrine** was discovered. It is easily identified by the sloping approach path paved with an intricate pattern of evenly matched cobbles, and the shrine itself, up three steps, is a small room with a ledge for cult objects. Here, a number of terracotta goddesses with arms raised were unearthed, as well as snake totems and other cult objects, now on display in the Iráklio Archeological Museum.

Pahiá Ámmos and around

PAHIÁ ÁMMOS (**Παχειά Άμμος**), a rather windswept little place 2km east of Gourniá, makes for a good lunch or coffee stop, with a string of waterfront tavernas. There's a grey, pebbly beach, protected by a floating boom from the worst of the plastic rubbish that blights this stretch of coast. To the south, a fast road heads across the narrowest part of the island towards Ierápetra, with the awesome slopes of the Thriptís range bearing down from the east.

Vasilikí

3km south of Pahiá Ámmos • Free

The Prepalatial settlement of **VASILIKÍ** (**Βασιλική**) dates from about 2650 to 2200 BC. The site may not be much to look at, but it's vitally important for the light that it sheds upon the hazy millennium preceding the period of Minoan greatness. Remains from this period occur at Knossós and other palaces but cannot be properly excavated because of the important buildings constructed on top of them: Vasilikí was found in pristine condition, having being abandoned after a fire around 2200 BC. The **pottery** known as Vasilikí ware – ochre or red with dark, blotchy decoration – is named after this site, where some fine examples on display in the archeological museums at Iráklio and Áyios Nikólaos were discovered.

The site contains two main buildings, originally surrounded by numerous smaller (and simpler) dwellings. The remains of the edifice nearest to the entrance, on the lower slope of the hill, are slightly earlier than those on the crown. The **Red House**, as the former is named, has a number of interesting features. It is oriented with its corners towards the cardinal points of the compass, a practice normal in Mesopotamia and the Near East but alien to Egypt and the Aegean (and thus possibly a clue to Minoan origins). In the southern corner, deep basement rooms allow you to gain an idea of early Minoan building techniques: holes to support the absent wooden beams are visible as well as large patches of hard, red lime plaster, the forerunner of what later artists were to use as the ideal background for the wonderful palace frescoes. On the southern flank of the Red House, excavations have revealed a bath, a stretch of roadway, more dwellings and quite a few hand-grindstones.

If you continue on up the lane into the **village** of Vasilikí, you'll find a friendly bar and a glimpse of traditional rural Crete well off the tourist trail.

Episkopí

Almost exactly halfway across the isthmus, **EPISKOPÍ** (**Επισκοπή**) makes a worthwhile diversion. Below the road, beside a raised platía where old men play *távli* in the shade of lofty eucalyptus trees, lies a charming **Byzantine church** dedicated to Áyios Yeóryios and Áyios Harálambos. The arched drum dome with elaborate blue-tile decoration, together with an unusual ground plan, make this church unique on the island. You may not be able to get in, but in any case it's the church's restored exterior that gives it its standing in Byzantine architecture.

The road to Sitía

The tawny bulk of the Ornó range of the Sitía mountains makes a formidable barrier to progress beyond the isthmus, and the road at first is carved into the cliff face, teetering perilously above the gulf. There's just one resort of any significance, at **Mókhlos**. Beyond here, lined in summer with a riot of pink and white oleander flowers, the road runs mostly a little further from the coast, toiling through villages clinging to the mountainside until the final approach to Sitía and a descent in great loops through softer hills. As you progress, the familiar olive groves are increasingly interspersed with **vineyards**, and there are some highly regarded local wines to be had in the village cafés, especially in **Mésa Mouliana** and its neighbour **Éxo Mouliana**. Most of the grapes, however, go to make sultanas; in late summer, when they are laid out to dry in the fields and on rooftops all around, the various stages of their slow change from green to gold to brown make a compelling spectacle.

Kavoúsi

KAVOÚSI (**Καβούσι**), less than 6km from Pahiá Ámmos yet already high above the coast, is a pleasant village with Byzantine churches and a main street lined with oleanders and mulberry trees; at the far end of the village a map shows walks to various nearby places of interest, including a Minoan farmhouse and a vast, ancient olive tree. Many of the tempting **beaches** visible from on high are inaccessible, but **Thólos** – a quiet pebble-and-sand beach backed by tamarisk trees and a chapel, 3km below the village – can be reached by a good paved road; there's a good taverna here too.

Plátanos

As you travel east, the views back across the Gulf of Mirabéllo become more expansive all the time, until at **PLÁTANOS** (**Πλάτανος**), some 6km from Kavoúsi, you reach a famous viewpoint, with a couple of tavernas – *Panorama* and *Pixida* – where you can look down on the island of Psíra or west across the gulf to Áyios Nikólaos, which is especially spectacular at sunset.

Mókhlos

MÓKHLOS (**Μόχλος**) lies way below the main road via 5km or more of dusty hairpin bends, but in a sleepy way it's a surprisingly developed spot. Small as it is, almost every house seems to advertise rooms for rent, and there are at least half a dozen good tavernas, and as many cafés. The whole place, in fact, is much fancier and more

PSÍRA

The island of **Psíra** (**Ψείρα**), in the Gulf of Mirabéllo west of Mókhlos, like Mókhlos, was first excavated in 1907 by an American, Richard Seager, who revealed a Minoan port, occupied from the early Minoan era, with the remains of a town a little like Gourniá built amphitheatrically around a natural harbour. In one of a number of substantial dwellings – many containing hearths and with walls still standing up to 2m high in places – a fine relief **fresco** was found depicting female figures wearing richly embroidered dresses, the only known example outside Knossós.

No palaces or obvious public buildings were discovered, but the site did produce rich finds of **painted pottery**. One jar, now on display in the Iráklio Archeological Museum, is noted for its decoration of bulls' heads interspersed with the double-axe symbol. The remains of what is thought to be an ancient **well** have also been found, although the island is completely dry these days; even in ancient times, the islanders must have been heavily dependent on trade, with mainland Crete and further afield. The site was another of those destroyed about 1450 BC, though the **Romans** later used the island for strategic and navigational purposes, and the remains of their **lighthouse** and military settlement survive on the island's crown. Very few people visit, but it is possible to come here in a private boat, or on a trip from Thólos beach (see page 169).

upmarket than you might expect, which is largely due to the presence of Minoan sites on two offshore **islets**. Not only do these attract tourists, but also American and Greek archeological teams, who often spend whole summers here.

There's not a great deal to do in Mókhlos – swim out to the islet from the rocky foreshore or hang out in the cafés – but it's a place where it's very easy not to do a great deal.

Mókhlos islet

Unrestricted access • http://mochlosarchaeologicalproject.org

When the weather is calm it's a reasonably easy swim across to the **islet of Mókhlos** – plenty of people do it – or you can arrange a ride across (see page 155). This barren rock, inhabited from the Prepalatial period, was in Minoan times almost certainly a much less barren peninsula, and the sandy spit linking it to the mainland would have been used as a harbour (anchorages which could be approached from either side were a great advantage for boats that could sail only before the wind). You can see remains of **late Minoan houses** on the south side of the island, and there are more below the current sea level where recent excavations have also identified remnants of the ancient harbour. But the important discoveries at Mókhlos were in the much more ancient **tombs** built up against the cliff. Here, very early seal stones were found (including one from Mesopotamia), as well as some spectacular gold jewellery now in the Iráklio Archeological Museum and a fine collection of marble, steatite and rock-crystal vases on display in the Áyios Nikólaos and Sitía archeological museums.

Myrsíni

MYRSÍNI (**Μυρσίνι**) is a resolutely traditional village whose attractive church is built around, and entirely encloses, a frescoed fourteenth-century chapel – fascinating, but you'll need to find the priest if you want to look inside; ask at the *Taverna Kathodon* (see page 156).

Hamézi and around

The sleepy village of **HAMÉZI** (**Χαμέζι**) spreads uphill to the north of the road some 10km west of Sitía. In the narrow streets (don't try to bring a car up here) plants are festooned over buildings and down whitewashed steps. The local **folk museum** (charge, 28430 29243) is worth a visit for its collection of ancient farm implements and rooms filled with furniture and utensils from the nineteenth century. To get there, walk up the main street, passing the brilliant-white **church**, and turn left up a charming stepped street. For the path through the Áyii Pándes Gorge (see page 155), ask for directions locally.

Hamézi Minoan House

1.5km west of Hamézi village, near the ruined stone windmills on the final crest before the Bay of Sitía, a track on the right is signed "Middle Minoan House"; follow this winding track (driveable, or about a 15min walk), keeping right at a restored windmill, to the site • Unfenced • Free

The grey-stone **Minoan house** at Hamézi, dating from the Prepalatial period (c.2000 BC), is the only known Minoan structure to have had an oval ground plan, possibly dictated by the conical shape of the hill. It was thought at first to be a peak sanctuary, but the discovery of a **cistern** made a dwelling, or even a fortress, seem more likely. The ground plan sketched out by the walls – remaining more than 1m high in places – consists of a number of rooms grouped around a central courtyard, where the cistern is located. A paved entrance is visible on the south side. Whatever the building's function, it certainly had a commanding view over the surrounding terrain from its spectacular hilltop setting. While you're taking this in, keep an eye out for the rare **Eleonora's**

falcon that breeds on the offshore island of Paximádha – the valley to the east is one of its favourite hunting grounds.

Moní Faneroméni

About 6km west of Sitía, immediately east of the village of Skopí, a track heads north towards the **MONÍ FANEROMÉNI** (**Μονή Φανερωμένη**). This partly asphalted 5km road leads, via some alarming hairpin bends, to a picturesque rocky cove lapped by a turquoise sea. From the cove, the track climbs inland to the monastery. If you're coming from Sitía, you can join this route by following the signs down a narrow lane shortly after you leave the town.

The charming **monastic church** stands at the heart of a tiny, isolated community, built into the rock on the very lip of a gorge. Standing as a metaphor for recent Cretan history, the church has been battered but still stands unbowed. In 1829, monastery and church were looted and burned by the local Muslims, and most of the frescoes destroyed. They're now blackened and graffitied, but the beauty of what was lost can be glimpsed in one remaining fragment, depicting a saint reading. Behind the church, shoals of silver *taxímata* (ex votos), hung on the icon of the Panayía in a small cave, attest to the continuing importance of the shrine.

ARRIVAL AND INFORMATION — THE ROAD TO SITÍA

By bus If you're hoping to get to Mókhlos by bus, be warned that you'll be dropped on the main road, a full hour's walk above the village (and a sweaty slog back up); there's a good chance of getting a lift, however. Seven daily buses from Áyios Nikólaos (1hr) bound for Sitía pass the entry road.

Tourist information is an informative local website.

ACTIVITIES AND TOURS

Boat trips Mochlos Boat Tours – a rather grand name for one tiny fishing boat – takes people to and from the islet for €5 per person. The boat and captain are usually in Mókhlos harbour; if not ask at one of the nearby tavernas. From Thólos beach, the Ferryman (6976 805 913) is a traditional fishing boat that runs various enjoyable day-trips, notably to the island of Psíra.

Walks and tours Anne le Brun and Yannis Petrakis (6976 313 506 or 6945 578 257, http://kastelas.com) run botanical guided walks in the vicinity (from €15–25 including lunch), as well as trail bike and 4WD tours (from €75/day); they also have accommodation.

ACCOMMODATION

KAVOÚSI

Tholos Rooms Halfway down the Thólos road, 1.5km from Kavoúsi, http://tholos-rooms.gr. There are several rooms places on the main road in Kavoúsi proper, but this modern block with simple, good-value rooms offers peaceful nights, isolated in the middle of nowhere. There's a decent restaurant, too, where you can get breakfast. €

MÓKHLOS

Blue Sea Coast road, less than 1km east of the village, https://blueseamochlos.com. Sparkling rooms and apartments with fridge, satellite TV and balcony overlooking the sea and small pool, with pool bar (open to non-guests). Peaceful location, friendly, family welcome, and an excellent breakfast available (extra). €

★ **Limenaria** On a rise overlooking the new harbour, 600m west of town, http://mochlos-crete.gr. A tranquil hideaway in flower-filled gardens with four attractive, fully equipped sea-view terrace apartments sleeping up to four; big balconies front and back allow you to appreciate the view. €

HIKES AROUND HAMÉZI AND MONÍ FANEROMÉNI

There are a number of attractive **hiking** possibilities in the area around Moní Faneroméni. A well-marked path leads from the coast (there's a parking area by the road), up the Áyios Pándes Gorge beneath the monastery, and eventually to Hamézi, from where you should be able to get a bus back to Sitía. You can also walk to Sitía in 2–3hr, or walk the whole way from Hamézi, via the gorge, to Sitía.

Meltemi By the road as you enter the village, 28430 94200. Attractive studios with kitchenette and sea view just above the village. The same owner has a couple of wonderful apartments right on the harbour, with full, modern kitchens (including washing machine) and big balconies looking over the action; get information at *Taverna Bogazi*. €

Mochlos Hotel Set back from the waterfront in the heart of the village, 28430 94240. Long-established, three-storey hotel with rooms, studios and a two-room apartment, most of which have had a complete refurb; a few simpler, older rooms are also available. There's also a charming plant-filled patio for breakfast or late-night drinks. €€

Mochlos Mare Coast road 500m east of the village, http://mochlos-mare.com. Peaceful, well-equipped one- and two-bedroom apartments with kitchen for up to six people, set back from the road in the midst of the owner's lovingly tended kitchen garden. There's a separate lounging area above the sea. €

Sofia On the harbour, 28430 94554. This friendly hotel has simple rooms with fridge, TV and sea views from the balcony, and is situated above a harbourfont taverna; they also rent studios and apartments nearby. €

To Kyma Beyond the harbour, 28430 94177. A purpose-built block of modern, good-value studios with kitchen, satellite TV and balcony, just round the corner from the harbour. Ask at Minimarket Anna, next door, for information. €

EATING AND DRINKING

MÓKHLOS

Food is excellent at almost all of Mókhlos' tavernas. Many places feature *ahinosálata*, something of an acquired taste, made from the roe of the sea urchins that flourish in the clear, unpolluted water here (most people wear plastic shoes or flippers, sold at the local minimarkets, when they swim).

★ **Mesostrati** On the harbour, 28430 94170. Traditional Cretan cuisine from family recipes, as well as fresh fish, served on a pretty seaside terrace; also good breakfasts and a weekly Cretan cooking demonstration Wed at 5pm. €

The Rocks Waterfront, east end of harbour, 6977 675 076. There's little in the way of nightlife in Mókhlos, but this easy-going cocktail and snacks bar-café is a prime spot for a sundowner on the terrace.

Ta Kohylia Mochlos, 2843 094432. *Ta Kohylia* is the oldest (founded 1902) establishment here, offering consistent quality and value, as well as being polite (unlike some of its pushy neighbours). A rather full menu features fresh artichokes in spring, little fishes, stews and daily changing *piáta iméras* (specials). €

★ **To Bogazi** On the harbour, 28430 94200. With an unbeatable seafront position, *To Bogazi* is run by a Greek-Swiss couple; the shortish menu, heavy on fish (caught by the taverna's fisherman, Stavros), includes interesting "specials" such as rabbit in wine, grilled octopus and a delicious *skoumbrí* (grilled mackerel). The mezédhes list has plenty of vegetarian options and the barrel wine is from noted Pezá grower Lyrarakis. There's live music Thurs & Sun evenings in summer. €€

MYRSÍNI

Taverna Kathodon Immediately above the road in Myrsíni, 28430 94766. A classic Cretan taverna whose menu has everything from snails and *souvláki* to burgers and baked aubergine, plus – on the mezédhes menu – a tasty *fáva*. Food is served on a terrace with stunning views across the coast – down to Mókhlos and out across the Gulf – where there are also tremendous sunsets. €€

Sitía and around

After the excesses of Mália or Áyios Nikólaos, arriving in **SITÍA** (**Σητεία**) can seem somewhat anticlimactic. But allow yourself to adjust to the more leisurely pace of life here and you may, like many other visitors before you, end up staying much longer than intended. An ideal base from which to visit the local attractions, Sitía hasn't entirely escaped the tourist boom; many of the visitors are French or Italian (as they are, in fact, throughout the far east of Crete), a legacy perhaps of the French troops who garrisoned the place under the Great Power protection at the end of the nineteenth century, and the Italians who occupied it during World War II.

The town is set on a hill tumbling down towards the western end of the picturesque **Bay of Sitía**. Its oldest sections, hanging steeply above the harbour, look east over the bay and the ribbon of newer development along the coast. For visitors, life concentrates on the **waterfront**. A seafront promenade crowded with the outdoor tables of rival tavernas and cafés spreads in either direction from Platía Iróon Polytehníou, in the corner of the bay; northeast towards the port and ferry dock, south towards the town beach. The narrow streets behind the seafront feature the everyday scenes of a Cretan provincial town: villagers stocking up on news and necessities, and stores catering to their every conceivable need, from steel drums to wooden saddles, seed to pick-up trucks.

Brief history

This area was settled, as Eteia, in Classical times, but may be identified with the **Minoan** *se-to-i-ja* inscribed on clay tablets found locally. That there was a substantial Minoan presence hereabouts is borne out by the excavations at **Petrás** (see page 159),

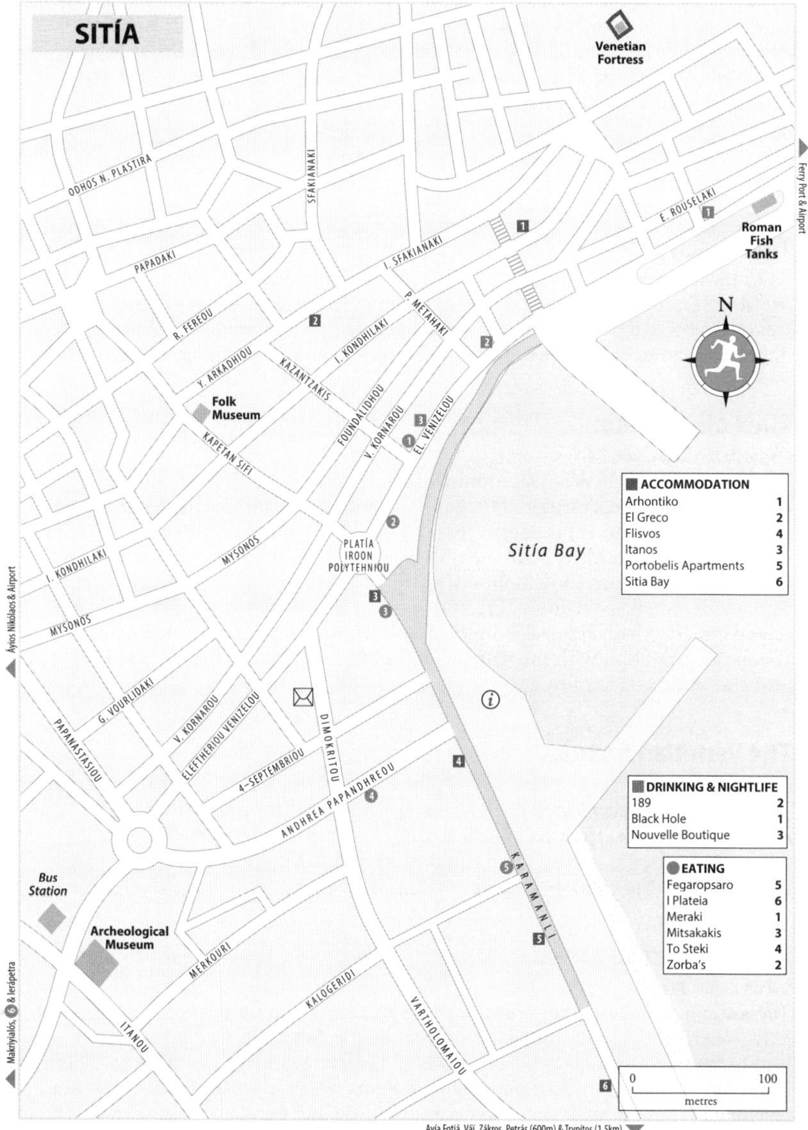

the town's southern suburb, where a settlement dating to the early second millennium BC has been unearthed and where, in the later Neopalatial period, there is evidence for what is believed to be a palace as well as a town with sophisticated buildings and roads. A couple of **Minoan villas** have also been excavated immediately south of the city (see page 160). Knowledge of the subsequent Greek and Roman settlements is sketchy, although a substantial chunk of **Hellenistic Sitía** has recently been discovered on the outskirts (see page 160). Apart from some tombs and fish tanks (now incorporated into an artificial pond on the harbour promenade), little tangible survives from the **Roman** town.

2

It was under the **Venetians** that the port really took off (they called it *La Sitia* – hence Lasíthi), as part of a conscious attempt to exploit the east of the island. For all their efforts, the area remained cut off by land from the rest of Crete and, although what was in effect a separate fiefdom developed here, it never amounted to a great deal. Perhaps the most significant event of this era was the birth of Vitzentzos Kornaros, author of the epic Cretan poem, the *Erotókritos*. More physical remains are few, due to earthquakes and the raids of **Barbarossa**. Where once there was a walled city, now you'll find only the barest remains of a fortress.

The beach

Sitía's **town beach** is surprisingly excellent; sandy, with beautifully clear water, and stretching far into the distance southeast of town. In summer the heat eventually seems to draw half the town's population down here by late afternoon, but it's never unbearably crowded, and there's room to escape if you walk far enough along.

The Folk Museum

Kápetan Sífi 28 • Charge • 28430 23917

The **Folk Museum** offers an entertaining look at traditional life, with displays of antique furniture, costumes, kitchenware and ceramics from the region, and above all textiles and embroidery. There's a working loom on which museum staff demonstrate; the finished items are on sale in the little shop. Another fascinating feature is a reconstructed schoolroom using desks and furniture acquired from a number of old village schools. The end result is disturbingly reminiscent of the school attended by Kazantzákis in the 1880s, to which his father (in *Report to Greco*) delivered him with the words "His bones are mine, his flesh is yours. Thrash him and make a man of him."

The Venetian fortress

On the hill above the harbour • Charge

The restored **Venetian fortress**, known as the Kazarma (from Casa di Arma) dominates the town from its hilltop setting. Now used as an open-air venue for concerts, theatre, lectures and exhibitions, it doesn't offer a great deal to see otherwise, but the views are superb.

The Roman fish tanks

Seafront, north of the centre

The seafront promenade north of the centre – heading towards the vast concrete ferry jetty – leads past the ruined remains of some **Roman fish tanks**: freshly caught fish were kept in these semicircular constructions until they were needed. The tanks have been incorporated into an artificial **pond** along the concrete promenade and are used as a preening perch by a resident colony of swans, ducks and geese.

The Archeological Museum

400m south of the centre on the Ierápetra road • Charge • 28430 23917

Eastern Crete is rich in ancient peak sanctuaries and Minoan villas or country houses. Many finds from these, as well as from the palace at Zákros and from excavations in and around Sitía itself, are gathered in Sitía's little-visited **Archeological Museum**, a modern building surrounded by construction and new development.

The museum's greatest treasure, the **Palékastro koúros**, is on display as you enter. This little male figure is an exquisitely delicate work dating from c.1500 BC, made from eight interlocking pieces of hippopotamus ivory; when complete it would have been decorated with a gold Minoan belt, bracelets and shoes. Note that the left leg is placed slightly forward, following the Egyptian convention for the portrayal of this form of statue.

Right from here – circling an atrium – the cases progress chronologically through the **Neolithic and Prepalatial periods**, including finds, such as jewellery and household goods, from cemeteries. Here also are a collection of seals found at the Petrás cemetery, some early ones made of hippopotamus ivory, and later ones made from agate, carnelian and jasper. Further cases display artefacts connected with peak sanctuaries and daily life, including a fascinating section on eating and drinking: look out for an oval-mouthed wine amphora from Mókhlos and terracotta grills used to prepare the ancient version of *souvláki*. In one excavated tripod pot were the remains of a hare stew (the bones of two hares were found inside as well as a lizard and sea snails); in the same pot was discovered a crystal lens that may have been used to start the fire.

A later case devoted to Minoan ritual and religion displays some intricate examples of Minoan painted decoration, depicting narcissus flowers, as well as the **Mókhlos pyxis**, an ivory jewellery case with a delicately carved representation of a Minoan goddess. There's also a case devoted to finds from a perfume workshop at Mókhlos and its intriguing production process, which involved using wool as a filter. Dotted around the museum are numerous painted Minoan burial chests, and great *píthoi* (earthenware jars) – many from the palace at Petrás – used for storage.

The **Protopalatial and Neopalatial** cases display tools from the palaces as well as weaving utensils and a set of weights conforming to a Minoan metric system. Later cases deal with the mysterious Linear A script, with inscribed clay tablets found at the Petrás and Zákros Minoan palaces. The visit concludes with the **Late Minoan and Eteocretan** periods, after which there is a small section devoted to **Hellenistic and Roman** Lasíthi.

Petrás Minoan Palace

Follow the Beach Road towards Vái–Tóplou for about 600m beyond the *Sitía Beach* hotel; the archeological site is about 500m up a road signed on the right • Charge

A little over a kilometre to the southeast of the centre are the remains of **Petrás (Πετράς) Minoan Palace**, which enjoys a typically beautiful setting on a low hill looking back over town. Excavations have been ongoing here since its discovery in 1985. The most important discovery is a palace structure – smaller in scale than the palaces at Zákros and Mália –built during the early second millennium BC. This building was destroyed by fire around 1700BC, along with many other Minoan palaces across the island, an event that ensured that the palace's hieroglyphic archive (written on clay tablets) was fired and preserved. The palace was subsequently rebuilt on a grander scale before suffering two further destructions, probably by natural causes, around 1500BC and in the mid-fourteenth century BC, when the palatial system collapsed. The palace seems to have served as an administrative, commercial and religious centre for the lands around the gulf of Sitía, and employed a large group of artisans producing stone vases, pottery and textiles. Many of the finds from the palace are displayed in Sitía's archeological museum (see page 159).

Access to the site is via a Venetian watchtower once owned by the sixteenth-century Cretan poet Vitzentzos Kornaros (see page 352). Information boards guide you around. The first structures are **House I and House II**, large two-storey Neopalatial buildings dating from the seventeenth century BC with typical Minoan architectural features such as light wells. The main **palace building** has many of the features associated with Minoan palaces elsewhere – central court, monumental staircase, complex drainage system, storage magazines, archives – but on a lesser scale. The **central court**, for instance, measures some 17.5m by 7.6m, less than half the area of the courts at Knossós, Festós or Mália. The court would have been enclosed on four sides with walls of fine ashlar masonry; as at other palaces these blocks bear masons' marks of double axes and stars. Excavation work continues both at the palace site and the remains of the town that once surrounded it.

Trypítos Hellenistic settlement

2km east of Sitía • Free • Off the main coast road, a signed track marked "Archeological Site" leads 100m to a farm building where you can park

The recently discovered remains of a **Hellenistic settlement**, at a site named **Trypítos**, dating from the third century BC and later, are substantial. Remains so far unearthed include easily identifiable ruins of dwellings, rooms and streets, and the remains of a remarkable 30m long "ship shed" with a sloping ramp for hauling ships ashore. Continuing excavations will no doubt add to these in the years ahead.

The Minoan graveyard

Ayía Fotiá, about 4km east of town: follow signs at the eastern edge of the village • Free

In 1971, the largest **Minoan graveyard** yet found in Crete was excavated, close to the sea on the edge of the village of Ayía Fotiá. More than 250 chamber tombs from the early Prepalatial period were revealed; among the outstanding finds of vases, fish hooks, daggers and stone axes (now in the Sitía and Áyios Nikólaos archeological museums) were a number of lead amulets, which suggests that these early Minoans regarded lead as a precious metal, as well as silver.

Piskokéfalo Minoan villa

Well signed 2km south of Sitía on the Ierápetra road • Free

Near the village of **Piskokéfalo**, the main road cuts straight through a **Minoan villa**. Dating from the late Neopalatial period (1550–1450 BC), it had two floors and is terraced into the hillside, with a well-preserved staircase giving access to an upper floor. The villa's view would have encompassed the river valley below the road, where its farmlands were probably located.

Zoú Minoan villa

6km south of Sitía • Unfenced • Free • From Piskokéfalo a road is signed to the village of Zoú; 2km before the village the Minoan villa (signed) lies on a high bank to the right of the road

The **Minoan villa** at Zoú, dating from the late Neopalatial period (1550–1450 BC), was excavated by Nikolaos Platon, the archeologist who unearthed the palace at Zákros. This one is more a farmhouse – cultivating the land in the valley to the east – than simply a country dwelling, with rooms that appear to have been divided between those for domestic life and others for work and storage of farm equipment. A pottery kiln (perhaps used for making olive-oil containers) was discovered in one room, while two deep pits near the entrance probably stored grain. On the south side there is a well preserved "L"-shaped bench.

ARRIVAL AND GETTING AROUND — SITÍA AND AROUND

By plane Sitía Airport (28430 24424, https://sitia-airport.gr) lies immediately north of town. There's no public transport, but it's a taxi ride of just 5min (less than €10). Although it is offficially an international one so far there's only the very occasional charter flight from northern Europe and none so far from the UK. Olympic (http://olympicair.com) flies to Athens (at least 6 weekly) and Thessaloníki; Sky Express (http://skyexpress.gr) to Alexandhroúpoli, , Kássos and Préveza (1–2 weekly).

By bus The bus station (28430 22272; timetables and online booking on http://ktelherlas.gr) is on the southwest fringe of the centre; head north along Odhós Venizélou to get into town. Most of the services below are restricted at weekends.

Destinations Ay. Nikólaos (6 daily; 1hr 45min); Ierápetra (4 daily; 1hr 30min); Iráklio (6 daily; 3hr 15min); Makríyialos (4 daily; 1hr); Palékastro (3 daily; 30min); Vái (3 daily in summer; 30min); Zákros (2 daily; 45min).

By ferry The ferry dock is 500m northeast of the centre. Just one ferry currently calls at Sitía, the *Prevelis* (28430 28555, http://anek.gr). It departs twice weekly in summer only) to Kássos (3hr), Kárpathos (5hr), Hálki (7hr) and Rhodes (9hr); and once or twice weekly to Iráklio (3hr), Santoríni (10hr), Mílos (14hr) and Pireás (19hr). Check timetables on http://openseas.gr or http://ferries.gr.

By car You're required to display a card to park anywhere in the centre Mon–Sat; cards (€1) can be purchased from kiosks and some shops. Most of the hotels on the Beach Road have off-street parking. For car rental, try Petras, Papandréou 8, a reliable local outfit (28430 24849; http://petras-rentals.gr) or Kazamias, Karamanlí 20 (28430 25037, http://kazamias-rent-a-car.gr), who also have scooters and bikes. There's also bike rental at the *Hotel Itanos*.

By taxi There's a rank at the corner of the harbour by the *Hotel Itanos*, or call 28430 22700.

INFORMATION

Tourist office The municipal tourist office, on the seafront along the Beach Road (May–Aug Mon–Fri 10am–2pm & 6–8pm, though in practice often closed; 28430 28300, https://visitsitia.gr but no English version at present) can supply accommodation lists, town maps and a free guide to the region that also describes some walking routes.

Tourist police Therísou 39 (28430 24200).

Travel agents Agents for ferry and airline tickets are mostly on Kornárou, one street inland from the harbour promenade. Try Tzortzakis Travel, with a branch on Kornárou at the corner of Kazantzáki (28430 29211, https://tzortzakistravel.com), or Sitian Holidays, Kornárou 83 (28430 28555, http://sitianholidays.gr). They can also help with accommodation, but the seafront *Porto Belis*, Karamánli 34 (28430 22370, https://portobelis-crete.gr) is better for apartments and villas.

ACCOMMODATION

SEE MAP PAGE 157

★ **Arhontiko** Kondhyláki 16, 28430 28172. The pick of the budget places, in a lovely, little-modernized traditional house with a shady garden. Only one of the rooms is en suite, but they're spotless and attractive with a charming proprietor. €

El Greco G. Arkadhíou 13, http://elgreco-sitia.gr. Charming small hotel in the upper town with an old-fashioned feel; simple balconied rooms have fridge and TV, and a couple have sea views. €

Flisvos Karamánli 4, www.flisvos-sitia.gr. Small hotel fronting the sea at the start of the Beach Road. Rooms with TV and fridge face either the sea or a patio garden behind; those at the back are larger and more modern, and cost the same as the sea-view option. Breakfast included. €

Itanos Platía Iróon Polytehníou, https://itanoshotel.com. This smart hotel just off the town's main square has light and airy balcony rooms, most with sea views either to the side or front (extra cost); all are equipped with plasma TV and fridge. There's also a lovely rooftop bar with the best views in town and a residents-only rooftop pool. Breakfast included. €

Portobelis Apartments Karamánli 34, http://portobelis-crete.gr. Studios and two-room apartments with kitchens for up to four people, plus some rooms. All are modern and well-equipped, and some have sea-view balconies, though most overlook a small garden. €€

★ **Sitia Bay** Trítis Septemvríou 8, https://sitiabay.com. Purpose-built apartment complex over-looking the town beach, with a respectably sized pool. Lovely modern studios and two-room apartments, all with sea-view balconies and fully equipped kitchens (restocked daily), plus a very warm welcome. Substantial discounts out of season. Studios €, apartments €€

EATING

SEE MAP PAGE 157

SITÍA

★ **Fengaropsaro** Karamanlí 20, 6976 447 052 or 6970 141551. Excellent little seafront ouzerí/taverna. It's not the most attractive spot on the front, but compensates with great-value fish; there's meat, too, like rabbit in wine sauce or lamb with artichokes; all washed down by good. barrel wine from Pezá. €

★ **Meraki** Venizélou 151, 28430 23460. The first of a

2

KORNÁRIA FESTIVAL

Sitía's **Kornária cultural festival**, from the beginning of July to mid-August, features concerts, dance and theatre by Greek and international performers. Many events take place in the castle, and there are also "traditional feasts" staged in nearby villages; ask at the tourist office (see page 161) for details.

group of fashionable *rakádhika* (like an ouzerí, but serving *raki*) on the seafront. You order (by ticking items off on a sheet) from a substantial menu combining modern and traditional dishes, but the best deal is to go for a drink with meze; it's not quite a meal, but you'll probably want another drink anyway, or you can order a few extras. The wine from Toploú monastery is also excellent. €

Mitsakakis Karamánli 6, at 4-Septemvríou, 28430 22377. Wonderful traditional *zaharoplastío* with a terrace facing the harbour, always busy with locals. Try their delicious *loukoumádhes* (dough fritters) with honey or ice cream; they also have sandwiches and crêpes. €

To Steki Papandréou 10, 28430 223857. Traditional place justifiably popular with locals for its excellent-value *souvláki*, grills and mezédhes, and above all home-made *mayireftá* (oven-baked dishes); lunchtime only unless there's any left over); maybe not the prettiest setting, but this is more than compensated for by the warm hospitality. There are more tables outside, on the grassy centre-strip of the road. €

Zorba's Venizélou 56, crnr Kazantáki 3, 28430 22689. Occupying a prime position in the corner of the harbour, this is the biggest and busiest place on the seafront, with far more authentic food than you might expect from its touristy appearance. Generous portions of simple home-style cooking (lamb in the oven, *moussakás*) as well as fresh fish and exceptional value set menus. €

PISKOKÉFALO

I Plateia Main square, 28430 22644. An excellent taverna 3km south of Sitía whose specialities include *kolokythóanthi* (stuffed courgette flowers), along with a good variety of mezéhes and traditional baked dishes. Sit on the terrace and watch village life go by. Central parking is difficult, so park on the village edge and walk in. €

DRINKING AND NIGHTLIFE

SEE MAP PAGE 157

189 Venizélou 189, 28430 20660. Big café-bar that's a favourite local hangout, open most of the day and night. By day there's coffee, snacks – burgers, sandwiches – and sofas for lounging, and at night you can enjoy cocktails and music, plus occasional special events.

Black Hole Karaveláki 7, on the continuation of Venizélou, 28430 20422. A meeting place for Sitía's alternative crowd, this is a rock music bar in an old harbour building with exposed stone walls. Loud rock and occasional live performances as the action moves inside from around 10.30pm.

Nouvelle Boutique Venizélou 161, 28430 26598 or 6909 619949. One of the liveliest bars in town, with a big dancefloor and a terrace, mainstream music, lurid pink decor and a young crowd.

SHOPPING

A colourful weekly **market** (Tues 7am–2pm) takes place along Odhós Itánou near the archeological museum. The **minimarket** at Karamanlí 22, on the corner of Kaloyerídhi, stocks foreign newspapers and paperbacks.

DIRECTORY

Banks and money There's a bank with ATM at the bottom of Kápetan Sífi, facing Platía Iróön Polytechníou, and others inland along Venizélou.

Hospital Off the Áyios Nikólaos road on the town's western edge (28433 40100).

Post office Dhimokrítou 10 (Mon–Fri 7.30am–2pm).

The northeast

Crete's northeast corner is among its most tempting destinations, at least if it's beaches and isolation you're after. You won't find much solitude at **Vái beach** which, with its famous grove of palm trees and silvery sands, features alongside Knossós, the Lasíthi plateau and the Samariá Gorge on almost every Cretan travel agent's list of excursions. But it remains a beautiful spot, and there are plenty of escapes roundabout. If you're planning to stay at this end of the island, **Palékastro** is a lovely small town within easy reach of many less well-known beaches, as well as some of Crete's best windsurfing.

There are also small **archeological sites** at Ítanos and Palékastro, as well as the ancient monastery of **Toplóu**, one of the most revered on the island.

Leaving Sitía, the road runs along the coast for about 10km, turning inland by the extraordinarily ugly and misguided *Dionysos Village* holiday complex. Here you start to climb into deserted, gently hilly country, the slopes covered in thyme, heather and sage with the occasional cluster of strategically sited beehives. In summer, the sweet-scented, deep-violet thyme flowers prove an irresistible attraction for the bees that feed on them almost exclusively, thus creating the much-sought-after **thymarísio méli** (thyme honey).

Moní Toplóu

15km east of Sitía • Charge • Not long after the main road leaves the coast a side road switchbacks steeply up to the left, signed to Moní Toplóú

Standing defiant in a landscape that is empty, save for a line of wind turbines along the ridge behind, **Moní Toplóu** (**Τοπλού**) looks more like a fortress than a religious institution. Which is appropriate: the name Toplóu is Turkish for "with a cannon", a reference to a giant device with which the monks used to defend themselves and uphold the Cretan monastic traditions of resistance to invaders. Highlights of the monastery's adventures include being sacked by pirates and destroyed in 1498; captured by the Ottomans during the 1821 rebellion, when twelve monks were hanged from the gate as an example; and serving as a place of shelter for the resistance in World War II. Forbidding exterior and grim history notwithstanding, Toplóu is startlingly beautiful within.

The monastery is reputed to be incredibly wealthy – it owns most of the northeastern corner of the island – which is no doubt how they can afford the extensive restorations that render the place so spotless. Stairways lead up from the flower-decked, cloister-like **courtyard** to arcaded walkways, off which lie the cells. The blue-robed monks stay out of the way of visitors as far as possible, and in quieter periods their cells and refectory (with spectacular modern frescoes) are left discreetly on view. In the **church** is one of the masterpieces of Cretan art, the eighteenth-century **icon** *Lord Thou Art Great* by Ioannis Kornaros. This marvellously intricate work incorporates 61 small scenes full of detail, each illustrating, and labelled with, a phrase from the Orthodox prayer that begins with this phrase. There's a small **museum**, too, and a shop where you can buy expensive reproductions of the famous icon, as well as postcards, books and the monastery's own wine and olive oil.

As you leave the church, take a look at the **inscription** set into the exterior wall. It records an arbitration by Magnesia, a city in Asia Minor, dating from the second century BC, concerning a territorial dispute between nearby Ítanos and Ierápytna (modern Ierápetra). At this time, when the Romans held sway over Crete, these deadly rivals clashed constantly, and finally Rome, unable to placate the two, called in the Magnesians to act as honest brokers. The inscription records part of their judgement (in favour of Ítanos) and was placed in the monastery wall at the suggestion of the English traveller and antiquarian Robert Pashley (see page 352), who found it being used as a gravestone in 1834.

Beyond Toplóu, the road descends towards Vái through the same arid, rock-strewn landscape as before. There's a chance here that you could spot the rare **Eleonora's falcon**, which breeds on the Dionysádhes islands to the north – Toplóu and Cape Sídheros (a closed military zone) are its regular hunting grounds.

Toplou Winery

Signed up the lane opposite Moní Toplóú • Free tasting, or larger sample plus meze (charge) • 28430 29630

The monastery has a long tradition of wine production, and now has a winery where you can get a quick tour of the vineyards before heading to the tasting and sale room to sample some of the products. The most famous Is a sweet red – possibly not to most modern tastes – but they also have dry reds and whites, and a good rosé. You can also buy the monks' olive oil and tsikoúdhiá here.

Vái

The beach at **VÁI** (**Βάι**), famous above all for its **palm trees**, makes for a thoroughly secular contrast to the spiritual tranquillity of Toploú – and the sudden appearance of what is claimed to be Europe's only indigenous wild date-palm grove (the palms here are a local species, Phoenix theophrasti present on Crete, a few of the Cyclades islands and southwestern Turkey for millennia) is indeed an exotic surprise. As you lie on the fine sand in the early morning, especially in early spring or late autumn, you could almost imagine yourself to be on a Caribbean island. Oddly, the palms seem to be immune to depredation by the red palm weevil (Rhynchophorus ferrugineus), which has devastated most iimported palms in Greece.

In summer, however, the beach fills to overflowing as buses – public ones from Sitía and tours from all over the island – pour into the car park (€2.50), and cars unable to squeeze in line the access road for hundreds of metres. On the beach itself, only the boardwalks guarantee a route through the mass of baking bodies. Pricey sun-loungers are available and a watersports centre offers waterskiing, ringos and other high-speed rides. There's a café and expensive taverna, and you'll pay again to have a shower or use the toilet. That said, for a couple of hours at each end of the day, you should be able to enjoy Vái the way it ought to be. For a bit more peace you can climb the steps cut into the rock behind the taverna to the less shaded cove to the south or, with rather more difficulty, clamber over the rocks to the north.

Ítanos

The sand may not be as good as at Vái, but the relative emptiness of the three small beaches at **ÍTANOS** (**Ίτανος**), 1.5km north of the turning to Vái, makes them far more enjoyable. There's still the odd palm tree scattered around here too, and you can explore the remains of the **ancient city** too; there are no facilities of any sort, however.

Ancient Ítanos

Scattered over the hill above the beach • Free

Inhabited from Minoan times, **ancient Ítanos** became important later, flourishing through the Classical Greek and Roman eras, when it vied with Ierápytna (modern

CAPE SÍDHEROS: A WILDERNESS UNDER THREAT

The wilderness of **CAPE SÍDHEROS** (**Σίδερος**), Crete's northeastern tip, lies to the north of Ítanos. At the end there's a naval base, strictly off-limits and no photography permitted, but you can drive quite a way up the excellent asphalted road towards it, across a wild and craggy peninsula where there are coves with tempting beaches and some likely places to snorkel. This area, owned by the Toploú monastery, is under threat from international developers who – with the consent of the monks and the Greek government – drew up plans for a mammoth 7000-bed **tourist "village"** with casinos, yacht harbour, golf courses and luxury hotels as long ago as 1991. Despite a chorus of protest from environmental and political groups, construction work was supposed to start in 2009. This was finally stalled when the Greek Supreme Court intervened at the eleventh hour, putting a stop to the project. In September 2012, however, the government used emergency powers introduced as a result of the financial crisis to give fast-track approval to a reduced development plan, involving 2000 beds. More appeals and opposition followed, but a presidential decree in 2016 appeared to give the project, known as *Cavo Sidero*, the final green light. At the time of writing, however, no construction had actually begun.

Ierápetra) for control of eastern Crete. One twenty-year squabble between these two led to the arbitration of Magnesia in 132 BC, part of the stone record of which is preserved at Toploú Monastery (see page 163). The settlement here remained prosperous until the medieval Byzantine era, when it was destroyed, most likely by Saracen pirates. All sorts of messy ruins strewn with potsherds survive beneath the twin acropolises, but little that retains any shape. You might be able to make out two early **basilicas** (one is signposted), as well as the beautifully cut lower courses of a **Hellenistic wall**, near a guardian's hut on the western hill.

Palékastro and around

A substantial village with easy access to numerous excellent beaches, and with plenty of accommodation both in town and in the surrounding area, **PALÉKASTRO** (**Παλαίκαστρο**) makes an excellent, quiet base. There are several good tavernas and just about every other facility you might need, but just one real sight, an interesting little **folk museum** (charge), housed in a restored traditional cottage. Inside, rooms are decorated with period furnishings, and there are the usual displays of tools and agricultural equipment plus an interesting video playing on traditional crafts and customs.

Angathiá

The hamlet of **ANGATHIÁ** (**Ανκαθιά**), barely ten minutes' walk east of Palékastro, is smaller and even quieter than its neighbour. There are good rooms and tavernas here, but little else – though it is convenient for Hióna beach, the Palékastro archeological site and the Petsofás peak sanctuary.

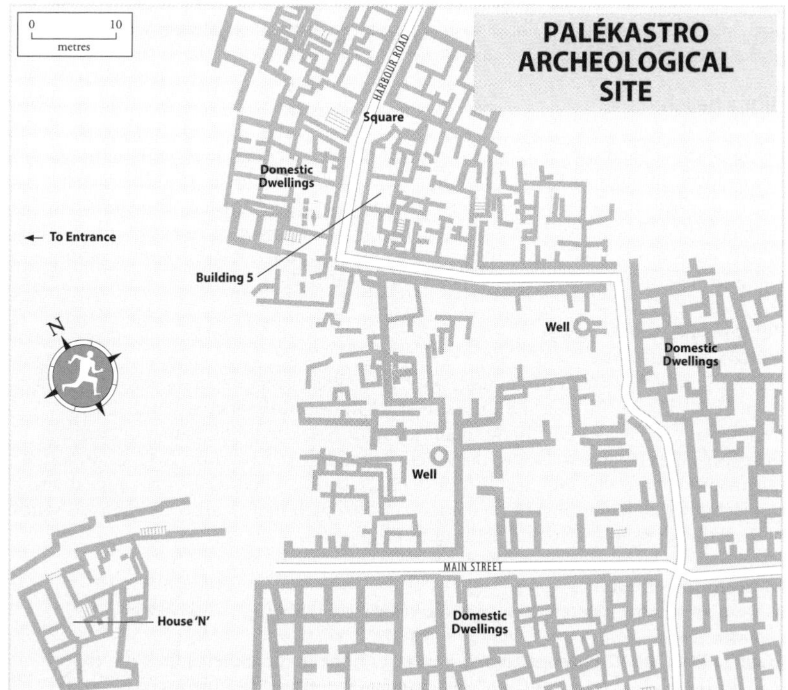

Ancient Palékastro

Close to Hióna beach, about a 20min walk from Palékastro village • Charge

2

For archeologists the Minoan site of **Palékastro** (aka Roussólakkos) is a very significant excavation: the largest Minoan town yet discovered and a rich source of information about everyday Minoan life. For an amateur it's less enthralling, especially when compared with the spectacular palace sites elsewhere on the island, but there's still plenty to see (though signage could be improved), and continuing excavation means that new finds are still coming to light. Recent explorations on the site's northern side, for example, have revealed a road leading from the town to the nearby harbour (no trace of which has yet been found), while beneath the olive groves to the south and west more of the Minoan town lies waiting to be revealed – geophysical surveys have indicated the existence of a very large building, maybe a palace.

Set on a fertile agricultural plain on a bay offering harbourage beneath the protection of the high, flat-topped bluff of Kastrí, this is an obvious place to settle – and indeed the area was extensively inhabited both before and after the Minoan era. Water was available too; the site is dotted with deep wells, so superbly constructed that they still contain water today. **Building 5**, now under cover to protect its plaster walls, lies at the heart of a complex of streets, dwellings and small squares around the harbour road. Here archeologists discovered the **Palékastro koúros** (see page 159), a stunning ivory statuette now in the Sitía archeological museum. To the south, the limestone-paved "**main street**" was the town's principal artery; around it a number of impressive dwellings with stone walls and column bases have been revealed, and the fine, Marine-style vases found in the ruins of some of them are evidence of the status and wealth of the owners. **House N**, at the site's western end, is dated to the late Neopalatial period, and excavations revealed horns of consecration and double-axe stands that had fallen from a shrine room on an upper floor. The room at the rear produced hundreds of cups as well as jars and cooking pots, suggesting that it may have been some form of communal eating club, or perhaps an early taverna.

Hióna beach

2km east of Palékastro

Hióna beach, a good stretch of blue-flag-rated pebble and sand, lies to the south of a flat-topped hill named Kastrí which dominates the coastal landscape. The closest beach to Palékastro, it's less than twenty minutes' walk via Angathiá. Though far from crowded, it is probably the most popular beach hereabouts: you can walk to still quieter coves around the bay to the south, following a rough track. A couple of the region's finest tavernas overlook the beach (see page 167).

Petsofás peak sanctuary

About 2km southeast of Palékastro

The summit of **PETSOFÁS (Πετσοφάς)** gives you a great overview of the ancient Minoan town of Palékastro, and was itself the site of a Minoan **peak sanctuary**, the most important in eastern Crete. Many small clay figurines were found here, representing the people that made offerings at the sanctuary, and these have provided a great deal of information about the dress and hairstyles of the period. Today there's not a great deal to see, but it's an enjoyable hike of some 3km on a path signed either off the road south of Angathiá or from the coastal path south of Hióna.

Koureménos Beach

2.5km northeast of Palékastro; there's a sandy track from Hioná, or from Palékastro head out on the Vái road and follow the signs; it's barely a 30min walk

KOUREMÉNOS BEACH (Κουρεμένος), north of Hióna on the other side of flat-topped Kastrí from Hióna, is one of Crete's top **windsurfing** spots. Not surprisingly, it can be windy (a funnel effect creates ideal windsurfing conditions; Hióna is far more sheltered), but it's a fine, long sand-and-pebble beach, with several tavernas and rooms places, a hotel well inland – even a bar – directly behind. There's also quite a community of camper vans in summer, and a couple of excellent windsurf centres, too.

GETTING AROUND — THE NORTHEAST

By bus There are 3 buses a day from from Sitía to Palékastro (45min) and to Vái (summer only; 30min).

By car Watch where you park in Palékastro – they give tickets for parking around the main square.

INFORMATION AND ACTIVITIES

Tourist information There's no tourist office, but a couple of excellent locally run websites have details of attractions and comprehensive accommodation listings: check out http://eastcrete-holidays.gr and http://palaikastro.com.

Bike and scooter rental and tours Moto Kastri (28430 61377), on the eastern edge of Palékastro along the Vái road, also has quad and mountain bikes. Freak Mountain Bike Centre (http://freak-mountainbike.com), at the edge of Palékastro on the Vái road, offers bike and e-bike rental, guided day-trips and cycle holiday packages.

Windsurfing There are two rival operations at Koureménos, both offering lessons and quality gear rental; Freak (6979 253 861, http://freak-surf.com; May–Nov) and Gone Surfing (6941 427 787, http://gonesurfing.gr).

Yoga Freak also have afternoon yoga classes on Koureménos beach.

ACCOMMODATION AND EATING

As well as plenty of **rooms** in Palékastro itself (you'll see signs throughout the village), there are many apartment complexes in the surrounding countryside and at the nearby beaches. July and August get very busy here, so advance booking is advisable. See also www. palaikastro.com and www.eastcrete-holidays.gr.

VÁI

Metohi Vai Village Taverna On the Palékastro road about 15min walk from the beach, 28430 61071. Former shepherds' shelters, owned by the Monastery of Toploú, have been converted to house an excellent garden taverna. There's good local food, with all the usuals plus some less obvious dishes like stuffed cabbage (a change from grape-leaf *dolmádhes*), *Skioufistá*, a home-made pasta, and *Xýgalo*, a local ewes' milk soft cheese. €

PALÉKASTRO

Hellas Hotel On the main square, 28430 61240. Simple rooms with balcony, TV and fridge; a little impersonal, but could hardly be closer to the action. There's a good traditional taverna, serving dishes such as lamb with lemon sauce and *soutzoukákia* (meat balls) on the terrace beneath the hotel, facing the square. €

House Margot Set back from the Sitía road on the edge of the village, www.palekastro.gr. Family-run accommodation in a garden setting, comprising en-suite, balconied rooms with fridge and air con. Clean, welcoming and good value, with an excellent breakfast available. €

Mythos On the main square, 28430 61243. This friendly, family-run taverna serves good traditional food at cheap prices on a streetside terrace, with meat and fish platters plus a vegetarian menu. €

Ostria Outskirts of the village on the Vái road, http://ostria-itanos.gr. An incongruously modern, brightly furnished hotel in a garden setting. The tile-floored rooms have fridge and balcony. €

Sticky Minds On the Zákros road, 50m from the square, http://stickyminds.cf. As wild as Palékastro's nightlife gets: a café-bar with a classic 60s and 70s rock soundtrack, strong cocktails and a courtyard shaded by mulberry trees. €

ANGATHIÁ

Taverna Vaios Up the hill from the bridge leading into the village, on the right, 28430 61043. A very popular place (you may need to book in high season), with traditional food and charcoal-grilled meats, plus mezédhes, oven-cooked daily specials and chicken on the spit served on a large roadside terrace. €€

HIÓNA

★ **Hiona** Hióna beach, http://hiona.gr. Stunningly beautiful seafood restaurant on a promontory at the northern end of the beach – it's a touch more formal than others in the area and a little pricier, but worth it. Try the *kakaviá* traditional fish stew. Often booked up in season. €€

Kakavia Hióna beach, 28430 61227. A less glamorous setting than nearby *Hiona*, but locals reckon that the fish here (priced per kilo) is even more expertly cooked. It's also marginally less expensive, and much more likely to have a table. €

Marina Village Hotel Off the Hióna beach road, about 600m from Hióna, 800m from Koureménos, https://marinavillage.gr. A peaceful haven with well-furnished balconied rooms surrounded by olive groves and a garden of bougainvillea and banana plants; there's a pool and tennis court too. They also rent a tiny house (for up to four people) right by Hióna beach. Buffet breakfast included. €

2

KOUREMÉNOS

Grandes Apartments Koureménos beach, https://grandes.gr. A small group of smart apartments with attractive terraces, right behind the beach. Each can sleep up to four, with bedroom, sitting area with sofabeds, and kitchen. There's a taverna out front. €

Kouremenos Beach Apartments Koureménos beach, http://kouremenosbeach.gr. A couple of small studios for two in the olive groves immediately behind the beach, as well as some larger apartments for up to six people, all with TV and fridge; the larger ones have a separate kitchen. They have a second apartment complex, with pool, in the countryside towards Hióna beach. €

★ **Kouremenos Villas/Panorama Apartments** On the hillside beyond Koureménos beach, https://palaikastro.com/kouremenos_apts. A glorious setting with great views over the beach and countryside as well as an exceptionally friendly welcome make this place special; very comfortable apartments with modern kitchen, satellite TV, and a pool. €

Porto Heli apartments Inland from the Vái road, 1km from Palékastro, 450m from Kourémenos, http://porto-heli-crete.gr. Two-room apartments, sleeping up to five, in a tranquil garden setting (no. 5, with sea view, is a peach), with a/c, TV and well-equipped kitchen. Four-night minimum stay in season. €

To Votsalo Kourémenos beach, 28430 61282. The pick of several tavernas behind the beach, *Votsalo* serves good Cretan dishes, fish and grills on a large terrace facing the sea, shaded by tamarisk trees. €

SHOPPING

Terra Elaía Not far from Palékastro's square on the road signed to Zákros and Hióna, 28430 61305. This shop sells high-class souvenirs, the arty photos of co-owner Manolis Tsantakis and regional products plus books, guides, maps and foreign press.

Zákros and around

South of Palékastro, a winding road offers a beautiful drive through countryside where the soil is a strange pinkish-purple colour, as if indelibly stained with grape juice (although actually it's olives that are responsible, which grow around here). The few hamlets you pass along the way are so tiny that they make **Áno Zákros** seem positively urban when finally you get there. This is the point where you turn off for **Káto Zákros**, the tiny seaside village that's home to the magnificent **Minoan palace of Zakros** (see page 169), either walking down the gorge or by a spectacular cliff road.

Hokhlakiés Gorge

Halfway between Palékastro and Áno Zákros

For a fine **gorge walk**, make a stop at tiny **HOKHLAKIÉS** (**Χοχλακιές**), from where you can follow a well-signed route through **Hokhlakiés Gorge** to Karoúmes Bay and beach, 3km below. From the bottom you can either return up the gorge or strike out along the coast in either direction; north to Palékastro, south to Káto Zákros, each about 6km further. To do the walk one-way, you could get dropped at Hokhlakiés by the Zákros bus; drivers in small cars (only a small car will squeeze through the village streets) can follow a track 200m from the main road to a parking place at the start of the trail.

Áno Zákros

A slow-moving little country town, **ÁNO ZÁKROS** (**Άνω Ζάκρος**) – "Upper" Zákros – boasts three or four tavernas around its central square which, throughout the summer at weekends, host numerous wedding feasts accompanied by dancing to *bouzoúki* and *lyra*; should you arrive then, you'll most likely have a glass of wine thrust into your hand by one of the multitude of smartly dressed revellers filling the square. The little trade these establishments see the rest of the time, however, is almost exclusively passing through, since the far more obvious attractions of Káto ("Lower") Zákros and the celebrated palace are on the coast 8km further southeast.

Locally, Áno Zákros enjoys a certain fame for the numerous **springs** that feed the lush vegetation hereabouts and which were also an attraction for the Minoans. If you follow the sign up to the right as you come into the town, or simply climb the hill from the centre, you'll reach a little **chapel** from where, in five minutes' walk, a path leads beside the stream to its source and some shady picnic spots. Information on how to get to it or to reach the start of the "Gorge of the Dead" walk is available from the town's small central hotel, the *Zakros*.

The Gorge of the Dead

There are plenty of ways to get to Káto Zákros, but perhaps the most satisfying is to walk, in about two hours altogether, via a beautiful ravine known as the **Gorge of the Dead** (but just as likely to be signed "Zákros Gorge" or "Dead's Gorge"). This path is also the final stage of the E4 trans-European footpath, so it's pretty well marked, at least once you get out of Áno Zákros. The easiest way to get on to it is to follow the signs from the south end of the village, opposite the *Napoleon* taverna. Alternatively there's a parking place beside the road about halfway to Káto Zákros, from where a steep path plunges down into the gorge, cutting off half the distance but still giving you the most spectacular portion of the hike.

Leaving from Áno Zákros, the first half-hour or so is through olive groves and lovingly tended smallholdings, gradually becoming lonelier and wilder as the valley closes in. The trail for the most part is easy to follow beside the stream bed, marked by the usual red waymarks and the occasional signpost in case of confusion. It's a solitary but magnificent walk, brightened especially in spring by plenty of plant life. High in the cliff walls you'll see the mouths of **caves**: it is these, used as tombs in Minoan times and earlier, which give the ravine its name. At the bottom you join a dirt road, which runs through groves of bananas and olives past the palace and into Káto Zákros.

Káto Zákros

From the first spectacular view as you approach along the clifftop road, **KÁTO ZÁKROS** (**Κάτω Ζάκρος**) – "Lower" Zákros – is a delight. There's a pebbly sand beach, half a dozen waterfront tavernas and café-bars, and a few places offering rooms and apartments; plus a tiny harbour with a few fishing boats, this is about all the place amounts to. It's best to bring cash and anything else you might need: they'll change money and offer local information in the tavernas, but there's no shop, or anything else much. If it's laidback tranquillity you're after, you've come to the right place.

The Palace of Zákros

500m inland from Káto Zákros • Charge • 28430 26897

Though the **Palace of Zákros** is small, it is full of interest, and can match any of the more important Minoan centres for quality of construction and materials. It's also much easier to understand than many of the other sites: here, the remains are of one palace only, dating from between 1600 and 1450 BC. Although there is an earlier settlement at a lower level, it is unlikely ever to be excavated – mainly because this end of the island is gradually sinking. The water table is already almost at the palace level, and anything deeper would be thoroughly submerged. Even the exposed parts of the palace are marshy and often waterlogged: there are terrapins living in the green water of the cistern. When it's really wet, you can keep your feet dry and get an excellent view of the overall plan of the palace by climbing the streets of one of Zákros's unique features: the **town** – a place very like Gourniá (see page 150) – that occupied the hill above it.

The destruction of the palace appears to have been very violent, with only enough time for the inhabitants to abandon it, taking almost nothing with them. This

2

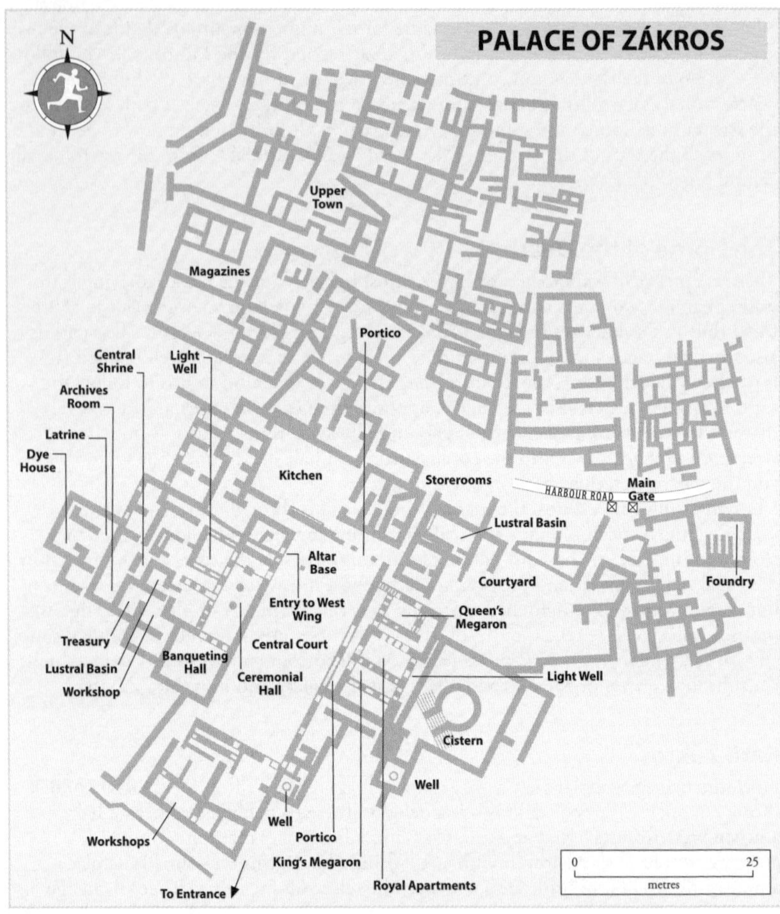

contributed to the enormous number of artefacts found here, but more importantly the nature of the destruction, in which the palace was flattened and burned, is an important prop in the theory that it was the explosion of Thíra (see page 325) that ended the Minoan civilization. Large lumps of **pumice** found among the ruins are supposed to have been swept there by the tidal wave that followed the eruption. However, many archeologists take issue with this hypothesis and question both its chronological accuracy and the type of destruction, seeing the palace's demise as more consistent with human than natural causes.

The harbour road

The **site entrance** is on the south side, but the following description starts on the **east side** along the harbour road. This would have been the traditional approach used by visitors to the palace who arrived by sea. Following the road west leads to the palace's main gateway. The **harbour**, now lost beneath the sea, was the chief reason why a palace existed here at all; this must have been a significant port, the first landfall on Crete for trade from Egypt's Nile Delta and the Middle East. Among the ruins were found ingots of copper imported from Cyprus, elephant tusks from Syria, and gold and precious materials from Egypt.

Before entering the palace, the harbour road passed various dwellings on each side as well as a **foundry** dating from the Protopalatial period; the remains stand beneath a protective canopy on the left. The road (part of which has been reconstructed) then curves round into the town, passing the palace entrance on the left.

The Central Court

As you enter the **palace**, the **main gate** leads to a stepped ramp, followed by a **courtyard** that may have served as a meeting place between the palace hierarchy and the townspeople. Here, in the northeast corner beneath another canopy, is a **lustral basin** where visitors to the palace may have been required to wash or purify themselves before proceeding. To the west of the courtyard lies the main or **Central Court**, a little over 30m by 12m, or about a third the size of that at Knossós. Crossing the north edge of the court, you come to an **altar base**, with the lower courses of the west-wing wall in grey ashlar stone beyond.

The west wing

The **west wing** (actually the northwest, as Zákros is not truly aligned north–south), entered between two pillars, is where, as usual, the chief ceremonial and ritual rooms were located. A **reception room** leads into a colonnaded **light well**, the hallmark of Minoan architecture. The light well's black-stone crazy paving survives, as do the pillar bases and a drain in the northwest corner. It was here that the excavators unearthed what was arguably Zákros's single most important find: the **Peak Sanctuary Rhyton**, a carved stone vase depicting a peak sanctuary with wild goats, from which valuable information about Minoan religion was gleaned. The light well illuminated the **Ceremonial Hall**, beyond which lay the **Banqueting Hall**, originally a lavish room with frescoed walls and an elaborate floor. Platon gave the room this name because of the large number of cups and drinking vessels discovered scattered about the floor.

At the heart of a complex of rooms behind the Banqueting Hall is the **Central Shrine** (with a canopy), which contains a ledge and niche, similar to the shrine at Gourniá, where idols would have been placed. Nearby is the **lustral basin**, necessary for purification before entering the shrine. Here, too, was the **Treasury** – probably the most important discovery from the excavators' viewpoint as it is the only one so far positively identified. In a number of box-like compartments (which have been partially restored), almost a hundred fine stone jars and libation vessels were discovered, including the exquisite rock crystal rhyton with its delicate crystal bead handle and collar – found crushed into more than three hundred fragments – that the Iráklio Archeological Museum is so proud of (see page 57).

Next to the Treasury, in the **Archives Room**, hundreds of Linear A record tablets were stored in wooden chests. Sadly, only a handful of the top layers survived the centuries of rain and flooding; the rest solidified into a mass of clay, depriving the archeologists

EXCAVATING ZÁKROS

The valley behind Káto Zákros was explored by a British archeologist, **David Hogarth**, at much the same time as the other great Cretan palaces were being discovered, around the beginning of the 20th century. But Hogarth gave up the search, having unearthed only a couple of Minoan houses, and it was not until the 1960s that new explorations were begun by a Cretan archeologist, **Nikolaos Platon**. Platon found the palace almost immediately, just metres from where Hogarth's trenches ended. The Palace of Zákros thus benefited from modern techniques in its excavation and, having been forgotten even locally, it was never looted. As a result, the site yielded an enormous quantity of treasures and everyday items, including a religious treasury full of stone vases and ritual vessels, and storerooms with their giant *píthoi* still in place.

of potentially priceless clues in their attempts at deciphering the script. On the opposite side of the treasury is a **workshop** where pieces of raw marble and steatite were found. The remaining stone slabs probably supported a craftsman's workbench. More workshops and storerooms lay to the west of the shrine – one of these has been identified as a **dye-house** – and a **latrine** with a cesspit outside the wall was found nearby. Further west, beyond the palace confines, new excavations are still going on.

The kitchen and south wing workshops

On the north side of the Central Court was the palace **kitchen**, the first to be positively identified at any of the palaces. Bones, cooking pots and utensils were found strewn around the floor both here and in the storeroom or pantry next door. The south wing was devoted to **workshops**: for smiths, lapidaries, potters and even, according to Platon, perfume-makers – possibly a borrowing from Egypt. The **well** that serviced this area still flows with drinkable water, and an offering cup was found close by, containing olives preserved by the waters. Platon and his team devoured the 3500-year-old olives, which shrivelled upon contact with the air, and said that they tasted as fresh as those in the nearby tavernas.

The royal apartments

Two large rooms regarded as **royal apartments** flank the east side of the Central Court behind a portico. The larger of the two, to the south, is called the King's Megaron or chamber and the smaller is described as that of the queen. However, one of these may have been the throne room, and there would have been elaborate rooms on the upper floor, possibly with verandas overlooking the courtyard below, where the rulers may have lived. Next to a light well in the eastern wall of the King's Megaron lay the colonnaded **Cistern** with eight steps leading down to water contained in a plaster-lined basin, which may have served as a royal aquarium or even a swimming pool (if so, the only one known). It is ingeniously designed to maintain the water at a constant level, with the excess draining into the well to the south, which, being outside the palace wall, was probably used by the townsfolk. The water from the spring was, as at Knossós, piped throughout the palace, and traces of the pipework can still be seen.

Residential areas

Beyond the royal apartments lay other **residential areas**, though much has been destroyed by centuries of ploughing combined with frequent waterlogging of the land, partly caused by the silting up of the cistern's outflow. In the steep **upper town** more survives and, close to the perimeter fence, a **narrow street** running east to west passes an impressive doorway and gives you some idea of how the town may have looked when twin-storey buildings overlooked these narrow thoroughfares. Quite a few grindstones found in the excavations are to be seen here, and nearby there's also a charming **stone bench**, now exposed, which would have looked into a light well. It's not hard to imagine someone sitting here, enjoying the cool shade of a summer evening. Near to the bench, there's a well-preserved stairway climbing tantalizingly a couple of metres towards the now disappeared second storey. Both the stairway and the bench are close to the perimeter fence on the eastern (or seaward) side of the upper town.

ARRIVAL AND INFORMATION — ZÁKROS AND AROUND

By bus Buses run from Sitía to Áno Zákros three times a day.
On foot The gorge walk between Áno and Káto Zákros (see page 168), about 2hr each way, is just the start of the local hiking possibilities: the owner of *Terra Minoika*, qualified mountaineer Ilias Pagiannidis, has waymarked several other 3–4hr walks in the surrounding hills; information is available both here and at *Stella's*. A good map to bring if you're thinking of doing a lot of walking is the *Anavasi* 1:25,000 Zákros–Vái-Sitía map, widely available from bookshops on Crete and at Orange Books on the square in Áno Zákros.

Tourist information *Taverna Akrogiali* is a handy source of local information, and acts as agent for a number of rooms places nearby.

ACCOMMODATION AND EATING

The most attractive places to eat are in Káto Zákros. If you have trouble finding somewhere to stay – August can be very busy – try at the various waterfront tavernas, especially *Akrogiali*, which act as agents for many of the local places, or check out www.eastcrete-holidays.gr.

★ **Akrogiali** End of the beach road, www.kato-zakros.gr. The last of the places on the waterfront, with a particularly attractive waterfront terrace away from the road. Excellent, simple Greek food and the friendly owner, Nikos, is a fount of information; he also acts as an agent for several room options nearby. €

Coral & Athina On the rise immediately beyond Taverna Akrogiali, www.kato-zakros.gr. Rooms right above the beach, with great sea views from large communal terraces; clean and simply furnished, with fridge and TV. Information at *Akrogiali*; breakfast included. €

Katerina Apartments About 500m inland, beyond the palace, www.kato-zakros.gr. Lovely, stone and wood apartments with fine views from their balconies; a couple have galleried beds, others can sleep up to four. Well fitted out, and a friendly welcome. €

★ **Kato Zakros Palace Apartments** On the entry road above the village, www.katozakros-apts.gr. Perched high above the coast with spectacular views of the gorge, palace and beach; rooms and studios equipped with TV, fridge, kitchen (in studios) or kettle, plus communal library and laundry. Expect an exuberant welcome and gifts of fresh produce grown right outside. €

★ **Stella's Traditional Apartments** About 500m inland, beyond the palace, https://stelapts.com. Large, elegantly decorated, stone-built studios, with hammocks and lovely views in the verdant gardens. Exceptionally well equipped, well run and friendly, if not cheap. €€

Terra Minoika Boutique Resort On the entry road above the village, https://terraminoika.com. A complex of stone-built luxury suites (sleeping up to four) with terraces; the upper apartments have particularly fine views. Each apartment features a fully equipped kitchen, tiled floors, beamed ceilings, top-quality furnishings and satellite TV. There's a small gym too. €€€

Yiannis Retreat About 500m inland, beyond the palace, http://katozakros-rooms.com. Sharing a site with sister *Stella's*, *Yianni's* offers simpler, smaller studios, with slightly less magical views, though they're still classily fitted out. €

2

The southeast

Few tourists venture south of Zákros, and indeed there's little in the way of habitation in the whole of the southeastern corner of the island, and barely any public transport. The effort of getting to these remote parts is rewarded with a barren, empty landscape and numerous excellent **beaches** – mostly deserted. Along the road from Áno Zákros to **Xerókambos**, agricultural country of olive groves and plastic greenhouses gradually gives way to a harsher mountain environment until finally you emerge high above the coast, and a brilliant turquoise sea and white sandy beaches divided by rocky outcrops appear below. Beyond Xerókambos you can circle back round to Sitía, taking in an archeological site at **Presós** along the way, or carry on towards the south coast.

Xerókambos

Straggling across a little coastal plain in the lee of the Sitían mountains, the tiny hamlet of **XERÓKAMBOS** (**Ξερόκαμπος**) is not especially attractive, but it's as isolated and peaceful as you could wish for. There's no real centre, just a street along which, between fields of olive groves, are spaced some houses, a few tavernas and a couple of basic minimarkets, with rooms and apartment places scattered along the road and down by the beach. Despite the stirrings of development, this **main beach** is more than long enough to find seclusion if you want it, and there are isolated coves either side where you might never see another soul. The crystal-clear waters here are great for **snorkelling** too – the minimarkets sell the basic equipment.

Away from the sea, you could stretch your legs with a walk to the tiny chapel on a low hill to the south of the beach. Surrounding this are the ruins of an extensive **Minoan settlement** not yet fully explored or documented.

Hamétoulo

A good paved road – populated by herds of goats who, despite the arrival of the asphalt, still regard it as their domain – switchbacks up into the barren, desolate mountains behind Xerókambos, offering dramatic views before heading down towards Zíros. Almost at the highest point lies the primitive hamlet of **HAMÉTOULO** (**Χαμαίτουλο**), a piece of living Cretan folklore with twenty dwellings, a cobbled street and a church. Beyond here all views are dominated by a giant radar dome on the mountaintop, and the road itself is dotted with "No Photography" signs – this is a military zone and NATO's main intelligence-gathering post for the eastern Mediterranean.

Zíros

The farming village of **ZÍROS** (**Zίρος**), in the midst of a high inland plain, is the administrative centre of this region. That doesn't amount to a great deal, but it's a fair-sized place, tumbling down a hillside towards a neat platía circled by acacia trees with whitewashed trunks. Facilities here include banks and fuel, and should you come in late July you might be lucky enough to catch the annual **festival**, when the women of the village produce huge trays of delicacies that are laid out on tables in the square and washed down with gallons of *rakí* to the accompaniment of *bouzoúki* and *lyra*. For quieter times, there are sixteenth-century frescoes to be seen in the church of **Ayía Paraskeví**, or you may prefer simply to soak up the atmosphere with a drink at a table in the square. In the early evening, when the rocky heights seem to crowd in on all sides, places like Zíros feel like the real heart of Crete.

Handhrás

The olive groves and vineyards around Zíros are said to be among the best on the island; the villages are still prosperous, though you feel that their best days are several hundred years behind them. **HANDHRÁS** (**Χανδράς**), another tidy farming village, is entered past its sail-less and derelict irrigation windmills whose modern counterparts – a phalanx of mammoth wind turbines spaced out along the ridge above the village – make a surreal addition to the landscape.

Etiá

At **ETIÁ** (**Ετιά**), a **Venetian mansion** (free) stands in memorial to the glory days of that Italian city's power in Crete. Built by the Di Mezzo family (whose arms decorate the doorway) in the late fifteenth century, this once elegant edifice was badly damaged in 1828 when the local populace vented their rage on the Muslims who had been using it as an administrative base, and later fell into almost complete ruin, along with the rest of the village. The completely refurbished mansion – often used for concerts and exhibitions – is one of the very few Venetian buildings to survive outside the cities. Around it is effectively a ghost town of one-room stone shacks; the last of what were once over five hundred permanent residents left in the 1970s. Only a seasonal roadside taverna, a Byzantine chapel and the church of **Ayía Katerína** (open daily during daylight hours), with an elegant carved stone belfry, show any signs of life.

Voilá

The ruined medieval village of **VOILÁ** (**Βοιλά**) is signed up a lane just outside Handhrás. With its Gothic arches and silent paved streets, this is a distinctly eerie place to wander round; two ornamental drinking **fountains** with beautiful brass taps still function, one at each end of the village, an Ottoman contribution to this Venetian stronghold. The only building still standing with a functional roof is the twin-naved **Áyios Yeóryios** church (open daylight hours), inside which you can see an interesting sixteenth-century gravestone fresco. The church and a tower of the Ottoman period dominate the site; you can also climb to a ruined Venetian fort above the village.

Ancient Presós

6km northwest of Handhrás • Free • From the centre of the village of Néa Presós, opposite a *kafenío* with a raised terrace, a dirt road is clearly signposted downhill; after about 2km you'll come to a signed gate for the "Archeological sites", where you can park

The archeological site of **PRESÓS** (**Πραισός**) is another of those sites where what you see – in this case very little – cannot begin to match the interest and importance of the history. When eventually it is excavated it will undoubtedly become one of the most important sites in the east of the island. But even without ruins, it would be worth taking the walk around the site for the **scenery** alone.

Brief history

Presós first came to light in 1884, when the Italian archeologist Federico Halbherr turned up a large number of clay idols and some unusual inscriptions written in an unknown tongue – very likely the same as that of the Linear A tablets – using Greek characters. Set out with lines reading alternately right to left and left to right, these **Eteocretan** (true Cretan) inscriptions are now believed to be evidence of the post-Bronze Age Minoans who fled from the Dorian invasions to remote locations in the east of the island in an attempt to preserve their civilization. Presós seems to have been one of their principal towns, controlling the sanctuary of Dhiktean Zeus at Palékastro, probably an earlier Minoan shrine. With harbours on the north and south coasts of the island, its power eventually led to conflict with the leading Dorian city of the region, Ierápytna (modern Ierápetra). Following final victory about 155 BC, Ierápytna razed Presós to the ground and the city was never rebuilt. With this defeat, the long twilight of Minoan civilization, lasting more than a thousand years after the palaces had fallen, came to an end.

The site

From the entrance, follow the signed path west to a saddle between the two hills where the ancient city lay; the defensive wall that encircled these two hills can still be made out in places. On the summit of the **First Acropolis** are the foundations of a temple. Further on, the path forks and to the right – on the western slope of the same hill – are the remains of a substantial **Hellenistic house**. Dating from the third century BC, the outer walls of superbly cut stone define the main living rooms at the front of the house, with workrooms at the rear. In the largest workroom, an olive press was found together with a stone tank for storing the oil. A stairway to the left of the main door led down to a cellar. Turning left at the fork brings you – after a hundred-metre walk across the saddle – to the **Second Acropolis** where cuttings in the rock on the south side formed the foundations of dwellings.

ARRIVAL AND GETTING AROUND — THE SOUTHEAST

By bus A twice-daily bus runs from Sitía to Zíros and back, and that's about it for public transport in this region.

By car Approaching the region directly from Sitía, the main road across the island to the south coast cuts high between the east and west ranges of the Sitía mountains. Along the way are a number of sturdy agricultural hamlets where you can stop for a snack and a drink, and short detours will take you to Presós or Etiá, and to Zíros beyond. From Xerókambos there are three potential routes. On the outskirts of Zíros, a paved road heads directly for the south coast at Goúdhouras (see page 178), through very lonely country. Continue through Zíros and the older road divides at Handhrás, both picturesque branches continuing to meet the main Sitía–Ierápetra road; the southerly route, the logical direction if you're heading for Makríyialos, Ierápetra and the south coast, goes via Etiá; the northerly, back toward Sitía, passes Voilá and ancient Presós.

On foot The E4 path passes through Handhrás and Zíros, before turning northeast to end at the Gorge of the Dead and Káto Zákros.

ACCOMMODATION AND EATING

The only reliable accommodation in the region is at **Xerókambos**, where it's scattered across the countryside behind the beach; many local options are listed at www.xerocamboscreta.com and www.eastcrete-holidays.gr.

XERÓKAMBOS

2

Akrogiali On the beachfront, at the south end, 28430 26777. This taverna serves up fresh fish, seafood, salads and Cretan dishes on a large terrace set back from the beach with good sea views. €

Asteras In the hills above the main road, http://asterasapartments.gr. Set in their own garden above the olive groves, these modern studio rooms and two-room apartment all come with kitchenette, fridge and good sea views. €

Faros On the main road, http://faros-apts.gr. Pleasant rooms, studios and apartments with TV, and some with sea view. There's also a bar, and a garden with children's play area. €

Lithos Main road towards the south end of Xerókambos, http://lithoshouses.gr. The village's most luxurious option, with elegantly furnished stone-built sea-view apartments (bedroom upstairs, living quarters below) – all come with kitchen, satellite TV, sound system and woodburner for winter. Free olive oil, wine and *rakí* are provided. €€

★ **Liviko View** On main street, near the turn-off to the beach and chapel, https://livikoview.gr. These excellent rooms, run by a couple of retired Greek-Australians, come with a/c and sea view from the balcony; there are also some very well-equipped apartments sleeping up to four. Breakfast included. €

ZÍROS

Taverna Karkionakis Main street, opposite the dhimarhío (town hall), 28430 91266. Superb and friendly village taverna with an atmospheric bar-dining room. This is meat country, and the succulent *païdhákia* are a bargain (lamb chops). Meze includes *loukánika* (spicy sausage) and *spanakopitakia* (spinach pies). €

The south coast

There are three main approaches to Lasíthi's south coast: the long haul across the centre of the island from Iráklio via Áno Viánnos to approach from the west; the short cut across the isthmus from Pahiá Ámmos to **Ierápetra**; or the road south from Sitía that emerges on the coast at **Pilalímata**, close to **Makríyialos**.

Makríyialos and around

At first sight, **MAKRÍYIALOS (Μακρύγιαλος)** seems just another example of ruinous strip development, and even on better acquaintance it's never wildly attractive. However, it does have its compensations: the development is almost exclusively along the road, so get away from that and there are some quiet corners and congenial places to stay; there's an attractive little harbour, and right in town is one of the best **beaches** at this end of Crete, with sand that shelves so gently you might imagine you could walk the 320km to Africa. There are plenty of other beaches nearby, too, and attractive walks into the hills behind.

Much the most appealing part of town is in the west, where the **harbour** shelters under a little bluff, just off the main road. There's a patch of beach right by the harbour, and another around the corner of the bluff, to the west, but the main sands stretch out eastwards, where Makríyialos transitions almost imperceptibly into **Análipsi**.

Makríyialos Roman villa

On the bluff above the harbour, at the western end of the village • Free

The extensive and impressive remains of Makríyialos's **Roman villa** are a reminder that this was an important trading port in Roman and Byzantine times. The trade was based on **Koufonísi**, an island to the southeast that's currently off-limits, and on the murex, a type of sea-snail found there from which valuable purple dye was extracted. As you stroll around the neglected site enjoying the sea views you can make out the remains of mosaic floors and – at the southern end – an elaborate suite of bathing rooms complete with hypocaust and furnace to provide underfloor heating. In other rooms, traces of plasterwork are visible on the walls along with fragments of the original marble that would have covered them. On the villa's west side, an atrium or ornamental garden underlines the fact that the owner was a person of elevated status.

Beaches around Makríyialos

Should the town beaches get too crowded, there are plenty of alternatives nearby. To the west, the village of **Koutsourás** is effectively part of the same resort (albeit the poor relation), and though its beach may not be the most attractive, it does offer some excellent places to eat right by the water. Better places to swim and to escape the crowds lie to the east. The first of them, **Dhiaskári**, is at the eastern edge of town just beyond the *Sunwing Hotel*, an easy walk. The taverna here rents out little shelters with hammocks for a truly sybaritic experience, or walk further along the sand to get away from people altogether. Further east, there are numerous attractive little coves along the road to Moní Kapsá; to find them, simply look out for where the locals have parked alongside the road. A couple of the better ones are at **Kaló Neró**, where there are two small cafés, not far beyond the large *Dragon's Cave Taverna*, whose signs you can't miss.

2

Péfki Gorge

Directly behind the eastern edge of Makríyialos; follow the track past *White River Cottages* (see page 179)

The hike up the **Péfki Gorge** to the village of Péfki is the most straightforward of several gorge walks you can make from Makríyialos, and the easiest. It starts up the valley of the Áspros Potámos (White River), towards the eastern edge of town. Where the track ends, the gorge starts, and though rocky in places it's a relatively straightforward hike that should see you at the top in around two hours. **PÉFKI** itself (**Πεύκοι**) is a lovely village, where a number of houses have been bought and done up by foreigners. There are relaxing places to sit and eat, drink and take in the views and, right at the top of the village, a little **folklore museum** (charge) is housed in the former schoolhouse, full of traditional artefacts including a working loom.

Moní Kapsá

8km east of Makríyialos • Free • Modest dress required

MONÍ KAPSÁ (**Μονή Καψά**) enjoys an abiding reputation for miracles as well as a spectacular setting on a ledge in the cliffs where a gorge emerges into the sea (see page 177). You can easily imagine the isolation of this place when no real coast road existed, and even the paved road and extensive restoration can't entirely destroy the romance. The original monastery, probably founded early during ithe Venetian period, was destroyed by **Turkish pirates** in 1471. It was rebuilt, but most of the present buildings were constructed in the nineteenth century, thanks to the energies of **Yerontoyiannis**, a monk who earned himself a name as a Robin Hood-style hero as well as a healer. Locally he is revered as a saint, and although he never conducted a single service due to his illiteracy and is denied canonization by the Church, Cretans flock to leave offerings beside his silver-encased cadaver and skull in the monastery chapel. You can also visit a **cave** behind the church to which he often retreated and from where there's a fine view towards the island of Koufonísi.

Pervolákia Gorge

8km east of Makríyialos

The **Pervolákia Gorge** emerges at the sea by Moní Kapsá (see page 177) where there's a tiny pebble beach offering a chance to cool off. This is the deepest and most spectacular of the gorges around Makríyialos, and one of the more challenging hikes; two hours for the 3.5km up to the village of **Káto Pervolákia** (**Κάτο Περβολάκια**), a little less back down. Since there's no transport at either end, you'll need to walk both ways or arrange a taxi to take you up, or from the *Kafenío Aposperida* (see page 180) when you reach the village. The gorge walk combines neatly with a visit to the monastery.

Goúdhouras

The village of **GOÚDHOURAS (Γούδουρας)** marks the end of the coast road east of Makríyialos, though you can turn inland here towards Zíros (see page 174). Numerous grandiose modern villas in finest mock-Classical style attest to a recent local economic boom, thanks in part to the dusty plastic greenhouses scattered along the coast, and in part to the small fishing fleet, but above all to the new oil- and gas-fired power station in an isolated spot 5km further round the coast, at Atherinolakós. There's a long stretch of pebbly, rather windswept beach.

2

Butterfly Gorge

5km west of Makríyialos

West of Koutsourás, keep an eye out on the right for the poorly signed **Koutsourás Communal Park.** This is at the bottom of **Butterfly Gorge**, and the start of a three- to four-hour walk up to the village of Orinó. Despite the name, the butterflies (Red admirals, predominantly) have not been much in evidence in recent years, perhaps because the slopes higher up and the gorge itself were devastated by a massive fire in 1993. Although the woodland has grown back since then, and butterflies have been spotted, they have not yet recovered to the numbers preceding the blaze. Some believe that the fire was not the accident it appeared at the time; many of the nearby villagers would prefer to see olives planted here or some other "sensible" use of the land.

It's easy enough to stroll a short way into the park (which, since it's on the main Ierápetra road, can be reached by bus), but the finest scenery, flora and fauna are to be found further up. In effect there are two gorges here: set out from the park through the first one, then across flatter, cultivated land to a final steep climb. In this last section there are waterfalls (in spring these can become torrents that make the way impassable, so check before setting out) and spectacular mountain scenery.

Orinó

The village of **ORINÓ (Ορεινό)** lies 2km further up the road from the top of Butterfly Gorge – you can also drive up there, on a road west of the park. Surrounded by lush greenery and wildflowers and at a height of nearly 1000m, the village is noticeably cooler than the coast; there's an excellent *kafenío* as well as a couple of rustic bars where you can slake your thirst after the climb.

THE FIRES OF CRETE

Forest fires are an all-too-common occurrence in Crete. Understandable, perhaps, given the summer heat and tinderbox conditions but, depressingly, not all are the accidents they seem to be. Figures from the Greek Agricultural Ministry attribute no less than 57 percent of all fires to unknown causes or arson; the number also increases prior to elections. This, of course, is when the politicians – in a desperate scramble for votes – are willing to recognize the claims to land of those who may have started the fires in the first place. Under Greek law, there is no organized system of land registry for publicly owned land, which means that if an area of woodland is burned down, the barren territory left behind becomes a no-man's-land that can be illegally claimed under squatters' rights. Once olives or other crops have been planted, a foothold towards possession has been attained, with local politicians often smoothing over any obstacles to the land transfer. This callous attitude to the environment, where trees are little regarded for their beauty and their environmental benefits ignored or not understood, has a long history. In his book *Wild Flowers of Crete*, biologist George Sfikas writes of the Greek view that "a green wood is useless because the trees drink valuable water and don't produce anything". Attitudes are slowly changing as environmental awareness grows, especially among the young, but for now fires continue to plague the island.

Ayía Fotiá

AYÍA FOTIÁ (**Αγία Φωτιά**) is almost exactly halfway between Makríyialos and Ierápetra, where a poorly signposted turning (hazardously situated halfway round a bend) leads down to an excellent small, sandy **beach** hidden from the road in a wooded valley. The tiny resort here is quiet at night, but the beach can get very crowded on summer weekends, when parking is also a nightmare. Nearby **Ahliá**, with a taverna and other facilities, is another lovely cove beach.

ARRIVAL AND DEPARTURE

MAKRÍYIALOS AND AROUND

By bus Four buses a day run in each direction between Sitía (1hr away) and Ierápetra (30min), stopping at various points on the main road behind the beach in Makríyialos; get off at the harbour for the western end of town, or near the *Villea Village Hotel* for Áspros Pótamos and places at the eastern end of town.

By boat In summer, there are daily trips from the harbour to Gaidhouronísi – Hrissi Island (see page 183) – with Cretan Daily Cruises (€25, half-price for kids; www.cretandailycruises.com) on the *Sofia* (6974 409 511).

ACCOMMODATION

Thanks to its popularity with the package holiday market (generally the more exclusive end of it), Makríyialos is not overflowing with accommodation for anyone on a modest budget. There are some very good midmarket choices, though; many more can be found on http://makrysgialos.com.

MAKRÍYIALOS

★ **Aspros Potamos Traditional Houses** Signed off the Pefkí road, www.asprospotamos.com. A group of tiny stone houses has been delightfully converted into studios and apartments at this back-to-nature accommodation, slightly further up the valley from the *White River Cottages*; you can walk down the valley to town in about 20 min. There's only solar power here; rooms have a fridge, single bathroom light and LED reading lamp (plus solar hot water), and in reception there's wi-fi and power for chargers, otherwise you are reliant on oil lamps and candles for lighting, and a fireplace to warm you in winter (extra charge for firewood). €

Asteria Studios Beachfront west of the harbour, close to the Roman villa, https://rlaxincrete.com. English-run air con studios right by the beach: bright, airy and exceptionally well kitted out with everything from toasters to hairdryers. €

Maria Tsankalioti Apartments Seaward side of the main road, halfway through town, http://makrigialos-crete.com. In an unbeatable beachfront position, run by a super-friendly family, these slightly old-fashioned but immaculately kept studios and apartments have kitchenette, a/c and TV; some also have big balconies overlooking the sea. €

Miramare Studios Eastern end of the town beach, down a track opposite the turning to Áspros Pótamos, http://miramare-studios.gr. Bright, blue-and-white a/c studios with kitchenette, TV and large balconies directly above the beach, where they have free sunbeds. €

Oasis Studios Beachfront west of the harbour, close to the Roman villa, 28430 51918. Spacious, simple and clean studios with kitchenette, fridge, terrace and balcony with sea view (extra for a/c), right on the beach. Easy parking. €

★ **The White Houses** On the harbour, www.makrigialos.com. Three houses and two apartments in beautifully restored harbour buildings, each one architect-designed and unique. Equipment includes everything from washing machine to champagne glasses. April–Oct. Apartments €€, houses €€€

White River Cottages 500m up a signed track at the eastern end of town, http://whiterivercottages.com. An abandoned hamlet of traditional stone dwellings has been restored as a warren of studios and apartments (for up to four people) around a small pool. Built partly into the rocks, with the original stone floors and whitewashed walls, they come with kitchens and private terraces. Minimum three-night stay. €€

AYÍA FOTIÁ

Markos Studios Built into the cliff on the east side of the bay, overlooking the beach, http://markos-agiafotia.com. Modern studios and apartments for up to four people, with kitchenettes and balconies affording awesome views. Studios €, apartments €€

Taverna Agia Fotia Right by the beach, http://agiafotia.gr. Simple but good value studios set back a little from the beach, behind the taverna. This is also the best of the places to eat here, with a great location and busy beach bar. Breakfast included. €

EATING AND DRINKING

The majority of **tavernas** in Makríyialos itself offer fairly standard, touristy food; options improve if you're prepared to travel a bit further. There's not much in the way of nightlife, but a number of **bars** on the harbour play soft music and serve cocktails.

2

MAKRÍYIALOS

Cafe Olympio Overlooking the beach beside the harbour, 28430 52135. Friendly bar-café that's a good source of local information, with sunbeds on a sandy strip of beach. Breakfasts, light lunches, and draught beer in the daytime give way to creatively named cocktails ("Bloody Troika" and "Lost in Crisis" are typical) after dark. €

Faros Overlooking the beach beside the harbour, 28430 52456. Big taverna in a great position, with everything from pizza and pasta to octopus and calamari; good fish from their own boat too. €

Helios Overlooking the beach beside the harbour, 28430 51280. Housed in a refurbished carob warehouse, this bar-café serves breakfast but is better later on, when it's the perfect place for a sundowner. €

Mina's Place Overlooking the harbour near the White House, 28430 51949. Friendly and economical little taverna which uses the harbour jetty as its terrace. Fresh fish is the house speciality – try the tasty *gávros* (fried anchovies) – but they also do meat grills and a range of mezédhes. Your order will probably be supplemented by "on the house" offerings from "Mama" in the kitchen. €

★ **Olive Tree** Overlooking the beach beside the harbour, 6973 240 181. Modern taverna with a pleasant waterfront terrace and slightly smarter ambience. The bread, dips and mezédhes are all superb; they also do fresh fish and a full menu – try the *païdhákia* or risotto with scallops. €€

KOUTSOURÁS

★ **Kalliotzina** Towards the western end of the village, 28430 51207. A classic old-fashioned taverna, serving home-cooked food and excellent fish on a tree-shaded terrace right by the sea. There's no written menu, so check out what's on offer in the kitchen or listen carefully as the day's dishes are reeled off at speed. There's often music on summer weekends. €€

Votsalakia In the middle of the beach by the mouth of the stream, 250m east of Kalliotzina, 28430 51247. Looking for an unpretentious, locally patronised place in or near Makrýgialos? Look no further than this sympathetic spot with the sound of the waves bashing the *votsalákia* (little pebbles) of the rocky shore below. The seafood is cheap, and there are exceptional grilled vegetables, *myzithrópittes* (mini-soft-cheese-pies) and meat platters if desired. Only the *rakí* could be faulted as it left a headache the next day. €

PERVOLÁKIA

Aposperida Káto Pervolákia, 28430 31010 or 6937 819 269. Arriving at this *kafenío* – a simple place run by ex-sea captain Manolis Contolemakis and his wife Antonia – is a worthwhile reward for climbing the Pervolákia Gorge. It's a good place for a drink and a few mezédhes or Antonia's home-cooked food (including a delicious "village chicken" with tagliatelle). Call ahead to check they're open; they can arrange a taxi for the gorge walk (see page 177). €€

PEFKÍ

★ **Piperia** Upper part of the village, 28430 52471. A lovely spot under a spreading pepper tree, with authentic, traditional food and great views over the coast. Mains like *païdhákia*, okra with lamb or rabbit in wine sauce are well worth a try; they also have live Greek music some summer evenings (with a set menu), and sell their own jams, olives and liqueurs. €€

Ierápetra and around

IERÁPETRA (**Ιεράπετρα**) has various claims to fame – the southernmost town in Europe, the most hours of sunshine, the largest town on the south coast of Crete, the westernmost town of Afghanistan, after the main ehnicity of thousands of immigrants who staff the local agricultural industry – but charm is not really one of them. Though there's an excellent Blue Flag **beach**, it's a big, sprawling place and a major supply centre for the region's numerous farmers who have grown rich on the year-round cultivation of cucumbers, tomatoes and peppers in the plastic greenhouses that scar the landscape along this coast. In recent years some resources have been devoted to smartening the town up, and, on the **seafront**, where a string of restaurants and bars stretches out in either direction, Ierápetra can be genuinely picturesque. However, tourism seems very much an afterthought, and things to do by day – apart from lie on the beach – are limited.

Brief history

Although you'd hardly know it to look at the town today, Ierápetra has quite a history. Early knowledge is sketchy, but it's almost certain that there was a settlement here, or at least a port, in **Minoan** times. A look at the map suggests a link across the isthmus with Gourniá, and it was probably from Ierápetra and other south-coast harbours that the Keftiu, as the Egyptians called the Cretans, sailed for the coast of Africa.

However, it was as a **Doric** settlement that **Ierápytna**, as the place was then known, grew to real prominence. By the second century BC it occupied more territory than any other Cretan city and had become a bastion of the Greek Dorians against their bitter enemies the Eteocretans: the final victory over Eteocretan Presós in 155 BC ended the last Minoan presence in eastern Crete. Only Ítanos, near Vái, now stood between Ierápytna and the complete domination of the eastern end of the island. Prolonged wars and disputes rumbled on for almost a century, and were finally brought to an end only by Rome's ruthless conquest of the entire island. Even then, Ierápytna stubbornly resisted to the last, becoming the final city to fall to the invading legions.

When **Rome** then joined Crete to Cyrene in northern Libya, forming the province of Cyrenaica, Ierápytna embarked on a new career as an important **commercial centre**, trading with Greece and Italy as well as Africa and the Near East. During this period, much impressive building took place – theatres, amphitheatres, temples – of which virtually nothing survives today, save for piles of fractured pillars and column capitals scattered in odd corners around the town.

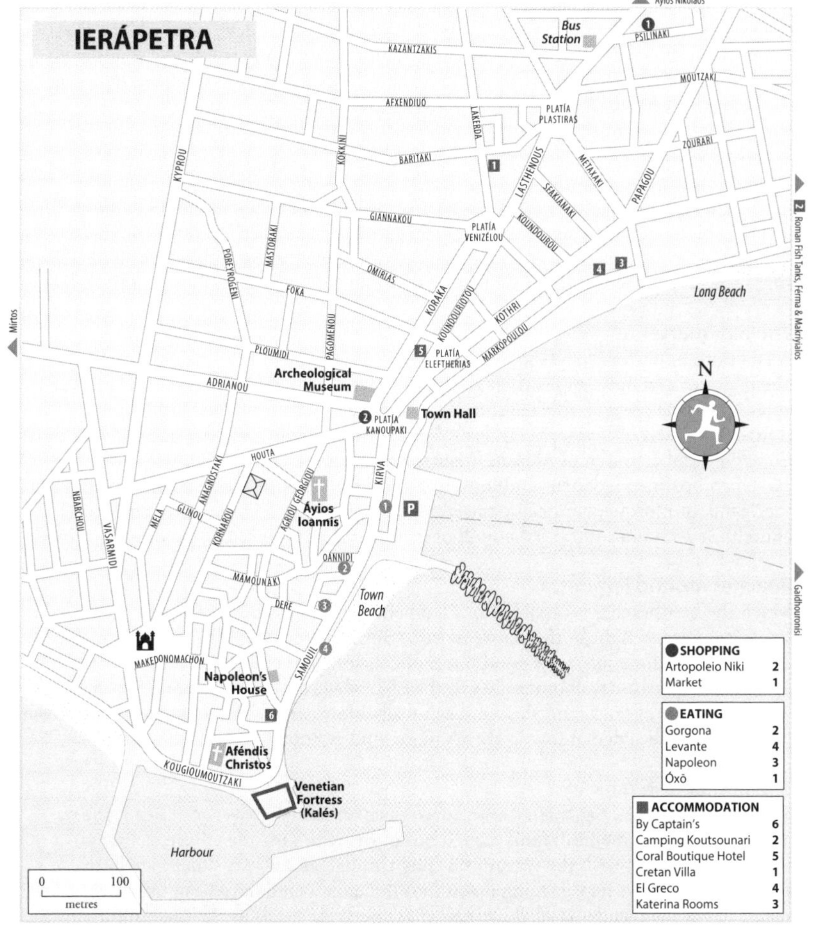

From the Romans to the tourists is a chronicle of steady decline. The Venetians (who favoured Sitía as their administrative centre in the east) left behind a small **fortress**, now restored, defending the harbour entrance. The Ottomans, under whom Ierápetra languished as a backwater, are represented by a nineteenth-century **mosque** and nearby inscribed fountain.

The Archeological Museum

2

Just off Platía Kanoupáki • Charge • 28420 28721 • Temporarily closed at the time of writing due to renovation work

Ierapetra's **Archeological Museum**, housed in a former madrassa or Koranic academy, is poorly labelled and doesn't take long to see, but does boast some high-quality exhibits. Among the highlights are numerous Minoan **lárnakes**, or clay coffins, the finest example of which was excavated at nearby Episkopí. Dating from the very end of the Neopalatial period (c.1300 BC), it has fascinating painted panels, one of which depicts a mare suckling her foal; other scenes revel in the stalking of the *kri-kri*, or wild ibex, by hunting dogs. Look out too for some interesting **Vasilikí ware** (see page 152), including typical jugs and vases, as well as some potters' turntables from the early Minoan settlement at Fournoú Korýfi (see page 185). The Greek and Roman section contains a selection of statuary, mostly headless because iconoclastic Christians tended to regard the stone craniums as places where the spirit of the devil was lurking. One more recent discovery, a wonderful second-century statue of **Persephone**, holding an ear of corn in her left hand, managed to hang on to hers, which is crowned by a small altar encoiled by two serpents, symbols of her divinity.

The Kalés

East side of the harbour • Free

A restored fortress known as the **Kalés** guards the harbour. Reputedly built by the Genoese pirate Pescatore in 1212, the present structure is basically a seventeenth-century Venetian defence, later used and modified by the Ottomans. Atmospheric as it is, it's simply an empty shell, with no signage or anything else apart from some public toilets.

The old quarter

A labyrinth of narrow streets inland from the harbour constitutes the **old quarter**. You'll almost certainly get lost here, but it's so tiny that a couple of minutes later you'll emerge at some recognizable landmark. Places to look out for include **Napoleon's House** (Káto Merá 9), where Napoleon Bonaparte allegedly spent a night in 1798, and the twin-domed church of **Aféndis Hristos**, a fourteenth-century building with a fine carved and painted wooden témblon . In a small square opposite a Turkish fountain, the **Tzami**, or mosque, has been painstakingly restored (it had been converted to a church). It retains a substantial chunk of its minaret and – inside – the original mihrab.

Beaches around Ierápetra

Much the best beaches accessible from Ierápetra are on Gaidhouronísi, but there's a small **town beach** right in the centre in front of the old quarter, and more along the coast in either direction, with good bus services along the main road behind them. Most of the tourist development lies to the east, where aptly named **Long Beach**, a windswept line of sand (and the wind can really blow here) stretches virtually unbroken for 5km from the edge of town. There's more sand at **Koutsonári**, just beyond.

The Roman fish tank

Between Koutsonári and Férma, about 9km east of Ierápetra • Look for a sign for "Roman Fish Tanks" in front of the *Kakkos Bay Hotel*

The remarkable **Roman fish tank**, carved out of the rock near the village of Férma, is some 4m square, with the sea still sloshing through an ancient sluice gate in the bottom. The carved steps leading down into the tank would have been used by the fish sellers to net the fish demanded by their customers; the pools in the surrounding rocks were no doubt used for the fish to be sold that day, while the smaller ones could be fattened up in the larger tank below.

Gaidhouronísi

The most popular way to escape Ierápetra's often stifling summer temperatures is to take a boat trip to **GAIDHOURONÍSI** (**Γαιδουρονήσι**) – Donkey Island, more often known locally as **Hrissi** – some 6 nautical miles offshore. A little over 4km in length, with a fine cedar forest and a couple of tavernas, Gaidhouronísi has some excellent sandy **beaches**, which these days are very highly commercialized and busy. It's not too hard to escape, though: there's a waymarked **walking route** around the island on which you should spot quite a few examples of the varied flora and fauna, as well as fossils and the fabulous "**Shell Beach**" (Belegrina), covered with discarded shells from countless generations of molluscs (no souvenir-taking allowed). Beach shoes are recommended for getting in and out of the water, as it's rocky in places.

ARRIVAL AND DEPARTURE — IERÁPETRA AND AROUND

By car Ierápetra has a complex one-way system and the usual shortage of parking. The easiest plan is to follow the signs to the "Archeological Collection" and from there to the seafront, where there's a large car park.

By bus The bus station (28420 28237) is on Lasthénous – the Áyios Nikólaos road. The centre lies to the southwest, a 5min walk away. Most of these services are slightly less frequent at weekends; timetables and online booking at http://ktelherlas.gr.

Destinations Ay. Nikólaos (8 daily; 1hr); Iráklio (8 daily; 2hr 30min); Makríyialos (7 daily; 30min); Mýrtos (Mon–Fri 4 daily, Sat 2; 30min); Sitía (4 daily; 1hr 30min).

GETTING AROUND AND INFORMATION

By boat Two competing companies, Chrysi Cruises (28420 20008, http://cretandailycruises.com) and Zanadu (6937 811 095), run daily trips to Gaidhouronísi, on large boats with on-board bars, from the jetty on the seafront (May–Oct; peak-season departures 10.30am, 11am & 12.30pm, returning 4pm, 5pm & 6pm; 55min). Tickets are sold by agents throughout town, or at the boat; officially they cost €25 return but off-season, or if you bargain with the agents, you may get them for much less. From the harbour, small boats offer more personalized trips and private charters, for not a great deal more; they include a traditional fishing *kaïki* (the *Nefeli*; 6942 791 474, www.nefeliboat.com) and a fast modern motor-yacht (the *Nautilos*; 6972 894 279, http://www.nautiloscruises.com).

By taxi There's a taxi rank on Platía Kanoupáki, or call 28420 26600.

ACCOMMODATION — SEE MAP PAGE 181

By Captain's Stratígou Samouíl 54, 28420 26672. Studios above a seafront souvenir shop, in a great location close to the town beach, with TV, modern kitchenette, and big seafront balconies in a couple; those at the back are less attractive. €

Camping Koutsounari Koutsounári, off the coast road 7km east, http://camping-koutsounari.gr. The only campsite on this stretch of the south coast, with a taverna, store and pool, and although the ground is a bit gritty there's a good beach and plenty of shade. €

Coral Boutique Hotel Platía Eleftherías 19, https://coralhotelcrete.gr. Swish small hotel with luxuriously decorated and furnished balcony rooms and suites (the higher ones come with sea views), kitted out with fridge, plasma TV and tea-making facilities. They also have refurbished apartments, and free public parking, nearby. €€

★ **Cretan Villa** Lakerdhá 16, www.cretan-villa.com. Close to the bus station on a pedestrianized street, this is a gem offering sparkling rooms with TV and fridge overlooking the flower-bedecked patio of a beautifully restored eighteenth-century stone house. They also have modern apartments, some with sea views, nearby. €

El Greco Kothrí 42, 28420 28471, http://elgreco-ierapetra.gr. Refurbished beachfront hotel with harmoniously toned rooms and suites; balconies at the front have great sea views (extra), while inland-facing rooms are cheaper. Also has its own café and restaurant (discounts for guests). Breakfast included. €€

Katerina Rooms Markópoulo 95, on the seafront behind the in-town beach, 28420 28345. A former seafront hotel that's been done up to offer studios and apartments with TV and cooking facilities, though the building itself can feel neglected. Those at the front have tremendous sea views. €

EATING AND DRINKING — SEE MAP PAGE 181

Along Markópoulou, the seafront promenade stretching behind the beach northeast of the town hall, there's a string of **café-bars** with outdoor seating, many of which serve breakfast. Samouíl, the promenade south of the

2

ferry terminal, has a number of more traditional **tavernas** facing the sea. In town itself there are plenty of more basic café and fast-food options between Platía Kanoupáki and Platía Eleftherías. Nightlife is pretty quiet, though there are lots of late-opening **bars** in the centre, especially around Platía Kanoupáki, by the Archeological Museum and south along Kírva.

Gorgona Stratígou Samouíl 12, 28420 26619. Near the harbour and fort, directly on the beach, this reliable, well-known and locally popular taverna serves good fish and seafood, along with all the standards. €

Levante Ierápetra waterfront (officially Stratigoú Samouíl 38), about 150m shy of the castle, https://levante-taverna.gr. The most reliable and oldest (since the 1930s) of Ierápetra's castle-view tavernas, with a great line in country-style dishes, plus seafood delicacies. Try the *omathiés* (rice-and-offal sausages particular to eastern Crete) or the *hohlií bourbouristí* (snails sauteed delicately with lemon and rosemary – the waiter will give you extraction lessons). An ideal lunch or dinner venue after a visit to Ierápetra's small but sweet archaeological museum or a cruise to Hrysí islet. €€

★ **Napoleon** Stratígou Samouil 26, 28420 22410. Another of Ierápetra's oldest tavernas, usually busy with locals; except during summer at lunchtime, when it may close. Freshly cooked dishes include oven-baked mountain lamb, and there's a good choice of mezédhes – try a mixed plate of their cheese and vegetable pies or delicious courgette fritters. The wholemeal bread – baked daily by the proprietor's wife – is outstanding. €€

Óxō Kýrva 15, 28420 22484. This colourful *rakádhiko* (like an ouzerí, but with *rakí as tipple instead*) is packed late at night with young locals; it's one of a number of fashionable restaurants here, with tables looking out towards the harbour jetty. Good, inexpensive mezédhes, plus *souvláki*, *panséta* (pork ribs) and meat or mushroom pies. €€

SHOPPING SEE MAP PAGE 181

Artopoleio Niki Houtá 2, 28420 27566. Foreign newspapers are available from this bakery facing the archeological museum.

Market Psilinaki to the northeast of the centre. An excellent Saturday street market and farmers' market with plenty of fruit and veg, plus local cheeses and spicy sausages (*lasithiotika*) as well as clothes, tools and flowers. Sat 8am–2pm.

Mýrtos and around

The coastline west of Ierápetra is, even more than usual, swathed in plastic, and holds plentiful signs of the wealth this form of agriculture has brought to the region: gleaming new car and kitchen showrooms line the road. At the end of this stretch **MÝRTOS (Μύρτος)** lies just off the main road, which here turns inland, heading up towards Áno Viánnos. Razed to the ground by the German army in 1944 as a punishment for resistance activities, Mýrtos today is an unexpected pleasure after the drabness of what has gone before; a charming, white-walled village with a long shingle beach. Even in August, when the place can get pretty full, the pace of life remains slow, the atmosphere pleasantly laidback. It's a suntrap all year round, claimed to be the one place around the Mediterranean when the swallows and house martins stay put in winter, not migrating south. part from topping up your tan, swimming, renting a boat or lingering over a drink, there's not a great deal to do in Mýrtos, but the surrounding countryside offers a couple of important **Minoan sites**, as well as the opportunity for foothill **hikes**. Above the beach at the western edge of the village there's evidence of a **Roman-era settlement**: a brick-built circular tank construction that may be part of a Roman baths complex, walls and, closer to the water, harbour installations – all awaiting archeological investigation.

Mýrtos Museum

Western side of the village, beside the church • Free

Mýrtos Museum was put together by a much-loved and respected local schoolmaster, Yiorgos Dimitrianakis, who taught most of the older folk in the village prior to his death in 1994. Throughout his life, he spent much of his free time wandering the fields and hills around Mýrtos collecting a wealth of finds, including ancient statuettes and vase fragments, and it was he who brought the Fournoú Korýfi and Pýrgos sites to the attention of archeologists. Inside are minor finds from those sites, as well as a folklore section with tools, kitchen and farming implements once used by the villagers. There's also a superb clay model of the site at Fournoú Korýfi created by John Atkinson, a British potter who now looks after the museum.

Pýrgos

Immediately east of Mýrtos, just beyond the bridge over the Mýrtos River; take the signed track and follow a waymarked footpath to the right, which climbs to the site, atop a low hill

The Minoan villa at **PÝRGOS** (**Πύργος**) was inhabited, like nearby Fournoú Korýfi, in the early Prepalatial Period (c.2500 BC) and destroyed by fire around 2200 BC. Unlike Fournoú Korýfi, however, Pýrgos was reoccupied and rebuilt following its destruction, when it appears to have incorporated the former's lands. By the time of the Neopalatial Period (c.1600 BC), the community occupying the lower slopes was dominated by a two- or three-storey country villa spread over the crown of the hill.

The path up circles around the back of the hill and past the remains of an enormous plastered **cistern**, the largest found in Minoan Crete, dating from the Prepalatial era (c.1900–1700 BC). When it burst over the northern side of the hill in ancient times, it was not repaired. Beyond this, a fine stretch of **paved road** survives from the early period: this led to a burial pit, now excavated. Continuing up, a **stepped street** flanked by some well-cut lower courses of the villa's outer wall leads into a **courtyard**, partly paved in the purple limestone of the region. At the rear of the villa (furthest away from the sea) on the west side, it's possible to make out a **light well** floored with the same purple limestone. Many of the walls carry marks of the ferocious blaze which destroyed the villa around 1450 BC, lending credibility to the Thíra explosion theory (see page 325), especially since volcanic material was discovered amid the rubble. But it now seems that while the villa was burned, the surrounding settlement was untouched – another puzzle to contemplate as you savour the magnificent sea view from the courtyard.

Fournoú Korýfi

Signed inland a couple of kilometres east of Mýrtos, near the village of Néa Mýrtos • The gate is generally left open • The site is on the peak, reached by scrambling up a gully (signed), then heading towards a stand of pine trees just before which a path heads to the right across a flat expanse of brush towards a hill, where the fenced site is clearly visible

At **FOURNOÚ KORÝFI** (**Φουρνού Κορύφι**) – Kiln Hill, also known as **Néa Mýrtos** – a Minoan site excavated in the 1960s by a British team yielded important evidence concerning early Minoan settlements. The excavations – which are not always easy to make sense of – revealed a **stone-built village** of nearly one hundred rooms, spread over the hilltop. Probably typical of numerous other settlements sited on the coast of eastern Crete during the early Prepalatial Period (c.2500 BC), these rooms contained stone and copper tools, carved seals and over seven hundred **pottery vessels**. Some of these were Vasilikí-type jugs (see page 152), and many were no doubt used to store the produce of the surrounding lands, then less arid than today.

In a room in the southwest corner of the site was located the oldest known Minoan domestic shrine, which produced the most important of the finds here: the **goddess of Mýrtos**, a clay idol with a stalked neck carrying a ewer (it's now in the Áyios Nikólaos museum, along with most of the other finds from this site and Pýrgos). Around the goddess, broken offering vessels were strewn about the floor, many of them charred by the fire that destroyed the site in about 2200 BC. The riddle of the fire, which seems to have left no casualties and provoked no rebuilding, is yet another unresolved Minoan question.

ARRIVAL AND INFORMATION — MÝRTOS AND AROUND

By bus There are 5 buses to and from Ierápetra on weekdays, just two on Sat (8am & 1pm) and none on Sun.

Travel agencies Several travel agencies in Mýrtos offer local information and help with rooms, villas for rent, money exchange, car rental and the like. Perhaps the most helpful is the friendly Prima Tours (28420 51530, http://sunbudget.net), on a side street near the beach towards the eastern end of the village where the bus timetable and lots of other information is posted; they also run a used book exchange and have information on local hiking routes. There's also useful information on the town website (www.mirtoscrete.gr).

ACCOMMODATION

Big Blue Apartments West side of village, http://big-blue.gr. Lovely rooms with fridge, studios with kitchenette, and larger two-bedroom apartments offering stunning views ("Heaven" and "Myth" are the ones to go for), all with sea-view balconies in an unimproveable stunning position high above the beach. Doubles or studios €, apartments €€

Hotel Myrtos On the main street behind the beach, 28420 51227. Friendly and good-value little hotel in the heart of the action. Refurbished rooms come with fridge and balcony, and some of those on the second floor have a sea view. There's an excellent taverna below, too. €

Myrthe Apartments Towards the back of the village near the church, https://myrthe.gr. Pretty apartment complex where the ample ultra-modern two-room apartments (sleeping two to five people) come with terrace, marble bathrooms and kitchen. Facilities include a/c and satellite TV. The minimum stay is seven days but this may be negotiable in slacker periods. €

Nikos House At the heart of the village near Hotel Myrtos, 28420 51116. Very simple studios and two-room apartments with kitchenettes; the upstairs studio, especially, is lovely, and you feel very much part of village life here. €

Panorama At almost the highest point at the west end of the village, above Big Blue, 28420 51556. Simple studios with kitchenette, TV and balconies; there are exceptional sea views from those at the front. €

★ **Villa Mala** Malés village 12km north, https://villamala.gr. Very pleasant rural luxury hotel in Malés (see page 186), whose extremely comfortable and tastefully furnished beamed rooms come with four-poster beds, snazzy bathrooms and terrace balconies. There's heating (for winter lets) and it's located next to a very good taverna. Half-price or less deals sometimes available online. Breakfast included. €€€€

Villa Nostos Eastern edge of the village, signed as you enter from the main road, https://villanostos.nl. Welcoming garden complex, right behind the beach, with plain but very good-value studios and apartments plus a couple of self-contained cottages, some with sea view. A/c is available for an extra charge. €

INLAND ESCAPES FROM MÝRTOS

The **mountainous terrain** behind Mýrtos offers plenty of opportunity to escape the crowds and heat of the coast, or to stretch your legs, as well as some spectacular scenery. If you're driving to or from Ierápetra, the route through **Mýthi** and **Máles** to Gra Ligiá offers a beautiful, if extremely slow, alternative to the plastic-strewn coast road. From Gra Ligiá you could also head north to Kalamáfka (see page 169).

SARAKINÁS GORGE

The scenic, 150m-deep **Sarakinás Gorge** starts close to the village of **Mýthi**, some 5km north of Mýrtos. To reach the start of the walk, drive or take a taxi to the village and then follow the signs to the gorge; there's a small parking place five minutes downhill, just before the bridge, where the walk begins. Depending on the rains, the water level in the gorge may mean you'll have to do some wading in parts, so waterproof footwear would be useful. It's about 2km or one hour's climb to the top of the gorge and a little less coming back down, by which time the *kafenío* in Mýthi will be an irresistible stop. Should you not wish to repeat the scramble back down, it's possible to pick up an asphalt road back to Mýthi by following the river a further 300m upstream from the top of the gorge to where it's feasible to wade across. A path heads off from the opposite bank to meet the road.

MÁLES

Above Mýthi, with transport, you can continue to climb to **Máles**, a village clinging to the lower slopes of the Dhíkti range. The climb takes in some stunning rock formations and as you get higher there are magical views of Hrissi Island far out to sea, as well as the expanse of plastic greenhouses along the coastal strip. Máles would be a good starting point if you wanted to take a **walk** through some stunning mountain terrain (the E4 Pan-European footpath passes just 3km north of here) and it has a comfortable hotel and taverna (see page 186).

EATING AND DRINKING

Beach Café Western end of the promenade, 28420 51527. The last spot at the western end of the village, right above the beach, where they offer loungers to customers. It's all too tempting to linger here for hours over a drink; they also serve breakfast and full meals. €

Myrtos Taverna Main thoroughfare, ground floor of the Hotel Myrtos, 28420 51227. An excellent, economical family-run taverna offering a range of *mayireftá* home-cooked dishes – try the *kounéli krasáto* (rabbit stewed in wine) – as well as fresh fish and tasty mezédhes, with outdoor tables on a pleasant terrace. €

Votsalo Seafront in the middle of the beach, 28420 51457. A likeable place with a great position at the centre of the beachfront promenade; hand-painted menus detail a good traditional set of dishes, washed down with home-produced wine. They also do breakfast, and coffee and drinks throughout the day. €€

Tértsa

The narrow coast road west from Mýrtos runs for some 6km, past some tempting cove beaches, to the tiny resort of **TÉRTSA** (**Τέρτσα**). Technically this is in Iráklio province, and there is a paved road that winds inland to meet the main Áno Viánnos road, but practically everyone who gets here has come from Mýrtos. There's an excellent long beach, partly nudist, a couple of fine tavernas, and some get-away-from-it-all apartments.

ACCOMMODATION, EATING AND ACTIVITIES — TÉRTSA

Lambros Apartments Set back down a side road from the centre of the village, http://tertsa.gr. Modern studios and apartments with kitchenette and TV, in a rural setting at the back of the village. In-person information is available from *Lambros Taverna*. €

Lambros Taverna Seafront in the centre of the village, http://tertsa.gr. Family-run taverna with a beachside terrace serving home-made traditional food plus daily fresh fish, a good meze selection and veggie options. There's also a Sunday barbecue with *souvláki* and lamb on the spit. The taverna acts as an unofficial rooms information centre and provides free sunbeds on the beach for customers. €€

Yoga There are Ashtanga yoga sessions on the beach most days in summer. Details at www.tertsaretreat.com.

1600
RaKi Ba RaKi

Réthymno

OLD TOWN OF RÉTHYMNO

Réthymno

3

The province of Réthymno has something for everyone. The island's intellectual and cultural capital, Réthymno itself is a relaxed university town overlooked by one of the most imposing Venetian fortresses on the island. It also retains a picturesque old quarter, redolent of traditional urban life, plus a fine beach. Probably the greatest attraction of the province, however, is its interior, dominated by mountains that provide stunning vistas at almost every turn. The provincial borders are defined by the island's loftiest peaks; in the east the looming mass of Psiloritis, Crete's highest mountain, and to the west the far reaches of the Lefká Óri, the White Mountains. The villages ranged around the Psiloritis massif provide ideal bases for spectacular wilderness hikes, highly recommended for casual ramblers and committed hikers alike.

The peaks themselves are approached most easily from **Anóyia**, a high mountain town known for its sheep-breeding, weaving and embroidery. From here, you can hike across to the south side of the mountains or down, via the summit of Psiloritis, to the pretty villages of the lushly fertile **Amári valley** – some of the least visited and most traditional places in Crete. Southwest of Réthymno town you're on the fringes of the Lefká Óri, studded with traditional hill villages such as **Aryiroúpoli** and **Así Goniá**, surrounded by more magnificent **hiking** country. In both directions, the mountains and valleys also offer spectacular **driving routes** across the island.

Not far out of Réthymno, en route to the Amári valley, is the revered **Moní Arkádhi**, a beautiful, ancient monastery whose history makes it the emblem of Crete's nineteenth-century struggle for independence against theOttomans. The main road towards the south, meanwhile, heads via the Minoan cemetery at **Arméni** to the attractive hill town of **Spíli**, another centre for walkers with many fine hikes in the surrounding hills.

Réthymno's **south coast** has no fancy hotels, but if all you want is sea and sand it's a far more attractive prospect than the north. There are two sizeable resorts, crowded **Ayía Galíni** and its more easy-going rival, **Plakiás**. Along the coast between them is a string of secluded pockets of sand – sometimes with a village attached – often hard to access but well worth it for a few lazy days. One of them, **Palm Beach**, is among the most picturesque on Crete, though far from undiscovered. Above it is **Moní Préveli**, an illustrious seaside monastery that played a pivotal role during the Battle of Crete.

Réthymno town

Although it's the third largest town in Crete, **RÉTHYMNO** (**Ρέθυμνο**) never feels like a city, as Haniá and Iráklio do. Instead, it has an easy-going provincial air; it's a place that moves slowly and, for all the myriad bars springing up along the seafront, the **old town** still preserves much of its Venetian and Ottoman appearance. Here the streets are a fascinating mix of **architectural eras**, the Venetian buildings largely indistinguishable from the Ottoman and all of them adapted by later generations. Ornate wooden doors and covered balconies – the locally famed *kióskia* –and ancient stonework crop up everywhere, and there are a number of mosques and elaborate Ottoman calligraphically inscribed **fountains** hidden in obscure corners of the old town. A few traditional stores survive too, where craftsmen still make *lyras* (the Cretan "spike fiddle") or sharpen knives by hand. Arriving, especially if you approach from the east in the evening,

TRIÓPETRA BEACH

Highlights

❶ **Réthymno** The provincial capital has fine Venetian and Ottoman monuments and an atmospheric old quarter, as well as a great in-town beach, fine food and buzzing nightlife. See page 190

❷ **Moní Arkádhi and Moní Préveli** Two of Crete's most important monasteries, the imposing Moní Arkádhhi and the seaside Moní Préveli are inextricably bound up with the island's history. See pages 203 and 226

❸ **Margarítes** A major centre of ceramics production, this is the place to buy anything from an egg cup to a massive Minoan-style *píthos*. See page 206

❹ **Mount Psiloritis** Dominating the province, Crete's highest peak provides some challenging hikes. See page 209

❺ **Amári valley** White-walled villages with frescoed Byzantine chapels surrounded by orchards, vineyards and olive groves, all with a spectacular mountain backdrop. See page 211

❻ **Triópetra** A gorgeous south coast beach, isolated yet accessible, with development if you want it and plenty of room to escape if you don't. See page 221

❼ **Mountain roads** West of Réthymno, the mountain roads to the south coast offer some of Crete's most enthralling drives. See page 228

HIGHLIGHTS ARE MARKED ON THE MAP ON PAGE 192

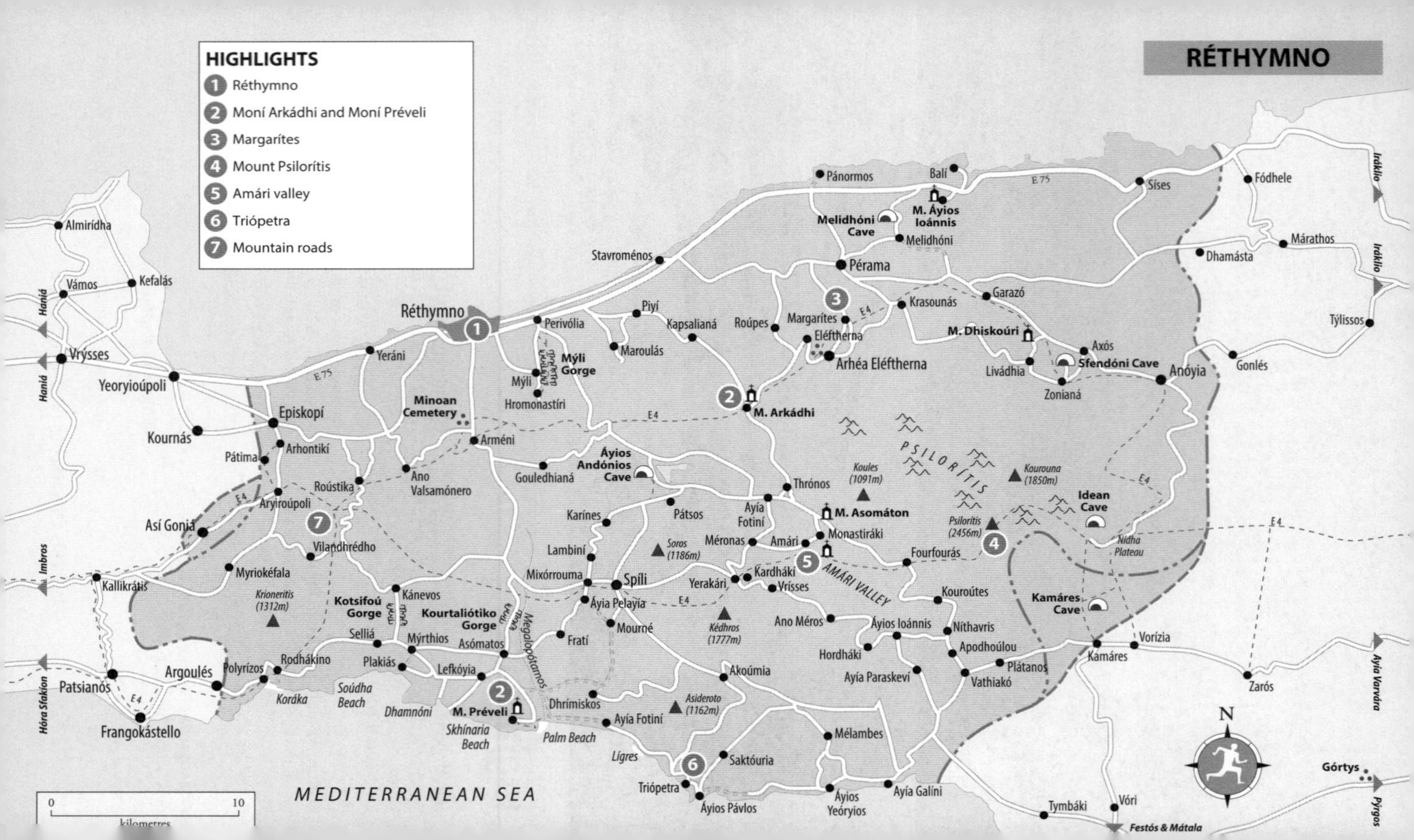
RÉTHYMNO
HIGHLIGHTS
1 Réthymno
2 Moní Arkádhi and Moní Préveli
3 Margarítes
4 Mount Psiloritis
5 Amári valley
6 Triópetra
7 Mountain roads
Réthymno
Almirídha
Vámos
Kefalás
Vrýsses
Yeoryioúpoli
Kournás
Episkopí
Yeráni
Pátima
Arhontikí
Roústika
Aryiroúpoli
Así Goniá
Vilandhrédho
Myriokéfala
Kallikrátis
Krioneritis (1312m)
Patsianós
Frangokástello
Argoulés
Polyrízos
Rodhákino
Koráka
Soúdha Beach
Dhamnóni
Plakiás
Selliá
Kotsifoú Gorge
Kánevos
Kourtaliótiko Gorge
Mýrthios
Asómatos
Lefkóyia
M. Préveli
Skhínaria Beach
Palm Beach
Megalopótamos
Dhrímiskos
Ayía Fotiní
Lígres
Triópetra
Áyios Pávlos
Saktoúria
Áyios Yeóryios
Ayía Galíni
Mélambes
Asideroto (1162m)
Akoúmia
Minoan Cemetery
Arméni
Ano Valsamónero
Perivólia
Mýli Gorge
Mýli
Hromonastíri
Piyí
Maroulás
Kapsalianá
Roúpes
Margarítes
Eléftherna
Arhéa Eléftherna
M. Arkádhi
Stavroménos
Pérama
Pánormos
Bali
M. Áyios Ioánnis
Melidhóni Cave
Melidhóni
Krasounás
Garazó
M. Dhiskoúri
Livádhia
Axós
Sfendóni Cave
Zonianá
Anóyia
Síses
Fódhele
Dhamásta
Márathos
Týlissos
Gonlés
Gouledhianá
Áyios Andónios Cave
Karínes
Pátsos
Lambiní
Mixórrouma
Spíli
Áyia Pelayía
Mourné
Fratí
Soros (1186m)
Thrónos
Ayía Fotiní
Méronas
Amári
Monastiráki
M. Asomáton
Yerakári
Kardháki
Vrísses
Amári Valley
Kédhros (1777m)
Ano Méros
Koules (1091m)
Psiloritis
Kourouna (1850m)
Psiloritis (2456m)
Idean Cave
Nídha Plateau
Fourfourás
Kouroútes
Áyios Ioánnis
Níthavris
Hordháki
Apodhoúlou
Ayía Paraskeví
Plátanos
Vathiakó
Kamáres Cave
Kamáres
Vorízia
Zarós
Tymbáki
Vóri
Górtys
Festós & Mátala
Pýrgos
Ayía Varvára
Iráklio
Iráklio
Haniá
Haniá
Ímbros
Hóra Sfakion
E 75
E 75
E4
E4
E4
E4
E4
E4
MEDITERRANEAN SEA
N
0
10
kilometres

RÉTHYMNO CITY CENTRE ORIENTATION

Réthymno **city centre**, at least as far as tourists are concerned, is the largely pedestrianized old town bordered by the fortress, harbour and beach in the north, and the traffic-filled streets that run through the busy **Platía Tessáron** to the south. The fortress also delineates the northwestern limit of the ancient streets, while to the east the beach and main roads converge around **Platía Stratióti** and the marina. The major thoroughfares are **Ethníkis Andistásis**, the **market** street, leading from the heart of the old town south to the **Porta Guora**, the only surviving remnant of the city walls, and **Arkadhíou**, running parallel to the shore but a block inland, a more commercial and touristy shopping street.

the town looks exactly as it does in old engravings or in Edward Lear's watercolours – dominated by the bulk of a colossal **Venetian fortress**, the skyline picked out with delicate minarets.

All of this is increasingly under commercial threat – there are hundreds of tavernas, bars, cafés and clubs – but on the whole the big hotels are out of town, stretching away along the shore to the east. The town centre remains a very enjoyable place to spend some time, with a wide, sandy **beach** and palm-fringed promenade in front of the tangled streets of the old town.

The harbour

The Venetian or inner **harbour** is the most attractive part of Réthymno's waterfront, although these days its elegant sixteenth-century lighthouse looks down on a line of quayside fish tavernas, rather than the sailing ships and barges of bygone eras. The impressive breakwaters delineating the outer harbour see little use: ever since the Venetians built the harbour it has had an unstoppable tendency to silt up, and few big ships now call here. The inner harbour and the marina under the eastern breakwater are instead given over to small fishing *kaïkia*, pleasure craft and tourist cruise boats.

The old town

Wandering through the old town is a large part of the pleasure of visiting Réthymno; there's little specifically to visit, but plenty to look out for as you stroll. At its heart are two Venetian survivals – the seventeenth-century **Rimóndi fountain**, whose lion-head spouts look out over **Platía Petiháki**, one of the liveliest areas in town, and the sixteenth-century **Loggia**, now serving as a museum replica shop. Not far away is the restored **Nerantzés Mosque** (originally a church, now used for concerts but not otherwise open to the public), whose iconic minaret dominates the skyline.

The Archeological Museum

Ayíou Frangískou, off Ethnikís Andístasis • Charge • http://archmuseumreth.gr

Rethýmno's **Archeological Museum** occupies the church of St Francis, a beautiful building that was once part of a Venetian monastery, later incorporated into the Nerantzés mosque complex – a gorgeous archway beyond the museum opens into Platía Mikrasiatón, behind the mosque. This is supposed to be a temporary home for the museum, after it was evicted from its former premises up in the old jail though it seems likely to stay here for the foreseeable future. The collection, all of it from Rethýmno province, is exceptionally rich, ranging from stone axe-heads over 100,000 years old, through fine Minoan pottery and jewellery and Roman-era statuary and glass, to Byzantine and Arab items including rescued frescoes and mosaic floors. Among the highlights are Minoan pottery, jewellery, swords and sarcophagi from **Arméni** (see page 216) and an unusual unfinished Roman **statue of Aphrodite**, with

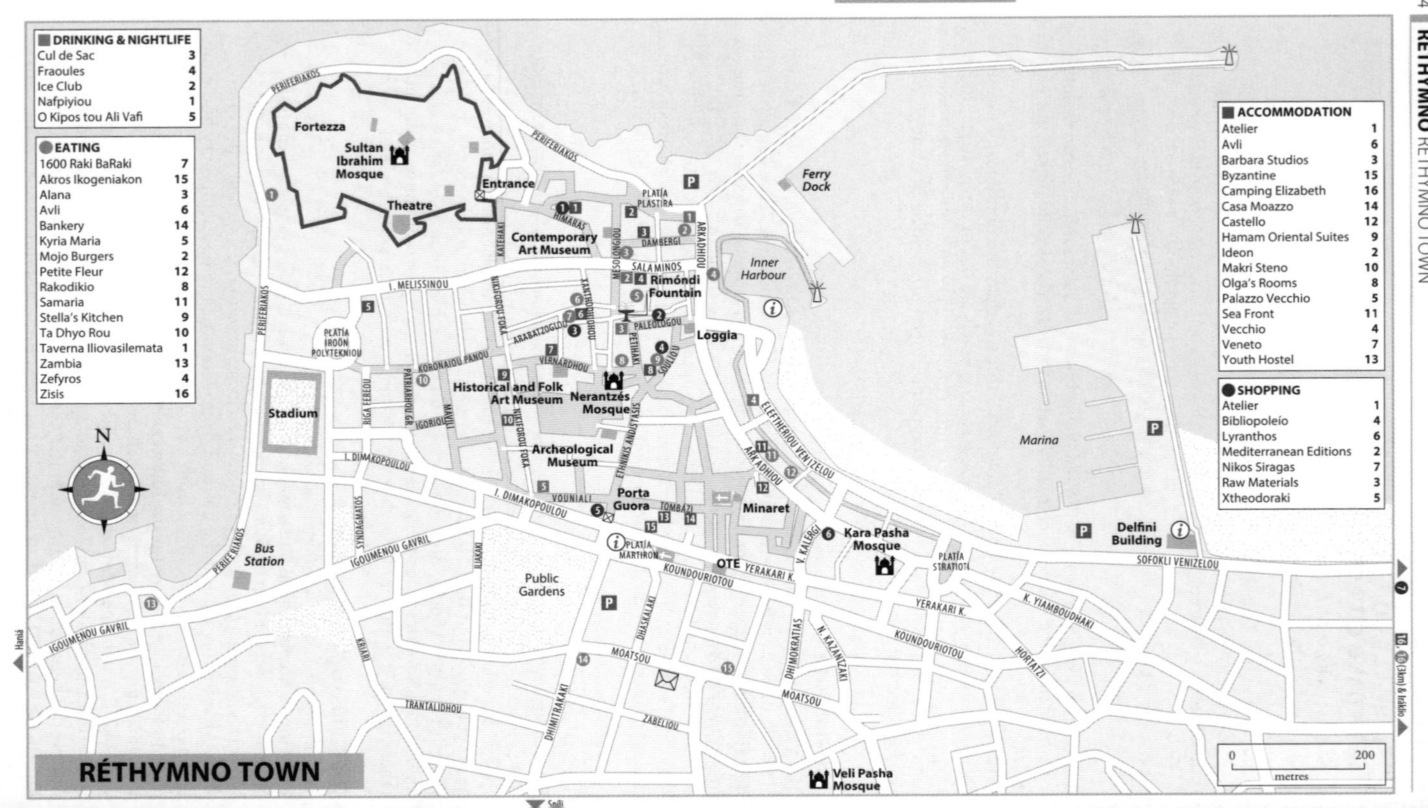
RÉTHYMNO TOWN
DRINKING & NIGHTLIFE
Cul de Sac 3
Fraoules 4
Ice Club 2
Nafpiyiou 1
O Kipos tou Ali Vafi 5
EATING
1600 Raki BaRaki 7
Akros Ikogeniakon 15
Alana 3
Avli 6
Bankery 14
Kyria Maria 5
Mojo Burgers 2
Petite Fleur 12
Rakodikio 8
Samaria 11
Stella's Kitchen 9
Ta Dhyo Rou 10
Taverna Iliovasilemata 1
Zambia 13
Zefyros 4
Zisis 16
ACCOMMODATION
Atelier 1
Avli 6
Barbara Studios 3
Byzantine 15
Camping Elizabeth 16
Casa Moazzo 14
Castello 12
Hamam Oriental Suites 9
Ideon 2
Makri Steno 10
Olga's Rooms 8
Palazzo Vecchio 5
Sea Front 11
Vecchio 4
Veneto 7
Youth Hostel 13
SHOPPING
Atelier 1
Bibliopoleío 4
Lyranthos 6
Mediterranean Editions 2
Nikos Siragas 7
Raw Materials 3
Xtheodoraki 5
0 200
metres
N
16, 16 (3km) & Iráklio
7
Haniá
Spíli
Fortezza
Sultan Ibrahim Mosque
Theatre
Entrance
Contemporary Art Museum
Historical and Folk Art Museum
Nerantzés Mosque
Archeological Museum
Rimóndi Fountain
Loggia
Porta Guora
Minaret
OTE
Kara Pasha Mosque
Veli Pasha Mosque
Delfini Building
Inner Harbour
Ferry Dock
Marina
Public Gardens
Stadium
Bus Station
PLATÍA PLASTIRA
PLATÍA IROON POLYTEKNIOU
PLATÍA MARTIRON
PLATÍA STRATIOTI
ARKADHIOU
ELEFTHERIOU VENIZELOU
SOFOKLI VENIZELOU
PERIFERIAKOS
I. MELISSINOU
I. DIMAKOPOULOU
IGOUMENOU GAVRIL
KOUNDOURIOTOU
YERAKARI K.
MOATSOU
DHIMITRAKAKI
DHIMOKRATIAS
N. KAZANTZAKI
HORTATZI
K. YIAMBOUDHAKI
NIKIFOROU FOKA
ETHNIKIS ANDISTASIS
PALEOLOGOU
PETIHAKI
MESOLONGIOU
SALAMINOS
DAMBERGI
XANTHOUDHIDHOU
VERNARDHOU
ARABATZOGLOU
KORONAIOU PANOU
MAVILI
PATRIARHOU GR
RIGA FEREOU
IGORIOU
SYNDAGMATOS
KRIARI
TRANTALIDHOU
ILIAKAKI
ZABELIOU
DHASKALAKI
TOMBAZI
VOUNIALI
SOULIOU
HIMARAS
KATEHAKI
V. KALERGI

the sculptor's chisel marks still plain to see, allowing you to glimpse the goddess's features – never completed – emerging from the stone.

The Historical and Folk Art Museum

Vernádhou 28 • Charge • 28310 23398

The little-visited **Historical and Folk Art Museum**, in a beautifully restored seventeenth-century Venetian mansion near the Nerantzés Mosque, is among the best of its kind. Starting with the inevitable Independence and Battle of Crete weaponry and memorabilia, it moves on to an exceptional depiction of traditional life, including a comprehensive weaving and embroidery display, a reconstructed sitting-room with all its furnishings, musical instruments (including the *lyra* of Nikos Piskopakis, one of its greatest-ever exponents), basketry, farm tools, traditional costumes, jewellery, pottery and more. At the back is a recreation of a typical city street including a *kafenío*, pharmacy, barber, tailor and blacksmith. It's a fascinating insight into the island's fast-disappearing lifestyles, many of which had survived virtually unchanged from Venetian times to the 1960s.

The Contemporary Art Museum

Mesolongíou 32 • Charge • http://cca.gr

Réthymno's **Contemporary Art Museum** has a small permanent collection of works by Greek and Cretan sculptors and painters, with oils and watercolours by Réthymno-born artist Lefteris Kanakakis (1934–85) forming the core of the collection. Mostly, though, they stage challenging special exhibitions, both in the main building and at other venues across town, including places you might not otherwise be able to visit, such as the Kara Pasha mosque inside the Fortezza.

The Fortezza (Fortétsa)

Entrance from Odhós Kateháki • Charge • 28310 28101

Looking down on the old town from higher ground at the western end of the seafront stands the massive **Fortezza** or **Venetian Fortress**. Although much is ruined now, the fort remains thoroughly atmospheric (even more so if you catch an evening concert here), with **views** from the walls over the town and harbour, or in the other direction along the coast to the west. The chief impression once you're close up, inside or out, is of its vast scale – the fortress was designed to be large enough for the entire population to take shelter within its walls.

Brief history

Said to be the largest Venetian castle ever built, the Fortezza was a response, in the last quarter of the sixteenth century, to a series of **pirate raids** (by Barbarossa in 1538 and Uluch Ali in 1562 and 1571) that had devastated the town. Designed by the Italian engineer Sforza Pallavicini, the mammoth edifice took a full ten years to build, at crippling cost. Whether it was effective is another matter; in 1645 the Venetian city fell to the Ottomans in less than 24 hours (the latter simply bypassed the fort), and when the English writer Robert Pashley visited in 1834 he found the guns, some of them still the Venetian originals, to be entirely useless.

Within the walls

As you walk through the impressive gateway in the walls you pass what must have been some sort of **guardhouse** within the bastion, and then emerge into the vast open interior space, dotted with the remains of barracks, arsenals, officers' houses, earthworks and deep shafts. At the centre is a large domed building which was purpose built as a mosque by the Ottomans in honour of the reigning sultan Ibrahim and is in fact the largest domed structure in Greece, with superb acoustics taken advantage of for occasional performances. Once a **church** and later – following the fall of the town to the Turks – converted into a **mosque** dedicated to the then ruling sultan. The renovated interior has a truly fabulous **dome** and a pretty, polychrome mihrab (a niche indicating the direction of Mecca). Just north of the church/mosque are some fine arched foundations and a **stairway** leading down to a gate in the seaward defences. Among the most impressive remains are the **cisterns** where rainwater would have been collected: they are deep and cool, and dimly lit by slits through which shafts of sunlight penetrate.

The beach

Réthymno's **beach** is an invitingly broad swathe of tawny sand, right alongside the old town. There are showers and cafés, and the waters protected by the breakwaters are dead calm (and ideal for kids). Sadly, they're also crowded and often none too clean. Outside the harbour, less sheltered sands stretch for kilometres, only marginally less crowded but with much cleaner water and all sorts of watersports. Interspersed among the hotels along here is every facility you could need – travel agents, bike rental, bars and restaurants.

ARRIVAL AND DEPARTURE — RÉTHYMNO TOWN AND AROUND

BY BUS

Bus station The bus station in Réthymno is by the sea to the west of the town centre; from the station, it's about a 10min walk to the harbour; local bus #20 runs through the centre and east along the coast to the hotel zone. Info, timetables and tickets at http://e-ktel.com.

Destinations Amári (Mon–Fri 2.30pm; 1hr); Anóyia (Mon–Fri 5.30am & 2pm; 1hr 30min); Arkádhi (4 daily; 50min); Ay. Galíni via Spíli (5 daily; 1hr 20min); Haniá (17 daily; 1hr 15min); Hóra Sfakíon (change at Vrísses; 3 daily; 2hr); Iráklio (16 daily; 1hr 30min); Moní Préveli (9am & 11am; 1hr); Omalós (daily at 7am; 1hr 45min); Pánormos and hotels en route (at least 20 daily; 1hr); Plakiás (5 daily; 1hr).

BY CAR

Parking is even more tricky in Réthymno than elsewhere, especially as most of the old town is pedestrianized. Some hotels have spaces, or try the streets near Platía Plastíra by the outer harbour (where there is also a public pay car park), around the public gardens (with another pay car park) or in the streets surrounding Platía Stratióti at the east end of the seafront.

BY FERRY

In summer, there's a twice-weekly fast catamaran to Santoríni (2hr 15min), Íos (3hr), Náxos (4hr) and Mýkonos (5hr). It leaves early and returns the same evening: any local travel agent can sell you a day-trip package to Santoríni (including a tour and meals) or book direct with SeaJets (http://seajets.gr).

BY PLANE

The nearest airports to Réthymno are at Haniá (60km, see page 244) and Iráklio (78km, see page 67).

GETTING AROUND AND INFORMATION

By bus Once in Réthymno you'll mostly be walking, but if you're staying in the hotel strip east of town, you can take advantage of the excellent bus service along the coast road (every 30min 7.30am–midnight), and there are local buses, too, to nearby villages, detailed in the text where relevant.

By taxi There are ranks in Platía Tessáron Martýon and Platía Stratióti, or call 28310 25000 or 28310 35000.

By bike There's an e-bike hire system in Réthymno (https://bikeazy.gr): download their app and you can use bikes at an hourly, daily or weekly rate.

Car and bike rental Arkadi, Venizélou 22 (28310 29134, www.arkadi-rental.com/), have good modern cars, scooters and bikes. There are plenty of others nearby on this section of the seafront close to the marina, many with pedal bikes too.

City tours Open-top bus and "Little Train" tours of the city are generally a waste of time, as they can't go into the old town; some do take you a long way out into the countryside, though, and can be handy for hikes or visiting villages. One way you can explore the old town is on a Segway, with BestRide, Venizélou 4 (6948 175 785, http://bestride.gr).

Tourist information The main Tourist Information office (Mon–Fri 8am–2.30pm, 28310 29148) is at the back of the Delfini building, on the seafront east of the centre. In summer, info booths can also be found at the corner of the old harbour and in Platía Tessáron Martýron (June–Sept Mon–Fri 9am–2pm, but unreliable). The municipal websites, https://rethymno.guide and https://rethymno.gr, are dated but still useful.

Travel agents There are numerous travel agents in the

centre, especially on Venizélou near the marina. Good options for tours and tickets are Cool Holidays, Melissinoú 2 in the old town (28310 35567, http://coolholidays.gr), and Panayotis Klados Travel, Platía Tessáron Martýron 13 (28310 54428, http://kladostravel.gr).

TOURS AND ACTIVITIES

Boat trips Dolphin Cruises (28310 57666, http://dolphin-cruises.com) runs a variety of day-trips and short cruises from the marina, including a "pirate" boat, fishing trips and sunset cruises. There are also day-trips to Santoríni with Seajets (http://seajets.gr).

Diving Paradise Dive Center (28310 26317, https://diving-center.gr), 10km west of town off the E75 highway, offers PADI-certificated scuba courses for beginners and outings facilities for certified divers. They will collect you and return you to your hotel. Kalypso Dive Centre (28310 74687, http://kalypsodivecenter.com) also offers PADI beginners and advanced courses. Prices include transfers to and from their dive centre near Plakiás on the south coast.

Mountain climbing The local EOS mountain climbing club is at Dhimokratías 12 (28310 57766, http://eosrethymnou.gr; office open Tues 9–11pm); besides offering advice on climbing, it also organizes walking tours and easy climbs that anyone can join.

Walking tours The Happy Walker, Tombázi 56 (28310 31390, http://happywalker.com; office daily April–Oct 10am–2pm, closed weekends in July & Aug), a long-standing Dutch operation near the youth hostel, offers walking tours from one to ten days. Single-day guided walks, available every day except Sunday, cost €32 (lunch and any entry fees extra), including transport to and from your hotel to the start point.

3

ACCOMMODATION

SEE MAP PAGE 194

The greatest concentration of **rooms** lies in the tangled old town streets west of the inner harbour, though there are also quite a few places on and around Arkadhíou, behind the town beach, while the resort hotel zone stretches for kilometres eastward along the coast.

AROUND THE HARBOUR AND FORTRESS

Atelier Himáras 25, 28310 24440. This small place near the fortress is run by a talented potter, above her workspace and shop. The attractive rooms come with kitchenette and satellite TV. €

★ **Avli** Xanthoudhídhou 22, https://avli.gr. Luxury apartments and suites from the people who also run a couple of great local restaurants. They have several locations at various prices, but the best are within a couple of lovingly restored old townhouses, with a rooftop terrace and hot tub; a superb breakfast is included. €€

★ **Barbara Studios** Dhamvérgi 14, https://barbarastudios.gr. Beautifully done-up, well-equipped rooms, studios and apartments in a rambling old building, sharing a roof garden and communal areas. Great location and an exceptionally friendly welcome. €

★ **Hamam Oriental Suites** Nikifórou Foká 86, http://hamamsuites.com. A stunning conversion of a Turkish hamam into five luxury suites. The Hamam Suite (Cyclamen) occupies the main, domed room and has a private steam bath; the top-floor Ottoman Suite (Hyacinth) is a fully-equipped two-room apartment with mini sauna and tiny pool; the others are slightly less fancy (and cost less). Breakfast included. €€

Ideon Platía Plastíra 10, http://hotelideon.gr. Traditional-style hotel in an excellent location just north of the harbour – try to get a balcony room with a sea view. There's an internal garden courtyard with a decent-sized pool. Breakfast included. €

Makri Steno Nikifórou Foká 56, https://makristeno.gr. A somewhat chaotic but welcoming and nicely renovated mansion, its airy studios with TV, huge roof terrace, and washing machine for guests' use. Some slightly more expensive apartments are also available. €

Palazzo Vecchio Corner Iróon Polytehníou and Melissinoú, www.palazzovecchio.gr. A delightful small boutique hotel in a restored Venetian mansion, where the elegantly furnished suites and maisonettes all come with cooking facilities; there's also a small pool. Breakfast included. €€

Vecchio Daliáni 4, http://vecchio.gr. Hidden away in a narrow alley close to the Rimóndi fountain, this Venetian mansion was one of the city's first boutique hotels, and remains a haven of peace. Balcony rooms are set around a courtyard pool; they're showing their age, but this is reflected in the price. €

Veneto Epiménidhou 4, https://venetohotel.gr. Venetian-era monastery lovingly converted to a boutique hotel and restaurant. Each room or suite is unique, but most are furnished with antiques and have hefty, beamed ceilings; one, in the basement, occupies a stone monk's cell. €€

EASTERN OLD TOWN

Byzantine Vospórou 26, https://hotelbyzantine.com. Big, if rather basic, rooms in a renovated Byzantine palace, which also has a tranquil patio bar and a roof terrace hidden away down an alley, which also has a tranquil patio bar and a roof terrace. Breakfast included. €

Casa Moazzo Tombázi 57, http://casamoazzo.gr. Delightful boutique hotel offering six luxurious and stylish suites with king-size beds, jacuzzi, plus coffee- and tea-making facilities. Breakfast included. €€

Castello Karaolí ke Dhimitríou 10, https://castello-rethymno.gr. A very congenial small *pension* in a 300-year-old Muslim mansion; rooms come with fridge and TV, and there's a delightful patio garden for taking breakfast, plus a tiny subterranean jacuzzi pool. €

Olga's Rooms Soulíou 3557, http://rethymnoguide.com/olgas. Redolent of an earlier era, though a/c, tv and wi-fi have been added, this basic, but exceptionally friendly and good value hotel has a tranquil patio bar and a roof terrace. They also have more modern studios in a separate building nearby. Excellent breakfast served nearby at *Stella's Kitchen*. €

Sea Front Arkadhíou 159/Venizélou 45, http://rethymnohotel.adminbs.com. Attractive rooms and studios in a waterfront house, some with sea-view balconies (well worth the extra money), and all with fridge and TV. The welcoming owners also have a number of excellent sea-view apartments nearby. €

★**Youth Hostel** Tombázi 41, http://yhrethymno.com. Long-established, friendly and popular hostel with the cheapest beds in town, in six- to eight-bunk dorms. Each bed has power and a locker, with modern bathrooms and there's a communal kitchen and washing machines, plus a sociable café for breakfast, juices and drinks. €

CAMPSITE

Camping Elizabeth About 3km east of town, near the highway junction, www.camping-elizabeth.net. A large, appealing beachfront site with all facilities, plenty of shade, and regular connections to the city using the hotel zone bus. €

3

EATING

SEE MAP PAGE 194

Immediately **behind the town beach** are arrayed the most obvious of Réthymno's restaurants, all with illustrated menus out front and most with waiters who will run off their patter in a variety of languages. These places sometimes provide reasonable value – especially if you hanker after an "English breakfast" – but they are all thoroughly touristy. Around the inner harbour there's a cluster of rather more expensive and intimate fish tavernas. The more authentic and inviting places are generally found in less obvious parts of the old town.

OLD TOWN AND HARBOUR

1600 Raki BaRaki Arabatsóglou 17, 28310 58250. Big, modern meze place from the people who run *Avli* (the hotel and very fancy restaurant next door). It's pricier than some, but the food is very good, the ambience welcoming, it's open all day and there's a huge amount to choose from, whether its cheese pie with *apáki* (smoked pork), aubergine and filo rolls with goat cheese, grilled sardines or *moussakás*. €€

★**Alana** Salamínos 15, https://alana-restaurant.gr. An attractive, tree-filled courtyard provides the setting for an elegant restaurant serving both traditional and updated Cretan dishes. Among the former, try lamb *tsigariasto* (a traditional, slow-cooked stew), the latter includes the likes of sea bass cooked sous-vide with citrus sauce. Also, good wine and a range of bottles. €€

★**Avli** Xanthoudhídhou 22, http://avli.gr. Upmarket restaurant with a glorious, elegant courtyard setting with a well as a focal feature. Traditional Cretan dishes are updated with wider Mediterranean touches: for lunch try the *moussakás* or *Avli* salad, or if you're settling in there are excellent four to six-course menus; mains such as lamb stuffed with graviera cheese or grilled garlic prawns with cabbage risotto. There's also an extensive wine list. €€€

Kyria Maria Moskhovítou 20, 28310 29078. Tucked down an alley behind the Rimóndi fountain, this popular little taverna serves tasty mezédhes and good-value, well-cooked fish and meat dishes (chicken *souvláki*, rabbit in lemon sauce, set menu for two with wine); after the meal, everyone gets a couple of Maria's delicious *tyropitákia* with honey, on the house. €€

Mojo Burgers Dhamvérgi 38, 28310 50550. If you need a break from Greek food, *Mojo* serves up excellent burgers (go for an "Elvis" with cheese, bacon and syrup) and hot dogs in a diner-style space. €

Petite Fleur Venizélou 36, http://petitefleur.gr. Very different from the bulk of seafront places, with a modern Greek-Mediterranean menu and bistro atmosphere. They have delicious salads (fig & pomegranate, for example), snacks or starters like stuffed mini-pitas, and mains ranging from pasta to their speciality huge steaks. €€

Rakodikio Vernádhou 7, 28310 54437. Modern *mezedhopolío*, very popular with locals (especially students), on a street with a few other similar places. Interesting salads (spinach, apple and pomegranate, for example), and plenty of classic Greek dishes too (*moussakás*, *saganáki* prawns). €

Samaria Venizélou 40, 28310 24681. One of the few seafront places patronized by locals, especially late at night, this place offers simple Greek food, specializing in charcoal-grilled meat (pork fillet or lamb chops) and *mayireftá*. €€

★**Stella's Kitchen** Soulíou 55, 28311 03402. A great-value and welcoming little diner run by the eponymous and ebullient proprietor. Stella serves up half-a-dozen fresh, home-made daily specials (at least two are vegetarian; when they're gone, they're gone); it's also a good spot for breakfast. €

Ta Dyo Rou Pánou Koronéou 28, 6936 500892. This *inomageirío* (wine-and-cooking shop) in a less frequented part of the old town delights with its *stamnagáthi* (chicory greens), *anginâres me koutsiá* (artichokes with broad beans, in springtime), *askordouláki* (tassel hyacinth bulbs), *keftédes* (superior meatballs), imám-style eggplant, melt-in-the-mouth *soupiés* (cuttlefish) stewed with fennel, and *yaprákia* (stuffed vine leaves), accompanied by excellent whole-grain

RÉTHYMNO'S SUMMER FESTIVALS

The **Cretan Diet Festival** is a week of celebration of Cretan food and wine, along with traditional music and dancing, held in the public gardens at the beginning of July – it's a fun event with plenty to eat and drink. Later on, at the end of August or early September, the **Renaissance Festival** (http://rfr.gr) sees the fortress and venues around the old town host folk and classical music concerts and theatrical events, as well as performances of Classical tragedies and comedies.

bread and mezédhes. The interior is a de facto photo gallery of bygone times; blues, 1940s jazz and Horace Silver, on the sound system. 'Ta Dyo Rou' stands for RouRou, the nickname of the proprietor's wife, in case you were wondering about the odd name. €€

Zefyros Inner harbour, 28310 28206. If you're determined to eat by the water, *Zefyros* is one of the more reliable of the harbourside fish tavernas, offering reasonably priced (for this location) fish and seafood such as sole fillet stuffed with prawns or fisherman's spaghetti. €€

NEW TOWN

Akros Ikogeniakon Moátsou 40, 28310 55403. Modern-style *estiatório*, entirely off the tourist trail, serving hearty daily specials that you choose from the heated trays behind a glass display. Busiest at lunchtime. €

Bankery Dimitrakaki 2, 2831 026004. A trendy café-restaurant that can satisfy every craving or mood; here you will find delicious pastries, hearty brunch options and all-day dishes like pasta, burgers or pizzas. The bar also serves excellent coffee. €€

Taverna Iliovasilemata Periferiákos, 28310 23943. The *Sunsets Taverna* is frequented more for its spectacular sunset views than its food, but the meals aren't bad value, there's usually a decent selection of fish, and often freshly caught octopus drying on the line. The terrace tables are right by the shore, and it's an ideal place for an ouzo and mezédhes at sunset with the breakers splashing over the rocks below. €€

Zambia Stamathioudháki 20, 28310 24561. Popular – and good-value – local taverna with a seafront terrace, specializing in fish and serving delicious lunchtime *mayireftá* (traditional baked dishes). €€

★ **Zisis** Mákhis Krítis 63, Misíria, on the main road in the hotel zone 3km east of town, 28310 28814, http://taverna-zisis.gr. *Zisis* is one of the great Rethymnian institutions, where local families get together for celebrations, especially at Sunday lunchtimes, when booking is advised. The place is large and elegant with real table linen, *mayireftá* (traditional baked dishes) laid out in heated display cabinets and a menu filled with other tempting fish and meat dishes; and its exceptionally good value. It's a short taxi or bus ride from the centre. €

3

DRINKING AND NIGHTLIFE

SEE MAP PAGE 194

Réthymno's **bars and nightlife** are concentrated on the seafront – especially either side of the inner harbour around Venizélou and Platía Plastíra – and up Salamínos and Melissinoú heading inland. The café-cum-cocktail places around the Rimóndi fountain are great for people-watching, but the cacophony of late-evening noise from competing bars is less than relaxing. Summer-only **clubs** operate to the east, among the big hotels, and it's also worth looking out for posters advertising beach parties.

Cul de Sac Platía Petiháki, 6946 341 161. Prime people-watching spot on the busy corner by the Rimóndi Fountain. They serve brunch, sandwiches and burgers but mostly it's a place to drink – coffees by day, pitchers of beer and cocktails later, when there's sometimes a DJ or live band.

Fraoules Venizélou 62, 28310 24525. One of several lively all-day bar-cafés on this stretch of Venizélou that are especially busy late in the evening with a pre-club local crowd. Good value breakfasts, burgers and sandwiches by day, strong cocktails and occasional events or live music.

Ice Club Salamínos 22, 6985 946 247. One of half a dozen clubs around the junction of Salamínos, Mesolongíou and Melissinoú, *Ice* is popular with young locals and open year-round; mixed Greek and international playlist.

Nafpiyiou Arkadhíou 254, 6946 227 117. Music bar/club, open all day, with a terrace overlooking the water, but mainly a late-night place, with house and techno DJs.

O Kipos tou Ali Vafi Vounialí 65, 28310 23238. A vaulted tunnel off the street leads to a hidden garden and a cool café-bar bearing the former owner's name with shisha pipes, board games, and events including live Cretan music on Sunday afternoons. They also serve good food.

SHOPPING

SEE MAP PAGE 194

There are interesting **shops** throughout the old town; in general crafts and touristy stores cluster in the area around the Rimóndi fountain and along Ethníkis Andistásis, with boutiques and leather goods on and around Arkadhíou.

There's a big **flea market** every Thursday in the car park by the Platía Tessáron Martýron, and on Mondays in the suburb of Kallithéa, just beyond the bus station.

Atelier Himáras 27, 28310 24440. Studio-workshop selling creative modern ceramics from local potter Frosso Bora.

Bibliopoleío Souliou 43, 28310 54307. A handy place for secondhand English-language books in the old town.

Lyranthos Arkadhíou 66, http://liranthos.com. Réthymno is a centre of *lyra* and *laoúto* (lute) production, and this is the shop of craftsman Mihailis Katsantonis; they sell CDs of traditional music and gifts as well as musical instruments.

Mediterranean Editions Paleológou 41, 28310 21440. A good selection of books in English, as well as many foreign newspapers.

Nikos Siragas Petalioti 2, https://siragas.gr. Gallery-shop of an internationally recognized wood-turner who produces creative sculptures in olive, eucalyptus, walnut and carob woods, as well as plenty of smaller items at souvenir prices. He also runs wood-turning classes.

Raw Materials Arabatsóglou 40, 28310 58250. The elegant speciality Cretan and Greek food shop of the *Avli hotel* group stocks many of the island's best wines and olive oils in addition to herbs, cheeses and lots more; all beautifully packaged, if at premium prices.

Xtheodoraki Ethníkis Andistásis 22, http://xtheodoraki.gr. Interesting contemporary Greek jewellery from young designers at affordable prices, as well as accessories such as bags made from antique Cretan materials.

3

DIRECTORY

Banks ATMs can be found throughout the centre, but bank branches are mainly in the new town, especially along Koundouriótou east of the Platía Tessáron Martýron.

Laundry Iris, Melissinoú 36 (daily 9am–8pm, service wash from €8; 28311 04444).

Post office The main post office (Mon–Fri 7.30am–8pm) is on Moátsou, opposite the *Brascos* hotel.

East of Réthymno: the coast road

Leaving Réthymno to the east you can strike almost immediately onto the **coastal highway**, which runs fast, flat and dull along the coastal plain, or follow the old road, squeezed into the narrow gap between this and the sea. On the latter route you'll pass through a string of village suburbs, connected now by almost continuous hotel development for some 10km. In the hills behind the resort zone a few attractive villages survive, above all **Hromonastíri**, where the nearby **gorge at Mýli** offers one of the best walks in the region. Around 15km from Réthymno the nature of the coast changes as you approach the Psiloritis massif: here the small resorts of **Pánormos** and **Balí** occupy coves beneath the road.

Hromonastíri and around

In summer, half a dozen daily buses from Réthymno bus station head to Mýli and Hromonastíri, and several of the bus and Little Train tours of Réthymno also wind their way up here daily; the Rethymno City Tour bus (http://rethymnocitytour.gr), for example, is a hop-on, hop-off service that passes through several times a day

One of the most attractive drives you could take out of Réthymno is to Mýli and **HROMONASTÍRI (Χρομοναστήρι)**, hill villages to the southeast of town, with the chance to walk down the Mýli gorge on the way back. The road up to Hromonastíri winds attractively up the side of the gorge to arrive at the ancient and beautiful village. Its sights include **Prinari's mill** (charge), an old olive mill restored as a tiny folk museum, a couple of Byzantine churches, and the **Villa Claudio**, a striking Venetian mansion now run by the Greek army as a **military museum**, with all sorts of hardware parked outside (charge).

The Mýli Gorge

The entry to the **Mýli Gorge** is signed off the road below Hromonastíri, just beneath the village of Mýli. Considering that you're barely 5km from the centre of Réthymno here, the gorge is pretty impressive, though it can't compare with the great south-coast ravines. Starting the descent to the bottom of the gorge, you'll find a friendly café-snack bar from where the path down is well signed. In the early sections you'll see the abandoned buildings of an old hamlet, including the mill from which the gorge and village takes

SAVE THE TURTLES

The beaches east of Réthymno make up the second largest nesting area in the Mediterranean for the endangered **loggerhead sea turtle**. Loggerheads, once common throughout the Mediterranean, are today under serious threat from the damage wrought by tourism and industry on their breeding habitats.

A seagoing creature for most of its life, the turtle must return to a beach – always the same one – in order to lay its eggs. Unfortunately, nesting occurs from early June to the end of August, coinciding with the high tourist season. Once the female has buried her eighty to a hundred eggs on a nocturnal visit to the beach, the eggs must then remain undisturbed for a period of two months before the hatchlings emerge to head for the sea. But even if they avoid being skewered by a beach umbrella or crushed by the feet of bathers – both common hazards – further dangers lie ahead for the newborn turtles. When they emerge, many of them, instead of heading for the sea, are lured inland by artificial lights from hotel and tourist developments. Emblematic of Crete's and Greece's problem of balancing tourist development and the needs of the environment, it remains to be seen whether the loggerhead turtle will avoid the fate of the dodo.

For **information** on programmes to protect the turtle, making donations or becoming a volunteer, contact the Sea Turtle Protection Society of Greece (6937 352 379, http://archelon.gr); volunteers also run information booths in the harbours at Réthymno and Haniá.

their name; there's plenty of water in the stream, so this is a lush and shady walk. After about an hour, you arrive at the bottom. Here you can either walk back up, or if you walk about twenty minutes more, taking minor roads along the bottom of the gorge, you will come to the main road outside Perivólia, where you can pick up a bus or taxi.

Pánormos

PÁNORMOS (**Πάνορμος**), 22km east of Réthymno, marks a distinct break in topography: to the west is a long stretch of level coastline, to the east a spectacular, swooping mountain drive on the E75 highway which continues virtually all the way to Iráklio. The village is just a short (poorly signed) detour off the road, a pretty little place with pedestrianized streets and a tiny harbour, with a couple of small beaches either side. Perhaps because the beaches don't amount to much, Pánormos does not attract big crowds even in high season, and as a result holds on to its appealing tranquillity; many visitors rent apartments and stay for weeks or months. The better of the beaches is to the west of the harbour, with a bar-café and sunbeds. Surprisingly, Pánormos is also an ancient settlement (a minuscule river runs through to the sea) with the ruins of what was once a large sixth-century **basilica**, probably destroyed in the ninth-century Saracen invasion, and of a later **Genoese** or possibly Venetian castle.

ARRIVAL AND ACTIVITIES — PÁNORMOS

By bus The Réthymno hotel zone bus runs as far as Pánormos (at least 20 daily; 1hr); there are also faster highway buses.

Boat trips and tours Most of the boat trips from Balí call at Pánormos (see page 203); buy tickets at the harbour or from travel agents in town. There's a tourist train that runs to villages way up in the hills, including Margarítes (see page 206).

ACCOMMODATION

Asterion On a low hill above the village, www.asterion-panormo.gr. Modern, purpose-built studio and apartment complex on the edge of the village; a family-run, family-friendly place with pool and comfortable units, all with kitchen, balcony and TV. €

Captain's House On the harbour, http://captainshouse.gr. Comfortable seafront studios and apartments with the best location in town, directly above the water, though those on the harbourside can be noisy; there's also a beautiful luxury three-bedroom apartment. €

Lucy's Pension In the middle of the village, http://lucy.gr. Excellent and good-value a/c studios, apartments and two-bedroom "maisonettes", all well-equipped with cooking facilities, balcony and TV. The friendly eponymous proprietor lives in an apartment below, and they have a fabulous five-bedroom luxury villa nearby, with pool and sea views (7-night minimum). Studios or maisonette €, villa €€€

EATING AND DRINKING

Places round the harbour have a lovely setting but are mostly very touristy, with international menus; on the whole you'll eat better for less at places on the small section of pedestrianized street immediately inland.

Angyra East side of the harbour, 28340 51022. The classiest of the harbour tavernas, *Angyra* (anchor) specializes in fresh fish but also has plenty of more straightforward Greek and international food. €€

Geronymos Pedestrianized street, directly up from the harbour, 28340 51338. Popular taverna serving good-value quality Cretan food on an atmospheric street terrace. Try the *tsigariastó* (slow-sauteed lamb) or mixed grill. €

Oasis Pedestrianized street, by Steki tou Sifaki, 28340 51390. This very pleasant garden café makes an ideal place for breakfast or a nightcap. They show occasional original-version films on a screen in the garden and host frequent live guitar music. €

★ To Steki tou Sifaki Pedestrianized street, east of the centre, 28340 51230. Good taverna with an attractive terrace serving delicious family-style traditional food such as stuffed peppers with meatballs or lamb baked with potatoes in lemon sauce. €

3

Balí

BALÍ (**Μπαλί**) is a resort set around a series of little coves, 9km east of Pánormos. The place is much bigger than it first appears, especially as the streets are winding and hilly – it's a couple of kilometres from the main road to the village, more to the best beach. Sadly, although the beaches are spectacular, they're very much overrun, and Balí has become a package resort too popular for its own good. It's lively and friendly, but only really tempting out of season, when there are bound to be bargains given the number of rooms.

Balí's beaches

The first beach, immediately below the road, is **Livádhi** (aka Paradise Beach). An extensive stretch of sand, with a row of bars and tavernas behind, it's the biggest, most recently developed and busiest of the beaches, lively at night as well. Balí proper is centred around three west-facing **coves** with pebbly beaches on the promontory beyond. The first is known as **Varkótopos**, with an inflatable fun park offshore and good bars behind; the second, at the centre of the old village, is itself divided in two by a rocky outcrop into **Limáni**, where the harbour is, and Limanákia beaches; a long loop of road then winds round to the final cove (there are short cuts if you walk), generally known as **Evita Beach** after some apartments behind it. This is barely developed and much the most pleasant place to swim – with a patch of sand and, on either side, crags of rock with level places to sunbathe – but still very crowded and overlooked. Two shady **tavernas** just above the beach make reasonable lunch stops.

Moní Áyios Ioánnis

Reached by turning inland on a good road (though a dangerous exit from the E75) that turns off the highway a short distance west of the resort

A wonderful viewpoint to appreciate Balí's setting is the tiny, part-restored seventeenth-century **Moní Áyios Ioánnis**. The monastery church has some fragmentary seventeenth-century frescoes and mosaics and there's a serene garden fronting the monks' cells (only a couple of monks now remain), but its reputation among Cretans today is for its energetic role in the struggle against Muslim rule, for which it was bombarded in 1866 by the Ottoman navy.

ARRIVAL AND DEPARTURE — BALÍ

By bus Buses will drop you by a large service station at the junction with the road into town. It's quite a walk to the centre, so it may be worth considering a taxi (€5; 28340 23000 or 6987 963 238) or jumping on the tourist train that meets many of the buses and trundles into town.

INFORMATION AND ACTIVITIES

Boat trips and watersports There are all sort of day-trips and cruises available from the harbour, including regular excursions to Réthymno via Pánormos, sailing trips and sunset cruises, plus motorboat, kayak, pedalo and jet ski rental. Most can be booked on the spot, or through many travel agents in town.

Diving Just behind the harbour, Hippocampos (28340 94193, www.hippocampos.com) is a PADI dive centre offering courses, trial dives and more.

ACCOMMODATION

Bali Blue Bay Hotel On the ridge between Varkótopos cove and Limáni, http://balibluebay.gr. Friendly, family-run, modern hotel with great views from most rooms and even better ones from the rooftop pool. Buffet breakfast included. €

Dimitris Apartments High above the north side of the harbour, 6973 352 714, https://apts-dimitris.gr. Simple but well-equipped modern studios and two-room apartments, with good views from their balconies. €

Mira Mare Above Varkótopos cove, 28340 94256. Handily located above a supermarket, these traditional rooms with fridge and sea views from the balcony are basic but excellent value. €

EATING AND DRINKING

There are supermarkets, cafés and tavernas throughout the resort. A couple of the best **tavernas** are in the old village by the harbour. **Nightlife** tends to consist of late-night drinks at a number of music bars behind the beaches.

Baboo La Vida Loca Livádhi Beach, 6980 219 001. Beach bar at the end of the beach where they can make some noise; free loungers for customers by day and a busy dancefloor at night, with some wild parties.

Panorama In the old village by the harbour, 28340 94217. Occupying a renovated old warehouse, with a superb view from its terrace overlooking the water, *Panorama* has an international menu, though you're best sticking to Greek standards. Specialities include good-value assorted mezédhes plates and grilled fresh octopus. €€

Porto Paradiso Varkótopos cove, 28340 94201. A good spot for an early or late-evening cocktail, with the waves lapping the shore a mere 20m from the terrace tables.

Valentino In the old village by the harbour, 28340 94501. Pleasantly situated harbourfront taverna with a lively terrace serving up the usual standards as well as fresh fish. €€

The foothills of Psilorítis

Taking the old roads east from Réthymno, through the **foothills of the Psilorítis** range, there are a variety of routes to choose from or combine. On the whole, the higher you head, the more interesting and scenic the road, though also more twisty and tortuous. The low road, through Dhamásta, has least to offer, though it's a pretty enough drive and takes you close to the historic cave at **Melidhóni**. If you head inland earlier, the **monastery of Arkádhi** is an obvious first stop – gateway both to the highest roads around the northern edge of the massif, and to the route south through the Amári valley (see page 211) on its western flank. This will take you through the potters' village of **Margarítes** and past **Arhéa Eléftherna**, where there's a striking museum and a number of archeological sites, before continuing towards **Anóyia** via the remarkable caves at **Sfendóni**. The northern branch of the **E4 footpath** winds through this area, offering numerous attractive short walks.

Moní Arkádhi

25km southeast of Réthymno • Charge • http://arkadimonastery.gr

MONÍ ARKÁDHI (**Μονή Αρκαδίου**) is, for Cretans, a shrine to the struggle for independence. Historical resonance apart, the monastery's striking architecture and highly scenic location are reason enough to visit. It won't take you long to see the place: you can peer into the roofless **vault** beside the cloister where the 1866 explosion took place, and wander about the rest of the well-restored grounds. The bulk of the buildings were relatively unscathed by the explosion and Arkádhi is still a working monastery. Of the surviving buildings the **church** is the most impressive, its rich mix

3

A SHRINE TO CRETAN INDEPENDENCE

Historically, Arkádhi was one of the richest monasteries in Crete and a well-known stopover for travellers, as well as a centre of resistance. In the 1820s eighty Muslims, who had occupied the monastery to pacify local rebels, were captured and put to death; in retaliation, many of the buildings were burned.

It is the events of **1866**, however, which guarantee Arkádhi a place in history. In the rebellion of that year the monastery served as an Othodox stronghold in which, as Cretan Musloims took the upper hand, hundreds of Cretan guerrillas and their families took refuge. Here they were surrounded by a regular Ottoman Turkish army until, after a siege of two days, the defences were finally breached on November 9, 1866. As the attackers poured in, the ammunition stored in the monastery exploded – deliberately fired, according to the accepted version of events, on the orders of the abbot. Hundreds were killed in the initial blast, Orthodox and Muslim alike, and most of the surviving defenders were put to death by the enraged assailants. This incited a wave of international sympathy for the cause of **Cretan independence**. Figures as disparate as Victor Hugo, Garibaldi and the poet Swinburne were moved to public declarations of support, and in Britain money was raised for a ship (the *Arkádhi*) to run the Ottoman blockade of the island. Although Crete's liberty was still some way off at that stage, the monastery remains the most potent symbol of the struggle (and the anniversary of the blast is commemorated on November 7–9 each year). More recently the monastery lent assistance to guerrilla fighters during **World War II**: George Psychoundakis (see page 351), for example, describes handing over supplies from a parachute drop to the monks.

of styles placing it among the finest Venetian structures left in Crete. The rest of the monastery is mainly seventeenth-century (though it was originally founded as early as the eleventh). A small **museum** and Gallery of Cretan Warriors (wielding rifles and fierce moustaches) is devoted to the exploits of the defenders of the faith, with a variety of mementoes and tributes, blood-stained clothing and commemorative medals. Opposite the monastery (next to its cafeteria-taverna) is a monumental **ossuary** where skulls and bones of a few of the explosion's victims are displayed behind glass.

ARRIVAL AND DEPARTURE

By bus From Réthymno there are 4 daily buses (2 at weekends and out of season; 40min), as well as countless tours.

By car If driving, watch out for the road layout: the Réthymno–Amári road passes the monastery on one side, the route east towards Anóyia starts on the other; they're connected only by the unpaved track through the monastery's car park.

ACCOMMODATION AND EATING — MONÍ ARKÁDHI

Food is available from the monastery's cafeteria-taverna, and there are plenty of picnic spots nearby, but more attractive places to eat can be found in almost any direction, especially in the Amári valley (see page 214), Eléftherna (page 206) or Margarítes (page 206). Nearby is a unique hotel, though.

Kapsaliana Village Hotel Kapsalianá, 4km north of Arkádhi, http://kapsalianavillage.gr. The monastery's former olive oil factory, abandoned in 1955, along with most of the homes of the hamlet that grew up around it, have been transformed into a chic boutique hotel. Luxurious rooms and suites, each unique, feature plenty of exposed beams and stonework, and are surrounded by gardens containing a pool and high-class restaurant. €€€

Eléftherna

From Arkádhi a lovely, lonely road winds through the village of Néa Eléftherna to the far more interesting hamlet of **ARHÉA ELÉFTHERNA** (**Αρχαία Ελεύθερνα**) and the spectacular remains of ancient **Eléftherna**. Occupation of this area appears to have begun as early as the third millennium BC, and continued right through to the 1330s, when the Venetians evacuated the population following a revolt. The city reached its apogee as one of the most important centres of eighth- and seventh-century BC Dorian Crete; still powerful when the Romans came in search of conquest in 67 BC, it put up a stiff resistance, and later flourished as the seat of a Christian bishop. A great deal of work has been going on here in recent years to open up the numerous sites surrounding the village to visitors; there are impressive looking facilities and lots of new signage and paths between sites. Apart from the Acropolis and the magnificent new museum, however, these were not regularly open at the time of writing, though you could get close to most of them – check the current situation at the museum. But you may assume 10am–6pm opning for 'minor attractions.

Museum of Ancient Eléftherna

On the road between Néa and Arhéa Eléftherna • Charge • https://mae.uoc.gr

The futuristic-looking **Museum of Ancient Eléftherna** is a fabulous introduction to the area, and definitely worth making your first stop. It concentrates on the period from around the ninth- to the sixth-century BC, the time when the city flourished and also a time of which relatively little is known – the Homeric era, and something of a dark age in terms of historical and archeological knowledge. The museum is therefore almost unique in the world. It's an excellent display in a fine building, clearly explained and with some entertaining audio-visual elements. Much of what you see came from the necropolis and from the funeral pyres there; there's gold jewellery and high-quality bronze-work, above all a fine bronze shield with a boss in the form of a lion's head, displayed alongside a shiny modern cast.

Acropolis of Eléftherna

Signposted from the centre of the village • Free

The **acropolis of Eléftherna** enjoys a magnificent defensive position on a steep-sided spur of rock surrounded by narrow ravines. It is approached via a narrow, natural causeway, carved in ancient times to resemble paving stones, at the end of which a hefty *pýrgos* or **tower** (which in large part still stands) protects the narrow entrance to the acropolis itself. The E4 path (which seems blocked on the east side) climbs out of the western valley onto the acropolis – immediately below the point where it joins the main path, remarkable **Roman cisterns** are carved into the hill's west side, with enormous pillars of solid rock supporting a cavernous interior. Further out along the promontory (it's a good fifteen-minute walk to the end) are numerous scattered fragments of massive walls and ancient buildings, not always easy to make sense of, as well as the roofless ruined ancient church of **Ayía Ánna**, still revered as a shrine by locals.

Other sites

Below the village and acropolis • No reliable hours

In the valley below the acropolis you can see both the **main site of ancient Eléftherna**, to the east, and, to the northwest, its **necropolis**. Both have impressive-looking visitor facilities and, when they are open, may well charge an entry fee. At the necropolis, archeologists made a potentially very significant discovery: traces of a **human sacrifice** made in front of the funeral pyre of some local magnate. It apparently dates from the late eighth century BC, about the same time that Homer was describing very similar sacrifices of Trojan prisoners in front of the funeral pyre of Achilles. The victim, who was bound hand and foot before ritually having his throat cut, may well have been expected to serve the dead man in the next world: also found in front of the pyre were sacrificed animals and offerings of perfume and food. Other cremations on the site (some twenty have been found, though only one human sacrifice) had offerings including gold, jewellery and fine pottery, as well as four tiny, superbly crafted **ivory heads** which are among the best work of their time (c.600 BC) yet discovered anywhere.

Sotíros Hrístos

Signed where the road from Margarítes heads out of Arhéa Eléftherna • Usually unlocked in daylight hours

Sotíros Hrístos is a beautiful tenth-century Byzantine chapel in a picturesque setting beside a spring-fed pool. Inside there's a fine twelfth-century *Pandokrátor* in the dome, the only surviving **fresco** of what must once have been a glorious painted interior.

The Hellenistic bridge

On the river north of the acropolis • Easiest approach is from Néa Eléftherna, where a track and the E4 path head steeply downhill towards the Necropolis archeological site; from here on foot you can follow the track north along the valley for 15min or so to the bridge; the track can also be reached on the E4 descending from the acropolis

The remarkable stone-built **Hellenistic bridge**, standing 5m high and 3m deep, dates from roughly 300 BC. Its vaulted arch is almost perfectly intact and still capable of carrying traffic across the river. Beneath the arch is a washing and bathing place cut into the rock, probably dating from the same era.

3

ARRIVAL AND DEPARTURE — ELÉFTHERNA

By bus In season two buses a day head from Réthymno, via Arkádhi, Eléftherna (45min) and Margarítes to Pánormos, from where they turn round and go back the same way. If you catch the same bus on its return journey, you get about 1hr 45min here. There are also tours.

ACCOMMODATION AND EATING

Kafenio Filio Arhéa Eléftherna, on the main road opposite the acropolis entrance, www.kafeniofilio.gr. A welcoming café/taverna with delicious, inexpensive home cooking. Look out for the fresh dish of the day, or there are classics like *souvláki*, rabbit and an excellent house salad with rocket, peppers, nuts and local cheese. €

Margarítes

A very pretty place on the edge of a ravine, with views back towards the coast, **MARGARÍTES** (**Μαργαρίτες**) has a long tradition of making **pottery**. A hundred years ago there were as many as eighty sizeable workshops here, producing all sorts of items for everyday and agricultural use. Today, smaller artisan producers are scattered throughout the village, and you can buy their work in a dozen or more outlets along the steep main street. Off the village's lower square, a well-signed path leads to **Moní Sotíros Hrístos**, or Áyios Gedeón, a ruined monastery that has been partly restored by its last remaining monk. The ancient church is usually open and the beautifully tended grounds are a flowery haven of peace and birdsong (from caged songbirds) – all the work of the same monk.

ARRIVAL AND DEPARTURE — MARGARÍTES

By bus On weekdays there are two daily buses to and from Réthymno (40min), at 6.15am and 1.15pm, returning as soon as they arrive. In season two slower buses a day also head from Réthymno, via Arkádhi, Eléftherna and Margarítes to Pánormos, from where they turn round and go back the same way. If you catch the same bus on its return journey, you get about 1hr 30min here. There are also plenty of tours.

ACCOMMODATION AND EATING

★ **Kouriton House** In the hamlet of Tzanakianá, immediately north of Margarítes, www.kouritonhouse.gr. An eighteenth-century stone-built house, creatively converted to rented rooms, each unique and furnished in traditional style. Owner Anastasia is an expert on the local area – which she promotes as an open-air "ecomuseum" – and also runs activities including local walks, cookery classes and harvesting olives. Wonderful Greek breakfast included. €

★ **Taverna Mantalos** Main square, 28340 92294. On the village's attractive upper platía, this great little taverna has a shady terrace offering fine views over the valley. The friendly proprietors cook up tasty traditional Cretan food including delicious *kolokythóanthi i yemistá* (stuffed courgette flowers). €€

Taverna Velanidhia Just above the village, almost opposite the Tsikalario shop, http://belanidiahotel.gr/en. Good-value rooms with balcony, fridge and TV in a tranquil, leafy setting, and a very good taverna with views over the gorge. €

SHOPPING

E&A Main street just below the main square, http://eaceramicstudio.com. Arty, handcrafted earthenware based on a modern interpretation of traditional forms.

Kerameion Main street above the main square, http://keramion.gr. Creative potter Yiorgos Dalamvelas derives inspiration for his traditionally made ceramics from Minoan and Byzantine originals; lovely plates and bowls with fish and olive motifs.

Tsikalario Just above the village, by the road junction, https://tsikalario.gr. The workshop of Nikos Kafgalakis is one of the largest and most traditional in town, turning out enormous *píthoi*, similar to those found in the Minoan palaces and still used throughout agricultural Crete today, as well as plenty of smaller and more decorative items.

The Melidhóni Cave

Signposted from the village of Melidhóni, 4km from the substantial town of Pérama, on the lower road • Charge • www.melidoni.gr

The **Melidhóni Cave** was the setting for one of the most horrific **atrocities** in the struggle for Cretan independence (see page 204). In terms of sheer size, it is also one of the most impressive on the island, and one can easily imagine the refugees sheltering in its cathedral-like space. Mythology holds that the cave was the home of **Talos**, a bronze giant who protected the coasts of Crete by striding around the island hurling rocks at unfriendly ships; the Argonauts were greeted thus when they approached. Excavations in the cave have shown that it was inhabited during the Neolithic period and later was an important shrine for the **Minoans**, who may have worshipped their fertility goddess Eileithyia here. The Greeks and Romans transformed it into a shrine to the god **Hermes Tallaios**, evidenced by thousands of inscriptions etched into the walls of one of the cave's inner chambers.

Today, the awesome **central chamber** shelters a shrine and ossuary commemorating the victims of the massacre, along with petrified "draperies", spectacular curtain-like folds formed by the calcium deposits, and hefty stalagmites and stalactites, though most of the latter have long since been broken off. Outside, the owners of the site run a friendly café.

The Sfendóni Cave

Signed from the village of Zonianá, or from Axós on the lower road • Charge • https://sfentoni-cave.com

The **Sfendóni Cave**, also known (and signposted) as the Zonianá Cave, is the largest cave complex in Crete that's open to the public: local legend has it that the cave was discovered by an eight-year-old girl who, lured away by fairies, was later found dead in its darkest recesses. Today, enthusiastic and knowledgeable guides conduct you along walkways through a series of caverns, extending some 500m into a spur of Mount Psilorítis. There are magnificent displays of stalactites, stalagmites and petrified waves,

THE MELIDHÓNI MASSACRE

In 1824, during one of the early rebellions against Ottoman dominance, around three hundred villagers took refuge in the Melidhóni Cave, as they had often done before at time of war. This time, however, the Muslim commander demanded that they come out. When the Cretans refused, and shot two messengers sent to offer safe conduct, he tried to force them out by blocking the mouth of the cave with stones and cutting off the air supply. After several days of this, with the defenders opening new air passages every night, the troops changed their tactics, piling combustible materials in front of the cave and setting light to them; everyone inside was asphyxiated. The bodies were left where they lay for the cave to become their tomb; ten years later traveller and historian Robert Pashley, one of the first to enter after the tragedy, found "the bones and skulls of the poor Christians so thickly scattered, that it is almost impossible to avoid crushing them as we pick our steps along". This grisly event was far from unique: numerous other caves around the island have similar histories, although none claimed so many victims.

many more than five million years old. At the entrance there's a giant visitor centre with a café and shop, where you may have to wait some time for a tour.

Anóyia

ANÓYIA (**Ανώγεια**), a small town perched beneath the highest peaks of the Psiloritis range, is the obvious place from which to approach the **Idean Cave** (see page 209) and, for the committed, the **summit of Psiloritis** itself (see page 210). The weather, refreshingly cool when the summer heat lower down is becoming oppressive, is one good reason to come, but most people are drawn by the proximity of the mountains or by a reputation for some of the best woven and embroidered **handicrafts** in Crete. The last is greatly exaggerated but this exceptionally friendly town still makes a pleasant break from the coast. The town also has a reputation as a centre of **lyra** playing and has a buoyant **sheep farming** sector; don't miss the local cheese, or the spit-roast lamb if you're carnivorously inclined.

On first impression it seems that Anóyia has two quite distinct halves: coming from the west you enter what appears to be the older, lower town, before the road takes a broad loop around to re-emerge near the upper town's large, modern-looking **Platía Meídani**, lined with youthful bars. The upper town has almost all the accommodation as well as the bank (with ATM) and post office, police and most of the non-tourist stores. In many ways this appearance is deceptive. A series of steep, sometimes stepped alleys connect the two directly, and however traditional the buildings may look, closer inspection shows that most are actually concrete. This reflects a tragic history – the village was one of those destroyed in 1944 as a reprisal for the abduction of **General Kreipe** (see page 334), when all the men who could be rounded up here were executed. Their names are chillingly recorded on the war memorial by the upper town's church.

ARRIVAL AND DEPARTURE — ANÓYIA

By bus Three buses a day (one on Sun) run between Iráklio and Anóyia (1hr), and on weekdays there are two daily buses to and from Réthymno (1hr 30min).

ACCOMMODATION AND EATING

Anóyia sees a lot of day-trippers, but most stay only an hour or so. Linger a while, or stay overnight, and it's surprisingly uncommercial. It shouldn't be hard to find a **room** in the upper town, where the best places line the ring road (Periferiákos) that climbs parallel to the main road on the east side of the village. The speciality of most local tavernas is huge, fatty cuts of lamb (and other meats), grilled outdoors over wood or charcoal. This is best at lunchtime – in the evening you'll be eating whatever is left over.

Aetos Main street, upper village, 28340 31262. Excellent local taverna with a wood-fired grill and spacious terrace. Specialities include *souvláki* and goat dishes as well as rotisserie chicken and a mouth-watering *ofto* (wood-fire-roasted lamb). €€

Arodamos Upper village, on the Psiloritis road, 28340 31100. Exceptionally friendly place with a limited menu of local dishes, all of it sourced locally and some from their own farm and dairy; great lamb, and be sure to try some of their own cheese. €€

★ **Hotel Aristea** Periferiákos Dhrómos, http://hotel

EMBROIDERY IN ANÓYIA

Shops and stalls bedecked with local embroidery line the streets leading off **Platía Livádhi** in the lower town. This local handicraft tradition arose in part from bitter necessity, with so large a proportion of the local men killed in 1944. As a way of surviving it seems to have worked, and a few elderly widows (accompanied now by their daughters and granddaughters) remain anxious to subject any passing visitor to their aggressive sales techniques. The traditional feel of the lower town is reinforced by the elderly men, baggy trousers tucked into their black boots, moustaches bristling, who sit at the *kafenía* tables around the square.

THE LYRA IN ANÓYIA

Anóyia is a noted centre of **lyra music** – many of the greatest performers on the instrument have come from here. Among them, the late, self-taught Nikos Xylouris was a shepherd who made his own *lyra*, and whose performances and compositions made him a Cretan legend in the 1960s and 1970s. The house where he was born, on Platía Livádhi, is now the tiny *Kafenion Xylouris*, where you can get a glass of *rakí* or house wine, and here, or more frequently in the music cafés of the upper town, you may well have the chance to hear local performers.

aristea.gr. Lovely room and apartment complex run by the irrepressible Aristea, her daughter and granddaughter (both also called Aristea). There's a beautiful maisonette for up to six people, as well as family duplex apartments and simpler rooms, all with sensational views. Good-value breakfast available. Doubles and small studios €, large family or group-sized apartments €€

Hotel Marina Periferiákós, Dhrómos 28340 31817. Three-star modern hotel with studio rooms sporting kitchenettes; most with fabulous views from their balconies. Enquire at *Rooms Aris* if no one's around. €

Mihalos Platía Livádhi, 28340 31396. Tavernas in the lower town are not great value on the whole, but this retro *kafenío* right on the square is a perfect people-watching spot serving breakfast, drinks, snacks and delicious *galaktoboúreko* (traditional custard pie, here made with fresh ewes' milk). €

3

Mount Psiloritis

At 2456m, **MOUNT PSILORÍTIS** (Ψηλορείτης), also known as Mount Ida or Ídhi, is the highest mountain in Crete. It's 21km from Anóyia to the **Nídha plateau** (1400m) at its base – a steady climb most of the way, along a road travelled little except by the shepherds who pasture their sheep up here. In late spring, as the snow recedes, you'll see myriad wildflowers and, at all times, quite a few birds, including vultures and magnificent golden eagles. The *mitáta* or stone huts near the roadside – many of them ruined – are former shepherds' dwellings; many are now used as dog kennels and chicken coops.

Somewhere near the highest point a signed road leads off left for 3km to the **Skínakas Observatory**, sitting atop the peak of the same name (open on occasional weekends in summer – dates should be posted on a board at the start of the road. A little further along, a track to the right goes to the **ski area**, which sees plenty of snow in some winters but has never supported a proper ski resort. Soon after, the small plateau and its bare summer pastures fan out below you, and the road drops to skirt around its western edge. At the end of the road, overlooking the plain, stands a crumbling and abandoned **visitor centre**.

The Idean Cave

A 15min climb on a well-signed path at the end of the paved road • Visitor facilities have been built at the cave, but have never opened and show no sign of doing so; for the moment you can approach the mouth for free, but not go far in; in spring, and even early summer, the entrance can be blocked with snow

The celebrated Idhéon Andhrón (**Idean Cave**) rivals that on Mount Dhíkti (see page 145) for the title of **Zeus's birthplace**. Although scholarly arguments rage over the exact identity of the caves in the legends of Zeus, and over interpretation of versions of the legend, locals are in no doubt that the Idean Cave is the place where the god was brought up, suckled by wild animals. Certainly, this hole in the mountainside, which as Cretan caves go is not especially large or impressive, was associated from the earliest times with the cult of Zeus, and at times ranked among the most important centres of pilgrimage in the Greek world. Pythagoras visited the cave, Plato set *The Laws* as a dialogue along the pilgrimage route here, and the finds within indicate offerings brought from all over the eastern Mediterranean. First signs of occupation go back as far as 3000

BC, and though it may then have been a mere place of shelter, by the Minoan era it was already established as a shrine, maintaining this role until about 500 AD.

Climbing Psiloritis

The derelict visitor centre marks the start of the way (now forming a stretch of the E4 path) to the **summit of Psiloritis**. Though it's not for the unwary or unfit, the climb should present few problems to experienced, properly equipped hikers, and there are also **guided ascents** (including by moonlight) from Thrónos (see page 212) and elsewhere. The route, which diverts from the path to the Idean Cave just beyond the small spring and chapel, is marked with red arrows in addition to the E4 waymarkers – a guide who knows the mountain would be useful, since it's not always obvious which is the main trail, but is by no means essential. The *Anavasi Psiloritis* map is the best available for this area and clearly marks the routes described here. Don't attempt the ascent alone, however, as you could face a very long wait for help if you were to run into trouble. If you do make the climb, allow for a six- to eight-hour return trip to the chapel at the summit, and be prepared in spring for thick snow to slow you down. Carry enough food, water and warm gear to be able to overnight in one of the shelters should the weather turn; a night at the top, with the whole island laid out in the sunset and sunrise, is a wonderful experience.

3

Only in the last twenty minutes or so of the climb does the peak of Psiloritis itself become visible and the ground start to fall away to reveal just how high you are. The **summit** is marked by a shelter and the chapel of **Tímios Stavrós** ("Holy Cross" – a name by which the peak is sometimes known locally), inside which Nikos Kazantzakis famously claimed to have lost his virginity. Nearby there's water in a cistern, which you should boil or purify before drinking. On a (rare) clear day the spectacular **panoramas** from the summit – including the Lefká Óri (White Mountains) rising in the west and the Dhíkti massif to the east – make the climb well worthwhile.

Alternative routes

There are any number of **alternate routes** up and down the mountain. From the west the obvious departure point is Fourfourás in the Amári valley, along the route of the E4. This is relatively straightforward in the sense that you can see the peak almost all

THE DESCENT FROM NÍDHA TO KAMÁRES

While most people are here to climb **Psiloritis**, there is also a good 5hr hike down from Nídha to Kamáres, via the huge **Kamáres Cave**, where the first great cache of the elaborate pottery known as Kamáres ware was found. You can either follow the E4 towards the summit for around an hour and a half, until you reach a basin (Kollita) where the trails meet, and descend south from there, or you can take the track which heads south from the end of the paved road. This is a much flatter route, but also significantly harder to follow in the later stages, so you're advised to check directions first; get it right and you will eventually approach the cave (a short detour off the E4) from the east. The track initially leads to a gully, which shortly after becomes a considerable ravine. Here, large red arrows direct you towards Kamáres and the cave. For **Vorízia**, follow the ravine for about an hour until a faint trail climbs out on the left (soon after this, the stream bed becomes impassable). Above the ravine there are fine views and a heady drop for another hour, when you must turn left (east) again. This is not obvious, but you should begin to see signs of life – goat trails and shepherds' huts. You cut past the top of a second, smaller ravine to a stone hut and then descend, zigzagging steeply, to a dirt road and Vorízia village.

Neither Kamáres nor Vorízia has a lot to offer when you arrive. In Kamáres the trail emerges at the eastern end of the village, opposite a very basic taverna. Ask here and you may be able to find a room; the only other facilities are a couple of old-fashioned *kafenía*. Vorízia has neither food nor accommodation.

THE WILDEST CAT IN CRETE

In Cretan myth and legend there have long been told tales of the **fourokattos** ("furious cat"), a mountain wildcat. Although in 1905 two skins from such a beast were bought at the market in Haniá by a British woman attached to a scientific mission, for most of the last century scientists regarded the existence of such a creature as unlikely. They also dismissed the stories of shepherds and goatherds who claimed to have seen this wild cat.

Then, in 1996, an Italian university team studying the carnivores of the Cretan mountains were astonished when they returned to their traps one morning to find they had snared a 5.5-kilo wildcat. The news created a sensation as the beast was taken to the University of Crete for study before being released back into the wild equipped with a radio tracking device. Tawny and with small lynx-like tufts, the cat does not belong to the subspecies of cats on the mainland of Greece and the rest of Europe; its nearest relative is a species inhabiting North Africa and Sardinia. Scientists believe that it is an extremely reclusive, nocturnal animal, which explains why it is so rarely seen.

The cat's discovery not only proved generations of Cretans right, but turned the zoological history of the island upside down. Recent research has produced evidence of more wildcats, but there are serious concerns for the future as its natural environment is encroached upon by development. Scientists are now puzzling over how the animal got to Crete in the first place – was the cat perhaps brought over as a domesticated beast by the ancestors of the Minoans, or has it been on Crete since the island became separated from the closest mainland?

the way, though it can be hard to find the start of the path, or to work out which is the main trail at times, despite the waymarking: it's also much further, a 2000m ascent and at least five or six hours climbing. There's a mountain hut about halfway up, run by the EOS in Réthymno (see page 197). The proprietors of the *Windy Place* taverna-rooms in Fourfourás (see page 216) can provide details of a short cut, which involves taking your car a good way up the mountain. With care you can take a vehicle to the tree line (about 1hr), from where it's about a three-hour trek to the summit, two hours back down. South of the mountain, **Kamáres** is another possible trailhead, on yet another branch of the E4. Again, this is a much more substantial ascent than from the plateau, starting from around 900m, and with some stiff climbing in the early stages.

The Amári valley

The **Amári valley** is one of those areas, like Sfakiá, which features prominently in almost everything written about Crete – especially in tales of **wartime resistance** – yet which is hardly explored at all by modern visitors. Shadowed by the vast profile of Psiloritis, its way of life survives barely altered by the changes of the last twenty or even fifty years. Throughout the valley, isolated hamlets subsist on the ubiquitous olive, with the occasional luxury of an orchard of cherries (especially around Yerakári), pears or figs, and throughout there are a startling number of richly frescoed **churches**. It's an environment conducive to slow exploration, with a climate noticeably cooler than the coast, and in midsummer the trees, flowers and general greenery make a stunning contrast to the rest of the island.

Coming from Réthymno you can take the slightly more circuitous route via the monastery at Arkádhi (see page 203), but the main route turns south at the first highway junction, passing the Amári reservoir and a lovely short walk through the **Pátsos Gorge** (see page 211). There are two **roads** through the valley, too, one following the **eastern** side and clinging to the flanks of the Psiloritis range, the other tracing the edge of the lesser Kédhros range on the south**western** side. Both are scenically spectacular, but the eastern route probably has the edge in terms of beauty. On a day-trip, of course, you can do a complete circuit of both routes.

Thrónos and around

The first of the real Amári villages, at the head of the valley and close to the junction of both the routes in, is **THRÓNOS** (**Θρόνος**). Thrónos stands on the site of ancient Syvritos, and like so many of these villages seems lost in the past, with its beautifully frescoed eleventh-century **church of the Panayía** and majestic views. In the Byzantine era this was the seat of a bishop (hence *thrónos*, throne) and these early Christian days are recalled by the remains of the mosaic floor of the much larger original (fourth-century) church which spreads around the current building, with brightly-coloured traces both inside and out. Someone will usually appear with the key as soon as you start to take an interest in the church; if not enquire at one of the nearby *kafenía* or at *Aravanes*.

The acropolis of Sývritos

On the hill above the village are the remains of the **acropolis of ancient Sývritos**, easily reached by following a path signed on the left beyond the church. Founded in the twelfth century BC in the troubled Late Minoan period, the original settlement seems to have been more a refuge from mainland invaders (similar to those at Karfí and Présos in eastern Crete) than a real town. Most of the remains visible today, however, date from the substantial Greco-Roman town that flourished from the fifth century BC into the early Byzantine period, when the modern resort of Ayía Galíni served as its port. The town was destroyed by the Saracens in the ninth century. At the top of the hill is a radio mast and plenty of ancient ruins, but above all there are spectacular views in all directions.

3

Moní Asomáton

Outside Thrónos, a confusing slew of roads converge at a junction by **Moní Asomáton**, just a couple of kilometres away. The *Kafenio Klados* here is a wonderfully old-fashioned place, full of local farmers. A palm-lined drive leads into an agricultural school (which occupies the monastery's lands) and the abandoned monastery, mostly crumbling but whose church has a beautiful carved and painted témblon(altarpiece). Between Thrónos and Asomáton you'll see signs to the "**Monumental Olive of Jenna**", an olive tree said to be well over two thousand years old, and to the church of **Ayía Paraskévi**, a beautiful dome-in-cross church now isolated in the middle of nowhere. Both are in fields off a very rough track, and most easily reached on foot.

Monastiráki archeological site

Just outside the village of Monastiráki, 3km from Asomáton • Charge

HIKES FROM THRÓNOS

The proprietor of *Aravanes* (see page 215) conducts **guided treks** to the peak of **Mount Psilorítis** (€120, including meals). Although he does take groups up in the daytime, his preferred approach is during the full moons of June, July and August, which avoids the extreme summer temperatures. Phone in advance for details; it's not a difficult climb, but you'll need sturdy footwear and a sleeping bag. On the **night walks**, the summit is reached at around dawn, and the sunrise is always spectacular. On the route down, you'll visit a goatherd's *mitáto* (stone mountain hut) where you can sample delicious cheese made on the spot.

You can also get details at *Aravanes* of other **hikes** from Thrónos; again, guided tours are available (€20/hr). These include a relatively easy route north through the foothills in a couple of hours to the monastery of **Arkádhi** (see page 203). The first half of this follows the road, before you head off cross-country to the east. South from Thrónos an extremely easy stroll on a paved road runs into the main valley via **Kalóyeros**. Fifteen minutes' walk beyond Kalóyeros, a narrow path on the left leads uphill to the small stone church of **Áyios Ioánnis Theológos**, whose fine but decayed frescoes date from 1347 – the church should be open. This walk can be extended into a two-hour trek back to Thrónos.

The archeological site of **Monastiráki**, though little known or visited, is an important and substantial one: a Middle Minoan settlement that may have been an important trading and agricultural centre. Indeed the archeologists currently working here apparently believe that it may even have been a palace to rival Knossós or Festós – though little of their work has so far been published. At any rate it has a gorgeous setting beneath Psiloritis and there's plenty to see, including a maze of little rooms or storage areas, hefty walls, lime-plastered floors and some larger, later Hellenistic buildings. In the village of **MONASTIRÁKI** (**Μοναστηράκι**) stands a giant plane tree allegedly blessed by Zeus never to lose its leaves, and beneath it an ancient washing-place and a cistern full of frogs.

Amári

The village of **AMÁRI** (**Αμάρι**) lies right at the heart of the valley, easily reached from either the eastern or the western roads, and has a fair claim to be the valley's prettiest: it looks like nothing so much as a perfect Tuscan hill village – note the steeply sloping roofs to cope with the winter snows, and the chimneys for wood fires. There's very little to do here – though the café on the central platía serves good, simple food – but there are scintillating views across to Psilorítis and west towards Méronas. For a bird's-eye view, climb the **Venetian clock tower** that dominates the narrow alleyways (the door is always open). Just outside the village, the church of **Ayía Ánna**, reached down a lane on the western edge opposite the police station, has some extremely faded **frescoes** – dating from 1225, they are among the oldest on Crete.

3

The eastern Amári valley

The eastern side of the valley, with the peak of Psilorítis almost directly above and the softer lines of Mount Kédhros facing you, is much less populated than the west. After Asomáton there's little on the road until you reach **Fourfourás**, some 10km away, a substantial village with facilities including an ATM and a friendly, excellent-value **taverna** and **rooms** place. From here the E4 heads up to the summit of Psilorítis (see page 210) and it's also the trailhead of some arduous hikes to the lesser peaks. Another just about driveable track heads up towards the peaks from tiny **Kouroútes** – this one going to the mountain hut at Prínos, the halfway point of the E4.

At the small village of **Níthavris**, 4km south of Kouroútes, the road divides. South, you can continue to **Apodhoúlou** (a worthwhile 3km detour even if you're not continuing this way) and then on to circumnavigate Psilorítis or cut down to the south coast and Ayía Galíni. Head west and you can again choose to head to Ayía Galíni, or curve round to complete a circuit of the Amári valley. These roads divide at the hamlet of **Áyios Ioánnis**; on the route south, **Ayía Paraskeví** has fine sixteenth-century **frescoes** in the small **church of the Panayía**. The road to Hordháki, on the western side of the valley, is narrow, winding and neglected.

Apodhoúlou

On the way into the village of **APODHOÚLOU** (**Αποδούλου**) there's a Late Minoan **passage tomb**, signed on the left, with its lintel still intact. Beyond here – opposite a fountain – lies an interesting, partly ruined mansion known as the **House of Kalitsa Psaraki**.

The church of **Áyios Yeóryios**, signed from the village centre, lies around 1.5km from the village along a lane and dirt track (the latter is best done on foot, and takes about ten minutes). Inside are some damaged but wonderful **frescoes** from the fourteenth century by Iereas Anastasios, one portraying George vigorously slaying the dragon, while outside are perfect vistas of the south coast and the high mountains. Around 1km beyond the turn-off for the church the **Minoan site of Apodhoúlou** with its protective metal canopies can be seen; sometimes there is an attendant, but the gates

THE HOUSE OF KALITSA PSARAKI

Apodhoúlou's once substantial **House of Kalítsa Psaraki** gets its name from the daughter of a local official who, in the 1821 rising against Ottoman rule, was abducted by Muslims and sent to the slave market at Alexandria. By chance she was seen there by Robert Hay, a wealthy Scottish gentleman traveller and Egyptologist, who secured her freedom and – after he had paid for her to be educated in Britain – proposed. They married in Malta, after which Kalitsa accompanied him on his archeological trips to Egypt. Later, when they returned to Crete, an overjoyed family built this house for them to live in. Now a crumbling pile, it's nevertheless possible to see evidence of former grandeur. The stone lintel of a window facing the road bears both Hay's and Psaraki's initials and the date of 1846, when the house was completed.

seem to be left open even when he's absent. With no signage or information it's hard to make out what you're looking at, but excavations here have revealed impressive remains of a settlement dating from the early second millennium BC, with substantial dwellings and all the familiar features of Minoan architecture, including light wells, benches and narrow corridors.

The western Amári valley

The **western** side of the Amári valley is more populous, but the traditional-looking villages here are in fact almost entirely **modern** – rebuilt after their deliberate destruction during World War II (see page 215).

Méronas

Arriving from the north, **MÉRONAS** (**Μέρωνας**) is the first substantial village you reach. Here, the soft-pink Venetian-style **church of the Panayía** shelters frescoes from the fourteenth century. It takes time for your eyes to adjust to the dim interior and take in the painstaking detail of the artwork, darkened with age: a torch would allow you to see a great deal more than the candles or nightlights that usually provide illumination. There's an excellent **taverna** here too (see page 215), and a side road that cuts across the valley through Amári.

Yerakári and around

YERAKÁRI (**Γερακάρι**) is a bigger, more modern and prosperous-looking village than most, with several places to stop for a drink, food and accommodation. The village's delicious **cheeses**, *thimarísio méli* (thyme honey) and pickled cherries are all for sale on the main square. A spectacular road heads west from here to Spíli (see page 216), offering tremendous views along a valley between the heights of Kédhros and Sorós towards the distant Lefká Óri. Continuing south, though, the road beyond Yerakári narrows and is increasingly neglected. Just outside the village is the unusual thirteenth-century church of **Áyios Ioánnis Fótis**, with a spreading oak tree providing shade for a tapped spring – a beautiful spot to stop for a breather, or a picnic. The church has been painstakingly repaired and restored and its remaining **frescoes** preserved for posterity. Traces of the medieval stone road on which the church was originally aligned can still be made out behind it.

ARRIVAL AND DEPARTURE — THE AMÁRI VALLEY

By bus On weekdays there are two daily buses from Réthymno along the western edge of the valley to Áno Méros; there are also early-morning buses to Amári and to Apodhoúlou, calling at various villages en route.

ACCOMMODATION AND EATING

Alexander Hotel Main street, Yerakári, 28330 51160. Indubitably the poshest place in the valley, this sprawling

WAR IN THE AMÁRI

The Amári villages suffered gravely during **World War II**, particularly towards the end of the German occupation in the latter part of 1944 when – with an Allied victory assured – the occupiers carried out many wanton atrocities. George Psychoundakis (see page 351) watched the outrage from a cave on the slopes of Psiloritis:

I stayed there two or three days before leaving, watching the Kedros villages burning ceaselessly on the other side of the deep valley. Every now and then we heard the sound of explosions. The Germans went there in the small hours of the twenty-second of August and the burning went on for an entire week. The villages we could see from there and which were given over to the flames were: Yerakari, Kardhaki, Gourgouthoi, Vrysses, Smiles, Dryes and Ano-Meros. First they emptied every single house, transporting all the loot to Retimo, then they set fire to them, and finally, to complete the ruin, they piled dynamite into every remaining corner, and blew them sky high. The village schools met the same fate, also the churches and the wells, and at Ano-Meros they even blew up the cemetery. They shot all the men they could find.

Other villages around Psiloritis, from Anóyia to Kamáres, were also burned and destroyed. Officially these atrocities were in reprisal for the kidnap of General Kreipe, four months earlier. But Psychoundakis, for one, believed that it was a more general revenge, intended to destroy any effective resistance in the closing months of the German occupation. Today the villages of Méronas, Elénes, Yerakári, Kardháki and Vrísses mark the southward progress of the German troops with etched stone **memorials** dated one day apart. Áno Méros has a striking war memorial of a woman wielding a hammer and chisel as she carves the names of the dead into the monument.

3

four-star hotel complex is full only in August. Out of season it's an extraordinary bargain, if eerily deserted. Built by a local boy made good, it hopes to become an outdoor activity (including hiking) centre and there's a large pool (open to all for the price of a drink) and tennis court in its ample grounds. It also has its own bar and taverna. Breakfast included. €

Aravanes Thrónos, http://aravanes.com. The stone-built *Aravanes* has stunning panoramic views across the valley to Mount Psiloritis. The rooms are modern with wood-burners (and central heating for winter), flat-screen TV and fridge; there's also a family apartment, and a pool. The managingf amily run the attractive taverna below, together with a small shop selling mountain herbs and homemade honey; they also organise activities including grape harvesting, *rakí* distillation and hiking (see page 212). €

Elia Hotel Above Méronas, signed from the northern edge of the village, http://eliameronas.gr. Incongruously fancy apartment complex with fabulous views, pool and bar. Well-equipped rooms, studios with kitchens and two-bedroom apartments; all with air/con and heating, some with working fireplaces. Breakfast included. €

★ **Moskhovolis** Main street, Merónas, 28330 22526. Excellent taverna offering a limited range of dishes served with organic veg from their own smallholding; there's no menu, just a few daily specials. €

Patsos Escape Pátsos, https://patsosescape.com. An excellent traditional taverna with simple rooms; some directly above the taverna, others in the village. There's wonderful home cooking, with fresh dishes every day, while the proprietor, a veteran of the Greek special forces, can advise on walks in the area or act as a guide; above all,

FESTIVITIES AND DANCE IN THE AMÁRI VALLEY

Whenever you come to the Amári valley, but in July or August especially, you may be lucky enough to stumble on a village wedding or a **festival** in honour of a local saint, the harvest or some obscure historical event; the latter are worth going out of your way for, so keep an eye out for notices pasted in *kafenío* windows. Beginning with a distorted cacophony of overamplified Cretan music, *lyra* and *laoúto* to the fore, the celebrations continue until the participants are sufficiently gorged on roast lamb and enlivened by wine to get down to the real business of **dancing**. Cretan dancing at an event such as this is an extraordinary display of athleticism and, as often as not, endurance – and if the party really takes off, locals will dig out their old guns and rattle off a few rounds into the sky to celebrate.

there's a beautiful, easy walk through the Gorge of Pátsos to the reservoir; and you can also visit the cave where the kidnappers of General Kreipe (see page 334) hid out for two nights on their journey to the south coast. €

★ **Windy Place Taverna and Rooms** Fourfourás, 2833 041000. The taverna on the northern edge of the village serves up hearty meals on an attractive terrace, while the cosy rooms are in another building in the village proper. The proprietors can describe a short cut (with your own vehicle) to the Psiloritis peak (see page 210) and advise on a 15km gorge walk along the Plátis river valley to Ayía Galíni; they can even collect you from there to return you to Fourfourás. €

South from Réthymno

The main road south from Réthymno heads via Arméni and Spíli to Ayía Galíni (see page 218); for Plakiás (see page 222) and the western half of the south coast, you turn off a little over halfway across the island.

3

Arméni Minoan cemetery

Signed just before the village of Arméni, 10km south of Réthymno • Charge

The little-visited but fascinating **Minoan cemetery** at **ARMÉNI** (**Αρμένοι**) features more than two hundred rock-cut tombs dating from the Late Minoan period, after the fall of the great palaces. Most of the tombs, pleasantly sited today in a shady oak wood, are of the *drómos* (passage) and chamber type; each probably a family mausoleum. One large tomb under a cover on the south side of the site has a particularly spectacular *drómos* and finely cut chamber and may well have belonged to a royal personage. Many others are almost as impressive, although at some only the *drómos* has been cut, and work seems for some reason to have been abandoned. A number of important discoveries were made here, including many *lárnakes* (clay coffins) and rich grave goods – weapons, jewellery, vases and a rare helmet made from boar's tusks – now on display in the archeological museums at Réthymno and Iráklio. One mystery is still to be solved: the location of the sizeable settlement that provided this necropolis with its customers.

EATING — ARMÉNI

Goules Taverna Main square, Gouledhianá, about 4km east of the main road, south of Arméni village, http://goules.gr. An outstanding country taverna that uses local ingredients to create traditional Cretan cuisine, often with an inventive twist, with good meat, fish and vegetarian options; the pork in wine and honey is a perennial favourite. It also serves Brink's beers (see page 216). €€

Spíli

The pleasant country town of **SPÍLI** (**Σπίλι**), tucked into the folds of the Mount Kédhros foothills 30km south of Réthymno, doesn't look much as you drive through, although

GERMAN BEER COMES TO CRETE

When German Bernd Brink decided to build a **brewery** after marrying a local girl, many thought he had bitten off more than he could chew. But using tact, diplomacy and not a little tenacity, he started work on what is now **Brink's Brewery** (6932 194 989, http://bricksbeerhouse.gr) in 2001. Today this glittering stainless steel model of Teutonic efficiency receives orders from as far away as Cyprus and Denmark. He produces two very tasty brews, a blonde and a dark – both organic and made in accordance with sixteenth-century German beer purity laws. Unfiltered and unpasteurized, they are made only with water, hops, yeast and malt. You pass the brewery on the main road south of Arméni; sadly Greek bureaucracy means it's no longer open for visits, but the beer is widely available in bars and tavernas throughout Réthymno and Haniá provinces (often under the name Rethymnian Beer).

WALKS AROUND SPÍLI

Plenty of challenging **hikes** start in Spíli. Heracles, the proprietor of the **Heracles** hotel (see page 218) can advise on many of the local walking possibilities, has maps of some, and can help with route information. Both here and the nearby *Green Hotel* can book taxis back to Spíli (around €25 from either Yerakári or Moní Prevéli, for example). None of the available **maps** have enough detail to be really useful.

TO THE AMÁRI VALLEY VIA MOUNT KÉDHROS

The direct route to **Yerakári** in the Amári valley is on the paved road, but there's also a spectacular walk there on the E4 (which passes through Spíli). This heads south, initially along the road, to the village of Kissós and then up via the summit of Kédhros (1777m). A slightly easier route bypasses the summit, but this is still a tough, all-day, 19km trek with plenty of climbing.

SPÍLI CIRCULAR LOOP

An easy 2hr **loop walk** via the ancient chapel of Áyio Pnevma This sets out from Spíli's health centre, up a side road on the left, 200m south of the centre (a road to the right just before the health centre leads 75m to the site of the Venetian fountain that once stood in Spíli's central platía), and meanders into the hills to meet the Spíli–Yerakári road, from where you can descend along narrow lanes to the central square; Heracles has details and a map.

3

NORTH FROM MIXÓRROUMA

West of Spíli, the E4 follows the road for 4km to the village of **Mixórrouma**, where you can loop back either north or south of the main road. The northern route is all on roads, initially signed for Karínes. This climbs steeply to the pretty village of **Lambiní** and its domed Byzantine **church of the Panayía**, the scene of a terrible massacre in 1827 (marked by a plaque) when the Muslims locked the congregation inside the church before setting fire to it. From here it's 5km further climbing to **Karínes**, another attractive village with a friendly *kafenío*, followed by a 7km descent to **Pátsos**. A turn on the left 1km before **Pátsos** leads for ten minutes to the **Áyios Andónios Cave**, which was a Minoan and later Dorian and Roman sanctuary, close to a beautiful gorge. From Pátsos it's less than 10km to Thrónos in the Amári valley (see page 211), or about 7km back to Spíli.

SOUTH FROM MIXÓRROUMA

The southern route from Mixórrouma, via **Fratí** and **Mourné**, takes in some superb scenery and four ancient churches. It's probably easier tackled in the other direction – by road from Spíli to Mourné (4km), cross-country from there to Fratí (8km; you'll need directions), then an easy route above the Kíssanos river valley to Ayía Pelayía and Mixórrouma (4km).

TO MONÍ PRÉVELI

You can also walk the 15km southwest from Spíli to **Moní Préveli** and **Palm Beach** (see page 226). Head to Mourné, from where a track leads south towards **Dhrímiskos**; just before the village a cross-track heads west to the Megalopótamos River. Follow the river to reach the beach.

the mountainside which towers over the houses is impressive. If you get off the main road, however, into the white-walled alleys that wind upwards towards the cliff, it can be very attractive. Plenty of people break their journey briefly here, but only a few stay, mostly ramblers and botanists: it's the trailhead for a series of attractive country **hikes**.

A sharp curve in the road marks the centre of town, by a small platía overlooked by lofty plane trees. Just above this there's a prodigious 25-plaster-spouted **fountain**, a replacement for the elegant carved Venetian original. Beyond the fountain begins a steep labyrinth of cobbled lanes and shady archways, full of flowered balconies, giant urns and whitewashed chimneypots. Spíli can become quite crowded – many of the bus tours passing along the road make a brief stop here, usually for lunch – but between times and in the evenings it is quiet and rural.

ARRIVAL AND DEPARTURE — SPÍLI

By bus The main road passes right through the centre of Spíli, and the Réthymno–Ayía Galíni bus (5 daily each way; 40min) will drop you in the heart of town.

ACCOMMODATION AND EATING

Fabricafe Fountain square, 28320 22766. One of several places around the fountain, this modern bar-café is lively at night, and serves Brink's beers (see page 216).

Green Hotel Main road, 100m north of the square, http://maravelspili.gr. Lovely, great-value rooms place with fabulous views across the valley if you get a room at the back. The owners have a large herb garden outside town, and they organize herbal and botanical walks as well as other activities. Breakfast available. €

3

★ **Heracles** Just off the main road, below the Green Hotel, 28320 22111, http://heracles-hotel.eu. Friendly *pension* boasting spotless balcony rooms with TV and fridge, plus an excellent breakfast (extra). The genial proprietor can advise on walks in the surrounding hills, and rents out mountain bikes. He also has exceptionally well-equipped apartments, sleeping up to four, in his grandparents' converted house in the older part of town. €

Platia Fountain square, 6979 226 668. Pleasant café with an elevated terrace above the fountain and a small but excellent selection of dishes, such as chicken in tomato sauce and home-made cheese or spinach pies. €

Yannis Main road, 50m south of the square, 28320 22707. Close to the heart of things, this is a decent, straightforward taverna for solid Cretan cooking served on a streetside terrace; they also offer breakfast. €

Ayía Galíni

Fifty years ago, **AYÍA GALÍNI** (**Αγία Γαλήνη**) must have been an idyllic spot: an isolated fishing community of some five hundred souls nestling in a convenient fold of the mountains which dominate this part of the **south coast**. Although this was the port of ancient **Syvritos** (see page 212), the modern village is barely a hundred years old, its inhabitants having moved down from the mountain villages of Mélambes and Saktoúria as the traditional threat of piracy along the coast receded.

Catch it out of season and the streets of white houses, crowded in on three sides by mountains and opening below to a small, busy **harbour**, can still appeal. But this is a face which is increasingly hard to find, especially given a surprising number of long-term expat residents. Crowded throughout the season, and confined by the limits of its narrow situation, the village has seen many of its older houses squeezed out by apartment buildings and uninspiring hotels. And for a place that bills itself as the province's major resort, the **beach** here is surprisingly small. If you're looking for strands with space to breathe you'll need to use the resort as a base for trips to nearby beaches or opt for a shorter stay. Nonetheless there's something about Ayía Galíni that

AYÍA GALÍNI ORIENTATION

Few of the streets in Ayía Galíni village are named and such names as there are seem rarely used. The streets which run steeply down to the harbour form the heart of the place: the first of these (**Venizélou**) is a continuation of the main road into town, ending at the harbour; along it you can take care of all the practicalities, from banks to car hire, English-language books and newspapers, laundry, pharmacies and even a doctor. Parallel to this to the east are a series of narrow, pedestrianized and sometimes stepped alleys; the first (known locally as "**Shopping Street**") is lined with stores, jewellery shops, bars and travel agencies; further in is "**Taverna Street**", named for obvious reasons – though the name actually applies to a number of alleys rather than a single street. All of this falls within a very small area where nothing is more than a couple of minutes' walk away.

attracts a loyal following, and there are certainly plenty of excellent restaurants and bars, well-priced rooms and a friendly atmosphere that survives and even thrives on all the visitors. The only real sight is a tiny **Folk Art Museum** (free, donations accepted) in a cave above the harbour.

The beach

The **beach** at Ayía Galíni lies to the east of the village, ten minutes' walk on a narrow path that tracks around the cliff from the harbour, or by a path that descends from the top of the town. You can also drive round and park behind the beach. Walking round by the cliffs, you'll pass **caves** that during World War II served as gun emplacements. The sandy beach is bisected by the River Platys (spanned by a footbridge) and backed by cafés, tavernas and rooms places; various **watersports**, from waterskiing to jet skis and pedaloes, are available.

ARRIVAL AND DEPARTURE — AYÍA GALÍNI

By bus Buses terminate at the upper of two platías on Venizélou, about 250m above the harbour.

Destinations Réthymno via Spíli (5 daily; 1hr 20min); Iráklio via Míres (8 daily, fewer at weekends; 2hr 15min).

By car Coming in by car, head for the large car park on the harbour. Numerous travel agencies and car rental places line Venizélou; reliable operators include Alianthos (28320 32033, http://alianthos-group.com), Auto Galini (28320 91241, www.autogalini.com) and Motor Holidays (28320 91373).

ACTIVITIES

Boat trips Most people who stay here end up making regular excursions elsewhere. In season, the *Sactouris* (6976 693 729; €30 return) runs to Áyios Pávlos and Palm Beach at Préveli (see page 226); the *Elizabeth* (6936 848 445) offers a day-trip to Áyios Yeóryios (€15) and fishing day-trips (€30, including barbecue lunch); and the *Agia Galini* goes to the Paximádhia islands, 12km offshore, which have wonderful fine-sand beaches but little shade (6930 979 864; €40 including on-board meal; reservation essential). All have booths open at the harbour in the evening and before departure; details can be found on https://gogalini.com.

ACCOMMODATION

There are so many **rooms** in Ayía Galíni that you'll find exceptional bargains for much of the year – though perhaps not in August when many are pre-booked by tour operators. Dozens of places, including almost all of those that we review here, are represented on http://agia-galini.com.

Camping No Problem Behind the beach, on the far side of the river, 28320 91239. Big campsite with a pool, shop and restaurant, with sandy, tree-shaded pitches. €

Hariklia Entry road from Réthymno on right just before the descent, http://hotelhariklia.gr. Delightful, spotless *pension* with refurbished rooms with fridge. The communal balconies have fine views and guests also have use of kitchen to prepare breakfasts and snacks. €

★ **Minos** Entry road from Réthymno on left, http://minoshotel.gr. Welcoming hotel with comfortable, modern rooms with fridge and TV; there's also a small family apartment and studio – other rooms have use of a shared kitchen. Many of the rooms enjoy the best sea views in town (well worth the extra money). Superb breakfast available. €

Palazzo Greco Entry road from Réthymno on left, http://palazzogreco.com. Immaculate boutique hotel done up in bright colours with marble floors, designer bathrooms and gorgeous sea views from many rooms; the suites (an extra cost) are fabulous, the standard rooms a little cramped for the price. It also squeezes in a small pool. €€

Tropica Club Behind the beach, far side of the river, 28320 91351. Run by an Anglo-Greek couple, these studios and apartments right behind the beach have the added attraction of a big seawater pool. Studios have TV and fridge, while the more spacious apartments also have a kitchen; the more modern units come with sea views and handmade wooden furnishings. Beachfront bar/taverna (breakfast available) and poolside yoga sessions, too. €€

EATING AND DRINKING

Ayía Galíni's vast range of **food** and **drink** – one major and undeniable benefit of the resort's popularity – is often excellent and, thanks to the competition, not overpriced. There's a good bakery opposite the post office.

RESTAURANTS

Faros Shopping St, 6944 773 702. The resort's best and most unpretentious fish restaurant, with a small street terrace, where the friendly family who run it serve up what they catch themselves. The catch of the day is chalked up on a blackboard and they also specialise in *astakomakaronada* (lobster flaked into spaghetti). €€

Madame Hortense Overlooking the harbour, above Zorba's bar, 6932 989 538. Named after Zorba the Greek's floozy in the classic novel, *Madame Hortense* is a little pricier than the competition. Its upstairs timber-floored dining room offers arguably the town's best harbour view (worth booking for a ringside seat), and a slightly eccentric short menu with pasta and curry as well as Greek dishes; rabbit in a lemon and wine sauce and Thai chicken curry. €€

Platía On a small square slightly south of the bus stop, 28320 91185. This café is famed for its breakfasts. and later in the day also does snack meals and mezédhes. €

Romantika Romantika Hotel, behind the beach, on the far side of the river, 28320 91388. One of several enjoyable bar/tavernas behind the beach, with a mixed, international menu taking in breakfast, omelettes and pizzas, as well as simple Greek dishes like chicken *souvlaki*. €

3

★ **To Petrino** Just off the bus stop platía, 28320 91504. Friendly little gem of an ouzerí whose proprietor is an ex-sea captain. Serves breakfast and coffee plus excellent mezédhes later in the day, and retains some of the flavour of the pre-tourist days. €€

CAFÉS AND BARS

Balloon Cocktail Harbourfront, 2832 091184. An all-day café right by the harbour that serves great coffee in the morning and delicious cocktails by night.

Kafenío Elpida Shopping St, 28320 91557. This good-value traditional *kafenío* has been given a modern makeover, but still attracts locals and serves bite-size mezédhes with every drink; delicious ewes' milk ice-cream too.

Miro Music Café Taverna St. Bar/café with a jazz, blues and rock soundtrack, catering to the local long-hairs and tourists reliving their youth.

Zorba's Overlooking the harbour, 6932 989 538. A pleasant place for an early-evening drink, with a veranda overlooking the harbour, as well as a dartboard and a shrine to the Beatles. It changes character later, when the dancing starts around midnight.

West of Ayía Galíni

In high summer visitors seeking breathing space tend to head west to the beaches of **Áyios Yeóryios**, **Áyios Pávlos** and beyond. Both of these first two have boat trips from Ayía Galini, and you can also walk to Áyios Yeóryios. If you're aiming for the more isolated beach settlements further west, at **Triópetra**, **Lígres** or **Ayía Fotiní**, you'll need your own transport. On clear days, the island of Gávdhos (see page 314) looms on the horizon.

Áyios Yeóryios

Less than 4km west of Ayía Galíni, the seaside hamlet of **ÁYIOS YEÓRYIOS** (**Άγιος Γεώργιος**) is fairly easily reached on foot, by a marked and well-trodden path that leaves town from the top of the main street, near the *Hotel Ostria*. The beach is almost two hours away, a shingle cove with a taverna. Daily boat trips from Ayía Galíni also visit, and you can drive here, on a paved road that turns off the Ayía Galíni–Mélambes road (accessed from the highway north of Ayía Galíni). When you get here, though the water is startlingly clear, the beach is not especially attractive, and has little shade (although loungers and umbrellas can be rented). If you have a car you're better off heading further west.

Áyios Pávlos

A driveable road, paved about half the distance, follows the coast 8km east from Áyios Yeóryios to **ÁYIOS PÁVLOS** (**Άγιος Πάυλος**), though if you're coming direct from Ayía Galíni you're better off following the main highway north for about 10km before taking the road down via Saktoúria. It's an attractive spot, with some striking rock formations around a sheltered bay, and excellent snorkelling. The lovely **beach** can be subject to strong winds, which you can escape by climbing over the headland to the west, where you can scramble down a sandy slope to two fine-sand beaches, one very sheltered, one nudist. In addition to the visitors arriving by car from the surrounding hinterland, Áyios Pávlos is home to a colony of New Age practitioners who run **yoga** and related courses at their centre, Yoga Plus (bookable in advance only; http://yogaplus.co.uk).

West of Áyios Pávlos

West of Áyios Pávlos it's possible to drive all the way to Palm Beach (see page 226). Most of this is on paved roads, and though they can be steep, winding and narrow in places (and the route not always obvious), it's not an especially hard drive – by far the toughest section comes after you reach Palm Beach, where the road around the back of the beach is very rough, though this is also much the busiest part of the route. Along the way are a series of long beaches, with only the first stirrings of development. If you're coming from the north, these can also be reached by direct turnings off the Spíli road.

Triópetra

TRIÓPETRA (**Τριόπετρα**) – Three Rocks, named for the great crags offshore – is very close to Áyios Pávlos though the road winds around inland. If you just wanted to hole up for a couple of days in a tranquil haven, with a lovely small cove and a huge but exposed beach beyond it, this would be as good a choice as any. There's another excellent yoga retreat here (http://yogaholidaysgreece.com) and a couple of good tavernas with rooms. Quite a lot of daytrippers make it here and there are several tavernas to cater for them, with sunloungers for guests, but there's more than enough room to absorb them all If you want to escape.

3

Lígres and around

To drive from Triópetra to **LÍGRES** (**Λίγρες**), 4km west, simply follow the beach; it's not obvious at first, but quickly becomes a paved road again. Another isolated grey-sand beach here seems to stretch for miles, with a couple of unexpectedly popular taverna-rooms places. Finally, a couple of kilometres beyond Lígres lies **Ayía Fotiní**, a still simpler place with a less attractive, pebbly beach. This is the last stop before the celebrated Palm Beach; the final section of coast road is unpaved.

ACCOMMODATION AND EATING — WEST OF AYÍA GALÍNI

There are relatively few rooms on these beaches, and they're popular, so you'll need to book ahead at pretty much any time of year.

ÁYIOS YEÓRYIOS

Nikos http://aggeorgios.gr. A great taverna where the eponymous proprietor serves his daily seafood catch, including langoustine and lobster (priced per kilo), on a beautifully sited terrace above the sea. They also have simple, comfy rooms. €

ÁYIOS PÁVLOS

Ayios Pavlos Hotel http://agiospavloshotel.gr. A great place to stay, with lovely sea-view rooms and some cheaper, more basic options; they also have other apartments and rooms nearby. The café-restaurant boasts a terrace on the rocks directly above the sea, with a late-night bar in a cave below it. €

TRIÓPETRA

Apanemia On the eastern cove, www.apanemiatriopetra.gr. A very good, chilled taverna, right on the beach with free loungers for patrons, serving breakfast and a standard Greek menu (*kléftiko*, *moussakás*) with an unexpectedly extensive wine list. Just a few simple rooms with fridge and balcony. €

Pavlos' Place On the eastern cove, http://triopetra.com.gr. Appealing air con rooms with fridge and balcony above a little harbour; also a taverna, though this can be dominated by the yoga courses (mostly German-speaking) that the hotel also hosts. €

★ **To Yiroyiali** Behind the western beach, 6976 430 145. Taverna with an attractive terrace overlooking the beach and a short menu of daily specials such as rabbit *stifádho*. There are free loungers on the beach for clients and guests, and very pleasant rooms with fridge and TV in a separate two-storey block overlooking a garden. €

LÍGRES

Ligres Beach http://ligres.gr. Simple rooms with fridge, somewhat oddly decorated in an attempt to make them "designer", with sea-view balconies, above a reliable taverna serving fresh fish. €

Villa Maria 6949 477 081. A slightly incongruous stone building beside a rushing stream houses simple but welcoming rooms and studios with TV and fridge as well as some great two-room apartments. The taverna offers good food (they catch their own fish) and icy spring water from the waterfall outside. €

AYÍA FOTINÍ

★ **Taverna Agia Fotia** 6937 124 600. A lovely, isolated

and tranquil option that's a throwback to the Crete of forty years ago; the excellent taverna, with a terrace out front, offers a range of traditional Cretan dishes as well as fresh fish. Upstairs are four simple but spotless rooms overlooking the sea. Breakfast included. €

Plakiás and around

PLAKIÁS (**Πλακιάς**), 35km south of Réthymno, is a well-established resort, though it's a long way from the big league. Commercialized as it is, Plakiás has a very different feel to anywhere on the north coast, or even Ayía Galíni – the accommodation is simpler, less of it is booked up in advance, the beaches are infinitely better and it attracts a younger crowd. Don't come for sophisticated nightlife or for a picturesque white Greek island village: what you'll find is a lively, friendly place that makes a good base for **walks** in the beautiful surrounding countryside and trips to some great **beaches**.

The gorges

Approaching Plakiás from the main Réthymno–Ayía Galíni road you've a choice of routes, each of which passes through a spectacular gorge. The first turning, via the tiny settlement of **Kánevos** (where there's an excellent taverna) passes through the narrow **Kotsifóu Gorge**; the second approaches via the still more impressive **Kourtaliótiko Gorge**. Either way, it's worth pulling over to take time to appreciate the scenery and the wildlife, from snakes by the water to vast birds of prey soaring above. If you're coming from the south you can also turn off at Mixórrouma, from where you can join the Kourtaliótiko gorge route.

The beaches

Getting from town to the beach can involve no more than a two-minute walk. The town is set at the western end of the bay, and to the east the grey sand of the **town beach** curves around in an unbroken line to the headland a kilometre or more away, with an increasing amount of development behind it. This beach generally looks better from a distance than from close up, however – the long open sweep of the bay means it can be exposed and gusty, and the strong summer **winds** seem to affect Plakiás more than other places along this coast. There's plenty of space, especially towards the far end, but you'll find better sands beyond the headland – riddled with caves and wartime bunkers and gun emplacements – at Dhamnóni, or to the west at Soúdha Beach, with its own grove of Cretan palms.

Soúdha Beach

Soúdha Beach is just over half an hour's walk west of Plakiás, with places to stop for a swim along the way and a couple of good tavernas when you get there. The sand may be a little gritty, but there's plenty of room and the water at the far end is sheltered by rocks; closer to town, where there are fewer people and less development, it's largely nudist.

Dhamnóni

To reach the beaches on foot, about a 40min walk, follow the main road east and turn right along a track which leads through the olive groves; by car, continue east towards Lefkóyia and turn down at the sign for Dhamnóni or, further on, for Amoúdhi

Just east of Plakiás lie some of the most tempting beaches in central Crete, albeit a very poorly kept secret. On arrival you'll find three splashes of yellow sand, divided by rocky promontories, that go by the general name of Dhamnóni. **Dhamnóni beach** itself is the first of them, and the only one that has so far really seen much development: the western half is dominated by a Swiss-owned holiday village, *Hapimag*, while the road down to the sand has an increasing number of **rooms** places. The **beach**, though, is a wonderful long strip of yellow sand and super-clear water with a couple of **tavernas** and seasonal *kantínas*. At the far end you're likely to find a few people who've dispensed with their clothes, at least out of season, and the little cove that shelters the middle of the three beaches (a scramble over the rocks, or a very rough track) is almost entirely **nudist**. This enclave can get very crowded, but they're a good-humoured bunch and, unusually, often include quite a few Greek naturists too. The water is beautiful and there are caves at the back of the beach and rocks to dive from, with some great snorkelling to be had. The third of the coves is **Amoúdhi beach**, where there's a rather more sedate atmosphere and another **taverna** attached to the *Ammoudi Hotel*.

Skhínaria

Skhínaria beach is almost adjacent to Amoúdhi, but to get there you have to drive several kilometres round, via Lefkóyia. Another fine, sandy cove, it's popular with Greek families at holiday times and weekends, and occasionally hosts groups learning to scuba dive, but is otherwise delightfully quiet. There's a taverna open here during the day.

Mýrthios

The village of **MÝRTHIOS** (**Μύρθιος**) hangs high above Plakiás, with wonderful views over the bay exploited by some excellent tavernas and rooms places. There are few other facilities, though, so you really need transport if you're staying here. It's easy enough to walk to Plakiás, about twenty minutes steeply downhill, or to any of the nearby beaches, but the walk back up is considerably tougher.

ARRIVAL AND DEPARTURE — PLAKIÁS AND AROUND

By car If you've taken the Kourtaliótiko Gorge route you turn right for Plakiás, passing through Asómatos and Lefkóyia (continue straight and you'll follow the course of the Megalopótamos river all the way down to Préveli); the Kotsifoú Gorge route emerges on the main coast road west of Plakiás where you turn right for Selliá (see page 227), left for Mýrthios and Plakiás. Either way, the main road enters Plakiás from the east and heads straight into the heart of things along the seafront; virtually everything in Plakiás lies along or just off this main street, running beside the sea, or on one of the lanes connecting it to the single parallel street that runs inland. Continuing through town, the coast road ends after 3km or so at Soúdha, though you can turn off to head up to Selliá and the road west via a vertiginous series of narrow hairpin bends.

By bus Buses arrive and depart from a stop just east of the little bridge, roughly halfway along the seafront opposite the big Forum supermarket; the timetable is usually pinned up and is also displayed at nearby travel agencies.

Destinations Réthymno (5 daily; 1hr), Préveli (June–Sept 4 daily; 20 min).

GETTING AROUND

Bike and car rental There are car rental outlets all along the seafront; Alianthos (28320 32033, http://alianthos-group.com) is excellent, or try Anso Travel (28320 31444, https://ansotravel.com), who also have mountain bikes.

By taxi There's a taxi office at the bottom of the street to the post office, or try Taxi4you (6932 281 995, https://taxi4you.gr).

INFORMATION AND ACTIVITIES

Travel agencies There are plenty of travel agencies on the seafront, including Anso Travel (28320 31444, http://ansotravel.com). Elena Tours (28320 20465, http://crete-tourist-information.com), in an alley up from the harbour, offers all the usual services plus interesting local small-group tours.

Boat trips and fishing In season, several boats a day head to Palm Beach (some via Dhamnóni), and at least once a week further afield to Triópetra and Áyios Pávlos, or west to Frangokástello and Loútro; information and tickets at the harbour, or from the bars opposite. They also offer fishing trips – for information on *Tassos* boat enquire at the *Tassomanolis* taverna (6977 750 458, http://plakiasboattours.gr); for the *Finikas* at the *Smerna* bar (28320 31971).

Diving Some of Crete's best diving is near Plakiás, and there are also easy beaches for learners. Dive2gether is a Dutch company with an office on the front, east of the bridge (28320 32313, https://dive2gether.com); Kalypso Rocks Dive Centre (28310 74687, https://kalypsodivecenter.com) organizes dives at the nearby *Kalypso Cretan Village* resort and also has an office in town.

Horseriding The country around Plakiás is great to explore on horseback; the Horse Riding Center (28320 31196, https://cretehorseriding.com) is out of town opposite the turning to Dhamnóni, with horses for every ability and also donkey rides and a mini-zoo; for information, ask at the *Alianthos Beach Hotel*.

ACCOMMODATION

While there are scores of **hotels** and **rooms** in Plakiás – indeed at times it seems there's little else – you may have difficulty finding a vacancy in high season. The places on the backstreets lack sea views but are quieter and usually the last to fill, and there are also lots of studio-apartment complexes on the road as you approach town and along the coast towards Soúdha Beach to the west. An excellent **list** of local accommodation can be found at http://plakias-filoxenia.gr.

3

PLAKIÁS

Alianthos Beach At the start of the seafront road, https://alianthosbeach-plakias.com. Friendly hotel above a good taverna, with use of the pool at the next door *Alianthos Garden*. Rooms are simple but comfy; those at the front have balconies overlooking the beach. Breakfast included. €

★ **Anna Plakias Apartments** Inland, towards the youth hostel, https://anna-plakias.gr. Classy modern apartments and studios, plus a suite with a tiny private pool, in a quiet spot shaded by palm trees. There's a small, shared rooftop pool and sundeck. €

Gio-ma Western end of the seafront, http://gioma.gr. In a prime position overlooking the harbour, these simple but fabulously located rooms (with fridge and flatscreen TV) sit above the taverna of the same name, right on the water. Over the road are studios and two-room apartments, also refurbished, also with sea views. Great value. €

Limani Apartments Inland immediately behind the port, http://plakiaslimani.gr. Modern two-room apartments on the height above the harbour, with good balcony views. The same owners have two more apartment complexes a little further inland. €

★ **Morpheas Apartments** On the seafront, above Plakías Market, http://morpheas-apartments-plakias-crete-greece.com. Fine modern rooms, studios and galleried apartments with balconies overlooking the beach (although not all have sea view). They're double-glazed against the potentially noisy location, with TV, fridge and, in the larger apartments, even a washing machine Three-night minimum at peak times. €

Oasis Apartments About 1km east of town, on the main road near the Dhamnóni turnoff, https://oasis-plakias.gr. Spacious room and apartment complex with a pool and taverna (where they also serve breakfast) in pretty gardens. €

Phoenix Apartments 1.5km west, near Soúdha Beach, http://phoenix-plakias.com. Tranquil complex with a good-sized pool in a great spot, high above the sea. Studios and three-room apartments are all well equipped and good value. €

★ **Youth Hostel** Inland a little way behind town, http://yhplakias.com.The best hostel on Crete – friendly, relaxed and well run, in an attractively rural setting, with a terrace for breakfast and evening drinks and a busy social scene. Hot showers and wi-fi included; mixed and women-only dorms. March–Nov. €

AMOÚDHI BEACH

Ammoudi Hotel http://ammoudi.grA fabulous place for a complete getaway, its simple balconied rooms with fridge and TV, plus a couple of apartments, 100m from the shore. Meals, including breakfast, are available in their taverna. It also has a dive centre, and this is an ideal spot to learn. €

MÝRTHIOS

★ **Anna Apartments** Mýrthios, www.annaview.com. These classy apartments, built with traditional stone and wood, are beautifully furnished and have fantastic views over Plakiás Bay. Various configurations sleep from two to four, all come with kitchenette, balcony, satellite TV and wi-fi. €

★ **Village Apartments** http://village-apartments.gr. Large apartments and maisonettes (the latter with two bedrooms, living room and washing machine) with magnificent views that are great value for families and larger groups. €

EATING

Plakiás's seafront street is lined with **tavernas**, cafés and bars, but the prime spot is towards the harbour right at the centre of town, where a strip of places have tables next to the water. You'll pay a bit more here than at other places in the resort – but the setting is worth it. For breakfast, there are a number of **bakeries** along the seafront too, and many of the **cafés** open early. There are plenty of **supermarkets**, including a very large one on the edge of town by the *Alianthos Beach Hotel*, which has an excellent bakery and wonderful fruit shop, plus an organic mini-market, on an alley running inland from the harbour.

PLAKIÁS

Candia Bakery Between the hotels Livikon and Lamon on

the seafront. A good place for breakfast, and throughout the day for coffee and juices; choose a pastry from the bakery at the back to have with your drink. €

Christos Overlooking the harbour at west end of the seafront, 28320 31472. The longest-established and arguably the best located of the seafront places, with a pleasant tamarisk-shaded terrace. The menu changes daily, with fresh fish prominent, and includes the likes of home-smoked sea-bass, black spaghetti with calamari and lamb *tsigariasto*. Service can be slow, though. €

★ **Kri Kri** Near the bridge on the seafront, 28320 32223. Good pizza from a wood-fired oven as well as all the taverna standards such as *stifádho* and *kléftiko*. €

Medousa Inland, near the back of the Alianthos Garden hotel, 28320 31521. The fanciest place in town, in both appearance and menu. A beautiful room and great service, though the more inventive dishes can be a bit hit and miss; choose from standard Greek fare such as cumin-spiced meatballs and lamb with beans and tomato sauce, or more ambitious creations like calamari stuffed with chickpeas, citron, rose geranium, herbs and feta. There's a decent wine list, too. €€

★ **Tassomanolis** Facing west along the shore beyond the harbour, 28320 31229. Seafood is king here, most of it caught by the proprietor from his own boat and competitively priced by the kilo. €

Throumbi On the narrow street running inland, between the river and the harbour, 28320 31915. Family-run, traditional Cretan taverna serving up simple, inexpensive local food on a street-side terrace. Daily specials such as rabbit stew or *moussaka*. €

SOÚDHA BEACH

Taverna Galini Far end of the beach, 6982 286 973. On the beach is a beach bar with loungers for guests, while the taverna occupies a grassy space behind, serving all the standards plus some interesting daily specials, like rabbit in tomato sauce with walnuts and feta. There's live Greek music every Wednesday night. €

MYRTHIOS

Panorama Village square, 28320 31450. A decent alternative to next-door *Plateia* if you can't get in there, with equally fine vistas from its terrace and a slightly simpler, cheaper menu; it's also open for breakfast. €

★ **Plateia** Village square, 28320 31560. This long-established taverna with arguably the most spectacular terrace view on the island serves up tasty Cretan cuisine with the odd creative twist – dishes include red lamb, rabbit in lemon sauce and vegetarian lasagne. It can get busy, especially at Sun lunchtimes, so turn up early if you don't want to wait; they don't accept bookings. €€

3

KÁNEVOS

Iliomanolis Kánevos, 7km north of Plakiás, 28320 51053. An excellent and inexpensive rural taverna in a tiny settlement at the top of the Kotsifoú Gorge; there's no menu, so choose from the daily specials in the kitchen; they also have simple but beautifully-kept rooms. €

DRINKING AND NIGHTLIFE

Cozy Backyard Opposite Throumbi, on the narrow street running inland, between the river and the harbour, 6957 667 551. Cocktail bar with seating in a brightly coloured courtyard, well-priced, well-mixed drinks and a chilled but fun atmosphere.

Frame Central seafront, above the Forum supermarket. 6976 972 927. Stylish café-bar with panoramic windows overlooking the water; coffee by day, cocktails at night.

Ostraco On the waterfront, close to the harbour, 28320 32249. *Ostraco* has been here for ever, it seems, with a rock-based playlist and fun atmosphere. It's one of the best places in town, with two floors of bars and a balcony; the upstairs dancing bar opens at 9pm.

SHOPPING

Creta Earth Central seafront, 6987 031 831. Two stores next to each other, one selling crafts, the other products such as oils and herbs, all extremely good quality.

Forum Central seafront, 28320 31320. Supermarket that describes itself as a department store – which given that they stock everything you might conceivably need, from flip-flops to fishing gear, isn't far from the truth; also the best selection of maps, books and newspapers in town.

Savra Just inland from the harbour, 6907 489 003. Quality handmade jewellery and other crafts.

Préveli and Palm Beach

Some 10km east of Plakiás a paved road descends into the fertile valley of the Megalopótamos River, which, unusually for Crete, flows throughout the year. Where it meets the river, the road turns south to climb past the ruins of the **Monastery of Áyios Ioánnis**, also called Káto, or Lower, Préveli. This is the site of the original tenth-century monastery of Préveli, until it was left behind in the following century when the monks decided to move to the greater safety of the present site further uphill. Torched by Muslims during the nineteenth century and long abandoned, it has been meticulously restored this century and may be visited from dawn to dusk (small admission charge when somebody is around to collect it).

Moní Préveli

Charge • http://www.preveli.org

The celebrated **MONÍ PRÉVELI** (**Μονί Πρέβελη**), perched high above the sea, is justifiably proud of its role in centuries of Cretan resistance and famed above all for the shelter provided to Allied troops, many of them Australian, stranded on the island after the Battle of Crete in World War II. The monks supported and fed many soldiers and helped organize them into groups to be taken off nearby beaches by submarine. There's a startling **monument** to these events, overlooking the sea just before the monastery, depicting a life-sized rifle-toting abbot and an Allied soldier cast in bronze. More commemorative plaques decorate the monastery interior, and alongside the icons in the church are a number of offerings from grateful individuals and governments. The church also houses a cross said to contain a fragment of the True Cross; there's a small **museum** with other relics and religious vestments; and a fountain in the courtyard with the palindromic Greek inscription *Nipson anomemata me monan opsin* "Wash your sins, not only your face". There are also fine views out to sea towards the distant and chunky-looking Paximádhia islands, which take their name from the tooth-cracking lumps of twice-baked bread served up with mezédhes in the *kafenía*.

3

Palm Beach

A sand-filled cove at the mouth of the Kourtaliótiko gorge, where a stream feeds a little oasis complete with palm grove and cluster of oleanders, **Palm Beach** certainly looks beautiful – but for much of the year it's overwhelmed by visitors, with loungers, sun umbrellas and pedaloes diminishing the natural charm of the place. Behind the beach, you can escape up the palm-lined riverbanks on foot or take a pedalo through the icy water. Further upstream, before the gorge becomes too steep to follow, are a couple of deep pools nice to swim in. On the beach, a small **bar-taverna** provides basic food and sells drinks, snacks and a few provisions. It's strange to think, as you bask on the crowded sands, that from here, in 1941, many of the Allied soldiers who sought refuge at Moní Préveli (see page 226) were evacuated by submarine.

ARRIVAL AND GETTING AROUND — PRÉVELI AND PALM BEACH

By boat Day-trip boats from Plakiás and Ayía Galíni ply regularly to Palm Beach.

By bus In summer there are 2 buses a day from Réthymno (1hr) and 4 from Plakiás (20min) run to upper Préveli monastery.

By car Driving from Plakiás, after 9km the road bends right into the Megalopótamos river valley and shortly beyond this you'll pass an ancient-looking bridge (actually a nineteenth-century copy of a Venetian original), where a sign indicates a left turn to Palm Beach. Immediately across the river you turn right, soon crossing another cobbled Venetian bridge, beyond which the track leads – in 5km, but 15min of tortuous, rough driving – to the *Dionysos Taverna*. From here, Palm Beach is a 5min climb around the cliff via a stairway carved into the rock – and your first view of it as you reach the crest is quite stunning. An alternative, easier, route is to head towards upperPréveli and follow signs on the left to a car park (€2). From here a well-marked, stepped path with dramatic views heads steeply down over the rocks – a 10min descent to Palm Beach, and a sweaty, muscle-taxing 15–20min back up.

On foot If you arrive at the beach by boat, or the monastery by bus, you can easily walk between the two – 15–20min down, a strenuous 30min or so heading up.

ACCOMMODATION AND EATING

Dionysos Palm Beach, www.prevelicrete.com. The better of two places that offer food and rooms on the grey sand beach at the end of the road alongside Palm Beach. Rooms are simple but comfortable – only a couple have air/con (extra) – and the food served on the vine-shaded terrace is equally unfussy, but fresh and delicious mains. They also have a shop for basic supplies to take to the beach. €

Taverna Gefyra By the "Venetian" bridge on the Préveli–Palm Beach Road, 6944 986 740. A pleasant taverna on the way to Palm Beach serving mezédhes, snacks and drinks on a shady terrace, plus more substantial daily specials, such as goat in tomato sauce. €

West of Plakiás

West of Plakiás the terrain becomes more mountainous as you approach Sfakiá and the foothills of the Lefká Óri. Leaving town, it's a stiff climb up towards Mýrthios and then round, hugging the mountainside, to **Selliá**. You can also approach Selliá direct by an alarmingly steep, winding road climbing from the coast west of Plakiás. Much of the road to Frangokástello (see page 288) runs high above the coast, with spectacular views, but below are some very attractive small beaches.

3

Selliá

Looking up from Plakiás or across from Mýrthios you would imagine that **SELLIÁ** (**Σελλιά**) had the best views of all across this area, but if you drive through you see nothing: only the backs of the houses face out across the sea towards Africa. It's a pretty place, though, and if you want to stop and catch the view it's easy enough to find a path through; better still, pause for a drink or a bite to eat at the tiny taverna on the main street. There are also several excellent shops featuring work by local potters and artists. You can walk from the centre of the village down to Plakiás, a steep thirty minutes below, or you could include Selliá in a long circular hike from Plakiás via Mýrthios.

Rodhákino

Beyond Selliá the country changes and there's a real feeling of the approach of western Crete. The road runs high above a series of capes and small coves, where the only village of any size is **RODHÁKINO** (**Ροδάκινο**), whose two halves are set on steep streets divided by a dramatic ravine. Below is the sand-and-shingle beach of **Koráka**, where General Kreipe was finally taken off the island after his kidnapping in 1944 (see page 334). Some development has started on the coast around here, and if you want to get away from it all there are a few good **rooms** places.

Polyrízos and beyond

Immediately west of Koráka, in the next bay, is **POLYRÍZOS** (**Πολυρίζος**), where there are more rooms places and villas above a small sandy beach. Continuing west, the main road winds high above the coast, from where a number of beaches look tempting, though hardly any are accessible. Signs of development increase as you cross the provincial border into Haniá and approach Frangokástello; there are villas, a few isolated rooms places and even the odd taverna. New tracks connecting these places pop up all the time, which makes things confusing; however, if you drive towards the coast you can often find a way through, though the last bit may be on foot. Some of the best are found by following the sign from the main road to **Lákki beach** – follow this road as it heads back east and you'll reach a headland from which you can easily walk down to a couple of beautiful patches of sand.

ACCOMMODATION AND EATING **WEST OF PLAKIÁS**

SELLIÁ

★ **Elia** Main street, 28320 36002. Excellent little ouzerí-taverna where the home-cooked food is every bit as good as the stunning terrace view; there are daily specials on the board, and often some offbeat choices alongside the traditional – orange, fennel and cheese salad, for example, or simple *soutzoukákia*. €

RODHÁKINO

Arokaria Set back behind the beach, http://cleanthi-rooms.gr. A very good, friendly taverna with large, somewhat dated but quiet and comfy rooms with TV, kitchenette and great views. The taverna serves mainly grilled meat and fresh fish, or check out the kitchen for Sfakian specialities such as wild goat; and don't miss their home-made orange liqueur. €

Sunrise A short way up the hill above the beach, http://sunrise-hotel-crete.gr. Attractive rooms, studios and apartments with sea views, as well as a pool, bar and taverna. Breakfast available. €

POLYRÍZOS

Panorama Above the small sandy beach, 28320 31788. Aptly named for its raised position, *Panorama* has simple rooms (with TV and fridge), and a taverna serving just a few home-made specials each day – delicious and inexpensive. €

Polyrizos Hotel http://polyrizoshotel.com. A relatively large and fancy hotel complex, with a pool and good restaurant where any of the lamb dishes are worth a try. €€

3

West of Réthymno

Heading **west from Réthymno** the E75 main road is easy and efficient, but offers little in the way of diversion. The **highway** initially climbs above the coast before dropping back to sea level at **Yeráni**, 6km from Réthymno, with a rocky cove good for swimming. Beyond, after another brief flirtation with the hills, the road finally levels out beside the **Gulf of Almyrós,** where it traces the shore, flat and straight, all the way to Yeoryioúpolis (see page 259), alongside a long and windswept **sandy beach**. There are pockets of development but for the most part this beach, separated from the road by straggling bushes of oleander, is virtually deserted. There can be dangerous currents so don't venture too far out; it gets more sheltered as you approach the development at Yeoryioúpolis.

The scenic **old road** is by comparison quite populous. To join it, you can either head west from Réthymno, turning inland shortly after you leave the city, or south past the Minoan cemetery at Arméni (see page 216), just after which you can cut west into the hills. Either way, you'll pass through half a dozen prosperous little villages before arriving, after some 20km, at **Episkopí**, a local market centre with narrow, twisting hilly streets at its heart. Here you're approaching the foothills of the White Mountains, which rise with increasing majesty ahead. Beyond Episkopí the road soon divides, the main way descending steadily towards Yeoryioúpolis, a secondary route climbing through the village of Kournás (see page 261) and then dropping steeply to the lake. Alternatively you can head **south** from Episkopí towards **Aryiroúpoli**, **Así Goniá** and a series of small mountain villages, a rarely travelled route where the old life continues, and where there are good opportunities for **hiking** in the surrounding hills.

Roústika

A diversion of 5km or so from the Episkopí road will take you to **ROÚSTIKA** (**Ρούστικα**), whose **Church of Panayía and Sotíra** has some of the finest frescoes in Crete.

CROSSING THE ISLAND: SPECTACULAR DRIVES

If you enjoy driving on **Cretan mountain roads**, the trans-island routes west of Réthymno are among the finest on the island, though not for the faint-hearted.

There are a number of routes, paved all the way and emerging either at Plakiás or Frangokástello. The chief ones are: from Roústika or from Aryiroúpoli via Vilandhrédho to Kánevos at the head of the Kotsifoú Gorge (see page 222), and from there on to Plakiás; or from Aryiroúpoli via either Myriokéfala or Así Goniá (the latter in poor condition) to Kallikrátis, and thence a heart-stopping descent to Frangokástello.

ARYIROÚPOLI'S UPPER VILLAGE: A CIRCULAR TOUR

You can begin a **tour** of the upper village in the main square, opposite the church. Pass beneath a stone arch and keep straight ahead to find an elegant Venetian dwelling (perhaps part of the once extensive villa of the Clodio family) on the left, with a fine **portal** bearing the legend *Omnia Mundi Fumus et Umbra* (All Things in This World are Smoke and Shadow). The street eventually climbs and the houses become brilliant white. This is not a tourist village, however, and discreet glances inside open doorways will reveal the everyday work of the village women – rolling *bourekákia* pastries for the evening meal, peeling corncobs, or embroidering and repairing family clothing. The route will lead you past more crumbling Venetian houses, some being refurbished, to a superb **Roman mosaic floor** beneath a canopy on a street corner. Part of a third-century bathhouse, its quality is not only an indication of the wealth of the ancient town, but also of how much still lies buried beneath the modern village. Following the same street around the hill leads back to the arch and the main square.

3

Follow the signs to the left as you enter the village, and narrow streets lead to a square and the elegant, twin-aisled, Byzantine church. Inside (the key is kept at the café next door) are wonderfully preserved fourteenth-century frescoes, principally of scenes from the life of Christ.

Aryiroúpoli

ARYIROÚPOLI (**Αργυρούπολη**), 6km south of Episkopí, is a strikingly scenic village filled with rushing water, which historically was exploited by a series of watermills. Its **springs** made it a prosperous place throughout history: it was the site of the prestigious Greco-Roman city of **Lappa** and an important commercial centre through Byzantine and Venetian times. Today, with lovely views over the Mousélias river valley and surrounded by some fine **walking** country in the foothills of the White Mountains, it attracts plenty of day-trippers and coach parties, but out of hours reverts to being a peaceful backwater, a refreshing escape from the summer heat.

The springs

Below the village, down a right-hand fork as you come in, gushing **spring water** cascades in every direction. Vegetation is abundant in this fertile environment and the roar of water impressive; there's so much of it here that it supplies the whole of Réthymno town. Around the streams, shaded by great chestnut and plane trees, are half a dozen **tavernas** specializing in trout, kept in ponds, and barbecued meat. Also here are the remains of ancient **waterworks and mills**, some of the most obvious below the *Palios Mylos* taverna, accessed through its grounds. There's a restored Byzantine chapel fronted by a Roman pillar, and not far away by the stream a remarkable seventeenth-century **Venetian fulling mill** (used for shrinking, beating and preparing cloth), whose wooden machinery is rapidly crumbling away. Nearby are the scanty remains of the **Roman baths** of ancient Lappa.

The upper village

Aryiroúpoli itself centres on a tranquil square overlooked by the elegant seventeenth-century Venetian church of **Áyios Ioánnis**. This segment of the village is built over ancient **Lappa**, parts of which can be seen near the church; archeologists have been busy over recent years excavating and documenting the city's ancient necropolis in the valley to the north, where they have unearthed a wealth of grave goods. Beyond the church, the village's **folk museum** is also worth a look (free).

Heading downhill from the west side of the square along narrow, stepped streets, you come to a smaller square (the old **marketplace**), with a couple of tiny churches en route. At the northern end of the village, a pleasant walk will bring you to the delightful chapel of **Áyios Nikólaos**, dating from the eleventh century, with fourteenth-century frescoes by Ioannis Pagomenos (John the Frozen). To get there, take the signed track heading down into the valley to the right off the main road about 400m out of the village, then take the first track on the left and descend to the church (which is unlocked), some 300m further.

Ancient Lappa

3

Originally a Dorian settlement, **Lappa** was an ally of Lyttos (see page 83) in the latter's wars against Knossós. When it fiercely opposed the Roman invasion in 67 BC, the city was destroyed by the conquering legions. Later, when Lappa aided Octavian-Augustus in his struggle against Antony for the control of the Roman world, the victorious emperor permitted the Lappans to rebuild their town and gifted them a **water reservoir** in 27 BC which, incredibly, still supplies the village today. The city flourished for many centuries, even outlasting Roman rule, but was razed again by the Saracens in the ninth century. It recovered during the Venetian occupation and was an important centre, as is evident from the numerous villas left behind by Venetian landlords. You'll spot remnants from all periods of this history incorporated into houses throughout the village: classical inscriptions, ancient columns and bits of Venetian stone carving crop up in the most unlikely places.

The necropolis

Just over 1km north of Aryiroúpoli • Access is by a signed footpath from the village

Ancient Lappa's **necropolis** is located at a site known as the Five Virgins, after a nearby chapel. Hundreds of **tombs** – currently being investigated by archeologists – have been cut into the rock cliffs here, many of them with elaborate interior and exterior decoration. One, opened only a few years ago, after its discovery by a goatherd, was found to contain a stunning gold diadem. The chapel takes its name from five young women put to death by the Romans in the third century for secretly practising Christianity in the tombs. Nearby, alongside yet another spring, stands a gigantic 2000-year-old **plane tree** (claimed by locals to be the oldest in Crete), with a path cut through it.

ARRIVAL AND INFORMATION — ARYIROÚPOLI

By bus Buses (Mon–Fri only; final destination Myriokéfala) leave Réthymno at 6am and 2.45pm, and return at 6.45am and 3.30pm. There are also lots of tours from both Réthymno and Yeoryioúpolis.

Information Beneath the stone arch in the main square, Lappa Avocado (28310 81070), a shop selling local wine, herbs and olive oil as well as various avocado products, is a helpful source of information when they're not too busy. There are several other good craft shops nearby.

ACCOMMODATION

Arcus Suites Heart of the upper village, http://arcus.com.gr. A group of ancient village houses lovingly restored as luxury suites around a small pool. There's lots of exposed stone and wood, and excellent facilities including full kitchen; the largest family suite can sleep six. €€

Taverna-Rooms Zografakis 50m along the Miriakéfala road just off the main square, http://ezografakis.gr. Classic Greek-style rooms with fridge, TV and great views northwards from the balconies. above a decent taverna. Breakfast (extra) available. €

EATING AND DRINKING

The village's main cluster of restaurants is at the **springs**, where tavernas have all incorporated water features into their terraces – walls of tumbling water, oriental wooden water bells, water wheels and the like. The whole scene is especially magical at night. The **upper village** can't really compete for ambience but there are a couple of places well worth a try.

Bar Maria Main square, upper village. The village's main bar, which serves breakfast and snacks. A speciality is their avocado and tuna salad prepared with organic village-grown avocados. €

★ **O Kipos tis Arkoudenas** Just outside Episkopí on the

Aryiroúpoli road, 6946 753 544. Exceptional creative cooking in an unexpected setting, using local, organic ingredients in creative ways. There's a salad with 47 separate ingredients (home-grown or foraged) and mains such as pork stuffed with feta, and rabbit *stifádho*. €€

Palios Mylos At the springs, 28310 81209. Perhaps the most atmospheric of the many good tavernas at the springs, with its tables arranged around a gushing spout. Specialities include mountain goat, charcoal-roast lamb and fresh trout (sold by weight), and there are plenty of vegetarian options. €€

Taverna Arhea Lappa 200m along the Episkopí road below the village, 28310 81004. Good, inexpensive local taverna with an outdoor terrace specializing, like most here, in grilled meat; try the *kontosoúvli* (spit-roast pork) or *loukánika* (sausages). €

Myriokéfala

The road leading out of Aryiroúpoli's upper village beyond the church allows visits to more villages and interesting churches. After 7km – with possible stops en route to explore the hamlets of Marouloú and Arolíthi, just off the road to left and right – the road passes through **MYRIOKÉFALA** (**Μυριοκέφαλα**), whose former monastery church of the **Panayía Antifonitria** has ancient **Byzantine frescoes** depicting the Passion which are among the earliest examples on the island, dating from the eleventh and twelfth centuries. The tiny drum-domed edifice – in a courtyard at the bottom of the village (follow signs to the monastery) – also has an icon of the Virgin which is highly venerated locally.

3

Así Goniá

Beyond the springs at Aryiroúpoli, the road continues southwest for 6km through the verdant cleft of the Gipari Gorge, where trees thrust skywards from a riverbed flowing with water all winter, but which lies arid in the summer drought. This habitat breeds a profusion of **birdlife**: as well as blue rock thrushes, pipits and the ubiquitous tits, you may also spot griffon vultures and hawks hovering around the crags.

The road finally arrives in the broad platía of **ASÍ GONIÁ** (**Ασή Γωνιά**), an isolated and perpetually cloudy rustic settlement. You're now in Haniá province, and there is a real contrast here between the barren heights of the White Mountains to the west, and the softer green of the Aryiroúpoli side of the valley. The square is ringed by **busts** portraying Venizélou and associated village heroes, but curiously not its most celebrated recent son, **George Psychoundakis** (see page 351) who died in 2006 aged 85. From the square, the **main street** climbs uphill between simple stone dwellings, their yards piled with the firewood needed to stave off the bitterly cold winters here. A few of the men here still wear the traditional *saríki* black headdress, baggy *vraka* trousers and *stivánia* high leather boots, and almost all still dress in black.

Haniá

THE HARBOUR AND MOSQUE IN HANIÁ

Haniá

Haniá, Crete's westernmost province, is still its least visited, which is a significant part of its attraction. Although tourist development is spreading fast and has already covered much of the coast around the city of Haniá, the west is likely to remain one of the emptier parts of the island, partly because there are few beaches suited to large resort hotels, and partly because the great archeological sites are a long way from here. In their place are some of the island's most classic elements: scattered coves, unexploited rural villages, and a spectacular vista of mountains.

The city of **Haniá**, island capital until 1971, is unequivocally the most enjoyable of Crete's larger towns, littered with oddments from its Venetian and Ottoman past, and bustling with harbourside life. To either side, along virtually the whole **north coast** of the province, spreads a line of sandy beach – at times exposed, and increasingly developed, but still with numerous stretches where you can escape the crowds. Three peninsulas punctuate this northern coastline: **Akrotíri**, enclosing the magnificent natural harbour of **Soúdha Bay**; **Rodhopoú**, a bare and roadless tract of mountain; and, at the western tip of the island, **Gramvoúsa**, uninhabited and entirely barren. Akrotíri, ringed with air bases and naval installations, is well worth a day-trip, with a couple of excellent beaches and two beautiful monasteries. Most tourists stay to the west, on the coast between Haniá and Rodhopoú, in one of a number of former villages now linked by an ever-expanding strip of low-rise development centred on **Ayía Marína** and **Plataniás**, with the villas and apartments thinning out as you head further from the city.

The south is overshadowed by the peaks of the **Lefká Óri** – the **White Mountains** – whose grey bulk, snow-capped from January through to May or June, dominates every view in western Crete. Although marginally less high than the Psiloritis range, they're far more rewarding for walking or climbing. Along the south coast the mountains drop straight to the Libyan Sea, and the few towns here lie in their shadow, clinging to what flat land can be found around the bays. Through the heart of the massif there's no road at all, nor is there any driveable route along the south coast: unless you want to travel back and forth across the island you'll have to rely on boats, or on walking. The hike through the National Park in the **Samariá Gorge**, Europe's longest, is stunning, despite the summer hordes. With a little spirit of adventure and preparation you can take scores of other, deserted **hiking** routes.

The south-coast communities beneath the mountains see plenty of visitors, mostly gorge-trippers passing through, but none could really be described as a resort. **Ayía Rouméli**, the sometimes frenetic end-point of the Samariá Gorge walk, and serene **Loutró** can be reached only on foot or by boat. **Hóra Sfakíon**, the capital of the wild region known as **Sfakiá**, is a pleasant place to stay if you can handle the influx of day-trippers; more peace is to be found down the coast a little, at the superb beaches by the Venetian castle of **Frangokástello**.

The west end of the island, beyond Rodhopoú, is very sparsely populated. The port of **Kastélli** Kissámou is the only town of any size, and there's a small resort at **Paleóhora** in the south. **Soúyia** may be the next in line for development, but for the moment it seems in a rather charming state of limbo. The whole of the mountainous southwestern corner around Paleóhoa, an area known as **Sélinos**, is worth exploring, with rough roads leading to untouched mountain villages and little-known ruins and churches. On the west-facing coast – hard to get to but well worth the effort – are two of Crete's finest beaches, **Falásarna** and **Elafonísi**. Finally there's **Gávdhos**, an island some 30km

THE HARBOUR AT NIGHT IN THE TINY VILLAGE OF LOUTRÓ

Highlights

❶ **Haniá** The island's second-largest city is also its most enjoyable, with a delightful Old Town, scenic harbour, and great food, drink and nightlife. See page 237

❷ **Lefká Óri** Haniá's White Mountains offer a huge range of hiking opportunities, from easy gorge walks to serious mountain expeditions. See page 270

❸ **Loutró** Accessible only on foot or by boat, the tiny village of Loutró epitomizes the isolated appeal of the southwest coast. See page 277

❹ **Frangokástello** A stunning seaside castle with a stunning backdrop of stark mountains. See page 288

❺ **West coast beaches** Crete's little-known west coast boasts two of the island's finest beaches. See pages 296 and 300

❻ **Byzantine churches** Ancient churches, many of them with remains of original frescoes, are found throughout the region, particularly in Sélinos. See page 303

❼ **Paleóhora** The only real resort in the southwest, with a great beach, lively atmosphere and an enjoyable end-of-the-road feel. See page 305

❽ **Gávdhos** If you truly want to get away from it all, this island off Crete's south coast is about as far as you can go. See page 314

HIGHLIGHTS ARE MARKED ON THE MAP ON PAGE 236

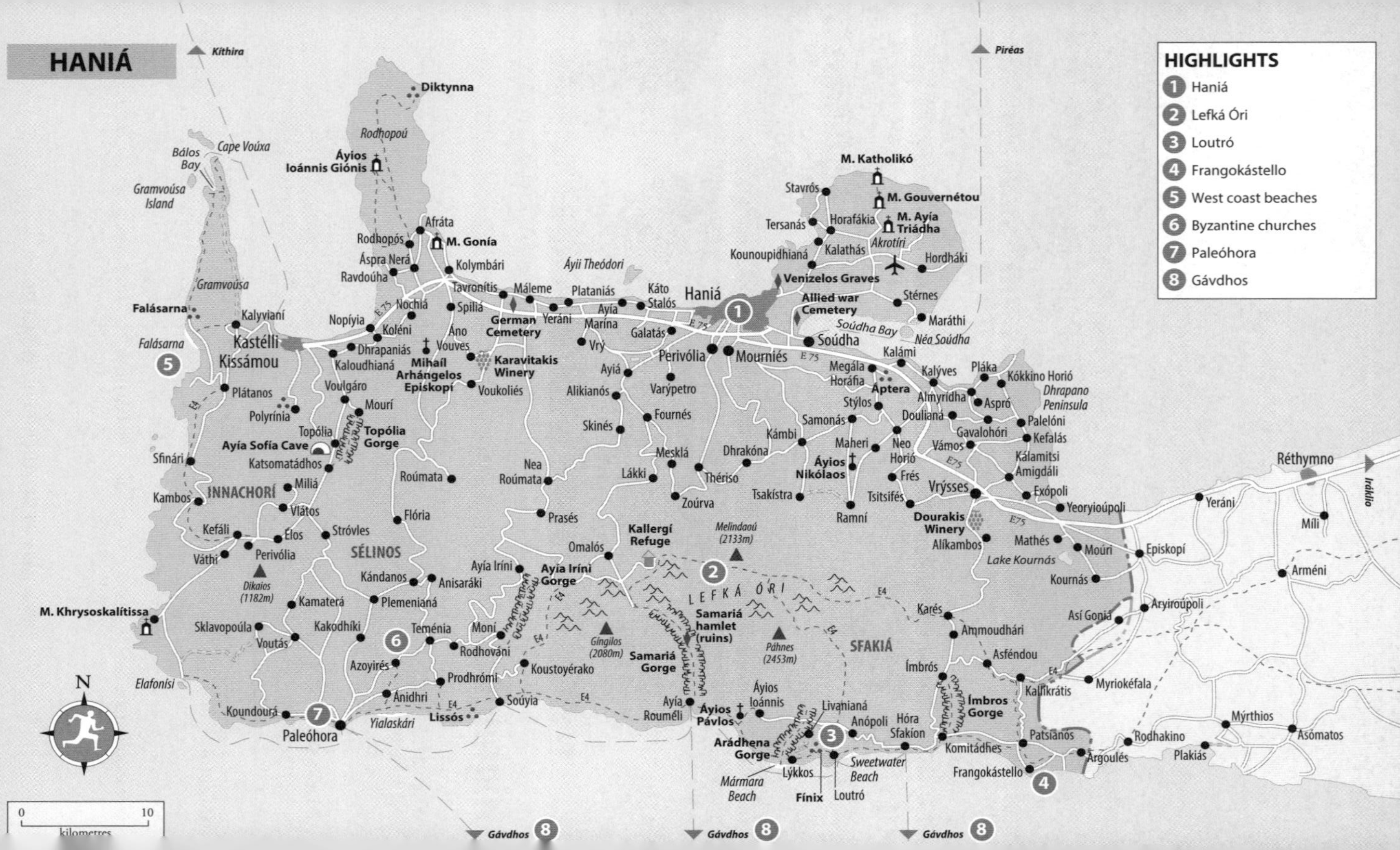

HANIÁ
HIGHLIGHTS
1 Haniá
2 Lefká Óri
3 Loutró
4 Frangokástello
5 West coast beaches
6 Byzantine churches
7 Paleóhora
8 Gávdhos
Kíthira
Piréas
Iráklio
Gávdhos
Diktynna
Rodhopoú
Áyios Ioánnis Giónis
Cape Voúxa
Bálos Bay
Gramvoúsa Island
Gramvoúsa
Falásarna
Kastélli Kissámou
Kalyvianí
M. Katholikó
M. Gouvernétou
M. Ayía Triádha
Stavrós
Tersanás
Horafákia
Kalathás
Akrotíri
Kounoupidhianá
Hordháki
Venizelos Graves
Allied war Cemetery
Stérnes
Maráthi
Soúdha Bay
Néa Soúdha
Soúdha
Haniá
Káto Stalós
Áyii Theódori
Afráta
M. Gonía
Rodhopós
Áspra Nerá
Ravdoúha
Kolymbári
Tavronítis
Máleme
Plataniás
Ayía Marína
Yeráni
German Cemetery
Nochiá
Spiliá
Nopíyia
Koléni
Dhrapaniás
Kaloudhianá
Áno Vouves
Mihaíl Arhángelos Episkopí
Karavitakis Winery
Voukoliés
Vrý
Galatás
Perivólia
Mourniés
Ayiá
Alikianós
Varýpetro
Fournés
Skinés
Meskla
Lákki
Thériso
Zoúrva
Dhrakóna
Kámbi
Samonás
Stýlos
Megála Horáfia
Áptera
Kalámi
Kalýves
Pláka
Kókkino Horió
Dhrapano Peninsula
Almyrídha
Aspró
Paleloni
Douliana
Gavalohóri
Kefalás
Vámos
Maheri
Neo Horió
Áyios Nikólaos
Frés
Kálamitsi
Amigdáli
Exópoli
Tsakístra
Ramní
Tsitsifés
Vrýsses
Dourakis Winery
Yeoryioúpoli
Réthymno
Yeráni
Míli
Alíkambos
Mathés
Moúri
Lake Kournás
Kournás
Episkopí
Arméni
Aryiroúpoli
Así Goniá
Myriokéfala
Kallikrátis
Asféndou
Ammoudhári
Karés
Ímbrós
Ímbros Gorge
Komitádhes
Patsianós
Argoulés
Frangokástello
Rodhakino
Plakiás
Mýrthios
Asómatos
Hóra Sfakíon
Anópoli
Livanianá
Sweetwater Beach
Loutró
Fínix
Lýkkos
Áyios Ioánnis
Áyios Pávlos
Arádhena Gorge
Mármara Beach
Ayía Rouméli
SFAKIÁ
Páhnes (2453m)
LEFKÁ ÓRI
Samariá hamlet (ruins)
Samariá Gorge
Melindaoú (2133m)
Kallergí Refuge
Omalós
Gíngilos (2080m)
Ayía Iríni Gorge
Ayía Iríni
Nea Roúmata
Prasés
Koustoyérako
Soúyia
Moní
Rodhováni
Teménia
Prodhrómi
Anisaráki
Kándanos
Plemenianá
Ánidhri
Lissós
Yialaskári
Azoyirés
Kakodhíki
Kamaterá
SÉLINOS
Stróvles
Flória
Roúmata
Topólia
Topólia Gorge
Mourí
Voulgáro
Ayía Sofía Cave
Katsomatádhos
Miliá
Vlátos
Élos
Perivólia
INNACHORÍ
Polyrínia
Plátanos
Sfinári
Kambos
Kefáli
Váthi
Dikaios (1182m)
M. Khrysoskalítissa
Sklavopoúla
Voutás
Elafonísi
Koundourá
Paleóhora
E75
E4
N
0
10
kilometres

off the south coast that is Europe's southernmost point, caught somewhere between the eighteenth and the twenty-first centuries.

Haniá town

HANIÁ (**Χανιά**), as any of its residents will tell you, is spiritually the capital of Crete, even if the formal political title was long ago passed back to Iráklio. With its shimmering waterfront, crumbling masonry and web of alleys, it is an extraordinarily attractive city, especially if you can catch it in spring when the Lefká Óri's snow-capped peaks seem to hover above the roofs. Although it is for the most part a modern place, whose permanent population – fast expanding into hill and coastal suburbs – always outnumbers the visitors, you might never know this as a tourist. Surrounding the harbour is a wonderful jumble of Venetian streets, a maze-like **old town** contained by ancient city walls and littered with **Ottoman**, **Byzantine** and **Minoan ruins**. Highlights include the **Venetian harbour** itself and a quartet of **museums**, but the greatest pleasure of all, perhaps, is to be had simply wandering the narrow streets and stepped alleyways. Add plentiful accommodation and tavernas, excellent **markets**, shopping and nightlife, and you'll almost certainly want to stay longer than you intended.

Brief history

Haniá is one of the longest continuously inhabited city sites in the world, though its convoluted and often violent history has left it with relatively little to show for it. Only recently has the arrival of **tourism**, amid a rare period of peace and prosperity, inspired the will – if not the resources – to save the city's crumbling architectural heritage.

4

Ancient Kydonia and La Canea

Ancient **Kydonia** was an apparently substantial **Minoan** community about which little is known: only scattered remnants have so far been brought to light, but many believe that there was a major palace here, probably beneath the modern buildings in Kastélli, overlooking the harbour. After the collapse of the Minoan palace culture, Kydonia grew into one of the island's most important cities – well enough known for its citizens to warrant a mention in Homer's *Odyssey* – and remained so through the Classical Greek era. When **Rome** came in search of conquest, the city mounted a stiff resistance prior to its eventual capitulation in 69 BC, after which it flourished once more. The Kastélli hill served as the Roman city's acropolis, but dwellings spread at least as far as the extent of the walled city that can be seen today: Roman mosaics have been discovered beneath Cathedral Square and up near the present-day market hall.

In early **Christian** times Kydonia was the seat of a bishop, and under the protection of Byzantium the city flourished along with the island. As the Byzantine Empire became increasingly embattled however, so did its further outposts, Kydonia included, suffered

HANIÁ ORIENTATION

Haniá's **old city** clusters around the harbour, and most tourists confine themselves to this area or the fringes of the **new town** up towards the bus station. You may get lost wandering among the alleys, but it's never far to the sea, to one of the main thoroughfares or to some other landmark. The major junction at the top of Hálidhon marks the centre of town as well as anywhere. If you stand facing north at this junction, everything in front of and below you is basically the old, walled city; behind is Platía 1866 and the newer parts of town. To the east, **Odhós Yiánnari** leads past the market and on towards the Akrotíri peninsula and airport, or out to the main highway, while to the west, **Skalídhi** leads out of town towards the closest beaches, and eventually to the highway west and Kastélli Kissámou.

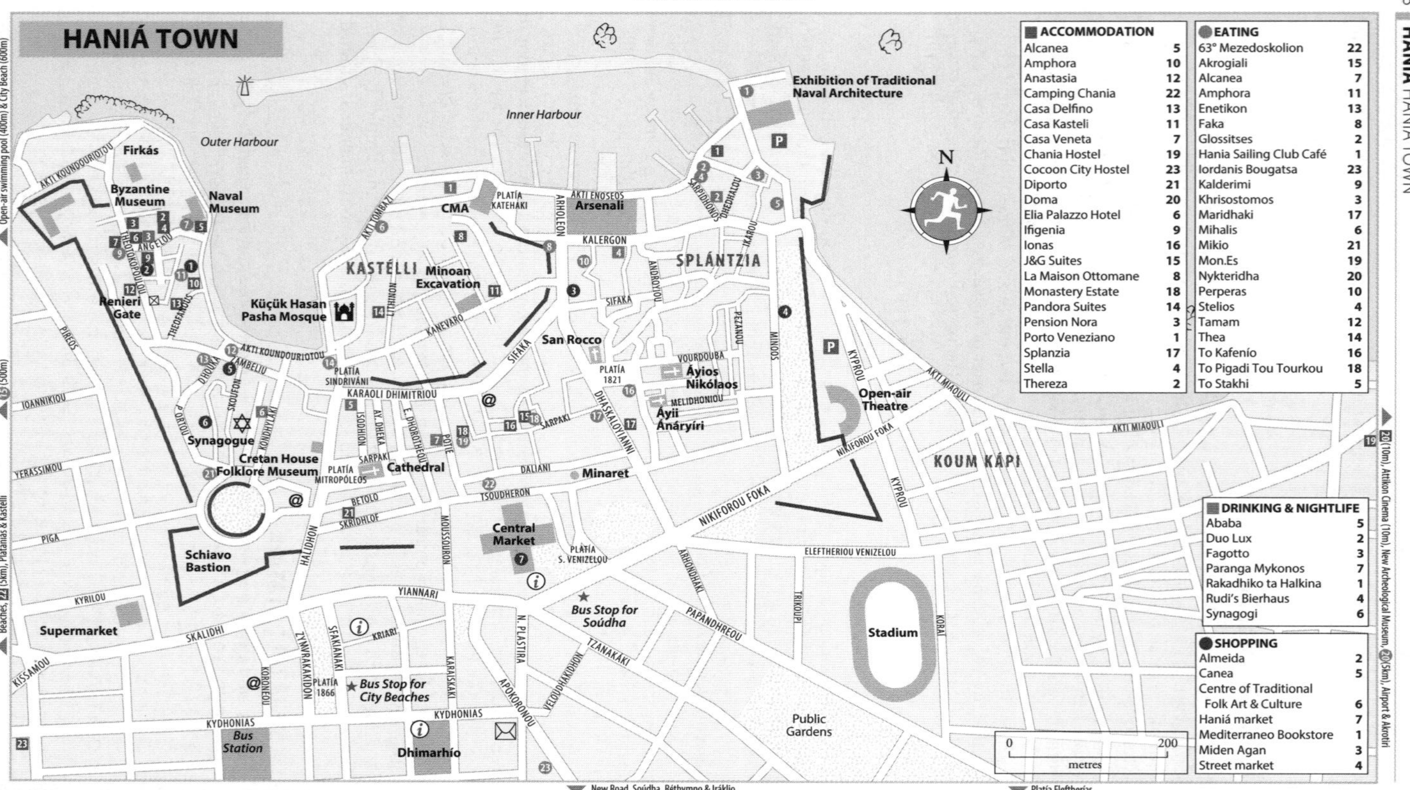
HANIÁ TOWN
ACCOMMODATION
Alcanea 5
Amphora 10
Anastasia 12
Camping Chania 22
Casa Delfino 13
Casa Kasteli 11
Casa Veneta 7
Chania Hostel 19
Cocoon City Hostel 23
Diporto 21
Doma 20
Elia Palazzo Hotel 6
Ifigenia 9
Ionas 16
J&G Suites 15
La Maison Ottomane 8
Monastery Estate 18
Pandora Suites 14
Pension Nora 3
Porto Veneziano 1
Splanzia 17
Stella 4
Thereza 2
EATING
63° Mezedoskolion 22
Akrogiali 15
Alcanea 7
Amphora 11
Enetikon 13
Faka 8
Glossitses 2
Hania Sailing Club Café 1
Iordanis Bougatsa 23
Kalderimi 9
Khrisostomos 3
Maridhaki 17
Mihalis 6
Mikio 21
Mon.Es 19
Nykteridha 20
Perperas 10
Stelios 4
Tamam 12
Thea 14
To Kafenío 16
To Pigadi Tou Tourkou 18
To Stakhi 5
DRINKING & NIGHTLIFE
Ababa 5
Duo Lux 2
Fagotto 3
Paranga Mykonos 7
Rakadhiko ta Halkina 1
Rudi's Bierhaus 4
Synagogi 6
SHOPPING
Almeida 2
Canea 5
Centre of Traditional Folk Art & Culture 6
Haniá market 7
Mediterraneo Bookstore 1
Miden Agan 3
Street market 4
0 200
metres
Outer Harbour
Inner Harbour
Exhibition of Traditional Naval Architecture
Firkás
Byzantine Museum
Naval Museum
CMA
Arsenali
KASTÉLLI
Minoan Excavation
SPLÁNTZIA
Küçük Hasan Pasha Mosque
Renieri Gate
San Rocco
Áyios Nikólaos
Áyii Anáryiri
Open-air Theatre
KOUM KÁPI
Synagogue
Cretan House Folklore Museum
Cathedral
Minaret
Central Market
Schiavo Bastion
Supermarket
Bus Stop for Soúdha
Bus Stop for City Beaches
Bus Station
Dhimarhío
Stadium
Public Gardens
AKTI KOUNDOURIOTOU
ANGELOU
THEOTOKOPOULOU
THEOFANOUS
AKTI TOMBAZI
PLATÍA KATEHAKI
AKTI ENOSEOS
ARHOLEON
KALERGON
ANDROYIOU
SARPIDHONOS
DHEDHALOU
IKAROU
LITHINON
KANEVARO
SIFAKA
PEZANOU
MINOOS
VOURDOUBA
MELIDHONIOU
KYPROU
AKTI MIAOULI
PIREOS
ZAMBELIU
DHOUKA
SKOUFON
KONDHYLAKI
P. ORTOU
PLATÍA SINDRIVÁNI
KARAOLI DHIMITRIOU
ISODHION
AY. DHEKA
E. DHOROTHEOU
POTIE
SARPAKI
PLATÍA 1821
DHASKALOYIANNI
PLATÍA MITROPÓLEOS
DALIANI
TSOUDHERON
NIKIFOROU FOKA
BETOLO
SKRIDHLOF
HALIDHON
MOUSSOURON
PLATÍA S. VENIZELOU
ELEFTHERIOU VENIZELOU
ARHONDHAKI
PAPANDHREOU
TRIKOUPI
KORAI
IOANNIKIOU
YERASSIMOU
PIGA
KYRILOU
KISSAMOU
SKALIDHI
YIANNARI
KRIARI
ZYMVRAKAKIDON
SFAKIANAKI
PLATÍA 1866
KARAISKAKI
N. PLASTIRA
TZANAKAKI
VELOUDHAKIDHON
APOKORONOU
KORONEOU
KYDHONIAS
Open-air swimming pool (400m) & City Beach (600m)
(500m)
Beaches, 22 (5km), Plataniás & Kastélli
New Road, Soúdha, Réthymno & Iráklio
Platía Eleftherías
20 (10m), Attikon Cinema (10m), New Archeological Museum, 20 (5km), Airport & Akrotiri

neglect. Not much is heard of the place again until the thirteenth century, when the **Genoese** seized the city from the Venetians and held it from 1263 to 1285.

When the **Venetians** finally won the city back they turned **La Canea** (as it was now known) into a formidable bulwark, as well as probably the island's most beautiful city. The city walls were built in two stages: in the fourteenth century Kastélli alone was fortified; in the sixteenth century, new walls were constructed as a defence against constant raids by pirate corsairs – in particular against the systematic ravages of Barbarossa. It is these defences, along with the Venetian harbour installations, that define the shape of Haniá's old town today.

Occupation and resistance

In 1645, after a two-month siege with terrible losses (the Turkish commander was executed upon his return home for losing as many as forty thousand men), Haniá fell to the **Ottomans.** It was the first major Cretan stronghold to succumb, becoming the Turkish island capital. Churches were converted to mosques, the defences more or less maintained, and there must have been at least some new building, though today it is barely possible to distinguish Venetian from Ottoman workmanship.

For the rest, it is a history of struggle. In the **independence** campaign, the city's most dramatic moment came in 1897, following the outbreak of war between Greece and the Ottoman Empire, when the Great Powers (Britain, France, Russia and Italy) imposed peace and stationed a joint force in the waters off Haniá. From here, they bombarded Cretan insurgents attempting prematurely to raise the flag of Greece on the hill of Profítis Elías (see page 249). When the Ottomans were finally forced to leave, Prince George, the high commissioner chosen by the powers, established his capital here for the brief period of his regency.

During **World War II**, with most of the German landings and the bulk of the fighting on the coast immediately west of the city, Haniá suffered severe bombardment, the destruction eventually compounded by a fire, which wiped out almost everything apart from the area around the harbour.

The harbour

The **harbour** area is at its busiest and most attractive at night, when the lights from bars and restaurants reflect in the water and the animated crowds – locals as much as tourists – parade in a ritualistic volta of apparently perpetual motion. Stalls sell everything from seashells to henna tattoos, and buskers serenade the passers-by. By day, especially in the hot, dozy mid-afternoon, it can be less appealing – often deserted and with the occasional whiff of decay from the rubbish washing up against the quayside. From waterfront Platía Sindriváni, almost always known simply as **Harbour Square**, Aktí Koundouriótou circles to the left around the outer harbour, crowded with outdoor cafés and tavernas, while straight ahead Aktí Tombázi heads past the mosque towards the inner harbour.

Küçük Hasan Pasha Mosque

Aktí Tombázi

The curious, domed profile of the **Küçük Hasan Pasha Mosque**, also known as the Yáli (Seaside) mosque, dominates the Harbour Square view. Built in 1645, the year Haniá fell to the Ottomans, it is the oldest building on the island, and has been well restored – apart from the jarring concrete dome. Currently without a fixed function, it is usually open for temporary exhibitions while a more long-term plan is considered. In the mainly bare interior, the most striking feature is the **mihrab** (a niche indicating the direction of Mecca) complete with Koranic inscription.

The Naval Museum

Aktí Koundouriótou • Charge • http://mar-mus-crete.gr

The hefty Firkas Bastion at the western end of the outer harbour houses Crete's **Naval Museum**. Although largely of specialist interest, the enthusiasm here is infectious, and the model ships, maquettes of the town in Venetian times, old maps and working exhibits like the old harbour light are hard to resist.

Whether visiting the museum or not, it's worth going through the main gate (usually open in daylight hours) to see the compound of the small naval garrison. Here you can climb onto the renovated seaward fortifications of the **Firkás**, as this part of the city defences is known. It was on this spot that the modern Greek flag was first officially raised on Crete – in 1913 – and there are fine sea views.

The inner harbour

Around the sheltered **inner harbour** pleasure boats, private yachts and small fishing vessels are moored, while sixteenth-century Venetian arsenals look out towards the breakwater across a cluster of waterfront restaurants and bars. Many of the arched **Arsenali** are still in a ruinous state, but others have been sensitively restored: one, the sixteenth-century Great Arsenal, is occupied by the **Center for Mediterranean Architecture** (CMA), with offices, a café and a glitzy space for temporary exhibitions (times and prices vary).

At the eastern end of the inner harbour and in the tangled, atmospheric alleys behind there are more signs of regeneration and refurbishment; this is now a fashionable part of town. A pleasant stroll follows the outer sea wall around for some 600m as far as the minaret-style **lighthouse**, with excellent views back over the city.

The Exhibition of Traditional Naval Architecture

Inner harbour • Charge • http://mar-mus-crete.gr

One of the Arsenali, at the extreme eastern end of the harbour, houses the Naval Museum's **Exhibition of Traditional Naval Architecture**, the highlight of which is a reconstruction of a fifteenth-century BC **Minoan ship**, the *Minoa*. This was rowed to Athens for the start of the 2004 Olympics and, together with the vast boatshed itself, it easily outshines the rest of the exhibits.

Odhós Halídhon and the old town

Odhós Halídhon, climbing from the harbour to the new town, is perhaps the most commercially touristy street in Haniá, especially around its junction with animated **Odhós Skridhlóf** ("Leather Street"). Here, traditionally, leather-makers plied their trade and although many inventories are now geared entirely to tourists, prices for leather sandals, bags and the like remain some of the best in Crete. In this direction, east of Hálidhon and behind the cathedral, commercial streets blend into the new town and towards the market; to the west, behind the outer harbour, are some of the busiest alleys of the **old town**.

Platía Mitropóleos

Haniá's cathedral square, **Platía Mitropóleos**, opens off Halídhon about halfway up. The **cathedral** itself is a modest 1860s structure with little architectural merit, but it's an attractive space, surrounded by outdoor cafés – more peaceful if you head round to the back of the building. There's a fine statue of Anagnostis Mandakas, a nineteenth-century insurgent who raised the first official Greek flag on Crete, in 1913.

New Archeological Museum

Skra 15 • 2821 023315

Following the closure of the old site in a Venetian-built church in September 2020, Haniá's **New Archeological Museum** has moved to its new home in a spectacular new building in the eastern suburb of Halepa. Designed by renowned Greek architect Theofanis Bobotis, the new edifice has far more exhibition space and provides library and laboratory facilities for researchers. At the time of writing, it is still undergoing its finishing touches and has not yet opened its doors, so be sure to check with the tourist office (see page 244) for the latest news on prices and opening hours.

Many of the pevious site's artefacts are expected to be on display at the new location, such as a large group of Classical **sculptures**, a case full of Greco-Roman **glassware**, some third-century Roman **mosaics** and a large collection of **Minoan metalwork and pottery**, including a few huge storage jars or *píthoi* and a collection of Minoan clay coffins (*lárnakes*), one containing two small skeletons. For archeologists, the most significant items will be the **inscribed tablets** excavated in Kastélli; this is the only place other than Knossós where examples of Linear A and Linear B script (see page 326) have been found together – more evidence supporting the existence of a major palace here. Another important find from the Kastélli excavations is the **"Master Impression" seal.** Dating from the Late Minoan period (1500–1450 BC), it is almost unique in depicting a townscape – a long-haired male figure in Minoan loincloth, holding a sceptre, is shown standing over a great complex of multi-storey buildings (the Kastélli hill?) with a rocky seaside landscape below.

The Cretan House Folklore Museum

Hálidhon 46B • Charge • 28210 90816

The **Cretan House Folklore Museum** is a cluttered collection of artefacts, tapestries and traditional crafts equipment set out in a replica of a "traditional" house (though few can have been quite so packed). Embroidered cloths and tapestries made on site are for sale. On your way out, take a look at Haniá's elegant **Roman Catholic church** in the same courtyard, an interesting contrast to the city's Orthodox churches.

Evraïki

Between Halídhon and the Renieri Gate (see page 241), the **Kondhyláki** street, was the medieval Jewish ghetto, a quarter still officially known as **Evraïkí.**

Etz Hayyim Synagogue

Párados Kóndhylaki • Free • www.etz-hayyim-hania.org

Signed at the end of a small alley off the west side of Kóndhilaki is Haniá's fifteenth-century Etz Hayyim **synagogue**, renovated by a fraternity of local Christians, Muslims and Jews after falling into ruin, working under the supervision of the late Nikos Stavroulakis. All but one family of the city's Jews were rounded up by the Nazi occupation forces in June 1944; they met their end (along with around seven hundred Greek and Italian prisoners of war) when the transport ship *Thanais* taking them to Pireás (en route to Auschwitz) was torpedoed by a British submarine, which mistook it for a Nazi supply craft, off the island of Mílos. The single family, warned of what awaited them, fled before that on a motor-less fishing boat which only sailed at night and successully reached Athens after some weeks. The synagogue is entered through the original Venetian doorway, and its garden, *mikveh* (purification bathing pool), reconstructed interior and *bimah* (speakers' platform) have been sensitively restored. The names of the 276 Jews who perished in the ship are remembered on a plaque in a garden cemetery at the rear.

The city walls

Corralling the western edge of the Old Town lies much the best-preserved stretch of the **city walls**, impressive, weighty and threatening. On the outside, Odhós Pireós traces them all the way from the new town's Skalíddhi Street to the sea. Following them on the inside is rather trickier, but far more enjoyable. This is where you'll stumble on some of the most picturesque little alleyways and finest Venetian houses in Haniá, and also where the pace of renovation and gentrification is most rapid. The arch of the Gate on the **Renieri Mansion** is particularly elegant. There are also interesting art and craft stores around here, along Theotokopóulou and the many alleys that run off it down towards the harbour.

The Byzantine Museum

Theotokopóulou 78 • Charge • 28210 96046

The **Byzantine Museum**, in the Venetian chapel of San Salvatore, has a tiny but beautifully displayed collection of mosaics, icons, jewellery, coins, sculpture and everyday objects, giving a fascinating insight into an era that's largely overlooked – the entire period from early Christianity to the end of the Venetian occupation in the seventeenth century.

Kastélli

The bluff that rises behind the mosque and the inner harbour, known as **Kastélli**, was the site of the first habitation in Haniá. Favoured from earliest times for its defensive qualities, this little hill takes its name from a fortress that originally dated from the Byzantine era. Later it was the centre of the Venetian and of the Ottoman towns. Little survived a heavy bombardment during World War II, though there are traces everywhere, with houses built against and from the ancient walls, a few surviving sections of which are being restored.

Walking up Kanevárou from Platía Sindriváni you'll pass various remains, including a couple of fenced-off sites where **Minoan Kydonia** is being excavated. The Swedish-Greek archeological team have traced the outline of substantial buildings engulfed by a violent fire in about 1450 BC, similar to that which destroyed Knossós. Many believe that this could be the site of the **palace** long thought to have existed here – if so, it would complete a pattern across the island – but as yet no trace of a "Central Court", the defining feature of Minoan palaces in Crete, has come to light. Trial excavations in the nearby Odhós Dhaskaloyiánni at the end of Kanevárou revealed the whole area to be covered with Minoan remains, so there remains a real possibility that a Minoan palace could lie somewhere here. In the period following the Minoan demise it is also likely, given its proximity to the mainland, that this may well have been the focus of Mycenaean power on Crete.

Among pottery finds were some dating back to the Neolithic era, but the greatest prize uncovered was an archive of clay tablets bearing Minoan Linear A script (see page 326), the first to be found so far west in Crete. All around the Kastélli hill various other **trial excavations**, usually on vacant lots between existing houses, reveal further tantalizing glimpses of the substantial Minoan conurbation that lies beneath the modern town, and there are plans for much more extensive excavations once all the relevant property has been acquired. The alleys up to the left, onto the rise, end up going nowhere, but it's worth exploring up here for the traces of the old city that survive, and tantalizing glimpses of the views that the old buildings afford. Lithinón, for example, has various Venetian doorways and inscriptions and, at the top, a fine old archway, beyond which the rather derelict hilltop area allows fine **views** over the harbour and out to sea.

Splántzia

Inland from Kastélli, you can head through the backstreets towards the **market**. This area, still known by its Ottoman name **Splántzia**, is full of unexpected architectural delights, with carved wooden balconies and houses arching across the street at first-floor level. Many of the streets between here and the inner harbour have been recobbled and refurbished, and they're among the most evocative in the old town.

Platía 1821 and around

The tranquil **Platía 1821** features the refurbished church of Áyios Nikólaos, whose **minaret** is missing its top. Built by the Venetians, the church was converted to a mosque under Sultan Ibrahim and reconverted back after Crete's reversion to Greek authority. The square itself – whose name recalls the date of one of the larger rebellions against Ottoman authority, following which an Orthodox bishop was hanged here – is a shady space set

HANIÁ'S BEACHES

Haniá's closest beaches lie west of town. The town beach can be reached on foot, while the others are accessible by bus #21 from Platía 1866.

Néa Hóra The city beach is about a 10min walk from the old harbour, round past the Naval Museum and on by the city's open-air swimming pool and a small fishing-boat harbour. The beach has clean sand and sheltered water, showers, and usually crowds of people. Cafés and restaurants line the seafront, while offshore (a longer swim than it looks) rises a tiny islet with a sandy beach large enough for about five people at a time.

Áyii Apóstoli Around 3km west of Néa Hora – about 20min on foot. A good long stretch of yellow sand, behind which is the city's campsite and a low-key cluster of development; the only drawback (as at most of these beaches) is the crashing breakers, which can become vicious.

Hryssí Aktí Some 2km beyond Áyii Apóstoli. Hrissí Aktí (Golden Beach) has more good sand, which has attracted the apartment-builders. But it's not overcrowded, has some good tavernas and is popular with locals.

Oasis beach and Kalamáki Beyond the Hryssí Aktí headland lies a tiny sand cove, another small promontory, and then the long curve of Oasis Beach running on round to Kalamáki. This is justly crowded – the swimming is probably the best in the area, with a gently shelving sandy bottom and a fossil-covered (and very sharp) rocky islet/reef that fends off the bigger waves. There's a string of cafés and tavernas, and other facilities including windsurf rental and lessons. Kalamáki is the furthest beach accessible by city bus, and it's right by the main road.

Further afield There are even finer beaches at Ayía Marína (see page 262) to the west, or Kalathás and Stavrós (see page 250) out on the Akrotíri peninsula, all of which can be reached by KTEL bus from the main station.

4

with café chairs. Nearby are two more old churches: San Rocco, at the square's northeast corner, is small and old-fashioned, while south of the square **Áyii Anáryiri**, which retained its Orthodox status throughout the Ottoman occupation, has some very ancient icons.

The modern town

Modern Haniá sprawls in every direction, encircling the old town. The areas southwest of the **market**, on the way to **Platía 1866** and the bus station, have an attractively old-fashioned commercialism about them, full of stores stocking life's essentials.

The public gardens

Between Odhós Tzanakáki and Odhós Papandhréou, southeast of the market

Laid out by a Muslim pasha during the nineteenth century, the **public gardens** include a few caged animals – Cretan wild ibex, or *kri-kri*, ponies, loud monkeys and birds – a fine traditional café where you can sit under the trees and a children's play area. The open-air auditorium is often used as a cinema, and also hosts local ceremonies and folklore displays, including many events for the town's main annual **festival**, the commemoration of the Battle of Crete, around May 20.

Platía Eleftherías and around

At the end of Papandhréou, about 500m southeast of the public gardens, **Platía Eleftherías** has a statue of Venizelos in the centre and an imposing court building along the south side, which was originally the government building of Prince George's short-lived administration (see page 333). **Iróon Polytehníou Poly** runs due north from Platía Eleftherías down to the sea. A broad avenue divided by trees and lined with large houses, interspersed with several expensive garden restaurants and a number of fashionable café-bars, it makes for an interesting walk in a part of the city very different from that dominated by the tourist crowds around the medieval harbour.

ARRIVAL AND DEPARTURE

HANIÁ TOWN

BY BUS

Bus station Odhós Kydhonías, within easy walking distance of the centre; there's a left-luggage office. Information, booking and timetables at 28210 93052, www.e-ktel.com/en/home.

Destinations Airport (at least one hourly, 5am–10pm; 30min); Almyrídha (4 daily; 40min); Ayía Marína (at least half hourly, 6am–11pm; 15min); Bálos (summer only 4 daily; 1hr 30min); Elafonísi (1 daily, 9am; 2hr 15min); Falásarna (3 daily; 2hr); Hóra Sfakíon (4 daily; 1hr 40min); Iráklio (17 daily; 2hr 45min); Kalýves (6 daily; 30min); Kastélli (14 daily; 1hr); Kolymbári (at least half hourly, 6am–11pm; 40min); Máleme (at least half hourly, 6am–11pm; 30min); Omalós, for the Samariá Gorge (Daily at 7.45am & 8.45am; 1hr 30min); Paleóhora (4 daily; 2hr); Plataniás (at least half hourly, 6am–11pm; 20min); Réthymno (22 daily; 1hr); Soúyia (3 daily, 5am, 8.45am & 1.45pm; 1hr 45min); Stavrós (via Horafákia; 6 daily; 30min); Vámos (5 daily; 40min); Yeoryioúpoli (17 daily; 40min).

BY FERRY

4

Ferry dock At the port of Soúdha (see page 252), 10km east of Haniá. Frequent local buses (every 20min; 20min; €1.70) will drop you by the market on the fringes of the old town, or you can take a taxi (about €12; prices to other destinations posted); KTEL buses to Réthymno and Kastélli Lissámmou also meet the ferries.

Ferry tickets Available from most travel agencies or direct from ANEK (office on Venizélou opposite the market; 28210 27500, http://anek.gr) or Minoan (28210 81276, http://minoan.gr).

Destinations Departures to and from Pireás (9hr) every evening year-round, plus daytime sailings at peak summer periods.

BY PLANE

Haniá airport About 15km northeast of the city, in the middle of the Akrotíri peninsula. Buses run to Haniá (every 30min for most of the day, 6.30am–11.45pm; 30min; €2.50) and to Réthymno (6 daily; 1hr 30min): a taxi to the city costs about €20. The driving route into Haniá is pretty clear: for all destinations other than the city, it's quicker and easier to take the left turn signed to Soúdha at the roundabout some 7km from the airport; this will take you down past the head of Soúdha Bay and out onto the main E75 highway, bypassing Haniá's congestion.

Airlines Olympic (http://olympicair.com), Ryanair (http://ryanair.com) and Sky Express (www.skyexpress.gr) (http://ellinair.com) offer domestic flights; Easyjet, Ryanair, British Airways, and Tui also have scheduled flights to the UK throughout the summer (see page 25).

Destinations Athens (4–8 daily with Olympic, occasionally on Ryanair); Thessaloníki (4 a week on Ryanair

BY CAR

Parking Driving can be a nightmare once you hit the harbour area and get tangled up in the one-way system and no-parking zones. As a car is near-useless inside the old walled city and distances are easily walkable anyway, the least stressful solution is to park outside the old town and walk in. Longer-term parking places can usually be found along Aktí Kanári to the west of the Naval Museum near the seafront, or on the side streets off Pireós leading down there, and to the north of the open-air theatre on the east side of the old town; there are also signposted pay car parks in the new town. Much of the old town is off-limits to vehicles, and parking within the walls is almost impossible in high season – get advice from your hotel if you are driving, as they may help you with your luggage, or have a temporary space where you can unload.

GETTING AROUND

By bus The terminus for most city buses, especially those heading west (including the beaches; bus #21), is at Platía 1866; for Soúdha (bus #13) and the eastern side of town you may find it easier to get on at one of the stops by the market. Timetables at http://chaniabus.gr; fares are €1.10 within the city and €1.50 further afield, if you buy your ticket in advance; €2 or €2.50 on the bus. Longer-distance buses, including those to the coastal resorts around Plataniás (see page 262), run from the main bus station (see page 244).

By car and bike For car rental try around the top of Halídhon, where Tellus, Hálidhon 108 (28210 91500, http://rentacarchania.gr) is one of many. Alianthos is another reliable outlet (28320 32033, http://alianthos-group.com), with offices at the airport and in Plataniás. Summertime, Dhaskaloyiánni 7 and other local branches (28210 33316, http://strentals.gr), has a vast range of wheels, including cars, motorbikes and good bikes.

By taxi The main taxi rank is in Platía 1866, with smaller ones nearby at the bus station and on Venizélou near the market. For radio taxis call 18300 or 28210 94300, http://chaniataxi.gr.

INFORMATION AND ACTIVITIES

Tourist offices The helpful municipal tourist office is at Mylonoyiánni 53, at the side of the *Dhimarhío* (town hall; Mon–Fri 8.30am–3pm; 28210 41665, http://chania tourism.com). They have timetables for buses, sites and museums, as well as details on excursions. In summer they also run an information booth in front of the market (July & Aug daily 10am–2pm). The Greek National Tourist Office is nearby at Kriári 40, just off Platía 1866 (Mon–Fri 9am–2pm; 28210 92943), and there's also an office at the airport in summer (July–Sept Mon–Sat 9am–9pm).

Travel agencies Concentrated around the top end of Halídhon and on Platía 1866, as well as around the bus station. Try Tellus Travel, Halídhon 108 (28210 91500, www.tellustravel.gr), or Kyriakakis, Yiánnari 78 (28210 27700, www.kyriakakis.gr).

Boat trips A number of boats run trips from the outer harbour (typically €15–20), mainly to the nearby islands of Áyii Theódori and Lazarétta, for swimming and *kri-kri* (ibex) spotting: you're unlikely to escape the attentions of their touts around the harbour. Alternatives include sunset cruises and all-day trips to the Rodhopoú peninsula. On the inner harbour, smaller boats offer sailing and private charter excursions.

City tours There's a hop-on, hop-off city bus tour (€15) that won't show you much of the old town, but does take in the town beach and new town, and heads out to Soúdha and the Venizélos Graves (see page 249); one way to see the old city is on a Segway or bike with Chania Segway Tours, Khrysánthou Episkópou 25 (28210 08695, https://chaniasegwaytours.com; from €39).

Climbing and walking The local EOS mountaineering club, Tzanakáki 90 (28210 44647, https://eoshanion.gr), provides information about climbing in the Lefká Óri and takes reservations for the mountain refuge at Kallergí, near the Samariá Gorge (see page 273). They also organise various events, walks and climbs while maintaining and marking a number of hiking trails, described very schematically on their website.

Cycling Hellas Bike (28210 60858, http://hellasbike.net), in nearby Ayía Marína (see page 262), offers bike tours around the area, from easy to challenging (€42/half-day; €72/full day, including pick-up from your accommodation).

Diving There are numerous dive shops in Haniá; Chania Diving Center, Kanevárou 1 (28210 58939, http://chaniadiving.gr), is a quality outfit.

Water park The expansive Limnoupolis (May–Sept adults €25/€17 after 3pm, kids €18/€14; http://limnoupolis.gr) is near to the village of Varýpetro, 8km southwest of the city; there are four buses a day from the bus station.

4

ACCOMMODATION

SEE MAP PAGE 238

In and around Haniá there's a huge range of accommodation, from simple **rooms for rent** to elegant **boutique hotels**. The popularity of the latter has led to anyone with a room near the harbour to tart it up, call it boutique, and attempt to rent it out at a ridiculously inflated price. Perhaps the most desirable rooms are those overlooking the **harbour**, which are sometimes available at reasonable rates: this is often because they're noisy at night. Most are approached from the streets behind; those further back from the water are likely to be more peaceful. Theotokopoúlou and the alleys off it make a good starting point. The best of the more expensive places are here, too, equally set back but often with views from the upper storeys. In the **addresses** below, Párodhos means side street or alley, so 2 Párodhos Theotokopóulou, for example, is the second alley off Theotokopóulou. Dozens of small rooms places, accross the entire province can be found at www.chaniarooms.gr.

HARBOUR AREA: WEST OF HÁLIDHON

★ **Alcanea** Angélou 2, 28210 75370. Gorgeous eight-room boutique hotel in a historic building beside the Naval Museum. Rooms come with all facilities including satellite TV and iPod docks, with coffee machines and traditional teas in the communal areas. The pricier rooms (around twice the price of the most basic) have stunning views and balconies. Excellent breakfast included. €€

★ **Amphora** 2 Párodhos Theotokopóulou 20, http://amphora.gr. Set in a beautifully renovated fourteenth-century Venetian building, with spiral staircases, wooden floors and four-poster beds. Balcony rooms (such as Room 20) with harbour view are the best value; those without a view are cheaper. €€

Anastasia Theotokopóulou 21, http://anastasia-apartments.com. Attractive, fully equipped apartments plus some simpler rooms in buildings on each side of this atmospheric street. €

Casa Delfino Theofánous 9, http://casadelfino.com. Over-the-top hotel offering designer rooms and big, deluxe suites with elegant decor, marble or polished-wood floors, satellite TV and jacuzzis; there's also a small spa. €€

Casa Veneta Theotokopóulou 57, http://casa-veneta.gr. Very well-equipped, comfortable studios and apartments run by a helpful, friendly proprietor, with kitchenette, TV and (some) balcony sea views behind a Venetian facade; the large duplex apartment is particularly attractive. Studios €, apartment €€

Ifigenia A. Gámba 23, http://ifigeniastudios.gr. A small empire of rooms, suites and apartments at various prices, in old Venetian buildings scattered across the old town. Most have elegant, quirky decor (one has a jacuzzi bath right in the middle of the room), and some buildings have roof gardens and views. Doubles €, apartments €€

Elia Palazzo Hotel Theotokopoulou 54, www.eliahotels.com. An elegant mansion converted to a classy modern hotel, retaining some of the original wood-beamed ceilings and old wooden floors. Good-sized rooms, most with balconies, plus a roof terrace with harbour views and tasty breakfasts (included). This hotel group has at least a dozen more classy boutique hotels and apartment places scattered around the Old Town, though some are a little pricey. €€

Pension Nora Theotokopóulou 60, www.pension-nora.com. Charming, old-fashioned a/c rooms in a refurbished Ottoman house with wooden floors, rickety wooden staircase and a communal kitchen. Also, appealing studios (same price) in a building nearby. €

Stella Angélou 10, http://pension10stella.wixsite.com/stella-rooms-chania. Creaky, eccentric old house above an eclectic gift shop, with a wide variety of rooms equipped with a/c and fridge. The cheapest are very small; no.4 is airy, with a fine view, but more expensive. €

Thereza Angélou 8, http://pensiontheresa.gr. Beautiful old *pension* in a great position with stunning views from its roof terrace and some rooms; it has characterful traditional decor and a kitchen (with breakfast ingredients supplied) for guests' use. They also have a three-bedroom house around the corner. Very popular, so book ahead. €

EAST OF HALIDHON

★**Casa Kasteli** Kanevárou 39, http://kastelistudios.gr. Comfortable, modern, reasonably priced pension, very quiet at the back. The proprietor is very helpful and also has studios and a couple of beautiful apartments to rent nearby. Studios €, apartments €€

4

Diporto Betólo 41, http://todiporto.gr. The "Two Doors" runs between Betólo and pedestrianised Skridhlóf: the balcony rooms over the latter, especially, are quiet. Friendly and good value, with TV, fridge and coffee machine in the rooms, which include singles and triples. €

Ionas Sarpáki, corner of Sórvolou, http://ionashotel.com. Small boutique hotel in a lovingly restored Venetian mansion, with very comfortable rooms and beautiful architectural detail, though service is occasionally lacking. €

J&G Suites Sarpáki 41, http://jgsuites-crete.gr. Newly renovated suites inside a Venetian house with a restored Ottoman frontage; all have basic cooking facilities. €

★**La Maison Ottomane** Párodhos Kanevárou, http://lamaisonottomane.com. Stunning boutique hotel with just three luxurious apartments, opulently decorated in Ottoman pasha style, with objets d'art sourced from markets in Crete, London and the Middle East. Modern comforts include flatscreen TV and Nespresso machines, plus a superb breakfast. €€€

★**Monastery Estate** Párodhos 4, Kalliníkou Sarpáki 40, http://monasteryestate.com. Glorious ultra-modern conversion of a Turko-Venetian mansion, with glass panels in the floor revealing ancient remains found during restoration. The suites, each unique, are minimalist in style, but with everything you need. Excellent breakfast in the courtyard restaurant. €€

Pandora Suites Lithínon 29, https://pandorasuites.com. Well set-up rooms and studios, plus a larger apartment at the back, some of which enjoy arguably the finest view in Haniá, from high above the harbour (for a small premium, well worth paying). All rooms have cooking facilities, and all guests can take in the view from the spectacular roof garden. Breakfast included. €€

Porto Veneziano Overlooking the inner harbour, http://portoveneziano.gr. Very plush traditional hotel, with elegant rooms and all facilities, if a little business-class in atmosphere. The best rooms (extra cost) have balcony views over the harbour. Breakfast included. €€

★**Splanzia** Dhaskaloyiánni 20. Attractive and friendly boutique hotel in an elegantly refurbished Venetian mansion, with stylish rooms, each unique, some with four-posters, and extraordinary lighting. Breakfast (included) is served in a pretty courtyard. €€

THE MODERN TOWN

Chania Hostel Venizélou 116, next to the Attikon cinema, 28210 44955. Exceptionally friendly backpacker-style hostel, run by Cretan-Australian Angeliki. Great atmosphere and plenty of activities, though facilities, from chunky home-made wooden bunks to lack of air/con, are fairly basic, and it's about a 15-minute walk from the harbour. Continental breakfast included. €

Cocoon City Hostel Kydhonías 145, http://cocooncityhostel.com. Designer-style backpackers with classy, custom-furnished four- and six-bed dorms, with individual lockers and power points. Also, two double rooms, one with private bath. It's about three blocks from the bus station, a 10-minute walk to the harbour. €

★**Doma** Venizélou 124, https://hotel-doma.gr. Elegant seafront hotel inside a late nineteenth-century building that served as the Austrian Embassy and later the British consulate until it was taken over by the Germans during World War II. There are fine sea views from some rooms and a serene patio garden. The comfortable rooms (and more expensive suites) are tastefully furnished, and the hotel is filled with fascinating photos of old Haniá. Delicious breakfast included. Parking nearby. €€

CAMPSITE

Camping Chania Behind the beach in Áyii Apóstoli, 5km west of the city, https://camping-chania.gr. A rather small site, hemmed in by new development, but with a pool and all the usual facilities, just a short walk from some of the better beaches. €

EATING

SEE MAP PAGE 238

Evenings in Haniá for most visitors centre around the harbour, and you need not stray far from the waterfront to find a cocktail before **dinner**, a meal, a late-night **bar** and a **club**. These places tend to be pricey, however, and the quality at many leaves a lot to be desired. Away from the water, there are plenty of more interesting, attractive, and often slightly cheaper restaurants and tavernas. The abundant **cafés** round the harbour tend to serve cocktails and fresh juices at exorbitant prices, though breakfast can be good value. There are more traditional cafés by the cathedral, at the market – where you also find a couple of good *zaharoplastía* (one on Tsoudherón, the other, *Kronos*, on Mousoúron, down the steps from the side entrance of the market) – and along Dhaskaloyiánni, where Platía 1821 is a delightfully tranquil oasis. For **fast food**, head for the new town, especially Platía 1866.

CAFÉS

Alcanea Angélou 2, 28210 75377. Appealing terrace bar with a great harbour view beneath the hotel of the same name; it's good for breakfast, coffee and mezédhes and, after sunset, cocktails and Cretan wines. Occasional live acoustic music at night. €

Hania Sailing Club Café Aktí Enóseos, 28210 40265. Occupying the outermost of the Arsenali, and with tables outside with great views over harbour and town, this is a great place for breakfast, for a coffee, juice or sandwich, or for a cocktail in the evening. There are more tables in the echoing interior, where the sailing club boats are stored at the back and there are frequent art exhibitions. €

Iordanis Bougatsa Apokorónou 24, 28210 88855. Specializes in delicious traditional *bougátsa* (creamy sweet or savoury cheese pie served warm and sprinkled with sugar and cinnamon), and nothing else, to eat in or take away. €

Thea Sindriváni, 28210 73377. Café-bar overlooking the harbourside crowds from a first-floor terrace – a great spot for people-watching in peace. €

To Kafenío Platía 1821, 28210 43755. Perhaps the best of the relaxing cafés on this wonderful old square, and the closest thing to a traditional *kafenío* in central Haniá; good prices, too, and in the evening a great place for ouzo and meze. €

TAVERNAS AND RESTAURANTS

63° Mezedoskolion Hatzimihali Daliáni 63, 28213 05080. The "School of Meze" is a fashionable modern *mezedhopolío* (meze plates) with a literal old-school theme – you sit at old school desks, chalky blackboards are everywhere, and you tick off your order on paper in the style of a multiple-choice exam. Packed with young locals late at night, as is this entire street. €

★ **Akrogiali** Aktí Papanikoli 19, Néa Hóra, 28210 73110. Opposite the city beach, with a summer terrace, this excellent, reasonably priced fish and seafood taverna is well worth the 15min walk or short taxi ride away. Whole fish are priced by the kilo, or there's seafood spaghetti, cuttlefish in ink with rice, sardines and even a few meat dishes. Always packed with locals, so may be worth booking – though there are plenty of alternatives along the same street. €€

Amphora Aktí Koundouriótou 49, outer harbour, 28210 71976. Excellent option among the touristy places on the outer harbour, with good, plain Greek food and no hard sell. Check the blackboard for the day's specials and fresh fish – or the lamb *stamnagáthi* (with local greens) is always good. €€

Enetikon Zambelíou 57, 28210 88270. A very good taverna whose proprietor is a wine buff: the house wine comes from the excellent Lyrarakis vineyard in Pezá. The food is also top-notch and anything with lamb is recommended: try the *arní me stamnágathi* (lamb with wild chicory). €€

★ **Faka** Arholéon 15, 28210 42341. Set back from the harbour, so significantly less touristy than many near neighbours, *Faka* serves good traditional local food, often with live Greek music. Check out the daily specials, made using seasonal ingredients, such as stuffed courgette flowers or choose a mixed meze for two. €€

Glossitses Aktí Enóseos, inner harbour, 28210 59074. Modern Greek restaurant on the waterfront serving classic dishes with a delicious twist; chicken in yoghurt sauce, cuttlefish *pilaf*, plus good daily specials and fresh fish. €€

Kalderimi Theotokopóulou 53, 28210 76741. A little gem of a place serving traditional Cretan dishes such as lamb *tsigariastó* with fried potatoes, *moussakás* or local pasta with shrimps. Occasional live traditional music too. €€

Khrisostomos Dhefkalíona and Ikárou, 28210 57035. Sfakian restaurant – the original branch was an isolated taverna at Mármara beach (see page 279) – serving interesting and delicious Cretan food. The setting may not be the most attractive, but the fact that it's always full (booking recommended) attests to the quality; meat from Sfakiá is a speciality in dishes like goat *tsigariastó* (a rich stew), rabbit in white wine sauce and roast lamb or suckling pig with baked potatoes. €

Maridhaki Dhaskaloyiánni 33, 28210 08880. Exceptional fish and seafood, keenly priced, at this on-trend place at the heart of a newly fashionable area, where young locals hang out at a series of bars, restaurants and ouzerí. Go for the catch of the day (sold by weight), and they also sell most fish by the portion as well as the likes of octopus with *fáva* and some meat dishes. €€

Mihalis Aktí Tombázi, 28210 58330. Arguably the best waterfront place on the outer harbour, with a varied menu (make sure you get the proper menu, not the plastic picture version) and a good selection of Cretan specialities and mezédhes, though it's seafood that they do best; fish priced per kilo, a seafood selection for two or vast seafood platter. There are also meat and meze selections for two, and a good wine list. €€

Mikio Skoufón 24, 6945 861 641. A tiny place with just half a dozen tables set outside in an alley, shaded by a vine. There's simple home-cooking such as lamb *tsigariastó*, snails or chicken in red sauce, washed down with Brinks beer. €€

Mon.Es Párodhos 4 Sarpáki, 28210 52129. The restaurant of the *Monastery Estate* hotel (see page 247) is tucked away in a back-street courtyard, but well worth seeking out for great food and sleek, Scandi-style design. It's a lovely lunch spot, with sandwiches and salads, while also having excellent vegan fare (beetroot roasted with cumin, with green beans and walnuts) plus regular fish and meat dishes. €€

★ **Nykteridha** 5km east of town off the Akrotíri road, http://nykterida.gr. Founded in 1933, this upmarket and stylish taverna is a Haniá institution, with a Greek/Mediterranean menu and stunning views over Soúdha Bay. It's a huge place, so can lack atmosphere when not full. €€€

Perperas Kapsokalývon 6, behind the Arsenali, 28215 00057. Fine little taverna set back off the street, with a shady terrace, serving well-prepared and economical Cretan dishes with good local wine. €

Stelios Aktí Enóseos, 28210 54240. Simple, old-fashioned seafood place towards the far end of the inner harbour. Very few frills, but excellent fish, squid and the like, especially if you order what's fresh that day. The stuffed kalamári is delicious as is the fish soup, and fish priced by the kilo goes for less than anywhere else around the harbour. The "small" seafood platter will easily feed four combined with a few meze. €

★ **Tamam** Zambelíou 49, 28210 96080. Popular place where the adventurous, basically Greek menu includes much vegetarian food, with added spices giving an oriental flavour to dishes such as Smyrnian rabbit or Iranian rice. The original restaurant is housed in an old Venetian public bath, while opposite is a less atmospheric, newer annexe. The tables squeezed into the alley between the two are very cramped, and you're likely to be jostled by the passing crowds. €€

To Pigadi Tou Tourkou Sarpáki 1, 28210 54547. The "Well of the Turk" is a Greco-Moroccan fusion restaurant with an interesting menu combining the two cuisines as well as adding a few dishes from the wider Middle East – think Armenian *lahmatzoun* – with plenty of vegetarian choices. Expect the likes of lamb with preserved lemons, aubergine meatballs or Arab bread with spinach, *myzíthra*, nuts and raisins. €

To Stakhi Dhefkalíona 5, 28210 42589. Organic vegetarian and vegan restaurant serving a wide range of tasty daily specials including soups, meze and mains like *yemistá* (stuffed tomatoes and peppers) and *bouréki* (Cretan veggie and cheese bake). Also fresh juices, herbal teas, and organic beer and wine. €

4

DRINKING, NIGHTLIFE AND ENTERTAINMENT

SEE MAP PAGE 238

As you might expect, the harbour area contains plenty of beautifully set but touristy **bars**. Locals tend to congregate instead behind the inner harbour and up into Splántzia; here streets like Kalergón and Daliáni are boisterously jammed around midnight. In the early hours, the action may move on to the **clubs**, and where these are depends on the time of year. In summer, many of the downtown venues close and the action moves to the pulsing scene at **Plataniás** and **Ayía Marína** on the coast west of town (see page 264).

Ababa Isodhíon 12, 6937 965 936. Funky bar with childishly colourful decor, open all day, offering snacks, books and board games; chilled sounds and cocktails in the evening through to the early hours.

Attikon Venizélou 118, http://cineattikon.gr. A great open-air cinema near the city stadium; in winter showings move round the corner, where they have a couple of cosy indoor screens.

Duo Lux Sarpidhónos 8, 28210 52515. Comfy café-bar in a street just off the inner harbour; regular DJs and club nights after midnight, and occasional live bands.

Fagotto Angélou 16, 28210 71877. Cosy, atmospheric backstreet jazz bar housed in an impressively restored Venetian mansion. Great cocktails, and high-quality live performances in season.

Paranga Mykonos Potié 32, 6947 003 848. Achingly trendy café-bar surrounded by similar places in a newly fashionable area. There's coffee and food by day, but it really comes into its own at night, with cocktails and chilled sounds.

★ **Rakadhiko ta Halkina** Aktí Tombázi 29–30, http://chalkina.com. Live Cretan music every evening, though the place doesn't really liven up till well after midnight, when the locals start to dance. There's also good foodand wine, but it's the traditional music everyone comes for. Hugely popular, but they can usually squeeze you in somewhere.

Rudi's Bierhaus Kalergón 16, 28210 20319. Haniá's beer shrine: Austrian – and longtime Haniá resident – Rudi Riegler's bar stocks more than a hundred of Europe's finest brews, plus excellent mezédhes to accompany them. Other, more fashionable, bars crowd this street. Daily 6pm–2am

Synagogi Párodhos Kondhylaki, between Kondhyláki and Skoufón, 28210 95242. Taking its name from the restored Jewish synagogue next door, this is a beautiful bar set in the roofless, jasmine-scented remains of a bombed-out Venetian mansion. Good music and cocktails, and coffee, salads and sandwiches during the day.

SHOPPING

SEE MAP PAGE 238

Stores aimed at tourists are mainly found in the old town, especially on HáliHalidhon and in the streets behind the outer harbour: Kanevárou, Zambelíou, Kondhiyáki and Theotokopoúlouóulou. The **leather** goods on Skridhlóf are excellent value, while north of here along Sífaka the traditional shops of Haniá's cutlers will sell you fearsome **Cretan knives** with goat-horn handles or something less vicious for the kitchen. In the new town, around the junction of Hálidhon and Yiánnari and down towards the market you'll find pharmacies, newspaper stores, photographic shops and banks, and there's a sizeable **supermarket** at the top of Pireós. The major thoroughfares heading south off Yiánnari – Apokorónou, Tzanakáki and Papandreou – are full of clothes and furniture stores, car rental places and more banks, while the streets around Platía 1866, especially towards the town hall and market, have more interesting local shops, from food and fashion to pet shops and printers. English and other foreign-language **newspapers** are sold at a number of places, including a couple around the junction of Halídhon and Yiánnari.

Almeida Theotokopóulou 50, 28210 93184. Lovely modern jewellery at prices that won't break the bank, mostly created on the premises.

Canea Zambelíou 45, 28210 98639. Designer gift shop with classy souvenirs, including T-shirts, bags, ceramics and more.

Centre of Traditional Folk Art & Culture Skoufón 20, 28210 92677. A wonderful place that feels more like a museum than a shop, displaying the astonishing embroideries made by the owner, some of which fetch thousands of euros.

Haniá market Odhós Yiánnari, with another entrance on Tsoudherón. Haniá's market, an imposing and rather beautiful cross-shaped structure, dating from around 1900, is in full swing on weekday mornings, when it's a wonderful kaleidoscope of bustle and colour, and there are some good souvenirs to be had among the stalls of meat, fish and veg.

Mediterraneo Bookstore Aktí Koundouriótou 57, near the Naval Museum, 28210 86904. Impressively stocked book and magazine store with lots of English-language titles, maps and guides.

Miden Agan Dhaskaloyiánni 70, 28210 27068. Deli with a big selection of Greek and Cretan wines, as well as elegantly packaged olive oils, spices and the like.

Street market Minöos. There's a fabulous weekly street market inside the eastern medieval wall, where local farmers sell their produce. Sat mornings.

DIRECTORY

Banks The main branch of the National Bank of Greece, with ATMs, is opposite the market. There's a cluster of banks with more ATMs around the top of Halídhon, and lots of out-of-hours exchange places on Halídhon, in the travel agencies.

Hospital For an ambulance, dial 166. The main hospital is in the village of Mourniés, 1.5km south of the centre (28210 22000).

Laundry Service washes at Old Town Laundromat, Karaóli Dhimitríou 40 (Mon–Sat 8.30am–2.30pm & 5.30–8.30pm); or there's cheap self-service at easywash, Dhaskaloyiánni 8 (daily 7am–midnight).

Pharmacies Several on Yiánnari between the market and Platía 1866; others up Tzanakáki.

Post office The main post office is on Odhós Perídhou just off Kydhonías (Mon–Fri 7.30am–8pm, Sat 9am–1pm).

Tourist police Iraklíou 23 (emergency 100, 28210 28750 or 28210 25931), some way south of the centre in the new town.

4

The Akrotíri peninsula

The hilly peninsula of **Akrotíri** loops round to the east of Haniá, protecting the magnificent anchorages of the **Bay of Soúdha**. It's a somewhat strange amalgam, with a couple of developing **resorts** along with burgeoning suburbs and a new university on the north coast, several ancient **monasteries** in the northeast, and military installations and the airport dominating the centre and south. This is very much apartment and villa country, geared to families and longer-term stays.

The Venizélos Graves

Off the main Akrotíri road at the top of the hill as you leave Haniá • Bus #11 and others from Haniá market (about 20min); the city tour bus also stops here

The **Venizélos Graves** are the simple stone-slab tombs of Eleftherios Venizélos, Crete's most famous statesman, and his son Sophocles. The immaculately tended garden setting, looking back over Haniá and the coast for miles beyond, is magnificent and also historic – the scene in 1897 of an illegal raising of the Greek flag by rebels led by Venizélos in defiance of the Ottomans and the European powers. The flagpole was smashed by a salvo from the European fleet, but the Cretans raised their standard by hand, keeping it flying even under fire. Two stories attach to this: one that the sailors were so impressed that they all stopped firing to applaud; the second that a shell fired from a Russian ship hit the little church of Profítis Elías, which still stands, and that divine revenge caused the offending ship itself to explode the next day.

EATING AND DRINKING — THE VENIZÉLOS GRAVES

Koukouvaya 28210 27449. Excellent, elegant café with a fabulous view over Haniá from its terrace. They specialize in cakes and tarts (try the walnut cake) as well as sandwiches, salads, teas and coffees.

The north-coast beaches

The road by the Venizélos Graves divides: straight ahead takes you east across the peninsula towards the **airport**, while the left fork heads north to Horafákia and the north-coast beaches, culminating at **Stavrós**.

Kalathás

Just beyond the village of **Kounoupidhianá**, the road suddenly plunges down and emerges by the **beach** at **KALATHÁS (Καλαθάς)**, two little patches of sand divided by a rocky promontory, with a bar and taverna right on the sand. This makes a fine place to spend a lazy day, marred only slightly by the proximity of the road: there's an offshore island to which you can swim, and good snorkelling.

Horafákia and around

HORAFÁKIA (Χωραφάκια), inland, a little over 1km beyond Kalathás, has the bulk of the local facilities, including shops and car rental. From here a road leads down to the coast at **Tersanás** where there's a tiny cove beach, shallow and safe for small children, as well as a couple of tavernas.

4

Stavrós

Some 3km beyond Horafákia, you finally reach **STAVRÓS (Σταυρός)** and its near-perfect beach, an almost completely enclosed circular bay. The sea is dead calm with gently shelving sand underfoot, making it ideal for kids. It's an extraordinary-looking place, too, with a sheer, bare mountainside rising just 100m away from you on the far side of the bay. This is where the cataclysmic climax of *Zorba the Greek* was shot (the hill is known locally as Zorba's Mountain) and is also the site of a **cave**, whose entrance can just about be seen from the beach, in which there was an ancient sanctuary.

Stavrós beach is often crowded – sometimes unpleasantly so as it doesn't take many people to fill it up – but even so it's a great place to bask for a few hours. There's a far less visited patch of sand facing directly out to sea if you do find it oppressive.

ARRIVAL AND DEPARTURE — THE NORTH-COAST BEACHES

By bus There are services to Stavrós via Kalathás and Horafákia from Haniá's bus station (6 daily, fewer at weekends; 30min).

ACCOMMODATION AND EATING

Accommodation is widely scattered in the flat plain lining the coast between Stavrós and Tersanás, so you'll ideally need your own transport here, though all of the options below are within walking distance of town and beach. There are plenty of tavernas near the beaches, serving perfectly good standard Greek food, but few that stand out.

KALATHÁS

Giorgi's Blue Apartments Signed from the road, immediately west of Kalathás, Very comfortable one- and two-bedroom apartments with pool and bar beautifully situated above a rocky coastline; steps lead down to what is in effect a private cove. Breakfast included. €€

Lena Beach Directly above the beach, http://lenabeach.gr. Slightly old-fashioned hotel immediately above the beach; rooms have every facility and great views, and there's a pool and a path directly down to the sand. €

Skalakia Just above the beach, 2821 049361. Good taverna for Cretan classics and fresh fish (priced per kilo for the day's catch), with a terrace above the water. Try the *kontosoúvli* (spit roast pork) or *katsikáki yemistá* (stuffed goat). €€

HORAFÁKIA

Bahar Outside Horafákia, on the road to Stavrós, 28210 39410. One of the few restaurants on the peninsula having any pretensions, with a varied Cretan and Mediterranean menu served amid somewhat eccentric modern decor. Their "Aphrodisiac" plate – mussels, prawns and lobster bisque with pasta – is a bargain for two. There's also an excellent wine selection, and a house wine from noted Pezá grower Lyrarakis. The attached bar hosts live music (jazz, soul, Greek) on Saturday nights. €€

STAVRÓS AND AROUND

Almyriki Behind the beach, 28210 29489. Attractive taverna with tables spread beneath the shady tamarisk tree that gives it its name, beside a windmill. Specialities include a range of mezédhes as well as Cretan dishes such as *bouréki* (veggie and cheese bake) and stuffed tomatoes. €€

Blue Beach Apartments On the seafront at the western edge of Stavrós, http://bluebeach.eu. Very large apartment complex with everything from studios to three-bedroom apartments with a tiny sand beach, small pool and a seaside terrace where meals are served. Studios €, apartments €€

★ **Georgia-Vicky Apartments** About 1km west of Stavrós, http://georgia-vicky.com. Excellent-value, welcoming, well-equipped studios and apartments, all with stunning views from terraces and balconies over a rocky shore. There's a large seawater pool and kids' playground too. €

Kavos Hotel About 1km west of Stavrós, http://kavosbeach.gr. Attractive, modern apartment complex with a large pool, pool bar and well-equipped studios and split-level maisonettes. Breakfast included. €

Moní Ayía Triádha

5km east of Horafákia, 2km north of the airport • Charge

The monastery of **AYÍA TRIÁDHA** (**Μονή Αγίας Τριάδας**), often known as Moní Zangarólon after its founding family, was established in the seventeenth century and built in Venetian style. Today, while not exactly thriving, it is one of the few Cretan monasteries to preserve real monastic life to any degree. Its imposing ochre frontage is approached through carefully tended fields of vines and olive groves – all the property of the monastery, which now bottles and markets its own wine and organic olive oil.

You can walk right through the complex and sit on benches shaded by orange trees in the patio. The **church**, which appears strangely foreshortened, contains a beautiful old gilded altarpiece and, around the walls, ancient wooden stalls; like most of the monastery it is built from stone that glows orange in the afternoon sun. By the entrance a small **museum** exhibits silver chalices, vestments, relics and manuscripts, mostly dating from the eighteenth or nineteenth centuries, and a few icons that are considerably older. In the courtyard there's a water cooler; in quieter times, if you're lucky, the traditional hospitality might extend to a glass of *rakí* and a piece of *loukoúm* (Turkish delight) in the hall where you sign the visitors' book.

Moní Gouvernétou

4km north of Ayía Triádha • Charge • The monastery is enclosed within a compound; leave any transport at the gate and approach via a path through a garden (around 100m)

The lonely road to **MONÍ GOUVERNÉTOU** (**Μονή Γουβερνέτου**) ascends through a biblical landscape of rocks and wild olives; the final section is paved but horribly rutted as it twists through a steep rocky gully. Older than Ayía Triádha (a Greek inscription above the entrance is dated 1573), the monastery is fortress-like from the outside, with two towers standing guard; inside there's the usual refreshingly shaded patio, ancient frescoes in the church and a tiny museum. Despite its remote location, Gouvernétou feels like a thriving community: beautifully renovated and with carefully tended flowerbeds and chapel. Nevertheless, the stark surroundings help to give a real sense of the isolation that the remaining monks must face for most of the year, and their life is contemplative and strict; visitors are expected to respect this.

St John the Hermit's cave

500m beyond Gouvernétou monastery

Immediately above Gouvernétou is a simple marble war memorial. Beyond this, you can follow (on foot) a path that heads down towards the sea; after about ten minutes you reach the cave in which **St John the Hermit** is said to have lived and died. This large, low cavern – stark, dank and dripping – features hefty stalactites and stalagmites and a substantial bathing tank, probably for baptisms. Excavations revealed that this had been an important Minoan shrine too, and in the Greek period it became a sanctuary dedicated to the goddess Artemis.

Moní Katholikó

About 1km north of Gouvernétou monastery

Descending beyond St John the Hermit's cave the path deteriorates as the going gets steeper, rockier and sharper. After some 500m you reach the amazing **ruins** of **MONÍ KATHOLIKÓ (Μονή Καθολικού)**, built into the side of, and partly carved from, a craggy ravine of spectacular desolation. This older monastery, founded in the eleventh century and one of the oldest on the island, was abandoned more than three hundred years ago when the monks, driven by repeated pirate raids, moved up to the comparative safety of Gouvernétou. The valley sides are dotted with caves, which formed a centre of still-earlier Christian worship, at least one of which (just before the buildings) you can explore if you have a torch.

Spanning the ravine by the ruins is a vast **bridge** leading nowhere, evocatively captured by Edward Lear in one of his Cretan watercolours (see page 351). Cross it and you can scramble down to the bottom of the ravine and follow the stream bed for about another fifteen minutes to the sea. There's a tiny natural **harbour**, a fjord-like finger of water pushing up between the rocks, where remains of a port can still be made out. Hewn from the rock, and with part of its roof intact, is what appears to be an ancient boathouse or slipway. There's no beach, but it's easy enough to lower yourself from the rocks straight into the astonishingly clear green water. The walk back up takes perhaps an hour in all – and is much more strenuous than it might have seemed on the way down.

Soúdha Bay

Much of the **south side** of the Akrotíri peninsula, and the area round the airport, is a **military zone**, with naval installations in the bay and the air force on land. There are good beaches at **Maráthi**, beyond the airport to the south, extremely popular with locals at weekends and hence with some excellent tavernas, and a spectacular tiny cove at **Seitán**, on the peninsula's east coast, accessed via the village of Hordháki followed by a scary scramble down the cliff. Boat trips from resorts across the bay occasionally run to the little harbour at Maráthi, only adding to the crush for space on the beach; driving here affords some of the best views of **Soúdha Bay** and above all, of the fortified islet (**Néa Soúdha**) defending the entrance, bristling with Venetian and Ottoman fortifications which, from a distance at least, appear miraculously well preserved. Long-haul ferries and some boat trips operate from the town of **SOÚDHA (Σούδα)**, in the bay's innermost, southwest corner. If you are hanging around here you can find just about everything you need on the square right by the ferries, but it's not an attractive place.

The Allied war cemetery

1km northwest of Soúdha, signed off the main road towards the peninsula • The Haniá city tour bus stops here

Surrounded by eucalyptus trees and beautifully sited at the water's edge with Soúdha Bay stretching away beyond, **the Allied war cemetery** is a melancholy and moving spot. With its row upon row of immaculately tended headstones, many of them to unknown soldiers and very young men, the serene and dignified cemetery brings home with some force the scale of the calamity of the Battle of Crete in which most of them perished (see page 335). A grave in row 10E on the cemetery's northern side is that of the distinguished archeologist John Pendlebury, who took over at Knossós after Arthur Evans retired; he died fighting alongside Cretans during the German assault on Iráklio in 1941.

ARRIVAL AND DEPARTURE **SOÚDHA BAY**

By bus Frequent local buses run between Soúdha and the market in Haniá (every 20min; 20min), or you can take a taxi (€12; prices to other destinations posted); KTEL buses to Réthymno and Kastélli also meet the ferries. Five buses a day run from Haniá's bus station to Maráthi (30min).

By ferry ANEK (28210 27500, http://anek.gr) and Minoan (28210 81276, http://minoan.gr) both have departures to Pireás every evening; at peak summer periods there are also daytime sailings (9hr).

East from Haniá to Yeoryioúpoli

Heading east out of Haniá you can either make your way through the new town to pick up the main E75 road on the south side of town, or follow the buses and most of the other traffic along the old road to **Soúdha**, beyond which the routes merge. The new road is fast, but you'll see little through the screen of trees and flowering shrubs until you emerge on the coast at **Yeoryioúpoli**. If you're in no hurry, or you simply want an attractive circular drive, then the minor roads that head inland or out onto the **Dhrápano peninsula** have much more to offer.

Megála Horáfia

Some 6km east of Soúdha, and 1km (and a steep climb) inland, the village of **MEGÁLA HORÁFIA (Μεγάλα Χωράφια)** – which has officially changed its name to Áptera, though no one seems to pay this much attention – is a popular spot for villa holidays, with numerous houses and apartments (many with pool) offering spectacular hilltop views. Just 2km away, signed from the main square, is the archeological site of **Áptera**.

4

Áptera

Signed off the E75 highway, 2km above Megála Horáfia • Charge

The archeological site of **ÁPTERA (Άπτερα)** occupies the table top of a mesa-like hilltop, high above Soúdha Bay. This location appears in Linear B inscriptions, and therefore seems to have been **continuously occupied** from as early as the fourteenth century BC right up to 1964, when the monastery here was finally abandoned. From the fifth century BC into early Christian times Áptera was one of the island's most important cities. Work on the extensive remains is continuing, so new areas may be opened up, or others fenced off for excavation; the site has little shade and can be very hot in high summer – visit in the early morning if you can.

The main entrance is by the **Monastery of Áyios Ioánnis Theológos,** the most obvious building at the site. Here the biggest of the fenced areas includes the monastery, the cisterns, a bath complex and, right by the entrance, a fifth-century BC Classical Greek **temple** marked by huge stone slabs. The Roman **cisterns**, brick-lined and mainly underground, must be among the largest surviving – an awesome, cavernous testament to Roman engineering genius. Below spreads an extensive **Roman bath** complex, all of which raises the question of just how enough water to fill the vast cisterns and feed the baths was collected on what is now a barren hilltop, although it could be that long-gone aqueducts were the source.

Numerous other remains are scattered around the immediate area, mostly signed but not all accessible. Check the map at the site entrance (or there may be a leaflet). Many are reached by a well-signed path on the opposite side of the car park from the monastery (and outside the fenced site). There are remains of a small **theatre** here, and of a **Roman villa** full of collapsed pillars. To reach the latter head along a path through the olives for 150m in a roughly southwest direction. When you reach them, the remains of the first- or second-century peristyle villa are impressive and the size of the collapsed stone columns show how grand it must once have been. You also pass a World War II machine-gun post, which, if it weren't signed, could easily be mistaken for another restored Roman ruin. The path continues down towards Megála Horáfia and ends, right on the edge of the village, by a substantial section of the ancient city **wall**, complete with defensive tower and gate. In the other direction, you can also take a paved road from the site entrance to a magnificent (but locked) **castle** on a point overlooking the defences at the entrance to the Bay of Soúdha.

ACCOMMODATION AND EATING — MEGÁLA HORÁFIA

Aptera Apartments On the road leading to the Áptera site, http://aptera-apartments.com. Attractive, fully equipped studios and apartments with a large pool and spectacular views over Soúdha Bay. €

Taverna Aptera Centre of the village, 28250 31313. Very good rural taverna, one of several around the crossroads at the heart of Megála Horáfia, serving heartily traditional home-cooked daily specials; the likes of spinach with rice, or stuffed courgette flowers. €

Stýlos and around

South from Áptera you can follow minor roads inland to circle round via the Dhrápano peninsula, a very attractive drive. The first place of any size is **STÝLOS** (**Στύλος**), which is where the Australian and New Zealand rearguard made their final stand during the Battle of Crete (this was then the start of the main road south), enabling the majority of Allied troops to be evacuated while they themselves were mostly stranded on the island. Many found refuge in the villages in the foothills around here and were later smuggled off the island – the Germans destroyed some of these villages in retribution. Today Stýlos is an attractive old place on a rushing river, whose excellent tavernas are a popular outing for city-folk from Haniá. The local spring water is bottled under the Samariá brand (it comes in jugs at the restaurants here), and there's a very ancient church, Áyios Ioánnis Theológos, usually open, with damaged frescoes inside.

4

If you enjoy driving on Crete's **mountain roads**, head from Stýlos up towards **Samonás**, a twisting and turning ride of 4km, offering better views at every turn. Beyond, you can continue on a still more tortuous route via **Kámbi** (from where there's a good road back to Haniá) to **Dhrakóna** and **Thériso** (see page 267). At Samonás you can also take a diversion to visit the isolated Byzantine church of Áyios Nikólaos at **Kyriakosélia**.

Áyios Nikólaos

To arrange a visit head for the *kafenío* in Samonás – preferably in late afternoon after siesta – and they'll phone for a keyholder who'll accompany you to the church; they don't accept money for their time, but a contribution towards the upkeep of the church is unlikely to be refused

The beautiful restored church of **Áyios Nikólaos**, nestling in a valley outside the village of Kyriakosélia, boasts **medieval frescoes** as good as any on Crete. Painted in the thirteenth century, these have not been touched by the restorers – at least not recently – and are patchy and faded against their deep-blue background, but parts still seem as vivid as the day they were created. A *Madonna and Child*, at eye level on the left-hand side, and a dramatic *Christ Pantokrátor* in the drum dome stand out.

EATING AND DRINKING — STÝLOS AND AROUND

★ **Moustakia** Main road in Stýlos, 28250 41190. The pick of the tavernas in Stýlos, with fountains, geese and ducks along the river, and terrace tables set beneath giant plane trees. Simple food, mainly grilled, but everything is as fresh as it can be; try the Greek salad topped with *myzíthra* sheep's cheese (a meal in itself) or the spit-roasted lamb – the chips, too, are gourmet standard. €

The Apokóronas

The **Apokóronas** region, east of Haniá, is rich agricultural land, a countryside of rolling green, wooded hills interrupted by immaculately whitewashed, and obviously wealthy, villages. The **Dhrápano** peninsula, on the coast, has a couple of popular resorts, though many once beautiful coastal villages here have been blighted by a real estate boom – prior to the economic crisis – which saw villas thrown up on any piece of land with a view. **Inland**, while there are few attractions to detain you long, there's a multitude of excellent roads criss-crossing the region, almost all of them scenic and well surfaced. Everywhere there are *kafenía* where you can sit and wonder at the rural tranquillity away from the main-road traffic, and there are a number of excellent restaurants too.

The Dhrápano coast

On the **north coast** of the Dhrápano peninsula are two sizeable resorts, **Kalýves** and **Almyrídha**, both with decent sandy beaches. Away from these, and especially on the peninsula's east-facing coast, low cliffs mean that there are few places where the water can be easily accessed, though there are glorious sea views from many of the villages – the more popular of which have been overrun by expats and unattractive villas.

Kalýves

KALÝVES (Καλύβες) is both a resort and an agricultural market centre of some size. As you approach, you pass a long sandy beach in the lee of Áptera's castle-topped bluff, which looks attractive but is hard to reach. The main **beach** stretches in both directions from the centre of the village, best at the eastern end where it curves round to a small harbour in the shelter of a headland. The village itself is not particularly attractive at first sight, a rather straggly development lining the main road for over 2km. It's very much a package resort, although the mainly low-rise apartments and studios keep it low-key; along with Almyrídha, Kalýves has become a focus for the largely British villa-owning community in the surrounding hills and there are a number of businesses and bars with English names.

The centre of town is marked by a small square with a church, just to the east of which a river runs through to the sea. The most attractive parts are round here, especially if you cut down to the seafront just one block away. Just about everything you might need, from banks with ATMs to a launderette and travel agencies, can be found along the main street through town, within walking distance of the centre.

Almyrídha

ALMYRÍDHA (Αλμυρίδα), the next village along the coast from Kalýves, is smaller, marginally more of a resort, and considerably more attractive. The beach, lined with tavernas and cafés, is a popular spot for **windsurfing**, with a fairly reliable breeze once you're slightly offshore. It's worth looking at the remains of an **early Christian basilica** dating from the fifth century, with a wonderful mosaic floor. It lies beside the road as it enters the western end of the village, close to the *Lagos* taverna.

Pláka and around

Beyond Almyrídha the coast becomes increasingly rocky, with cliffs almost all the way round to Yeoryioúpoli denying access to the sea. The roads and the signage also deteriorate if you go this way, but as you climb the views become increasingly worthwhile. The first place you reach, immediately east of Almyrídha and these days almost a suburb, is **PLÁKA (Πλάκα)**, a beautiful but overdeveloped hamlet, with tempting tavernas and cafés on a sleepy central platía; nearby *Sunset Taverna* has fabulous views back over Almyrídha and the coast.

Further around the coast, there are great views if you take the deserted coastal road via **Kefalás**, an absurdly pretty place perched above the sea with spectacular views towards Réthymno. Pretty much the only place to get down to the water, though, is at **Palelóni**, where a narrow road leads down to a rocky cove alongside a small naval base.

ARRIVAL AND GETTING AROUND

By bus There are regular buses connecting Haniá with both Kalýves (6 daily; 30min) and Almýridha (4 daily; 40min), but no public transport around the region.

Car and bike rental Flisvos Travel (28250 31100, http://flisvos.com), at the bottom of the inland road in Almyrídha and on the main road west of the centre of Kalýves (28250 31337), has cars, scooters and bikes, and can also help with accommodation, money exchange and excursions; there's even an ATM in Almyrídha.

ACTIVITIES

Watersports UCPA (2825 032 062), at the heart of the seafront in Almyrídha, rents out windsurfers (€10/hr), kayaks (€8/hr) and pedalos. Dream Adventure Trips, with a desk under the tamarisks at the eastern end of the seafront (6944 357 383), runs speedboat and snorkelling trips to inaccessible parts of the nearby coast (both €22). Omega Divers (28250 31412, www.omegadivers.com), on the seafront at the junction of the inland road, offers diving excursions and dive courses.

ACCOMMODATION

KALÝVES

Blue Sea Apartments Eastern end of the seafront, http://bluesea-kalyves.com. Almost the last building as you head east along the beach, *Blue Sea* has a great, quiet position and big roof terrace with wonderful views. All the apartments have cooking facilities and at least indirect sea views; a couple are directly above the beach. €

Garifalo On the seafront east of the Kalyves Beach Hotel, 28250 32718. Excellent-value modern two-room apartments with kitchen, most with great sea views. Good for families, and they have their own loungers and umbrellas on the beach. €

Kalyves Beach Hotel On the seafront in the centre of town, beside the river, www.seacretehotels.com. Occupying the prime central beachfront position, the renovated *Kalyves Beach Hotel* is also much the largest in town, with facilities including indoor and outdoor pools, beach bar and a tiny gym. Only a few rooms have direct sea views, though. Breakfast included. €€

ALMYRÍDHA

Almyrida Resort In the centre, http://almyridaresort.com. The centre of town is marked by two incongruous modern hotels: the four-star *Almyrida Residence* and slightly more downmarket *Almyrida Beach* which, together with the suites and family rooms at beachfront *Almyrida Studios*, are all under the same management and share facilities, including several pools and a bowling alley. Rates include breakfast. €€

Rooms Pothoulakis Near the bottom of the Pláka road, 28250 32132. Bright pink building in a lush garden with simply decorated studios and apartments (all with flat-screen TV and kitchen). There can be a bit of traffic noise. €

PLÁKA

★ **Betreat-Inn** Pláka, http://betreat-inn.com. Family-run hotel that has been beautifully renovated in designer style – each room colourful and individual. There's a lush garden, a small pool and playground, plus a bar. €€€

Studios Koukouros Pláka, 28250 31145. Pleasant rooms with balcony and fridge, and a stunning garden filled with palms, cacti and bougainvillea. €

EATING AND DRINKING

KALÝVES

Cafe Arena y Mar Eastern end of the beach. Café-bar with TV sport, free wi-fi and free sunbeds on the beach for customers; one of the livelier places in town. €

Il Forno Eastern end of the beach, 28250 32520. Excellent pizza from a wood-fired oven, plus less tempting pasta and Greek dishes, and free sunbeds for customers. €

Kritiko In the centre of town, on the main road between the square and the river, 28250 31096. Probably the fanciest place in town, with its own beach bar, garden and beachfront terrace. Pricier than most, too, but only marginally so, and worth it for dishes like roast lamb with lemon and aromatic herbs, smoked in a wood oven or rabbit in muscat wine with olives and cheese. €€

Potamos Overlooking the river close to the square. *Kafenío* serving snacks and drinks in an attractive waterside setting. €

Provlita Seafront promenade west of the centre, 28250 31835. Almost the last taverna as you follow the seafront west from the centre, with an attractive seafront terrace and a reputation for perfectly cooked fish that makes it popular with locals. Go for whatever's fresh, such as *skathári* black bream or sea bass. Good wine list. €€

ALMYRÍDHA

Café Françoise Towards the eastern end of the seafront, 28250 32591. Vibrant little café-patisserie serving a wide range of tasty snacks including salads, sandwiches, omelettes and burgers. They also do a mammoth "English breakfast", as well as pastries and ice cream, plus cocktails in the evening. €

Dimitri's In the centre of the seafront, 28250 31303. Long-established, traditional taverna, open from breakfast until late at night. Good salads and traditional Greek dishes including a tasty mixed meze, *païdhákia* (lamb chops) and *moussakás*. €

Nikita's Place On the seafront next to Dimitri's, 6944 857 509. All-day café-bar with music and cocktails at night on a lovely waterfront terrace – their karaoke night is about as wild as the local nightlife ever gets. €

O Lagos On the main road at the western edge of the village, 6977 391 778. "The Hare" taverna has an attractive garden setting and a meaty, traditional menu (*soutzoukákia*, rabbit *stifádho*), plus excellent *kalitsoúnia* (cheese pies) and stuffed peppers. €

Thalami Central seafront, http://thalami-almyrida.gr. One of the most popular of the waterfront tavernas, with a slightly upmarket menu and atmosphere. There's a wide range of fish dishes, plus the usual meat and vegetable options. €€

PLÁKA

Sunset Taverna At the entrance to the village coming from Almyrídha, 28250 32047. It's really all about the views and – of course – sunsets at family-run *Sunset*, but the food is pretty good too, with a scattering of international items like spareribs to attract the expats. €

Inland Apokóronas

Good roads head inland from both Kalýves and Almyrídha, and this is lovely country to explore if you have a car or bicycle, with interesting driving, plenty of alternative routes, and numerous villages worth a brief stop on the way. **Vámos** is the heart of the region and its main town – all roads seem to lead here in the end – while **Vrýsses** is the gateway to the road south into Sfakiá, and also to some far less visited villages on the south side of the E75 highway.

4

Aspró

Immediately inland from Almyrídha you pass below **ASPRÓ** (**Ασπρό**), a tiny, ancient hamlet looking down over the coast. This is the old Greek village as you've always imagined it, with lots of bougainvillea-draped backstreets and dozing dogs stretched out in the road. A handful of foreigners have snapped up any empty houses and it seems only a matter of time before the remaining local residents decide to cash in, too.

Doulianá

DOULIANÁ (**Ντουλιανά**), a couple of kilometres southwest of Aspró as the crow flies but a few more along the back roads you're forced to take to reach it, is a delightful hamlet. Overflowing with plants and flowers and crisscrossed by winding lanes lined with fine old houses, it's yet another place where time seems to stand still.

Gavalohóri

The evidence that **GAVALOHÓRI** (**Γαβαλοχώρι**), 2km south of Aspró, is an ancient settlement is scattered throughout the village's narrow, winding streets: there are Byzantine wells and Roman tombs on the outskirts, and on the corner by the museum you can see the cleverly preserved remains of a Muslim coffee shop. In a pedestrian area just off the main street, housed in a beautifully restored Venetian building with Ottoman era additions, Gavalohóri's small but excellent **folklore museum** (charge) documents the history and culture of the village. Of special interest are the examples of stone-cutting, woodcarving and *kopanéli* (silk lace made by bobbin-weaving), which is being revived in the village. The mulberry trees planted around here by the Muslims still produce silk from the silkworms that feed on their leaves – although the worms themselves are now imported from Japan and China.

Vámos

The main agricultural centre of the peninsula and the capital of the Apokóronas district, **VÁMOS** (**Βάμος**) is hard to miss – from all over the region signs direct you to the local health centre. It's worth coming here, too, for a couple of excellent tavernas and for **Vámos Village** (see page 258), a co-operative founded to promote ecotourism and to rebuild and restore houses in the village. While you're here, make sure to see the upper part of the village, which is where most of the population lives; it's easy to get the idea that the co-operative's half is all there is. The upper village's main square has a number of quiet *kafenía* with street terraces.

Vrýsses

VRÝSSES (Βρύσες), on the south side of the E75 highway, was a major junction on the old road and is still at the crossroads for the route south to Hóra Sfakíon (if you're coming from Réthymno or anywhere else to the east, you usually have to **change buses** here), though nowadays bypassed by much of the traffic. Set on the banks of the Almyrós A River, Vrýsses is a wonderfully shady little town, its streets lined with huge old plane trees and busy with the life of a local agricultural centre. On the riverside are a number of inviting cafés and **tavernas**.

ARRIVAL AND ACTIVITIES — INLAND APOKÓRONAS

By bus There are regular buses connecting Haniá with Vámos (5 daily, fewer at weekends; 40min), while many (but not all) of the Haniá–Réthymno and Hóra Sfákion services call at Vrýsses, but there's no public transport between villages.

Vamos Village 75m from the Sterna Tou Bloumosifi tavern in Vámos, up a road alongside it, http://vamosvillage.gr. Helpful tourist information as well as walking tours, cookery courses and all sorts of excursions and seasonal activities; they also sell an excellent local walking guide, *Discover Vamos On Foot*, detailing seven walks between 7 and 10km.

4

ACCOMMODATION AND EATING

DOULIANÁ

Iliopetra On the edge of the village by Ta Douliana, http://iliopetra-milopetra.gr. Small complex of modern studios and one-bedroom maisonettes designed to blend into the village, well-equipped with kitchens and washing machines; there's also a small pool. Studios €, maisonettes €€

★ **Natalia's Houses** Signed in the heart of the village, 28250 23356, http://nataliashouses.gr. Four new but traditionally built houses, exceptionally thoughtfully fitted out and beautifully furnished, with an excellent taverna and welcoming hosts. €€

Taverna Douliana Signposted down a narrow track on the southern edge of the village, 28250 23380. A friendly taverna with tables on a leafy terrace. Their fried chicken livers are a favourite, as are simple lamb or chicken casseroles, and they also make good pizza in a wood-fired oven, available for delivery to local villas. €€

GAVALOHÓRI

Arismari In pedestrian alley by the museum, 28250 84066. A lovely spot, with tables outside under a venerable plane tree. Go for the freshly-made specials from the seasonal menu; there are lots of vegetarian choices such as home-made local pasta with cheese or stuffed courgette flowers. Occasional live Greek music. €€

VÁMOS

★ **Sterna Tou Bloumosifi** Main road, near the centre of the lower village, 28250 83220. Outstanding taverna with a tree-shaded terrace dedicated to traditional Cretan cuisine. The menu changes with the seasons; excellent salads and mezédhes are followed by the likes of chestnut stew with mushrooms , goat with wild greens or pork with wine and goat buttermilk. They have a decent wine list, and the hýma (barrelled house wine, red and white) is pretty good, too. €€

★ **Vamos Village** 75m from the Sterna Tou Bloumosifi taverna, http://vamosvillage.gr. A range of carefully restored traditional cottages, mostly in Vámos, some in the surrounding countryside, all fully equipped with everything you might need. Some have pools. €€

VRÝSSES AND AROUND

O Progoulis Centre of town, on the north side of the river, Vrýsses, 28250 51086. With a terrace overlooking the river and its pools filled with entertaining ducks and geese, *Progoulis* specializes in grilled meats, with a wood-fired barbecue. €

★ **Taverna Tzitzifias** In the tiny hamlet of Tzitzifés, off the road between Vrýsses and Frés, 28254 00190. A wonderful rural taverna, rich with the smell of wood-smoke and with its own *rakí* still in the back yard. Locals from Haniá and Réthymno pack the place at weekends, lapping up the friendly, traditional atmosphere. There's a long menu from which only a few items are available on any given day, but on the whole it's the local meat barbecued over wood you should go for – village sausages or pork with marjoram;

HIKING AROUND YEORYIOÚPOLI

If you want to do some walking in the area around Yeoryioúpoli, pick up a copy of the excellent local walking guide, *Discover Kavros and Georgioupolis On Foot*, widely sold locally. As a taster, you could try hiking up the Almyrós valley towards Vrýsses or tackling the steep climb to Exópoli, where there are some wonderfully sited tavernas with magnificent views. Hikes to and around Lake Kournás (see page 261) are another possibility.

if you call in advance they'll roast a whole joint for you. Getting here is part of the fun – though well-signposted, *Tzitzifés* is down terrifyingly narrow roads in the middle of nowhere. €

Yeoryioúpoli

YEORYIOÚPOLI (**Γεωργιούπολη**) – or Georgioupolis – lies at the base of Cape Dhrápano where the Almyrós Stream flows into the sea. It's named after the ill-starred Prince George, a son of the Greek king who was appointed High Commissioner to Crete in 1898 (see page 333). These days, the place has a distinctly split personality: on the one hand is a pretty **old town** by the river, its approaches shaded by ancient eucalyptus trees; on the other is a lively **package resort**, with development spreading further east every year along the beach beyond town. For the moment the two sides maintain a comfortable balance and Yeoryioúpoli remains a pleasant place to spend a few days: small-scale, yet with plenty of action, and with the freshwater **Lake Kournás** an easy trip away.

4

Yeoryioúpoli beaches

The main course of the river runs into the sea on the northern edge of Yeoryioúpoli, by a small harbour protected by a long rocky breakwater, and there are numerous smaller streams crossing the **beach** all around, some of which have wooden bridges to let you cross without getting your feet wet. These can make swimming cold in places, and they also create little quicksands, mostly only ankle-deep. This area is also a favoured nesting ground of the loggerhead **sea turtle** (see page 348). Close to town it can be hard to find space between the sunloungers, but several **beach bars** offer these for free as long as you pay for the odd drink; the best of these is probably the *Tropicana Beach Café*, at the start of the long eastern stretch. Beyond *Tropicana* a large stream crosses the beach, and more beach bars and hotels stretch into the distance; you may find more space here, but you should swim close to a lifeguard as there are **dangerous currents** in places: don't venture too far out, and take heed of any warning notices.

A second, much more sheltered beach,**i Kalyváki**, lies to the north of the river in a small bay. Swimming here is safer and there are generally fewer people, but the water can be extremely cold.

ARRIVAL AND INFORMATION — YEORYIOÚPOLI

By bus All buses between Haniá and Réthymno call at Yeoryioúpoli, so there's an hourly dedicated service in each direction throughout the day. They drop you on the highway, just a couple of minutes' walk from the square and crossroads at the centre of town – a booth here sells tickets for onward buses.

Travel agencies Ethon Tours on the square (28250 61432, https://ethon.gr) offers everything from car, mountain and motorbike rental to its own ATM.

TOURS AND ACTIVITIES

Boat trips Sofía Cruises (28250 61100) runs boat trips (June–Sept) from the river just below the bridge, including a daily trip to Maráthi, at the mouth of Soúdha Bay (see page 252). You'll find fishing trips on offer here too.

Horseriding Horseriding and tuition are offered by Zoraïda's (28250 61745, https://zoraidas-horseriding.com); trips include beach rides and excursions up to Lake Kournás.

Train tours Two tourist trains transport visitors along the seafront and to various places of interest inland, including the lake, and even as far as Aryiroúpoli (see page 229).

Watersports There's usually at least one watersports operation on the main beach, offering banana rides, jet skis and the like, while Turtle River (6985 786 361), at the mouth of the river on the Kalyváki side, rent pedalos and kayaks for trips upstream.

ACCOMMODATION

There are **rooms to rent** everywhere in Yeoryioúpoli, it seems, and only at the height of season are you likely to have any trouble finding a vacancy. The competition generally keeps prices low. **Mosquitoes** can be a problem if you're staying near the river (as can noisy geese), but the wildlife on the banks is some compensation and kingfishers are regular visitors. With your own transport, the nearby hill village of **Exópoli** becomes a viable alternative to staying in town. The big hotels are mostly out to the east, especially in and around the village of **Kavrós**. The best thing you can say about Kavrós, which is almost entirely purpose-built, is that it has plenty of nightlife, and there's a frequent tourist 'train' into Yeoryioúpoli.

Andy's Rooms Near the church, on the road towards the beach from the south end of the square by the supermarket, http://andys.georgioupoli.net. This friendly place shaded by trees has good-value rooms, simple but spotless, with big balconies and fridge, plus a couple of well-equipped apartments. €€

Anna's House Just across the river from town, on the Exópoli road, https://annashouse.gr. Lovely, 1990s-built studios and apartments with well-equipped kitchens and modern decor, around a full-size pool; a short walk to town or Kalyváki beach. Studios €, apartments €€

Eligas On the first cross street below the square, heading towards the beach, https://eligas.gr. Simply furnished but well-maintained studios, plus one apartment, in a bougainvillea-draped building; upper floors have good views from the back. €

Georgioupolis Beach Hotel On the seafront at the bottom of the road from the north corner of the square, http://gbhotel.gr. Good value considering the enviable seafront location and excellent facilities – rooms and small apartments with beach views and satellite TV, plus a pool and tiny spa. Breakfast available. €€€

★ **Marika Apartments** In the hill village of Exópoli, 3km northwest of town, http://marika-exopoli.com. Attractive place with lovingly tended a/c studios and apartments around a pool with a truly spectacular view; it's worth paying a little extra for the sea-view apartment, if it's available. €€

Sofia Seafront near the mouth of the river, http://riverside.gr. Refurbished apartment complex with modern two-room apartments with kitchen and TV, most with sea views. The same owners run the adjacent Riverside Hotel, with similar facilities but inland views (and some cheaper rooms), and have other places nearby and in the hills. €€

Sunlight Seafront, just east of the centre, http://sunlightgeo.gr. Modern apartment complex that's ugly from the outside, but friendly and comfortable within, with good sea-view balconies and rooms for two to six people. €

4

EATING AND DRINKING

There are plenty of restaurants and tavernas in Yeoryioúpoli, mainly between the square and the river or along the waterfront; the square itself is ringed by cafés. There are a number of tavernas up in the hill village of **Exópoli** too, with stunning views over the coast. In terms of **nightlife**, Yeoryioúpoli itself is pretty quiet, though there are plenty of **bars** open late. There are regular Greek dance nights and other events at the *Tropicana Beach Café*, and look out for posters for weekend beach parties and the like – there are also several clubs in Kavrós.

Babis On the first cross street, 28250 61819. Traditional taverna with good-value, simple Cretan food; try their excellent rabbit *stifádho*. €

Blue Moon Overlooking the river, just upstream from the bridge, 6972 705 310. Café-bar with a riverside terrace for breakfast or a sundowner, plus snacks and drinks all day. €

Corissia Park On the seafront in the centre of town, 28250 83010. Pool-bar and restaurant. One of the best locations in town makes up for a somewhat bland menu, and customers can use the pool and loungers on the beach for free; there's a breakfast buffet, burgers and snacks by day, and a more formal atmosphere in the evening. Frequent live music. €

Efthymis On the road heading east out of town, parallel to the highway, 28250 61886. Friendly little taverna serving good wood-oven pizza and decent Greek dishes. Some good house wine too. €

O Fanis Main street near the bridge, 6984 436 380. Grill house offering the freshest catch from the quayside, 30m away, with fish dishes and good meat dishes. €

Paradise Down by the river west of the square, 28250 61313. Reliable taverna in an attractive garden setting. Their Cretan kitchen turns out a range of popular standards from *biftéki* to shrimp *saganáki*. €

Poseidon Taverna Hidden away down a lane southwest of the square; look for the signs off the road to the highway, 28250 61026. Hidden away in a shady courtyard, *Poseidon* serves "every day fish from our own boat" at reasonable prices. There's no menu, and nothing but fish, seafood and chips; choose your fish carefully (it's sold by weight) to avoid a nasty surprise when the bill arrives. €€

Syrtaki Main street near the bridge, 28250 61382. Excellent taverna-ouzerí with a raised terrace serving well-prepared mezédhes, traditional dishes (*yemistá*) and delicious grilled meat and fish. €

Lake Kournás and around

Crete's only freshwater lake, **LAKE KOURNÁS (Λίμν Κουρνά)**, shelters in a steep bowl of hills 4km inland from Yeoryioúpoli. As lakes go, it's small and shallow, but it nevertheless makes for an interesting excursion. Its appearance varies greatly according to when you visit: during the day its colours change remarkably as the sun shifts around the rim of the bowl, and its size alters over the course of a year. In late summer the level drops to reveal sand (or dried mud) beaches all around, and a number of popular camping spots. Earlier in the year, the water comes right up to the tidal ring of scrubby growth and it's much harder to find anywhere to camp on or to swim from. The lake and the surrounding hills are also a good place to seek out some of the more unusual island wildlife. In summer it's possible to make a circuit of the lake using a path and the dried mud beaches where this runs out – about an hour's walk.

On the lakeshore where you arrive it can be extremely crowded, with **tavernas** competing for your custom and pedaloes and canoes for rent; take one to the centre of the lake where the water is cleaner, and dive in – a short stroll will usually find you a quieter spot. The nearby hamlet of **Mathés**, some 2km away on a back road to Yeoryioúpoli, is more peaceful still, with fine coastal views from an excellent taverna, and some lovely rooms.

Kournás

The village of **KOURNÁS (Κουρνάς)**, a charming hill settlement fanning out around its inclined main street, is a stiff 4km climb beyond Lake Kournás. The church of **Áyios Yeóryios** here is a fine old Byzantine structure with Venetian additions and some impressive fresco fragments. If it's locked, ask around and someone should be able to produce a key.

4

ARRIVAL AND DEPARTURE — LAKE KOURNÁS

There's no public transport to the lake, but there are **tours** from many nearby resorts. To get to the lake from Yeoryioúpoli you could take the **tourist train** or rent a **bike**, or it's an easy **walk**. The best route is via the hamlet of Mathés (cross the highway at the crossroads in Yeoryioúpoli and a quiet road leads straight ahead). From here there's a waymarked rambling route to the lake's northern edge, linking in with the route around it – ask the villagers at **Mathés** to direct you to the path, should you have difficulty.

ACCOMMODATION AND EATING

KOURNÁS

★ **Kali Kardia** Main street in the heart of the village, 28250 96278. Great, inexpensive taverna with some of the best lamb and sausages in the province, together with tasty *souvláki* and super salads – and don't miss their *galaktoboúreko* dessert, a lemony egg-custard pudding. €

Villa Stella On the right as you come in from the lake, 6932 959 156. Beautiful apartments sleeping two to four in a sensitively restored old mansion; lots of exposed beams and traditional furniture, plus fabulous views towards the sea. €

MATHÉS

Taverna Mathes Centre of the village, 6997 487 494. Excellent food on a fine terrace with a stunning panoramic view. They specialize in charcoal-grilled and rotisserie meats, though there are also plenty of veggie dishes; try the *kalitsoúnia* (cheese pies), or suckling pig. €

★ **Villa Kapasa** www.villa-kapasas.com. Delightful old place with simple rooms overlooking the leafy garden of an ancient, restored house. It's high above the village so has fabulous views; they also do meals. €

West of Haniá

West of Haniá, the E75 speeds you towards Kastélli with little to see along the way. The **old road**, meanwhile, also served by buses, follows the coastline more or less consistently, through a string of small towns and growing resorts, all the way to the **Rodhopoú peninsula**. Occasionally it runs right above the water, more often 100m or so inland, but never more than easy walking distance from the sea. As you drive along the coast everything may seem entirely modern, but in most cases there is a real village up in the hills behind, where traditional life survives to a remarkable degree. This area was also a crucial battlefield in the 1941 **Battle of Crete**, and the bridgehead from which the Germans established their domination.

The hotel zone

There are hotels and apartments the whole way from Haniá to Kolymbári at the base of the **Rodhopoú peninsula**, but the first real resort area starts at **Káto Stalós**, which runs into **Ayía Marína** and then into **Plataniás** without a break, creating the most built-up, touristy strip in the west of the island. This is better than it sounds: it's all fairly low-rise, there's a decent beach almost all the way along (with facilities including jet skis, windsurfers and parascending) and, by resort standards, it's pretty quiet. Beyond Plataniás development thins out, though there are still plenty of hotels and apartment complexes and one or two more concentrated resort clusters such as **Yeráni**. These on the whole are pleasantly low-key, but the beach is rarely that great, being very open to wind and waves and with rather gravelly, grey sand.

Ayía Marína

AYÍA MARÍNA (**Αγία Μαρίνα**) is distinguished by a beautiful beach, curving round a little promontory with a fine view of the sunset and of **Áyii Theódori**, an offshore islet that's a sanctuary for *kri-kri* or wild ibex (you're not allowed to go ashore). From the west of the island a great cave gapes like the jaws of a beast; legend has Áyii Theódori as a sea-monster which, emerging from the depths to swallow Crete, was petrified by the gods. Remains found in the cave suggest that it was a place of Minoan worship, while in more recent times the Venetians turned the island into a fortress. As for Ayía Marína itself, there's every facility and tour you could want on offer; uphill and inland the original village still retains some of its traditional character.

4

Plataniás

Seamlessly adjoining Ayía Marína to the west, **PLATANIÁS** (**Πλατανιάς**) is an even busier place boasting a delightful old quarter perched high on an almost sheer bluff above the road. At the top of this hill, under the church, a volunteer-run **World War II museum** (Mon–Sat 10am–noon & 5–8pm; free) occupies tunnels dug by Cretan forced labour; the extensive tunnel system was used for weapons storage and as access to German defensive positions on the hillside.

Máleme

MÁLEME (**Μάλεμε**) is a place with significant historical resonance. This was the site of the **airfield** (still operational) that saw much of the early fighting in the Battle of Crete and where the German invasion began on May 20, 1941; the loss of this airfield in controversial circumstances was crucial to the German success (see page 335). There are also Minoan remains nearby.

German war cemetery

Signposted up a narrow lane from the coast road just beyond Máleme

On a hillside below the ridge known as Hill 107, which played a pivotal role in the struggle for the nearby airfield, the **German war cemetery** overlooks the battleground where so many of the four and a half thousand remembered here lost their lives. The lines of flat headstones, each marking a double grave, lend a sombre aspect to an otherwise peaceful scene. In an instance of almost grotesque irony, the cemetery's keepers were for many years the resistance heroes George Psychoundakis, author of *The Cretan Runner*, and Manolis Pateraki, who played a leading role in the capture of General Kreipe (see page 334).

Late Minoan tomb

Follow the lane down from the cemetery to the first left bend, where a track (signed) on the right leads 100m along a terraced hillside to the tomb on the right

The discovery in 1966 of a splendid **Late Minoan tomb** near Máleme demonstrated that this area had already been a graveyard for more than three thousand years. The *dhrómos* or entrance passage of the stone-built tomb and its enormous heavy lintel are well preserved.

ARRIVAL AND DEPARTURE

By bus There's an excellent bus service along the coast from Haniá, stopping frequently at all the resorts, with peak-season services at least half-hourly throughout the day, and in peak summer season hourly through the night as far as Plataniás.

ACTIVITIES

Bike tours Hellas Bike, in Ayía Marína (28210 60858) https://www.hellasbike.net offers bike rental and easy bike tours (€42/half-day; €72/full day, including pick-up from your accommodation) around this area and into the mountains.

Boat trips and watersports All sorts of boat trips depart from the little harbours in Ayía Marína and Plataniás, and there are watersports operators at regular intervals along the beach.

ACCOMMODATION

The best accommodation deals on the coast are invariably on **packages**; there are a few old-fashioned rooms places but, out of season at least, you'll be better off at one of the many modern, well-appointed apartment complexes (most have pools). Outside July or August there may well be bargains available. Any of the travel agencies along the main street should be able to arrange a deal.

AYÍA MARÍNA

Villa Life Upper village, beyond the highway, https://villa-life.gr. Welcoming, purpose-built one- and two-bedroom balcony apartments around a pleasant pool, from where there's a great view down over the coast; some traffic noise from the nearby highway, however. €€

PLATANIÁS

Effi Apartments On the beach, www.effiapartments.com. Lovely designer-style studios and apartments with contemporary furnishings in a garden setting right on the beach, plus an exceptionally friendly welcome. €€

Ermis Suites On the beach, http://ermis-suites.gr. Fairly simple studios and apartments, many with sea view and all with balcony or veranda. The larger apartments have two rooms and a fully equipped kitchen. Studios €, apartments €€

Pelagos Holiday Apartments Halfway up the hill above the main square, 28210 60075. Modern, exceptionally well-fitted-out duplex apartments with designer furnishings (including Scandinavian beds), all with balcony sea views, kitchenette and satellite TV. €€

4

EATING

A number of **tavernas** in Plataniás attract evening and weekend visitors from Haniá. The best views are from the eagles' eyries right at the top of the village, including the terraces of *Vigli* and *Astrea*. The best food, however, is down below.

AYÍA MARÍNA

Manolis Taverna In the heart of the upper village, 6974 814 737. Excellent little family taverna away from the seafront maelstrom, with a shady outdoor terrace. Solid Cretan cooking includes dishes like *bouréki* and *kounéli stifádho* (stewed rabbit) and there's an outdoor charcoal grill plus a decent selection of reasonably priced bottled wines. €€

PLATANIÁS

★ **Mylos tou Kerata** Main road, just west of the centre, 28210 68578. A restaurant of repute that opened its doors in 1960, *Mylos* is expensive by Cretan standards, but worth it. Specialities include *kontosoúvli* – pork cooked on a spit over charcoal – and pricey steaks, plus a variety of salads. You eat in a delightful walled garden with an old millstream running through it. €€

★ **Taverna Drakiana** Just outside the hamlet of Dhrakianá, 3km inland on the road beside O Mylos, 28210 61677. The food – organic and based on traditional recipes – may not be quite up to the same standard as *Mylos*, but the prices are more palatable and the riverside setting, in wooded surroundings, couldn't be more romantic – especially at night. It's an easy walk inland, or they offer a free minibus from Plataniás that will also bring you home after you've eaten; simply call ahead. There's Cretan dancing every Wednesday evening. €

DRINKING AND NIGHTLIFE

PLATANIÁS

Mylos Main road, just west of the centre, http://myloschania.com. For most young people in Haniá, Plataniás means clubs, and a great exodus from the city takes place in summer at around midnight. This is the top place, with a beach bar by day and club at night, but there are plenty of other beach bars and bar-clubs open much of the day and most of the night.

The Rodhopoú peninsula

Half a dozen villages cluster near the base of the **Rodhopoú peninsula**, in an area that is relatively newly developed for tourism. The peninsula itself is for the most part a barren, harsh landscape, with no roads penetrating northwards; if you want to explore towards the tip, you'll have to do so on foot or come by boat. **Inland**, a road heads south from Kolymbári through Spiliá, tracking the valley of the Spiliákos river and offering an opportunity to see an impressive **cave** and a trio of superb **churches**.

Kolymbári

KOLYMBÁRI (**Κολυμπάρι**), just off the main road, is much the most developed village on Rodhopoú, but still has far more appeal than anything that has preceded it along the north coast. If there were a sandy beach, it would be a perfect resort; as it is, there's a long strip of pebbles and clear water looking back along the coast towards Haniá in the distance. There's every facility you might need, including boat trips and car rental, but it's little spoiled, and from the narrow main street, where there are a couple of good tavernas, you can walk through to a seafront promenade lined with more restaurants and cafés. Nearby, a vast moden concrete harbour is entirely deserted most of the time. Some villas and apartments are in the old village on the hill above, where the views compensate for the ten-minute walk up.

4

Moní Gonía

1km north of Kolymbári • Charge • Respectable dress required

A short walk from Kolymbári on the main road out onto the peninsula, the seventeenth-century **Gonía Monastery** (**Μονή Παναγίας Οδηγήτριας Γωνιάς**) occupies a prime site, with stupendous views and a scramble down to a sandy cove – rumoured to be the monks' private beach. Every monk in Crete can tell tales of a valiant heritage of resistance to invaders, but here the Turkish cannonballs are still lodged in the walls to prove it, a relic of which the good fathers seem far more proud than any of the icons. That said, the church has a splendid series of seventeenth- and eighteenth-century icons (plus a few modern examples); Áyios Nikólaos, in a side chapel, is particularly fine. More are kept in the small **museum**, along with assorted vestments and relics.

Afráta

A scenic road extends up the peninsula's east coast as far as **AFRÁTA** (**Άφράτα**), a tiny place with a couple of tavernas and the first stirrings of development. Keep right here, down an increasingly steep, narrow road, and after little more than 1km you'll reach a rocky **cove** at the far end of the gorge you can see from the village. There's a seasonal taverna here and the exceptionally clear water offers great swimming, although it's a tiny space and can get crowded.

Ravdoúha

RAVDOÚHA (**Ραβδούχα**) is the only place on the peninsula's west coast accessible by road, either directly from the highway or an attractive drive from Afráta on good roads via **Astrátigos** and **Áspra Nerá**, with a turn-off to the village of **Rodhopós**, all pleasant if unremarkable settlements with places to eat and drink. Much the same might be said of Ravdoúha itself, the difference being that from here you can head down to the shore, passing the ancient church of **Ayía Marína** with some fine fresco fragments and, next to it, an old communal washing place, evoking a Crete long gone. **Ravdoúha beach**, a dizzying drop below the village, is something of a misnomer, but there are patches of rocky foreshore to swim from, and an isolated taverna with rooms.

The tip of the peninsula

Towards the tip of the peninsula you'll find no easily driveable roads, although a rough track (for which you'll need a 4WD) heads north out of Rodhopós up the spine of the peninsula to ancient Diktynna, 20km distant. There are, however, a couple of sites you might consider taking a major hike or a **boat trip** to reach. The latter is certainly the easier option – in summer the terrain is frighteningly hot, barren and shadeless.

Diktynna

There are regular boat trips to **Diktynna**, almost at the top of the peninsula above a little bay on the northeast side. An important Roman sanctuary to the goddess of the same name, this was probably built over more ancient centres of worship, and though it has never been properly excavated there's a surprising amount to be seen. The boats come here mainly because it's a sheltered spot to swim (when the sea is rough, fishing boats often shelter here too), but they allow plenty of time to explore.

Church of Áyios Ioánnis Giónis

If you've come to Diktynna by boat, there's a challenging 14km hike over to the isolated **Church of Áyios Ioánnis Giónis** on the western side of the peninsula, from where you could continue back to Rodhopós (7km) or Kolymbári (a further 7km); but let the boatmen know your plans to save them sending out a search party. On August 29, the church plays host to a major pilgrimage and a mass baptism of boys called Yiannis, marking one of the most important festivals of the Cretan religious calendar. At this time the two- to three-hour walk (each way) from Rodhopós among crowds of people is definitely worth it.

Spiliá and around

A little over 3km south of Kolymbári lies the rural village of **SPILIÁ** (**Σπηλιά**). Signs from the southern edge of the village lead to the charming, finely restored fourteenth-century church of the **Panayía**, raised on the lower slope of a hill and ringed by junipers. Inside (the church is usually left open) the dark interior is decorated with fine fourteenth-century **frescoes**, though here the restoration of the building is rather crude. Several other fine churches can be found in the countryside surrounding Spiliá.

Cave of Áyios Ioánnis Ermítis

North of, and high above, Spiliá, close to the hamlet of Marathokefála • Usually open daylight hours • Free

The **Cave of Áyios Ioánnis Ermítis** (St John the Hermit) is a sizeable grotto with an eleventh-century church, dedicated to the evangelist, built inside it. There's a terrace with fine coastal views and a café and museum, open on weekends and holidays when this is a popular outing for locals.

Áyios Stéfanos

Signposted from the road just over 2km south of Spiliá, beyond the village of Dhrakóna • Usually open daylight hours • Free

The **chapel of Áyios Stéfanos** is an extraordinary, tiny, tenth-century white-walled chapel squatting in a grove of mature trees. Inside you'll find the hefty stone walls decorated with exquisite **frescoes** dating from the period following the Arab conquest, when the Christian faith was being triumphantly restored.

Mihaíl Arhángelos Episkopí

4km southwest of Spiliá on the outskirts of Episkopí • Free

The most impressive church in the area around Spiliá, and one of the oldest in Greece, is the remarkable **Mihaíl Arhángelos Episkopí**, whose concentric stepped **dome**, unique in Crete, gives the structure its local name, "The Rotunda". The church was, as its official name suggests, a bishop's seat during the Venetian period, but the edifice is much older than this. The core rotunda section dates to the first Byzantine period, completed perhaps as early as the sixth century, and originally stood alone; the rest of the building was added after the end of the Arab occupation in the tenth century. Recent excavations in the adjoining graveyard yielded evidence that the present church was built over the remains of a still earlier Christian basilica, with various layers of burials from all periods of the church's history. The exterior has arguably been over-restored – inside, fragmentary **frescoes** dating back to the tenth century include a poignant head and partial wing of Arhángelos Mihaíl, the church's patron. There are also impressive mosaic floor fragments (some thought to date to the earliest period), and a fine double-seated marble **font**.

Karavitakis Winery

Near Pondikianá, not far from Áno Voúves; extensively signed throughout the area • Charge • www.karavitakiswines.com

The **Karavitakis Winery** is a good exemple of the new wave of Cretan winemaking, a serious boutique operation with 150 acres of vineyards growing both traditional indigenous and introduced grape varieties. There's an informative short tour of the process, including the attractive, traditional-looking modern buildings where the wine is made, followed by a tasting of some of their award-winning wines.

4

ARRIVAL AND DEPARTURE — THE RODHOPOÚ PENINSULA

By bus The Haniá hotel zone bus terminates at Kolymbári, with services along the coast at least half-hourly throughout the day; in addition, almost all buses between Haniá and Kastélli stop here (15 daily; 30min either way).

ACCOMMODATION AND EATING

KOLYMBÁRI

Aphea Village On the road to the upper village, https://aphea-village.gr. Sizeable modern apartment complex with a big pool and great views. The two- and three-bedroom a/c apartments are large and have everything you need, but feel somewhat spartan. Simple breakfast and a home-style evening meal are available around the pool. €

★ **Argentina** Main street, behind the harbour, 28240 22243. One of the best tavernas in the village, with a sea-view terrace. There's generally a big variety of fresh fish to choose from, plus the usual meat dishes and salads and very good house wine. €€

Diktina Main street, behind the harbour, 28240 22611. With a terrace at the rear overlooking the old harbour, this good taverna serves fresh fish (priced per kilo) and seafood (cuttlefish, shrimp spaghetti) along with the usual standards. €€

Grand Bay Beach Resort At the eastern end of the beach, http://grandbay.gr. Classy adults-only hotel in a fabulous position right on the water. There are several pools and a swim-up bar; it's probably worth paying extra for the excellent sea view. €€€

THE WORLD'S OLDEST OLIVE TREE

Áno Voúves, well-signed 4km east of Episkopí, has become famous throughout Greece as the location of one of the oldest olive trees in existence. Having seen the zenith of Minoan Crete and being seriously venerable at the time of Christ, the gnarled and contorted tree looks every one of the 4000-plus years attributed to it by experts from the University of Crete (the 3000 years quoted on information boards at the site is thought to be a conservative estimate). Still vigorously producing foliage and fruit, the ancient tree has become a source of huge pride for Áno Voúves, and there's a café and museum (https://olivemuseumvouves.com) for visitors. In 2004 a branch from the tree was carried to Athens on a reconstructed Minoan boat (see page 240) and two victory wreaths fashioned from its leaves were used to honour the first and last winners of events in that year's Olympic Games.

Palio Arhontiko Overlooking the beach, 28240 22124. Highly popular taverna with more pretensions to style than any of its neighbours and a few more elaborate dishes (Gruyère pies with fruit sauce; squid stuffed with cheese and peppers), as well as plenty of standard Greek fare and somewhat pricey fresh fish. €€

★ **Polichna Traditional Apartments** Upper village, 6945 232 288. Delightful two-storey a/c apartments, extremely well-equipped (most with washing machine) and thoughtfully furnished in traditional style. There's a tiny outdoor jacuzzi pool too. €

AFRÁTA

Tis Litsas ta Kamomata On the crossroads in the centre of the village, 6976 228 778. Lovely place on a raised terrace serving coffees, snacks and drinks – including Brinks beer (see page 216) – throughout the day and delicious, simple home-made food at lunchtime and in the evenings. €€

RAVDOÚHA

Ravdoucha Beach Studios Ravdoúha Beach, http://ravdouchabeachstudios.gr. Tucked away behind *Waves on the Rock* in a position that guarantees utter tranquillity, these modern two-room a/c studio apartments have great views from their balconies; meals are available at *Waves on the Rock*, run by the same family. €

★ **Waves on the Rock** Ravdoúha Beach, http://wavesontherock.eu. An excellent, out-of-the-way taverna fronting a pebble beach shaded by tamarisks, serving up tasty Cretan dishes and fresh fish. They also have five inexpensive, basic studio rooms, but the same family has newer apartments next door. €

South of Haniá

The area immediately inland from Haniá, around **Thériso**, is one that's little explored by tourists, though plenty of local visitors head up here for the mountain air, rural tavernas, and associations with the revered Cretan statesman **Eleftherios Venizélos** who, as prime minister of Greece for most of the period from 1910 to 1932, finally brought Crete into the modern Greek nation. Further west, roads through **Alikianós** head south towards Omalós, the Samariá Gorge and the heart of the White Mountains, and also to Soúyia on the south coast. This is agricultural country, growing oranges above all, and paying little heed to tourism, though again there's a wealth of history here. Most recently this area was the scene of some of the fiercest fighting in the **Battle of Crete** (see page 335), though many of the villages also have a much longer history of resistance.

4

Thériso and around

One of the most attractive trips you can make around Haniá is the 14km drive up to the traditional country village of **THÉRISO (Θέρισο)**, one of the cradles of Cretan independence and hometown of Eleftherios Venizélos's mother. Here in 1905 the Revolutionary Assembly was held (all baggy black shirts and drooping moustaches, as depicted in so many Cretan museums) that ousted Prince George and did much to precipitate union with Greece. Venizélos's family home is now a tiny **folklore museum** (signposted off the main street; charge; www.venizelos-foundation.gr/) and, with its plaque commemorating the famous son, is all but obligatory for Cretans – the village is frequently crowded with busloads of schoolkids. There's also a **Museum of National Resistance 1941–45** (signposted off the main street; charge; 28210 78004) and numerous **tavernas**, some of them huge, mostly empty except at weekends and holidays.

Thériso Gorge

The route up to Thériso passes through the **Thériso Gorge**. In terms of spectacle it can't, of course, compare with Samariá and, in any case, the bed of the ravine is given over to the road. But it is exceedingly pretty in the lower reaches, gentle and winding with the stream crossed and recrossed on concrete bridges, and surprisingly craggy towards the top where the walls are cracked and pocked with caves. There are plenty of opportunities to pull over and explore.

South of Thériso

South of Thériso, spectacularly heady mountain roads skirt the foothills of the White Mountains in two directions. East, you can head through the hamlet of **Dhrakóna**, where there are a couple of excellent places to eat, and then circle back to Haniá or continue east on still narrower byways towards Stýlos (see page 254). To the west you climb over what feels like an impressively lofty ridge to **Zoúrva**, a cluster of whitewashed houses with a lovely taverna and stupendous views over the surrounding valleys, and from there can continue down via Mesklá to the Alikianós road. This route makes a wonderful long **hike**, occasionally traversed by rambling groups but quite possible on your own if you arrange for a taxi pick-up at the other end.

Mesklá

MESKLÁ (**Μεσκλά**) is another beautiful village, set on a swift-flowing brook and surrounded by lush agricultural land and orange groves. Under the Venetians, Mesklá was a place of considerably more importance than it is now, as indicated by the tiny chapel of **Metamórphosis Sotírou** (Transfiguration of the Saviour), which lies at the bottom of the village – cross the bridge and it's signed up a track. The restored, barrel-vaulted church preserves some truly impressive fourteenth-century **frescoes**, many of which have also been restored; there are some particularly striking scenes of the Last Judgement. At the top of the village there's another chapel dedicated to the **Panayía** (next to a large modern church of the same name), which was constructed in the fourteenth century over a fifth-century basilica which had, in its turn, been raised over a Roman temple to Aphrodite.

Alikianós and around

ALIKIANÓS (**Αλικιανός**) is a historically important village astride the main road south into the mountains. Just outside town, which is nowadays bypassed by the main roads, is a junction where you can head directly south towards Omalós and the heart of the mountains, or southwest towards Soúyia and the south coast. Beside this turning there's a large **war memorial**, commemorating local members of the irregular forces that defended this area, known as "Prison Valley", in the Battle of Crete (you can't miss the prison; it's the big white building bristling with aerials). Cut off from any other Allied units – who believed that resistance here collapsed on the first day of the battle – the Greeks fought on even as everyone else was in full retreat. By doing so they prevented the Germans getting around the mountains to cut the road and guaranteed that the evacuation from Hóra Sfakíon could go ahead. In much earlier history, Alikianós was also the site of the wedding massacre that ended the Kandanoleon revolt.

The village itself has a couple of churches worth a look. Follow the lane signed to Koufós and you'll reach the small fourteenth-century church of **Áyios Yeóryios**, on the northern edge of the village, whose frescoes were destroyed during World War II. Continue along the same road, out of the village, for 1km to find **Áyios Ioánnis** (also signed as Zoödóhos Píyi), down a track into orange groves on the right. An impressively large fourteenth-century building on the site of at least two previous churches dating back to the sixth century, the domed church employs parts of the previous basilica in the construction of its apse. Inside, surviving **frescoes** depict the Ascension as well as a number of saints.

Galatás

About 5km out of Hanía on the Alikianós road, a turn-off to the right is signed to the hilltop village of **GALATÁS** (**Γαλατάς**) one of the major battlegrounds in the Battle of Crete, when poorly armed villagers and a contingent of New Zealand soldiers stood

THE KANDANOLEON REVOLT

The village of Mesklá (see page 268) was the centre of one of the great legends of Cretan resistance, the **Kandanoleon revolt**. According to the story (which is certainly not historically accurate, though probably has some basis in fact), much of western Crete rose against the Venetians early in the sixteenth century. They elected as their leader one George Kandanoleon, who established a base in Mesklá and from here ran a rebel administration, controlling much of the west. In order to legitimize his authority, Kandanoleon arranged for his son to marry the daughter of a Venetian aristocrat, Francesco Molini. During the wedding celebrations Kandanoleon and several hundred of his supporters ate and drank themselves into a stupor – at which point, by pre-arranged signal, a Venetian army arrived and captured the Cretans as they slept. Their leaders were hanged at villages around the countryside, and the revolt was over.

You can visit the alleged scene of the massacre in Alikianós. Ask directions to the ruins of the **Da Molini castle**, in an orange grove over the road from the church of Áyios Yeóryios. To reach the castle, with your back to the church gate turn right to a new porticoed building on the left. Follow a narrow alley to the left of this for 50m: the castle ruins lie in an orange grove off to the right. Impressive walls still stand, festooned with weeds, and the overgrown entrance lintel carries the inscription *Omnia Mundi Fumus et Umbra* ("All in the World is Smoke and Shadow"), a sentiment to which the Venetians were particularly attached, and which ultimately turned out to be grimly accurate regarding their Cretan possessions.

between Haniá and the might of the German army. Heroically, and against all odds, they held back the German army for almost a week with huge loss of life. The village today is a pleasant and fair-sized place, with a tiny, one-room **Battle of Crete museum** dedicated to the events of 1941 (usually daily 9am–2pm; free). Sited on the main square, it's basically a collection of rusty guns, helmets, photos and newspaper cuttings, but fascinating nevertheless. Outside is a memorial to those who died here, including 145 New Zealand soldiers. If the museum is closed, enquiries at any of the nearby *kafenía* should soon produce the key (and possibly a guided tour).

The Ayiá Reservoir

On the edge of the village of Ayiá

The **Ayiá Reservoir** is arguably the best **bird-watching** spot on Crete. This marshland is home to a rich variety of species, including crakes, avocet, marsh harrier, spotted flycatcher and squacco heron in season. The kingfishers are a particular delight and not at all put off their diving tricks by human visitors. Terrapins too, are resident here and when not squelching around in the marshy pools they can often be spotted sunning themselves on a raised mud bank. The best sightings should be in the early morning or a couple of hours before dusk, though there's plenty of birdlife year-round, at almost any time of day; binoculars are helpful. There are a number of walkways around the lake, and a couple of upmarket and rather incongruous cafés on the banks. The *Limni* café is signed off the main road, and has a terrace with views over the water, but for the best access to the lake you are better off continuing into the village, where a swan-shaped sign will take you to the *Erasma* café and lakeside walkways.

ARRIVAL AND DEPARTURE — SOUTH OF HANIÁ

By bus Although there are a couple of daily buses from Haniá to Thériso, and a single daily bus to some of the other villages, it's not really practical to explore this area by bus. The one place that has a regular service is Alikianós, with seven buses a day from Haniá (4 at weekends; 20min).

By car There are some lovely drives in this region, and several circular routes; most obviously up to Thériso, returning via Mesklá and Alikianós. From Mesklá there's also a short cut directly up to the Omalós road, for those heading for the mountains.

ACCOMMODATION AND EATING

THÉRISO

Andartis Main street, near the village centre, 28210 78833. Huge taverna set up for feasting, with Cretan dishes including spit-roasted lamb, *sýnglino* (cured pork), *stifádho* and *sfakianó* (lamb casserole). €€

Madares Taverna-Rooms Main street, near the village centre, 28210 92127. These rustic rooms are more like mini-apartments, with beds in a gallery under the eaves, a fireplace as well as a/c (this is also a winter destination, when rooms cost more to cover the cost of firewood), and kitchenette. The speciality in the inexpensive taverna below is tasty charcoal-grilled *arní* (lamb). €

DHRAKÓNA

★ **Dounias** Right at the top of the village, 28210 65083. *Dounias* slow-food taverna is an exceptional place set up by a professional chef who decided to move home to his village. Everything is sourced locally and cooked in the traditional manner on wood-burning stoves or in wood-fired ovens, down to the home-made bread. Don't expect glamour – you eat at rickety wooden tables on an earth-floored outdoor terrace and choose your food from burnt pots in the smoky kitchen – but the daily specials (such as pork with orange, or lentil stew) are authentic, delicious and inexpensive. Best not to come too late as when the food is gone, it's gone. Fabulous views too. €€

ZOÚRVA

Apirathes Houses Centre of the village, https://apirathes-zourva.gr/?lang=en. Impressive traditional-looking modern stone building offering superbly equipped and furnished maisonettes (sleeping 2–6), all with tremendous views. €€

Emilia Entrance to village, 2821 067060. Very appealing, good value taverna with a terrace. Much of the food is home-grown or raised; specials might include *tsigariastó* (goat sautéed in rich sauce) or charcoal-grilled lamb. €

MESKLÁ

Taverna Halaris At the top of the village beyond the modern church, 28210 67480. A fine little taverna in a woodland setting with tables shaded by plane trees. The traditional cooking uses many home-grown ingredients, with specialities including *bouréki*, *stifádho* and – according to proprietor Manolis – the best *païdhákia* in the province. €€

4

Sfakiá and the Lefká Óri

Just a couple of metres short of the highest point of the Psiloritis range, the **Lefká Óri** (White Mountains) are in every other way more impressive mountains: barer, craggier and far less tamed. Along with the coast to the south and east they form the heart of **Sfakiá** – a region that for all its desolation and depopulation is perhaps the most famous, and certainly the most written about, in Crete. It is an area notorious for its fierceness: harsh living conditions, unrelenting weather and warlike people. Historically the region was cut off and barbaric, almost a nation apart which, as occupying armies came and went, carried on with life – feuding, rustling, rearing sheep – pretty much regardless. Many of the great tales of Cretan resistance, of *pallikári* fighters and mountain guerrillas, originate in Sfakiá.

Stealing was a way of life and so was feuding and revenge – with vendettas on a Sicilian scale continuing well into the twentieth century, and occasionally rumoured even now. The Venetians had plans to pacify the region, but their castle on the coast at **Frangokástello** was rarely more than an isolated outpost. The Ottomans did more, imposing taxation for example, but they also provoked more violent reaction, notably in the revolt of Dhaskaloyiannis (see page 282) and many that succeeded it. The mountains were always a safe refuge in which bandits and rebels could conceal themselves while opposing armies took revenge on the lowlands. In World War II Sfakiá resumed this traditional role: when the Germans invaded, King George of Greece was rushed across the island and down the Samariá Gorge to be evacuated, and it was from the region's tiny capital, **Hóra Sfakíon**, that the bulk of the Allied forces were evacuated. Throughout the war, the mountain heights remained the realm of the resistance.

Nowadays all of this seems romantically distant. There are frequent **buses** to Hóra Sfakíon and Omalós and a constant stream of people trekking between the two, but you don't have to get far off this path to realize how the reputation grew, and why it still holds such sway. Anyone who spends any time at all here is eventually taken with the urge to explore, whether it's an arduous mountain trek, or simply getting a boat to a nearby beach. And even now there is just one road into the heart of the area, climbing up to the cold, enclosed plateau of **Omalós** in the heart of the mountains. From here the most spectacular, and spectacularly popular, way to the south coast is on foot, through the great cleft of the **Samariá Gorge**. Famous as it is, this is just the largest of a series of ravines by which streams make their escape to the coast. Far less beaten tracks lead, for example, down the **Ímbros Gorge** towards Hóra Sfakíon, or from **Ayía Iríni** to Soúyia. With more preparation you could also go climbing among the peaks or undertake an expedition right across the range, though bear in mind that this is a genuinely wild mountain zone – venture nowhere alone or without adequate equipment. In the south, the mountains drop steeply to a **coastline** dotted with hard-to-reach **coves and beaches**, with further enticing opportunities to **walk** between them.

The Omalós plateau

From Hanía the road up to Omalós forks at Alikianós (see page 268) and then, beyond the substantial and prosperous village of **FOURNÉS** (**Φουρνές**), begins to climb in earnest to the Lefká Óri through a series of sweeping great loops with increasingly alarming drops. After eighteen steeply ascending kilometres you eventually reach the **Omalós plateau** at more than 1000m elevation – a cold, flat expanse dotted with stunted vegetation, and with the enclosing ring of stone peaks clearly visible all around.

4

Fournés Botanical Park

4km south of Fournés on the Omalós road • Charge • http://botanical-park.com • A couple of buses a day run directly here from Haniá bus station, via Plataniás

When the four Marinakis brothers lost their olive groves in a disastrous fire in 2003, instead of replanting the olives they decided to create a **botanical park** on the land to enable Cretans to understand and learn to care for the natural environment. Making use of the steep site's unique set of microclimates they imported plants and trees from all over the world; there are separate areas for fruits, vegetables, cacti and many more, as well as a lake and mini-zoo. You can race round in as little as an hour, or linger and spend half a day here. There's an excellent **taverna-café** using produce from the gardens, and they also sell honey and other farm goods.

Lákki

LÁKKI (**Λάκκι**), the only village of any size on the climb up towards the plateau, has stupendous views from its leafy churchyard, to the rear of a small platía. A bracingly exposed place, it makes an ideal base for walking in the surrounding hills, especially in spring when wildflowers abound.

Omalós

OMALÓS (**Ομαλός**), at the heart of the Omalós plateau, is largely unaffected by the daily dawn procession in summer when up to fifty buses pass through, transporting walkers from all over the island to the Samariá Gorge entrance. Once the hordes have gone it settles back into the tranquil rustic settlement it remains for most of the year. Walk out into the plain in almost any direction and within five minutes you'll have left all traces of modern life behind, with only the jingling of the occasional goat's bell or the deliberate piling of stones to remind you of human presence. Few people live here year-round: in winter everything is deep in snow and deserted. In spring the land is marshy and waterlogged – almost becoming a lake if there's a sudden melt. Only in summer do most residents move here full-time,

HIKING AROUND OMALÓS

The area around Omalós is excellent for **walking**. The paths into the hills surrounding the plateau (a branch of the E4 Pan-European footpath crosses the southern edge of the village) are strewn with wildflowers in season, birdlife is profuse year-round and temperatures even in high summer are refreshingly cool. Despite this, as so often in places like this in Crete, you'll usually find that most of the excellent, good-value accommodation is empty throughout the season.

The obvious walk from Omalós is to the Samariá Gorge and then down to the coast, but there are dozens of alternatives. If it's the coast you're after, you can also hike **to Soúyia**, starting either from the top of the gorge or from Omalós and descending via the Ayía Iríni Gorge (see page 313) or on a slightly tougher, higher route through Koustoyérako (see page 312). These are alternative branches of the E4, so reasonably well signposted – though take care not to miss the point where you turn off the road. Either route is a full day's walk and both are detailed on the excellent *Anavasi* 1:30,000 Samariá, Soúyia Paleóhora map.

SCALING THE PEAKS

The **Kallergi Refuge** (see page 273) acts as the base for climbing into the highest peaks, and the staff here are the best source of information on doing so. As well as the high-mountain treks from the hut, there are also walks to the west of the Samariá Gorge. Most impressively, you can tackle the climb to the peak of **Mount Gíngilos** (2080m), beginning from the top of the gorge. Its north face, the one everyone sees, is a near-vertical slope of solid rock; round the back, though, you can reach the summit with only a little scrambling. It's hard work and you need confidence with heights, especially if it's windy, but no special mountaineering skills are necessary. A large yellow sign points the way from the back of the *Tourist Lodge* and the path should be easy enough to follow for the two and a half hours to the top. The final ascent is signalled with red paint blobs – stick to the path as there are hidden hazards and even the official route needs hands as well as feet. The rewards are an all-round panorama from the summit and, with luck, the chance to spot some of the rarer animal life that the crowds have driven from the gorge itself.

coming up from Lákki and other villages on the lower slopes to pasture sheep and goats or to cultivate, on a small scale, cereals and potatoes.

ARRIVAL AND DEPARTURE — THE OMALÓS PLATEAU

By bus There are two daily buses from Haniá to the Botanical Park (30min), and two early-morning services (the ones that continue to the gorge) to Omalós (1hr 10min).

ACCOMMODATION AND EATING

FOURNÉS

Botanical Park taverna Entrance to the Botanical Park, 6976 860 573. You don't need to pay the entry fee to visit the Botanical Park's taverna, where much of the food is sourced from the park's plants and the rest is mainly local and organic. Interesting salads, plenty of vegetarian options and excellent fresh lemonade. €€

OMALÓS

Hotel Exari Omalós village, https://exari.gr. Impressive, modern but stone-built hotel offering comfortable balconied rooms with TV and a decent restaurant; breakfast is included. €

Hotel Neos Omalos Omalós village, www.neos-omalos.gr. Perhaps the pick of the hotels in Omalós, and certainly the busiest taverna, this has pleasant balconied rooms with central heating and satellite TV. €

Taverna Xyloskalo Gorge entrance, 28210 67237. Perched above the gorge entrance, with magnificent mountain views from its terrace, this is a good place to take breakfast or lunch before heading down the gorge (though not open for early starters). They also have comfortable modern stone-built apartments, *Samaria Village*, on the road approaching the gorge. €

THE KALLERGI REFUGE

If you are staying on the Omalós plateau for a couple of days a hike to the wonderful **Kallergi Refuge** (www.kalergilodge.gr; charg) is a bracing introduction to the high mountains. Perched high over the eastern edge of the Samariá Gorge at 1680m, it's a fairly easy (if unrelenting) ascent for 5km from the Omalós plain and once you're there makes an excellent base for many other mountain treks.

To get to the hut from Omalós, follow the road towards the gorge entrance for 3km, then turn left onto the dirt track signposted to the hut, a 90min climb (with a 4WD vehicle you can also drive this, along – in the early stages – a badly rutted dirt road); alternatively, from the top of the Samariá Gorge a signed path leads up, also in about 90min. From Kallergi you can peer down into the gorge, looking exceptionally impressive from the isolation of the bare stone peaks up here, a slash of rich green in an otherwise remorseless landscape of grey and brown. On clearer days both the Libyan and Aegean seas can also be seen from the hut, while the nights are spectacular, with the whole dome of the starry heavens arranged above you.

There's usually no problem finding a bed at the refuge (although it's best to ring ahead) and the hut is comfortably equipped with wood-burning stoves and space for 45 people in cosy four-bed dorms or a larger group bunk loft. There's also excellent **food**. With advance warning they can also collect you from the plateau and arrange guided climbs and **hikes**. Walking routes include the 6hr circular waymarked route to **Melindaoú peak** (2133m) via Mount Psarí (1817m), or the 16hr hike to Anópoli via **Mount Páhnes** (at 2453m, just 3m short of Psiloritís for the title of loftiest in Crete: Haniot mountaineers regularly add stones to the cairn on the peak in an attempt to catch up) with an overnight stop at another refuge en route. Both follow the E4 much of the way.

4

The Samariá Gorge

Charge • http://samaria.gr

The one trip that every visitor to Crete – even those eminently unsuited to it – feels compelled to make is the hike down the **SAMARIÁ GORGE** (**Φαράγγι Σαμαριάς**) which, at 16km, is claimed to be the **longest in Europe**. Protected as a National Park since 1962, this natural wonder was formed by a river flowing between Mount Volakiás to the west and the towering bulk of the heart of the Lefká Óri to the east. In summer the violent winter torrent reduces to a meek trickle and this is when the multitudes descend. If you're expecting a wilderness experience, think again; Friday and Saturday are the days attracting fewest visitors. Bear in mind that this is not a gentle stroll to be lightly undertaken; especially in spring when the river is roaring, or on a hot midsummer day, it can be a thoroughly gruelling test of fitness and stamina. The mules and helicopter standing by to rescue the injured are not mere show: anyone who regularly leads tours through the gorge has a stack of horror stories to regale you with – broken legs and heart attacks feature most frequently. To undertake the walk you need to be reasonably fit and/or used to lengthy walks, and you should have walking boots or sturdy trainers that will stand up to hot, sharp rocks – flip-flop wearers need not apply.

The gorge hike itself is some **18km long** (the final 2km to reach the sea from the mouth of the gorge) and the **walk** down takes between four and seven hours, depending on your level of fitness and how often you stop to admire the scenery, bathe your feet and take refreshment. Be wary of the kilometre markers – these mark only distances within the park, not the full extent of the walk.

The Samariá Gorge hike

The gorge begins, with startling suddenness, on the far side of the Omalós plateau. After the dull tranquillity of the plain you are faced with this great cleft opening beneath your feet and, across it – close enough to bounce stones off, it seems – the

FLORA AND FAUNA IN THE SAMARIÁ GORGE

Gorge **wildlife** means most famously the **kri-kri** (variously the *agrimi*, *Capra aegagrus*, the Cretan wild ibex), for whose protection the park was primarily created. You are unlikely to see one of these large, nimble animals with their long backswept horns, though you may well see ordinary mountain goats defying death on the cliff faces. In addition, almost four hundred varieties of **birds** are claimed to have been seen here, including owls, eagles, falcons and vultures; birdwatchers after a coup should look out for the endangered lammergeier (or bearded vulture). On the ground lizards abound, there's also the odd snake and you may just spot a beech marten, spiny mouse or weasel.

The multifarious **trees** – Cretan maple, pine and cypress – provide the backdrop to an often dazzling array of **wildflowers**; the purple *Tulipa saxatilis* and rock plants such as aubretias, saxifrages and anemones stand out, and there are wild irises and orchids too. **Herbs** are also in abundance; besides the aromatic thyme and rosemary, common sage and oregano, there are half a dozen species that exist exclusively here. Also to be found – and usually growing in the most inaccessible places – is **Cretan dittany**, a celebrated medicinal herb referred to by Aristotle and Hippocrates and taken by women in ancient times as a method of abortion.

Two **books** on the gorge can prove useful and are portable enough to take along. *The Samariá Gorge Yesterday and Today* (Toubis, Athens; also from online booksellers) documents the history of the gorge and includes an illustrated guide to its flora and fauna, while *The Gorge of Samariá and its Plants* by Albertis Atonis (Albertis, Iráklio) provides a step-by-step description of the flora. Both are available from bookshops on the island, though the latter is becoming rare.

gaunt limestone face of Mount Gíngilos. The descent starts on the **Xylóskalon** ("wooden stairway"), a stepped path cut from the rock and augmented by log stairs and wooden handrails, which zigzags rapidly down to the base of the gorge, plunging 350m in the first 2km or so of the walk. Near the bottom the chapel of Áyios Nikólaos stands on a little terrace of coniferous trees where there are benches from which to enjoy the view, and fresh water. Beyond, the path begins gradually to level out, following the stream bed amid softer vegetation which reflects the milder climate down here. In late spring it's magnificent, but at any time of year there should be wildflowers and rare plants (no picking allowed), including the endangered large white peony, *Paeonia clusii*. The stream itself is less reliable: there are places where you can be sure of icy fresh water and pools to bathe sore feet all year round (particularly in the middle sections), but what starts in spring as a fierce, even dangerous torrent has dwindled by autumn to a trickle between hot, dry boulders, disappearing beneath the surface for long stretches.

The abandoned hamlet of **Samariá** lies a little under midway through the walk, shortly before the 7km marker. One of the buildings here has been converted to house the wardens' office, another has been pressed into (inadequate) service as a public toilet, but for the most part the remains of the village are quietly crumbling away. Its inhabitants, until they were relocated to make way for the park in 1962, were predominantly members of the Viglis family, who claimed direct descent from one of twelve aristocratic clans implanted locally from Byzantium. Certainly this settlement, as isolated as any in Crete and cut off by floodwater for much of the year, is a very ancient one – the church of **Óssia María**, from which both gorge and village take their name, was founded early in the fourteenth century.

After Samariá the ground is more level, the walls of the gorge begin to close in and the path is often forced to cross from one side of the stream to the other, on **stepping stones** which at times may be submerged and slippery. Beside you, the contorted striations of the cliffs are increasingly spectacular, but the highlight comes shortly after the Hristós resting point with the **Sidherespórtes** (Iron Gates) where two rock walls rise sheer to within a whisker of a thousand feet: standing at the bottom, one can almost touch both at once. For this short stretch, there's a wooden walkway raised above the stream, whose swirling waters fill the whole of the narrow passage. Almost as suddenly as you entered this mighty crack in the mountain you leave it again, the valley broadens, its sides fall away, and you're in a parched wilderness of rubble deposited here by the spring thaw.

Before long you reach the fringes of **Ayía Rouméli**, where there's a gate by which you leave the park and a couple of stalls selling cool drinks at crippling prices. Frustratingly, however, this is not the end of the walk: old Ayía Rouméli has been all but deserted in favour of the new beachside community, a further excruciatingly hot, dull twenty minutes away. A **shuttle bus service** (€1.50) means that you can now avoid this final rather tedious stretch if you wish; the bus drops you in the coastal settlement.

Ascending the gorge

Starting from the bottom, the hike **up the gorge** to **Omalós** is not as hard as some imagine, though it will take rather longer – six to seven hours at a reasonable, steady pace. Few people do it all the way, which means that at the top you may well find the gorge almost empty; on the way up, however, you'll have had to pass the hordes charging down. You could also walk a short way up and come back – an outing offered as a day-trip known as "Samariá the Lazy Way". This will show you the Iron Gates, the most spectacular individual section, but none of the almost alpine scenes nearer the top.

ARRIVAL AND DEPARTURE — THE SAMARIÁ GORGE

4

WITH A TOUR

The vast majority of people who walk through the gorge do so as part of a day-trip: a very early bus to the top, walk down by early afternoon, boat from Ayía Rouméli to Hóra Sfakíon or Soúyia and bus from there back home. Most go with one of the guided tours offered by every travel agent on the island – certainly if you're staying in a hotel anywhere in the east of Crete this is much the simplest method, and probably the only way of doing it in a single day. Most tours will include all bus and ferry connections, but not food or the park entrance fee. They can be very good value, adding only €5–10 to the cost of doing it yourself (from Haniá, the cost of bus, ferry and entry tickets adds up to about €30). If you're planning to stay on the south coast, the tour bus can save you the effort of carrying your bags; simply stow them underneath and retrieve them in Hóra Sfakíon. Do let them know your plan, though, both to guard against an unexpected switch of bus and to prevent search parties being sent out.

BY PUBLIC TRANSPORT

Buses to the gorge from Haniá From Haniá there are departures daily at 7.45am and 8.45am, arriving at the top about 1hr 15min later. You'll normally be sold a return ticket, including the return leg from Hóra Sfakíon (which needn't necessarily be used the same day), so if you don't want this you'll have to make your intentions very clear; the bus station is chaotic when the first buses leave. There's a lot to be said for taking the earlier bus: more of the walk can be completed while it's still relatively cool, there's no need to force your pace, and if you're planning to stop over anywhere at the bottom you've more chance of being among the first to arrive. On the other hand, everyone does this – there's often a procession of as many as four full buses leaving Haniá, there are queues and confusion when you arrive, and you're unlikely to escape from crowds the whole way down. It may be hotter, but it's also quieter if you set out later.

Buses from other destinations The first couple of buses of the day from Iráklio and Réthymno allow you to connect in Haniá for the journey to Omalós. There are also services from Paleóhora (6.15am) and Soúyia (7am); these meet in Ayía Iríni from where one continues to the gorge and the other direct to Haniá, so you may have to change.

Ferries from Ayía Rouméli Having reached the south coast you can continue to walk in either direction, but it's a great deal easier to get around by boat. There's a kiosk selling tickets just above the end of the jetty, in the centre of the village; ferries (http://anendyk.gr) run to Loutró/Hóra Sfakíon (May–Oct at least 3 daily; 40min/1hr) and Soúyia/Paleóhora (May–Oct daily at 5.30pm; 45min/1hr 20min).

Return buses Return bus journeys from Hóra Sfakíon (at 6.30pm) or Soúyia (at 6.15pm) are timed to coincide with the ferries and will wait for them – theoretically, no one gets left behind, but it makes sense to hurry off the ferry and grab a seat.

INDEPENDENT TRAVEL

If you want to see the gorge using your own transport, or while staying in Omalós, it's possible to walk down (the hotels will take you to the gorge entrance for free if you're a guest), take the boat to Soúyia, and then get a taxi back up to Omalós or the gorge parking area from there – Soúyia taxis generally charge about €60 for this; there should also be an evening bus from Soúyia to Omalós, but check the schedule. Should you plan to stay longer on the coast, the Omalós hotels can also (by prior arrangement and for a fee) put your luggage on the morning ferry in Soúyia, so that it's waiting for you at the bottom of the gorge.

Ayía Rouméli

For most people **AYÍA ROUMÉLI** (**Αγία Ρουμέλη**) is nothing more than the end of the Samariá Gorge walk, a place to eat and drink your fill, then rest up on the beach before leaving on one of the afternoon ferries. If you have walked here, the place at first has an almost mirage-like quality, where you face an agonizing choice between plunging into the sea or diving into a taverna for an iced drink, likely to live in the memory as the most refreshing ever. Once your senses adjust, you'll find that the village isn't all that appealing, but while it's far from the most attractive place on this coast, it is wonderfully peaceful at night, and locals are making strenuous efforts to develop alternative attractions to persuade people to stay longer. Most obviously this involves other **hikes** – there are smaller but more challenging gorges to both east and west, as well as coastal paths to various beaches – but there are also

4

SAMARIÁ GORGE PRACTICALITIES

Be aware that the gorge is **regularly closed** for safety reasons; generally in spring and autumn if there's a risk of flash floods, or in extremely hot weather in mid-summer. If in any doubt check in advance to save a wasted journey.

PARK REGULATIONS

There is a whole series of national park **rules** (posted at the entrance), of which the most important are: no camping, no fires (or smoking outside the designated areas), no alcohol, no hunting and no interfering with the wildlife or collecting plants. Wardens patrol to ensure these rules are obeyed, that no one wanders too far from the main path, and that no stragglers are overtaken by nightfall. At the entrance, you'll be given a **date-stamped ticket** in return for your entrance fee, which you should hand in at the gate when you leave; this, too, is partly to check that nobody is lost inside, and partly to make sure no one tries camping.

SUPPLIES

Carry the minimum possible. A **water bottle** is essential (there are springs at regular intervals and ice-cold water in the stream, but for long periods you'll find neither – especially over the last, hottest hour) and something to munch on the way definitely worthwhile, as is some means of carrying clothes you discard en route (7am at the top feels close to freezing; 1pm at the bottom may hover around 38°C/100°F).

FACILITIES

Near the gorge entrance there's a **café** and stalls for hot drinks, bottled water and snacks (all open early), as well as the *Taverna Xyloskalo* (see page 272), while Ayía Rouméli is more than equipped to feed everyone arriving at the bottom; there are **toilets** at regular intervals along the walk. The nearest **bed** you can get to the entrance is in Omalós (see page 271) or at the excellent *Kallergi Refuge* (see page 273). Even here you'd have to be up early to steal a march on the first arrivals from Haniá. Nonetheless, it does make quite a change to stay up here and freeze for a night, and of course it gives you the opportunity to explore more than just the gorge. Staying on the south coast for a night or more after your exertions makes more sense: in addition to Ayía Rouméli, there are rooms at Loutró (see page 277) and Hóra Sfakíon (see page 284) or westwards in Soúyia (see page 311) and Paleóhora (see page 305).

boat trips and kayaks for hire. You can find details of many of these, and a walking map, at the *Calypso* taverna.

There was an ancient settlement on this site – **Tarra**, inhabited probably from the fifth century BC through to the fifth AD – and more or less constant later habitation, though very little remains to be seen. Tarra straddled the stream where it ran into the sea, just to the east of the present village – the only obvious remains are the foundations of an early Christian basilica by the present **church of Panayía**, around which you may also spot a few tiny fragments of mosaic. This, supposedly, was the site of a much earlier temple of Apollo.

ARRIVAL AND DEPARTURE — AYÍA ROUMÉLI

By ferry Ferries run east to Loutró and Hóra Sfakíon (May–Oct 3 daily; 40min/1hr) and west to Soúyia and Paleóhora (May–Oct daily at 5.30pm; 45min/1hr 20min). There are also a few weekly departures to Gávdhos (July–Aug–Oct Thur, Fri, Sat, Sun morning, Mon & Wed 10.30am, less ofen spring/autumn; 3hr). A kiosk selling tickets is just above the end of the jetty, in the centre of the village; timetables at https://anendyk.gr.

On foot The majority of people who get to Ayía Rouméli have done so on foot, down the Samariá Gorge. You can also get here, or leave, along the coastal path, part of the E4. East to Loutró or Anópoli is challenging but relatively straightforward (see page 280); west to Soúyia is a very tough two-day hike – don't attempt it without checking conditions locally, as the route can be blocked by rockfalls.

ACCOMMODATION AND EATING

There are often people camping on the beach east of the village, where there are showers and toilets, or in the caves nearby. The bigger beachfront tavernas often offer free loungers to clients, and a couple have bars on the beach, but these tend to be packed with huge tour groups.

Hotel Calypso Western side of the village, not far from the jetty, http://calypso.agiaroumeli.gr. Friendly, family-run taverna with rooms. The taverna has good fresh seafood from their own boat as well as local goat and all the usuals. They rent kayaks on the beach and have a wall map of local kayaking and walking routes. The comfortable rooms have fridge, balcony and sea view. €

Pachnes Bed & Breakfast 200m inland, off the path from the gorge, http://pachnes.gr. Great value, rustically furnished rooms in a quiet position just outside the main village, popular with serious hikers – they can advise on local walks and exploration. Breakfast included. €

Taverna Tarra Seafront by the jetty, 28250 91231. Some of the best views in town from both the taverna and rooms upstairs above, situated directly above the water. Fine local meat dishes, such as lamb in the oven, and home-grown veg. The rooms are simple, but more than adequate. €

4

Loutró and around

Of all the south coast villages, **LOUTRÓ** (**Λουτρό**) perhaps best sums up what this coast ought to be all about. It's a soporific place, where there's nothing to do but eat, drink and laze – and where you fast lose any desire to do anything else. There are few facilities and no ATM, so you should bring sufficient cash to see you through your stay (though at a pinch your hotel or rooms place may change money). The big excitements of the day are the occasional arrivals and departures of the ferries. Little happens all summer long to interrupt this easy-going idyll, but if you're here for the great **feast of the Panayía** on August 15 the small church is the place to head for. From early dawn the formidable local priest conducts the service, which lasts until after midday. The small churchyard then fills up with all those who had intended to come earlier – and each of whom receives a disapproving glare from the *papás* – as biblical quantities of *arní*, *psomí* and *krasí* (lamb, bread and wine) are doled out and everyone enjoys a great feast.

The waterfront

The short **waterfront** arching around a beautiful little bay consists of a row of perhaps a dozen tavernas and cafés and a similar number of rooms places and small hotels; the mountains rise immediately behind. There's no road in – everyone here has either come on the boat or walked, which helps to keep things very low-key, prices reasonable, big groups rare and the people genuinely friendly. Although the transparent blue water is always inviting, perhaps Loutró's main drawback is its lack of a real **beach**. There's an overcrowded stretch of pebbles in front of the tavernas and a much smaller, more private beach immediately beyond the last of the buildings. But the sheltered bay is otherwise ideal for **swimming**, clear and warm, and people bask nude on the rocks around the point, far enough out to avoid offence. Other excellent beaches are within walking distance, with small boats or rented canoes ferrying visitors to the best, at **Sweetwater** to the east, and **Mármara** to the west (see page 279).

Sweetwater Beach

East of Loutró, **Sweetwater Beach** lies in the middle of a barren coastline, approximately halfway to Hóra Sfakíon. From the sea, as you pass on one of the coastal boats, it appears as a long, extremely narrow slice of grey between sheer ochre cliffs and a dark, deep sea. Closer up, the beach seems much larger, but there's still a frightening sense of being isolated between unscaleable mountains and an endless stretch of water.

The beach takes its name from the small springs that bubble up beneath the pebbles to provide fresh, cool drinking water. You can dig a hole almost anywhere to find water, but take care not to pollute the groundwater with soap. Daily boat services bring in quite a few people, but so far these have not spoilt the place – the beach is easily big enough to absorb everyone – and the nudist campers who once had Sweetwater practically to themselves remain, doing a good job of keeping things pristine: signs warn against leaving rubbish, and people domake an effort to pick up any junk that is left behind.

The long-term residents (including local goats) tend to monopolize the only shade, in the **caves** at the back of the beach, but you can always escape the sun at the small **bar-taverna**, which also rents out sun umbrellas.

Fínix

In the beautiful little bay immediately west of Loutró stood **ancient Fínikas**, now known as **Fínix** or Phoenix. This was a major town during the Roman and Byzantine periods, and a significant port long after that: it was the harbour at Fínix, a more comfortable place to wait out the winter storms than Kalí Liménes, which St Paul's ship was hoping to reach when it was swept away. A local story has the saint actually landing here and being beaten up by the locals he tried to convert. Today there is very little to be seen and, with nothing beyond a popular taverna and a small rooms place, it's hard to believe there could ever have been a population of any size here. Up on the headland, though, there's certainly evidence of later occupation, principally in the form of the **Venetian fortification** on the point. Nearby are traces of a Byzantine basilica and other scattered remains.

Lýkkos

West of Fínix, the path continues over cliffs to another, much longer bay, **Lýkkos**. Again there's very little here beyond a couple of very simple **taverna-rooms** places,

HIKING IN SFÁKIA

Sfákia can boast some of the finest walking country in Crete. Along the **coast**, a series of paths link Ayía Rouméli in the west with Hóra Sfakíon in the east; **Loutró**, accessible only on foot or by boat, lies close to the heart of this network. **Inland**, ancient paths and trails survive to give a variety of marvellous hikes, even the easiest of which can be demanding in the heat of high summer. You'll need, at the very least, decent boots or shoes to cope with rough, rocky terrain and a water bottle, which you should fill at every opportunity. You should also have a companion, since some of these paths are pretty isolated, and outside help cannot be relied upon.

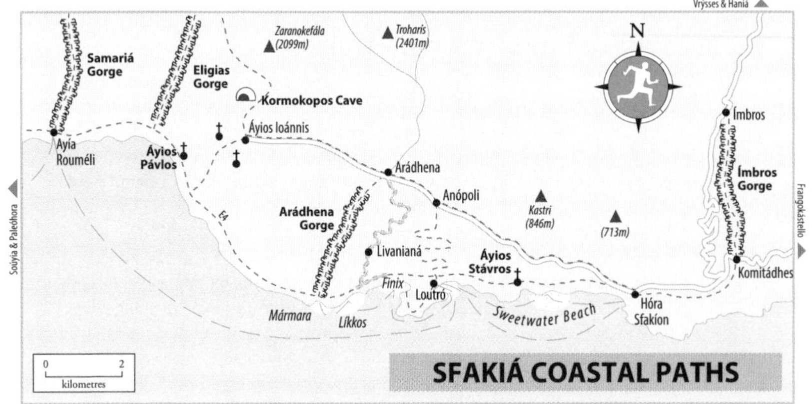

and far fewer people get this far, making it an escapist's paradise. One thing that is in bountiful supply is fresh, cool spring water, proudly served up (often with a home-made *rakí*) in the tavernas. The **beach** itself is rocks and pebbles, awkward to swim from unless you wear shoes, but with plenty of room to spread out. Behind, you can look up and see the village of Livanianá, perched on the eastern flank of the Arádhena Gorge (see page 283); there's a rough dirt road down from there, a scary drive, but one which any vehicle should be able to manage, with care.

4

Mármara Beach

The Arádhena Gorge (see page 283) emerges at the sea in the next bay west of **Lýkkos, MÁRMARA BEACH (Μάρμαρα)**, which takes its name from marble deposits visible near the jetty where you land. The small cove, with a sandy beach surrounded by interesting rock formations full of caves and slabs to dive from or sunbathe on, can get uncomfortably busy in summer, what with boats from Loutró and people walking down the gorge, but even when busy it's charming, with a simple **taverna-rooms place** to give the place focus, as well as providing sun umbrellas, loungers and tempting cool drinks.

ARRIVAL AND GETTING AROUND — LOUTRÓ AND AROUND

LOUTRÓ

By boat Ferry tickets are sold from a kiosk behind the dock at the western end of the seafront, which opens only for a few minutes before each departure. The timetable is seasonal, so check locally or online (http://anendyk.gr), but from May to October there are generally 6 daily departures to Hóra Sfakíon (20min) and 3 to Ayía Roúmeli (35min). In July/Aug there are also three crossings a week to Gávdhos (see page 314), taking 3hr. A taxi-boat to/from Hóra Sfakíon costs around €35 and can be arranged by any of the seafront tavernas in either village.

SWEETWATER BEACH

By boat Boats from Loutró and Hóra Sfakíon arrive once in the morning and again at 5pm; more frequently in peak season. A taxi-boat (one way) from Loutró costs around €15. Kayaking to the beach is also possible.

On foot It's a very hot and shadeless 45min walk from Loutró, an hour from Hóra Sfakíon – boats back to each leave at 5.30pm in summer. In Loutró the path runs behind the houses – climb the hill to find it.

FÍNIX

By boat A taxi-boat from Loutró will cost about €10 one way (look for signs, or ask at local tavernas), or you can kayak around to it. The boat from the *Old Phoenix* (see page 281) regularly collects groups for lunch, so you may be able to hitch a ride with them.

On foot To walk to Fínix by the most direct route, join the well-signed path – part of the E4 – that runs behind Loutró (head up behind the beachside kiosk, past *Taverna Stratis*). This will lead you straight up, past the castle and directly over the headland, in around 20min. It's also possible to get there by walking out past the last house in Loutró and

WALKING THE COASTAL PATH FROM LOUTRÓ

The **coastal path** – now part of the E4 Pan-European Footpath – is the most obvious hike from Loutró, the most frequently used by tourists and, in terms of not getting lost, the simplest to follow. There's not a great deal to see en route, however, nor is it an easy walk – the path is often frighteningly narrow and uneven as it clings to the cliff face, and in summer it is very, very hot, offering no shelter at all from the sun. In Loutró the path runs inland, behind most of the houses; to find it, climb up until you see the signs.

LOUTRÓ TO HÓRA SFAKÍON

Heading east from **Loutró to Hóra Sfakíon** is barely a problem: it's the most heavily travelled part, the whole walk takes less than two hours (8km), and there's a rest stop at Sweetwater Beach (see page 278) halfway. Loutró to Sweetwater is straightforward and fairly well trodden; beyond here the path clambers over a massive rockfall and then follows the cliffs until it eventually emerges on the Hóra Sfakíon–Anópoli road about thirty minutes' walk above Hóra. This is easy to find from the other direction too, the pathleaving the road to the left at the first hairpin bend.

LOUTRÓ TO AYÍA ROUMÉLI

Heading west, **Loutró to Ayía Rouméli** is an altogether tougher proposition. You can expect to be walking for at least four hours solid, a real sweat in high summer, and after the tavernas at **Lýkkos** and Mármara the only chance of refreshment is at Áyios Pávlos. After Mármara you climb again to track along the exposed cliff face for around an hour before reaching the first sign of civilization, a solitary cottage and a few trees. In about another hour, you'll arrive at the eleventh-century cruciform chapel of **Áyios Pávlos**, yet another site where St Paul is supposed to have landed. Here he allegedly christened locals in a spring close to the church (now only a trickle). The chapel itself is ancient and rather beautiful, set on a ledge above the water, and surrounded by dunes; inside are fresco fragments dated to the thirteenth century. You could cool off in the sea here before setting out on the final hour to Ayía Rouméli, and there is a simple **taverna** (June–Sept only), which also rents out tents for nearby camping.

Returning from Ayía Rouméli this path is well marked, heading east out of the village. Ten to fifteen minutes after Áyios Pávlos it splits, heading left to climb inland to Áyios Ioánnis and Anópoli, or right to continue along the coast to Mármara.

simply following the rocky coast around. This is twice as far but it does pass plenty of good rocks to swim from, and extensive remains of old buildings which you can imagine are, and may indeed be, ancient Fínikas.

By car It's just about possible to drive here, on a hair-raising barrierless dirt road that descends via Livanianá and Lýkkos .

LÝKKOS

By boat A taxi-boat from Loútro will cost about €15, or you may get a better deal by calling one of the íýkkos tavernas, assuming you plan to eat there.

On foot From Fínix the path heads up and over the headland to Lýkkos in about 20 minutes.

MÁRMARA BEACH

By boat A boat runs between Loutró and Mármara twice a day in summer; if you walk there, the return is at 5pm. A taxi-boat (one way) to or from Loutró costs around €15.

On foot From Lýkkos to Mármara takes around 25 minutes, a steep and occasionally scary clamber over the rocks and close to the cliff edge.

ACTIVITIES

Boat trips Small boats depart from Loutró's jetty daily at 11am (after the arrival of the ferry) to Sweetwater and Mármara beaches, returning at 5pm.

Kayak and boat rental You can rent kayaks in Loutró for expeditions to the nearby coves and beaches, and there are also pedalos (which can't leave the bay) and motor boats for hire. Taxi-boat numbers are widely advertised, or ask at the tavernas.

ACCOMMODATION

There's a huge amount of choice in Loutró, where the vast majority of the rooms are simple and traditional; a sea view is the one significant difference. The quietest places are generally the furthest round to the east, but nowhere is exactly loud or stays open late. If you're staying anywhere outside Loutró, the proprietors will pick you up by boat if you let them know when you're arriving. Almost everything here closes from November to March.

LOUTRÓ

★**Blue House** 2825 091035 One of the original places here, and still one of the friendliest and best. Good-value sea-view rooms with fridge and TV, plus superior rooms in a wonderful (more expensive) top-floor extension. €

Hotel Porto Loutro In the middle of the village above the beach, http://hotelportoloutro.com. Run by Anglo-Greek proprietors, this hotel – one of the few with any pretensions at all – is a lovely place whose white cubes fit in surprisingly well with the surroundings; as the rooms are pretty accurate reproductions of a simple Greek room you may question whether it's worth paying the extra. Breakfast included. €€

★**Nikolas** Eastern end of the seafront, 28250 91352. Virtually the last building in Loutró and probably the quietest you'll find; simple but comfortable rooms all with fridge and most with great views. Top-floor rooms cost more but are bigger, with large balconies and even finer views. €

Protopapas Inland, eastern end behind Taverna Limani, 28250 91400. Simple, good-sized rooms with fridge, some triples and quads; it's not right on the water, which keeps the prices down, and often has vacancies when others are full. Partial sea views from some rooms. €

★**Villa Niki** High above the centre of the village, http://loutro-accommodation.com. The classiest accommodation in town, with a beautiful three-bedroom apartment (the "villa") and some rather simpler two-bedroom apartments and studios. The smallest studios have no view. Studios and apartments €, villa €€

FÍNIX

Finikas Resort www.finikas-resort.net. Very simple rooms with fan and fridge, but an absolutely lovely, tranquil location on the side of the bay, not too close to the sometimes crowded *Old Phoenix*. €

LÝKKOS

★**Akrogiali** http://akrogiali-lykos.gr. For an absolute away-from-it-all experience you'd struggle to find a quieter spot than Lýkkos, and these are the more comfortable rooms here, purpose-built, with sea-view balconies. Also, great food and an enthusiastic welcome. €

Small Paradise http://thesmallparadise.com. Run by a friendly Irish-Cretan couple, *Small Paradise* offers simple balcony rooms above an excellent taverna with wood-burning oven. Only a couple of rooms have air/con. €

MÁRMARA BEACH

Chrisostomos https://chrisostomos.gr/en/. Simple cabins on the headland above the beach, with a generator providing power for lighting, water and fans. There's also an excellent affiliated taverna. €

4

EATING AND DRINKING

LOUTRÓ

Blue House Central seafront, 28250 91035. Arguably the best traditional taverna in Loutró, serving an array of Cretan specialities, plus fresh fish and plenty of vegetarian options; the owners, brothers Vangelis and Yiorgos, are among the village's friendliest characters. €€

Café Bistro Seafront at the western end of Loutró, beneath Sifis hotel, 28250 91346. Monopolizing most of the waterfront near the jetty, *Café Bistro* (aka *Christina's*), serves breakfast, juices and coffee, and beer and cocktails in the evening. Busy throughout the day. €

Ilios Eastern end of the seafront, 28250 91160. Good fresh fish caught from their own boat (priced per kilo) as well as a range of taverna standards served on a waterfront terrace. It's also a good breakfast stop, with overhead fans keeping temperatures down. €€

Notos Central seafront, 6932 490 907. Excellent range of mezédhes including plenty of vegetarian possibilities, plus some more unusual mains such as shrimp curry or chicken in mustard sauce, served on an attractive raised terrace. €€

Oasis Above the east end of town, where the E4 path arrives, 28250 91017. Pretty rooftop bar/café with fine views, which can be breezy when the waterfront is baking. They lure in walkers with chilled fresh lemonade. €

Stratis Inland from the centre of the seafront, 28250 91348. Superb charcoal-grilled meats from the mountains (go for whatever is on the outdoor grill), as well as traditional specialities including snails. €

FÍNIX

Old Phoenix 28250 91257, https://old-phoenix.com. Big hotel-taverna that can be too popular for its own good – there are often large tour groups shipped in, and the place can barely cope. At quiet times, though, it's lovely, with a shaded waterfront terrace serving fine traditional Greek food. €€

LÝKKOS

★**Akrogiali** 28250 91446. Shaded seafront terrace where excellent traditional Cretan food (daily specials such as meatballs in tomato sauce or oven-baked chicken with potatoes and vegetables) is washed down by jugs of fresh spring water (though there's plenty of good house wine and *rakí* too). €

Anópoli and around

ANÓPOLI (Ανώπολη), high above Loutró, is a quiet country village dominating a small upland plain with a few vestiges of rare forest. If you're hiking for its own sake, or for that matter if you want to take the easiest route from Ayía Rouméli to Hóra Sfakíon without necessarily calling at Loutró, then the inland trails centring on Anópoli have a great deal to be said for them: it also makes a good base for an exploration of the **Arádhena Gorge** and for walks into the heart of the White Mountains. The village itself, which straggles for some distance along the road, is a wonderful location to sample the simple delights of rural Crete, and except at the busiest local holiday periods you should have no problem finding somewhere to stay, away from the hustle of the coast.

Arádhena

West of Anópoli, a paved road continues northwest to the effectively abandoned hamlet of **ARÁDHENA (Αράδαινα)**, some 3km away. This also makes a pleasant forty-minute walk, with plenty of obvious short cuts close to the little-travelled road. With the coming of the paved road, one or two people have moved back and started to restore some of the settlement's crumbling buildings.

The bridge

4

The first thing to grab your attention in Arádhena is a steel **bridge** across a dramatic gorge – a remarkable construction, all the more so when you discover that it's a bridge to nowhere, as the road on the far side soon peters out at nearby Áyios Ioánnis (see page 283). Built in 1986 by the local Vardinoyiannis family, controllers of an international business empire, the bridge was a gift to provide a lifeline to the outside world without which their home village, Áyios Ioánnis, would probably have died out. Rumble across it in a car and the terrifying crack of the wooden boards against metal thunders around the gorge below. The **views** from the bridge down into the gorge – one of Crete's most precipitous – are vertiginously spectacular, and you can even take a **bungee jump** (charge, www.bungy.gr), plunging 138m into the ravine.

Mihaíl Arhángelos

Right on the rim of the Arádhena Gorge • The church is locked following a number of thefts; ask about access at the *kantína* at the bridge's northern end

The romantically picturesque Byzantine church of **Mihaíl Arhángelos**, with its curious "pepper-pot" dome, stands proud above the gorge with the Lefká Óri's heights as a backdrop. The white-walled church dates from the fourteenth or fifteenth century and was constructed on the ruins of a much earlier basilica. Inside, outstanding **frescoes** depict the life and crucifixion of Christ as well as the church's patron archangel. Scattered round about, beyond the nearly deserted village, are a few traces of ancient

DHASKALOYIANNIS

Anópoli was the home of the first of the great Cretan rebels against the Ottomans, **Dhaskaloyiannis** – the subject of a celebrated epic ballad. To cut a very long story extremely short, Dhaskaloyiannis, a wealthy ship-owner, was promised support by Russian agents if he raised a rebellion in Sfakiá, support which in the event never materialized. (The Russians hoped only to divert attention from their campaigns against the Ottoman Empire elsewhere.) The revolt, in 1770, was short-lived and disastrous for Sfakiá, which for the first time was brought well and truly under the Otttoman heel. Dhaskaloyiannis went to the Turks in an attempt to negotiate acceptable surrender terms; instead the Ottoman authorities seized him and took him to Iráklio, where he was publicly tortured, skinned alive and executed. There's a statue honouring him in the square at Anópoli.

LOUTRÓ TO THE ARÁDHENA GORGE: THE CIRCUIT

The **circuit from Loutró**, up to Anópoli, through the gorge and down to Mármara beach (see page 279), from where you can get a boat back to Loutró, is about 11km in total and will realistically take at least 6hr; significantly more if you make many stops along the way. Add an extra 3km (or 1hr 30min) if you walk back to Loutró from Mármara. You can cut out the hardest part (the initial climb), by taking a boat to Hóra Sfakíon and a taxi from there to Anópoli or Arádhena. A shorter but less spectacular route from Loutró would be to head out past Fínix and follow the road to Livanianá, clearly visible above you; from there a path descends into the lower reaches of the gorge.

The start of the **descent** into the gorge at Arádhena is not obvious: you need to turn right off the road just after you catch your first glimpse of the bridge, about 200m before the turn-off to Livanianá, following a narrow trail below a pine coppice. This will lead you to the unmistakable monopáti, the ancient stone path down to the bottom (this side should be used rather than the track on the far side, which is in much worse condition). The impressive stepped stone path and the relatively flat section as you head under the bridge conspire to lull you into a false sense of security: as it gets steeper further down, you find yourself jumping from rock to rock or taking narrow steps around dry cascades. Look out as you go for the paint marks indicating the route – these often seem to take you over unnecessarily tricky terrain, but you usually discover the reason further on when you reach an impassable portion. Fill up with water at every opportunity, as there's none towards the end of the gorge.

Araden, a still unexcavated Greco-Roman town from whose stones the church is said to have been built.

The Arádhena Gorge

Standing on the Arádhena bridge you can see the old path, negotiable only on foot or by pack animals, zigzagging down to the bottom of the **ARÁDHENA GORGE** and back up the other side. For well over two millennia this was the only way across the gorge, and it's still the path you take to follow the gorge down to the sea, a walk of around two and a half hours. This is a superb hike, and though it has been tamed in recent years and is fairly well trodden, it's still reasonably tough, with steep staircases and scrambles over rocks in places. Parts can be scary too, not helped by the ominous presence of picked-clean skeletons of goats, which presumably have either fallen from the top or been washed away in spring floods. The sense of achievement, however, is immense, and the gorge, though far smaller than that of Samariá, is in physical terms almost as impressive. There isn't much in the way of wildlife, but the rocky riverbed is forced into an extremely narrow gap between sheer walls almost all the way down – and there'll be hardly anyone else around.

Livanianá

Just before the bridge in Arádhena, a signed, mostly asphalted road on the left heads for **LIVANIANÁ** (**Λιβανιανά**), a hamlet perched above the lower reaches of the Arádhena Gorge, some 4km away. There are a few potholed patches, but the road is easily driveable as far as Livanianá. Beyond, a rough dirt road continues to Líkkos (see page 278) and Fínix (see page 278). In the village there's a path (signed "Mármara") down into the gorge. It starts beyond a gate just above the church and emerges fairly near the bottom of the gorge, having bypassed all the hardest bits. The red markings show you the best path down and you'll reach the beach after about 45 minutes.

Áyios Ioánnis

Beyond Arádhena, the paved road from the bridge climbs westward for about an hour on foot (5km) to **ÁYIOS IOÁNNIS** (**Άγιος Ιωάννης**), beneath the massed peaks of Páhnes,

Troharís and Zaranokefála. The village has a good rooms place, the *Alonia* hostel, and a couple of **Byzantine churches** with fourteenth-century frescoes; enquire at the hostel (see page 284) for information on getting in. There are also several impressively large **caves** nearby: a signed track leads up to the Kormokopos Cave, about an hour's climb above the village.

The onward path to Ayía Rouméli (see page 276) is also signposted, at least initially, though it becomes hard to follow for a while until it emerges on top of the cliffs. From here it loops down as a rough but obvious path to join the coastal trail before the chapel of **Áyios Pávlos**. You should be able to complete the approximately 17km walk from Anópoli to Ayía Rouméli in about four hours, though with rest stops and wrong turnings it could well take much longer; leave plenty of leeway if you need to catch a boat back. If you are undertaking this walk in reverse, start early so as to complete the climb of the cliffs before it gets too hot.

ARRIVAL, DEPARTURE AND EXCURSIONS — ANÓPOLI AND AROUND

By bus Buses head from Hóra Sfakíon to Anópoli (15min) and Arádhena (25min) daily at 9am and 2.30pm in summer.

On foot from Hóra Sfakíon There's a good road from Hóra Sfakíon to Anópoli, 12km away, but it's still a very steep climb; having to follow the road means it's not a very attractive walk, but there's no real alternative.

On foot from Loutró The climb up from Loutró looks terrifying – you can see the path tracking back and forth across an almost vertical cliff – but is not as bad as it appears, though it will take about 2hr, climbing steeply most of the way. This is best done very early, before the sun gets too hot. The path diverges from the coastal route immediately outside Loutró, by the gate at the edge of the village; near the top the old path has been disrupted by fencing and a farmers' track – the easiest course is to follow the latter to the paved road (the Hóra Sfakíon–Anópoli road), and turn left on that into the village. If you continue to climb you'll go right over the top of the ridge and into Anópoli from above.

By taxi A taxi from Hóra Sfakíon to Anópoli will cost around €25.

Tours From Taverna/Rooms Anopoli they offer four-wheel drive excursions into the mountains; they can take you about an hour up dirt tracks towards Páhnes, for example, leaving about two hours' climb to the peak.

4

ACCOMMODATION AND EATING

ANÓPOLI

Anopoli Main road, about 100m west of the square, https://www.anopolirooms.gr/en/rooms.html. Taverna with rooms serving excellent, inexpensive home-cooked food. Rooms are simple but modern and comfortable and management also offer mountain excursions. €

Taverna Plátanos On the main square, https://anopoli-sfakia.com. You'll get a warm Sfakiá welcome here, along with comfortable rooms offering heating, fridge and a wonderful mountain view. The busy taverna below, serving excellent breakfasts and hearty local food, is right at the heart of village life. €

Xenonas Main road, east of the square, http://xenonas-anopoli.gr. Very pleasant purpose-built modern studios and apartments, all with kitchen, heating and TV. The same family runs the superb bakery nearby (enquire there if there's no one around) – try their sweet sesame bread or Sfakian pie topped with honey. €

LIVANIANÁ

Taverna Livanianá Centre of village. The old village taverna reopened after years of closure; the German owner has great plans, but in the early days just cold drinks and snacks are available. There are lovely views, though, and it's a welcome break for hikers. €

ÁYIOS IOÁNNIS

★ **Alonia Mountain Hostel** Turn left as you enter the village, then left again, https://www.alonia.gr. Appealing mountain hostel with an "end of the world" feel, bigger than it first appears – it's tricky to find, so you may need to ask. The stone-built, two- and three-bed rooms are simply furnished with wood-burning stoves and rustic wooden furniture handmade by the talented owner, who is also a great source of information on local walking and climbing spots. €

Hóra Sfakíon

Squeezed between the sea and the mountains, **HÓRA SFAKÍON** (**Χώρα Σφακίων**) – often known simply as Hóra, meaning "chief town" – couldn't grow even if it wanted to.

Nevertheless it's a surprise to find the capital of Sfakiá quite so small. It is, though, a thoroughly commercial place: there's a post office and a couple of ATMs on the main square; restaurants cram the seafront promenade; and half the houses in town seem to display a large "Rooms" sign. That said, it's inexpensive and pleasant, relatively quiet by the end of the day, and a good base for local hikes and boat trips. The **beach** facing the harbour in front of town is rather pebbly; there's better swimming at Vríssi beach, just round the corner to the west.

There are just two pedestrian streets leading into town off the square: one along the waterfront, with an unbroken row of tavernas leading round to the old fishing harbour, the other just inland, lined with shops and rooms places. In the other direction from the square, more restaurants and snack bars line the road to the ferry jetty and the new harbour. For all the town's and region's history there's not a lot to show; several ancient-looking but locked **churches**, a **war memorial** on the eastern side of the bay commemorating the evacuation of some ten thousand Allied troops in 1941, and the **Cave of Dhaskaloyiannis**, one of several large caves in the cliffs west of Hóra. Always a hideout in times of trouble, this was where the rebel leader (see page 282) set up a mint to produce revolutionary coinage.

ARRIVAL AND DEPARTURE — HÓRA SFAKÍON

By car The road into Hóra Sfakíon ends at a small square just above the water. You have to pay to park here (€1/hr or €3/day), or anywhere on the road down towards the new harbour. You can park for free higher up, most obviously at the beginning of the Anópoli road; if you're staying, your hotel should also be able to find you a free space.

By bus Buses stop immediately above the square and there's a ticket booth on the square, which should be open before departures. Anyone who has walked the gorge and already has a ticket should get on the bus and secure a seat; the last bus waits for the evening ferry.

Destinations Anópoli and Arádhena (summer daily at 9am & 2.30pm; 15min/25min); Frangokástello (2 daily; 30min); Haniá (4 daily; 1hr 30min).

By ferry and boat Large ferries generally leave from the concrete jetty on the east side of the harbour, not far from the square; smaller vessels (including the *Neptune* to Loutró, operated by the Anendyk ferry company) and taxi-boats go from the new harbour beyond, a good ten-minute walk from most hotels, so leave plenty of time (the big ferries may also operate from here in poor weather). The Anendyk ticket booth at the top of the jetty opens about 1hr before departure; schedules are posted but are highly seasonal, so check in advance (28250 91221, http://anendyk.gr; summer schedules are quoted below, there are more at peak times and a reduced service runs year-round). Early departures generally wait for the arrival of the first bus from Haniá. Taxi boats and day-trips have ticket booths at the new harbour, and advertise widely in town; these include Gavdos Cruises, operating a fast boat to Gavdos (6981 920 076, https://gavdos-cruises.jimdofree.com).

Destinations Loutró (May–Oct at least 5 daily; 20 min) Ayía Rouméli (May–Oct 3 daily; 1hr); Gávdhos (June & Sept Tues & Fri 10.30am, July & Aug Tues, Fri & Sun 8.30am; 2hr 30min. Also morning departures with Gavdos Cruises 5 times weekly May–Oct); Sweetwater Beach (summer daily 10.15am, after the bus arrives; return 5.30pm).

By taxi There's a taxi office on the main square, also good for long-distance transfers (28250 91269, http://taxi-sfakia.com).

INFORMATION AND ACTIVITIES

Tourist information The bus ticket kiosk on the main square (erratic hours) can also provide information on ferries (but not tickets) and taxi-boats along with general information about the town and surroundings.

Travel agencies Sfakiá Tours (April–Sept daily 9am–10pm; 28250 91272, www.sfakia-tours.com), on the main square, is a useful source of local information, offering car rental and help with finding accommodation.

Diving Notos Mare is a good dive place at the new harbour (28210 08536, https://notosmare.com). They also run boat trips and a 24hr taxi-boat service.

Kayaking There's kayak rental on Vríssi beach (6972 690 139).

ACCOMMODATION

Hotel Stavris Follow the inland street around, or climb the steps behind the waterfront tavernas, https://stavris.com. A variety of rooms and studios, all with balconies, increasing in price as you add a/c, kitchenette, or sea views. The Perrakis brothers, who own and run the place, have more rooms elsewhere in town, and at Frangokástello. €

★ **Hotel Xenia** At the far end of the seafront promenade, just above the harbour, https://sfakia-xenia-hotel.gr. This former state-owned hotel, now refurbished, has the best location in town with amazing views across the Libyan Sea. All rooms have a fridge, satellite TV and balcony with sea view. Steps at the rear let you swim off the rocks, and the bar-taverna terrace is a great place to watch the harbour activity. There's a car park, and breakfast is included. €

Tria Adelfia Top of the inland street, above Vríssi beach, 28250 91450. Another place with a big variety of comfortable rooms and apartments, many of them overlooking Vríssi beach. €

EATING AND DRINKING

Finding food is never a problem in Hóra Sfakíon, and the excellent **seafront tavernas** have a good array of vegetarian options; almost everywhere here serves breakfast, too. There's little to choose between them, though you'll find cheaper **cafés** and takeaway places on the east side of the bay, towards the ferry jetty. The **supermarket** just above *Niki's Bakery* has better prices than those on the front.

Lefka Ori Corner of the harbour, 28250 91209. Probably the best of the waterfront tavernas for seafood, with a decent terrace by the water. Like everywhere on the seafront they have a tempting display of traditional dishes like *moussakás* or fish casserole, and also the hearty local speciality *kreatópita* (lamb and cheese pie). €€

Niki's Bakery On the inland street, 28250 91268. A Hóra institution, offering a superb range of breads, cookies and other sweet temptations. €

★ **Tria Adelfia** Overlooking Vríssi beach, 28250 91040. In a quiet spot, with a lovely terrace above the sea, this taverna serves good food with a wide range of salads, pasta and vegetarian dishes. Mezédhes include a tasty *melitzánes tiganites* (fried aubergine), while *kounéli stifádho* (rabbit stew) is just one of many Cretan specials. If you like smoked fish, don't miss their home-smoked local dorado. €€

Xenia At the far end of the seafront promenade, under the Hotel Xenia, 28250 91490. The hotel's taverna has a limited but well-prepared menu supervised by hotel manager and all-round good guy Yiorgos Lykoyiannakis. House specials include charcoal-grilled lamb, goat and pork, and the grilled fresh fish is excellent. €

4

From Vrýsses to Sfakiá

The easy way **into Sfakiá** from the north coast is by a good road that cuts south from Vrýsses (see page 258), almost immediately beginning to spiral up into the mountains towards the **plateau of Askífou**. The climb seems straightforward from a vehicle, but the country has a history as bloody as any in Crete: you pass first through a little ravine where two Ottoman armies were massacred, the first during the 1821 uprising, the second in 1866 after the heroic events at Arkádhi (see page 204); while the road itself is the one along which the Allied troops retreated at such cost in the final stages of the Battle of Crete. This chaotic flight has been described in detail in just about all the books covering the battle (and also in Evelyn Waugh's *Officers and Gentlemen*).

The final descent to the coast is stunning, running high above the **Ímbros Gorge** until the road breaks out of its confinement, way above the sea, and plunges down through a series of hairpin bends. Frangokástello can be made out on the broad plain to the east and ahead are immense vistas out towards Africa, with Gávdhos hazily visible on the horizon.

Dourakis Winery

Between Vrýsses and Alíkambos • Charge • https://dourakiswinery.gr

Part of the Cretan wine "revolution" which has seen the emergence of many prize-winning vineyards on the island in recent years, the **Dourakis Winery** was founded in the 1980s and produces red, white and organic wines. The visit (often guided by amiable owner Andreas Dourakis, or by the next generation of the family, who are gradually taking over the business) includes the impressive cellars and an explanation of the entire production process. Tours can be booked which include meals and tasting, or even night-time star-gazing and tasting.

Alíkambos

About 4km south of Vrýsses there's a turn-off to the ancient village of **ALÍKAMBOS** (**Αλίκαμπος**), which has a couple of *kafenía*. Just before the village, the **church of the Panayía** (signed "Kimisis tis Theotokou") is beautifully set in a steep valley. In its nave are outstanding, remarkably well-preserved **frescoes** by the fourteenth-century master, Ioannis Pagomenos; they depict the Panyía and Child, Áyios Yeóryios and Áyios Dhimítrios. The paintings around the altar are by a later artist. You can just about make the frescoes out even if the church is locked; if it is, the key should be available by askingin the village.

Askífou plateau

The **Askífou plateau** is dominated by a ruined Turkish castle on a hill – a hill so small and perfectly conical it almost looks fake, put there expressly to raise the castle above its surroundings. Chief among the several small villages up here, all bypassed by the main road, is **AMMOUDHÁRI (Αμμουδάρι)**, with a couple of small tavernas. There are more tavernas in nearby **KARÉS (Καρές)**, along with home-made signs to an equally home-made Battle of Crete **museum** (charge, www.warmuseumaskifou.com). Gathered in the home of the late Yiorgos Hatzidakis, who witnessed the German invasion as a child, this is a fascinating jumble of weapons, helmets, badges and photos, much of it picked up in the immediate area. Yiorgos' children and grandchildren seem a lot less keen on his collection than he was, however, and their tours can be perfunctory at best, at least until it comes to collecting your money.

The Ímbros Gorge

April–Oct 8am–sunset; Nov–March unstaffed • April–Oct charge; Nov–March free

On the far side of the Askífou plateau lies **ÍMBROS (Ίμπρος)**, the entry point for the Ímbros Gorge. Barely even a village, it consists primarily of a clutch of tavernas and rooms places strung out along the road. The **gorge walk** is clearly signed from here, and there are several ways down into it. Once in the gorge, you are following a **track** that was once the district's main thoroughfare; this well-trodden trail soon passes a booth where you will be charged the entry fee. The hike is easily enough done in less than three hours and provided you don't coincide with a tour bus (set out early), it can be wonderfully peaceful, certainly in contrast to the crowds at Samariá. In its own way the gorge is as interesting as its better-known rival, albeit on a smaller scale: narrow and stiflingly confined in places, speckled with caves in others and at one point passing under a monumental, natural stone archway. Through the ravine you simply follow the stream until, emerging at the lower end, an obvious track leads away again towards the

4

HIKING ON THE ASKÍFOU PLATEAU

For keen **walkers**, the most obvious hike from the plateau is the Ímbros Gorge, but there are also a couple of more serious treks into the Lefká Óri, most obviously on the E4 Pan-European footpath, which passes through Ammoudhári. To the west the E4 climbs into the foothills – initially easy walking with good opportunities for bird-spotting – before beginning to ascend seriously into the heart of the mountains. This little-travelled section eventually reaches the Kallergí Refuge (see page 273): a two-day trek with a possible overnight stop at the Katsiveli or Svourihti refuge (if open). In the other direction the E4 follows the road south across the plain to Ímbros, where one branch heads down the gorge to meet the coastal path while another climbs east to Asféndou (see page 289) and from there to Así Gonía (see page 211).

Alternative routes include a short-cut from Ammoudhári, via the nearby village of **Goní**, to Así Gonía, some 12km in all, or a long day's hike west to Anópoli (see page 282). For the latter you can either follow a track from Ímbros via Trikoukiá to the hamlet of **Kalí Láki** (abandoned but for the odd shepherd in summer) and thence south to Anópoli, or take a path from the village of Petrés, immediately south of Ammoudhári, to join this route at Trikoukiá. Though detailed on the pertinent *Anavasi map*, it's not an easy route to follow and you should get thorough tdirections locally before setting off.

village of **Komitádhes**, full of huge, usually empty, tavernas waiting for the occasional tour party to arrive.

ARRIVAL AND DEPARTURE THE ÍMBROS GORGE

There are numerous entry points to the gorge in Ímbros, where many of the tavernas offer parking and a service to pick you up from the bottom (around €20); the lowest of these is the *Taverna Porofarago* (see page 288).

By bus It's possible to walk the gorge as a half-day trip from Hóra Sfakíon (or Loutró, by getting the first boat from there): simply take the early bus to Haniá, and get off at Ímbros.

By taxi A taxi to the top from Hóra Sfakíon will cost around €20; if you don't have a number to call for a pick-up at the bottom, the tavernas in Komitádhes can order one for you – about €20 back to the top, €10 to Hóra Sfakíon.

On foot From the bottom of the gorge you can walk to Hóra Sfakíon easily enough, though this final 5km makes a hot, boring anticlimax to what has gone before.

ACCOMMODATION AND EATING

Tavern-Apartments Kalinorisma Ímbros, 6944 799 859. Lovely, large modern apartments with separate sitting area and full kitchen, above a taverna serving quality food on a terrace looking out towards the gorge. Parking and transfers available for walkers; hearty breakfast included for guests. €

Taverna Porofarago Ímbros, 28250 95450. A very good, friendly taverna with an attractive shady terrace overlooking the gorge. Sfakian specialities include goat stew and meat pie, and they're also open for breakfast. Parking and transfers available for walkers. €

Frangokástello

4

FRANGOKÁSTELLO (Φραγκοκάστελλο) lies 14km east of Hóra Sfakíon, about 3km south of the road heading east towards Plakiás (see page 222). A series of isolated dwellings dotted across a plain between the mountains and the Libyan Sea, it's a curious place, with a fabulous **beach** but no real centre, leaving you with little option but to head for the **castle** – the imposing silhouette of which comes into view long before anything else.

The castle

Centre of the village fronting the sea • Charge

The **castle**, so impressively four-square from a distance, turns out close-up to be a mere shell albeit one part consolidated restored since 2010; stable stairs now pemit safe ascent to the upper level. Nothing but the bare walls survives, with a tower in each corner and, over the seaward entrance, an escutcheon which can just be made out as the Venetian lion of St Mark. Still, it's some shell. The fortress was originally built in 1371 to deter pirates and in an attempt to impose some order on Sfakiá: a garrison was maintained here throughout the Venetian and Ottoman occupations, controlling the plain as surely as it failed to tame the mountains – even today, the orange-pink walls look puny when you see them with the grey bulk of the mountains towering behind. In 1828, Frangokástello was occupied by **Hatzimihali Daliani**, a Greek adventurer attempting to spread the War of Independence from the mainland to Crete. Instead of taking to the hills as all sensible rebels before and since have done, he and his tiny force attempted to make a stand around the castle. Predictably, they were massacred and their martyrdom became fuel for yet more heroic legends of the *pallikári*. Locals claim that to this day, on or about May 17, the ghosts of Daliani and his army march from the castle: they are known as *dhrossoulítes*, or dewy ones, because they appear in the mists around dawn.

The beach

For peaceful lassitude the **beach** at Frangokástello is among the best spots in Crete, with fine sand, crystal-clear water (with good snorkelling opportunities), and very little effort required either to get here or to find food and drink once you've arrived. If you want company you'll find it around the castle, where the best part of the sand is almost lagoon-like, sheltered and slowly shelving. For solitude, head west along the shoreline, where it's windier and the sand is less soft, but it's still very pleasant. There are beaches to the east too: follow the coastal path for ten to fifteen minutes and you'll arrive at the top of a low cliff overlooking perhaps 1km of beautiful, deserted sand and rocks.

ARRIVAL AND GETTING AROUND — FRANGOKÁSTELLO

By bus In summer there are two buses a day from Hóra Sfakíon (30min).

Vehicle rental You can rent cars from Drive Kreta (28250 92095, http://drivekreta.com) based at *Blue Sky* apartments, or Tracer (6979 091 339, http://tracercarrentals.com), based at *Paradisos*; for bikes and bike tours try Mountainbiking Frangokastello (6945 231 897), based at Babis & Popi.

ACCOMMODATION

Most of the **places to stay** and other facilities are strung out for some distance along the road that heads in from Hóra Sfakíon: a turn-off immediately before the castle leads to another little group of seaside rooms places and tavernas; and there are a couple more east of the castle. Wherever you stay, come prepared for **mosquitoes**. Pretty much everything here closes in winter, from November to March.

Babis & Popi Main road west of the castle, https://babis-popi.com. A range of accommodation from simple, old-fashioned rooms (not all a/c) above the popular taverna and mini-market, to very comfy, well-equipped studios and apartments in a purpose-built block a short walk from the beach, most with great sea views. Rooms and studios €, apartments €€

Blue Sky Apartments Signed inland off the main road, west of the castle, www.blue-sky-kreta.com/en. Very attractive modern two-room apartments (sleeping five) with a/c, kitchen and TV in a tranquil location; there's a large pool and a decent café/tavern too. €

Oasis Main road west of the castle, http://frangokastelloapts.com. A good taverna with very pleasant, generously sized studios and apartments surrounded by flowers, with a path to what is in effect a private beach, where they have their own umbrellas and sunbeds; the two-room apartments with full kitchen are particularly good value. €

Paradisos Signed off the road east of the castle, http://paradisos.gr. Large studio and apartment complex in a tranquil setting amid olive groves very near the sandy eastern beach; well-equipped accommodation with kitchen and TV, plus a tennis court, free bikes and communal washing machine for guests (some larger apartments have their own). €

EATING AND DRINKING

Babis & Popi Main road west of the castle, 28250 92093. Much the most popular place here, which means they have a wider choice than many, though also slightly higher prices than elsewhere. *Astakomakoronáda* (lobster flaked into spaghetti) is a house special, while Saturday, barbecue night, offers charcoal-grilled fish, meat and sausage. All served on a raised terrace with views out to sea. €

Kali Kardia Main road, almost next to the castle, 28250 92311. The "Good Heart" started life as the village's *kafenío* and is still the place you're most likely to see locals. Although they have a menu there's normally a limited selection available, so go with what they recommend; local goat is a favourite, and they also make a mean tomato soup. This is also a good stop for breakfast, drinks and snacks, including takeaway pizza. €

Mylos Side road by the castle, 28250 92162. Enjoying probably the best position in town, right on the waterfront between the beach and tiny fishing harbour, this is a reliable place for fresh fish and solid Greek cooking. Good wine list too. €

Sunrise Taverna On the clifftop east of the castle, 28250 92041. Great views from a position hanging above the shore (with steps down to a little-used part of the beach), and good food; all the meat (goat and lamb) comes from their own herds (try the tasty Sfakian lamb casserole). The mezédhes are recommended, too, and there are many vegetarian possibilities. €

Kallikrátis and around

The road from Frangokástello to **KALLIKRÁTIS** (**Καλλικράτης**), in the mountains directly above, is among the steepest, most winding and spectacular in Crete, which is saying something. It ascends beside the Kallikrátis Gorge to emerge on a rocky, high plateau – often ten degrees or more cooler than the coast, and a blessed relief in summer. There's a great café here as well as a couple of more traditional tavernas, and **onward roads** head west via the the village of **Asféndou** to join the main trans-island

4

route just above Ímbros (see page 287), or northeast via either Myriokéfala or (a much worse road) Así Goniá towards Aryiroúpoli (see page 229) and the north coast. There are also a couple of reasonably easy gorge walks that can be combined into a 17km all-day loop. The **Kallikrátis Gorge** is a branch of the E4, so relatively well marked; the path veers off near the bottom of the road up to Kallikrátis and the climb takes around two hours, though from the top of the gorge it's a good half-hour more to the village. The **Asféndou Gorge**, west of here, descends from Asféndou (where there's another café) to Áyios Nektários on the coast road. Again, it's about two hours up or down, much of it on the remains of an ancient *kalderími* (cobbled path) that was once a major thoroughfare. To combine the two there are short-cuts that cross the plateau from near the top of the Kallikrátis Gorge to Asféndou, but these are poorly marked and they also mean missing the village of Kallikrátis; it's a great deal easier to do this section on the road.

EATING AND DRINKING **KALLIKRÁTIS**

Kallikratis Café On the road as you come into Kallikrátis from the south, 6949 092 073, http://wildherbsofcrete.com. Skull-bedecked rustic café run by Babis and Danish-born partner Janina. It's a very basic place with only snack food, but wonderful Greek coffee, home-made lemonade (sipped through a literal straw, picked from the fields) and cold beers. They also collect and distil local herbs into essential oils, and these are on sale along with home-made preserves and excellent honey. Walkers in need of a place to stay can usually be catered for, and they can also help with hiking directions. €

4

Kastélli Kissámou and the far west

Crete's **far west** has, to date, attracted surprisingly little attention from tourists or developers, and though that is beginning to change, such development as there is consists of mostly low-key apartments and rooms rather than big hotels. The one town of any size west of Haniá is **Kastélli Kissámou**, a port with a ferry service to the Peloponnese, very regular buses to Haniá and a fine museum. To the northwest of Kastélli the long, slender finger of the **Gramvoúsa peninsula** reaches out into the Aegean with, on its western flank, the fabulous white-sand beach of **Bálos Bay**. Extending to the south of this peninsula, Crete's west-facing coast remains remote: there's little public transport and virtually nothing in the way of luxurious facilities. However, here you'll find two of the finest **beaches** on the island – **Falásarna** and **Elafonísi** – both of them, sadly, all too well known.

The Gulf of Kissámou

Kastélli lies some 20km beyond the crossroads at Kolymbári (see page 264) on the coast of the **Gulf of Kissámou**. If you're in a hurry to head west, the new highway is fast and efficient, taking you right to the edge of Kastélli, where it finally ends. The **old road** – always a beautiful drive – has been left behind as a little-travelled, delightful backwater. Going this way you wind steeply up a rocky spur thrown back by the peninsula and emerge through a cleft in the hills to a magnificent view of the Gulf of Kissámou, with Kastélli in the middle distance. Caught with the sun setting behind the craggy heights of **Cape Voúxa** at the far west of Crete, this is a memorable panorama.

Leaving the hills behind, both roads run parallel across the fertile **plain of Kastélli.** Almost as soon as you hit level ground you'll see turnings to the beach, a long stretch of grey sand which, while not the best in Crete, is at least clean and uncrowded. The old road, further inland, passes through a number of quite large, entirely unvisited villages, such as Nohiá, Koléni or Kaloudhianá, where you could stop for a drink or a bite to eat at a number of inviting tavernas. **Kaloudhianá** marks the turn-off for the inland route to Topólia and Elafonísi (see page 301).

ACCOMMODATION **GULF OF KISSÁMOU**

There are scattered rooms places on the plain of Kastélli, and two good **campsites**, right on the beach about 1km from the road. There's a regular bus service to and from Kastélli, and though the sites are popular with people arriving in Kastélli on the ferry, there should always be space.

Camping Mithimna Between Nopíyia and Dhrapaniás, http://campingmithimna.gr. Much the larger of the two sites, *Mithimna* takes its name from the ancient Minoan town of Mithymna, thought to have stood nearby. There's a taverna and mini-market, and they rent tents or cabins and also have studios and apartments (sleeping 4) to rent nearby. €

Camping Nopigia Near Nopíyia village, at the eastern extremity of the beach, http://campingnopigia.com. Attractive site in a tranquil spot close to the Ródhopou peninsula, with a pool and taverna; you can also rent a tent here. €

Kastélli Kissámou

KASTÉLLI KISSÁMOU (**Καστέλλι Κισσάμου**; the Castle of Kíssamos) rarely goes by its full name – it's either **Kastélli** or **Kíssamos**, which officially is the name of the region but more readily distinguishes it from the many other Kastéllis across Greece. It's a busy little town and port with a long seafront, a rather rocky strand to the east and a small sandy beach to the west. This very ordinariness has real charm: it's a working town full of stores used by locals and cafés not entirely geared to outsiders. **Kísamos** was the Greco-Roman city-state that stood here in ancient times, and ongoing excavations in the town centre – whose finds are displayed in an outstanding **museum** – are revealing just how important the ancient city was.

The Archeological Museum

Platía Tzanakáki • Charge • 28220 83308

Housed in the former Venetian governor's palace on the main square, the fine **Archeological Museum** is Kastélli's major attraction. The lower floor exhibits finds from

4

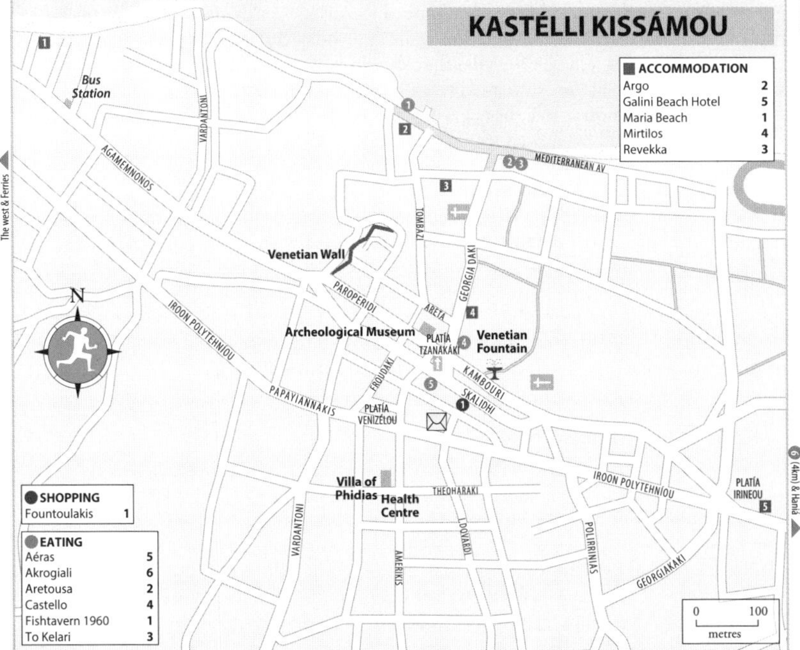

the prehistoric and Minoan periods, many of them from Polyrínia (see page 294) and Falásarna (see page 296), but the second floor – devoted to the Roman town – holds the highlights of the collection.

During the first and second centuries, when Kísamos thrived as an important municipality in the Roman Empire, many wealthy aristocrats embellished their luxurious villas here with sculptures, frescoes, inlaid marble floors (*opus sectile)* and fine mosaics. Many of these arts and crafts are exhibited in the museum, but it is the **Roman mosaics** that steal the show. Kísamos was a key centre of mosaic production, and at least a dozen other, equally splendid, mosaics have been discovered in excavations across the town, but the museum has no space to exhibit them. There are plans to open an extension on the Villa of Phidias excavation site nearby; if this ever happens the display would become one of Greece's most important museums of Greco-Roman mosaics.

Roman mosaics

The huge, polychromatic **Dyonysiac mosaic** covers most of the muaeum's Room 4 and depicts various scenes in a ritual devoted to the god Dionysos. Interestingly, the mosaic had been restored many times by the various owners of the villa that housed it. The museum's star exhibit, however, is **Horae and the Seasons**, displayed beside it. A brilliant work, its colours still remarkably vivid, this almost perfectly complete mosaic depicts a trio of dancing *horae* (goddesses of the seasons). There were only three seasons (spring, summer and winter) in the old Hellenic calendar but at the four corners the mosaicist has added depictions of the four seasons of later antiquity.

Archeological excavations

Originally the port of nearby Polyrínia, Kísamos grew to become the more powerful city; various **archeological excavations** have revealed substantial remains of the ancient town (and more mosaics). However, as the mosaics have been covered in sand and gravel to protect them until they are removed for display in the museum, all you can do is stare at the dirt, a few foundation walls and the odd stretch of ancient roadway, through a chain-link fence. One villa that should be opened to the public at some stage is the **Villa of Phidias**, so named from the owner whose name has been found on a mosaic. An enormous place, now partly covered by the town's health centre, it has six fine mosaics that will be viewed from a walkway.

The Venetian and Ottoman town

Immediately north of Platía Tzanakáki, where the ground falls sharply away towards the coast, are substantial **defensive bastions** connected with a Venetian castle here (which gave the town its name) and which was largely destroyed by Muslim pirates during the early sixteenth century. In the streets surrounding the square, particularly to the west, surviving sections of city wall from the same period can still be seen. There's also a beautiful old **Venetian fountain**, inscribed with the date 1520, about 100m east of the main square in a small courtyard to the left off Kamboúri.

KASTÉLLI ORIENTATION

On the eastern outskirts the old and new roads merge to head straight through town as Iróon Polytehníou, south of the centre. This is lined with stores and supermarkets, and there are cafés and banks on **Platía Venizélou**, where it passes through the centre of town. The heart of Kastélli's life, however, lies a couple of blocks towards the sea from here, around **Platía Tzanakáki** and the main street that runs through it, **Odhós Skalídhi**. There's a further cluster of development along the **waterfront**, directly down from the main squares, with an attractive promenade linking the town's **beaches** to the east and west.

ARRIVAL AND GETTING AROUND — KASTÉLLI KISSÁMOU

By bus The bus station is west of the centre, accessed from the main road via the car park at Carrefour; most buses make a stop in Platía Venizélou as they pass through. Timetables and online booking at http://e-ktel.com.
Destinations Bálos (May–Sept 4 daily; 1hr); Elafonísi (April–Oct daily at 10am, returning 5pm; 1hr 20min); Falásarna (May–Sept 6 daily, reduced service throughout the year; 40min); Haniá (14 daily; 1hr); Soúdha (daily to meet the ferries; 1hr 15min).
By ferry The ferry harbour, for ferries to Kýthira and the Peloponnese and day-trips to the island of Gramvoúsa and Bálos Bay, is 3km west of town – a bus runs daily from town to meet the Bálos boats or it's a cheap taxi ride; tickets are available from travel agencies in town, or before departure from a booth on the quayside. The Peloponnese ferry is operated by Avlemon (210 808 1967), once or twice a week to a complex schedule; check timetables at http://openseas.gr or http://ferries.gr.
Destinations Andikýthira (2hr 15min), Kýthira (4hr), Yíthio (7hr) Pireás (24hr).
By taxi The main rank is on Platía Venizélou, or try 28220 22324 or 28220 22069.
Bike and car rental For cars, motorbikes, scooters and mountain bikes try the longstanding and helpful Motofun/Autofun (28220 23440, http://rentacarkissamos.com) on Platía Tzanakáki; they offer remarkably cheap deals for a week's rental, and will also deliver to Haniá airport. Horeftakis Tours and others on Skalídhi also rent cars, while Balos Travel hire bikes.

INFORMATION AND TOURS

Boat trips Daily boat trips run from Kastélli port to the beautiful beaches at Gramvoúsa and Bálos Bay (see page 295). A public bus runs to the port before departure.
Hiking, cycling and other tours Strata Tours, opposite the archeological museum (28220 24249, http://stratatours.com), offers walking and wildlife tours of the beautiful country around Kastélli (spring and autumn only), as well as other special-interest activities. Balos Travel, Iróon Politehníou 131, opposite Platía Venizélou (28220 22900, http://balos-travel.com), runs cycling tours to Falásarna, Polyrínia and other areas, with picnic lunch and guide included. They can also organize Cretan cooking lessons and many other tours and activities.
Travel agencies Several along Skalídhi: Horeftakis Tours at no. 33 (6972 038 070, http://horeftakistours.com) sells ferry tickets and rents cars.

4

ACCOMMODATION — SEE MAP PAGE 291

Argo Central seafront, Given their great location, these refurbished, marble-floored balcony rooms, with fridge and TV, are a real bargain. Buffet breakfast included. €
★ **Galini Beach Hotel** On the eastern beach, just past the football pitch, https://galinibeach.com. Friendly hotel with light and airy rooms with TV and balcony, some with fabulous sea views. It also offers an excellent breakfast (extra) served on its seafront terrace, in front of which is what is effectively a private beach, with sunbeds and umbrellas. The helpful proprietor has lots of information on hiking in the area. €€
Maria Beach On the western beach, www.mariabeach.gr. Right on the sandy beach, family-run *Maria's* consists of two separate buildings housing some fairly plain rooms (some with fridge) as well as new, fully equipped sea-view studios (with kitchenette) and apartments (sleeping 5) with kitchen; breakfast is available. Rooms and studios €, apartments €€
Mirtilos Platía Tzanakáki, https://mirtilos.com Modern, stylish and well-equipped studio-apartment complex arrayed around a large pool, right off the main square. Studios can sleep up to 4, and there are a couple of larger apartments, plus a roof terrace with great views; breakfast is available. €
Revekka A block back from the seafront, www.kissamia.gr. Modern building housing simple, spacious, stone-floored balconied rooms with fridge and TV, plus a couple of larger apartments. €

EATING AND DRINKING — SEE MAP PAGE 291

There's no shortage of **places to eat** in Kastélli: in the evening the seafront promenade, which can have a listless, end-of-season air by day, comes to life. As well as the tavernas here, there are a few **café-bars** that carry on late into the night: *Babel* and *Aqua* are among the most popular. By day, for light meals and breakfasts, the area around Platía Tzanakáki is a better bet; there's also a good **bakery**, *Hairetakis*, nearby at the corner of Ameríkis and Skalídhi. Wherever you eat, you'll probably be offered the local **red wine**. Made from the *roméïko* grape, believed to have been brought to the island by the Venetians, it is as good as any produced on Crete, and there are a number of new wineries in the area.

★ **Aéras** Skalídhi 85, at the top of Platía Tzanakáki, 28220 22913. "Winds" is the town's oldest *kafenío* and meeting place, serving customers for over a century. Remarkably, it's still in the hands of the same family and remains a great place for a breakfast coffee in the atmospheric bar (with photos of old Kastélli) or a sundowner on its terrace on the square, beneath the spreading rubber tree. They also serve a full menu throughout the day, including a Cretan breakfast (with wine). €

★ **Akrogiali** Korfalónas Beach, about 4km east of town, 28220 31410. *Akrogiali* is the real deal, serving fresh seafood caught daily by the friendly proprietor from his own boat, accompanied by home-made bread, veg from their garden and wine from the family vineyards. It's not attractive as you approach (immediately east of a seafront soap factory whose chimney stacks are visible from some distance), but food is served on a terrace with the waves almost lapping the table legs. They also have cheap rooms. €

Aretousa Towards western end of the seafront promenade, 28220 23569. A family taverna with mum in the kitchen, dad on the grill and the younger generation serving, this is a good bet for simple, traditional dishes like pork *souvláki* or stuffed squid. Also has good mezédhes, a decent wine list and a nice terrace. €

Castello Skalídhi 98, immediately west of Platía Tzanakáki, behind the museum, 28220 24083. Highly popular place with cost-conscious locals who queue for tasty takeaway souvláki and *yíros*; there are also tables in a small garden for sit-down meals. €

Fishtavern 1960 Western end of the seafront promenade, 28220 22340. The best choice at this end of the seafront, an old-fashioned place where you can check out the day's offerings in the kitchen; also reasonably priced fish and seafood and courteous service. €

To Kelari Eastern end of the seafront promenade, 6974 092 913. One of the most popular places on the seafront, with a more adventurous menu than most. Try the likes of fish fillet cooked in paper with onions and tomato, *yogurtlu* (Turkish-style kebab with tomato and yoghurt sauce) or goat in white wine sauce. €€

SHOPPING

SEE MAP PAGE 291

Fountoulakis Skalídhi 53, 28220 22361. You can buy foreign-language newspapers at several of the supermarkets, but the best selection, along with some books in English, is at Fountoulakis, just off the square.

DIRECTORY

4

Banks There are several with ATMs on Platía Venizélou, and a couple more along Skalídhi.

Laundry Kissamos Laundry, Papayiannakis 45 between the two squares (28220 24066; Mon–Sat 8am–2.30pm & 5–9.30pm); service washes and dry cleaning.

Post office Iróon Politehníou (Mon–Fri 7.30am–2pm).

Polyrínia

7km south of Kastélli above modern Polyrínia village • Open daylight hours • Free

Substantial vestiges of the ancient city of **POLYRÍNIA** (**Πολυρρήνια**) can be seen in and around the village of the same name, inland from Kastélli. **Polyrínia village** is a beautiful place, scattered with ancient remains including an aqueduct. From here it's a hot climb to the **hilltop site**, where ruins are scattered across two horns of high ground that seem to reach out to enclose the Gulf of Kissámou. Originally an eighth-century BC Dorian colony occupied by settlers from the Peloponnese, Polyrínia – a name meaning "rich in lambs" – remained a prosperous city down to Roman times and beyond. One of its main claims to fame, however, would not endear it to most Cretans: an inscription found here and dated to 69 BC tells of how the Polyrinians created a statue in honour of the Roman conqueror of Crete, Quintus Metellus, referring to him as the "saviour and benefactor of the city". It seems that Polyrínia did not join in the resistance put up by Haniá and other cities to the Roman invasion, and as a result was spared destruction.

The most obvious feature, right at the summit, is the **Acropolis**, reached via a circuitous track starting east of the church. There are stunning **views** of the coast from here, and though much of what you see is in fact a Venetian defensive structure, the site is dotted with ancient remains including Roman **cisterns** and the vestiges of an **aqueduct**. Miscellaneous Roman and Greek masonry is incorporated into the **church** that now stands below the Acropolis. The church is itself constructed on the base of what must have been an enormously impressive Hellenistic building, possibly a fourth-century BC temple. The sheer amount of work involved in cutting and dressing these stone blocks and transporting them to places as inaccessible as this makes you wonder at the phenomenal scale of manpower at the service of these towns in antiquity. Just below the church are the remains of Hellenistic **dwellings** with cisterns and cave-like storage cellars. The site is extensive and widely scattered across a steep hillside; to explore properly you'll need a couple of hours at least.

ARRIVAL AND DEPARTURE — POLYRÍNIA

By taxi There's no public transport; you could taxi up from Kastélli (around €10) and walk back down.

By car Drivers wanting to go straight to the main site should follow signs to the *Acropolis Taverna*.

On a tour Walking, cycling and bus tours from Kastélli (see page 242) and elsewhere come here.

EATING AND DRINKING

Acropolis Taverna Above the village close to the site, 6949 476 239. A good lunch stop, serving simple but tasty food on a shady terrace; omelettes, chicken in red sauce, local veg dishes. They can also arrange a taxi back to Kastélli. €

Old Kafeníon Polyrínia village, on the way up to the site, 6975 719 342. Quaint small café serving snacks and drinks; they have information on the site, local walks and more. €

The Gramvoúsa peninsula

Leaving Kastélli Kissámou for the west, the main road follows the coast as far as the base of the **Gramvoúsa peninsula**, where it turns inland, cutting southwest into the hills. Along this first stretch there are plenty of signs of development, with new apartment blocks and small hotels. To get to **Bálos Bay**, you need to turn off towards **Kalyvianí**. This marks the start of a 10km road (only the first kilometre of which is paved) up the east coast of the peninsula. It's a slow, 25-minute drive, ending at a car park high up on the spine of the peninsula (with a seasonal drinks stall). From here a well-marked path leads across to west-facing **Bálos** (twenty minutes' walk down, thirty or more back up), where there's a really spectacular white-sand **beach** more or less opposite Gramvoúsa island. There are a couple of seasonal tavernas here, and sunbeds and umbrellas, though these soon run out once the boat trips arrive.

4

Hiking on Gramvoúsa

Walking on the extraordinarily barren and quite unpopulated peninsula is great – but lonely, so take plenty of water and all the other provisions you're going to need. Apart from the car park stall and a spring near the chapel of Ayía Iríni, about 6km out (neither of which it's safe to rely on), there's nothing to be had beyond Kalyvianí.

On the **eastern side**, the walk as far as the car park will take around three hours. From there you can drop down to the beach or continue to **Cape Voúxa** at the tip of the peninsula, on a reasonably well-marked trail. It's also possible to hike up the peninsula's **western side** from Falásarna, but this is a much tougher route and you'll need a head for heights. Head out past the Falásarna archeological site and the bay beyond it (see page 297) and you'll find yourself on an occasionally scary path above the coast, marked by blue paint and cairns. After about four and a half hours you reach

SOUTH OF KASTÉLLI: A WEST COAST CIRCUIT

Beyond Kastélli you've a choice of two roads. To the west, you cut through hills across the base of the Gramvoúsa peninsula to emerge high above the west coast and a spectacular **coast road** that heads all the way down to Elafonísi, where it ends; here you must either turn round to return the way you came or complete a circuit via the inland route. This **inland road** starts a couple of kilometres east of Kastélli at Kaloudhianá, heading down through the Topólia Gorge (see page 301). Further on you've a choice; fork left towards Paleóhora (see page 305) and the south coast, or continue round to join the coast road outside the village of Kefáli (see page 299). The two routes make a fascinating **contrast**: the coast harsh, sparsely populated and occasionally nerve-wracking to drive; the inland route passing dozens of villages, lush and beautiful in a far softer way.

a crest, the highest point on the walk, with breathtaking views over the islands. If you do try this, don't do it alone, and take plenty of water.

Gramvoúsa Island

Along with the fortified islands of Néa Sóudha and Spinalónga, the formidable **castle** on **Gramvoúsa Island** was one of the points that held out against the Ottomans long after the Cretan mainland had fallen. When the Venetians left, the fort was allowed to fall into disrepair until it was taken over by Greek refugees from other Turkish-occupied islands (notably Kássos), who used it as a base for piracy. It took a major Ottoman campaign to wrest the fortress back, and thereafter they maintained a garrison here. During the War of Independence it became a base for Ottoman ships attempting to maintain a blockade of the coastline.

Today boat trips call daily in summer, and the island is briefly overrun; there's a small seasonal café, and a beach with very little shelter. You can climb up to the fort (a gruelling fifteen- to twenty-minute ascent in high summer), walk around its well-preserved ramparts with stunning **views**, and examine the huge water cisterns and chapel. There are lovely wildflowers in season.

ARRIVAL AND DEPARTURE — THE GRAMVOÚSA PENINSULA

By boat Boat trips to Gramvoúsa Island and Bálos operate daily throughout the summer from the ferry harbour at Kastélli (May, June, Sept & Oct 10.20am & 10.40am; July & Aug 10.20am, 10.40am & 12.30pm; returning at 4.30pm, 5.45pm and, in July & Aug, 7.30pm; €27; 28220 22888, www.cretandailycruises.com). The boat trip takes about an hour. Coach tours from around the island connect with these boats.

By bus In summer, four buses a day (the first at 9.30am) head from Kastélli up the track to the car park above Bálos (45min).

On foot If you're walking it's worth setting out early to get to Bálos before the boats arrive. If you took a taxi to Kalyvianí, you could walk up and get the boat back to Kastélli, though it's worth checking in advance that there will be space. Alternatively the Bálos bus could drop you off en route, or a main-road bus could drop you at the turn-off, about 1.5km from Kalyvianí.

ACCOMMODATION AND EATING

Balos Beach Hotel 6km west of Kastélli, http://balosbeach.gr. An attractive hotel in an isolated spot above the sea at the bottom of the peninsula, offering well-equipped studios and apartments (sleeping 4) with balconies and fabulous sea views back towards Kastélli. Also has a bar, restaurant, pool and children's pool. Studios €, apartments €€

Kaliviani Traditional Hotel Kalyvianí, http://kaliviani.com. Hotel-restaurant on a raised terrace in the centre of the village. The thoughtfully refurbished rooms come with fridge, TV and queen-size beds, plus balconies with good views out towards the bay. Breakfast available. €

Mama's Dinner Kalyvianí, http://mamasdinnerkaliviani.com. The restaurant of the *Kaliviani Hotel*, open for breakfast and dinner, is far more cosmopolitan than you might expect in this out-of-the-way spot. The modern Greek/Mediterranean menu features excellent salads, risottos and pastas and adventurous meat and fish mains. €€

Falásarna and the west coast

The road along **Crete's west coast** is spectacularly scenic, winding for the most part high above the sea with magnificent coastal views. The further south you go, the finer the vistas, until eventually you begin to see the distant beaches of **Elafonísi** shimmering mirage-like in a turquoise sea. Around you, olives ripen on the terraced hillsides and the few villages seem to cling desperately to the high mountainsides, as if miraculously saved from some calamitous slide to the water, glittering far below. The great beaches at **Falásarna** and **Elafonísi** apart, there are few places to stop, though **Sfinári** and **Kámbos** do offer accommodation and food, and access to far less frequented sand.

Falásarna

The descent from Plátanos, 10km southwest of Kastélli, to the beautiful beach at **FALÁSARNA** (**Φαλάσαρνα**) is via a hair-raising series of hairpin bends above a narrow coastal plain where farmers grow tomatoes, melons and the like in plastic greenhouses. Below, you can see two main **beaches**, with several smaller patches of sand between – the southern one (enterprisingly named "Big Beach") is much bigger, but the best and most sheltered spot is reached by continuing to the end of the asphalt, where there's a car park, the bus stop and a couple of taverna/rooms places above a broad crescent of yellow sand lapped by turquoise waters. You can either head straight down to the sand here, or walk a bit further north, past the *Orange Blue* bar. Although the beach can occasionally be afflicted by washed-up oil, tar and discarded rubbish, and is often wind-lashed, this doesn't detract from the overall beauty of the place. When it gets too crowded (and on Sundays in summer it will, as half of Haniá seems to head here) you can find other patches of sand within easy walking distance in either direction.

Ancient Falásarna

1km north of the car park

The **ancient city** and port of Falásarna lies just to the north of the beaches. Following the (driveable) dirt track through olive groves you will pass a large stone "**throne**", at the edge of the archeological site, that has puzzled experts for over a century – there is still no satisfactory explanation for its function. There's evidence of habitation here in the Minoan era but what you see now, the remains of the westernmost of the cities of ancient Crete, was founded around the seventh or eighth century BC. The scattered remnants of the city are built around a large depression – its inner **harbour** – and the bed of a canal that once joined this to the sea. The harbour was defended by part of the city wall linked by a number of towers to a harbour mole, with the **South Tower**, the nearest to the sea, a formidable bastion built of huge sandstone blocks. More ruined structures can be seen ascending the acropolis hill behind, and near the chapel of Áyios Yeóryios a more recently excavated building (beneath a canopy) revealed a number of well-preserved **terracotta baths**.

The entire site is now high and dry, offering conclusive proof that Crete's western extremities have risen at least 8m over the last 24 centuries or so. Excavators discovered large stone blocks thrown across the entrance to the old harbour; current thinking suggests that this was carried out in the first century BC by the Romans to prevent pirates using the port as a base. On the southwest side of the site (after scrambling over rocks) you can see the impressive remains of the **Roman quarries** where the stone was hewn to build the harbour and surrounding town. Nearer the sea here you can also view huge **fish tanks** carved in the rock where captive fish were maintained alive until they were required.

If you continue on the best of the tracks past the archeological site, you pass under Cyclopean walls to emerge above a small bay. Tempting as it is, this is too sharp and rocky to be able to get to the sea, but it does give you **views** to the north, over Cape Voúxa, which are shielded from Falásarna itself. Towards the top you can see the island of Gramvoúsa (not to be confused with the uninhabitable rock of Pondikonísi, a more distant islet that can sometimes be seen from the beach at Falásarna).

ARRIVAL AND DEPARTURE — FALÁSARNA

By bus In summer there are direct services to and from Haniá via Kastélli (5 daily; 1hr 30min); they make stops at various points along the beach.

ACCOMMODATION

An increasing number of **rooms** places are scattered along the road behind Falásarna, many of them very comfortable; all of the following are well signposted, on or just off this road. Quite a few people also **camp** at the back of the beach, either in a couple of small caves or beneath makeshift shelters slung between a few stumpy trees. Pretty much everything here closes from November to March.

Golden Sun Near the end of the road, http://hotelgoldensun.net. Charming place with exposed stone walls where the rooms, studios and apartments come with balconies or terraces, many with fine views over the coast. The friendly proprietors can also provide food, and there's a

4

garden and a washing machine for guests' use. €

Magnolia Apartments Overlooking Big Beach, http://magnolia-apartments.gr. Modern studio and apartment complex with some of the area's finest views from the surrounding gardens and from many of the balconies; well-equipped and comfortable. €

Stathis & Anastasia Just off the road, above Golden Sun, http://stathisanastasia.com. A simple, family-run rooms place in a quiet spot. Rooms (some with sea views) come with fridge, balcony and an exceptionally warm welcome. €

Sunset By the car park, http://sunset.com.gr. With an enviable location, right above the beach, and a good taverna, the long-established *Sunset* has a lot going for it, though some of its rooms could do with modernization. They also have very basic seafront apartments and, nearby, luxurious two-storey stone villas, sleeping up to six, overlooking the sea. Apartments €, villas €€

EATING AND DRINKING

There are seasonal drinks stands and beach bars on the busier stretches of beach. For something more substantial to eat, the places immediately above the beaches are as good as any – all simple, and somewhat overwhelmed on busy weekends. There's an excellent, if rather pricey minimarket – with all the necessities and more – on the road by the junction to Big Beach. A couple of slightly bigger supermarkets and other facilities can be found in Plátanos.

Orange Blue Bar Signed from the car park near the Sunset hotel, 6943 627 803. A lovely, chilled-out spot above the water, with sandwiches, burgers and snacks by day, cocktails and a widely varied soundtrack at night; there's often live music at weekends and occasional bigger events. €

Sunset By the car park, 28220 41204. Simple food served on a terrace above the beach with views to die for, though the premium position does mean it can get crazily busy at weekends. The Sunset salad, with pomegranate, pistachio, figs and avocado, is excellent. €

Taverna Mouraki Outside Plátanos, right at the top of the road before it heads down to Falásarna, 28224 00076. Welcoming, excellent taverna with spectacular views over the whole coast. Lamb dishes are recommended, and house specials include stuffed cuttlefish; there are also great mixed meze plates. €

Sfinári

Some 9km south of Plátanos the road descends towards the sea at the village of **SFINÁRI** (**Σφηνάρι**), where a turnoff leads to its beachfront extension a kilometre away. This consists of a quiet pebble beach somewhat spoiled by greenhouses and derelict buildings too close to the water for comfort. It is, however, a very friendly place, with plenty of places to eat by the strand. The southern end of the beach is marginally less cluttered and here a cluster of **tavernas** gather beneath shady tamarisks; they positively encourage **camping**, and there are showers on the beach and free loungers for customers at the tavernas.

ACCOMMODATION AND EATING — SFINÁRI

Captain Fidias Southern end of the waterfront, http://captainfidias.com. The first taverna in line, this is a friendly place where you'll usually see octopus – the house speciality – hanging out to dry by the entrance. All the fish is caught from their own boat, and other tasty dishes include *kakaviá* (fish soup); all of this is priced by weight. They also have a couple of pleasant, fully equipped apartments in the upper village. €

Sunset Southern end of the waterfront, 28220 41627. Good taverna offering fresh fish – stuffed cuttlefish is a house special – along with locally sourced meat and veg. €

Kámbos

Beyond Sfinári the road climbs again for a sinuous 10km to **KÁMBOS** (**Κάμπος**). Less developed than its neighbour, there's a **beach** accessible below the village, albeit an hour's hike down a gorge inhabited by colonies of doves. The path, waymarked with yellow and blue dots, sets off from the church by the village square; alternatively there's a steep but driveable track down, apshalted until the last 100m or so. Isolation is the main attraction of the beach, which, close up, is rather stony.

ACCOMMODATION AND EATING — KÁMBOS

Taverna Hartzoulakis Main road, 28220 41445. Taverna with an attractive terrace hanging over a little gorge. Much of the produce, including the meat, is home-produced and organic. They also have simple rooms and a rather faded wall-map detailing walking trails around this coast. €

Kefáli

Shortly before **KEFÁLI** (**Κεφάλι**) the road turns inland and just beyond the village the road splits; south to Elafonísi or east towards Élos. Kefáli itself is a charming village, with a wonderful setting perched on a hill looking down the Tyflós valley towards the distant sea, closely linked to villages further inland – it is one of the so-called Innachorí, or "Nine Villages" (see page 302). There's a fine fourteenth-century frescoed **church**, Metamórphosis tou Sotiríou (Transfiguration of Christ), signed down a track off the Elafonísi road; it's not easy to find, so ask at one of the roadside tavernas. Inside, the fine **frescoes** depict the betrayal by Judas (whose face has been gouged) and the lowering of Christ from the cross. There is also some interesting and apparently genuine early graffiti, scratched across the paintings. An Englishman, Francis Lerfordes, has marked his contribution with the date 1553, while Muslims later inscribed their blasphemous thoughts along with the star-and-crescent symbol.

ACCOMMODATION AND EATING — KEFÁLI

Taverna-Rooms Panorama Main street, 6946 292 933. The best of several tavernas along the main road, this aptly named, welcoming place has a fantastic view from its terrace, where they serve reliable standards and changing daily specials. Just two well-appointed little rooms in an attractive stone-built house in the old village, with balconies and roof terrace. €€

Váthi

One kilometre south of Kefáli on the Elafonísi road, **VÁTHI** (**Βάθη**) has two ancient frescoed **churches**: thirteenth-century Áyios Yeóryios off the central square, and the century-older Mihaíl Arhángelos, just to the south. To reach the former take a track uphill facing the plane tree in the central platía to the left of a drinking fountain. Follow the track uphill for 200m, where it turns into a narrow *kalderími* (ancient cobbled footpath) that leads you to the sturdy, overgrown church. Inside, the frescoes are in good condition, with a sensitive portrayal of the Archangel Gabriel and an unusual image of the Mother of God and Child in the apse. Mihaíl Arhángelos, at the southern end of the village, has wonderfully preserved early fourteenth-century **frescoes** depicting the Emperor Constantine and his mother Helena, the Fall of Jericho, Christ entering Jerusalem, and a moving portrayal of the betrayal by Judas. Keys for both are kept at the wonderfully old-school *kafenío/pantopolío Kouneni*, just off the square; this generally closes for a siesta from 2–5pm.

4

Moní Khrysoskalítissa

10km southwest of Kefáli • Free • 28220 61261

MONÍ KHRYSOSKALÍTISSA (**Μονή Χρυσοσκαλίτισσας**; the Monastery of the Golden Step) is a weathered, white-walled nunnery beautifully sited on a rocky promontory above the waves. Today barely functioning, it has reduced from some two hundred residents to a solitary nun and one monk, whose main task seems to be keeping the place acceptable for tourists. The present church – containing a much-venerated thousand-year-old icon of the Panayía – dates only from the nineteenth century, but this is an ancient foundation: the first church was built in a cave here in the thirteenth century and recent investigations have turned up evidence of a much earlier Minoan settlement (or shrine) as well. A small **museum** has a few icons along with assorted religious paraphernalia. Look out for the ninety steps that lead to the top of the crag around which the place is built: one of them appears golden, the hrysíeysí (*hrissí skála*) to those who are pure in spirit – a fact that the authors of this guide are unable to verify.

ACCOMMODATION AND EATING — KHRYSOSKALÍTISSA

Glykeria Immediately north of Moní Khrysoskalítissa, http://glykeria.com. An excellent taverna with fine views from its terrace, plus a nearby modern block of lovely tranquil rooms whose balconies have if anything even better sea views. There's also a good-sized pool and gardens. €

Elafonísi

Just over 5km south of Moní Khrysoskalítissa, the tiny uninhabited islet of **ELAFONÍSI** (**Ελαφονήσι**) lies marooned on the edge of a gloriously scenic turquoise lagoon. The almost tropical waters sheltered by the islet boast white sand tinged pink by coral, aquamarine waters, salt-encrusted rock pools and bright-red starfish. The water is incredibly warm, calm and shallow and the islet itself is a short wade across the sand bar. There are more beaches on its far side (with waves), along with the odd ruined wall and a monument to Australian sailors shipwrecked here in 1907.

It's all too easy to get here, a fact reflected in the huge number of visitors who do so, and at peak times Elafonísi can be unbearably jammed. While the arrival of crowds has brought lines of sun umbrellas and loungers to the **beach**, there's little else in the way of infrastructure; the area is a national park, so no permanent structures can be erected. There are stalls selling cold drinks and basic food, and there are portable toilets and an incongruous phone box, but if you're here on a day-trip, the best option is to bring your own picnic, or resign yourself to lunching in the nearest tavernas (see below)

ARRIVAL AND DEPARTURE — ELAFONÍSI

By bus In summer there are daily buses from Haniá (9am; 2hr 15min), Kastélli (10am; 1hr 20min) and Paleóhora (10am; 1hr), with a return at the end of the day. There are also coach tours from all over the west of the island.

By boat In summer there's a daily boat trip from Paleóhora (10am, returning 4.30pm; 1hr).

By car For drivers the inland route is faster and easier, but a visit also gives you the chance to complete a circuit of the west (see page 295). Beware the well-signed route to Sklavopoúla, which is exceptionally tough going (see page 309).

4

ACCOMMODATION AND EATING

Elafonisi Resort On the approach road to the beach, http://elafonisi-resort.com. Probably the best choice here, with a good and balcony rooms and studios, many with sea views, dispersed across an extensive site. €

Panorama On the approach road to the beach, http://elafonisi-village.gr. The closest place to the beach, which means the taverna terrace has much the best views here – looking out over the beach – though the range of food is limited to salads, grills and frozen pizza. The rooms too, known as *Elafonisi Village*, are less enticing than they first appear. €

Inland from Kastélli

The **inland road** south of Kastélli Kissámou passes through some of the most fertile country on the island. Here, lush **woodland** watered by tumbling streams is a haven for a rich variety of flora and fauna, and in the sturdy farming villages there are plenty of opportunities to take in the local wildlife, or to do some walking in the oleander- and chestnut-wooded hills and along numerous gorges.

Voulgáro and around

VOULGÁRO (**Βουλγάρω**) is a large village astride the main road south, with an exceptional number of cafés, restaurants and stalls selling honey and olive oil. A minor diversion here allows you to stretch your legs in search of the ancient church of Áyios

WALKS FROM ELAFONÍSI

Continuing south from Elafonísi, the E4 **coastal path** to Paleóhora (about 17km away) is reasonably well marked, but it's a tough walk, especially in the early stages, with one hair-raising section above a sheer drop near the hill of Ktista (6km out), which is definitely not for the faint-hearted. Check the route before you set out, and don't venture this way alone, or without plentiful water. You could also hike up the track heading inland to **Sklavopoúla**, 13km away (see page 309), from where paved roads head on towards Paleóhora.

Nikólaos at **MOURÍ** (**Μουρί**), a hilltop village about 5km away, signed from the centre of Voulgáro. The chapel is further signed up a track as you enter the village; follow this for 500m and you crest a ridge, suddenly revealing fine views northwards over the Gulf of Kissámou. The whitewashed **church** (normally unlocked) sits alone in an entirely rural setting, surrounded by olive groves and vineyards, often with birds of prey soaring overhead. Inside, the **fresco fragments** – especially those of Áyios Pandeleímon and scenes from the Bible – are extremely fine.

Topólia Gorge

As you pass through **TOPÓLIA** (**Τοπόλια**), 3km beyond Voulgháro, it seems just another large village strung along the road. Pull over, however, and follow one of the many signs to the upper village, and in a few paces you feel as if you've stepped back fifty years; there's a dramatic change of pace as you suddenly find yourself in streets designed for pack-animals rather than cars, and surrounded by the little-changed life of rural Crete. One thing to seek out here is the twin-aisled **church of Ayía Paraskeví**, with **frescoes** from the late Byzantine period.

Beyond the village the road enters the dramatic **Topólia Gorge**, short, but in its way among the most imposing on the island. The road sticks high to the western edge, at one point passing through a single-file tunnel, controlled by lights. Far below, it's a relatively easy **walk** through the gorge, just an hour or so from Topólia to Katsomatádhos; black-and-yellow waymarks in Topólia village will lead you down into the valley and through the gorge. Keep an eye out for the vultures that nest in the surrounding cliffs.

4

Katsomatádhos

The hamlet of **KATSOMATÁDHOS** (**Κατσοματάδος**) marks the bottom end of the Topólia Gorge, with a couple of excellent tavernas (and even rooms) that make an enjoyable spot to break the journey. If you stay longer there are a number of potential hikes in addition to the gorge walk, many of which are signposted. The most obvious is the ten-minute path to the **Cave of Ayía Sofía** (daily 8am–8.30pm; free). You can also get here from the road through the gorge, where a well-signposted stairway cut into the rock offers a muscle-taxing short climb to the cave, one of the largest on Crete. Remains found here date its usage back to Neolithic times, and it now shelters a small chapel, along with stalactites, stalagmites and its present residents, a colony of bats. Other local walks include a path to Miliá, about an hour's climb, and the ascent of **Koproúla**, the highest peak hereabouts.

Miliá

A couple of kilometres south of Katsomatádhos, a beautifully scenic diversion would take you on backroads, through leafy hills and farming villages, along the western flank of the Tiflós valley via **Vlátos**, to rejoin the main road at Élos. Not far up here, a road is signed to the remarkable "eco-tourist" village of **MILIÁ** (**Μηλιά**). The precipitous track, only the first half of which is surfaced, climbs dizzily along the shoulder of Mount Kefáli for 5km, offering magnificent views over the chestnut- and olive-clad valley below. This eventually arrives at a car park, from where a path leads into a stunningly picturesque hamlet of stone houses, once occupied by farmers and shepherds. The isolation of the village eventually led to its abandonment around a century ago until, in the early 1980s, a relative of a former inhabitant proposed restoring the whole place as a working village and welcoming visitors. Other families who owned ruined houses joined in and a co-operative was formed, backed by EU money. Stonemasons skilled in building traditional dwellings were brought over from the Peloponnese and helped to recreate what you now see: an almost too perfect village with solid stone houses on many levels overlooking a verdant cleft.

You should soon locate the house that serves as the community centre and **bar-taverna** (see page 303). Visitors are welcome to get involved in the farming activities, including planting and sowing as well as chestnut-, olive- and apple-harvesting (Miliá means "apple tree" in Greek), and there are occasionally cookery courses and other activities – you can even help make *rakí* at the village's still. Otherwise you can **walk** in the nearby hills – the easier paths are signed – or simply contemplate the natural surroundings; nights up here are truly magical.

Élos

A kilometre beyond the turn-off for Vlátos and Miliá there's a turn on the left for Strovlés and Voutás, leading to the south coast resort of Paleóhora (see page 305). The main route continues southwest past slopes covered with magnificent stands of chestnut, plane and other deciduous trees. Chestnuts are a major local crop, and the picturesque village of **ÉLOS** (**Έλος**), 4km along, is the chief village of the **Innachorí** – the "Nine Villages" – at the centre of the **chestnut-growing** region. Even at the height of summer, this is a wonderfully refreshing place, and it's easy to forget just how high you are here – the mountains to the south rise to about 1200m. Behind the village's *Kastanofolia* taverna (see page 303) there is an impressive section of aqueduct, claimed to be Roman (though perhaps more likely Ottoman). A path leads up the stream here to the fourteenth-century Byzantine **chapel of Áyios Yeóryios**, whose damaged frescoes include an impressive *Pantokrátor* in the apse; if it's closed, the key should be available from the taverna. The great event in Élos's year is the annual **chestnut festival** in late October.

Perivólia

4

Some 5km southwest of Élos, a turn on the left indicates a sharp descent to the picturesque hamlet of **PERIVÓLIA** (**Περιβόλια**), tucked into the folds of a high gorge beneath the northern flank of Mount Áyios Díkeos Ióv (Jon the Just). The village is a verdant oasis with charming narrow streets punctuated by simple white-walled dwellings and smallholdings overflowing with vigorously sprouting vegetables. Park any vehicle where you cross a bridge at the foot of the descent and, turning right, continue on foot to the bottom of the village and a fountain, near a bust to one of the noted local *pallikári* (guerrilla fighters) of the nineteenth century, Anagnostis Skalidis.

Anagnostis Skalidis Museum

Near the fountain, Perivólia • Charge • 28220 61544

The small **museum** was assembled by one of Anagnostis Skalidis' descendants, Zacharia Skalidis. An amiable man who speaks only Greek, he will be delighted to show you around his collection, which includes lots of atmospheric photos from a Crete long gone, as well as old guns, letters and coins.

ACCOMMODATION AND EATING — INLAND FROM KASTÉLLI

KATSOMATÁDHOS

★ **Arhondas** Just below the main road, at the gorge entry, 6949 974 669. Like many of the best Cretan tavernas, *Arhondas* doesn't look special at all, with rickety wooden tables haphazardly spread over a concrete terrace and under trees in the garden. But the food, almost all of which is organic and from their or their neighbours' farms, bursts with flavour; a simple meal of grilled pork chops, accompanied by fried courgettes, Greek salad (with home-made *myzíthra* cheese), hand-cut chips and freshly baked bread, is a revelation. They also have clean and comfy rooms in an utterly rural setting, with use of a communal kitchen and washing machine; and they sell their own olives, olive oil and preserves. €

Taverna Oasis On the main road, 28220 83246. Pleasant rooms with views over the gorge. The taverna is good, too, offering local food including quite a few vegetarian possibilities. The proprietors can advise on walking routes in the area, and there's a track down into the gorge next to the taverna. €

VLÁTOS

Taverna Platania Down a track off the Vlátos road, about 1km from the turn-off, 28220 51406. A rural taverna, surrounded by venerable olive and vast monumental plane trees. With tables spread out beneath the planes, this friendly hideaway serves up good meat and mezédhes – the grilled lamb dishes are recommended – though at times it can feel very empty, as much of its business comes from mammoth wedding feasts. €

MILIÁ

★ **Miliá Eco Village** 3km above Vlátos village, http://milia.gr. The rustic accommodation in Miliá varies from small "semi-detached" cottages to houses for four, but all are delightful, with huge fireplaces (wood provided in winter) and stone ovens. There's solar hot water but no mains electricity – candles illuminate the rooms and the restaurant in the evening – and the only concession to modernity is a satellite internet connection in the bar. Everything served in the taverna (booking advised) is local, and much of it produced in the village; there are excellent traditional soups, stews and salads. Buffet breakfast included, featuring freshly baked bread with their own fruit, cheese and preserves. €

ÉLOS

Taverna Kamares In the centre of the village, 28220 61332. The *Kastanofolia* across the road tends to grab all the attention, but this is a very friendly and affordable alternative for traditional Cretan cooking, with valley views from the terrace; the lamb chops and goat dishes are recommended (served up with delicious potatoes and chestnuts). €

Taverna-Rooms Kastanofolia In the centre of the village, 28220 61258. Shaded by plane, eucalyptus and, of course, chestnut trees, *Kastanofolia* ("Chestnut Nest") is a lovely-looking place, with a terrace above the brook and ducks swimming by. However, it is often overrun by coach parties, when service can suffer badly; at quieter times the simple food is pretty good. They also have some fairly basic rooms. €

Sélinos

Despite its isolation from the north and centre of the island, the eparchy (province) of **SÉLINOS** (**Σέλινο**), stretching roughly from the village of Flória to the south coast, has played a significant role in the island's history since ancient times. As early as the third century BC several of the communities here were important enough to form a confederation with Górtys (see page 104) and Cyrenaica, in Libya, and under the Romans, cities such as **Lissos**, **Elyros** and **Syia** (modern Sóuyia) prospered greatly. This distinguished past laid the foundations for the communal pride that created the scores of frescoed **Byzantine churches** here, perhaps the main reason to visit inland Sélinos today. One of the glories of Crete, every village seems to offer at least one example, while some have as many as three or more. We have detailed some wonderful examples in this account, but many more small churches can be found throughout the whole area, particularly if you get off the road into the smaller villages. Few, if any, of them will be open when you arrive – but express an interest at the nearest *kafenío* or to a local passer-by and it rarely takes long to hunt out the priest or someone else with a key.

4

Flória

FLÓRIA (**Φλώρια**), roughly halfway across the island on the Paleóhora road, is divided into two halves: Káto (lower) Flória, straddling the road, and Apáno (upper) Flória above it. The upper village has the church of Áyii Patéres (the Holy Fathers), although here only fresco fragments remain. In the lower village, **Áyios Yeóryios** preserves thirteen panels of fine fifteenth-century frescoes. To reach it, entering from the north end of the village, go down a lane to the right of the second taverna you pass on the right. After about 600m you'll come to a small footbridge over a dry stream bed; cross

ROUTES TO THE SOUTHWEST COAST

Though you can approach from Kastélli, the fastest and most direct routes into Sélinos and to the south coast resorts start further east. For **Soúyia**, the direct approach is via Alikianós (see page 268), on a road that diverges from the north-coast highway immediately west of Haniá. For **Paleóhora** the main road turns off about 20km further west, outside Tavronítis, heading south via Voukoliés.

this and after 50m veer left at a fork to follow the path leading to the church. Near the first taverna (the better of the pair), two war memorials – one German, one Greek – face each other across the road, serving as grim reminders of the terrible atrocities that happened here during World War II.

Kándanos and around

KÁNDANOS (**Κάντανος**), 9km south of Flória and approached along a verdant valley planted with olives, is the chief village of Sélinos (though it's a great deal smaller than Paleóhora), and makes an appealing, quiet place to stop for coffee or a meal. Despite an ancient name that goes back to Dorian times and the existence of twenty or more Byzantine **churches** in the immediate vicinity (it was the seat of a bishop throughout the Byzantine and Venetian periods), the village buildings are almost entirely new, for the place was razed to the ground by the Germans in revenge for its role in the **wartime resistance**. In 1941, after the German army had taken Máleme (see page 262), troops were dispatched urgently along this road to prevent the Allies landing reinforcements at Paleóhora. The resistance fighters of Kándanos determined to stop them, and despite a ferocious pitched battle the Germans could not break through for two crucial days. In retribution the Germans utterly destroyed the village. The original sign erected at the time is today preserved in the museum (currently closed) but a copy stands on a war memorial in the square – in German and Greek it reads: "Here stood Kándanos, destroyed in retribution for the murder of 25 German soldiers, and never to be rebuilt again."

The village that arose defiantly from the ashes after World War II is today an easygoing place, with attractive cafés and tavernas around its main square. Here you may be able to pick up a copy of a free **map**, detailing local sights including all the churches in the surrounding area. On the outskirts is a waterworks, given to the village by the Germans after the war as an act of reconciliation. Many of the German military who served here have since returned to forge friendships with their erstwhile adversaries.

The Kándanos churches

Four Byzantine **churches** are within a couple of minutes' stroll of the main road through Kándanos. Approaching from the north there are good but damaged frescoes at the restored **Mihaíl Arhángelos**, signposted to the east up a lane on the northern edge of the village, and in the charming small white chapel of **Áyios Mámas**, 1km away through the olive groves, signed down a road by the petrol station, opposite the village's main road junction. **Ayía Ekateríni**, signed off the main street near the central platía, is a beautiful old building with faded fresco fragments. The best of all, though, is **Áyios Ioánnis**, another small white church with superb fresco fragments, signed downhill off the Paleóhora road on the southern edge of the village, around 1km from the road.

Anisaráki

A short detour from Kándanos climbs a couple of kilometres east to **ANISARÁKI** (**Ανισαράκι**), on a minor mountain road which is also a short-cut to Soúyia via Teménia (see page 311). Halfway up to Anisaráki, in the hamlet of **Koufalotós**, the chapel of **Áyios Mihaíl Arhángelos** has fourteenth-century paintings by the Cretan master Ioannis Pagomenos. The chapel is located down a track on the left, across a stream. Anisaráki itself has more fine frescoes in the fifteenth-century churches of **Ayía Ánna** (signed on the left in an olive grove as you enter), with a rare stone iconostasis, **Panayía** and **Ayía Paraskeví** (both signed from the centre).

South of Kándanos

Beyond Kándanos the main road south bypasses several more villages with frescoed churches: Áyios Yeóryios, in **Plemenianá**, has paintings dating from the fifteenth century, while **Kakodhíki**, known for its curative springs, has several churches nearby. These include the very ancient chapel of **Mihaíl Arhángelos**, probably early thirteenth-century, beside the modern church of Ayía Triádha, and the hilltop Áyios Isidhóros, with magnificent views and frescoes defaced by the Turks. **Kádhros**, some 9km south of Kándanos, has the churches of Ioánnis Hrysóstomos and the **Panayía** (reached via a downhill path beside a gaily decorated *kafenío*; key from the house near the church), whose fine fresco cycle is almost complete.

Paleóhora

PALEÓHORA (**Παλαιόχωρα**) was known originally as Kastél Selínou – the castle of Sélinos – and for much of its history was no more than that, a castle. Built by the Venetians in 1279, the fort was destroyed by Barbarossa in 1539 and never properly reconstructed even when the small port grew up beneath it. The ruins are still perched at the bulbous end of the headland now occupied by the settlement of Paleóhora – at its narrowest a bare four blocks across from the harbour on one side to the beach on the other.

Today, the village has become a small town and an enjoyably laidback, end-of-the-line resort, helped by superb and extensive sands and by the fact that there are no big hotels, and almost all the rooms and restaurants are still owned and run by local families. Warm right through the winter, this out-of-season backwater makes an excellent place to rent an inexpensive apartment long-term. Other than head for the beach, eat and drink, there's not a great deal to see or do here, which of course is a major part of its attraction. However, there are plenty of trips on offer (see page 307), as well as attractive **walks** inland, to charming villages like Ánidhri and Azoyirés (see page 310), or along the coast in either direction.

4

Paleóhora castle

In town you can check out the **castle**, for the views back over town, or walk right around the end of the promontory to return to the beach on the other side. Neither of these options is as appealing as it might be, since the fortress itself is little more than a hillock ringed with broken walls, while a new concrete marina and some unsightly harbour buildings dominate the point. Steps lead up from the church towards the castle, and along the way you'll see the oldest parts of town, to the south of the harbour.

The beaches

Of the beaches, the westerlyu **Sandy Beach** is more impressive: magnificently broad and sandy, lined with tamarisks and supplied with showers, on a bay with excellent, easy windsurfing. **Pebble Beach**, facing east, is at first sight a much less attractive proposition. However, this eastern side is far livelier at night, when the beachfront

PALEÓHORA ORIENTATION

The main road from Kándanos leads you into a eucalyptus-lined avenue that becomes Paleóhora's single main street, **Odhós Venizélos**, lined with taverna after café after bar. If you come from the west, on the roads via Voutás or Sarakína, you'll emerge on the road behind the sandy western beach, by the post office. Bisecting the village north to south, **Venizélos** is Paleóhora's vibrant soul, and on summer evenings its central stretch is closed to traffic, brightly illuminated and filled to overflowing as the bar and restaurant tables spill across the pavement and encroach onto the road. From the main street, nothing is further than a five-minute walk away: straight ahead (south) lies the **castle** with a virtually empty marina beyond it; to the left (east) is the aptly named **Pebble Beach**, with its harbour from where boats to Soúyia and Gávdhos depart; to the right (west) are the broad sands of the fabulous **Sandy Beach**, where you'll find quite a few hotels.

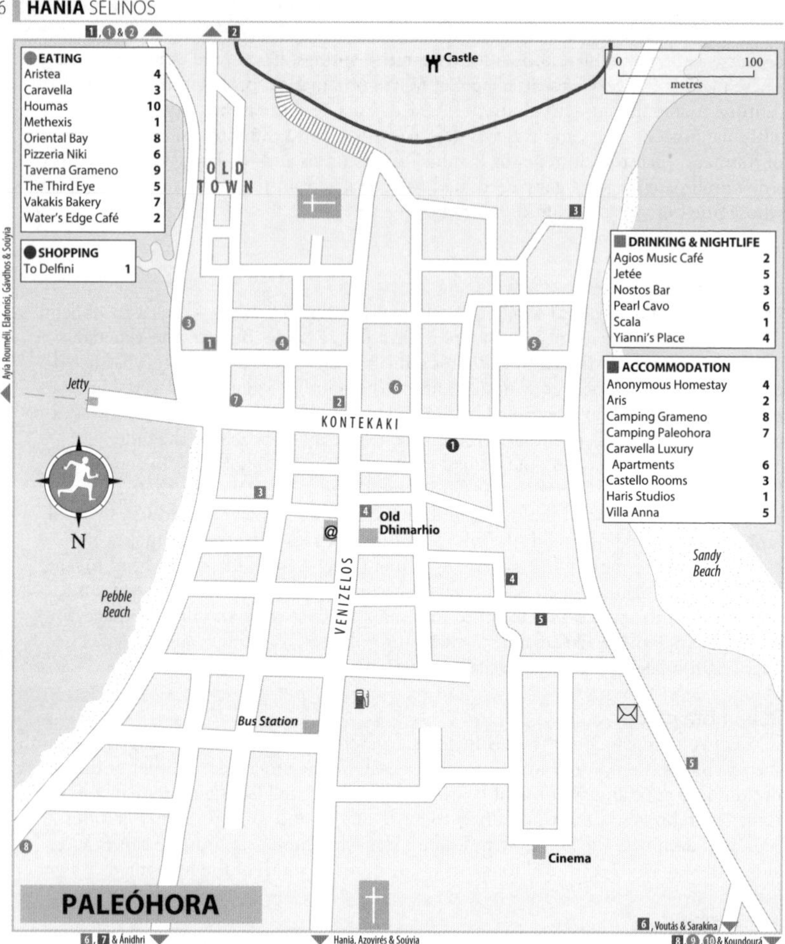

promenade rivals the main street for action and choice of eating; the cafés and restaurants over here have a stunning view of the moon rising over the mountains. The beach is also more sheltered when the wind is blowing, and if you venture far enough north, away from town, you'll even find some sand.

ARRIVAL AND GETTING AROUND — PALEÓHORA

By bus The bus terminus is at the northern end of Venizélos. The Omalós bus takes you to both the Ayía Iríni and Samariá gorges, and connects in Ayía Iríni with buses to Soúyia.

Destinations Elafonísi (May–Sept daily at 10am, returning 4pm; 1hr 20min); Haniá (4 daily; 2hr); Koundoúra (for local beaches to the west; 3 daily; 20min); Soúyia (3 daily; 6.15am bus continues to Omalós; 1hr).

By boat or ferry Ferries dock on the east side of town, at the jetty at the bottom of Pebble Beach, as does the smaller boat to Elafonísi and any tour boats. Summer schedules are below, but confirm times with any of the local travel agencies or online (http://anendyk.gr); the ferries run a restricted schedule year-round. From Ayía Rouméli there are onward ferries to Loutró and Hóra Sfákion.

Destinations Ayía Rouméli (April–Oct daily 8.30am; 1hr 20min) via Soúyia (30min); Elafonísi (April–Oct daily 10am, returning 4.30pm; 1hr); Gávdhos (April–Oct Mon & Wed 8.30am; 4hr 30min).

By taxi There's a taxi office just by the ferry dock (28230 41128, https://paleochora-taxi.com), and another at the top of Venizélos near the bus station (28230 41368).

Bike rental Nikos (daily 9am–3pm & 6–10pm; 6988

480 414), towards the northern end of Venizélos, has good mountain bikes, though you can also rent them from the Notos and Sabine travel agencies.

Car rental You can rent a car or motorbike at the Notos and Sabine travel agencies.

INFORMATION AND ACTIVITIES

Travel agencies Notos Travel (6976 436 044, http://notoscar.com), on Venizélos opposite the old town hall, has a finger in every pie, with a laundry and internet café as well as exchange, vehicle rental, accommodation tours and more. Sabine Travel (28230 42105, https://sabinetravel.gr, virtually next door, also has trips, exchange and vehicle rental, including well-maintained bikes and e-bikes. Selino Travel (28230 42272), on Kondekáki just up from the harbour, is a little less frenetic and good for the latest ferry updates.

Boat trips Local boat trips include dolphin-spotting cruises (though despite claims of 70 percent likelihood, these don't seem to have a very high success rate), plus excursions to Lissós, Elafonísi, Samariá and Gramvoúsa. Contact any of the travel agents.

Diving and adventure sports Nireas Adventures (6940 111 165, http://nireasadventures.com) can take you scuba diving or snorkelling, and also organize canyoning and hiking trips.

Walking There are organized gorge walks of Samariá and Ayía Iríni; enquire at one of the travel agencies. It's also easy to do these yourself by bus, with a service heading for Omalós via Ayía Iríni daily at 6.15am throughout the summer. You can then get the boat back from Ayía Rouméli or Soúyia in the late afternoon.

ACCOMMODATION

SEE MAP PAGE 306

Anonymous Homestay In a backstreet off Venizélos, http://anonymoushomestay.com. Among the least expensive places in town, and something of a travellers' meeting place. Simple rooms, with use of a communal kitchen, off a charming garden courtyard, plus two two-bedroom apartments. €

★ **Aris** Last place on the upper road at the south end of the peninsula, beneath the castle, http://arishotel.gr. Charming, welcoming and peaceful hotel, artistically renovated with particularly lovely handmade wooden headboards. All rooms have balconies, many with sea views, others over the lush gardens, along with fridge and tea- and coffee-making facilities (but no TV), and there's an excellent breakfast available. €

Camping Grammeno 4km along the coast to the west, http://grammenocamping.gr. Friendly campsite with youthful management, close to a truly beautiful beach and some good tavernas. €

Camping Paleohora 2km northeast of the centre, reached along the road behind Pebble Beach, http://campingpaleochora.gr. Attractively sited in an olive grove close to the beach, with plenty of shade. The only drawback here is the bone-hard terrain. €

Caravella Luxury Apartments Reached via the turn-off for Voutás at the northwest end of town, 28230 41131, http://caravella.gr. On a rise above the resort, these six ultramodern luxury apartments have large terraces or balconies with stunning views and come with marble floors, lounge (some with wood-burning stove) and satellite TV, plus a fully equipped kitchen. €€€

★ **Castello Rooms** Overlooking the southern end of Sandy Beach, 28230 41143. Exceptionally friendly place, most of whose simple rooms have balconies overlooking the beach with some of the best views in town; a few rooms at the back without view are less expensive (singles available too), and you can still enjoy the views from the terrace taverna. €

Haris Studios On the seafront below the east side of the castle, http://paleochora-holidays.com. A friendly Cretan-Scottish-run place with some simple studios close to the water, most with great sea views, and a newer block (*Yiorgos Studios*) of excellent, well-equipped modern studios and apartments with a garden, roof terrace and small pool (which all guests can use) set further back. €

Villa Anna In a broad side street off Sandy Beach near the post office, http://villaanna-paleochora.com. Somewhat pricey but very pleasant apartments for four to six people – large, nicely furnished, all with kitchen, and surrounded by wonderful lush gardens. €

4

EATING

SEE MAP PAGE 306

Aristea Backstreets one block inland from the jetty, 28230 41430. A lovely courtyard setting for delicious, home-style Cretan food. Take a look in the kitchen at the day's specials, which might include the likes of chicken *lemonato*, and there are all the usuals, including a good Greek salad. €€

★ **Caravella** Old town seafront, just south of the ferry jetty, 28230 41131. Paleóhora's best seafood restaurant, with a waterfront terrace. All the fish is caught locally (and sold by weight) and both cooking and service are excellent, as are their house wines, including a very tasty French-style muscatel dessert wine from the Sélinos village of Máza. They also serve some meat, plus a daily selection of *mayireftá* (pre-cooked dishes). €€

Houmas Graméno beach, 5km west along the coast road, 2823 041745. With an impeccable beachfront setting and loungers on the sand, *Houmas* is a place you can spend all day at. Luckily the food is excellent, especially simple things like *moussakás*, fresh kalamari and the daily specials. €€

Methexis Far southern end of the eastern seafront, 28230 41431. Hugely popular taverna above a tiny pebbly beach, where it has its own beach bar. Food (portions are big) is served on a terrace higher up and is traditional with a twist; daily specials might be goat with green beans, or rabbit with chestnuts and olives. Unusual dishes like goat with *askólymbri* (oyster thistle) or *tsigerosárma* (lamb-liver roulade) go quickly. Also good salads, inexpensive house wine and a decent bottled wine list. €€

★ **Oriental Bay** Northern end of Pebble Beach, 28230 41322. With an inviting, tamarisk-shaded terrace fronting the sea, *Oriental Bay* serves some of the best traditional food in town, with daily specials such as *arnáki kokkinistó* (lamb stewed with tomatoes, onion and garlic) stuffed courgette flowers or "granny's meatballs". There's occasional live music and also fresh juices and breakfasts. €€

Pizzeria Niki Off the south side of Kontekáki, 28230 41532. An attractive, bougainvillea-filled courtyard setting for excellent wood-fired pizzas, as well as pasta and salads. €

★ **Taverna Grameno** 5km west towards Koundourá along the coast road, near Gramméno beach, 28230 41505. Perhaps the area's most authentic Cretan restaurant, this is a friendly garden taverna with a play area for kids, and the cooking is outstanding – take a look in the kitchen for what is seasonal and fresh. €€

The Third Eye Inland from Sandy Beach, http://thethirdeye-paleochora.com. Excellent vegetarian restaurant run by a Greek-New Zealand family with flavours rarely seen on Crete, from curries to *gado-gado*, as well as more conventional Greek dishes: expect the likes of Cambodian curry, *yemistá* and interesting salads such as beetroot and walnut. €€

Vakakis Bakery Bottom of Kondekáki, facing the jetty, 28230 41850. This long-established bakery also has a café where you can enjoy their cakes, pies and pastries, as well as sandwiches, coffee and ice cream. It's a handy place to grab some breakfast if you're leaving on the ferry. €

Water's Edge Café On the seafront below the east side of the castle, at Haris Studios, 6938 098 976. As well as having a lovely sea-view terrace for breakfasts, snacks and drinks (big, all-day English breakfast; also breakfast cocktails), the *Water's Edge* serves dinner every evening, including fish of the day caught by the owner Haris (priced by weight, good value) and a great burger. €

4

DRINKING, NIGHTLIFE AND ENTERTAINMENT SEE MAP PAGE 306

Paleóhora clings to its village origins and has no pretensions to be anything other than a tranquil seaside resort with family appeal: if you're looking for all-night clubs and raucous bars you've come to the wrong place. Most **bars** keep their volume well down after dark; many of the most popular of these are shoehorned into the area around the Venizélos–Kont Kondekáki junction and down towards the harbour. Nightly showings at the open-air **cinema**, Cine Attikon, tucked away in the northern backstreets, are wonderfully atmospheric; most of their recent-release films are in English and programmes (advertised on billboards outside the cinema and along Venizélos) change daily.

Agios Music Café Corner of Venizélos and Kontekáki, http://agiosbar.gr. Café and central meeting place by day, cocktail bar at night, when there's decent music too.

Jetée Sandy Beach, right on the sand near the post office, 2823 041162. A classy, quiet spot to linger over a sundowner, with cocktails and a jazzy soundtrack, and often lively later on; occasional "beach party" events in high summer. Also open all day with a good breakfast buffet and snacks.

★ **Nostos Bar** Pebble Beach, 6947 562 654. The liveliest late-night joint in town, with a chilled club atmosphere and outside courtyard bar; doesn't really get lively until near midnight.

Pearl Cavo 1km or so from the north end of Pebble Beach, 28230 43127. Beach bar by day, with chilled sounds, but comes into its own by night, when it's far enough from town to be able to make some noise; occasional live music and DJ sets. In the evenings a beaten-up shuttle bus runs from the ferry jetty.

Scala By the ferry jetty, 28230 41793. This is one of the town's best spots for breakfast, and for burgers, snacks and smoothies during the day; later the drinks get stronger and there's often live music.

Yianni's Place Venizélos near the old Town Hall, 28230 41396. Café/ouzerí with tables spread across the main street, great for people-watching, whose eponymous proprietor (his children now run the place) is one of the town's characters.

SHOPPING SEE MAP PAGE 306

Supermarkets There are a couple of large supermarkets behind Sandy Beach.

To Delfini Kondekáki. This bookshop sells foreign newspapers, also available at the well-stocked *períptero* on Venizélos. *To Delfini* also has a good selection of books in English, including local walking guides.

DIRECTORY

Banks There are several banks with ATMs on Kondekáki west of Venizélos and on Venizélos itself, north of the town hall.

Laundry At Notos Travel (see page 307).

Post office On the road behind Sandy Beach (Mon–Fri 7.30am–2.45pm).

West of Paleóhora

The coastline **west of Paleóhora**, where you can get a bus as far as the farming centre of **Koundourá**, is an uneasy mix of tourist development and polytunnel agriculture, rarely very attractive but with a number of worthwhile little coves and beaches along the way. Much the best of the beaches is **Gramméno**, after about 5km, where a small peninsula shelters lagoon-like water and there's a glorious sandy beach with trees for shade. There are a couple of rooms places here, as well as some excellent tavernas and a campsite (see page 307). Beyond Koundourá, a driveable track continues, petering out shortly after aptly named, pebbly **Krýos** beach ("cold", which the water here generally is, thanks to freshwater seeps on the bottom). The E4 path to Elafonísi (see page 300) leads onward from here.

The Pelekaniotikós valley

Northwest from Paleóhora a lovely, deserted drive tracks the valley of the River Pelekaniotikós through a string of charming Sélinos hamlets. At **Voutás**, 12km northwest of Paleóhora, you can choose one of two routes to circle back to the coast. A left turn will take you to the isolated village of Sklavopoúla and its wonderful frescoed **churches**, from where you can drop directly down to the coast at Koundourá. Straight ahead, the road winds northwards through dramatic mountain scenery to join the route that cuts across from the far west to Paleóhora, a couple of kilometres south of **Stróvles**. Keep going north here and you'll reach the Élos road (see page 302); south takes you back towards Paleóhora and the main road from Haniá.

4

On the Sklavopoúla route, 1km before the village of Kítiros, the small fourteenth-century church of **Ayía Paraskeví** is worth a stop to see some faded frescoes on its rear wall; one has a remarkably lurid portrayal of hell with devils putting sinners into the flames while others are being crushed by serpents.

Sklavopoúla

SKLAVOPOÚLA (**Σκλαβοπούλα**), one of the remotest communities in the Sélinos at an altitude of 640m, is, unexpectedly, a place with a considerable history. The nineteenth-century English traveller Robert Pashley visited and identified Sklavopoúla as the site of Doulópolis, a Dorian city renowned for its military prowess. The village's present name ("Village of the Slavs") may stem from a resettlement of Slavs here by Nikiforos Phokas (see page 330) following his reconquest of Crete from the Saracens in 961. There are no less than seven **churches** in the vicinity, all with wall paintings. Beware the enticing road **signs to Elafonísi** near the southern edge of the village; a route also marked on many maps. It is just about possible to drive this in a regular car but it requires great care, and will take around 45 minutes to cover 13km.

THE SKLAVOPOÚLA CHURCHES

As you come in to the village of Sklavopoúla from the east you pass the church of **Áyios Yeóryios**, next to a school playground on the left, with some fine frescoes dating from the thirteenth century. To get the key go to the second house below the school, the home of Petros, the guardian. Continuing into the village, two other notable churches (usually open) are reached down a path next to the primitive **kafenío/village shop** – itself something not to be missed. Head downhill along a very rough ancient *kalderími* (cobbled track), running the gamut of chained dogs, for 200m or so, through a farm where if anyone is around you could ask further directions. The church of the **Panayía** is obvious, just beyond the farm, with frescoes including superb gospel scenes and a portrait of the donor. **Sotíros Christós** is less easy to find, hidden away in the fields.

East of Paleóhora

East of Paleóhora several routes head towards Soúyia, though if you want to follow the **coast** you'll have to do so on foot. Here a driveable dirt road continues beyond the *Camping Paleohora* campsite for a couple of kilometres to **Yialaskári** beach, an attractive spot with sunloungers and a seasonal *kantína*. Beyond, the **E4 path** (see page 310) traces the shore, passing a succession of grey pebble strips with fewer people clad in fewer clothes the further you venture.

Ánidhri

Some 6km east of Paleóhora, on the paved road that climbs beyond the campsite, **ÁNIDHRI** (**Άνιδρι**) is a particularly beautiful village, with a popular taverna. Just below this you'll find the fourteenth-century church of **Áyios Yeóryios**, which has an unusual double altar and fine **frescoes** depicting the lives of Christ and Áyios Yeóryios by Ioannis Pagomenos (John the Frozen), the most prolific of several painters whose signatures appear frequently around Sélinos. Beyond Ánidhri the road deteriorates beyond **Prodhrómi**, from where it's a tortuous drive round to Azoyirés; alternatively it's an easy walk from Ánidhri (see page 310).

Azoyirés

Heading north out of Paleóhora on the main road, you'll soon see signs to **AZOYIRÉS** (**Αζογυρές**), "Paradise Village". The road up to the village is set amid woods of cypress and pine, a lovely drive on good roads, and Azoyirés itself is set in a beautiful wooded valley above a rushing brook. Several short **walks** in the valley are well signposted, taking you past plenty of evidence that this was once a much bigger place; there's an ancient bridge, a monastery (still just about functioning), an abandoned school, an olive oil factory and more. All of this is recorded on a map which you can find on the back of the menu at the *Alpha* taverna – handily printed on paper so you can take it with you – and there's also a tiny one-room **museum** (officially Sat & Sun 9am–2pm; when closed enquire at the *Alpha*), delightfully located in the valley at the bottom of the village.

4

The Azoyirés cave

The biggest of several local **caves** is on an easy-to-miss road which (approaching from Paleóhora) heads off left just before the *Alpha* taverna, and winds steeply upwards for nearly 2km (keep climbing and turning where there's any doubt about the way). At the top you'll need to park any transport. From here there's an obvious path leading on – look up and you'll see a cross, some 200m above, which marks your destination. Approaching the cave you may disturb quail; the eerie sounds in the cave itself emanate

WALKS EAST OF PALEÓHORA

If you take a taxi up to Azoyirés (or the early-morning Omalós bus), you could easily hike back to Paleóhora or, more strenuously, on to Soúyia; taxis to Ánidhri or Yialaskári offer shorter versions of the same. It's a relatively easy, well-marked walk down the valley from **Azoyirés to Ánidhri** (1hr 30min or less) and from there down the verdant **Ánidhri Gorge** to the beach at Yialaskári, about an hour below. From Yialaskári you could head back into Paleóhora or follow the E4 towards **Lissós** and **Soúyia** (see page 311). Walking from Paleóhora to Yialaskári will take around 1hr 30min; it's a further 3 hours to Lissós, and 1hr 30min more to Soúyia; if you time it right you can return to Paleóhora on the evening boat from Soúyia. The **E4** is waymarked, but it doesn't simply follow the coast all the way, and there are one or two steep scrambles. Since the most scenic section is through the gorge between Lissós and Soúyia, it might be easier to head to Soúyia and do the shorter walk from there.

from more birds, mostly pigeons, amplified by the acoustics. A steep metal stairway and rock-cut steps descend 50m or so to a little shrine lit from above by dim, reflected light. If you have a powerful torch you can continue a fair way, although there's no proper path.

Teménia

Beyond Azoyirés it's 10km or so to **TEMÉNIA (Τεμένια)**, source of the drinks of that brand name sold throughout western Crete. Turn right at the edge of the village, downhill along the Rodováni road, and you'll pass a stone chapel atop a low hill to the left and see, about 200m further on, a sign on the right to **ancient Hyrtakína**. Head down this narrow track, and on your right you will soon see the charming, tumble-down church of **Sotíros Hristós**. Inside, a number of damaged **frescoes** include a stirring image of a mounted Áyios Yeóryios slaying the dragon. Of the ancient Doric city, on the hilltop high above, there's almost no trace, but there are fine views and it's a bracing walk, or teeth-rattling drive, up there.

ACCOMMODATION AND EATING — EAST OF PALEÓHORA

Alpha Azoyirés, http://azogires.com. Exceptionally friendly and helpful café-taverna with a limited menu and economical balconied rooms nearby, some with air/con and fridge. They also organize walking tours. €

Kafenío Sto Scolio Ánidhri, 28230 83001. "The Old School", tastefully converted, makes a good place to pause for a drink or a bite to eat. The cooking is good, with a range of mezédhes and specials chalked up on the blackboard (such as tomato fritters, pork leg with rosemary, lamb's liver with sage and Metaxa), and there's an inviting, shady terrace with views. It's worth booking in summer. €

Taverna Temenia Teménia, 6944 280 046. Welcoming rural taverna serving delicious Cretan traditional cuisine. All of the dishes are recommended, especially the home-reared lamb, village chicken and very tasty *loukánika* sausages. €

4

Soúyia and around

The south coast settlement of **SOÚYIA (Σούγια)** is a small village well on its way to becoming a resort. There are no big hotels, no major tour operators (and no bank or ATM, so bring cash), just lots of rooms, simple restaurants and bars, added to a couple of general stores which double as travel agencies. A rather unkempt little place – not particularly attractive at first sight – Soúyia tends to grow on you. Its best feature lies right at the end of the road: an enormous swathe of bay with sparklingly clean, clear sea and a long, pebbly **beach**. There's plenty of room to spread out here – even on summer weekends when it's popular with locals – there are beachfront cafés and restaurants, and you could **camp** under the few scraggly trees if you wanted, although you'd be advised to get as far away from the central beach as possible to be left in peace. Around at the east end of the bay there's something of a nudist camping community, known locally as the **Bay of Pigs**.

Lissós

4km west of Soúyia • You can walk or take a boat or taxi-boat from Soúyia (daily trip at 10am, returning 3.30pm, charge

The archeological site of **Lissós** is a great deal more rewarding than anything you'll see in Soúyia itself. Originally a Dorian city, Lissós grew through the Hellenistic and Roman eras and continued to thrive, along with its neighbours Syia and Elyrós, right up to the Saracen invasion in the ninth century, when they were all abandoned. Little is known of these places' history, although they did join together around 300 BC – along with Hyrtakína in the hills behind, Pikilássos on the inaccessible coast between here and Ayía Rouméli, and Tarra, at modern Ayía Rouméli – to form the **Confederation of Oreioi**, later to be joined by Górtys and Cyrenaica (the latter in North Africa).

The ideal way to visit is either to walk over early and get a boat back in the middle of the day (precarious embarkation), or have a taxi boat drop you here late in the

WALKS FROM SOÚYIA: LISSÓS AND OMALÓS

The walk from **Soúyia to Lissós**, a little over an hour (3km), is part of the pleasure of a visit to the ancient site: you set out on the road which heads west, behind the beach, and at the harbour turn right onto a track leading slightly inland. The route – also the path trodden by ancient pilgrims – is part of the E4 coastal path, so it's well marked with black and yellow splodges. It leads up a beautiful echoing gorge, which you follow for about thirty minutes, and then climb steeply out of towards the coast. After a short level stretch the sea comes into view, followed almost immediately by Lissós, below you at the back of a delightful little bay. If you're continuing the walk **west towards Paleóhora** (see page 305), the path is again pretty obvious; there may be a guard in the hut at the site who can help, but don't rely on it. The path back to Soúyia from the beach is easy to see as it climbs the steep hill on the east side of the archeological site.

Hiking from **Soúyia to Omalós** (or vice versa, which is slightly easier) is a far more arduous proposition, not to be undertaken alone or without proper preparation: although Omalós is only some 12km away, the country in between is mountainous, remote and almost entirely uninhabited; it's a very full day's climb. If you head east along the beach in Soúyia, you'll see signs for the trail to the **Polyfemus Cave** and Koustoyérako (see page 312). This part (4–5hr) is generally well marked (it's yet another E4 branch), with the cave, a little under halfway, to add interest (Polyfemus was the Cyclops who imprisoned Odysseus in this cave, and was blinded by him) and to provide a handy picnic spot. An easier way to do this would be to get a taxi up to Koustoyérako and walk down. **Beyond Koustoyérako** the terrain is marginally less steep but the path generally harder to follow. There are two alternative routes: more or less due north, to meet the road out of the plateau; or a turning to the east, heading for Mt Gíngilos and the top of the Samariá Gorge. You can also get to Omalós from the top of the **Ayía Iríni Gorge** (see page 313) on a path which heads east, cutting off a huge loop of the road. All of these walks (with the exception of the Polyfemus cave leg) are clearly marked on Anavasi Samaria Soúyia map.

afternoon, leaving time for a look around the site (you'll very likely have it all to yourself and it's just the place to open a chilled bottle of wine) before the walk back to Soúyia in the cool of the evening. There's a small pebble **beach** for a refreshing swim after your explorations.

The site

The remains at Lissós are mostly Classical Greek and Roman, the most important survival being an **Asklepion**, or temple of healing, built beside a curative spring against the cliffs on the east side of the site. The temple probably dates from the third century BC, although the **mosaic floor** (protected by a broken-down fence) that is its most obvious feature was added later, in the first century AD; it's a poignant ancient relic, depicting images of polychrome birds in its central section (including a quail) and elaborate and beautifully crafted geometric patterns on its outer borders. Notice also the marble altar-base that would have supported a statue, and the "snake pit" (or hole to place sacrifices) next to it. On the gentler, western slope of the valley, opposite, are a group of tombs that look like small stone huts, with barrel-vaulted roofs – hardly the best advertisement for the healing temple. You'll also find a small ruined theatre and two thirteenth-century churches, Áyios Kyriákos – with a nearby **spring** – and Panayía, which reused older material from the site.

Koustoyérako

About 5km northeast of Soúyia, a road cuts off from the main Hanía highway to the villages of Livadás and **KOUSTOYÉRAKO** (**Κουστογέρακο**). The latter is a very ancient village that is still the home of the Paterakis family, famed in the annals of resistance to the German occupation. Manoli Paterakis was one of those who took part in the capture of General Kreipe (see page 334); he died some years ago at the age of 73, when he fell while chasing a wild goat through the mountains. Today the village seems to be in steep decline, with the *kafenía* and school closed, though it does see a few passing **walkers**, with a branch of the E4 path passing through between Soúyia and the Omalós plateau (see page 312). At the top of the village, behind a pristine restored house, the tiny Byzantine chapel of **Áyios Yeóryios** contains some beautiful remains of frescoes, with sixteenth-century graffiti carved into them; the chapel itself may be as early as the tenth century in origin.

The Ayía Iríni Gorge

Charge, though often unattended • The gorge is an easy day-trip from Paleóhora (the early-morning Omalós bus passes through Ayía Iríni, and you can get the afternoon ferry back from Soúyia) or Soúyia (again, take the early Haniá/Omalós bus); you could also get a taxi to the top from either of these places

The **AYÍA IRÍNI GORGE (Φαράγγι Αγίας Ειρήνης)** descends from the village of **Ayía Iríni**, a green place shaded by venerable chestnut trees, to the coast at Soúyia, roughly 12km in all, though the last five are along the road – about a four-hour trek. It's an attractive hike, not too taxing and usually very quiet unless you're unlucky enough to coincide with one of the occasional tours (mainly from Paleóhora). The well-marked route down into the gorge can be picked up on the south edge of the village; for the first few kilometres it's easy walking, with plenty of water, shade and picnic spots, but it gradually becomes drier, tougher and hotter as you descend. There are places to eat and drink at the top, and the aptly named *Oasis* café at the bottom end of the gorge; from here, you could summon up a taxi to collect you from Soúyia, or you might well be able to beg a lift from a fellow traveller.

ARRIVAL AND INFORMATION — SOÚYIA AND AROUND

By bus There's no bus station: buses drive down the main road and drop passengers on the seafront, then park up halfway to the harbour. The early Haniá bus offers the opportunity to walk either the Ayía Iríni or the Samariá Gorge – it meets the early bus from Paleóhora in Ayía Iríni, and from there one continues to Omalós and the other to Haniá, so you may have to change. Tickets are sold at *Roxana's*, at the bottom of the main road.

Destinations Haniá/Omalós (3 daily, first at 7am; 2hr/1hr), Paleóhora (connecting to Elafonísi; daily at 9am; 45min).

By ferry The harbour is at the western end of the seafront, a 5min walk from the centre. Ferry tickets are sold from a booth here, which opens 1hr before each departure. Timetables are generally posted up locally, or check online (http://anendyk.gr); the ferries run a restricted schedule year-round.

Destinations Ayía Rouméli (April–Oct daily 9am; 45min); Gávdhos (April–Oct Mon & Wed 9am; 3hr 30min); Paleóhora (April–Oct daily 6.10pm; 30 min).

By small boat Taxi-boats can be arranged through the Pelican supermarket or direct from *Captain George* (6947 605 802) or Yiannis Paterakis (6973 220 472). These are handy for getting to isolated beaches along the coast or ancient Lissós (around €20 one way); they also offer a regular itineary to Lissós, leaving at 10am and returning at 3.30pm, for €5 each way.

By taxi A taxi kiosk almost opposite the seafront *Santa Irene* hotel (6977 745 160 or 6972 370 480) can arrange taxis to various destinations, including the Ayía Iríni Gorge (€30 one way).

Tourist information Soúyia has virtually no formal tourist infrastructure – boat trips, tours, car rental and the like are arranged through the shops, restaurants or hotels. The seafront taxi booth is a good source for general and travel information, as are https://sougia.info and www.visitsougia.com, but the most useful sources of local information are the two minimarkets: Idomeneas, halfway down the main street, and Pelican near the bottom. The latter also has newspapers and books in English.

ACCOMMODATION

Almost every building in Soúyia seems to offer **rooms**. Some of the best are off the main road at the top of the hill as it enters town; others, more expensive, are right on the seafront (mostly to the right from the seafront junction); while another cluster of cheaper rooms can be found by turning left along the seafront and left again before the stream. Details of many of the following (and more) can be found on https://sougia.info.

Captain George To the west of the main street, near the top, http://sougia.info/hotels/captain_george. Simple balconied rooms with fridge, TV and kettle, plus slightly pricier studios and apartments with kitchenette, in a garden setting. €

Idomeneas Apartments Main road, at the top of the hill, http://idomeneas-sougia.gr. Bright, comfortable, modern a/c studios and spacious apartments with kitchens, TV and balcony. €

Paradisos On the lane by the stream, left and left again at the seafront junction, http://sougia.info/hotels/paradisos. Old-fashioned but clean and very cheap rooms with fridge and kettle; most with air/con and balcony. €

Pension El Greco To the west of the main street, near the top, http://sougia.info/hotels/elgreco. Set back from the road in a quiet, semi-rural setting, these simple upper-floor rooms have a balcony, fridge and kettle; there are also a couple of ground-floor studios. €

Santa Irene On the seafront, http://santa-irene.gr. Smart, modern studios and apartments around a courtyard in a great waterfront location (though only a few have sea views), all with TV, kitchenette and balcony. €

Syia Main street, near the top, http://syiahotel.com. Incongruously chic, boutique-style hotel; the most comfortable studios and apartments in town, if not the most beautiful surroundings. Breakfast included. Studios €, apartments €€

Villa Galini Main road, at the top of the hill, www.galinisougia.com. Run by a friendly proprietor, *Villa Galini* has big, comfortable, good-value modern studios and apartments with balconies and satellite TV – one apartment has a hidden upper level, perfect for kids. €

EATING, DRINKING AND NIGHTLIFE

SOÚYIA

Fortuna On the main road north of town, 6977 423 023. Open-air club with frequent live music and party events; a great deal busier and wilder than you might expect down here. Look out for posters promoting special events.

4

Liviko At the western end of the seafront, 28230 51414. A good bet for traditional Cretan standards (lamb in the oven) as well as grills and fresh fish (priced by weight), often with live music in the evening. €

Lotos Seafront, at the corner of the main road, 2823 051142. Big breakfasts, followed by coffees and juices, crêpes and snacks by day, and drinks and music in the evening; there are numerous similar café-bars on the seafront. €

Omikron On the seafront east of the main road, 28230 51492. German-run restaurant with a more north European ambience; international menu – including pastas and risottos and numerous vegetarian choices. €€

Polifimos Set back from the main street, halfway up, 28230 51343. Long-standing Soúyia favourite run by Yiannis, one of the village's characters. He serves his own wine and cooks with home-grown (and pressed) olive oil. Tasty dishes include interesting salads, *kontosoúvli* (spit-roast pork), rabbit *stifádho* and shrimp spaghetti. There's live Greek music on Thursdays. €€

★ **Rembetiko** Halfway up the main street, 28230 51510. Served up on a shady garden terrace, the shortish menu here features home-cooked traditional dishes including plenty of vegetarian options such as rice-stuffed tomatoes and peppers, plus meat reared on their own farm (lamb chops). €€

Roxana's Bakery Bottom of the main street, 28230 51362. Great little bakery for breakfast, cakes and savouries like *tyrópita* and *spanakópita*, plus sandwiches and cold drinks to eat in or take away; they're open early for snacks for the bus (and to sell bus tickets). €

Gávdhos

GÁVDHOS (Γάυδος), the southernmost landmass in Europe, is the largest of Crete's offshore islands and the only one with any significant population. Gávdhos is small (about 9km by 7km) and barren, but it has one major attraction: the enduring **isolation** which its inaccessible position has helped preserve. The 50 nautical miles of rough sea – more than 3000m deep – separating it from the coast of Crete frequently proves too much for the small local ferries, which can leave visitors stranded for days when sailings are suspended.

If all you want is a **beach** and a taverna to grill your fish, this remains the place for you. Just don't expect luxury. There's a semi-permanent community of campers and would-be "Robinson Crusoes" on the island year-round, swelling to thousands in August – but just six indigenous families. **Water** is in short supply, and although most rooms on the island have showers and relatively modern plumbing, much of it is not drinkable. Few places have 24hr **electricity** either – most rely on candles, solar power or part-time generators, and even where there's enough power for lights, there's rarely air-conditioning. One huge benefit of this is an amazing **night sky**, when the few lights twinkling from the mainland are overwhelmed by the extraordinary brightness and density of the stars.

Brief history

Little is known of the island's early history and although evidence has been found of **Neolithic** and **Minoan** activity, it was most probably not settled until **Classical Greek** times when it was a dependency of Górtys (see page 104) and famous for its juniper berries. Despite Gávdhos's claim to be Calypso's island (visited by Odysseus in Homer's *Odyssey*), it only appears in verifiable record later as a place well known to the **Romans**, who christened it Clauda or Kaudos: the New Testament relates how St Paul was blown past Clauda in the storm which carried him off from Kalí Liménes (see page 118). During the Middle Ages, Gávdhos is said to have had eight thousand residents and a bishop of its own; it was also notorious as a **pirates**' lair. In more modern history the island was used by dictatorial governments as a place of **exile** for political opponents, and later was a hideout for members of the notorious November 17 terrorist group (which was broken up in 2003). Publicity generated by this is at least one of the reasons for a recent upsurge in visitors, but it's still a harsh place to live, and many locals leave to spend the winter on mainland Crete, especially at Paleóhora.

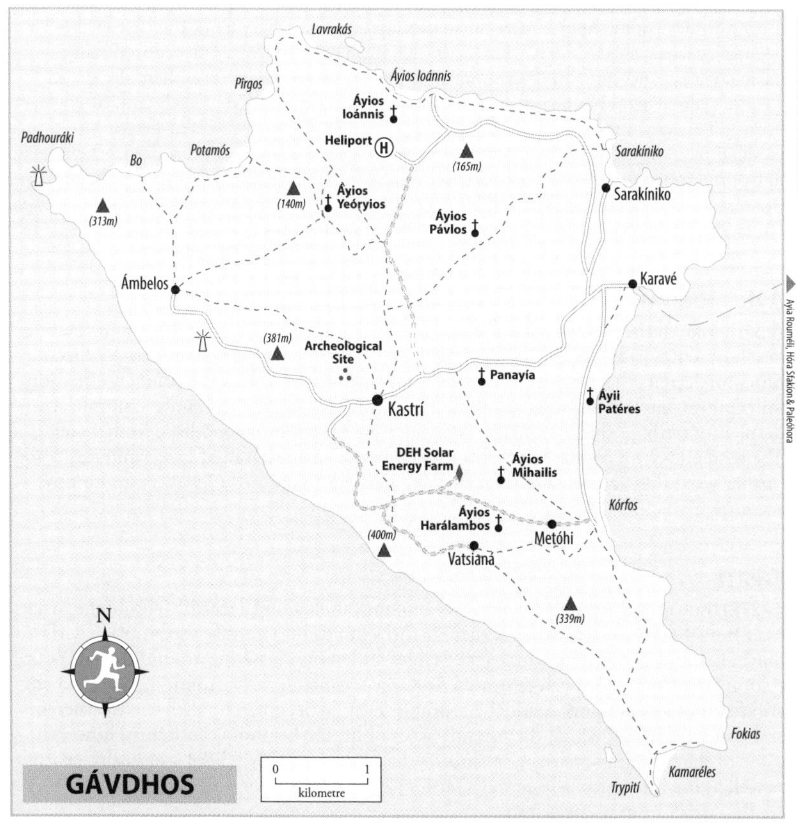

HIKING ON GÁVDHOS

It may be fiercely hot in summer, but Gávdhos is also small, so **hiking** from place to place is a realistic endeavour, especially as the roads are awful and there are few other transport options. Numerous trails have been well marked out across the island, and you'll find shelters with maps and information at the beginning of most of them. The maps pinpoint a number of **archeological sites** en route, though none with a great deal to see.

Karavé

As you approach Gávdhos, the harbour at **KARAVÉ** (**Καραβέ**) is hidden behind a headland, and the island looks totally uninhabited – only with binoculars might you pick out one or two isolated homes. For an hour or so either side of the ferry's arrival, Karavé is crowded and chaotic and the couple of cafés busy; the rest of the time, there's hardly anyone here at all. In front of the concrete harbour is an open space where everyone mills about as the ferry loads and unloads: somewhere here will be the buses to Sarakíniko and Áyios Ioánnis, and any other accommodation transport. On the heights behind the harbour squat a few dwellings and a small white church, alongside the modern municipal buildings.

Sarakíniko

4

SARAKÍNIKO (**Σαρακίνικο**) is Gávdhos's principal resort, with one of the best of the island's beaches, shaded by scattered juniper and tamarisk trees, half a dozen fairly basic tavernas and cafés, and a similar number of rooms places. Even here the broad strip of golden sand has a community of nudist campers settled at each end, often outnumbering those staying in the rooms (although the newly elected mayor has pledged to clamp down on the naturists and reclaim the beach for families). The largely ugly, unplanned architecture aside, this is a beautiful spot, with giant dunes sheltering the eastern end of the beach: each evening the setting sun illuminates and silhouettes Crete and the Lefká Óri on the horizon against a crimson sky.

Áyios Ioánnis

A 3km hike to the west of Sarakíniko (or a ten-minute bus ride) brings you to the fine beach of **ÁYIOS IOÁNNIS** (**Άγιος Ιωάννης**). There are high dunes here too, and a forest of miniature cedars that provide shade for an army of tents. This is the prime destination for campers, and the summer hangout of a substantial alternative nudist community, despite (or perhaps due to) the fact that there are few facilities and little fresh water. The road ends by a couple of **tavernas**, from where the beach itself is ten minutes' walk further west; there are usually stalls offering massage, handmade jewellery and hippy accoutrements.

Kastrí

KASTRÍ (**Καστρί**), the island "capital", is an hour's walk along a steadily climbing, paved road from Karavé. When you get there it turns out to be a ghostly sort of place with only a handful of dwellings, mangers, stables and barns clustering around the old police station and *dhimarhío,* both relocated to Karavé, while in the surrounding parched and arid fields older dwellings gradually crumble away to become one with the weathered and fissured rock on which they stand. Signs of life are beginning to return, however: some of the dwellings are being refurbished and there's a tiny school and health centre, as well as the incongruously snazzy *Gavdos Princess Apartments* (see page 318). There are fine views from up here, too.

Ámbelos and around

Climbing out of Kastrí the track heading west across the island reaches the ridgeline and divides. The right branch leads to the sparse hamlet of **ÁMBELOS** (**Άμβελος**), 3km north, from where there's a particularly fine view towards North Africa, over a sea lane ploughed constantly by enormous supertankers. On the way there you'll pass the impressive nineteenth-century **lighthouse,** bombed by the Germans in 1941 but fully restored with a café and **museum** depicting images, plans and sketches of other lighthouses throughout Greece (both have been closed for family reasons; check locally to see if they have reopened). A track north from Ámbelos leads to the scenic isolated beaches of **Potamós**, **Pýrgos** and, further east, **Lavrakás**; you are totally on your own here, there are no facilities, and you'll need to take along plenty of drinking water.

Vatsianá

Turning left at the junction beyond Kastrí leads, after 3km, to **VATSIANÁ** (**Βατσιανά**), a hamlet marooned in a rocky, almost lunar landscape. There's a chapel here, and half a dozen dwellings, one of which is a ramshackle **kafenío**, the last in Europe before you reach Africa. From Vatsianá you are in easy walking distance of Kórfos and its beach, to the east. Striking out more adventurously, there's also a path to the southernmost tip of the continent at Trypití, 3km to the south.

Kórfos

You can walk pretty much directly down from Vatsianá to **KÓRFOS** (**Κόρφος**), 2km away, where there's a good (but shadeless) sand and shingle beach and a couple of excellent places to stay. With a vehicle you'll have to head some way back for the track via Metóhi, or there's a paved road from Karavé.

4

Metóhi

The rooms place at **METÓHI** (**Μετόχι**) – see page 319 – is also host to a tiny **museum**. This two-room family collection won't take long to see, but it's a fascinating glimpse into traditional island life (or a pile of domestic junk, depending on your viewpoint): most was collected by the grandfather, Manolis Bikoyiannakis, who was the island's priest for many years; his son Stefanos now runs the island's car and bike rental from here, while his wife and children look after the rooms and taverna.

Trypití

TRYPITÍ (**Τρυπητή**), the most southerly point of Europe, can be reached in little over an hour on a well-marked path downhill from Vatsianá (thus a steep slog back up), or on a slightly longer trail from Kórfos. The beach here, **Kamaréles**, is pebbly with little shade but the water is brilliantly clear and a snorkeller's paradise, with plenty of aquatic life. When you need a break, you can do what everyone else comes here to do: climb the famous **three-holed rock**, sit in the **giant chair**, and dangle your feet off the edge of a continent.

ARRIVAL AND DEPARTURE — GÁVDHOS

By ferry There are ferries to Gávdhos the 50 nautical miles from Hóra Sfakíon year-round, and from Paleóhora from April to October; in summer many of them call at Ayía Rouméli and Soúyia. All, however, are dependent on the weather, which is unpredictable even in high summer; the high-sided, shallow-draft *Samariá* cannot handle even moderate winds and seas, while August is particularly dodgy given the frequency with which the *meltémi* blows. Be aware that you may be stranded on the island longer than you expect, and plan accordingly. Schedules change throughout the year, and at short notice if there are weather disruptions: details can be found online (http://anendyk.gr)

and are posted at the harbour in Karavé and at Sarakíniko. The Gavdos Cruises boat (http://gavdos-cruises.jimdo.com) is slightly less weather-dependent but is small, so may also be cancelled in rough weather. The following timings refer to the main summer season; these are the return journeys, so the ferry will have arrived from the mainland.

Timetables July–Sept Hóra Sfakíon (Anendyk Thur–Sun 12.30pm and or 2.30pm , returning 2.30pm, July & Aug also on Sun; Gavdos Cruises June–Sept daily at 9am, returning 5pm; 2hr 30min–3hr); Paleóhora via Soúyia and Ayía Rouméli (Mon & Wed 8.30am, returning 2pm; 3–4hr).

GETTING AROUND

By bus There are two buses, one run by KTEL, the other by Gavdos Tours (6942 480 815), at least one of which will meet every ferry and make the trip to Sarakíniko, Áyios Ioánnis and Kastrí (€2); there's a return trip from the beaches about 1hr before the ferry departs. Timetables are posted at Karavé, Sarakíniko and elsewhere; the schedule changes daily, but there's an evening round-island trip most days in summer (€5), starting from Sarakíniko, and often a lunchtime journey between the major centres. If you're staying anywhere other than Sarakíniko or Áyios Ioánnis, and have booked in advance, you should be met at the ferry by a minibus from your accommodation.

Vehicle rental Gavdos Travel (6940 813 613, http://metoxigavdos.wordpress.com; cash only), based at *Metoxi Rooms*, rents battered cars (around €35–40/day plus petrol) and elderly scooters (around €15–20/day including petrol); Kougios, based in Kastrí, has a few newer cars (6972 981 905); Odyssey (69488 377 985, nikoskaramarkos@gmail.com), based at *Gavdos Princess*, has reasonably new mountain bikes for around €10 a day. All will deliver the vehicle to you, which is a great deal easier than seeking them out.

ACCOMMODATION AND EATING

4

Many visitors to Gávdhos (the vast majority in peak season) still camp out by the beach, so most of the time there's no shortage of **rooms**. In August, however, the island is packed and prices are far higher; July and September are becoming increasingly busy too. Whenever you come, it would be foolish to turn up without having booked (unless you're happy to sleep under the stars), and there's the added advantage that many places will pick you up from the ferry; travel agencies in Paleóhora (see page 307) or Hóra Sfakíon (see page 285) can help if necessary. Very few places have effective **air-conditioning**; plenty of others have a/c units they can't use, because promised mains electricity never materialized. As for **food**, there are minimarkets in Karavé, Sarakíniko and Áyios Ioánnis, but they're pricey (almost everything is brought over on the ferry) and none is very well stocked – in particular there's little in the way of fresh fruit or vegetables. There's also an excellent **bakery**, on the road below Kastrí. Nonetheless it makes sense to bring some supplies with you, especially if you plan to camp out.

SARAKÍNIKO

Consolas Gavdos Studios By the road above the beach to the west, https://.gavdostudios.com. A breezy hillside setting for the island's largest apartment complex, which offers rooms, studios and "villas" (basically a single, huge room, with kitchenette and multiple beds); there are some very pleasant rooms, with terraces and views (plus fridge and something to cook on), but others are not so good, and there's a slightly regimented atmosphere. Wi-fi in the café, where they also serve breakfast (extra). A bus collects folk from the ferry. €

Haroto On the approach road. Describing itself as a café/bar/party space, *Haroto* is a makeshift place hidden away in the dunes that hosts party nights a couple of times a week: open-air affairs with fairy lights strung between trees and sand underfoot. Look out for posters and local publicity. Also open by day for drinks and snacks and in the evening for cocktails. €

Nykhterida Taverna-Rooms Beachfront, 28230 42120. Very pleasant, simple rooms right by the beach with power from a generator at night and a bottled gas cooker. They also have one of the better beachfront tavernas (with wi-fi) and the local minimarket stocking basic items and essentials. €

★ **Vailakakis (aka Gerti & Manolis)** Behind the beach, where the bus stops, http://gavdos-crete.com. Simple rooms (with 24hr generator power) and rather fancier stone-built houses, with full kitchen, for four to six people. It also has probably the best food on the beach, with excellent, good-value seafood caught daily by Manolis himself. €

ÁYIOS IOÁNNIS

Sofia Just above the car park, http://sofiaroomsgavdos.com. Lovely modern rooms with huge picture windows and spectacular terraces looking towards Crete. There's air-conditioning but only solar power, so it can only be used during the day. Also a friendly family bar-taverna. €

Taverna Ai Giannis At the end of the road, by the car park, 28920 42006. The closest place to the beach (there's another taverna and a minimarket almost next door), *Ai Giannis* serves excellent, simple food from a short menu, with daily specials and good breakfasts. €

KASTRÍ

Gavdos Princess Apartments Beside the road on the way into the village, 28230 41181. Some of the fanciest accommodation on Gávdhos – though that isn't saying a great deal and it's far from the best location – these modern-built studios and two-room apartments have a/c (Kastrí is one of the few places supplied by the island's solar power plant), terraces and kitchenettes. There's also a decent taverna, and a minibus to collect guests from the harbour. €

Stella's bakery On the road approaching Kastrí, 28320 41411. Super bakery with all sorts of delicious treats, from croissants to chocolate cake to home-made ice cream, as well as a range of traditional breads, biscuits and savoury pies. There's also a terrace to enjoy them all with a coffee or juice. €

★ **To Steki tis Gogos** Across the road from Gavdos Princess, 28320 41932. Simple taverna where Gogo, with her sister and daughter, prepares a limited range of local dishes every day, full of earthy rural flavour. There's a little terrace with lovely views. €

KÓRFOS

★ **Akroyiali** On the beach, http://gavdoshotel.com. Plain but comfortable rooms directly above the beach, so you're lulled to sleep by the sound of the sea; 24hr power from the island's solar plant means effective a/c and hot water, and the taverna serves good food on a seafront terrace. There's a minibus to pick guests up from the ferry, and which also does occasional tours of the island. €

Panorama On the hill down to the beach, www.gavdos-panorama.gr. Appropriately named place with stunning views from rooms and taverna. Rooms are simple but spotless, with 24hr power, and they'll collect you from the harbour if you ring ahead. The taverna serves excellent fresh fish (priced by weight) and other local dishes on a terrace overlooking the beach. €

METÓHI

Rooms Metoxi https://metoxigavdos.wordpress.com. Friendly family atmosphere and a good taverna with views. The rooms are rather run-down, with solar power for ceiling fans and fridge, and camping gas stoves. There's a small pool, but water shortages mean it's often empty. A minibus collects guests from the harbour. Free wi-fi in the taverna only. €

DIRECTORY

Doctor The health centre in Kastrí (28230 42195) is usually staffed by an intern opting out of military service.

Money There is no bank or official place to change money on the island: bring sufficient cash with you, remembering that, though life is simple, supplies are relatively expensive and you may be stuck here longer than expected should ferries be cancelled.

Police There is a police station (28230 41019) attached to the *dhimarhío* (town hall) above the harbour at Karavé.

WALL PAINTING, KNOSSÓS PALACE

Contexts

History

The people of Crete unfortunately make more history than they can consume locally.

Saki

The discovery of the Minoan civilization has tended to overshadow every other aspect of Cretan history; indeed it would be hard for any other period to rival what was, in effect, the first truly European civilization. It was in Crete that the developed societies of the East met influences from the West and North, and here that "Western culture", as synthesized in Classical Greece and Rome, first developed.

Yet this was no accident or freak one-off: Crete's position as a meeting place of East and West, and its strategic setting in the middle of the Mediterranean, has thrust the island to the centre stage of world history more often than seems comfortable. Long before Arthur Evans arrived to unearth Knossós, and for some time after, the island's struggle for freedom, and the Great Powers' inactivity, was the subject of Europe-wide scandal. The battle for the island when the Ottomans arrived had similarly aroused worldwide interest, and represented at the time a significant change in the balance of power between Islam and Christianity. In fact from Minoan times to World War II, there was rarely a sustained period when Crete didn't have some role to play in world affairs.

The Stone Age

Crete's first inhabitants, **Neolithic cave dwellers**, apparently reached the island around 7000 BC. They came, most probably, from Asia Minor (see page 147), or less likely from Syria, Palestine or North Africa, bringing with them the basics of Stone Age culture – tools of wood, stone and bone, crude pottery and simple cloth.

Development over the next three thousand years was almost imperceptibly slow, but gradually, whether through new migrations and influences or internal dynamics, advances were made. Elementary agriculture was practised, with domestic animals and basic crops. **Pottery** (the oldest samples of which were found beneath the palace at Knossós) became more sophisticated, with better-made domestic utensils and clay figurines of humans, animals and, especially, a fat mother-goddess or fertility figure. Obsidian imported from the island of Mílos was used too. And though caves continued to be inhabited, simple rectangular huts of mud bricks were also built, with increasing skill and complexity as the era wore on. One of the most important of the Neolithic settlements was at Knossós, where two remarkable dwellings have been revealed below the West Court, and there is abundant evidence that many other sites of later habitation were used at this time – Mália, Festós, Ayía Triádha, the Haniá area – as were most of the caves that later came to assume religious significance.

6000–2600 BC

Crete's first inhabitants arrive during the Stone Age when habitation starts in caves. Settlements grow at Knossós and elsewhere.

2600–2000 BC

New migration by the "first Minoans" brings more sophisticated culture and settlements: Vasilikí, Mókhlos and Mýrtos are among the best known.

2000–1700 BC

Evidence of a more formally structured society. First palaces built at most of the famous sites.

The Bronze Age: Minoan Crete

Minoan Crete has been the subject of intense and constant study since its emergence from myth to archeological reality at the beginning of the twentieth century. Yet there is still enormous controversy even over such fundamental details as who the Minoans were and what language they spoke. No written historical records from the time survive (or if they do, they have not yet been deciphered), so almost everything we know is deduced from physical remains, fleshed out somewhat by writings from Classical Greece, almost one thousand years after the destruction of Knossós. Nevertheless it is not hard to forge some kind of consensus from the theories about the Minoans, and this is what is set out below. Fresh discoveries may yet radically change this view.

One of the central arguments is over **dating**. The original system, conceived by Sir Arthur Evans, divided the period into Early, Middle and Late Minoan, with each of these again divided into three sub-periods – a sequence that has become extremely complicated and cumbersome as it has been further qualified and subdivided. Arcane distinctions between the pottery styles of Early Minoan IIa and IIb have no place in a brief history and a simpler system is used here (following the archeologist Nikolaos Platon) of four periods: **Prepalatial**, **Protopalatial** or First Palace, **Neopalatial** or New Palace, and **Postpalatial**.

However, as many archeological texts and guides, as well as numerous museums on the island use the Evans system, the approximate corresponding periods – Early Minoan **(E.M.)**, Middle Minoan **(M.M.)** and Late Minoan **(L.M.)** – are given in brackets.

Prepalatial: 3500–1900 BC (E.M.–M.M.I.)

Among the more important puzzles of Minoan society is its comparatively **sudden emergence**. During the centuries before 2600 BC, there were important changes on the island, and thereafter very rapid progress in almost every area of life. Villages and towns grew up where previously there had been only isolated settlements, and with them came craft specialists: potters, stonecutters, metalworkers, jewellers and weavers.

It seems safe to assume that these changes were wrought by a new **migration** of people from the east, who brought with them new technologies, methods of agriculture and styles of pottery, but most importantly perhaps, a knowledge of seafaring and trade. The olive and the vine – which need little tending and therefore help free a labour force – began to be produced alongside cereal crops. Copper tools replaced stone ones and were themselves later enhanced with the introduction of bronze. Art developed rapidly, with characteristic **Vasilikí ware** and other pottery styles, as well as gold jewellery, and stone jars of exceptional quality, based originally on Egyptian styles. Significantly, large quantities of seal stones have been found too, almost certainly the mark of a mercantile people. They were used to sign letters and documents, but especially to seal packets, boxes or doors as proof that they had not been opened: the designs – scorpions or poisonous spiders – were often meant as a further deterrent to robbery.

At the same time new methods of burial appear – tholos and chamber tombs in which riches were buried with the dead. These appear to have been communal, as, probably, was daily life, based perhaps on clan or kinship groupings.

c.1700 BC	**c.1700–1450 BC**	**c.1450 BC**
Earthquake destroys the palaces.	The Minoan Golden Age. Great palaces at Knossós, Festós, Mália and Zákros; thriving towns at Gourniá and Palékastro.	Final destruction of the palaces.

THE DISCOVERY OF BRONZE AGE CRETE

So ancient is **Minoan civilization** that even by Classical Greek times it had long disappeared into the mists of mythology and Homeric legend. The story of its rediscovery at the beginning of the twentieth century – dominated by two larger-than-life characters in **Heinrich Schliemann** and **Arthur Evans** – is almost as fascinating as that of the Minoans themselves.

HEINRICH SCHLIEMANN

Heinrich Schliemann, a wealthy, self-made, self-educated German, was determined to prove that Homer's stirring tales of prehistoric cities and heroes were true. In the 1870s and 80s, in the face of unremitting hostility from the archeological establishment, he discovered and excavated both Troy and Mycenae, revolutionizing our knowledge of the pre-Classical era. In 1887 he arrived in Crete, made a visit to the site at Knossós, and became convinced that a substantial palace lay waiting to be unearthed. But Crete was still under Ottoman subjection, and the local landowner refused to sell, and Schliemann never succeeded in getting permission to excavate the site.

ARTHUR EVANS AND KNOSSÓS

Arthur Evans, an independently wealthy British scholar who had been inspired by Schliemann, arrived in Crete for the first time on March 15, 1894. With the assistance of Joseph Hatzidhakis, president of the Cretan Archeological Society, Evans began to negotiate for the purchase of the land at Knossós with its Muslim owners. As Crete escaped the clutches of the Ottoman Empire, Evans succeeded in buying the site and excavation began in March, 1900. Within days, evidence of a vast and complex building had been revealed – elegant courtyards with sublime frescoes, pottery, jewellery and tablets bearing an undeciphered ancient script.

Evans was an autocrat whose personal ownership and financing of one of the major sites of antiquity – something that would be unthinkable today – allowed him extraordinary latitude. It was he who named the new civilization **Minoan** after the legendary Cretan king Minos. Far more controversially, he determined that he would not only reveal the palace of Minos but would also restore large parts of it to its original splendour. With the assistance of architects Theodore Fyfe and Piet de Jong, he roofed the Throne Room and reconstructed the grand staircase, replacing the tapered columns with his speculative concrete reconstructions (none of the wooden originals was ever found). Two French-Swiss artists then began to repaint the reconstructed walls with copies of the frescoes. An almost entirely conjectural upper storey, the Piano Nobile, was added using reinforced concrete, and the Central Court was extensively restored as the archeological dig became a building site. Evans argued that he wanted to recreate the "spirit" of the palace structure and decor rather than undertake a literal reconstruction. Few professional archeologists now would defend him, and certainly none would be allowed to carry out such work again, but there can be no doubt that it was the publicity Evans generated that brought Minoan culture to a worldwide audience.

In 1924 Evans donated the Knossós site and the Villa Ariadne, where he lived in style throughout the excavation, to the British School at Athens – it was only in 1952 that it was to become the property of the Greek government. His successor at Knossós – a young English archeologist, John Pendlebury – was killed in the early years of World War II, fighting alongside the Cretans during the German attack on Iráklio in 1941.

c.1450–1100 BC

Gradual revival under Mycenaean influence. Earlier sites reoccupied, with Kydonia the island's chief city. Eteo-Cretans keep Minoan culture alive at Présos and Karfí. Mycenaean control yields to Dorian.

c.1100–67 BC

Island divided into rival groupings, gradually emerging as constantly warring city-states. The most powerful include Láto, Kydonia, Knossós, Górtys and Ierápytna.

THE MINOAN ECONOMY

The extent and grandeur of the Minoan palaces themselves in this Protopalatial era are proof of the island's great prosperity at this time, and the artefacts found within offer further evidence. Advances were made in almost every field of artistic and craft endeavour. From this era came the famous **Kamáres** ware pottery – actually two distinct styles, one eggshell-thin and delicate, the other sturdier with bold-coloured designs. These remarkable works were enabled by the true potter's wheel (as against the turntable) now introduced for the first time, along with a simple form of hieroglyphic writing. Elaborate jewellery, seals and bronzework were also being produced.

Cretan bronze was used throughout the Mediterranean, and its production and distribution were dependent on a wide-ranging **maritime economy**. For though Crete may have produced some copper at this time, it never yielded tin, the nearest significant sources of which were as distant as modern Iran to the east, Central Europe in the north, Italy, Spain, Brittany and even Britain in the west. Nevertheless, Crete controlled the trade routes in the Mediterranean, importing tin, copper, ivory, gold, silver and precious stones of every kind, exporting timber from its rich cypress forests, olive oil, wine, bronze goods and its fine pottery, especially to Egypt. Minoan colonies or trading posts were established on many Cycladic islands as well as the island of Kýthira off the Peloponnese, Rhodes and the coast of Asia Minor; a fleet of merchant vessels maintained regular trade links between these centres and, above all, with Egypt and the east.

Protopalatial (The first palaces): 1900–1700 BC (M.M.I–M.M.II)

Shortly before 1900 BC, the first of the palaces were built, at **Knossós**, **Festós**, **Mália** and **Zákros** – these are the modern Greek place-names, the Minoan ones remain unknown. They represent another significant and apparently abrupt change: a shift of power back to the centre of the island and the emergence of a much more hierarchical, ordered society. The sites of these palaces were also no accident: Festós and Mália both dominate fertile plains, while Zákros had a superbly sited harbour for trade with the east. Knossós, occupying a strategic position above another plain to the south and west of Iráklio, was perhaps originally as much a religious centre as a base of secular power. Certainly at this time religion took on a new importance, with the widespread use of mountain-top sanctuaries and caves as **cult centres**. At the same time much larger towns were growing up, especially around the palaces, and in the countryside substantial "villas" appeared. Around 1700 BC, the palaces were destroyed for the first time, probably by earthquake, although raiders from the early Mycenaean Greek mainland may also have seized this opportunity to raid Crete while it was temporarily defenceless; this may well account for the wealth of gold and other treasure – much of it obviously Cretan – found in the later royal shaft graves at Mycenae.

The Neopalatial Period: 1700–1400 BC (M.M.II–L.M.I)

Although the destruction must have been a setback, Minoan culture continued to flourish, and with the palaces reconstructed on a still grander scale the society entered its golden age. It is these new palaces that provide most of our picture of Minoan life, and most of what is seen at the great sites – Knossós, Festós, Mália, Zákros – dates from this period.

c.300 BC	71 BC	69–67 BC
Cities on south coast form Confederation of Oreoi.	Failed Roman invasion.	Romans invade again and subjugate the island.

The **architecture** of the new palaces was of an unprecedented sophistication: complex, multistorey structures in which the use of space and light was as luxurious as the construction materials. Grand stairways, colonnaded porticoes and courtyards, brightly frescoed walls, elaborate plumbing and drainage, and great magazines in which to store the society's accumulation of wealth, were all integral, as were workshops for the technicians and craftsmen, and areas set aside for ritual and worship.

Obviously it was only an elite that enjoyed these comforts, but conditions for the ordinary people who kept Minos and his attendants in such style appear to have improved too: towns around the palaces and at sites such as Gourniá and Palékastro were growing as well.

Very little is known of how the society was organized, or indeed whether it was a single entity ruled from Knossós or simply several city-states with a common cultural heritage. However, in an intriguing reference to Crete in his *Politics*, Aristotle implied that a caste system had operated in the time of Minos. Clearly, though, it was a society in which **religion** played an important part. The great Corridor of the Procession fresco at Knossós depicted an annual delivery of tribute, apparently to a mother goddess; bull-leaping had a religious significance too; and in all the palaces substantial chambers were set aside for ritual purposes. Secular leaders were also religious leaders.

That Minoan society was a very open one is apparent too. There are virtually no **defences**, internal or external, at any Minoan site, and apparently the rulers felt no threat either from within or without, which has led scholars to emphasize a military strength based on sea power. As far as internal dissent goes, it seems safe to assume that the wealth of the island filtered down, to some extent at least, to all its inhabitants: the lot of a Minoan peasant may have been little different from that of a Cretan villager as little as seventy years ago.

Externally, **maritime supremacy** was further extended: objects of Cretan manufacture turn up all over the Mediterranean and have even been claimed as far afield as Britain and Scandinavia (amber from the Baltic certainly found its way to Crete). Behind their sea power the Minoans clearly felt safe, and the threat of attack or piracy was further reduced by the network of colonies or close allies throughout the Cycladic islands – ancient Thíea most famously but also at Mílos, Náxos, Páros, Mýkonos, Ándhros and Dílos – and in Rhodes, Kýpros, Syria and North Africa. Nevertheless, this appears to have remained a trading empire rather than a military one.

Destruction

Around 1600 BC the island again saw minor earthquake damage, though this was swiftly repaired. But in about 1450 BC came destruction on a calamitous scale: the palaces were smashed and (with the exception of Knossós itself) burned, and smaller settlements across the island were devastated. The cause of this disaster is still the most controversial of all Minoan riddles, and until recently the most convincing theory linked it with the explosion of the volcano of Thera in about 1500 BC – a blast that may have been five times as powerful as that of Krakatoa. The explosion threw up great clouds of black ash and a huge tidal wave, or waves. Coastal settlements would have been directly smashed by the wave, and perhaps further burnt by the overturn of lamps lighted on a day made unnaturally dark by the clouds of ash. Blast, panic and accompanying earth tremors would have contributed to the wreckage.

67 BC–395 AD

Roman rule with Górtys the chief city. Others include Lýttos, Áptera and Knossós. Public works constructed across the island.

67 BC

Crete merges with the Libyan kingdom of Cyrenaica to form a new province.

395 AD

Roman Empire splits; Crete falls under Byzantium, capital of the Eastern Empire.

CULTURAL ADVANCES IN THE NEOPALATIAL PERIOD

If the Neopalatial period was a high point of Minoan power, it also marked the apogee of arts and crafts in the island: again, the bulk of the objects you'll admire in the museums date from this era. The **frescoes** – startling in their freshness and vitality – are the most famous and obviously visible demonstration of this florescence. But they were just the highly visible tip of an artistic iceberg. It was in intricate small-scale work that the Minoans excelled above all. Naturalistic sculpted figures of humans and animals include the superb ivory bull-leaper, the leopard-head axe and the famous snake goddesses or priestesses, all of them on show in the Iráklio Archeological Museum. The carvings on seal stones of this era are of exceptional delicacy – a skill carried over into beautifully delicate gold jewellery. Examples of stone vessels include the bull's head rhyton from Knossós and the three black vases from Ayía Triádha, which are among the museum's most valuable possessions. And pottery broke out into an enormous variety of new shapes and design motifs, drawing inspiration especially from scenes of nature and marine life.

The other great advance was in writing. A new form of script, **Linear A**, had appeared at the end of the Prepalatial period, but in the new palaces its use became widespread. Still undeciphered, Linear A must record the original, unknown language of the Minoans: it seems to have been used in written form almost exclusively for administrative records – stock lists, records of transactions and tax payments. Even were it understood, therefore, it seems unlikely that the language would reveal much. The pieces that have survived were never intended as permanent records, and have been found intact only where the clay tablets used were baked solid in the fires that destroyed the palaces. It is probable that a more formal record, an abstract of the annual accounts, was kept on a more valuable but also more perishable material such as imported papyrus (the Minoans had strong trading links with Egypt) or even a paper produced from native date-palm leaves. There is evidence in the Iráklio museum of the use of ink to inscribe text on ceramic drinking cups that supports this proposition.

And then, as the ash fell, it apparently coated the centre and east of the island in a poisonous blanket under which nothing could grow, or would grow again, for as much as fifty years. Recent surveys by vulcanologists have traced ash from the explosion as far away as Greenland, the Black Sea and Egypt, suggesting that the thousands of tons of ash and pumice thrown into the atmosphere by the blast created a "nuclear winter" across much of Europe and beyond.

Only at Knossós was there any real continuity of habitation, and here it was with **Mycenaean Greeks** in control, bringing with them new styles of art, a greater number of weapons and, above all, keeping records in a form of writing known as **Linear B**, an adaptation of Linear A used to write in an early Greek dialect. In about 1370 BC, Knossós was itself burnt, whether by rebellious Cretans, a new wave of Mycenaeans or perhaps as a result of another natural disaster on a smaller scale.

Such at least is the prevailing theory. But it has its problems – why, for example, should Festós have been burnt when it was safe from waves and blast on the south side of the island? And why should the eruption that vulcanologists dated to 1500 BC have had such a dramatic effect only fifty years later – indeed there are signs that away from the worst effects of the devastation many areas on Crete experienced comparative prosperity after it. As the debate continues, the best that can be said

395–824

Crete ruled from Byzantium. Traces of early churches at Górtys, Soúyia and Thrónos.

824–961

Arab invasion and rule. Górtys sacked with al-Khandak, later Iráklio, the main Arab base.

961

Liberation by Byzantine general Nikephoros Phokas.

THE RIDDLE OF THE OLIVE BRANCH

The confusion surrounding theories about the end of the Neopalatial period was dramatically added to in 2005 when Danish vulcanologists working on Santoríni (modern Thíra) discovered an **olive tree branch** buried inside a rock face formed from volcanic debris. The researchers are convinced that the tree was alive when buried in the cataclysmic eruption. The branch's growth rings were intact and using radio-carbon dating the researchers were able to date the tree's death to between 1627 and 1600 BC. If this dating is correct it suggests that the eruption occurred at least 100 years earlier than previously thought. It has also plunged ancient Aegean chronology into confusion. Historians tend to rely on the Egyptian chronology (with its long history, king lists and 365-day years) for setting Minoan dates. Accepted thinking thus far is that Minoan civilization was contemporary with that of the Egyptian New Kingdom (dated c.1550–1050 BC). If the vulcanolgists' new dating is correct and Minoan civilization effectively collapsed c.1600 then this is wildly out of sync. As one Cretan archeologist put it: "We now have absolute chaos as far as giving years to events is concerned and something must give – this is likely to be Egyptian dates which are now out by up to two centuries."

currently is that the volcano theory fits the available evidence better than most of its rivals. But many scholars still claim that the facts are more consistent with destruction by human rather than natural causes.

The main counter-theory assumes an invasion by the Mycenaeans, and points to some evidence that Linear B was in use at Knossós before 1450 BC. But if the Mycenaeans came to conquer, they would have gained nothing by destroying the society already flourishing on Crete; nor would they have subsequently left the former population centres deserted for a generation or more.

A third theory attempts to answer these inconsistencies, suggesting that an **internal revolt** by the populace against its rulers (possibly in the wake of the chaos caused by the Thera eruption) could provide an explanation. This theory would fit the evidence from sites such as Pýrgos near Mýrtos on the south coast, where a villa dominating the site was burned down while the surrounding settlement remained untouched. Needless to say this theory does not find favour with those who see Minoan civilization as a haven of tranquil splendour, but it does fit with the later Greek tradition of a tyrannical Minos oppressing not only his own people but those abroad as well.

Post-Palatial: 1450–1100 BC (L.M.II–L.M.III)

From their foothold at Knossós, the Mycenaeans gradually spread their influence across the island as it became habitable again. By the early fourteenth century BC they controlled much of Crete, and some of the earlier sites, including Gourniá, Ayía Triádha, Týlissos and Palékastro, were **re-occupied**. It is a period that is still little known and that was written off by the early Minoan scholars almost entirely. However more recent excavations are revealing that the island remained productive, albeit in a role peripheral to the Greek mainland.

In particular **western Crete** now came into its own, as the area least affected by the volcano. **Kydonia** – the nearest port to the Mycenean heartland – became the chief city of the island, still with a considerable international trade and continuing, in its art

961–1204	**1204**	**1204–1669**
Byzantine rule returns. Small frescoed churches built across Crete.	Fourth Crusade. Byzantium sacked and occupied; Crete sold to Venice.	Venetian rule. Extensive early building includes churches and monasteries; later, major defence works at Iráklio, Réthymno and Haniá, plus castles at Frangokástello and on the fortified islets.

and architecture, very much in the Minoan style. But Kydonia lies beneath modern Haniá and has never been (nor is ever likely to be) properly excavated – another reason that far less is known about this period than those that preceded it. In **central Crete** the main change was in retreat from the coasts, a sign of the island's decline in international affairs and trade, and perhaps of an increase in piracy. Even here, however, despite the presence of new influences, much of the art is recognizably Minoan. Most of the famous clay and stone *lárnakes* (sarcophagi) – which were a distinctly new method of burial – date from this final Minoan era.

More direct evidence of the survival of Crete comes in Homer's account of the **Trojan War**, when he talks of a Cretan contingent taking part under King Idomenevs or Idomeneas (according to him, the grandson of Minos). The war and its aftermath – a period of widespread change – also affected Crete. In the north of Greece the Mycenaeans were being overrun by varied tribes (the so-called Sea Peoples moving down from the Balkans, in particular the **Dorians**. Around 1200 BC the relative peace was disrupted again: many sites were abandoned for the last time, others burnt. Briefly, Mycenaean influence became yet more widespread, as refugees arrived on the island. But by the end of the twelfth century BC, Minoan culture was in terminal decline, and Crete was entering into the period of confusion that engulfed most of the Greek world. Some of the original population of the island, later known as **Eteo-Cretans** (true Cretans), retreated at this time to mountain fastnesses at sites such as Présos and Karfí, where they survived, along with elements of Minoan culture and language, for almost another millennium.

Dorian and Classical Crete

By the end of the twelfth century, the bulk of the island had been taken over by the **Dorians**: there may have been an invasion, but it seems more probable that the process was a gradual one, by settlement. At any event, over the succeeding centuries the Dorians came to dominate the central lowlands, with substantial new cities such as Lato (Lató in modern Greek) near modern Áyios Nikólaos.

Dorian Crete was not in any real sense a unified society: its cities warred with each other and there may, as well as the Dorians and Eteo-Cretans, have been other cultural groupings in the west, at Kydonia and sites such as Falásarna and Polyrinía. Nevertheless the island saw another minor **artistic renaissance**, with styles now mostly shared with the rest of the Greek world; in the making of tools and weapons, **iron** gradually came to replace bronze.

Much the most important survival of this period, however, is the celebrated **law code** from Górtys. The code (see page 106) was set down around 450 BC, but it reflects laws that had already been in force for hundreds of years: the society described is a strictly hierarchical one, clearly divided into a ruling class, free men, serfs and slaves. For the rulers, life followed a harsh, militaristic regime similar to that of Sparta – the original population, presumably, had been reduced to the level of serfs.

As mainland Greece approached its **Classical Age**, Crete advanced little. It remained a populous island, but one where a multitude of small city-states were constantly vying for power. Towns of this period are characterized by their strong defences, and most observed the Górtys laws (Górtys remained among the most powerful of them) in tough oligarchical or aristocratic regimes. At best, Crete was a minor player in Greek

1453

Fall of Constantinople; renaissance of Byzantine art on Crete.

1541

The artist El Greco (Domenico Theotokópoulos) born in Crete; in 1577 moves to Toledo, Spain where he makes his name.

1587

Vitzentzos Kornaos, Crete's greatest poet and composer of the epic *Erotókritos*, born near Sitía.

affairs, increasingly known as the den of pirates and as a valuable source of mercenaries unrivalled in guerrilla tactics. The island must have retained influence though, for it was still regarded by Classical Athenians as the source of much of their culture, and its strict institutions were admired by many philosophers. In addition, many Cretan shrines and caves show unbroken use from Minoan through to Roman times, and those associated with the birth and early life of Zeus (the Dhiktean and Idean caves especially) were important centres of pilgrimage.

The multitude of small, independent **city-states** is well illustrated by the Confederation of Oreoi, an accord formed around 300 BC between Elyros, Lissos (modern Lissós), Hyrtakina, Tarra, Syia (modern Soúyia) and Pikílassos, six towns in a now barely populated area of the southwest. They were later joined in the Confederation by Górtys and Cyrenaica (in North Africa). Meanwhile Roman power was growing in the Mediterranean, and Crete's strategic position and turbulent reputation drew her inexorably into the struggle.

Conquest by Rome

From the second century BC onwards, **Rome** was drawn into wars in mainland Greece, and the involvement of Cretan troops on one or often both sides became an increasing irritation. The island was also a notorious haven for pirates that frequently preyed upon Roman merchant vessels. Hannibal was staying at Górtys at the time of one Roman attempt to pacify the island, around 188 BC. More than a century passed with only minor interventions, however, before Rome could turn its full attention to Crete – the last important part of the Greek world not under its sway.

In 74 BC Marcus Antonius (father of Mark Antony) attempted an invasion mainly aimed at chastising the pirates, but was heavily defeated by the Kydonians. A fresh attempt was made under **Quintus Metellus** (afterwards called Creticus) in 69 BC. This time a bridgehead was successfully established by exploiting divisions among the Cretans: Metellus was supported in his initial campaign against Kydonia by its rivals at Polyrínia. The tactic of setting Cretan against Cretan served him well, but even so it took almost three years of bitter and brutal warfare before the island was completely subdued in 67 BC. It was a campaign marked by infighting not only among the Cretans – Górtys was among those to take Metellus's side – but also between Romans, with further forces sent from Rome in an unsuccessful bid to curb Metellus's excesses and his growing power.

With the conquest complete, Crete was combined with Cyrenaica (in modern Libya) as a single province whose capital was at **Gortys**, and though there was little contact between the two halves of the province, both were important sources of grain and agricultural produce for Rome.

Through the first and second centuries AD, important public works were undertaken throughout Crete: roads, aqueducts and irrigation systems, important cities at Knossós, Áptera, Lýttos and others, as well as considerable grandeur at Gortys. **Christianity** arrived with St Paul's visit around 60 AD; soon after, he appointed Titus (Titos) as the island's first bishop to continue conversion in earnest. Around 250 AD, the Holy Ten – Áyii Dhéka – were martyred at Gortys, probably during the first great persecution of Christians initiated by the Emperor Decius.

1645	**1669**	**1669–1898**
Ottomans capture Haniá.	Iráklio surrenders to the Ottomans after a long siege.	Ottoman rule. Mosques and fountains constructed in the cities, especially Haniá, Réthymno and Ierápetra, but few public works undertaken elsewhere.

The Byzantine Age

With the split of the Roman Empire at the end of the fourth century, Crete found itself part of the Eastern Empire under **Byzantium**. The island continued to prosper – as the churches that were built everywhere testify – but in international terms it was not important. Byzantine rule, here as everywhere, imposed a stiflingly ordered society, hierarchical and bureaucratic in the extreme. Of the earliest churches only traces survive, in particular of mosaic floors like those at Soúyia or Thrónos, though there are more substantial remains of the basilica of Áyios Títos at Górtys.

Then in 824 Crete was invaded by a band of **Arabs** under Abu Hafs Omar. Essentially a piratical group who had been driven first from Spain and then Alexandria, they nevertheless managed to keep control of the island for well over a century. There was not much in the way of progress at this time but there was a fortress founded at al-Khandak, a site that later developed into Iráklio. At the same time Górtys and other Roman-Byzantine cities were sacked and destroyed.

After several failed attempts, the Byzantine general **Nikephoros Phokas** reconquered Crete in 961, following a siege at Khandak in which he catapulted the heads of his Arab prisoners over the walls. For a while the island revived, boosted by an influx of colonists from the mainland and from Constantinople, including a number of aristocratic families (the Arhontopouli) whose power survived throughout the medieval era. By now, however, the entire empire was embattled by Islam and losing out in trade to the Venetians and Genoese. Frescoed churches continued to be built, but most were small and parochial.

Ironically enough it was not Muslims who brought about the final end of Byzantine rule, but Crusaders. The **Fourth Crusade** turned on Constantinople in 1204 (at the instigation of the Venetians), sacking and capturing the city. The leader of this Crusade, Prince Boniface of Montferrat, ceded Crete to the Venetians for a nominal sum.

Venetian Crete

Before Venice could claim its new territory, it had to drive out its chief commercial rivals, the **Genoese**, who had taken control in 1206 with considerable local support. By 1210 the island had been secured, though for more than a century thereafter the Genoese pursued their claim, repeatedly siding with local rebels when it looked like there was a chance of establishing a presence on the island.

The Venetians, however, were not going to surrender their prize easily. Crete for them was a vital resource, both for the control of eastern Mediterranean trade routes that the island's ports commanded, and for the natural wealth of the agricultural land and the timber for shipbuilding. The Venetian system was rapidly and stringently imposed, with Venetian overlords, directly appointed from Venice, administering what were effectively a series of feudal fiefdoms.

This system was designed to exploit Crete's resources as efficiently as possible, and not surprisingly it provoked deep resentment from the beginning. There were constant **rebellions** throughout the thirteenth century, led as often as not by one or other of the aristocratic Byzantine families from an earlier wave of colonization. Certainly the wealthy had most to lose: it was their land that was confiscated to be granted to military colonists from Venice (along with the service of the people who

1770

Revolt against Turkish rule by rebel leader Dhaskaloyiannis in Sfakiá; he is defeated and executed at Iráklio.

1821

Greek War of Independence declared. Islanders repressed by Turkish and Egyptian troops with much bloodshed.

1828

Major battle between Cretans and Muslim forces at Frangokástello fort; more than a thousand killed.

lived on it), and their rights and privileges that were taken over by the new overlords. The rebellions were in general strictly noble affairs, ended by concessions of land or power to their Cretan leaders. But there were more fundamental resentments too. Heavy taxes and demands for feudal service were widely opposed – by the established colonists almost as much as by the natives. And the **Orthodox Church** was replaced by the Roman Catholic one as the "official" religion, the senior clergy expelled and much Church property seized. Local priests and monasteries that survived helped fuel antagonism: even from this early date the monasteries were becoming known as centres of dissent.

The **Middle Ages** were perhaps the most productive years in Crete's history, with exports of corn, wine, oil and salt, the ports busy with trans-shipment business and the wooded hillsides being stripped for timber.

After 1453, and the final fall of Constantinople, Crete saw a spectacular cultural renaissance as a stream of refugees arrived from the east. **Candia** – as the island and its capital were known to the Venetians – became the centre of exiled Byzantine art and scholarship. From this later period, and the meeting of the traditions of Byzantium and the Italian Renaissance, come the vast majority of the works of art and architecture now associated with the Venetian era. The great icon painter Dhamaskinos studied alongside El Greco in the school of Ayía Ekateríni in Iráklio; the Orthodox monasteries flourished; and in literature the island produced, among others, what is now regarded as its greatest work – the *Erotókritos* (see page 352).

But it was the growing **external threat** that stimulated the most enduring of the Venetian public works – the island's defences. Venice's bastions in the mainland Middle East had fallen alongside Constantinople, and in 1571 Cyprus too was taken by the Turks, leaving Crete well and truly on the front line. Large-scale pirate raids had already been common: in 1538 Barbarossa had destroyed Réthymno and almost taken Haniá, and during the 1560s there were further attacks. Across the island, cities were strengthened and the fortified islets defending the seaways were repaired and rebuilt. As the seventeenth century wore on, however, Venice itself was in severe decline: Mediterranean trade was overshadowed by New World commerce, a business dominated by the Spanish, English and Dutch.

Finally, in 1645 a Venetian attack on an Ottoman convoy provided the excuse for an all-out **Turkish assault** on Crete. Haniá fell after a siege that cost forty thousand attackers' lives, and Réthymno rapidly followed. By 1648 the Ottomans controlled the whole island except **Iráklio** , where they dug in for the long haul. For 23 years of siege the city resisted, supplied from the sea and with moral support at least from most of Europe. The end was inevitable, though, and from the Ottoman point of view there was no hurry: they controlled the island's produce, they were well supplied, and they enjoyed a fair degree of local support, having relaxed the Venetian rules – for example, they allowed Orthodox bishops back into Crete. By 1669 the city was essentially reduced, and in a final effort the pope managed to persuade the French to send a small army. After a couple of fruitless sorties involving heavy losses, the French withdrew in an argument over the command. On September 5, when Iráklio finally surrendered, close to 140,000 Ottomans, Cretans and Venetians had perished in the struggle for control of the city. Iráklio's fall left only the three fortified islets of Soúdha, Spinalónga and Gramvóusa in Venetian hands, where they remained until surrendered by treaty in 1715.

1864

Eleftherios Venizélos, Cretan revolutionary and statesman, born at Mourniés, near Haniá.

1866

Explosion at Arkádhi, a Cretan Orthodox guerrilla stronghold. Hundreds die in blast and international sympathy for Crete is aroused.

1883

Nikos Kazantzákis, Crete's most famous writer and creator of *Zorba the Greek*, born in Iráklio.

Ottoman Crete

It is arguable whether the Ottoman **occupation** was ever as stringent or arduous as the Venetian had been, but its reputation is far worse. In part this may simply be that its memory is more recent, but Ottoman rule was complicated too by the religious differences involved, and by the fact that it survived into the era of resurgent Greek nationalism and Great Power politics.

If on their arrival the Turks had been welcomed, it was not a long-lived honeymoon. Once again Crete was divided, now between powerful pashas, and once again it was regarded merely as a resource to be exploited. The Ottoman Empire was less strictly ordered than the Venetian, but it demanded no less: rather than attempt to take control of trade themselves, the Turks simply imposed crippling taxes. Imposition of local administration was left to local landlords and the local-convert **Janissaries** they controlled. At the local level, then, there was a further level of exploitation as these men too took their cut. Stultified by heavy taxes and tariffs, slowed by neglect, the island economy stagnated.

One way to avoid the worst of the burden was to become a Muslim and, gradually, much of the Christian population was converted to **Islam** – at least nominally. Conversion brought with it substantial material advantages in taxation and rights to own property, and it helped avoid the worst of the repression that inevitably followed any Christian rebellion. These Greek Muslims were not particularly religious, many were adherents of the Bektashi dervish order, which tolerated consumption of alcohol: even among the Muslims on the island, Islamic law seems to have been loosely interpreted, and many continued to worship as Christians in secret, but the mass apostasies served to further divide the island. For those who remained openly Christian the burden became increasingly heavy as there were fewer to bear it. Many took to the mountains, where Ottomans authority barely reached.

As the occupation continued, the Cretans strengthened their hold on the cities and the fertile plains around them, while the mountains became the stronghold of the Christian *pallikária*. The first major **rebellion** came in 1770, and inevitably it was centred in the recalcitrant region of Sfakiá. Under **Dhaskaloyiannis** (see page 282) the Cretans had been drawn into Great Power politics – drawn in and abandoned, for the promised aid from Russia never came. With the failure of this struggle, Sfakiá was itself brought under Ottoman control for a while. But a pattern had been set, and the nineteenth century saw almost constant outbreaks of rebellion.

The War of Independence

At the beginning of the nineteenth century the Ottoman Empire was under severe pressure on the Greek mainland, and in 1821 full-scale revolution, the **Greek War of Independence**, broke out. Part of the imperial response was to call on the pasha of Egypt, **Mehmet Ali**, for assistance: his price was control of Crete. By 1824, in a campaign that even by Cretan standards was brutal on both sides, he had crushed the island's resistance. When in 1832 an independent Greek state was finally established with the support of Britain, France and Russia, Crete was left in the hands of the Egyptians, but reverting to Otoman imperial control within ten years.

From now on guerrilla warfare in support of union with Greece – **énosis** – was almost constant, flaring occasionally into wider revolts but mostly taking the form of incessant raids and irritations. The Cretans enjoyed widespread support, not only on the Greek

1894	**1897**	**1898**
British archeologist Arthur Evans arrives in Crete and visits the site of Knossós, which would later bring him worldwide fame.	Great Powers occupy Crete after more uprisings; island divided into British, French, Russian and Italian sectors.	Riot in Iráklio sparks the end of the Ottoman rule. Autonomy follows, with Prince George of Greece acting under Ottoman suzerainty.

mainland but throughout western Europe, and especially among expatriate Greek communities. But the Greeks alone were no match for Ottoman fleets or armies, and the Great Powers, wary more than anything of each other, consistently failed to intervene. There was a major rising in 1841, bloodily suppressed, and in 1858 another which ended relatively peacefully in the recall of the imperial governor and some minor concessions to the Christian population.

In 1866 a Cretan Assembly meeting in Sfakiá declared independence and union with Greece, and Egyptian troops were recalled to put down a further wave of revolts bolstered by Greek volunteers. Again the Egyptians proved ruthlessly effective, but this campaign ended in the explosion at **Arkádhi** (see page 204), an act of defiance that aroused Europe-wide sympathy. The Great Powers – Britain above all – still refused to involve themselves, but privately the supply of arms and volunteers to the insurgents was redoubled. From now on some kind of solution seemed inevitable, but even in 1878 the Congress of Berlin left Crete under Ottoman dominion, demanding only further reforms in the government. In 1889 and 1896 there were further violent encounters, and in 1897 a Greek force landed to annexe the island. Finally, the Great Powers were forced into action, occupying Crete with an international force and dividing the island into areas controlled by the British, French, Russians and Italians.

Independence and union with Greece

The outrage that finally brought about the expulsion of Turkish troops from Crete in 1898 was a minor skirmish in Iráklio (see page 63) that led to the death of the British vice-consul. A local **national government** was set up, still nominally under Ottoman suzerainty, with Prince George, younger son of King George of Greece, as high commissioner; under him was a joint Muslim-Christian assembly, part elected, part appointed.

Euphoria at independence was muted, however, for full union with Greece remained the goal of most Cretans. A new leader of this movement rapidly emerged – **Eleftherios Venizélos**. Born at Mourniés, just outside Haniá, Venizélos had fought in the earlier independence struggles, and become a member of the Cretan Assembly and minister of justice under Prince George. Politically, however, he had little in common with his new master, and in 1905 he summoned an illegal Revolutionary Assembly at Thériso. Though the attempt to take up arms was summarily crushed, the strength of support for Venizélos was enough to force the resignation of Prince George. In 1908, the Cretan Assembly unilaterally declared *énosis* – much to the embarrassment of the Greek government. For, in the meantime, the "Young Turk" revolution looked set to revitalize the Ottoman Empire, and the Great Powers remained solidly opposed to anything that might upset the delicate balance of power in the Balkans.

The failure of the Greek government to act decisively in favour of Crete was one of the factors that led to the Military League of young officers forcing political reform on the mainland. With their backing, Venizélos became premier of Greece in 1910. In 1912 Greece, Serbia and Bulgaria declared war on the Ottoman Empire, making spectacular advances into its territory. By the peace of 1913, Crete finally and officially became part of the Greek nation.

Though Greece was politically riven by **World War I**, and succeeding decades saw frequent, sometimes violent changes of power between Venizelist and Royalist forces,

1898–1913	**1905**	**1908**
Quasi-Independence and emergence of Venizélos, who summons a Revolutionary Assembly at Thériso urging full union (*énosis*) with Greece.	The unpopular Prince George resigns.	Crete unilaterally declares *énosis*, which is opposed by the Great Powers.

THE KIDNAPPING OF GENERAL KREIPE

The Cretan resistance to the Nazi occupation had one spectacular success in 1944 when they kidnapped the German commander **General Kreipe** outside Iráklio, and succeeded in smuggling him over the mountains to the south coast and off the island to Egypt. Among this group were the author Patrick Leigh Fermor and Stanley Moss (whose *Ill Met by Moonlight* describes the incident in detail). The immediate result of this propaganda coup, however, was a terrible vengeance against the Cretan population, in which a string of villages around the Amári valley were destroyed and such menfolk as could be found were slaughtered. Harsh **retribution** against Cretan civilians, indeed, was the standard reaction by the German army to any success the resistance had.

Crete was little affected. On just one further occasion did the island play a significant role in Greek affairs before the outbreak of war in 1940: in July 1938 there was a popular uprising against the dictator Metaxas, but it was swiftly put down.

The island was, however, hit hard by the aftermath of the disastrous Greek attempt to conquer western Anatolia, including Constantinople, in pursuit of the "Great Idea" of reconstituting the Byzantine Empire. As part of the peace settlement that followed this military debacle, there was a forced **exchange of populations** in 1923: Muslims were expelled from Greece and Orthodox Christians from Turkey. In Crete many of these "Turks" were in fact Muslim Cretans, descendants of the mass apostasies of the eighteenth century. Nevertheless they left – some thirty thousand in all – and a similar number of Christian refugees from the new Turkish Republic took their place.

World War II and occupation

In the winter of 1940 Italian troops invaded northern Greece, only to be thrown back across the Albanian border by the Greek army. Mussolini's humiliation, however, only served to draw the Germans into the fight, and although an Allied army was sent to Greece, the **mainland** was rapidly overrun.

The Allied campaign was marked from the start by suspicion, confusion and lack of communication between the two commands. On the Greek side Metaxas had died in January, and his successor as premier committed suicide, leaving a Cretan banker – **Emmanuil Tsouderos** – to organize the retreat of king and government to his native island. They were rapidly followed by thousands of evacuees, including the bulk of the Allied army, a force made up in large part of Australian and New Zealand soldiers. Most of the native Cretan troops, a division of the Greek army, had been wiped out in defence of the mainland.

According to the Allied plan, Crete should by now have been an impregnable fortress. In practice, though, virtually nothing had been done to improve the island defences, there were hardly any serviceable planes or other heavy equipment, and the arriving troops found little in the way of a plan for their deployment.

On May 20, 1941 the **invasion** of the island began, as German troops poured in by glider and parachute. It was at first a horrible slaughter, with the invaders easily picked off as they drifted slowly down. Few of the first wave of parachutists reached the

1913

Following the First Balkan war by Greece and its allies against Ottoman Turkey, union of Greece and Crete is formally declared.

1923

Compulsory exchange of populations by confessional criteria between Greece and Turkey following Greek military debacle in the Greco-Turkish war; 30,000 Cretan Muslims expelled.

ground alive and many of the gliders crashed, while the main German force was smashed before it ever reached the ground. In the far west, however, beyond the main battle zone, they succeeded in taking the airfield at Máleme. Whether through incompetence (as much of the literature on the Battle of Crete suggests) or breakdown of communications, no attempt to recapture the field was made until the Germans had had time to defend it and, with a secure landing site, reinforcements and equipment began to pour in. Not long before the battle, the German codes had been cracked, and the Allied commander in Crete, General Freyberg, therefore knew in detail exactly where and how the attacks would come. However, because he was not allowed to divulge secret intelligence findings to his junior officers (who were not cleared to receive them), a fatal misunderstanding by the commander regarding the enemy's intentions contained in the intelligence led him to reduce his forces at Máleme. From now on the battle, which had seemed won, was lost, and the Allied troops, already under constant air attack, found themselves outgunned on land too.

Casualties of the **Battle of Crete** were horrendous on both sides – the cemeteries are reminiscent of the burial grounds of World War I victims in northern France – and the crack German airborne division was effectively wiped out, causing a devastated Hitler to erect the monument to it which still stands outside Haniá (although recently damaged by protesters). No one ever attempted a similar assault again. But once they were established with a secure bridgehead, the Germans advanced rapidly, and a week after the first landings the Allied army was in full retreat across the mountains towards Hóra Sfakíon, from where most were evacuated by ship to Egypt. On May 30, the battle was over, leaving behind several thousand Allied soldiers (and all the Cretans who had fought alongside them) to surrender or take to the mountains.

The resistance

One of the first tasks of **the resistance** was to get these stranded soldiers off the island, and in this they had remarkable success, organizing the fugitives into groups and arranging their collection by ship or submarine from isolated beaches on the south coast. Many were hidden and fed by monks while they waited to escape, most famously at the monastery of Préveli. In this and many other ways the German occupation closely mirrored earlier ones; opposition was constant and reprisals brutal. The north coast and the lowlands were, as in the past, easily and firmly controlled, but the mountains, and Sfakiá above all, remained the haunt of rebel and resistance groups throughout the war.

With the boats that took the battle survivors away from Crete came intelligence officers whose job it was to organize and arm the resistance; throughout the war there were a dozen or so on the island, living in mountain shelters or caves, attempting to organize parachute drops of arms and reporting by radio on troop movements on and around the island. How effective the sporadic efforts of the resistance were in wartime Crete is hard to gauge and it is questionable whether stunts such as the kidnapping of General Kreipe (see box) brought the end of the occupation any nearer.

At the end of 1944, the German forces withdrew to a heavily fortified perimeter around Haniá, where they held out for a final seven months before surrendering in mid-1945. In the rest of the island, this left a **power vacuum** that several of the resistance groups rushed to fill. Allied intelligence would no doubt claim that

1941

German invasion of Crete. A fatal blunder by the defenders allows invaders to take the airport at Máleme and establish a bridgehead.

1944

The island's German commander, Heinrich Kreipe, is kidnapped by the resistance. The German army carries out brutal reprisals against the islanders.

one of the achievements of their agents in Crete was the near-avoidance of the civil war that wracked the rest of Greece. On the mainland the organization of the resistance had been very largely the work of Greek Communists, who emerged at the end of the war as much the best organized and armed group. On Crete, groups in favour with the Allies had been the best armed and organized, and certainly in the latter stages of the war, Communist-dominated organizations had been deliberately starved of equipment.

Postwar and modern Crete

In avoiding the civil war, Crete was able to set about **reconstruction** some way in advance of the rest of Greece, and after 1945 it grew to become one of the most prosperous and productive regions of the nation. Politically, postwar Crete was deeply mistrustful of outside control, even from Athens, a situation that persists today. At the local level above all, loyalties are divided along clan and patronage lines rather than party political ones, and leaders are judged on how well they provide for their areas and their followers.

Cretan politicians at the local level (there is no overall island government, only three regional **administrations** based at Haniá, Iráklio and Áyios Nikólaos) continue to take an almost universal joy in standing up to central authority. **Rivalries** within Crete are fierce, too, most notably between Haniá, which was nominated as capital for a short period at the beginning of the century, and Iráklio, the traditional and present capital and nowadays the richer and politically more important city. This factionalism results in all sorts of anomalies and compromises: symptomatic was the rather impractical decision to spread the University of Crete across three campuses, at Iráklio, Réthymno (which has always considered itself the most cultured town in Crete) and the autonomous polytechnic of Haniá.

In **national politics**, the island presents a more unified front as the upholder of the liberal tradition of Venizélos. The 1967 anti-left coup in Athens that brought the junta of the Colonels to power was passionately opposed in Crete – one of the few areas of Greece to offer overt resistance to the regime. There followed seven years of repression during which all political activity was banned, the press heavily censored and Leftists arrested, imprisoned and tortured. In a referendum following the overthrow of the Colonels in 1974, Crete voted heavily against a restoration of the monarchy (the king had been indirectly implicated in the coup) and for a republican system. Then, in the succeeding presidential election, support for the right-winger Kostas Karamanlis (the winner) was less than half as strong on Crete as it was in the rest of Greece. Prior to the new millennium this became an abiding pattern: the socialist PASOK party consistently polled twice as many Cretan votes as the conservative ND, and still does well here even after the Syriza-led governments.

Into the new millennium

The dominant parties of the restored democracy, the conservative **Néa Dhimokratía** (New Democracy; ND) and socialist **Panhellenic Socialist Movement (PASOK)**, had both been founded in the aftermath of the dictatorship and alternated in power for four decades until the end of 2014. The dominant figures in both parties were their respective founders, **Konstantinos Karamanlis** of ND and **Andreas Papandreou** of

1945	1960s	1967–74	1981
Liberation. A war-shattered island begins the slow task of reconstruction.	Tourist boom begins.	Dictatorship of the Colonels. Following their overthrow, in a national referendum Crete votes heavily against any restoration of the monarchy.	Greece becomes a full member of the EU.

A GREEK TRAGEDY

The **debt crisis**, which began in 2009, saw Greece's economy nosedive. GDP shrank by over 25 percent between 2010 and 2017, the public sector was cut by 26 percent, and pensions and welfare payments were slashed by 70 percent. Unemployment reached 28 percent of the workforce (most of whom did not receive benefits), before falling back to around 20 percent, and was far worse among the young, with youth unemployment running around 43 percent. In the prolonged recession wages and pensions were slashed and a fifth of the nation were unable to meet their food needs, with a third below the poverty line. Since most of the bailout funds have gone to pay off creditors, almost nothing has been invested in economic recovery. To top it all, Greece's debt mountain amounted to almost twice the country's annual economic output.

Despite what seems to be a desperately bleak outlook, Greece does have the potential to be a successful economy. But to even start to get itself on a sound financial footing it will have to deal effectively with key issues such as **tax evasion** and **corruption** – often two sides of the same coin. The Greek debt crisis is, in short, the product of thirty years of budget deficits – racked up by the corrupt political dynasties of PASOK and Néa Dhimokratía – abetted by cripplingly low tax receipts. A survey by the Chicago Booth Business School in 2012 estimated that self-employed workers (Greece has proportionally more than any other EU country) had failed to report around €28 billion in taxable income in 2009 alone.

PASOK. The cause of many of Greece's current problems can be traced back to the first Papandreou administration, which came to power following an election victory in 1981, the same year that Greece entered the European Community. Promising "*allaghí*", the great change, he overturned the relatively cautious economic policies of previous governments and introduced sharp pay rises and an unprecedented increase of jobs in the public sector. This free-spending populist policy enabled PASOK to maintain power for most of the 1990s and early 2000s while the debts mounted. Following Papandreou's death in 1996 there was no change of direction by PASOK and the new leader, **Costas Simitis**, broadly followed the spendthrift policies of the Papandreou years. Simitis's major achievement was to steer Greece into the eurozone, although it later emerged that the accession criteria had not only not been met, but that the Greek government had falsified the figures relating to public debt and inflation to enable entry to go ahead.

The new ND leader, Konstantinos Karamanlis, namesake and nephew of the party's founder, did not oppose the policies of PASOK, but adopted an even more populist stance which enabled him to win the election of 2004. Ironically his victory was over the new leader of PASOK, **Yiorgakis (little George) Papandreou**, the son of PASOK's founder. However, the Karamanlis government proved little more successful than its predecessors in dealing with an ailing economy and rising unemployment, lurching from one crisis to another. A string of corruption scandals linked to the government rocked the administration, and in late 2008 riots broke out across the country, in a nationwide protest against the effects of the world economic downturn and frustration at the severely limited prospects for young people.

In September 2009, with the government barely clinging to power, Karamanlis called another election. Voters turned out to eject ND and **hand victory to**

1999

Greece joins eleven other EU states in creating the European Economic and Monetary Union (EMU) and a single currency, the euro.

2002

The drachma is replaced by the euro as Greece's official currency.

2004

Athens stages the Olympic Games, with some events held in Crete.

PASOK and its leader George Papandreou the Younger, often called Yorgakis to distinguish him from his politician grandfather.

The worst of times

Any chance the new government had of dealing with Greece's ongoing problems was capsized by the financial tsunami of the **government debt crisis** that overwhelmed the country at the end of 2009. Reports that Greece had been using dubious accounting practices to hide the scale of its borrowing triggered panic among overseas investors concerned that the country would be unable to meet its debt obligations. Following numerous revisions of the debt figures, in May 2010 the Greek deficit was again revised upwards to an estimated fifteen percent of GDP (against a eurozone limit of three percent), one of the highest in the world. Credit ratings agencies then downgraded Greek government bonds to junk status creating further alarm in financial markets. In order to avert a default by the Greek government, in May 2010 the IMF, European Central Bank and the European Commission (the so-called "troika") devised an urgent €45 billion **rescue package**, with a further €65 billion to follow. The price of this funding was a harsh series of **austerity measures** intended to bring the government's deficit under control. These measures – consisting of public sector workforce cuts and salary reductions, as well as labour and pension reforms – were opposed by large segments of the Greek populace, and a wave of **social unrest** swept across the country, with strikes and riots occurring in Athens and other cities.

Throughout 2011 Papandreou's government continued to grapple with the crisis, implementing more austerity measures as its popularity plummeted. In November, after failing to enlist the support of the other major parties to form a coalition administration, Papandreou **resigned as prime minister**. The PASOK and Néa Dhimokratía parties agreed to form an emergency government headed by former vice president of the European Central Bank, **Lucas Papademos**, until new elections could be held. In May 2012 the country went to the polls but the outcome was a stalemate: in a second election ND under its new leader, **Andonis Samaras**, gained the most seats and on June 20 formed a coalition with PASOK under its new leader, Evangelos Venizélos (a pseudonym; he is no relation to Eleftherios). The new coalition government had a workable majority over the other parties but, worryingly for the future, these included extreme left and neo-Nazi groups opposed to the financial strictures "imposed by foreigners".

The arrival of Syriza

In November 2012 the coalition government voted through a further round of severe austerity measures to receive the country's **second economic bailout** from the EU and IMF. The measures included pension cuts, increases in retirement age and wage cuts of up to thirty percent for civil servants and government employees. In the succeeding two years more cuts followed, plunging the country into deep economic distress. Now highly unpopular, the government fell, and new elections were announced for January 2015.

In the poll held on January 25, an electorate weary of the incompetent and corrupt dynastic parties PASOK and ND handed an historic victory to a coalition headed by left-wing **Syriza** that sent shockwaves through European capitals. Its young and charismatic leader, 41-year old **Alexis Tsipras**, vowed not only to end the old

2008

Crete is badly hit by the worldwide financial crisis.

2009–12

Greek government debt crisis and a possible default threatens the stability of the world's monetary system. Crete shares in severe austerity measures to cut the nation's deficit.

2013

Reopening of the Iráklio Archeological Museum, following a seven-year closure for reconstruction.

TOURISM: THE ISLAND'S FUTURE?

As falling prices for Crete's major agricultural products – olive oil, raisins and citrus fruits – mean they contribute less to the island's prosperity, Crete becomes more and more dependent on **tourism**. But at the same time the age of mass-market tourism is beginning to pall as the attractions of sun, beach and cheap booze along much of the coast attract mainly younger holidaymakers, who tend to move on when prices rise – as they have done as a consequence of the current financial calamity. The fallout from the global economic recession and the country's debt crisis has also taken its toll, but tourist arivals on Crete from overseas continue to be substantial, boosted by major overseas companies such as TUI.

Efforts to build a market in **green tourism** are in their infancy, held back by an indifference to environmental concerns by politicians, farmers and a populace that has yet to realize that environmentally organized tourism – for which the island, with its extended season, picturesque landscape and rich variety of flora and fauna is an ideal location – can be enormously profitable. The creation of an autonomous Cretan tourist authority in 2000, with a brief to promote the island, should also have been a force for change; its website motto – Sense the Authentic gives an idea of its approach.

The island has faced up to several invaders throughout its history, but the tourist invasion presents it with a new dilemma: to submerge its traditional ways in the pursuit of ever greater numbers or to try to raise the quality of its tourism and at the same time preserve Crete's unique character. The government in Athens has sent conflicting messages in recent years: on the one hand encouraging the Cretan authorities to do more to cater to ramblers, birdwatchers, naturalists and those interested in the island's archeology and history, on the other stating that funds would be available to support the development of conference centres (with golf courses attached), luxury hotels and casinos. The proposed Cape Sídheros project in eastern Crete (see page 164), where a wild and rugged coastal peninsula has been threatened with a huge resort complex, is a prime example of this confusion.

Given the island's serious economic plight, any ventures offering jobs are keenly supported by local politicians, often with little regard for the potential environmental consequences. It's to be hoped that the recent economic hurricanes faced by Crete and Greece will not lay waste to much good work in the area of sustainable tourist development done over previous decades.

Unfortunately due to the COVID-19 pandemic that hit the world in 2019, Crete had to shut its borders. Closing the island off for tourism had severe economic implications but luckily in May 2021 the island welcomed tourists back – showing the world that Crete is still perceived to be one of the safest destinations in Europe.

order but also "Greece's five years of humiliation and pain" by ditching austerity and renegotiating the country's €240 billion bailout. In a policy statement that harked back to the Andreas Papandreou governments of the 1980s he pledged to create 300,000 new jobs in the private, public and social sectors as well as promising substantial wage increases, and free electrical power and food subsidies to poor households.

In order to gain breathing space, Tsipras negotiated a four-month extension to the bailout and embarked on a public relations campaign to attempt to pressure Greece's creditors into watering down their austerity demands. However, the other members of the eurozone did not accept Greece's arguments and rejected a further extension,

2015

Left-wing Syriza party wins election victory and rejects EU's bailout terms; threat of ejection from the eurozone forces government to call another election to enable it to reverse its previous policy.

2020

Greece detects its first cases of COVID-19, a severe acute respiratory syndrome which became a worldwide pandemic. Greece closes its borders and announces a countrywide lockdown. COVID led to over 12,000 deaths in Greece alone.

effectively cutting Greece adrift. To prevent a flight of capital the Greek government **closed the banks** and imposed capital controls. Tsipras then declared that the bailout terms would be put to the people in a nationwide **referendum** on July 5. The predictable result was an overwhelming rejection of the creditors' terms by over sixty percent of voters.

Despite having recommended a "No" vote, Tsipras was now faced with a real danger that Greece would be forced out of the eurozone and into bankruptcy. Following several days of tense negotiations with Greece's creditors, he finally climbed down and backtracked on almost all of the reforms he had announced in his victory speech in January. A new agreement with harsher terms than had been on offer then was the price to secure a **third bailout** of €85 billion over three years. Tsipras's party split, with over forty deputies voting against the deal – which they condemned as "capitulation and treason" – in the Greek parliament. Tsipras replied by stating that for the nation it was a question of "staying alive or suicide", and got the vote through only with the support of pro-European opposition deputies.

Light at the end of the tunnel?

No longer able to command a majority in the Greek parliament, on August 20th, 2015 Tsipras resigned as prime minister and announced that the country would again go to the polls on September 20. In a historically low turnout of just over fifty percent, Syriza won the election and Tsipras was able to form a new government with the aid of a small nationalist party, **ANEL**. The second Tsipras administration embarked within a year on implementing another round of draconian reforms demanded by the international creditors in return for the third bailout.

By summer 2018, the new Syriza regime had not only survived, but had perhaps begun to come to the end of an eight-year bail-out nightmare. The economy was still in dire straits, and the population deeply disillusioned both with its own government and the European political elite, but there were signs of economic growth, an easing of the debt burden and an increase in the value of the Athens stock market. Most significantly, the country had achieved a healthy budget surplus, before interest on its debt. Eurozone member states agreed a plan to make the debt repayments (still vast) more manageable, a deal which the government was quick to hail as a return to normality, with the country regaining a measure of political and financial independence. This is by no means the end of the ordeal, and it took until August 2022 for Greece to exit special supervision by its creditors. However, 2024 saw positive forecasts, with the Greek economy expected to grow by nearly three percent.

2021

After several months of lockdown, Greece announces that it will ease these measures and open its borders to tourists from selected countries once again.

2023

Greece – and Crete – enjoy a record year for tourism, with around 30 million arrivals.

Crete in myth

Crete is intimately associated with much of ancient Greek mythology, and in particular with Zeus, who was not only brought up on the island, but according to some ancient Cretans was buried here as well. The Dhiktean Cave, a gash on the face of Mount Dhíkti, which soars above the Lasíthi plateau, has most claims to be the birthplace of the greatest god in the Greek pantheon, and symbolizes the potent influence of Minoan Crete on the land to the north.

The birth of Zeus

According to the earliest accounts of the myth, **Zeus** was the third generation of rulers of the gods. The original ruler, Ouranos (Uranus of the Romans), was overthrown by his youngest son Kronos. In order to prevent such a fate overtaking him, too, Kronos ate his first five children at birth. When she was bearing the sixth child, his wife, Rhea, took refuge in a Cretan cavern – a site much argued over, but most commonly assigned to the Dhiktean Cave (see page 145). Here Zeus was born, and in his place Rhea presented Kronos with a rock wrapped in blankets, which he duly devoured. Zeus was brought up secretly in the cave, his cries drowned by the **Kouretes**, who kept up a noisy dance with continuous clashing of shields and spears outside. The Kouretes, believed by Cretans to be the sons of the Earth Mother, were especially revered on the island as the inventors of beekeeping and honey as well as the hunting bow, and an inscription found at Palékastro suggests that they may well have a Minoan origin. The baby fed on milk from a mountain goat-nymph, Amalthea, one of whose horns he later made into a miraculous gift that a wish by the holder would fill with whatever was desired (hence the horn of plenty).

Having grown to manhood on Crete, Zeus declared war on Kronos and the Titans, a struggle that lasted ten years. Eventually, however, Zeus emerged as supreme ruler of the gods on **Mount Olympos** on the Greek mainland, and Kronos was banished to the Underworld. This myth has a precedent in Hittite texts of the second millennium BC that themselves had taken it over from the earlier Hurrians, a people who had settled in Syria and northern Mesopotamia. The Minoans passed it on to the Greeks.

The origin of the Cretans

The sexual prowess of Zeus led him into a bewildering number of affairs, one of which led to his best-known return to the island of his birth – with Europa – and the founding of the Cretan race. **Europa** was a princess, the daughter of King Phoenix (after whom Phoenicia was named), and Zeus lusted after her mightily. Approaching the shore of Phoenicia, Zeus saw her gathering flowers, and came to her in the guise of a **white bull**. Fascinated by the creature's docility Europa climbed onto its back, at which he leapt into the sea and carried her off across the sea to Crete. They landed at Mátala, travelled to Górtys (where one version of the myth avers that Zeus ravished her beneath a plane tree that has never lost its leaves since) and were married at the Dhiktean Cave. One of the presents Zeus gave to his bride was **Talos**, a bronze giant who strode around the island hurling boulders at approaching strangers. Jason and the Argonauts were greeted by a hail of stones from Talos when they approached Crete. Aided by their companion, the sorceress Medea, they brought about the giant's fall by piercing a vein on his ankle – his single vulnerable spot – thus allowing the *ichor*, a divine fluid that served as blood, to drain from his body.

Minos and the Minotaur

The Zeus of the Europa tale, taking the form of a **bull**, is almost certainly mixed up with earlier, native Cretan gods. The sun god of Crete also took the form of a bull, and the animal is a recurrent motif in the island's mythology.

In the story of **Minos**, a bull once again has a prominent role. Europa bore Zeus three sons – Minos, Rhadamanthys and Sarpedon – before eventually being abandoned. Later she married the king of Crete, Asterios, who adopted her children. Upon reaching manhood the three brothers quarrelled for the love of a beautiful boy named Miletos (a reflection of the mores and customs of the time). When Miletos chose Sarpedon, an enraged Minos drove him from the island. However, before boarding a ship to Asia Minor, Miletos killed King Asterios. Legend associates both Miletos and Sarpedon – who joined him in Asia Minor – with the founding of Miletos (see page 142), later an important coastal city in Greek and Roman times.

With Sarpedon removed, Minos claimed the throne and settled upon Rhadamanthys a third of Asterios' dominions. Rhadamanthys became renowned as a law-maker, appears in some tales as ruler at Festós, and every ninth year visited Zeus's cave on Mount Dhíkti to bring back a new set of laws. So great was Rhadamanthys's fame as a law-giver that Homer tells of how Zeus appointed him one of the three judges of the dead along with Minos and Aeakos.

Minos, meanwhile, was another ruler driven by lustful passions. He liaised with a succession of lovers including the Minoan goddess **Britomartis**, whom he chased relentlessly around the island for nine months until she threw herself into the sea off the end of the Rodhopoú peninsula to escape his attentions. Rescued from drowning by the net of a fisherman, she became known as Diktynna ("of the net"), and a great temple to her was erected on the site (see page 265). Minos's wife and queen, **Pasiphae**, incensed by her rakish husband's infidelities, put a spell on the king: whenever he lay with another woman he discharged not seed but a swarm of poisonous serpents, scorpions and insects that devoured the woman's vitals. News of his affliction (which bears a striking resemblance to venereal disease) apparently got around, and one of his bedmates Prokris, daughter of the Athenian king Erechthevs, insisted that he should take a prophylactic draught before their tryst which apparently prevented her invasion by serpents and scorpions.

Earlier, when he had gained the throne of his father, Minos prayed to Poseidon (or perhaps his father Zeus) to send a bull from the sea that he could offer as a sacrifice, thus signifying the god's recognition of the justice of his claim to the throne. When the radiant bull emerged from the sea, Minos was so taken by its beauty that he determined to keep it, sacrificing in its place another from his herds. Punishment for such hubris was inevitable, and in this case the gods chose to inflame Minos's wife, Pasiphae (a moon goddess in her own right – again the bull symbolizes the sun), with intense desire for the animal. She had the brilliant inventor and craftsman **Daedalos** construct an artificial cow, in which she hid and induced the bull to couple with her: the result was the **Minotaur**, a beast half man and half bull (probably human with a bull's head). To hide his shame, Minos had Daedalos construct the **labyrinth** in which to imprison the monster.

Theseus and Ariadne

The myth goes on to relate how Minos waged war on Athens after Androgeous, one of his sons by Pasiphae, had gone off to that city and won every event in the Panathenaic games, only to be slain on the orders of the outraged Athenian king, Aegeus. Part of the settlement demanded by the victorious Minos was that an annual tribute of seven young men and women be provided as sport or sacrifice for the imprisoned Minotaur. The third time the tribute was due, **Theseus**, the son of King Aegeus, resolved to end the slaughter and himself went as one of the victims. In Crete he met Minos's

THE DEATH OF ZEUS

The postscript to these Greek myths concerns **Zeus's death**. According to the Cretans, and reflecting the older Minoan idea of a fertility god who annually died and was reborn, Zeus was buried beneath Mount Yioúhtas near Knossós, in whose outline his recumbent profile can still be seen from the palace site. It was a purely local claim, however, and clashed with the northern Greek concept of Zeus as an immortal and all-powerful sky-god. The northern Greeks regarded the islanders' belief in a dying Zeus as blasphemy, and their contempt for the Cretan heresy may have given rise to the saying "all Cretans are liars".

daughter **Ariadne**, who fell in love with him and resolved to help him in his task. At the instigation of the sympathetic Daedalos, she provided Theseus with a ball of thread that he could unwind and, if he succeeded in killing the Minotaur, follow to find his way out of the labyrinth.

At first everything went to plan, and Theseus killed the beast and escaped from the island with Ariadne and the others. On the way home though, things were less successful. Ariadne was abandoned on a beach in Náxos (where she was later found by the god Dionysos and carried off to Olympus). Approaching Athens, Theseus forgot to change his black sails for white – the pre-arranged signal that his mission had succeeded. Thinking his son dead, King Aegeus threw himself into the sea and drowned.

Back on Crete, Minos imprisoned Daedalos in his own labyrinth, furious at Ariadne's desertion and his part in it, and at the failure of the maze. Locked up with Daedalos was his son, **Ikaros**. They escaped by making wings of feathers – from birds devoured by the Minotaur – held together with wax. Daedalos finally reached Sicily and the protection of King Kokalos: Ikaros, though, flew too close to the sun, the wing-wax melted and he plunged to his death in the sea. Still set on revenge, Minos tracked Daedalos down by setting a puzzle so fiendishly difficult that only he could have solved it: a large reward was promised to the first person who could pass a thread through a triton shell. When Minos eventually arrived in Sicily he posed the problem to Kokalos who said it would be easy. He then consulted secretly with Daedalos who drilled the shell at its point and tied a thread to the leg of an ant that was sent into the shell. When the insect emerged through the hole, Kokalos took the shell to show Minos. Now certain that Daedalos was hidden in the palace, Minos demanded that Kokalos hand him over. Kokalos appeared to agree to the request and offered Minos hospitality in the palace. There Minos met an undignified end when he was scalded to death in his bath by the king's daughters, urged on by Daedalos.

Wildlife

Although the south coast of Crete is closer to Libya than it is to Athens, the island's wildlife owes much more to mainland Greece than it does to Africa. This is because Crete lies at the end of the long range of drowned limestone mountains called the Hellenic arc which make up much of the southern Aegean sea, and you need to go a long way south into the Sahara before you again find mountains as high as the Cretan ones. Crete, then, has northern Mediterranean fauna and flora across a range of habitats.

Islands tend to be short on wildlife because of their isolation from the main bulk of species on the mainland. Not so Crete – it's rich in flora and fauna, and provides the full range of Mediterranean habitats. In fact, there are over two thousand species of **plants** in Crete, of which over 180 are endemic to the island, making up nearly a third of the Greek flora, and about as many as in the whole of Britain. With the wealth of plant life come far more **insects** than you get further north. The survival of Cretan wildlife in all its richness and diversity has been facilitated by the fact that agriculture remains fairly "undeveloped", although the pressures are mounting, in the form of widespread use of chemicals, increased water abstraction, road construction and tourist development. You won't find many birds or wildflowers among the hectares of polytunnels around Timbáki, but you will in the mountains where such methods remain uneconomic.

The only feature really lacking, as elsewhere in much of Greece, is **trees**. The Minoan civilization was a seafaring one, so as early as the Bronze Age there was a high demand for timber for shipbuilding. Some of the lower hills were perhaps deforested four thousand years ago, a process completed by the Venetians. Today, native forests exist only in remote uplands and gorges.

Crete's chief drawback, at least if you hope to combine nature with the rest of the island's sights and life, is the pattern of its **climate**. Because it's so far south, the summers are long and dry, and that period equates to our northern winters, when many plants shut down or die, with a corresponding decline in activity from all other wildlife. Trying to see wildflowers or birds in lowland Crete in August is a bit like going out for a nature ramble in Britain or Massachusetts in February.

Habitats

Rarely in Europe do you find such a wide range of habitats so tightly packed, or real "wilderness" areas so close to modern towns and resorts, as in Crete. Broadly speaking, you can divide the island into four major **habitats**: the coast; cultivated land; low hillsides less than 1000m; and mountains above 1000m. Crete is the only Greek island that is mountainous enough to have all four of these habitats.

Along the coast, sandy beaches and low rocky cliffs are the norm. Marshy river deltas or estuaries are rare (simply because Crete is a dry country and there aren't many rivers), but where you can find them, these wetland habitats are among the best places to look for birds.

Cultivated land is very variable in its wildlife interest, though look out for small market gardens – *perivólia* – often found on the edges of towns and villages, which are particularly good for small birds. Small hayfields can be a colourful mass of annual flowers and attendant insects in spring and early summer.

Low hillsides up to 1000m comprise much of Crete. Scrubby hillsides, loosely grazed by goats and sometimes sheep, are the most typical Mediterranean habitat, extremely rich in flowers, insects and reptiles. Botanically, they divide into two distinct types: the first is *phrýgana*, and consists of scattered scrubby bushes, always on limestone, especially rich in aromatic herbs and wildflowers. You can often find *phrýgana* by looking for beehives: Cretan beekeepers know where to find the thyme and rosemary that gives the local honey its wonderful flavour. The other hillside habitat is maquis, a dense, very prickly scrub with scattered trees. Of these two hillside habitats, *phrýgana* is better for flowers, maquis for birds.

Mountains over 1000m are surprisingly common: three separate ranges exceed 2000m, and they are responsible for much of the climate, creating rain and retaining it as snow for a large part of the year. The small upland plateaux among the mountains – Omalós or Lasíthi most famously – are a very special feature, with their own distinctive flora and fauna. Although the Cretan mountains don't as a rule have the exciting mammals of the mainland, they are very good for large and spectacular birds of prey.

Flowers

What you will see, obviously, depends on where and when you go. The best time is **spring**, which is heralded as early as January when the almond tree flowers, its petals falling like snow and carpeting the streets of small mountain villages. The season seriously gets under way in mid-February, however, in the southeast corner of the island, is at its peak during March over most of the lowlands (but continues well into April), and in the mountains comes later, starting in late April and going on through to June. In **early summer**, the spring anemones, orchids and rockroses are replaced by plants like broom and chrysanthemum; this ranges from mid-April in southern Crete to late July in the high mountains, though given global climate change these timings can vary – exceptionally by as much as a month.

Things are pretty much burnt out over all the lowlands from July to the end of September, though there are still some flowers in the mountains. Once the hot summer is over, blooming starts all over again. Some of the **autumn-flowering** species, such as cyclamens and autumn crocus, flower from October in the mountains to December in the southern flatlands. And by then you might as well stay on for the first of the spring bulbs in January.

Year-round, the best insurance policy is to be prepared to move up and down the hills until you find flowers – from the beginning of March to the end of June you are almost guaranteed to find classic displays somewhere on the island, and you'll see the less spectacular but still worthwhile autumn-flowering species from October to early December. If you have to go in July, August or September, then be prepared to see a restricted range, and also to go high up the mountains. The four habitats all have their own flowers, though some, of course, overlap.

Flower species

On the **coast** you might find the spectacular **yellow horned poppy** growing on shingled banks, and **sea stocks** and **Virginia stocks** growing among the rocks behind the beach. Sand dunes are rare but sometimes there is a flat grazed area behind the beach; these are often good for **orchids**. During early autumn, look for the very large white flowers of the **sea daffodil** (Pancratium maritimum), as well as **autumn crocuses** on the slopes behind the shore.

The trees and shrubs on **low hillsides** are varied and beautiful, with colourful brooms flowering in early summer, preceded by bushy **rockroses** – *Cistaceae* – which form a mass of pink or white flowers in spring. Dotted among the shrubs is the occasional tree; the **non-deciduous plane tree** is an endemic variety, and the **Judas tree** (*Cercis siliquastrum*) flowers on bare wood in spring, making a blaze of pink against green hillsides that stands out for miles. Lower than the shrubs are the **aromatic herbs** – sage, rosemary, thyme and lavender – with perhaps some spiny species of **Euphorbia**. Because

Crete is dry and hot for much of the year, you also get a high proportion of **xerophytes** – plants that are adapted to drought by having fleshy leaves and thick skins.

Below the herbs is the ground layer; peer around the edges and between the shrubs and you'll find a wealth of **orchids**, **anemones**, **grape hyacinths**, **irises**, and perhaps **fritillaries** if you're lucky. The orchids are extraordinary; the *Ophrys* species – have especially fascinating and unusual flowers.

Once spring is over, these plants give way to the early summer flowering of the brooms and aromatic herbs, as well as a final fling from the annuals that sense the coming of the heat and their own death. When the heat of the summer is over, the autumn bulbs appear, with species of **crocus** and their relatives, the **colchicums** and the **sternbergias**, and finally the **autumn cyclamens** through into early December.

Mountains are good to visit later in the year. The rocky mountain **gorges** are considered to be the elite environments for plants, and house the greatest biodiversity; this is because most gorges are generally left ungrazed and undisturbed and it's often possible to find at least ten Cretan endemics without too much difficulty. The gorges are the home of many familiar garden rock plants, such as the **aubretias**, **saxifrages** and **alyssums**, as well as **dwarf bellflowers** and **anemones**. Look for dwarf **tulips** in fields on the upland plateaux in spring. The mountains are also the place to see the remaining Cretan native pine **forests**, and in the woodland glades you will find **gentians**, **cyclamens** and **violets**. Above 1500m or so the forests begin to thin out, and in these upland meadows glorious **crocuses** flower almost before the snow has melted in spring – a very fine form of *Crocus seiberi* is a particularly early one. Autumn-flowering species of crocus and cyclamen should reward a visit later in the year.

Birds

More than 330 species of **birds** have been reported in Crete to date. Greece has a good range of Mediterranean species plus a few very rare ones such as the **Eleonora's falcon** and the **Ruppell's warbler**, which have their European breeding strongholds in Greece, particularly on Crete. The great thing about bird-watching in Crete is that, if you pick your time right, you can see both resident and migratory species. Crete is on one of the main fly-past routes for species that have wintered in East Africa, but breed in eastern and northern Europe. They migrate every spring up the Nile valley, and then move across the eastern Mediterranean, often in huge numbers. This happens from mid-March to mid-May, depending on the species, the weather, and where you are. The return migration in autumn is less spectacular because it is less concentrated in time, but still worth watching out for.

On the outskirts of towns and in the fields there are some colourful residents. Small predatory birds such as **woodchat shrikes**, **blackeared wheatears**, **kestrels** and migrating **red-footed falcons** can be seen perched on telegraph wires. The dramatic pink, black and white **hoopoe** and the striking yellow and black **golden oriole** are sometimes to be found in woodland and olive groves, and **Scops owls** (Europe's smallest owl) can often be heard calling around towns at night. They monotonously repeat a single "poo", sometimes in mournful vocal duets.

Look closely at the **swifts** and **swallows**, and you will find a few species not found in northern Europe: **crag martins** replace house martins in the **mountain gorges**, for example, and you may see the large **alpine swift**, which has a white belly. The **Sardinian warbler** dominates the rough scrubby **hillsides** – the male with a glossy black cap and an obvious red eye. These hillsides are also the home of the **chukar**, a species of partridge naturalised on Crete, after arrival from western Asia .

Wetlands and **coastal lagoons** are excellent for bird-spotting, especially at spring and autumn migration, although this habitat is hard to find. There's a wide variety of **herons** and **egrets**, as well as smaller waders such as the rare **avocet** and **marsh**

sandpiper and **black-winged stilt**, which has ridiculously long pink legs. **Marsh harriers** are common too, drifting over the reedbeds on characteristic raised wings. Scrubby woodland around coastal wetlands is a good place to see migrating smaller birds such as **warblers**, **wagtails** and the like.

The mountains hold some of the most exciting birds in Crete. Smaller birds like the **blue rock thrush**, non-migratory **cirl bunting** and **alpine chough** are common, and there is a good chance of seeing large and dramatic birds of prey. The **buzzards** and smaller eagles are confusingly similar, but there are also **golden eagles**, **Bonelli's eagles** and **vultures**. One very rare species of vulture, the **lammergeier** (or bearded vulture), is currently on the dramatically endangered list, although it used to be more common in Crete than anywhere else in Europe; you may be lucky enough to spot one of the island's thirty-five remaining birds (only seven breeding pairs) soaring above the Lasíthi or Omalós plateaux. It's a huge bird, with a wingspan of nearly 3m, and with narrower wings and a longer wedge-shaped tail than the other vulture you are likely to see, the **griffon vulture**.

Mammals

Cretan **mammals** are elusive, generally nocturnal, and very hard to see. Islands tend to have fewer species than the nearest mainland and in this Crete is no exception, with about half the species that you could expect to see on mainland Greece. Even such common animals as the red squirrel and fox have never made it across the water, nor will you find large exciting mammals like wolves or lynxes in the mountains, as you might (rarely) on the mainland.

However, there are some compensations. Islands often have their own endemic species, and one in Crete is the **Cretan spiny mouse**, which is found nowhere else; if you happen to be on a rocky hillside at dusk you may see this largish mouse with very big ears and a spiny back fossicking around. The other compensation in Crete is the ancestral **wild ibex** or *kri-kri*; a small population still exists in the White Mountains around the Samariá Gorge, and also on some offshore islands – but you'll be lucky if you see one outside the zoos. Apart from those, Crete has fourteen bat species, as well as **weasels**, **badgers**, **hares**, **hedgehogs**, **field mice**, **shrews** and **beech martens**.

One relatively recent addition to the zoological record was the rediscovery in 1996 of the **Cretan wildcat** – *fourógatos* (see page 211) – long thought to be either extinct or a folktale. Only a single specimen has ever been captured alive (in the Amári valley) and the population status of the animal is still unknown. A few years after the initial find an Amári valley shepherd claimed to have discovered a den containing five kittens.

There are several marine mammals that can occasionally be seen in offshore waters. The critically endangered and extremely rare **Mediterranean monk seal** breeds in a few sea caves around the island. The deep waters off the south coast of Haniá have recently become well known for a resident population of **sperm whales**. **Dolphins** – which so delighted the Minoans – can be seen all around the island but you'll be most likely to see them while on a boat or ferry.

Reptiles and amphibians

The hot, rocky terrain of Crete suits **reptiles** well, with plenty of sun to bask in and plenty of rocks to hide under, but the island's isolation has severely restricted the number of species occurring: fewer than a third of those that are found on the mainland. Identification is therefore rather easy. If you sit and watch a dry stone wall almost anywhere in the western half of the island you're bound to see the small local wall lizard, **Erhard's wall lizard**. A rustle in the rocks by the side of the road might be an **ocellated skink** – a bit like a lizard, but with a thicker body and a stubbier neck. In the bushes of the maquis and *phrgana* you may see the **Balkan green lizard**, a truly splendid bright-green animal up to 50cm long, most of which is tail – usually seen as it runs frantically on its hind legs from one bush to another.

At night, **geckoes** replace the lizards. Geckoes are small (less than 10cm), have big eyes and round adhesive pads on their toes that enable them to walk upside down on the ceiling. Sometimes they come into houses – in which case welcome them, for they will keep down the mosquitoes and other biting insects. Crete hosts three out of the four European species. The island is also one of only a handful of places where the **chameleon** occurs around the Mediterranean, although it is extremely rare and may hae died out locally since 2015); this may (or may not) be attributed to its camouflage skills. It lives in bushes and low trees, and hunts by day; its colour is greenish but obviously variable.

Tortoises, sadly, don't occur in Crete, but the stripe-necked **terrapin** does. Look out for these in any freshwater habitat – Lake Kournás and the Ayía bird sanctuary for example, or even in the cistern at the Zákros palace. There are also **sea turtles** in the Mediterranean: you might be lucky and see one while you're swimming or on a boat, since they sometimes bask on the surface of the water. The one you're most likely to see is the **loggerhead turtle**, which can grow up to a metre long. Crete has important breeding populations on beaches to the west of Haniá, around Mátala, and the largest (more than 350 nests) at Réthymno, but tourism and the associated development are threatening their future. Each year, many turtles are injured by motorboats, their nests are destroyed by bikes and jeeps ridden on the beaches, and the newly hatched young die entangled in deckchairs and umbrella stakes left out at night on the sand. The turtles are easily frightened by noise and lights too, which makes them uneasy cohabitants with freelance campers and nightclubs.

The Greek government has passed **laws** designed to protect the loggerheads, and the Sea Turtle Protection Society of Greece now operates an ambitious conservation programme, but local economic interests tend to prefer a beach full of sunbathing bodies to a sea full of turtles.

The final group of reptiles are the **snakes**, represented by four species, only one of which is poisonous – the **cat snake**. Even this is back-fanged and therefore extremely unlikely to be able to bite anything as big as a human, so you can relax a bit when strolling round the hillsides; most snakes are very timid and easily frightened anyway. One species worth looking out for is the beautiful **leopard snake**, which is grey with red blotches edged in black. It's fond of basking on the sides of roads and paths.

Only three species of **amphibian** occur in Crete. The **green toad** is smaller than the common toad, with an obvious marbled green and grey back. The **marsh frog** is a large frog, greenish but variable in colour, and very noisy in spring. T**ree frogs** are small, live in trees (examine the underside of leaves), and call very loudly at night.

Insects

There are around a million different species of insects in the world, and even in Crete there are probably a few hundred which have yet to be scientifically described or labelled. About a third of all insect species are beetles, and these are very obvious wherever you go. You might see one of the dung beetles rolling a ball of dung along a path like the mythological Sisyphus. If you have time to look closely at bushes and small trees, you might be rewarded with a stick insect or a **praying mantis**, creatures that are rarely seen because of their excellent camouflage.

The **grasshopper** and **cricket** family are well represented, and most patches of grass will hold a few. Grasshoppers produce their chirping noise by rubbing a wing against a leg, but crickets do it by rubbing both wings together. **Cicadas**, which most people think of as a night-calling grasshopper, aren't actually related at all – they're more of a large leaf-hopper. Their continuous whirring call is one of the characteristic sounds of the Mediterranean night, and is produced by the rapid vibration of two membranes, called tymbals, on either side of their body.

Perhaps the most obvious insects are the **butterflies**. Any time from spring through most of summer is good for butterfly-spotting, and there's a second flight of adults of many species in the autumn. Dramatic varieties in Crete include two species of **swallowtail**, easily identified by their large size, yellow and black colouring, and long spurs at the back of the hind wings. **Cleopatras** are large, brilliant yellow butterflies, related to the brimstone of northern Europe, but bigger and more colourful. Look out also for **Cretan Argus** – chocolate brown in colour and only found in the Psiloritis and Dhíkti mountain ranges, it is now thought to be increasingly threatened by human activity.

Books

From Homer on, Crete has inspired an exceptionally wide range of literature, and in Nikos Kazantzákis the island has also produced one truly world-class author. Though some of his work is out of print, most titles are still readily available online. In contrast to the proliferation of ancient history, there is no book in English devoted to modern Cretan history, though there's a good general account included in Hopkins's book on the island (see page 351).

The more specialist titles might also be found at a dedicated travel bookstore or a Greek-interest bookshop: in the UK, try the Hellenic Book Service, in Kentish Town, London (http://hellenicbookservice.com).

Books marked with the ★ symbol are particularly recommended.

ARCHEOLOGY AND ANCIENT HISTORY

Gerald Cadogan *Palaces of Minoan Crete*. Complete guide to all the major sites, with much more history and general information than the name implies.

John Chadwick *Linear B and related scripts*. A short version of *The Decipherment of Linear B*, in which the whole fascinating story is graphically told by Chadwick, who collaborated with Ventris, the English architect who made the crucial breakthrough. The same author's *Mycenaean World* vividly describes the society revealed by the tablets.

Leonard Cottrell *The Bull of Minos*. Breathless and somewhat dated account of the discoveries of Schliemann and Evans (see page 323); easy reading.

Costis Davaras *Guide to Cretan Antiquities*. A fascinating guide by the distinguished archeologist to the antiquities of Crete, from the ancient through to the Turkish eras. Cross-referenced in dictionary form, it has authoritative articles on all the major sites as well as subjects as diverse as Minoan razors and toilet articles, the disappearance of Cretan forests and the career of Venizélos. Widely available at museums on the island.

★ **Arthur Evans** *The Palace of Minos*. This four-volume work remains the seminal description of the discovery and excavation of the Knossós palace, and is fascinating to dip into.

Reynold Higgins *Minoan and Mycenaean Art*. Solid introduction to the subject with plenty of illustrations.

★ **J. Alexander Macgillivray** *Minotaur: Sir Arthur Evans and the Archaeology of the Minoan Myth*. Outstanding book by a Crete-based archeologist, which demonstrates how Evans fitted the evidence found at Knossós to his own preconception of the Minoans as peaceful, literate and aesthetic second-millennium BC Victorians. A superb read.

★ **J.D.S. Pendlebury** *The Archaeology of Crete*. Although published in 1933, this is still the most comprehensive archeological handbook, detailing virtually every site on the island. Pendlebury's *Handbook to the Palace of Minos* remains an excellent guide to the Knossós site by someone who – as curator after Evans's retirement – knew it inside out.

Nikos Psilakis *Byzantine Churches and Monasteries of Crete*. Locally published, this is a superbly illustrated and expert guide to over 150 of Crete's monasteries, churches and convents. As well as interesting background on all the monuments, there's also a fold-out map to locate them.

Paola Pugsley *The Blue Guide*. Excellent, detailed guide to the churches, archeological sites and museums across the island. However, some directions to remoter sights occasionally lack clarity and it is overdue for an update.

Peter Warren *The Aegean Civilizations*. A very good and concise introduction to Minoan and Mycenean Crete by one of the leading modern experts; good illustrations, but in need of a new edition.

R.F. Willetts *Everyday Life in Ancient Crete*. An interesting survey of Minoan daily life as lived in the towns, villages and farms, as well as the palaces.

MODERN HISTORY AND ARCHITECTURE

★ **James Angelos** *The Full Castastrophe*. Subtitled "a journey among the new Greek ruins," financial journalist Angelos uses character-driven narratives to bring to life the reality of Greece's current economic collapse. It's all here: the political chicanery, the corruption, the scams, an overburdened patronage system, endemic tax fraud and even the rise of the neo-Nazis. Riveting.

Michele Buonsanti & Alberta Galla *Candia Veneziana – Venetian Itineraries Through Crete*. Useful guide to the under-documented wealth of monuments surviving from La Serenissima's four and a half centuries of hegemony over the island. Widely available from bookshops on Crete.

Richard Clogg *A Concise History of Greece*. A rigorously historical account of Greek history from its emergence from

Ottoman rule to the present day, covering the wider aspects of Crete's struggle for independence and union with Greece.

★ **Adam Hopkins** *Crete, Its Past, Present and People*. Excellent general introduction to Cretan history and society with lots of interesting detail on topics as diverse as the Battle of Crete, daily life and diet, the arrival of mass tourism and medicinal wild herbs.

★ **John Julius Norwich** *Byzantium: the Early Centuries; Byzantium: the Apogee; Byzantium: Decline and Fall; A History of Venice; The Middle Sea*. The three volumes of Norwich's history of the Byzantine Empire are terrific narrative accounts, and much can be gleaned from them about Crete in this period. *History of Venice* relates the fascinating story of the rise and fall of the power that ruled Crete for four and a half centuries, while *Middle Sea* charts three thousand years of Mediterranean history, allowing the island's past to be seen in its wider geographical context.

★ **James Pettifer** *The Greeks: the Land and People since the War*. Excellent (if now somewhat dated) introduction to contemporary Greece. Pettifer roams the country and charts the state of the nation's politics, food, family life, religion, tourism and all points in between. Only passing references to Crete, however.

★ **Oliver Rackham & Jennifer Moody** *The Making of the Cretan Landscape*. A classic of its kind, this is an enthralling botanical and anthropological study of the Cretans in their environment, from antiquity to the present day, with sections devoted to the island's geological formation, vegetation, people and settlements. A seasoned champion of the Cretan natural environment, Oliver Rackham died in 2015.

WORLD WAR II

★ **Antony Beevor** *Crete: The Battle and the Resistance*. Relatively short study of the Battle of Crete, with colourful insights into the characters involved. Beevor dissects recent evidence to conclude that defeat was at least in part due to Cretan commander General Freyburg's fatal misinterpretation of an Ultra coded message leading him to divert troops away from the Máleme invasion site, critically weakening the Allied defences.

Alan Clark *The Fall of Crete*. Racy and sensational – but very readable – military history by the late maverick English politician. Detailed on the battles, and more critical of the command than you might expect from a former cabinet minister.

Wes Davis *The Ariadne Objective*. A fast-moving, novelistic account of the audacious kidnapping of the German commander Kreipe focused on the eccentric, larger-than-life characters (Leigh-Fermor, Moss et al) of the Special Operations Executive who pulled it off.

Patrick Leigh-Fermor *Abducting a General*. Posthumously published account of the kidnap of German general Kreipe by a leading participant. From his night parachute landing on the Katharó plateau to the departure with the captured general from Rodhákino beach a year later, it's a gripping tale. Fermor also gives due credit to the role of the Cretan "mountaineers" in the operation, whose contribution he felt had been downplayed in earlier accounts.

★ **Lew Lind** *Flowers of Rethymnon*. A gripping personal account of his part in the Battle of Crete and subsequent escape by a 19-year-old Australian soldier. The carnage of the battle is rivetingly described, and shining through the horror of it all comes the unflinching bravery of the Cretan villagers who put themselves in danger of German reprisals by helping servicemen trapped on Crete – such as Lind – escape to Egypt.

W. Stanley Moss *Ill Met by Moonlight*. This account of the capture of General Kreipe by one of the participants, largely taken from his diaries of the time, is a good *Boys' Own*-style adventure yarn. Moss also translated Baron von der Heydte's *Daedalus Returned* (o/p), which gives something of the other side of the story.

★ **George Psychoundakis** *The Cretan Runner*. Account of the invasion and resistance by a Cretan participant; Psychoundakis (who died in 2006) was a guide and message-runner for all the leading English-speaking protagonists. Great, although not much appreciated by many of his compatriots, who tend to dismiss him as an English lackey.

Tony Simpson *Operation Mercury: The Battle for Crete, 1941*. A very different way of looking at the subject, putting the campaign into an international context and relying heavily on oral history for details of the combat. Uncompromisingly critical of the command, and far more interesting than straight military history.

Evelyn Waugh *Officers and Gentlemen*; *Diaries*. Both include accounts of the Battle of Crete, and particularly of the horrors of the flight and evacuation.

TRAVEL WRITING

Michael Carroll *Greece: A Literary Guide for Travellers*. An excellent introduction to all the literary titans who have written about Greece, from ancient to contemporary, including a chapter on Crete.

Edward Lear *The Cretan Journal*. Diary of Lear's trip to Crete in 1864, illustrated with his sketches and watercolours. He didn't enjoy himself much.

★ **David MacNeil Doren** *Winds of Crete*. An American and his Swedish wife find enlightenment on Crete in the early 1970s, before the arrival of mass tourism. An amusing and well-observed travelogue documenting many of the island's customs and curiosities, in addition to some hair-raising brushes with Cretan physicians.

★ **Henry Miller** *The Colossus of Maroussi*. Miller's

idiosyncratic account of his travels in Greece on the eve of World War II includes a trip to Crete, where diarrhoea, biting flies and Festós palace all get bit-parts in the epic.

★ **Robert Pashley** *Travels in Crete*. Based on an extensive and punishing journey around Crete in the 1830s, Pashley is the original nineteenth-century British traveller, full of erudite observations, interesting anecdotes and outspoken attitudes. Recently republished in a pricey facsimile edition (two vols.) by the Cambridge University Press.

Dilys Powell *The Villa Ariadne*. The story of the British in Crete, from Arthur Evans to Paddy Leigh Fermor, through the villa at Knossós that linked all of them. Good at bringing the excitement of the early archeological work to life, but rather syrupy in style.

Pandelis Prevelakis *Tale of a Town* (Doric Publications, Athens). English translation of a native's description of life and times in Réthymno during the first quarter of the twentieth century. Widely available at bookshops on the island.

J.E. Hilary Skinner *Roughing It in Crete in 1867*. Great title for this account of another Englishman's adventures, this time with a band of rebels. Interesting on the less glamorous side of the independence struggle, since he spent the whole time searching for food or dodging Muslim patrols.

Christopher Somerville *The Golden Step*. Inspired by an epic (and extreme) long-distance gorge and mountain race from end to end of the island, Somerville set out to hike the same route, much of it along the haphazardly waymarked Pan-European E4 Footpath. Colourful descriptions of scrapes, scrambles and encounters en route make for an entertaining, perceptive and occasionally poignant tale.

★ **Capt. T.A.B. Spratt** *Travels and Researches in Crete*. Another nineteenth-century Briton who caught the Cretan bug while surveying the island's coastline, and left behind this account of its natural history, geology and archeology.

★ **Patricia Storace** *Dinner with Persephone*. Although not specifically about Crete, this is one of the best books ever written on the Greeks by a foreign author. Storace, an American poet, learned the language and went to live with, and travel among, the Hellenes for a year, delving deep into the psyche of this superficially attractive, but fiendishly complex people. Ideal holiday reading – you'll never look at the Greeks in the same light again.

Peter Trudgill *In Sfakiá*. In the 1970s British student Trudgill travelled to Crete, ending up in Hóra Sfakíon. It was the start of a forty-year love affair during which time the author – now a Greek socio-linguist – has returned annually to this coastal village. An astute and often witty portrait of rugged Sfakiá's customs, legends, history and its equally rugged people.

FICTION

Victoria Hislop *The Island*. The former leper colony of Spinalónga forms the backdrop to this novel about a young woman discovering her Cretan roots. A potentially good story is marred by the cloying and derivative manner of its telling. Oddly, the Greek film version – using locations near but not on the island which wasn't allowed – was much better.

Homer *The Iliad* and *The Odyssey*. The first concerns itself, semi-factually, with the Trojan War; the second recounts the hero Odysseus's long journey home, via Crete and seemingly every other corner of the Mediterranean. Homer's accounts were in some ways responsible for the "rediscovery" of Minoan Crete in the nineteenth century, so it seems appropriate to read them here.

★ **Nikos Kazantzákis** *Zorba the Greek*; *Freedom and Death*; *Report to Greco*. Something by the great Cretan novelist and man of letters is essential reading when on Crete. Forget the film that distorted the story's essentials: *Zorba the Greek* is a wonderful read on Crete that provides the backdrop to the adventures of one of the most irresistible characters of modern fiction. *Freedom and Death* is just as good, while *Report to Greco* is an autobiographical account of Kazantzákis' early years and later travels.

Ioannis Kondylakis *Patouchas*. The story of a Cretan shepherd on a journey of self-discovery; a wonderfully observed and humorous fictional sketch of Ottoman Crete during the nineteenth century by a little-known Cretan author.

Vitsentzos Kornaros (trans. Theodore Stefanides) *Erotokritos*. A beautifully produced English translation of the sixteenth-century Cretan epic poem, though now rare and hard to find.

★ **Mary Renault** *The King Must Die*; *The Bull from the Sea*. Stirring accounts of the Theseus legend and Minoan Crete for those who like their history in fictionalized form.

WILDLIFE AND GEOLOGY

Michael Chinerey *Collins Guide to the Insects of Britain and Western Europe*. This doesn't specifically include Greece (there's no comprehensive guide to Greek insects) but it gives a good general background and identification to the main families of insects that you're likely to see.

Charalampos G. Fassoulas *Field Guide to the Geology of Crete*. Excellent introduction to Crete's fascinating geology, explaining the island's geological evolution, paleography and paleontology. Superb colour photos and details of where to find many of the most interesting sites. Widely available at bookshops on the island.

John Fielding & Nicholas Turland *Flowers of Crete*. Coffee-table volume with 1900 colour photos of Cretan flora. A monumental work (in all senses), it runs to nearly 700 pages so is not for the backpack; useful for ID'ing your photos when you get back home.

Bob Gibbons and Martin Walters *Travellers' Nature Guides: Greece*. Good general guide to the ecology, flora and fauna of Greece, with a section devoted to Crete.

★ **Anthony Huxley & William Taylor** *Flowers of Greece*. Still one of the best books for identifying flowers in Crete, despite the taxonomy being obsolete.

★ **Mullarney, Svensson, Zetterstrom & Grant** *Collins Bird Guide to the Birds of Britain and Europe*. Outstanding guide to European birds covering most species you're likely to find in Crete. Superbly illustrated, too. Choose between a 2010 paperback edition, or a 2023 revised hardback.

George Sfikas *Wild Flowers of Crete*. Comprehensive illustrated guide to the island's flora.

Richard Lewington and Paul Whalley *The Mitchell Beazley Pocket Guide to Butterflies* (published in the US as *Butterflies*). A useful identification guide.

HIKING AND TOURING GUIDES

Anavasi *Crete Hiking Maps*. Excellent 1:25.000 scale hikers' map series with maps dedicated to the Lefká Óri, Samariá, Lasíthi and Sfakiá, as well as the Psiloritis range and the area around Zákros; check for future titles on https://anavasi.gr. Widely available at bookshops on Crete and through the website.

Luca Gianotti *The Cretan Way – A 28 Day Walk*. An account of a 28-day traverse of the island on the E4 path, including a description of the route with maps and downloadable GPS information, along with excerpts from Luca's daily journal and musings on the nature and culture of the land. Issued 2016 by Anavasi in Greece, still available.

Loraine Wilson *The high Mountains of Crete* Thorough and regularly updated guide, written by an experienced trekker and guide, to fifty-plus hikes in the Lefká Óri, with more recent sections added for Psiloritis and Mt. Dhíkti. Walks range between 3km and 20km, and routes can be linked for extended treks over several days.

FOOD AND DRINK

Konstantinos Lazarakis *The Wines of Greece*. A comprehensive survey of the rapidly changing Greek wine world, detailing what's new and where to find the rising stars.

Marianthi Mylona and Werner Stapelfeldt *Culinaria Greece*. Part of the enycyclopaedic Culinaria series, this is a great book for winter evenings in front of the fire, with plenty of stunning photos of Greek locations and food and drink. There's an entire chapter devoted to Crete, with articles on olive oil and how it's made, Cretan wine, herbs and teas, plus plenty of recipes.

★ **Maria and Nikos Psilakis** *Cretan Cooking*. Highly recommended guide to the Cretan kitchen – if only these dishes were generally available in the island's tavernas. The authors have gathered recipes from all parts of the island and interspersed with them illustrations not only of the food but of rural life past and present.

Language

So many Cretans have been compelled by poverty and other circumstances to work abroad, especially in the English-speaking world, that you'll find someone who speaks some English in almost every village. Add to that the thousands attending language schools or working in the tourist industry – English is the lingua franca of the north coast – and it's easy to see how so many visitors come back having learnt only half a dozen words between them. You can certainly get by this way, even in quite out-of-the-way places, but it isn't very satisfying.

Greek is not an easy language for English-speakers, but it is a beautiful one, and even a brief acquaintance will give you some idea of the debt western European languages owe to it. And the willingness to say even a few words will transform your status from that of *turístas* to the honourable one of *kséno*, a word which can mean stranger, traveller and guest all rolled into one.

Alphabet and grammar

On top of the usual difficulties of learning a new language, Greek presents the added problem of an entirely separate **alphabet**. Despite initial appearances, this is in practice fairly easily mastered and is a skill that will help enormously if you are going to get around independently (see box). In addition, certain combinations of letters have unexpected results. This book's transliteration system should help you make intelligible noises but you have to remember that the correct **stress** – marked in the book with an accent – is absolutely crucial. With the right sounds but the wrong stress people will either fail to understand you, or else understand something quite different from what you intended.

Greek **grammar** is more complicated still: nouns are divided into three genders, all with different case endings in the singular and in the plural, and all adjectives and articles have to agree with these in gender, number and case. (All adjectives are cited in the neuter form in the following lists.) Verbs are even worse. To begin with at least, the best thing is simply to say what you know the way you know it, and never mind the niceties. If you worry about your mistakes, you'll never say anything.

GREEK WORDS AND PHRASES

ESSENTIALS

Hello Yiásas/yiásou (polite/ informal) or Hérete
Good morning Kaliméra
Good evening Kalíspéra
Goodnight Kalíníkhta
Please parakaló
Thank you (very much) Efharistó (polí)
Yes né
No óhi
Certainly málista
OK, agreed endáksi
How are you? Ti kánis/ti kánete?
I'm fine Kalá íme
And you? Ke esís?
What's your name? Pos se léne?
My name is… Me léne...
I (don't) understand (Dhen) katalavéno
Speak slower, please Parakaló, miláte pió sigá
How do you say it in Greek? Pos léyete sta Eliniká?
I don't know Dhen kséro
Let's go Páme
See you tomorrow Tha se dho ávrio
See you soon Kalí andhámosi
Goodbye Adhío
Excuse me, do you speak English? Parakaló, mípos miláte angliká?
Please help me Parakaló, na me voithíste
Sorry/excuse me Signómi

THE GREEK ALPHABET: TRANSLITERATION

Set out below is the Greek alphabet, the system of transliteration used in this book and a brief aid to pronunciation.

GREEK TRANSLITERATION PRONOUNCED

Α, α a a as in father
Β, β v v as in *vet*
Γ, γ y/g y as in *yes* when before an e or i; when before consonants or a, o or ou it's a breathy, throaty g
Δ, δ dh th as in then
Ε, ε e e as in get
Ζ, ζ z z sound
Η, η i i sound as in ski
Θ, θ th th as in theme
Ι, ι i i as in b*it*
Κ, κ k k sound
Λ, λ l l sound
Μ, μ m m sound
Ν, ν n n sound
Ξ, ξ ks ks sound
Ο, ο o shortish o sound
Π, π p p sound
Ρ, ρ r rolled r sound
Σ, σ, ς s s sound, except like z' before 'g or 'm' sounds
Τ, τ t t sound
Υ, υ i i sound as in ski
Φ, φ f f sound
Χ, χ h/kh harsh h sound, like ch in lo*ch*
Ψ, ψ ps ps as in li*ps*
Ω, ω o shortish o sound

COMBINATIONS AND DIPHTHONGS

ΑΙ, αι e e as in get
ΑΥ, αυ av/af av or af depending on following consonant
ΕΙ, ει i i sound as in ski
ΟΙ, οι i i sound as in ski
ΕΥ, ευ ev/ef ev or ef depending on following consonant
ΟΥ, ου ou ou as in tourist
ΓΓ, γγ ng ng as in a*ngle*
ΓΚ, γκ g/ng g as in goat at the beginning of a word, ng in the middle
ΜΠ, μπ b/mb b at the beginning of a word, mb in the middle
ΝΤ, ντ d/nd d at the beginning of a word, nd in the middle
ΤΣ, τσ ts ts as in hi*ts*
ΣΙ, σι sh sh as in *sh*ame
ΤΖ, τζ tz j as in jam

Note: An umlaut or dieresis over a letter indicates that the two vowels are pronounced separately; for example *païdhákia* (lamb chops) is pronounced pah-ee-dhakia rather than peh-dhakia.

Cheers! Stiniyássas!/Yiámas!
Mr/Mrs/Miss Kírios/Kiría/Dhespinís
more perisótero
less ligótero
a little lígo
a lot polí

big/small megálo/mikró
cheap/expensive ftinó/akrivó
hot/cold zestó/krýo
with/without mazí/horís
quickly/slowly grígora/sigá

QUESTIONS

To ask a question, it's simplest to start with *parakaló*, then name the thing you want in an interrogative tone.
where? pou?
how? pos?
how many? póssi/pósses?
how much? póso?
when? póte?
why? yatí?
what time…? ti óra…?
what is/which is…? ti íne/pió íne..?

ACCOMMODATION

hotel ksenodhohío
a room éna dhomátio
We'd like a room Parakaló, éna dhomátio
for one/two/three people ya éna átomo/dhýo/tría átoma
for one/two/three nights ya mía/dhýo/trís vradhiés
with a double bed me megálo kreváti
with a shower me doús
hot water zestó neró
cold water krío neró
Can I see it? Boró na to dho?
Can we camp here? Boróume na váloume ti skiní edhó?
campsite kamping/kataskínosi
tent skiní
youth hostel ksenónas neótitos

SHOPPING AND SERVICES

How much (does it cost)? póso káni?
What time does it open/close? Tí óra aníyi/ klíni?
May I have a kilo of oranges? Parakaló, éna kiló portokália?
to eat/drink trógo/píno
bakery foúrnos, artopiío
pharmacy farmakío
post office tahydhromío
stamps gramatósima
petrol station venzinádhiko
bank trápeza
money leftá/hrímata
toilet toualéta
police astinomía
doctor iatrós
hospital nosokomío

ON THE MOVE

airplane aeropláno
bus leoforío
car aftokínito
motorbike, moped, scooter mihanáki, papáki
taxi taksí
ship plío/vapóri/karávi
bicycle podhílato
hitching otostóp
on foot me ta pódhia
trail monopáti
bus station praktorío leoforíon
bus stop stási
harbour limáni
What time does it leave? Ti óra févyi?
What time does it arrive? Ti óra ftháni?
How many kilometres? Pósa hiliómetra?
How many hours? Pósses óres?

GREEK'S GREEK

There are numerous words and phrases that you will hear constantly, even if you rarely have the chance to use them. These are a few of the most common.
Éla! Come (literally), but also Speak to me! You don't say! etc.
Oríste? What can I do for you?
Bros! Standard phone response
Ti néa? What's new?
Ti yínete? What's going on (here)?
Étsi k'étsi So-so
Ópa! Whoops! Watch it!
Po-po-po! Expression of dismay or concern, like French "O la la!"
Pedhí mou My boy/girl, sonny, friend, etc.
Maláka(s) Literally "wanker", but often used (don't try it!) as an informal form of address
Sigá sigá Take your time, slow down
Kaló taxídhi Bon voyage

Where are you going? Pou pas?
I'm going to... Páo sto...
I want to get off at... Thélo na katévo sto...
Can you show me the road to...? Parakaló, o dhrómos ya...?
Where is the bakery? Parakaló, o foúrnos?
near kondá
far makryá
left aristerá
right dheksiá
straight ahead katefthía
a ticket to... éna isistírio ya...
a return ticket éna isistírio me epistrofí
(sand) beach, shore ammoudhiá, paralía
cave spiliá
centre (of town) kéndro
church eklissía
sea thálassa
village horió

NUMBERS M/N/F)

1 énas/éna/mía
2 dhýo
3 trís/tría
4 tésseres/téssera
5 pénde
6 éksi
7 eftá
8 okhtó
9 ennéa
10 dhéka
11 éndheka
12 dhódheka
13 dhekatrís
14 dhekatésseres
20 íkosi
21 íkosi éna
30 triánda
40 saránda
50 penínda
60 eksínda
70 evdhomínda
80 ogdhónda
90 enenínda
100 ekató
150 ekatón penínda
200 dhiakóssies/ia
500 pendakóssies/ia
1000 hílies/ia
2000 dhýo hiliádhes
1,000,000 éna ekatomírio
first próto
second dhéftero
third tríto

TIME AND DAYS OF THE WEEK

now tóra
today símera
tomorrow ávrio
yesterday khthés
Monday Dheftéra
Tuesday Tríti
Wednesday Tetárti
Thursday Pémpti
Friday Paraskeví
Saturday Sávato
Sunday Kyriakí
What time is it? Ti óra íne?
One/two/three o'clock Mía/dhío/trís iy óra/
Twenty to four Tésseres pará íkosi
Five past seven Eftá ke pénde
Half past eleven Éndhekámisí
half-hour misí óra
quarter-hour éna tétarto

MONTHS AND SEASONS

You may see Katharévoussa, or hybrid, forms of the months written on timetables or street signs; these are the spoken forms.
January Yennáris
February Fleváris
March Mártis
April Aprílis
May Maïos
June Ioúnios
July Ioúlios
August Ávgoustos
September Septémvris
October Októvrios
November Noémvris
December Dhekémvris
summer schedule Therinó dhromolóyio
winter schedule Himerinó dhromolóyio

MENU READER

BASICS

aláti salt
avgá eggs
boukáli bottle
voútyro butter
fayitó food
(horís) ládhi (without) oil
hortofágos vegetarian

THE MINOAN DIET

Like today's islanders, the Minoans ate the wild plants and herbs that grow in the hills and mountains (known by modern Cretans as *hórta*), as well as a variety of grains and pulses. Lovers of **seafood**, they also fished the seas around the island's coast for many of the varieties familiar to modern diners in the island's tavernas: *tsipoúra*, *sargós* and *fangrí* (types of bream) plus safrídhi (horse mackerel), *okhtapódhi* (octopus) and *ahinosaláta* (sea urchins roe). Remains found at many Minoan sites indicate that lobster, crab, oyster, whelks and mussels were also highly regarded.

The Minoans' favourite **meats** (again as today) were sheep and goat, and the Cretan passion for *tsalingária* or *hohlí* (snails) was just as strong three and a half thousand years ago. Duck and partridge were also eaten, although chicken (and their eggs) were unknown in Minoan times. The **olive** was introduced in the Neolithic period and the great *píthoi* oil containers found in the Minoan palaces testify to the importance of oil at all levels of society. The Minoans were probably just as choosy about their olive oil as islanders today and each region – as now – was no doubt renowned for its subtle differences in taste and quality.

Almonds, figs, pears, plums and pomegranates were the Minoans' preferred **fruits**, and their **bread** – cooked on flat dishes using flour with little gluten (raising agent) – would be instantly recognizable to a modern Cretan as the flat *píta*, today a staple throughout Greece. Honey was the main source of sugar in Minoan times, and no doubt *thymárisio* (thyme honey) was as popular then as now. The Minoans were also enthusiastic **wine** drinkers: a four-thousand-year-old winepress discovered at Vathýpetro (see page 81), at the centre of a still-working vineyard, has a fair claim to being the oldest in the world.

kalambokísio corn
katálogo/lísta menu
koutáli spoon
kréas meat
ládhi, eleóladho olive oil
lahaniká vegetables
lemóni lemon
olikís aleseos whole-grain/whole-meal
o logariasmós the bill
mahéri knife
méli honey
neró enfialoméno bottled water
orektiká starters
pipéri pepper
piroúni fork
potíri glass
psári/psáriascaly fish (fishes)
psomí bread
siskalísio psomi rye bread
xýdhi vinegar
skórdho garlic
thalassiná seafood
thymárisio (méli) thyme (honey); highly prized on Crete
tyrí cheese
yiaoúrti yoghurt
záhari sugar

COOKING TERMS

liastó sun-dried
makaronádha spaghetti- or pasta-based dish
mayireftá oven-baked dishes
psitó roasted
skáras grilled
sti soúvla spit-roasted
sto foúrno baked
tiganitó pan-fried
tis óras grilled/fried to order
yemistá stuffed (squid, vegetables, etc)

STARTERS, SALADS AND MEZÉDHES

angourodomáta saláta cucumber and tomato salad, without cheese
avgolémono egg and lemon soup or sauce
bouréki, bourekákia courgette/zucchini, potato and cheese pie
dákos barley rusks soaked in oil and tomato, often sprinkled with cheese and oregano; base of the eponymous salad
dolmádhes/dolmadhákia stuffed vine leaves/small stuffed vine leaves
domatosaláta tomato salad
eliés olives
fasoládha bean soup
fáva purée of split yellow peas with onion, olive oil and perhaps a token olive
horiátiki (salatá) Greek salad (with olives, féta, etc)
kalitsoúnia pies filled with soft, sweet *myzíthra* cheese
keftédhes meatballs
kolokythakeftedhes courgette balls (fried)

kolokythákia tiganitá courgette/zucchini slices fried, usually in batter
kolokythoánthi yemistá stuffed courgette/ zucchini flowers, a delicious Cretan speciality
láhano-karóto saláta cabbage and carrot salad, offered during the cooler months, often overly heavy on the cabbage
maroúli saláta lettuce salad, common during springtime, ideally with *ánithos* (dill) and *frésko kremmýdhi* (green onion)
melitzanosaláta aubergine/eggplant dip; *nistísimo* or *ayiorítiko* is without mayonnaise
melitzánes tiganités aubergine/eggplant slices fried, usually in batter
paximádhia twice-baked Cretan rusks softened with water or oil and used in *dákos* or served with mezédhes
saganáki fried cheese, also a cheese-based sauce for seafood, especially shimp
soúpa soup, especially *psarósoupa* (fish soup)
spanakópita/spanakopitakia spinach pie/small spinach pies
taramosaláta fish roe pâté
tsalingária, hohlí snails
tyrópita/tyropitákia cheese pies/small cheese pies
tzatzíki yoghurt and cucumber dip
yígandes white haricot beans, almost always served *yahní* (in a red sauce)

VEGETABLES

ambelofásoula runner (green) beans, offered June–Sept, usually boiled plain, served as a salad with oil and lemon wedges
anginthe áres artichokes; *a la políta* are stewed with potato and carrot, served all year
angoúri cucumber
bámies okra
briám ratatouille of courgettes, potatoes, onions, tomato
domátes tomatoes
fakés lentils
fasolákia string beans
hórta greens (usually wild)
imám bayaldí stuffed, oven-baked aubergine/eggplant
kolokythákia courgette/zucchini, serve boiled with olive oil and lemon wedges
koukiá broad beans (fresh only in spring); otherwise rehydrated
kremmýdhia onions; *fréska kremmýdhia* are spring or green onions
ladhéra vegetables stewed/baked in oil
melitzána aubergine/eggplant
papoutsákia mince-stuffed aubergine/ eggplant
patátes potatoes
patátes limonátes potatoes baked with lemon and oil
piperiés peppers
radhíkia wild chicory
rízi/piláfi rice (usually with *sáltsa* – sauce)
saláta any salad
spanáki spinach
yemistá stuffed vegetables

MEAT AND POULTRY

arnáki me rízi ragout of lamb with rice
arní lamb
apákia smoked pork loin
biftéki hamburger
brizóla pork chop
spalobrizóla veal chop
hirinó pork
katsikáki kid (goat)
keftédhes meatballs
kléftiko meat, potatoes and veg cooked together in a pot or foil; a Cretan speciality traditionally carried to bandits in hiding
kókoras krasáto coq au vin
kokorétsi offal kebab
kotópoulo chicken
kounéli rabbit
loukánika sausages, often spicy
moskhári veal or yearling beef
moussakás baked aubergine/eggplant, potato and mince pie under bechamel sauce
païdhákia lamb chops
papoutsáki meat-stuffed version of *imám bayaldí* (see "Vegetables")
patsás tripe soup, often served at Easter
pastítsio macaroni pie baked with meat
sykóti liver
souvláki chunks of seasoned meat or fish skewered and chargrilled
stifádho meat (usually beef or rabbit) stew with tomato and onion
tsalingária garden snails
tsigaristó braised or sauteed lamb or goat stew from Sfakiá, with vegetables
tzoutzoukákia meatballs baked in tomato sauce
vodhinó beef
yíros sliced, spit-roasted seasoned pork or lamb
yiouvétsi meat casserole with *kritharáki* pasta (similar to Italian orzo)

FISH AND SEAFOOD

ahiní sea urchins; the briny orange roe is much esteemed as *ahinosaláta*
astakós slipper lobster
barbóunia red mullet
fangrí common bream, red porgy

garídhes prawns
gávros large frying anchovy; *gávros marinátos* (raw marinated ones) are a popular starter
glóssa sole
gópa bogue
kakaviá bouillabaisse-style fish stew
kalamária/kalamarákia squid/baby squid
koliós chub mackerel
lavráki sea bass
marídhes picarel; fried and served whole
melanoúri saddled bream
mýdhia mussels
okhtapódhi octopus; either grilled or *krasáto* (wine stewed)
sardhélles sardines
sargós white bream
sinagrídha dentex
skáros parrotfish
skathári black bream, most common spring/early summer
skorpína scorpion fish
skoumbrí Atlantic mackerel
soupiá cuttlefish
strídhia oysters
tónnos tuna
tsipoúra sea bream
xifías swordfish

DESSERTS, FRUIT AND NUTS

baklavás honey and nut pastry
banána banana
bougátsa creamy cheese pie, sweet or savoury sprinkled with powdered sugar and cinnamon; a tasty speciality of city market places and some bakeries
fistíkia pistachio nuts
fráoules strawberries
galaktobóureko custard-cream fiylo pie
halvás sesame-based sweetmeat
karydhópita walnut cake
karpoúzi watermelon
kataífi "angel hair" pastry filled with walnuts and soaked under syrup
kéik western-style cake
kerásia cherries
loukoumádhes dough fritters served hot with honey or cinnamon; similar to French beignets
loukoúmia Turkish delight
míla apples
milopita/milopitákia apple pies
pagotó ice cream
pastéli sesame and honey bar
pepóni Persian melon
portokália oranges
ryzógalo rice pudding
rodhákino peach
sýka figs, fresh or dried
stafýia grapes
yaoúrti yoghurt; superb in Crete and often served with honey as a dessert

CHEESE

anthótyros soft, full-fat unsalted cheese, similar to *myzíthra*
graviéra gruyère-type hard cheese
kasséri semi-hard sheep's milk cheese
kefalotýri salty, hard sheep's or goat's milk cheese
ladhotýi hard cheese matured in oil
manoúri mild, soft sheep's milk cheese
myzíthra sweet or savoury ricotta-style goat's or sheep's milk cheese

DRINKS

býra beer
frappé cold instant coffee shaken with condensed milk until it gets a frothy head, served with ice; a Greek institution
gála milk
gálakakáo chocolate milk
gazóza generic term for any non-alcoholic fizzy drink
hýma (krasí) bulk wine served by the quarter, half or full litre
kafés coffee
koniák brandy
krasí wine
áspro white
mávro/kókkino red
rosé/kokkinéli rosé, light red
limonádha lemonade
neró metalikó mineral water
oúzo distilled grape spirit; the national drink of Greece
portokaládha orangeade
rakí (pronounced ratchi) grape pomace distillate, unflavoured; the national drink of Crete
tónik tonic water
tsáï tea
tsikoudhia/rakí highly popular grappa- style firewater; the vast majority of islanders make their own which is of course "the best in Crete"
tsípouro distilled spirit; similar to *rakí*

Glossary

acropolis ancient, fortified hilltop
agora market and meeting place of an ancient city
amphora tall, narrow-necked jar for oil or wine
áno upper, as in upper town or village; eg Áno Zákros
apse curved recess at the altar end of a church
Archaic period Late Iron Age, from around 750 BC to the start of the Classical period in the fifth century BC
arsenali arsenals; a term used rather loosely for many Venetian defensive and harbour works
asklepion sanctuary dedicated to Asklepios, the Greek god of healing, where the sick sought cures for their ailments
atrium central altar-court of a Roman house
áyios/ayía/áyii saint or holy (m/f/pl), common place-name prefix (abbrev. Ag. or Ay.): Áyios Nikólaos is St Nicholas; Ayía Triádha is the Holy Trinity
basilica colonnaded "hall-type" church
Byzantine empire created by the division of the Roman Empire in 395 AD, this was the eastern half, ruled from Byzantium or Constantinople (modern Istanbul). There are many Byzantine churches of the fifth to the twelfth century on Crete, and Byzantine art flourished again after the fall of Constantinople in 1453, under Venetian rule, when many artists and scholars fled to the island
central court paved area at the heart of a Minoan palace
Classical period from the end of the Persian Wars in the fifth century BC to the unification of Greece under Philip II of Macedon (338 BC)
dhimarhío town hall (modern usage)
dhomátia rooms for rent in private houses, now more often in separate purpose-built blocks
Dorian civilization that overran the Mycenaeans from the north around 1100 BC, and became their successor throughout much of southern Greece, including Crete
eparhía the smallest subdivision of a modern province
Eteo-Cretan literally true Cretan, the Eteo-Cretans are believed to have been remnants of the Minoan people who kept a degree of their language and culture alive in isolated centres in eastern Crete as late as the third century BC
Geometric period Post-Mycenaean Iron Age, named for the style of its pottery: beginnings are in the early eleventh century BC with the arrival of Dorian peoples – by the eighth, with the development of representational styles, it becomes known as the Archaic period
Hellenistic period the last and most unified Greek empire, created by Philip II and Alexander the Great in the fourth century BC, finally collapsing with the fall of Corinth to the Romans in 146 BC
hóra main town of a region; literally it means "the place"
horns of consecration Minoan religious symbol imitating the bulls' horns that decorated Minoan palaces and shrines
iconostasis screen between the nave of a church and the altar, often covered in icons
ipnákos Greek version of the siesta, (also called mikró ýpno) which is widely practised in Crete, especially during the hot summer months. It usually lasts from around 1.30pm to 5.30pm with a legal requirement that requires silence from 3–5pm. Many stores and businesses close during these hours
janissary member of the Turkish Imperial Guard: in Crete under the Turks a much-feared mercenary force, often forcibly recruited from the local population
kafenío coffeehouse/café: in a small village the centre of communal life and probably the bus stop, too
kaïki caïque, or medium-sized boat, traditionally wooden. Now used for just about any coast-hopping or excursion boat
kámbos fertile agricultural plateau, usually near the mouth of a river
kapetánios widely used term of honour for a man of local power – originally for guerrilla leaders who earned the title through acts of particular bravado
kástro medieval castle or any fortified hill
káto lower, as in lower town or village; eg Káto Zákros
kernos ancient cult vessel or altar with a number of receptacles for offerings
krater large, two-handled wine bowl
lárnakes Minoan clay coffins
lustral basin a small sunken chamber in Minoan palaces reached by steps; perhaps actually some kind of bath but more likely for purely ritual purification
megaron principal hall of a Mycenaean palace
meltémi north wind that blows across the Aegean in summer (can be vicious in Crete). Its force is gauged by what it knocks over – "tableweather", "chairweather", etc
Minoan Crete's great Bronze Age civilization which dominated the Aegean from about 2500 to 1400 BC
Minos mythical ruler after whom Arthur Evans named Minoan society; more likely the title of a dynasty of priest-kings like the Egyptian "Pharaoh"
moní monastery or convent
Mycenaean mainland civilization centred on Mycenae c.1700–1100 BC: probably responsible for the destruction of Minoan civilization. Mycenaean

influence pervaded Crete in the late and post-Minoan periods

Neolithic the earliest era of settlement in Crete, characterized by the use of stone tools and weapons together with basic agriculture

néos, néa, néo new

Neopalatial The zenith of Minoan civilization c.1700–1400BC when the palaces were rebuilt on a luxurious scale following destruction

nomós modern Greek province: Crete is divided into four

odeion small amphitheatre used for performances or meetings

paleós, paleá, paleó old

pallikári Literally "brave man": in Crete a guerrilla fighter, particularly in the struggle for independence from the Turks, also a general term for a tough young man

Panayía the Virgin Mary

paniyíri festival or feast, the local celebration of a holy day

Pandokrátor literally "The Almighty", a stern figure of Christ or God the Father frescoed or in mosaic on the dome of many Byzantine churches

paralía seafront promenade

peak sanctuary mountain-top shrine, often in or associated with a cave, sometimes in continuous use from Neolithic through to Roman times

períptero street kiosk

peristyle colonnade or area surrounded by colonnade, used especially of Minoan halls or courtyards

píthos (pl. píthoi) Large ceramic jar for storing oil, grain etc, very common in the Minoan palaces and used in almost identical form in modern Cretan homes

platía square or plaza. Kentrikí Platía means the main square

Prepalatial The period of Minoan history c.3500–1900BC preceding the era of the palaces

Propylea portico or entrance to an ancient building

Protopalatial The period of Minoan history c.1900–1700BC when the first palaces were built

rhyton vessel, often horn-shaped, for pouring libations or offerings

sistrum ancient percussion instrument producing a maraca or tambourine sound

stele upright stone slab or column, usually inscribed

stoa colonnaded walkway in Classical-era marketplace

témblon screen, either plaster, stone or wooden, between the church sanctuary and the congregation, always studded with icons

theatral area open area found in most of the Minoan palaces with seat-like steps around; may have been a type of theatre or ritual area

tholos conical or beehive-shaped building, especially a Minoan or Mycenaean tomb

Acronyms

ELTA Greek postal service

EOS Greek Mountaineering Federation, based in Athens with branches in Haniá and Iráklio

EOT Ellinikós Organismós Tourismoú, the National Tourist Organization

KKE The Communist Party, unreconstructed.

KTEL National syndicate of bus companies, divided by province. The term is also used to refer to bus stations themselves

ND Néa Dhimokratía, the Conservative party, currently in power until the next elections in 2027, and probably thereafter; referred o as `nu `dhou, after its Greek initials

PASOK Socialist party (Pan-Hellenic Socialist Movement)

SYRIZA (Synaspismós tis Rizopastikís Aristerás) A eft-wing rainbow coalition including Maoist, Trotskyist and Green elements; currently in opposition

XA (Hrysí Avgí (Golden Dawn") Ultra-nationalist neo-Nazi party, now proscribed but with active epigones

Small print and index

A ROUGH GUIDE TO ROUGH GUIDES

Published in 1982, the first Rough Guide – to Greece – was a student scheme that became a publishing phenomenon. Mark Ellingham, a recent graduate in English from Bristol University, had been travelling in Greece the previous summer and couldn't find the right guidebook. With a small group of friends he wrote his own guide, combining a contemporary, journalistic style with a thoroughly practical approach to travellers' needs.

The immediate success of the book spawned a series that rapidly covered dozens of destinations. And, in addition to impecunious backpackers, Rough Guides soon acquired a much broader readership that relished the guides' wit and inquisitiveness as much as their enthusiastic, critical approach and value-for-money ethos. These days, Rough Guides include recommendations from budget to luxury and cover more than 120 destinations around the globe, from Amsterdam to Zanzibar, all regularly updated by our team of roaming writers.

Browse all our latest guides, read inspirational features and book your trip at **roughguides.com**.

Rough Guide credits

Editor: Beth Williams
Cartography: Carte
Picture Manager: Tom Smyth
Layout: Pradeep Thapliyal
Head of DTP and Pre-Press: Rebeka Davies
Head of Publishing: Sarah Clark

Publishing information

Thirteenth edition 2025

Distribution
UK, Ireland and Europe
Apa Publications (UK) Ltd; sales@roughguides.com
United States and Canada
Ingram Publisher Services; ips@ingramcontent.com
Australia and New Zealand
Booktopia; retailer@booktopia.com.au
Worldwide
Apa Publications (UK) Ltd; sales@roughguides.com

Special Sales, Content Licensing and CoPublishing
Rough Guides can be purchased in bulk quantities at discounted prices. We can create special editions, personalised jackets and corporate imprints tailored to your needs. sales@roughguides.com.
roughguides.com

Printed in Czech Republic

This book was produced using **Typefi** automated publishing software.

A catalogue record for this book is available from the British Library

Help us update

We've gone to a lot of effort to ensure that this edition of **The Rough Guide to Crete** is accurate and up-to-date. However, things change – places get "discovered", transport routes are altered, restaurants and hotels raise prices or lower standards, and businesses cease trading. If you feel we've got it wrong or left something out, we'd like to know, and if you can direct us to the web address, so much the better.

Please send your comments with the subject line "**Rough Guide Crete Update**" to mail@uk.roughguides.com. We'll acknowledge all contributions and send a copy of the next edition (or any other Rough Guide if you prefer) for the very best emails.

ABOUT THE AUTHOR

Marc Dubin divides his time between Greece and Essex, and first went to Crete in 1978, returning since then on numerous occasions.

Photo credits

(Key: T-top; C-centre; B-bottom; L-left; R-right)

Georgios Tsichlis/Shutterstock 12, 13TR, 13B, 14T, 17T, 17BL, 18T, 20, 22, 50/51, 126/127, 129, 188/189, 191, 232/233, 235
iStock 53, 320
Liquid Bungy 11T
Pantelis Mathioudakis 23
Shutterstock 1, 2, 4, 7, 9, 11B, 13TL, 13C, 14B, 14C, 15T, 15B, 16T, 16B, 17BR, 18B, 19T, 19C, 19B, 24

Cover: Knossos **Honza Hruby/Shutterstock**

Index

M

N

O

P

Map symbols

The symbols below are used on maps throughout the book

- Provincial boundary
- Chapter boundary
- Major road
- Minor road
- Unpaved road
- Pedestrian road
- Steps
- Ferry route
- Path
- Wall

- Post office
- Information office
- Parking
- Petrol station
- Point of interest
- Internet access
- Fountain
- Castle
- Archeological site
- Mountain hut

- Cave
- Lighthouse
- Gorge
- Mountain peak
- Mountain range
- Mosque
- Synagogue
- Monastery/convent
- Gate/entrance
- Winery

- Airport
- Heliport
- Bus stop
- Church (regional)
- Church (town)
- Building
- Stadium
- Park/forest
- Beach
- Cemetery

Listings key

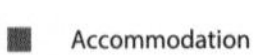

- Accommodation
- Eating
- Drinking/nightlife
- Shopping